The Platonian Leviathan

LEON HAROLD CRAIG

The Platonian Leviathan

UNIVERSITY OF TORONTO PRESS
Toronto Buffalo London

© University of Toronto Press Incorporated 2010
Toronto Buffalo London
www.utppublishing.com
Printed in Canada

ISBN 978-1-4426-4106-8

Printed on acid-free paper

Library and Archives Canada Cataloguing in Publication

Craig, Leon H., 1941–
The Platonian Leviathan / Leon Harold Craig.

Includes bibliographical references and index.
ISBN 978-1-4426-4106-8

1. Hobbes, Thomas, 1588–1679. Leviathan.   2. Political science – Philosophy.
3. Political science – Early works to 1800.   4. State, The.   I. Title.

B1247.C69 2010   320.1   C2009-905245-8

This book has been published with the help of a grant from the Canadian
Federation for the Humanities and Social Sciences, through the Aid to
Scholarly Publications Program, using funds provided by the Social
Sciences and Humanities Research Council of Canada.

University of Toronto Press acknowledges the financial assistance to its
publishing program of the Canada Council for the Arts and the Ontario
Arts Council.

University of Toronto Press acknowledges the financial support for its
publishing activities of the Government of Canada through the
Book Publishing Industry Development Program (BPIDP).

For my former students

The Ancients when they writt the Lives of ancient Philosophers, used to in the first place to speake of their Lineage. And they tell us, that in processe of time, severall great Families accounted it their Glory to be branched from such or such a Sapiens. Why now should that Method be omitted in this Historiola of our Malmesbury Philosopher? Who though of no Illustrious family but of Plebian descent, his Renowne haz and will give Brightnesse to his name and Familie: which hereafter may arise glorious and flourish in Riches, and may justly take it an honour to be of kin to this worthy Person, so famous, for his great Parts, both at home and abroad.

...

The Lord Chancellour Bacon loved to converse with him. He assisted his lordship in translating several of his essays into Latin, one, I well remember, is that 'Of the Greatness of Cities'. The rest I have forgott. His Lordship was a very Contemplative person, and was wont to contemplate in his delicious walkes at Gorambery, and dictate to Mr Thomas Bushell or some other of his Gentlemen, that attended him with inke and paper ready, to sett downe presently his Thoughts. His Lordship would often say he better liked Mr Hobbes's taking his Notions, then any of the other, because he understood what he wrote, which the others not understanding my Lord would many times have a hard taske to make sense of what they writt.

It is to be remembered that about these times, Mr Thomas Hobbes was much addicted to Musique, and practised on the Base-Violl.

John Aubrey, *The Life of Mr Thomas Hobbes of Malmesbury*

Contents

Acknowledgments

It is fitting that I dedicate this book to my former students, since it was in the course of over three decades of teaching both political philosophy and the history and philosophy of science that I formed my own understanding of the metaphysical and epistemological issues treated herein, and of their bearing on political life. I have other, more specific debts to acknowledge, however. First of all, to Sue Colberg, award-winning book designer, who has provided another winning design for my book; she is a wonder and delight to work with. Next, to the editorial staff of the University of Toronto Press: to Lennart Husband, History and Philosophy Editor, who somehow secured approval for publishing a manuscript of truly leviathanic proportions; to Wayne Herrington, my Managing Editor, especially for securing the services of a superb copy-editor, Jim Leahy, whose meticulous scouring of my text improved it in a myriad of ways. But before he ever laid eyes on it, it had been revised a couple more times in light of many helpful criticisms submitted by the two anonymous assessors who judged it worthy of publication; for their efforts I am truly grateful, as I am for several other friends and colleagues who read parts of the book and offered their advice. I am especially indebted, however, to Heidi D. Studer, who not only read and critiqued the entire text, but provided a draft version of the index – service beyond all call of duty – and I trust she knows how much I value her friendship.

But my most special thanks go to Kent Cochrane, who has been intimately involved throughout the eight years that I have been working on this book. Broadly conversant with our philosophical tradition and classical literature, and possessing in particular an extensive knowledge of Hobbes's writings and of Hobbesian scholarship, he has assessed all successive versions of the manuscript, correcting, enriching, augmenting, and refining my text in countless ways. There is scarcely a page I've written on Hobbes that is not the better for his tireless efforts. He is entitled to presume a proprietary interest in the result.

Last to thank, but always first in my heart, is my wife Judith Ann, who for forty years has generously indulged my clumsy flirtations with Sophia.

Prelude

As chance would have it, this book was begun in the month immediately following the infamous deeds of 11 September 2001. The ostensible motives behind that appalling crescendo of terrorism should, like nothing in the preceding century, awaken sympathy for Hobbes's view of the potential political problems posed by dogmatic religious fervour: how readily the credulous are manipulated, even to the point of self-sacrifice, by those who have somehow acquired religious authority in their eyes ('So easie are men to be drawn to believe any thing, from such men as have gotten credit with them; and can with gentlenesse, and dexterity, take hold of their fear, and ignorance' – XII/19, 56).[1] However, if ignorance and the fears to which it gives rise were the sole source of these problems, they would in principle be eradicable by education, including so far as necessary a rationally enlightened religious education. But as the events of that black day proved, the problems derive not simply from the possibility that 'crafty ambitious persons abuse the simple people' (II/8, 8) – that is, from the exploitation of ignorant rustics by clever, cynical pursuers of worldly power. For among the perpetrators of those suicidal attacks were college-educated men, amply familiar with modern liberal society, including the endless wonders generated by the scientific technology to which it is devoted – the form of society envisioned by Hobbes – but who rejected it root and branch, exploiting its freedom and technological vulnerability to attack it with multiple effectiveness.[2]

Perhaps, in the final analysis, one must conclude that their actions were profoundly, atrociously irrational; in which case, they reveal with sobering clarity the limits of the power of reason over the behaviour of certain people, including some supposedly well-educated. Alternatively, perhaps the conception of reason whence the preceding judgment would be rendered is deficient, its calculations neglecting if not excluding important concerns and constituents of human nature that are more adequately, or at least more readily, addressed by 'religion.' That is, addressed from within an understanding of this world as properly subordinate to another, promulgated by whoever, however, on whatever basis, exercises intellectual and moral authority in the name of something higher than (mere) human desire, will, or reason. But whether one regards suicidal terrorists as besotted acolytes of fanatical madmen or inspired heroes of their faith, their very existence today suggests that a thorough reconsideration of Hobbes's political prescription is very much in order.[3] And all the more urgently needed, one may add, insofar as some approximation of a Hobbesian regime is – practically speaking – the only kind regarded as legitimate by the vast majority of educated people alive today.[4]

However, to be truly thorough, such a reconsideration cannot be confined to Hobbes's own texts, even if that would seem the best place to begin. Correctly interpreting those texts might entail a comprehensive examination of the historical context in which Hobbes lived and wrote, including the effects of previous and contemporaneous philosophizing – to say nothing of the vast amount of extant scholarship on his life and thought. Moreover, judging the comparative advantages and liabilities of Hobbes's prescription would require giving fair consideration to alternative understandings of political life. This would necessitate re-examining the past history of political philosophy, perhaps even present speculations about future philosophy. Altogether, the work of several lifetimes, surely. Confronted with the limitations inherent in mortality, compromises must be made.

In the compromise presently before you, the focus is primarily on Hobbes's greatest book, *Leviathan*, the work of his maturity that best provides an overview of the world as he would have us see it. By way of both deepening and enriching a critical re-examination of this masterpiece, I have of course drawn upon the resources of many other minds, some doubtless abler than mine. These include, however, a pair that to professional scholars are apt to seem strange, but that I have found especially valuable: Herman Melville and Joseph Conrad. Both their strangeness and their value reflect their being known as neither philosophers nor scholars, but novelists. Obviously, I regard them as more – much more – than mere story-tellers; they are among the very greatest novelists precisely because they were first of all philosophers in the original, literal sense of the word: lovers, hence hunters and pursuers, of wisdom. Moreover, I suspect Hobbes, a liberally educated man with a lifelong fondness for fine literature (and even a dabbler in poetry himself), might well have regarded their 'prose poems'[5] as more insightful and interesting than but a fraction of conventional scholarly works. Be that as it may, I find them so, and herein attempt to show why.

Moby-Dick is the source of my book's title (and to that extent of its thesis), a conjunction of terms – 'Platonian Leviathan' – that in itself gives some small indication of Melville's unconventional mind.[6] Judging from his writings, he was on friendly terms with much of the philosophical tradition; one encounters allusions – some overt, others more subtle – to works by Aristotle, Machiavelli, Montaigne, Rousseau, Bacon, Descartes, Spinoza, Bayle, Locke, and Kant, among others. But his genius drew on four sources in particular: the Bible, Plato, Shakespeare, and 'Hobbes of Malmsbury, the paragon of perspicuity.'[7] This is particularly evident in Melville's most imposing masterpiece, alternatively entitled *The Whale*, wherein he offers various observations, ventures certain speculations, and points to philosophical relationships that, to my knowledge, have heretofore gone unconsidered – or at least undiscussed publicly. Especially significant, however, is his depicting a political possibility latent in the 'Popular' version of a Hobbesian commonwealth: Caesarism.

Conrad's *Heart of Darkness*, on the other hand, provides the basis for a radical reconsideration of Hobbes's account of the State of Nature – or rather, *States* of Nature. While ratifying the essentials of Hobbes's view, Conrad nonetheless indicates certain problems with it – or rather, with the usual interpretation of it – while adding much-needed depth and complexity to Hobbes's sketchy (not to say simplistic) psychology. Of not least consequence, we are obliged to consider the Male-Female distinction in both contexts: that of the States of Nature, and of Civil Societies. Thus Conrad's story can be seen as both an augmentation and a corrective to Hobbes's portrayal of mankind in these radically different conditions. More cautiously put, it suggests a set of questions to be borne in mind upon returning to Hobbes's text, inviting one to imagine how our Malmesbury philosopher might respond. From this Conrad-inspired rereading, there emerges a more profound, more substantial understanding of the danger implicit in the ever-possible return to the Hell that Hobbes characterizes as the State of Nature. And insofar as that threat is the foundation of his political science, one necessarily revises one's overall understanding of Hobbes's revolutionary project.

Thus, the form and content of this book. But in order that my reader proceed with suitably modest expectations, I must disclaim at the outset any intention of presenting an exhaustive interpretation of Hobbes's *Leviathan*, offering comment on every significant detail, the countless 'atoms' of which this endlessly rich text is composed. I am primarily interested in uncovering what Hobbes would call its 'main Designe.' Doing so, however, is first and foremost a matter of mastering Hobbes's rhetoric, thereby penetrating the seemingly plain-spoken, logical, but nonetheless somewhat perplexing veneer (basis of the textbook under-standings and controversies) within which he has concealed a far more radical and ambitious teaching. For Hobbes must be one of the most subtle, crafty, bold – and droll – truly *political* philosophers who have ever turned their thoughts into books.

However, in referring to Hobbes's rhetoric, I do not mean mainly his deft employment in *Leviathan* of the various tried and true rhetorical devices and techniques recommended by teachers and practitioners of rhetoric since antiquity (e.g., redescription, invocation of familiar maxims, ridicule, novel tropes, etc.). This has been exhaustively analysed, and certain of its implications explored, by others.[8] What I have in mind is more comprehensive, affecting the entire style and tone of *Leviathan*, and crafted for purposes other than making it immediately persuasive with the majority of potential readers. To give some preliminary indica-tion of what I mean, consider: Hobbes presents his new science of poli-tics in such a manner that virtually everyone – at least on first reading, and typically forever thereafter – assesses it exclusively from the perspective of one of the ruled, as a subject of the Sovereign.[9] How he accomplishes this rhetorical feat is instructive, but more to the point is the question of why he does so. What effect does Hobbes intend it to have on various readers' understandings of, hence emotive reactions towards, his teach-ing? This is perhaps the most obvious of several stylistic features of *Leviathan* that can bear profoundly on its interpretation, and which thus must be explicitly addressed if an interpretation is to be adequate, but which almost never is.

I referred above to the fact that most people today who regard themselves as both modern and educated (two terms meaning practically the same thing: modernly educated) think, judge, and live within an essentially Hobbesian understanding of political life. But speaking more precisely, this is only partially true. Contemporary thought and practice accept most of Hobbes's prescription: recognition of some sort of human equal-ity, beginning with equality before the law, as the only legitimate basis for a political association; the existence of certain rights inhering in humans as such, independent of and 'prior' to any and all particular polities, rights which limit what policies and practices are morally acceptable in such polities;[10] that sovereignty ultimately rests on the consent of the governed, this being the basis of both governmental legitimacy and political obligation; that, practically speaking, justice in a given polity is defined by its laws; that the primary purpose of a political association is the protection of the lives of its composing members (as opposed to promoting a particular conception of what constitutes the good life, there being no single way of life that actually is best for everyone); that what is not expressly forbidden is permitted, liberty thus resulting mainly from the silence of the law, and understood as an absence of external constraints; and since citizen-subjects should be allowed maximum liberty in order to pursue a good life as each sees fit (so far as doing so is compatible with civil peace), there should be no laws unnecessary to the true purpose of political association.

But what is of paramount importance, most educated moderns tacitly accept the distinctly modern conception of Nature – the non-teleological, materialistic-mechanistic conception advanced by Bacon, Galileo, Descartes, and other architects of the Scientific Revolution – the same conception that Hobbes adopted as the ostensible basis for an empirically sound, truly scientific understanding of politics. Partly as a consequence, moderns also accept the view that the natural, and not merely the historical, human condition is pre-political, more akin to the natural state of animals, and that accordingly the political association is profoundly artificial (i.e., that the very idea of it is a human invention, as are of course the particulars of each polity's design and construction). And with life in polities being indubitably a vast improvement over living in the primitive natural state, the artificial is generally seen as superior to the natural (scattered romantic protests to the contrary notwithstanding). Thus, Nature – far from providing the ultimate standards of right and wrong, good and bad, noble and debased – is itself to be judged by standards humans somehow devise from and for themselves. Judged, and generally found wanting, one must add, hence in need of artificial improvement, enhancement, correction, transformation, pacification, rational management.

Moreover, virtually all educated people today recognize, though without necessarily understanding the why or the how of it, what was clear to Hobbes from the outset: that the most important practical consequence of organizing polities in accordance with his prescription is its making possible the advancement of a technologically oriented science that would relieve the toil and suffering and insecurity of human life, transforming science from the 'small Power' it was in Hobbes's day (X/14, 42) to the great power it is in ours. The discoveries of modern science, fed into a free market economy, yield steadily increasing, widely shared prosperity: the universal means for the wide variety of 'good lives' people may pursue as they choose. In comparison with life in a primitive natural state (which one imagines would offer independence, but otherwise be poor, nasty, brutish, and short), interdependent life in a well-ordered Hobbesian commonwealth can be rich, gracious, humane, and long. It is also becoming clear to an increasing proportion of educated people today that the uncontrolled and now largely uncontrollable scope of scientific discovery, resulting in an ever-expanding range of technological powers available to be used and abused, itself presents unprecedented political problems. But this has not shaken the general faith in modern science. If science itself generates problems, most people nurtured in science-saturated societies remain convinced that the solutions are to be found through still more science, not less.

There are two important respects, however, in which modern liberal regimes depart from Hobbes's political prescription. And the rejected provisions are ones that Hobbes would insist are essential to the long-term viability of a civil society. One concerns the relation of Church and State, and presumes that the 'seeds' of religion 'can never be so abolished out of humane nature, but that new Religions may againe be made to spring out of them, by the culture of such men, as for such purpose are in reputation' (XII/23, 58). The only protection against novel, impolitic religions arising is provided by a politic religion being already firmly established, that there be no 'religious vacuum' such as human nature abhors. In choosing instead to keep religious matters separate from publicly sanctioned business – leaving religion largely unregulated (permitting, in effect, a 'competition' among various religions, which may include fanatically dogmatic religions, intolerant not merely of each other but of secular authority as such), while enshrining freedom of, or from, religious practice and expression as a fundamental civil right of each individual citizen (rather than merely acknowledging religious belief, or unbelief, as the private matter it inherently is) – in separating rather than integrating Church and State, one allows the seeds of a particularly implacable kind of civil strife and/or sedition to be sown. And what is perhaps equally important, one thereby forgoes the support for both political unity and moral education that a common religion can provide. Or so Hobbes argues.

The other departure from a strictly Hobbesian regime concerns censorship. Hobbes treats the regulation of whatever communications enter the public space as the central right of the Sovereign power:

> [I]t is annexed to the Soveraignty, to be Judge of what Opinions and Doctrines are averse, and what conducing to Peace; and consequently, on what occasions, how farre, and what, men are to be trusted withall, in speaking to Multitudes of people; and who shall examine the Doctrines of all bookes before they be published. For the Actions of men proceed from their Opinions; and in the wel[11] governing of Opinions, consisteth the well governing of mens Actions, in order to their Peace, and Concord.[12] (XVIII/9, 91)

The principal point is indisputable: people act mainly on the basis of what they believe, not only concerning their physical environment, but also with respect to what is morally acceptable, decent, respectable, successful, rewarded, admired, fashionable, necessary, desirable, deserved, respectful, justifiable, tolerated, and so on. And for the most part, people's beliefs do not originate with themselves, but from what they are taught in schools and places of worship, and from what they see and hear – largely, that is, from what they are told and shown, including in the various media of popular entertainment.

Because I believe contemporary liberal democracies are facing grave crises – not simply from terrorists or from the resurgence of dogmatic religious fanaticism, serious as these threats so clearly are, but also from two other burgeoning sets of problems that practically intertwine with them – I also believe that we need to reconsider the wisdom of these departures from Hobbes's political prescription. If it is to work as its designer intended, a Commonwealth or 'Leviathan' is reliant upon a general respect for reason, truth, and moral rectitude on the part of its composing individuals – especially of those who occupy any sort of leading role, be it commercial, martial, or governmental, but most especially of those charged with serving as its highest intellectual authorities.[13] Thus, one set of problems results from evolving political thought and practice in the context of moral decay and a loss of faith in reason in liberal societies themselves. This contributes indirectly to both nihilistic terrorism and the growing appeal of religious fundamentalism. The other set of problems arises from the spectacular success of Hobbes's political design for promoting modern science. The ever-accelerating growth of scientific technology that has resulted is increasingly unmanageable, presenting unprecedented ethical and practical quandaries, mortal dangers, and socio-economic vulnerabilities (which further magnify the terrorist threat).

I shall speak a bit more substantively about these problem areas in my Postlude, indicating why I believe they radically challenge the continuing viability of the liberal democratic regime in its current form. And why, consequently, minor structural and procedural alterations – introduced piecemeal as various manifestations of this or that problem are recognized, but without a coherent political configuration clearly in view – are unlikely to suffice. However, before considering what remedial changes might enhance our capacity to cope with the compound predicament confronting Western civilization at the outset of the twenty-first century, we need a sound understanding of this regime as its architect envisioned its actual functioning. For with a better grasp of Hobbes's underlying rationale, we will – whatever else – be less complacent regarding our deviations from his prescription. (We might even see merit in Hobbes's arguments favouring a rational Monarchy!) What, then, did Hobbes really have in mind as he wrote, revised, enriched, and polished the book that gave political shape to modernity, his *Leviathan*?[14] It is not simply what it is usually taken to be.

Being only too aware of my book's daunting size, let me conclude its Prelude with a few remarks that may be useful to some among the likely diversity of readers. First, concerning the basic structure of my argument for a 'Platonian Leviathan': it consists of both a 'negative' and a 'positive' part. The former (Part One: 'The Problematical *Leviathan*') consists of a sequence of chapters that critically examine what are widely regarded to be the basic principles upon which Hobbes has built his political prescription. These chapters are intended to show, not only that every one of these principles are problematic to the point of insupportable, but also (not surprisingly, then) that Hobbes did not in fact subscribe to them himself. This being so – that Hobbes entertained no doctrinal commitments which would *preclude* his agreeing with Plato concerning anything fundamental to a sound understanding of philosophy or politics – the way is open to my presenting the positive case for just such an agreement, which I undertake in Part Two ('The Platonic *Leviathan*').

Second, I confess that among my many old-fashioned views is a faith in the utility of substantial endnotes. Mine serve a variety of purposes, sufficiently enhancing the overall value of the book as to justify their inclusion (or so I believe), while allowing the argument of the main text to proceed in a more straightforward manner. But since most of the material thereby relegated is strictly supplementary, readers pressed for time, or who as a matter of principle object to long endnotes, or for whatever reason find them annoying, are cordially invited to ignore them.

Third, readers interested solely in focused analyses of Hobbes's *Leviathan* may confine their attention to the book's two main parts, as the chapters they comprise provide what I regard as most essential to my interpretive effort. Withal, I have tried so far as practical to fashion each chapter as intelligible unto itself. They are mutually reinforcing, however. Nor is their order arbitrary, as the overall strength of this very different interpretation builds step by step. Nor do I mean to suggest that the Melville and Conrad sections are not integral to the book's governing intention. They include many observations about Hobbes and his *Leviathan* that are not provided elsewhere in my text. And, as I attempt to show, these authors afford a kind of illumination of Hobbes's doctrine that neither I – nor anyone else, so far as I know – otherwise provides. Moreover, they do so in a manner that engages, hence educates, a reader's entire soul, the passions as well as reason, thereby furnishing a psychic experience that no purely rational analysis can match. And by implicitly inviting readers to generalize from my employing these two literary classics to further an understanding of Hobbes's doctrine, I hope a broader collateral purpose might be served as well: that of encouraging the study of other such works, open to the possibility of their having genuine philosophical value.

Finally, about my citing of extant scholarship: there is an enormous amount of it, it has been growing vigorously of late, and I have been able to consult but a fraction of it. Consequently, I am sure that I remain ignorant of some that is quite valuable. Based on what I have consulted, however, I am persuaded that most of it is, at best, tangential to my effort here, precisely because my reading of Hobbes is so very different from anything I have encountered elsewhere. And since I see no point in repeatedly registering these many differences with other scholars' interpretations – whether small, or more typically, very large – my citations consist mainly of works that, one way or another, are informative relative to my own. As these are the basis of my bibliography, it is but a partial reflection of all works consulted.

The Platonian Leviathan

A Melvillian Overture:
Moby-Dick and Philosophy

The whale, like all things that are mighty,
wears a false brow to the common world.

By way of concluding his provocatively titled chapter 'Of the Monstrous Pictures of Whales,' Melville's Ishmael provides the following summary caution:

> Though elephants have stood for their full-lengths, the living Leviathan has never yet fairly floated himself for his portrait. The living whale, in his full majesty and significance, is only to be seen at sea in unfathomable waters; and afloat the vast bulk of him is out of sight, like a launched line-of-battle ship;[1] and out of that element it is a thing eternally impossible for mortal man to hoist him bodily into the air, so as to preserve all his mighty swells and undulations. And, not to speak of the highly presumable difference of contour between a young sucking whale and a full-grown Platonian Leviathan ... it is one of the more curious things about this Leviathan, that his skeleton gives very little idea of his general shape ... For all these reasons, then, any way you may look at it, you must needs conclude that the great Leviathan is that one creature in the world which must remain unpainted to the last. True, one portrait may hit the mark much nearer than another, but none can hit it with any very considerable degree of exactness. So there is no earthly way of finding out precisely what the whale really looks like. And the only mode in which you can derive even a tolerable idea of his living contour, is by going a whaling yourself.[2]

A full-grown *Platonian* Leviathan? To a reader familiar with the standard scholarly views of Plato and Hobbes, the very idea must seem a philosophical oxymoron. Nonetheless, surely it is possible that a thoughtful nineteenth-century novelist, himself born and bred in the regime that more than any other owes its character to the vision of Thomas Hobbes, could have noticed and pondered certain peculiarities in that philosopher's presentation of his political prescription – having 'considered it himselfe, without the help of any interested, or envious Interpreter' – and so detected subtle hints pointing to its deeper interpretation, intimations that have been passed over, unappreciated, by virtually all other readers. Doubtless, stranger things have happened in the long twilit history of political philosophy.

Might Melville, then, be right: that all the standard portrayals of the Hobbesian regime are more or less inadequate – perhaps because the skeleton its author has provided provides 'very little idea' of the 'shape' it takes on in actual political life? More precisely, and more intriguing still, is there a 'Platonic' interpretation of Hobbes's prescription, or even a Platonic version of the regime itself (whatever either of these possibilities might substantially mean) that has gone unattended by scholars and statesmen alike? It would seem the only way to answer such questions is, as our author insists, to 'go a whaling oneself.' That is, to undertake a radical re-examination of the book whereby the name 'Leviathan' entered our political lexicon, keeping a careful lookout for anything that might lend credence to Melville's unorthodox, not to say heretical, suggestion.

Or is there not a prior question that must be settled, namely, whether there is any reason for paying serious attention to Melville on this of all matters? One may concede that *Moby-Dick*[3] is a rich and rewarding novel in all sorts of respects, a masterpiece even, yet never for a moment presume it to be a source of interpretive insight with respect to Hobbes, Plato, or any other philosopher worth naming. What evidence is there that Melville's famous story about whaling was crafted with, whatever else, philosophical intentions in mind – and in particular, with Hobbes's *Leviathan* in mind? Quite a lot, actually. To be fair, a conclusive demonstration would require a comprehensive treatment of Melville's whole elaborate tapestry and likely be more voluminous than the text it addresses. For one would have to depict its overall design, as well as anatomize all of its pertinent parts, much as Ishmael does the Sperm whale. Needless to say, nothing remotely that ambitious is intended here – nor required, I hope, simply to arouse the interest of a moderately open-minded reader in the philosophical dimensions of *Moby-Dick*, and a corresponding respect for the philosophical insight of its author. For that modest purpose, assembling some of the passages explicitly referring to philosophy and philosophers, and adding a few of the more intriguing tacit allusions, should do the trick.

One might begin, however, by reflecting on Melville's profligate use of the term 'Leviathan.' For as a result of Hobbes's disinterring it to title his controversial magnum opus, and as one name for the regime delineated therein, the word comes trailing clouds of political implications. Nor can there be any doubt but that Melville is fully aware of these associations. A quote from the philosopher's treatise – 'By art is created that great Leviathan, called a Commonwealth or State–(in Latin, Civitas) which is but an artificial man' – figures as the twenty-first of the some eighty 'Extracts' that preface the text of the novel.[4] Also, the very final extract, supposedly a *'Whale Song,'* would seem to point straight to the heart of Hobbes's political teaching:

> Oh, the rare old Whale, mid storm and gale
> In his ocean home will be
> A giant in might, where might is right,
> And King of the boundless sea.

Hobbes explicitly acknowledges that he lifted the name from the forty-first chapter of Job,[5] 'Leviathan' being the sobriquet for that crocodilian sea monster whose description suited Hobbes's rhetorical purpose to a tee, especially the concluding two verses (nos. 33 and 34), which he quotes: *'There is nothing,* saith he, *on earth, to be compared with him. He is made so as not to be afraid. Hee seeth every high thing below him; and is King of all the children of pride.'*[6] However, Job is a biblical text that also figures prominently in *Moby-Dick* (as does the Old Testament generally). Indeed, the 'Epilogue' of the book begins with a rather awkward but otherwise nondescript line, pointedly identified as a quote from Job (it is a portion of Job 1:15; 'And I only am escaped alone to tell thee.').

That Melville was himself well-versed in the source of Hobbes's usage – thus well knew that in its original context the name referred, not to a whale, but to some enormous super-crocodile or dragon-like creature of the sea – is made clear in several ways, beginning with his Sub-Sub-Librarian's second extract: 'Leviathan maketh a path to shine after him; / One would think the deep to be hoary.' This is from Job 41:32 – the verse that *immediately precedes* the two that Hobbes himself quotes (though Melville has taken the liberty of replacing the Bible's 'He' with its antecedent, 'Leviathan'). And in chapter 32 of *Moby-Dick*, the narrator, reflecting upon the scale of the Baconian task he has taken upon himself (that of providing 'some systematized exhibition of the whale in his broad genera'), laments: 'What am I that I should essay to hook the nose of this leviathan! The awful tauntings in Job might well appal me. "Will he (the leviathan) make a covenant with thee? Behold the hope of him is vain!"' These remarks are adapted from Job 41, verses 1–2, 4, and 9. Most significant, however, is the set of ironic questions that Melville's Job-absorbed narrator poses in the centre of chapter 81, musing on a harpooned whale writhing deep below the three whaleboats that are secured to him:

Seems it credible that by three such thin threads the great Leviathan was suspended like the big weight to an eight day clock. Suspended? and to what? To three bits of board. Is this the creature of whom it was once so triumphantly said – 'Canst thou fill his skin with barbed irons? or his head with fish-spears? [cf. Job 41:7, as per the King James translation] The sword of him that layeth at him cannot hold, the spear, the dart, nor the habergeon [Job 41:26]: he esteemeth iron as straw [Job 41:27; the narrator has omitted '*and* brass as rotten wood,' and slightly altered the punctuation]; the arrow cannot make him flee [Job 41:28; omitted 'sling stones are turned with him into stubble,' and altered punctuation]; darts are counted as stubble; he laugheth at the shaking of a spear!' [Job 41:29; altered punctuation] This the creature? this he?' (356)

The correct answer to this thrice-asked, pseudo-rhetorical question is: 'No! – definitely not!' The creature as described in Job, and which served Hobbes so appropriately as the epithet for the form of polity he envisioned, is clearly *not* a whale (it has scales, a neck, nostrils, a nose – whereas, 'the whale has nothing that can properly be called a neck,' and 'the Sperm Whale ... has no proper nose'; ch. 70, 310, and ch. 79, 345). But no matter. As a simultaneous allusion to Hobbes, Scripture, and (by quoting the most intriguing clause in the King James Bible) to Shakespeare, the passage is brilliant. Here is the main point, however: Melville *knows* that the creature referred to in Hobbes's source is not a whale, and yet it still serves *his* purpose to assimilate – not crocodiles or sea dragons to whales – but Hobbes's book about a great 'Leviathan' to his own.

Melville's use of 'Leviathan' and 'Whale' interchangeably is more than a little strange, as his collection of extracts itself suggests. True, the name 'Leviathan' occurs several times in the Bible, apparently referring to various monsters of the sea – including whales such as gulped Jonah (this being the usual interpretation of his being swallowed by a 'great fish,' cited in the third extract) – as well as symbolically representing the formless Sea itself, Chaos, the Serpent, Satan, the whole Fallen World.[7] Especially interesting is Melville's fifth Extract quoted (from Isaiah), since it is so closely akin to the description of Leviathan in Job: 'In that day, the Lord with his sore, and great, and strong sword, shall punish Leviathan the piercing serpent, even Leviathan that crooked serpent; and he shall slay the dragon that is in the sea.'[8] Likewise the thirteenth: 'The great Leviathan that maketh the seas to seeth like boiling pan,' which would seem to have been adapted directly from Job 41:31, though the prodigiously well-read Melville rightly attributes it to *Lord Bacon's Version of the Psalms* (Bacon having appropriated the line from Job for his own purpose).[9]

The Extracts, however, are said to be a set of 'whale statements,' albeit of uncertain veracity, and presented 'higgledy-piggledy.'[10] The term 'Leviathan' appears in only nine of the eighty (in at least one instance, courtesy of Melville's amending the source), and in only three or four of those nine does 'Leviathan' refer to a *whale* (nos. 23 and 24, from Milton; no. 26, from Dryden; and perhaps no. 51, from Montgomery). Moreover, the inclusion of 'mad' Hamlet's contemptuous teasing of Polonius as to what a certain *cloud* looks like ('Very like a whale,' no. 16), and Edmund Burke's 'somewhere' characterizing *Spain* as 'a great whale stranded on the shores of Europe' (no. 43), are sufficient indications that the ruling purpose in selecting these extracts *cannot* be simply, as implied, to provide 'a glancing bird's eye view of what has been promiscuously said, thought, fancied, or sung of Leviathan' (supposedly meaning 'whale'). Similarly suspect are Melville's culling from Boswell the jibe Goldsmith directed at Johnson ('If you should write a fable for little fishes, you would make them speak like great whales,' no. 38); and Eckermann's report of his and Goethe's learning from a Berlin newspaper 'that whales had been introduced on the stage there' (no. 57). For that matter, the line 'extracted' from Hobbes's Introduction to *Leviathan* ('By art is created that great Leviathan') is equally impertinent as an indication of 'what has been promiscuously said, thought, fancied, or sung' about actual creatures of the sea, however conceived.

Suffice it to say, Melville's apparently indifferent use of 'Leviathan' for 'Whale' is at least unusual, but all the more interesting in that *The Whale* is his book's alternative title.[11] Seen in light of his persistent interest in the peculiar problems of the American regime, however – especially those arising from the anomalous institution of slavery and the threat it posed to civil peace – it is not so unlikely that Melville would have Hobbes, philosophical grandfather of this regime, in the back of his mind throughout the writing of *Moby-Dick*.[12] Melville's lifelong preoccupation with the American regime is well attested and widely recognized by scholars.[13] It is the subject of much of his poetry; his *Battle Pieces* is an album of poems chronicling the Civil War from John Brown's raid to Lincoln's assassination.[14] *White-Jacket* (1849), the novel that immediately preceded *Moby-Dick*, is set upon an American frigate, and amounts to Melville's exposé of the un-American character of the Navy's hierarchical structure of power and privilege; also, in treating flogging as a symbol of man's inhumanity to man, 'he contributed to the escalating debate about slavery.'[15] His later historical novel, *Israel Potter*, set during and after the American Revolution, both satirizes and laments the discrepancy between the high ideals of that great historical event and the political reality that too soon resulted. *Benito Cereno* (the best known of his *Piazza Tales*, first published separately in 1855, i.e., four years after *Moby-Dick*), is an elaborate psycho-political allegory woven from an actual encounter of a naive and almost wilfully obtuse New England sea captain with a Spanish vessel that had been seized by the slaves it was transporting.[16] Melville's wonderfully comic *The Confidence Man* has been shown to be, whatever else, a satire on the leading American politicians of the day.[17] Given the constancy of Melville's absorption with the enduring problems of politics, and in particular with those most affecting the modern liberal democratic regime,[18] it is no wonder that he would have a commensurate interest in the writings of political philosophers. And inasmuch as the relationship between philosophy and politics is itself foremost among the enduring problems for political philosophy, it is no more surprising that he would have an interest in philosophy per se, as his masterpiece amply proves.

'*Call me Ishmael.*' So begins the narrator of this tale, told some indefinite number of years after the adventure it recounts ('never mind how long precisely'), and thus told with whatever benefit his further intellectual maturity might impart to the telling. Evidently his name is of some importance. It is, of course, an Old Testament name, hence freighted with the connotations associated with his biblical namesake. And to be sure, the story of Ishmael (Genesis 16–25) is a most extraordinary one, having endless historical significance if taken at face value, and philosophical significance even if not.

Briefly, Ishmael was the son whom Abraham fathered, at his barren wife's suggestion, on her Egyptian maid, a slave named Hagar. Once pregnant, however, Hagar behaved contemptuously towards her mistress (Sarai, or Sarah, as she eventually became known). When the wife complained of this, her husband said, 'Behold, thy maid *is* in thy hand; do to her as it pleaseth thee.' In response to Sarai's resulting harsh treatment of her, Hagar fled into the wilderness. There an angel of the Lord found her resting by a spring of water and counselled her, 'Return to thy mistress and submit thyself under her hands ... I will multiply thy seed exceedingly, that it shalt not be numbered for multitude ... Behold, thou *art* with child, and shalt bear a son, you shalt call his name Ishmael [i.e., 'God hears']; because the LORD hath heard thy affliction.' Subsequently, God cured Sarai's barrenness, who then bore a son named Isaac. As for Abraham, God assured him, 'behold, my covenant *is* with thee, and thou shalt be a father of many nations.' Later, Sarah, alarmed at the sight of Hagar's son playing with Isaac, and angered at the thought that her son might have to share his inheritance with his half-brother, insisted that the mother and son be cast out. Abraham was displeased, but God consoled him: 'And also of the son of the bondswoman will I make a nation, because he *is* thy seed.' So Hagar and Ishmael were sent away and wandered in the wilderness of Beer-sheba, where they would have perished of thirst had God not responded to the cries of young Ishmael (one of His angels again providing directions to Hagar):[19] 'And God was with the lad; and he grew, and dwelt in the wilderness, and became an archer.' Somehow Ishmael and Isaac eventually met again, as both were present at the burial of their father. Ishmael himself died at the ripe age of 137. However, his descendants the Ishmaelites later became enemies of God's chosen people, the Israelites descended from Isaac (and in the Israelites' eyes at least, enemies of God as well, judging from Psalms 83:2–6).[20]

'Call me Ishmael.' Fair enough, although almost no one in his story ever does.[21] But Melville's Ishmael has a philosophical streak unremarked of his biblical namesake, a trait moreover that seems to become more pronounced as his story unfolds, though it is subtly hinted in almost the first words he speaks. He explains his going to sea as his way of escaping from a growing morbid and aggressive discontent on land, such that he 'requires a strong moral principle' to restrain him from gratuitously knocking off the hats of everyone he meets: 'then, I account it high time to get to sea as soon as I can. This is my substitute for pistol and ball. With a philosophical flourish Cato throws himself upon his sword; I quietly take to the ship.'

However, Ishmael assures us that when he feels the urge to go to sea, he goes as neither Captain nor Cook, much less as a paying passenger ('there is all the difference in the world between paying and being paid'),[22] but 'as a simple sailor,' prepared to be ordered about, unpleasant though this be at first: 'It touches one's sense of honor,' especially if one comes from an old established family on the land, or has been (say) 'lording it as a country schoolmaster': 'The transition is a keen one, I assure you, from a schoolmaster to a sailor, and requires a strong decoction of Seneca and the Stoics to enable you to grin and bear it.' As for being ordered to sweep the deck by some old hunk of a sea captain, there is no indignity in that, seen from a divine perspective. 'Who ain't a slave' in one way or another, 'either in a physical or metaphysical point of view?' (ch. 1, 5–6).

But having previously been a merchant seaman, why did he decide this time round to ship on a whaler? Ishmael admits, 'I cannot tell why it was exactly that those stage managers, the Fates, put me down for this shabby part of a whaling voyage, when others were set down for magnificent parts in high tragedies, and short and easy parts in genteel comedies, and jolly parts in farces.' As for his conscious motives, 'Chief among [them] was the overwhelming idea of the great whale himself. Such a portentous and mysterious monster roused all my curiosity.' And the very perils of hunting it were attractive.[23] A further inducement was that its environs were so far removed from familiar locales: 'I am tormented with an ever-lasting itch for things remote. I love to sail forbidden seas, and land on barbarous coasts' (ch. 1, 7).

Upon deciding to go awhaling, Ishmael sets out for Nantucket, original home of American whalers. But missing the ferry packet to the island, he finds himself marooned in New Bedford, more recently become the effective capital of the whaling business. Obliged to find cheap lodging, he fixes upon The Spouter-Inn, where he ends up sharing a bed with an expert harpooner, the heathenishly tattooed 'cannibal' from the South Seas named Queequeg – destined to become his partner, teacher, and 'bosom friend.' Ishmael describes Queequeg as a man whose character was formed in what Rousseau at least would acknowledge to be a State of Nature, and who thus remains essentially an alien amid New England civilization ('He was just enough civilized to show off his outlandishness in the strangest possible manner'; ch. 4, 27). But almost from the beginning of their acquaintance, Ishmael credits this experienced whale hunter and exemplary 'Pagan' with qualities that are as revealing about Ishmael as Queequeg:

[S]avages are strange beings; at times you do not know exactly how to take them. At first they are overawing; their calm self-collectness of simplicity seems a Socratic wisdom. I had noticed also that Queequeg never consorted at all, or but very little, with the other seamen in the inn ... All this struck me as mighty singular; yet, upon second thoughts, there was something almost sublime in it. Here was a man some twenty thousand miles from home, by the way of Cape Horn, that is – which was the only way he could get there – thrown among people as strange to him as though he were in the planet Jupiter; and yet he seemed entirely at his ease; preserving the utmost serenity; content with his own companionship; always equal to himself. Surely this was a touch of fine philosophy; though no doubt he had never heard there was such a thing as that. But, perhaps, to be true philosophers, we mortals should not be conscious of so living or so striving. So soon as I hear that such or such a man gives himself out for a philosopher, I conclude that like the dyspeptic old woman, he must have 'broken his digester.' (ch. 10, 50)

Ishmael tells of visiting the Whaleman's Chapel in New Bedford, where he has the opportunity to contemplate the marble plaques memorializing men lost in the whale fisheries. He muses that most people's attitudes towards their dear Departed are paradoxical, in that they grieve for them, while nonetheless claiming that they dwell in 'unspeakable bliss.' He admits to entertaining heterodox views: 'Methinks we have hugely mistaken this matter of Life and Death. Methinks that what they call my shadow here on earth is my true substance. Methinks that in looking at things spiritual, we are too much like oysters observing the sun through the water, and thinking that thick water the thinnest air. Methinks my body is but the lees of my better being. In fact take my body who will, take it I say, it is not me' (ch. 7, 37). What is especially interesting about both his conclusions and the images he uses to express them (significantly in chapter 7),[24] is that they are lifted more or less directly from Plato's *Phaedo*, wherein is depicted Sokrates's final conversation – also concerning mortality and the human soul – preceding his death by hemlock.[25] This is the very dialogue Ishmael refers to in his later warning the 'ship-owners of Nantucket' to beware of enlisting any lad 'given to unseasonable meditativeness; and who offers to ship with the Phaedon instead of Bowditch in his head' (ch. 35, 158).[26] Melville's Ishmael, it seems, is something of a Platonist, 'all [his] curiosity' aroused by 'the overwhelming idea of the great whale himself.'

Thus, by a quarter of the way into Ishmael's narrative, the ground has been prepared for a philosophical confession. It comes in the thirty-fifth chapter, entitled 'The Masthead.' Ishmael is taking his turn on lookout for whales, perched high atop the mainmast of the ship. It provides him an occasion for reflecting on masthead manning through the ages, 'ashore or afloat,' beginning with the Egyptians ('a nation of mast-head standers') and before them 'the builders of Babel' whose efforts were frustrated by the wrath of God.[27] Compared with the Ancients, the Moderns don't fare so well: 'Of modern standers-of-mast-heads we have but a lifeless set; mere stone, iron, and bronze men;[28] who, though well capable of facing out a stiff gale, are still entirely incompetent to the business of singing out upon discovering any strange sight' (154–5).

Ishmael admits that, from a practical point of view, he was a sorry guardian of the ship's primary business: 'With the problem of the universe revolving in me, how could I – being left completely to myself at such a thought-engendering altitude – how could I but lightly hold my obligations to observe all whale-ships' standing orders, "Keep your weather eye open, and sing out every time."' Here, then, Ishmael, speaking with an authority that only personal experience can establish, admonishes the ship owners to beware of enlisting 'any lad with lean brow and hollow eye [and] given to unseasonable meditativeness':

Beware of such a one, I say: your whales must be seen before they can be killed; and this sunken-eyed young Platonist will tow you ten wakes around the world, and never make you one pint of sperm the richer. Nor are these monitions at all unneeded. For nowadays, the whale-fishery furnishes an asylum for many romantic, melancholy, and absent-minded young men, disgusted with the carking cares of earth, and seeking sentiment in tar and blubber ... Very often do the captains of such ships take those absent-minded young philosophers to task, upbraiding them with not feeling sufficient 'interest' in the voyage; half-hinting that they are so hopelessly lost to all honorable ambition, as that in their secret souls they would rather not see whales than otherwise. But all in vain; those young Platonists have a notion that their vision is imperfect; they are short-sighted; what use, then, to strain the visual nerve?[29] They have left their opera glasses at home ...

[B]ut lulled into such an opium-like listlessness of vacant, unconscious reverie is this absent-minded youth by the blending cadence of waves with thoughts, that at last he loses his identity; takes the mystic ocean at his feet for the visible image of that deep, blue, bottomless soul, pervading mankind and nature; and every strange, half-seen, gliding, beautiful thing that eludes him; every dimly-discovered, uprising fin of some undiscernible form, seems to him the embodiment of those elusive thoughts that only people the soul by continually flitting through it. In this enchanted mood, thy spirit ebbs away to whence it came; becomes diffused through time and space; like Wickliff's sprinkled Pantheistic ashes, forming at last a part of every shore the round globe over.

There is no life in thee, now, except that rocking life imparted by a gently rolling ship; by her, borrowed from the sea; by the sea, from the inscrutable tides of God. But while this sleep, this dream is on ye, move your foot or hand an inch, slip your hold at all; and your identity comes back in horror. Over Descartian vortices you hover. And perhaps, at midday, in the fairest weather, with one half-throttled shriek you drop through that transparent air into the summer sea, no more to rise forever. Heed it well, ye Pantheists! (158–9)

As in this passage, Platonic and Sokratic allusions season Ishmael's story throughout, along with references to other philosophers and philosophy. He once describes the condition of his ship as being as 'top-heavy ... as a dinnerless student with all Aristotle in his head' (ch. 110, 476). And his avowal, 'I am one of those that never take on about princely fortunes, and am quite content if the world is ready to board and lodge me' (ch. 16, 76), has a distinctly Sokratic ring, reminding one of the reward the old philosopher claimed for having been the city's greatest benefactor: its gadfly.[30] Similarly Sokratic – and Hobbesian – is Ishmael's concern for essential definitions: 'To be short, then, a whale is *a spouting fish with a horizontal tail*. There you have him. However contracted, that definition is the result of expanded meditation' (ch. 32, 137; cf. *Leviathan* IV/12–13, 15). The traditional philosophical attitude, depreciatory of mere mortal concerns,[31] hence more inclined to the Comedic than the Tragic view of life, is well captured in the curiously named chapter, 'The Hyena' (no. 49). Having just been rescued from a near brush with death, Ishmael muses:

There are certain queer times and occasions in this strange mixed affair we call life when a man takes this whole universe for a vast practical joke, though the wit thereof he but dimly discerns, and more than suspects that the joke is at nobody's expense but his own. However, nothing dispirits, and nothing seems worth while disputing. He bolts down all events, all creeds, and beliefs, and persuasions, all hard things visible and invisible, never mind how knobby; as an ostrich of potent digestion gobbles down bullets and gun flints. And as for small difficulties and worryings, prospects of sudden disaster, peril of life and limb; all these, and death itself, seem to him only sly, good-natured hits, and jolly punches in the side bestowed by the unseen and unaccountable old joker. That odd sort of wayward mood I am speaking of, comes over a man only in some time of extreme tribulation; it comes in the very midst of his earnestness, so that what just before might have seemed to him a thing most momentous, now seems but a part of the general joke. There is nothing like the perils of whaling to breed this free and easy sort of genial, desperado philosophy; and with it I now regarded this whole voyage of the Pequod, and the great White Whale its object. (226)

Ishmael expresses a companion view on a later occasion, again meditating on the dangers of whaling in the broader context of human life: 'All men live enveloped in whale-lines. All are born with halters round their necks; but it is only when caught in the swift, sudden turn of death, that mortals realize the silent, subtle, ever-present perils of life. And if you be a philosopher, though seated in the whale-boat, you would not at heart feel one whit more terror, than though seated before your evening fire with a poker, and not a harpoon, by your side' (ch. 60, 281).[32]

And who but a philosophical initiate would – or *could* – propose the analogy Melville has Ishmael express upon the occasion of the *Pequod*'s crew happening to have captured both a Right whale and a Sperm whale. They moored them (as per the standard practice) on opposite sides of the ship. In first hoisting the head of the Sperm, the ship heeled far over to one side, then in hoisting the Right's head it leaned the opposite way: 'by the counterpoise of both heads, she regained her even keel; though sorely strained, you may well believe.' Having summoned that image, Ishmael observes, 'So, when on one side you hoist in Locke's head, you go over that way; but now, on the other side, hoist in Kant's and you come back again; but in very poor plight. Thus, some minds for ever keep trimming boat. Oh, ye foolish! throw all these thunderheads overboard, and then you'll float light and right' (ch. 73, 327).

The naturally dialectical Ishmael treats the immediate adjacency of the two whales' heads as offering an ideal 'chance to study practical cetology.' The terms of his comparison speak volumes about him:

Can you catch the expression of the Sperm Whale's there? It is the same he died with, only some of the longer wrinkles in the forehead seem now faded away. I think his broad brow to be full of a prairie-like placidity, born of a speculative indifference as to death. But mark the other head's expression. See that amazing lower lip, pressed by accident against the vessel's side, so as firmly to embrace the jaw. Does not this whole head seem to speak of an enormous practical resolution in facing death? This Right Whale I take to have been a Stoic; the Sperm Whale, a Platonian, who might have taken up Spinoza in his latter years.' (ch. 75, 335)

Nor is it irrelevant that throughout his tale, Ishmael stresses that it is this Platonian whale, the Sperm, that is the most powerful, fearless, hence dangerously warlike of the whales. And in speaking of those 'ponderous profound beings' whose heads, like those of broaching whales, Ishmael is somehow sure give off 'a semi-visible steam while in the act of thinking deep thoughts,' the first such thinker that comes to his mind is Plato (followed by Pyrrho, the Devil, Jupiter, and Dante; ch. 85, 374).

However, it is an episode near the centre of his narrative that leads to Ishmael's – hence indirectly Melville's – most self-revealing statement. The story effectively begins (appropriately enough) in chapter 77 with his description of the huge cavity in the sperm whale's battering-ram head, which 'contains by far the most precious of all his oily vintages; namely, the highly-prized spermaceti, in its absolutely pure, limpid, and odoriferous state.' He likens this chamber to the famously enormous Great Heidelburgh Tun. When a sperm whale has been killed and its body towed to the ship, it is decapitated and the head suspended vertically alongside. With a full-grown specimen measuring some eighty feet long, and its head being a third of its length, 'you have more than twenty-six feet for the depth of the tun' (340). An opening is carefully cut in the top of the head to admit a bucket whereby the precious fluid can be extracted, a bucketful at a time, the bucket being guided down and ever deeper into the chamber on the end of a pole wielded by a sailor poised at the hole for that purpose.

On the occasion in question, the man executing this delicate task was one of the harpoonists, a 'wild Indian' named Tashtego. After some eighty or ninety buckets of spermaceti had been hoisted out, a series of accidents brought about a near disaster. Tashtego lost his grip or his footing and 'dropped head-foremost down into this great Tun of Heidelburgh, and with a horrible oily gurgling, went clean out of sight!' Meanwhile, the head of the whale bobbed 'just below the surface of the sea, as if that moment seized with some momentous idea.' Then the suspended head broke loose and began to sink, Tashtego trapped inside. He was saved by the quick action of Queequeg, who dove into the sea and cut open a breech in the sinking head. Ishmael, in describing the action, likens the extraction of Tashtego to a complicated birthing of a baby: 'And thus, through the courage and great skill in obstetrics of Queequeg, the deliverance, or rather, delivery of Tashtego, was successfully accomplished … which is a lesson by no means to be forgotten. Midwifery should be taught in the same course with fencing and boxing, riding and rowing.' Midwifery of the soul, assisting others to give birth to the ideas tumbling about in their heads, is precisely the skill Sokrates claims to practise through dialogue,[33] which he sometimes likens to verbal wrestling, boxing, or other sorts of combat training.[34] Ishmael concludes his account of this remarkable entombment and rescue by observing:

Now, had Tashtego perished in that head, it had been a very precious perishing; smothered in the very whitest and daintiest of fragrant spermaceti; coffined, hearsed, and tombed in the secret inner chamber and sanctum sanctorum of the whale. Only one sweeter end can be readily recalled – the delicious death of an Ohio honey-hunter, who seeking honey in the crotch of a hollow tree, found such exceeding store of it, that leaning too far over, it sucked him in, so that he died embalmed. How many, think ye, have likewise fallen into Plato's honey head, and sweetly perished there? (ch. 78, 344)

With respect to such 'sweet perishing,' it is worth recalling the maxim passed down from antiquity – and credited to Sokrates in particular – that to philosophize is to learn how to die.[35]

To summarize: Melville's Ishmael displays a practitioner's intimacy with philosophy in its various garbs and colours, and a depth and breadth of familiarity with philosophic literature more than adequate to qualify his creator as a possible source of philosophical insight and inspiration. And while a multiplicity of philosophic problems and doctrines figure in his story, they all tend to coalesce around a central theme – and that not a surprising one, given the shadowy presence of both Plato and Hobbes that haunts this tale.

The political interpretation of *Moby-Dick*, based largely upon linguistic, symbolic, and analogic associations,[36] is not the whole story, perhaps not even the main story, Melville means to tell in this whale of a book. But as Ishmael observes, having set out to compose his own whale book, 'To produce a mighty book, you must choose a mighty theme. No great and enduring volume can ever be written on the flea, though many there be who have tried it.' (How true on both counts!) What, then, *is* the mighty theme of *Moby-Dick*, if not Man and the State and whatever is entailed in understanding them? As for just what *is* entailed, the greatest works of political philosophy, such as Plato's *Republic* and Hobbes's *Leviathan*, provide substantial exemplifications. Works of this stature necessarily range beyond the 'political' as it is usually (that is, more or less narrowly) conceived. For a genuine understanding of political life requires an adequate grasp of the larger, trans-political setting, the embracive natural order in which all political living proceeds, as well as of the human capacity for understanding per se. Thus Ishmael-as-Aspiring-Author pleads:

One often hears of writers that rise and swell with their subject, though it may seem but an ordinary one. How, then, with me, writing of this Leviathan? ... Friends, hold my arms! For in the mere act of penning my thoughts of this Leviathan, they weary me, and make me faint with their outreaching comprehensiveness of sweep, as if to include the whole circle of the sciences, and all the generations of whales, and men, and mastodons, past, present, and to come, with all the revolving panoramas of empire on earth, and throughout the whole universe, not excluding its suburbs. Such, and so magnifying, is the virtue of a large and liberal theme! (ch. 104, 456)

Ishmael had prefaced this with the admission that 'Applied to any other creature than the Leviathan ... portly terms might justly be deemed unwarrantably grandiloquent. But when Leviathan is the text, the case is altered.'

'When Leviathan is the text'; when one is dealing with 'a large and liberal theme' – suggestive phrases, to say the least. Given the pattern of allusions (only some of which I have cited thus far), the possibility that *Moby-Dick* is, whatever else, a Hobbes-inspired political allegory cannot be blithely dismissed.[37] Moreover, there is ample evidence that Melville in crafting such an allegory was capable of bringing a Platonic perspective to bear on Hobbes's handiwork. But as I conceded at the outset, proving this (or any other interpretive thesis) in a comprehensive way would be a mighty task, and not to the purpose of this book. I shall return to the allegorical interpretation of the *Pequod* as a Hobbesian Commonwealth, though only by way of a Coda, since the elaboration I provide there presupposes the deeper understanding of Hobbes's political teaching I argue for in the intervening chapters. For now, let me simply conclude this Overture to my own 'whale cantata' by citing a few considerations that add further plausibility to the possibility.

First, there is the fact that the term 'leviathan' was used pejoratively by writers in the debates that preceded the American Civil War. For example, Theodore Parker, writing in 1848 (three years before the publication of *Moby-Dick*), warned, 'It is not to be supposed that the Leviathan of American slavery will allow himself to be drawn out of the mere in which he made his nest ... without some violence and floundering.'[38] The political intractability of the slavery problem, despite the deep philosophical contradiction it posed for the American version of a Hobbesian regime, figures persistently in Melville's published writings, albeit often esoterically, as, for example, in his allegorical novel *Mardi* (1848), wherein Melville has his Babbalanga observe: 'Humanity cries out against this vast enormity: – not one man knows a prudent remedy. Blame not, then, the North; and wisely judge the South.'[39]

There can be little question that Melville generally favoured an esoteric treatment of matters that he regarded as politically or morally sensitive, and that he had a keen eye and nose for esotericism in the practice of other writers he admired, including Hobbes.[40] As he wrote, anonymously, about his friend Nathaniel Hawthorne (to whom *Moby-Dick* is dedicated) and about Shakespeare (the philosopher-poet he most revered), and implicitly about Hobbes's view of human nature:

Certain it is ... that this great power of blackness in [Hawthorne] derives its force from its appeals to that Calvinistic sense of Innate Depravity and Original sin, from whose visitations, in some shape or other, no deeply thinking mind is always and wholly free. For in certain moods, no man can weigh this world, without throwing in something, somehow like Original Sin, to strike the uneven balance ... This blackness it is that furnishes the infinite obscure of his background, – that background against which Shakespeare plays his grandest conceits, the things that have made for Shakespeare his loftiest, but most circumscribed renown, as the profoundest of thinkers.[41] For by philosophers Shakespeare is not adored as the great man of tragedy and comedy ... But it is those deep faraway things in him; those occasional flashings-forth of the intuitive truth in him; those short, quick probings at the very axis of reality; – these are the things that make Shakespeare, Shakespeare. Through the mouths of the dark characters of Hamlet, Timon, Lear, and Iago, he craftily says, or insinuates the things, which we feel to be so terrifically true, that it were all but madness for any good man, in his own proper character, to utter, or even hint of them ... And if I magnify Shakespeare, it is not so much for what he did do, as for what he did not do, or refrained from doing. For in this world of lies, Truth is forced to fly like a scared white doe in the woodlands; and only by cunning glimpses will she reveal herself, as in Shakespeare and other masters of the great Art of Telling the Truth, – even if it be covertly, and by snatches.[42]

As this statement makes clear enough, Melville well appreciated that the Truth, the whole Truth and nothing but, is not suited for everyone. That far from being life-enhancing for most people, who are not indiscriminate lovers of the truth whatsoever it be – not philosophers, that is – certain truths about human existence would prove an intolerable burden to them, or at least to the better sort: those with some depth of soul. And that as such, it is irresponsible, indeed misanthropic, to pronounce, plainly and bluntly, all that one knows, or thinks, or believes, or even merely suspects, regardless of how dispiriting the effects may be for non-philosophical souls.

Esotericism serves more than prophylactic purposes, however. Melville understands that it can contribute positively to philosophy insofar as the challenge of comprehending it actively engages the reader, exercising (thus strengthening) his various rational powers: of observation, analysis, imagination, memory, and synthetic judgment. To that extent, esotericism encourages the naturally thoughtful reader to experience philosophizing first-hand, perhaps thereby awakening and afterwards sustaining an expanding philosophical interest. It is to this end that Melville hints, for example, of the special significance of the elaborate tattooing that adorned Queequeg:

[It] had been the work of a departed prophet and seer of his island, who, by those hieroglyphic marks, had written out on his body a complete theory of the heavens and the earth, and a mystical treatise on the art of attaining truth; so that Queequeg in his own proper person was a riddle to unfold; a wondrous work in one volume; but whose mysteries not even himself could read, though his own live heart beat against them.' (ch. 110, 480–1)

Thus we are invited to attempt to unfold the riddle of Queequeg – not, however, by deciphering tattoos left to our imaginations, but in the same way that Ishmael claims to have resolved a certain historical question: 'If, then, you properly put statements together, and reason upon them a bit' (ch. 45, 210). Indeed, one may regard this promoting of philosophical *activity* in readers naturally suited for it as the defining characteristic of genuinely philosophical writing (not, that is, the conveying of doctrines, so-called 'philosophies'). Consequently, philosophers have been among the most ingenious inventors and clever employers of the various means of esoteric communication – and none more adeptly, I shall argue, than Thomas Hobbes.[43] But Melville also, who aspired to be a philosopher in the old mould,[44] practised esoteric writing for the same reasons philosophers always have.

Melville's Ishmael several times alludes to there being awful truths, but does so mostly in such elliptical or formal terms as will pass most readers by without much effect. One example is in chapter 23, where Ishmael is musing about the man at the helm named Bulkington:

Know ye, now, Bulkington? Glimpses do ye seem to see of that mortally intolerable truth; that all deep, earnest thinking is but the intrepid effort of the soul to keep the open independence of her sea; while the wildest winds of heaven and earth conspire to cast her on the treacherous, slavish shore?

But in landlessness alone resides the highest truth, shoreless, indefinite as God – so, better it is to perish in that howling infinite, than be ingloriously dashed upon the lee, even if that were safety! (106–7)

As all students of *Leviathan* are aware, the incorrigible indefiniteness of God is a cardinal doctrine also preached – repeatedly – by Hobbes (e.g., III/12, 11; XXXI/28, 191; XXXIV/4, 208; XLVI/23, 374).

Later in Ishmael's odyssey (ch. 96), a brush with disaster moves him to conclude: 'The truest of all men was the Man of Sorrows, and the truest of all books is Solomon's, and Ecclesiastes is the fine hammered steel of woe. "All is vanity." ALL. This wilful world hath not got hold of unchristian Solomon's wisdom yet' (424). Parenthetically, this praise of 'unchristian Solomon's wisdom' is but one strand in a pattern of evidence suggesting that Melville endorses Bacon's treatment of Solomon as the Bible's version of a philosopher-king.[45] Melville shares with Bacon, Shakespeare, Hobbes, and Nietzsche a strong preference for the Old Testament perspective over that of the New.

Melville's more substantial indications of terrible but possible truths he has placed in the mouth of Captain Ahab, who (Ishmael repeatedly assures us) is mad – but mad in a peculiar way. For Melville has cast Ahab as a deranged perversion of the philosophic nature, the natural order of his soul inverted, with the result that his wilful spirit – seat of his voracious desire for vengeance – commands his reason.[46] Choosing to name the monomaniacal Captain of his whale hunters' Ship of State after the seventh King of Israel constitutes still another important link to Hobbes's *Leviathan*. Not that Melville has anything less than the full biblical story of King Ahab in mind (I Kings 16:29–22:40), of whom Scripture says, 'Ahab the son of Omri did evil in the sight of the LORD more than all that *were* before him,' and 'Ahab did more to provoke the LORD, the God of

Israel, to anger than all the kings of Israel who were before him' (16:30, 33). Although Hobbes refers to only one episode in Ahab's story – Micaiah's contradicting the pro-war advice of the four hundred, warning instead of Ahab's defeat and death – he does so no less than three times (XXXII/7, 196–7; XXXIV/8, 209; XXXVI/19, 231). By such an emphasis, Hobbes too, then, may intend to summon to a thoughtful reader's mind other notable features of King Ahab and his disastrous reign, to say nothing of the pernicious influence of Jezebel, his idolatrous Queen (having conveniently provided the relevant Scriptural citation).

Suffice it to say, there is no shortage of features woven into *Moby-Dick* that are suggestive of Hobbes's *Leviathan* – for instance, Ishmael's reasoning that his version of the 'Golden Rule' ('to do to my fellow man what I would have my fellow man do to me') is simply 'the will of God' (ch. 10, 52). No less than seven English variations and one Latin version of this same rule figure in Hobbes's text, who likewise contends that this formula summarizes the Laws of Nature, which are 'dictates of Reason' and as such may be understood to be 'the word of God' (XV/35 and 41, 79–80).[47] As for God and gods, Melville, like Hobbes, comes perilously close to claiming divine status for his leviathan: '[I]n the great Sperm Whale, this high and mighty god-like dignity inherent in the brow is so immensely amplified, that gazing on it, in that full front view, you feel the Deity and the dread powers more forcibly than in beholding any other object in living nature' (ch. 79, 346). Hobbes likewise attributes godlike status to his creation: 'This is the Generation of that great LEVIATHAN, or rather (to speak more reverently) of that *Mortall God*' (XVII/13, 87).

Indeed, could there be a more obvious Hobbesian echo than Ishmael's observation, 'Long exile from Christendom and civilization inevitably restores a man to that condition in which God placed him, *i.e.* what is called savagery' (ch. 57, 270)?

The curious parallels between these two great books, Melville's *The Whale* and Hobbes's *Leviathan*, could be multiplied (and will be in my Coda). But I presume my basic point has been made with those for whom it is possible to make it: that there is reason enough to regard Melville as a serious student of our intellectual tradition, and of the writings of Plato and Hobbes in particular, to treat his elliptical suggestion of a Platonian Leviathan as a hypothesis worth exploring. The possibility is the more intriguing in that the seemingly straightforward interpretation of Hobbes's treatise, however persuasive to practically minded readers, presents so many theoretical puzzles, paradoxes, implausibilities, and apparent contradictions as to render incredible the idea that a man as brilliant as Hobbes could have himself shared this exoteric understanding. That being the case, one can only assume its purpose is either rhetorical-political, or pedagogical, or both (as the writings of political philosophers typically are), and so proceed to understand the function of this carefully crafted surface in light of a more philosophically credible teaching which presumably underlies it. The balance of this book records the results of my attempt to do just that.

At a Grand Committee some days ago, this important discovery was made by a certain curious and refined observer: that seamen have a custom when they meet a *whale*, to fling him out an empty *tub* by way of amusement, to divert him from laying violent hands upon the ship. This parable was immediately mythologized; the whale was interpreted to be Hobbes's *Leviathan*, which tosses and plays with all schemes of Religion and Government, whereof a great many are hollow, and dry, and empty, and noisy, and wooden, and given to rotation. This is the *Leviathan* whence the terrible wits of our age are said to borrow their weapons. The *ship* in danger is easily understood to be its old antitype, the Commonwealth. But how to analyze the tub was a matter of difficulty.

– Jonathan Swift, 'Preface' to *A Tale of a Tub*

PART ONE

The Problematical *Leviathan*: Κακοφονία

There is a certain Philosophia prima, *on which all other Philosophy ought to depend; and consisteth principally, in right limiting of the significations of such Appellations, or Names, as are of all others the most Universall.* (XLVI/14, 371)

Although Hobbes involves himself with metaphysical matters from the very first sentence of his *Leviathan*, only near its conclusion – specifically in its penultimate chapter – does he first mention by name that 'on which all other Philosophy ought to depend.'[1] While this is stated in the context of discussing 'Vain Philosophy' derived mainly from Aristotle, it clearly is Hobbes's view. As he explains, the term 'Metaphysiques' bears two overlapping meanings: it is a synonym for First Philosophy in general; but it also refers to the treatises in which is presented Aristotle's own First Philosophy (whence Schoolmen derived the generic name: *meta-physica*, 'over-and-above Nature'). Hobbes's quarrels are all with the particulars of 'Aristotelity.' He would have his readers believe (or, to speak more cautiously here, have most of his readers believe) 'that scarce any thing can be more absurdly said in naturall Philosophy, than that which now is called *Aristotles Metaphysiques*' (XLVI/11, 370). But as regards the former, 'universal' meaning of the term, anyone who can think and who knows what sort of conceptions the name refers to must grant the logical priority of Metaphysics. This is so, whether or not one agrees with Hobbes's claim that *philosophia prima*, like all knowledge other than that of particular facts, is primarily, even exclusively, a linguistic matter. Moreover, given sufficient experience with the challenge of gaining an adequate Metaphysical view, one sees that the problems of First Philosophy, surely in practice if not in principle as well, are inextricably bound up with what has since come to be called 'Epistemology': knowledge about knowing and everything related thereto (e.g., perceiving, learning, remembering, reasoning, imagining, speculating, hypothesizing, believing, doubting – but especially language and its relation to both thought and things).

Hobbes indicates expressly what sorts of 'most Universall' terms are comprised by Metaphysics: 'the Definitions of Body, Time, Place, Matter, Forme, Essence, Subject, Substance, Accident, Power, Act, Finite, Infinite, Quantity, Quality, Motion, Action, Passion, and diverse others, necessary to the explaining of a mans Conceptions concerning the Nature and Generation of Bodies' (XLVI/14, 371). However, his emphasis on the literally fundamental importance of 'First Philosophy' simply underlines the puzzle posed by the manifest inadequacy of Hobbes's explicit treatment of the metaphysical issues he chooses to address. What is even more perplexing is the absence of any analysis whatsoever regarding other topics equally fundamental to the metaphysical position upon which he professes to base his political science. Most conspicuous by its absence from his list of Universals is 'Cause,' just as an analysis of causation is missing from the entire treatise.[2] Also missing is any mention here, or analysis anywhere, of Fortune or Chance or Luck (which, as Aristotle reminds us, people often speak of as if it were a cause of some things, or even of all things: that 'everything is due to chance').[3] And while Hobbes includes both Matter and Form in his list, he never provides any account of how either is to be properly defined, hence understood – this despite the treatise's subtitle 'The Matter, Forme, and Power of a COMMON-WEALTH.' Nor, consequently, does he address the question of what constitutes the 'natures' of various things (i.e., in what do their respective natures inhere, and how so), or how Nature as a whole is to be conceived. Merely asserting that 'the World' or 'the *Universe*' is 'the whole mass of all things that are' in no way suffices to explain the 'admirable *order*' of Nature that Hobbes himself refers to (XI/25, 51). His declining to address this question is the more perplexing, given his curious definition of 'admiration': '*Joy*, from apprehension of novelty, ADMIRATION; proper to Man, because it excites the appetite of knowing the *cause*' (VI/38, 26).

With respect to all of these topics – Cause, Chance, Form, Matter, Nature (among others) – Aristotle's *Metaphysics* remains rationally persuasive, if not simply definitive. Thus, reviewing his analyses is a particularly useful way of revealing some of the more glaring deficiencies of the metaphysical position Hobbes has staked out in the early chapters of his *Leviathan*. Moreover, clarity on these and other such issues – especially as they bear on materialism, determinism, hedonism, egoism, and the character of science – truly is, as Hobbes claims, of fundamental importance for philosophy in general, and not least of all *political* philosophy. For these issues enter directly into everyday political practice. People's opinions of what is real; of the ground of what is right and good, honourable and decent (the status of their so-called values); of the extent to which they are free and thus responsible for their actions; of their own relation to some enduring Whole – views about such matters impact political life profoundly.

I have reason to believe, however, that the majority of scholars who work in the field of political theory do not devote much time to probing these issues. Thus, studying Hobbes's masterwork has this special virtue, if one will but take advantage of it: it provides a convenient opportunity to consider, or reconsider, the most important metaphysical views that have shaped modernity. To be sure, the problems raised are challenging ones and have been of interest to philosophers since antiquity. Each has accordingly generated an extensive scholarly literature, most of it written in the past century or so by academic specialists. I have attempted to engage Hobbes on his own terms, however, which means assessing the inherent strengths and weaknesses of his own claims and arguments mainly in light of common sense, as augmented by the views of his philosophic predecessors as I understand them. Despite the fact that in taking up these questions of First Philosophy I am merely following Hobbes's lead, I, like him, must 'ask pardon of those who are not used to this kind of Discourse' (XLVI/15, 371), and who, being primarily interested in politics – especially Hobbes's account of politics – remain sceptical of any need for extensive excursions into the abstruse realm of metaphysicians. As for digressive expositions of Aristotle, such readers are apt to anticipate little more than tedium. By way of apology, I can offer only a confession and a promise.

First, the confession: judging from what I have read of recent Hobbes scholarship, including some of the most influential, I cannot help suspecting that many of its contributors lack sufficient familiarity with Aristotle's views to assess Hobbes's supposed rejection of them, or even to understand what is at stake. This can significantly limit, if not distort, one's interpretation of Hobbes's larger project. For example, he grossly misrepresents Aristotle's analysis of Chance and Fortune ('And in many occasions they [i.e., the Aristotelian Schoolmen] put for cause of Naturall events, their own Ignorance; but disguised in other words: As when they say, Fortune is the cause of things contingent; that is, of things whereof they know no cause'), then snidely adds, 'If such *Metaphysiques*, and *Physiques* as this, be not *Vain Philosophy*, there never was any' (XLVI/29–30, 375–6). That would be a fair judgment if Aristotle's account of Chance were as vacuous as Hobbes says. But his claim could not be further from the truth – as I presume he knew full well. Thus, to appreciate what a scarecrow opponent Hobbes has created whereby favourably to contrast his supposedly 'no-nonsense' First Philosophy, one must re-examine Aristotle's own analysis of chance phenomena. For 'the Role of Chance' can seem so pervasive and influential in political life as to render doubtful the very possibility of any *science* of politics. However, as intimated above, the idea of Chance, and its sub-species Fortune (or Luck), are explicable only in conjunction with an understanding of causation. So, too, as it turns out, are Form, Matter, Nature, and 'free will' (arguably, the most vital problem philosophy confronts, where metaphysics intersects psychology, theology, and morality – and which Hobbes treats as an oxymoron, a prime example of absurd, nonsensical speech; V/5, 19). I have endeavoured to keep my expositions of Aristotle to a minimum consistent with the purpose of better understanding Hobbes, simple but not simplistic.

As for the promise: though I will be at pains to indicate some of the political implications of these metaphysical issues in the course of my discussing them, my discussions, like Hobbes's, are but preliminary to addressing directly the essentials of his political prescription. I am reasonably confident that a suitably patient reader will be rewarded in the end with a deeper understanding of Hobbes, or at least one which differs greatly from that with which he began. As I shall endeavour to show, a careful, detailed analysis of Hobbes's entire text leads one to conclude that his actual views must be *very* different from those he has led most readers to ascribe to him.[4] This, of course, raises the question as to why he would wish to be so widely misunderstood – or (to speak less categorically), understood so superficially by the vast majority of his readers. Answering it carries one deep into his political wisdom.

The abiding puzzle, however, is a comprehensive one: is there a coherent interpretation of *Leviathan* that somehow explains, or otherwise accounts for, what I in this First Part attempt to show are quite inadequate, even incoherent treatments of issues that Hobbes acknowledges to be of fundamental importance – an interpretation, that is, which is *not* problematic? I presume that there is, and that it is Hobbes's own interpretation, which I venture to expound in a Second Part entitled 'The Platonic *Leviathan*.'

1

Curiosity about Causes
and the Problem of *Religion*

It is important to recognize from the outset how fundamental, according to Hobbes, causal analysis is to science and philosophy. There are nearly three hundred direct references to causation in *Leviathan*. It heads the list of the 'Speciall uses of Speech': 'to Register, what by cogitation, wee find to be the cause of any thing, present or past; and what we find things present or past may produce, or effect' (IV/3, 13). Science, 'the Knowledge required in a Philosopher; that is to say, of him that pretends to Reasoning' (IX/1, 40), is knowledge of causes, and correspondingly 'Want of Science [is] Ignorance of causes' (XI/17, 49). He insists, however, that 'ignorance of causes' is preferable to people 'relying on false rules, and taking for causes of what they aspire to, those that are not so, but rather causes of the contrary' (V/19, 21). Presuming such ignorance to be self-conscious, one may agree that, generally speaking, it is preferable to false belief, while inferior to knowledge. One may nonetheless wonder, however, where it ranks in comparison with a fourth category: *true* belief. Perhaps that would depend on whether one's interest was primarily practical, philosophical, or devotional.[1] Be that as it may, Hobbes defines Curiosity as the '*Desire*, to know why, and how ... such as is in no living creature but *Man*.' Hobbes equates it with 'the care of knowing causes; which is a Lust of the mind, that by a perseverance of delight in the continuall and indefatigable generation of Knowledge, exceedeth the short vehemence of any carnall Pleasure' (VI/35, 26).[2] This immediately precedes Hobbes's concise (if suspiciously impish) definitions pertaining to religion: '*Feare* of power invisible, feigned by the mind, or imagined from tales publiquely allowed, RELIGION; not allowed, SUPERSTITION. And when the power imagined, is truly such as we imagine, TRUE RELIGION.'

Not coincidentally, then, Hobbes's most concentrated reference to knowledge of causes (hence, Science) and ignorance of causes (i.e., 'Want of Science') is with respect to Religion. For some reason, Hobbes's treatment of this freighted topic begins with the final few paragraphs of Chapter Eleven, which, despite its curious title ('*Of the Difference of* MANNERS'), is not about etiquette, but 'those qualities of man-kind, that concern their living together in Peace, and Unity' (XI/1, 47). As such, this preceding chapter is of singular importance for understanding Hobbes's view of both politics and philosophy, hence of both religion and science, and the constellation of relationships among them. Perhaps by providing a preliminary sketch of his account – a much-expanded treatment of which follows immediately in the chapter expressly devoted to Religion – Hobbes means to suggest that the most politically significant factor causing 'difference in manners' of living, differentiating not only individuals but whole peoples, are their religious views:

Want of Science, that is, Ignorance of causes, disposeth, or rather constraineth a man to rely on the advise, and authority of others. For all men whom the truth concernes, if they rely not on their own, must rely on the opinion of some other, whom they think wiser than themselves, and see not why he should deceive them. ...

Ignorance of remote causes, disposeth men to attribute all events, to the causes immediate, and Instrumentall: For these are all the causes they perceive ...

Ignorance of naturall causes disposeth a man to Credulity, so as to believe many times impossibilities: For such know nothing to the contrary, but that they may be true; being unable to detect the Impossibility. And Credulity, because men love to be hearkened unto in company, disposeth them to lying: so that Ignorance it selfe without Malice, is able to make a man both to believe lyes, and tell them; and sometimes also to invent them.

Anxiety for the future time, disposeth men to enquire into the causes of things: because the knowledge of them, maketh men the better able to order the present to their best advantage.

Curiosity, or love of the knowledge of causes, draws a man from consideration of the effect, to seek the cause; and again, the cause of that cause; till of necessity he must come to this thought at last, that there is some cause, whereof there is no former cause, but is eternall; which is it men call God. So that it is impossible to make any profound enquiry into naturall causes, without being enclined thereby to believe there is one God Eternall; though they cannot have any Idea of him in their mind, answerable to his nature. For as a man that is born blind, hearing men talk of warming themselves by the fire, and being brought to warm himself by the same, may easily conceive, and assure himselfe, there is somewhat there, which men call *Fire*, and is the cause of the heat he feeles; but cannot imagine what it is like; nor have an Idea of it in his mind, such as they have that see it: so also, by the visible things of this world, and their admirable order, a man may conceive there is a cause of them, which men call God; and yet not have an Idea, or Image of him in his mind. (XI/17, 49; /22–5, 50–1)

Since this analogy of the Blind Man and the Fire has implications beyond illustrating the point for which it is ostensibly introduced – very far-reaching implications indeed, of which Hobbes was surely aware – it is worth making them explicit. One should first recall, however, that Fire is widely regarded as a natural symbol for technical power, and figures as such in the myth of Prometheus that Hobbes refers to in the following chapter. Second, understanding the nature of fire – what fire *is* – presents a challenging *scientific* problem, one that exercised a special fascination for Francis Bacon. Whereas Aristotle and other ancient thinkers treated fire as one of the four basic elements, Bacon suspected that fire is what we now know it to be: a physio-chemical *process*. It is not unreasonable to suppose that Hobbes shared Bacon's suspicion.

We might begin unpacking the analogy at this point, bearing in mind that it treats Fire as the analogue of God, Who is supposedly unknowable. One supposes various blind men would entertain various fanciful conceptions of fire, given their limited awareness of its sensory effects – which almost surely would include being pained rather than comforted upon venturing too close to it. That the effects of fire might be something they could manipulate and use for even the most basic technical purposes would not occur to blind men. Fire being invisible to them, and impalpable, but not inaudible, it might seem a purely 'spiritual' force. And we can well imagine the power, and consequent authority, that would be wielded among blind men by someone who managed to persuade them that he possessed special knowledge of how to control fire.

But it is what is *dis*-analogous in Hobbes's analogy that is especially provocative. The Blind Man is the exception; Sighted Men are the rule: the latter all know (as do we) what is of first importance: that fire *exists*! They know how it looks (they certainly *do* have an 'Idea, or Image of it' in their minds); they know what it 'feeds on' and what extinguishes it (what fire does and does not 'like'); they presumably have some valid opinions of what the power of fire can *do*, they know how to 'make' – *cause* – fire themselves, and of how to *use* it for their own purposes. Whereas with respect to knowledge of *God*, Blind Men are the norm, quite possibly the only kind of men there are; if there *is* a Sighted Man, *he* is exceptional. Moreover, must we not presume that Hobbes, like his mentor, believed that modern science would arrive at a full understanding of fire, of what it *truly* is, and of *how* it does whatever it does – that there is nothing 'spiritual,' nothing *super*natural about it? And that, consequently, the generations of pre-scientific Blind Men who worshipped the God of Fire would give way to Sighted Men, determined to understand 'the visible things of this world, and their admirable order' in terms of sequences of *natural* causes – though perhaps for the sake of logical completeness, some may acknowledge as God an utterly abstract conception of an Eternal First Cause (without any 'Idea, or Image' of it in their minds)? But for all *practical* purposes, the world as humans experience it would be understood as ruled through natural laws ascertainable through human Reason, the God of First Cause being totally irrelevant.

Before and until that time, however, men remain subject to the superstitious modes of thought that result in various religious beliefs, which in turn are subject to political exploitation.

And they that make little, or no enquiry into the naturall causes of things, yet from the feare that proceeds from the ignorance it selfe, of what it is that hath the power to do them much good or harm, are enclined to suppose, and feign unto themselves, severall kinds of Powers Invisible; and to stand in awe of their own imaginations; and in time of distresse to invoke them; as also in the time of unexpected good successe, to give them thanks; making the creatures of their own fancy, their Gods. By which means it hath come to passe, that from the innumerable variety of Fancy, men have created in the world innumerable sorts of Gods. And this Feare of things invisible, is the naturall Seed of that, which every one in himself calleth Religion; and in them that worship, or feare that Power otherwise than they do, Superstition.

And this seed of Religion, having been observed by many; some of those that have observed it, have been enclined thereby to nourish, dresse, and forme it into Lawes; and to adde to it of their own invention, any opinion of the causes of future events, by which they thought they should best be able to govern others, and make unto themselves the greatest use of their Powers. (XI/26–7, 51)

The incomprehensibility of God – first broached in the third chapter (III/12, 11), its implications analysed in sixteen paragraphs of chapter 31 (XXXI/13–28, 190–1), and repeatedly emphasized throughout the book (e.g., XXXIV/4, 208; XXXVI/13, 228; XLVI/12, 370; /22–3, 374; R&C/12, 394) – would seem to render otiose Hobbes's distinction between Religion and True Religion. As for his own strictly relativistic distinction between Religion and Superstition, its flippancy is sufficiently obvious on the face of it (I should think) to intimate the spirit of scepticism with which Hobbes views all so-called religious or supernatural phenomena.[3] As both his definitions and his subsequent discussion make clear, there is no *natural* difference between religion and superstition. The same phenomenon will be differently *named*, dependent simply upon the perspective whence it is viewed: in the State of Nature by each individual according to what he 'feigns' in his own mind; in a Civil Society, at least in one ordered as per Hobbes's prescription, according to what is officially recognized by law, i.e., the will of the Sovereign.

However viewed, the prevalence of religion and superstition throughout human history requires an explanation. The only valid explanation of recurrent phenomena is a scientific one, that is, an explanation in terms of natural causes. This is the task Hobbes undertakes in chapter 12, 'Of Religion'[4] – the chapter burdened, in effect, with explaining why his *Leviathan* is necessarily occupied with the 'theological-political problem,' literally from first page to last.[5]

Hobbes begins with an observation pertinent to causal analysis generally: if some effect is unique to one kind of thing, its cause must also be peculiar to that thing. Hence: 'Seeing there are no signes, nor fruit of *Religion*, but in Man onely; there is no cause to doubt, but that the seed of *Religion*, is also onely in Man; and consisteth in some peculiar quality, or at least in some eminent degree thereof, not to be found in other Living creatures.' Notice, in this case 'there is *no cause* to doubt,' implying were the 'signes' different, there might well be 'cause to doubt' (the observation being pointless otherwise). One would expect Hobbes's view of causation to inform his own linguistic usage, which here seems ordinary enough. And given the density of the term's occurrence in this chapter, reflective of its centrality to his analysis of religion, one would presume each mention of 'cause' to be guardedly self-conscious. In this case, and in virtually any conceivable use of 'cause to doubt,' the word might be replaced by 'reason' and the apparent meaning of the phrase be preserved: in the matter at issue (whether the '*seed* of Religion' is unique to man), 'there is no *reason* to doubt'; with respect to other matters, perhaps including some taken up in this very chapter, there may be reason, or 'cause,' to doubt. *Reasoning*, then, can be a proximate cause – though, to be sure, it is not independent of that about which one reasons. But neither is the *power* of Reason itself *reducible* to the 'ingredients' of reasoning.[6]

Having established the presumption that the cause of religion is to be sought in some feature or features unique to human nature, Hobbes immediately focuses attention on one, curiosity: 'And first, it is peculiar to the nature of Man, to be inquisitive into the Causes of the Events they see, some more, some lesse; but all men so much, as to be curious in the search of the causes of their own good and evill fortune' (XII/2, 52). Yet earlier in his treatise, he had adduced another peculiar human capacity, without which curiosity would be largely frustrated: hypothetical reasoning. In chapter 3, '*Of the Consequence or* Trayne *of Imaginations*,' we are told:

The Trayn of regulated Thoughts is of two kinds; One, when of an effect imagined,[7] wee seek the causes, or means that produce it: and this is common to Man and Beast. The other is, when imagining any thing whatsoever, wee seek all the possible effects, that can by it be produced; that is to say, we imagine what we can do with it, when wee have it. Of which I have not at any time seen any signe, but in man onely; for this is a curiosity hardly incident to the nature of any living creature that has no other Passion but sensuall, such as are hunger, thirst, lust, and anger. (III/5, 9)

While some animals may display a very limited capacity for the first kind of causal reasoning – as when a dog 'imagines' being free to roam, and seeks a way to escape his kennel; or a laboratory rat 'imagines' a food pellet, and pushes the right pedal to cause one to be dispensed (if we grant, dubiously, such to be the psychic process) – the human capacity for 'traynes' of reasoning whereby to produce, *cause*, imagined effects (walking on the moon, say, or an encyclopedia, or a full-employment economy) is of such an 'eminent degree' as to constitute a qualitative difference. And that quantitative increase can result in qualitative change is obvious to anyone who has ever boiled water. This first kind of causal reasoning is the same as that whereby one attempts to *explain* causally all actual, already produced effects – as Hobbes purports to with respect to Religion: explain its existence. Of this sort of thing, too, there is no 'signe, but in man onely.' The second form of reasoning – tracing out all of the implications of anything posited – is unquestionably unique to human beings, being most wondrously exemplified in Geometry, 'the onely Science that it hath pleased God hitherto to bestow on mankind' (IV/12, 15), and ostensibly the paradigm upon which it pleased Hobbes to bestow on mankind a new science of politics.

As reflection on the entirety of Hobbes's account reveals, *both* of man's unique qualities, each essential to the utility of the other – the

capacity for causal reasoning in either temporal direction being acti-
vated and sustained by curiosity – are necessary to explain this third
uniquely human thing, religion. But so, too, is still another power
unique to man, though not credited as such in Hobbes's manifestly
inadequate account of it: Imagination – essential to foresight, to
wishing, hoping, and dreading; to invention and creation; to empathetic
understanding; and to all hypothetical reasoning (whatever else). To fear
invisible powers 'feigned by the mind, or imagined from tales
publiquely allowed' obviously requires what *we* mean by 'imagination,'
an active faculty of infinitely greater power than any 'imaging' that may
be happening in animals.

The basis of Hobbes's scientific explanation of religion is presented in
the first few paragraphs of the chapter devoted to it:

And first, it is peculiar to the nature of Man, to be inquisitive into the Causes of
the Events they see, some more, some lesse; but all men so much, as to be curious
in the search of the causes of their own good and evill fortune.

Secondly, upon the sight of any thing that hath a Beginning, to think also it had
a cause, which determined the same to begin, then when it did, rather than sooner
or later.

Thirdly, whereas there is no other Felicity of Beasts, but the enjoying of their
quotidian Food, Ease, and Lusts; as having little, or no foresight of the time to
come, for want of observation, and memory of the order, consequence, and
dependance of the things they see; Man observeth how one Event hath been produced by another; and remembreth in them Antecedence and Consequence; And
when he cannot assure himselfe of the true causes of things, (for the causes of
good and evill fortune for the most part are invisible,) he supposes causes of them,
either such as his own fancy suggesteth; or trusteth to the Authority of other men,
such as he thinks to be his friends, and wiser than himselfe.

The two first, make Anxiety. For being assured that there be causes of all things
that have arrived hitherto, or shall arrive hereafter; it is impossible for a man, who
continually endeavoureth to secure himselfe against the evill he feares, and
procure the good he desireth, not to be in a perpetuall solicitude of the time to
come; So that every man, especially those that are over provident, are in an estate
like to that of *Prometheus*. For as *Prometheus*, (which interpreted, is, *The prudent
man,*) was bound to the hill *Caucasus*, a place of large prospect, where, an eagle
feeding on his liver, devoured in the day, as much as was repayred in the night: So
that man, who looks too far before him, in the care of future time, hath his heart
all day long, gnawed on by feare of death, poverty, or other calamity; and has no
repose, nor pause of his anxiety but in sleep. (XII/2–5, 52)

Thought about, this reference to Prometheus seems so inapt (and apparently unnecessary) for Hobbes's ostensible point that one must presume it to have an ulterior purpose. Perhaps, then, it is intended to prompt a patient reader to consider how the original myth might bear on the matters Hobbes is here treating.

Prometheus ('Forethought') was chained to the Caucasus for having stolen Fire from the Olympian Gods and given it to mankind, thereby providing the means of much – and symbol of all – technical power to cause effects. In this respect, Prometheus would seem to represent the modern scientific project that Hobbes's political prescription is designed to promote. But his reference makes no mention of this, the *reason* for Prometheus being bound, instead vaguely implying that it was a punishment for being 'over provident.' The mere mention of the name, however, invites the reader to reflect on the point of the original myth: that Prometheus – moulder of man out of clay, and bringer of heat, light, and the technical arts whereby Nature may be transformed in ways useful to man – was humankind's greatest benefactor, but at the expense of his own prolonged suffering of divine displeasure.[8]

Everyone's anxiety would be extreme in the insecurity of the State of Nature, but neither does worry about the future disappear within Civil Society despite all of the advantages the modern reorientation of Science may produce. Indeed, will any amount of technological power fully and finally allay that anxiety? Or must one find some other way to come to terms with the natural conditions of mortality? Perhaps Hobbes provides a clue in the continuation of his explanation of Religion:

This perpetuall feare, always accompanying mankind in the ignorance of causes, as it were in the Dark, must needs have for object something. And therefore when there is nothing to be seen, there is nothing to accuse, either of their good, or evil fortune, but some *Power*, or Agent *Invisible*: In which sense perhaps it was, that some of the old Poets said, that the Gods were at first created by humane Feare: which spoken of the Gods, (that is to say, of the many Gods of the Gentiles) is very true. But the acknowledging of one God Eternall, Infinite, and Omnipotent, may more easily be derived, from the desire men have to know the causes of naturall bodies, and their severall vertues, and operations; than from the feare of what was to befall them in time to come. For he that from any effect hee seeth come to passe, should reason to the next and immediate cause thereof, and from thence to the cause of that cause, and plunge himselfe profoundly into the pursuit of causes; shall at last come to this, that there must be (as even the Heathen Philosophers confessed) one First Mover; that is, a First, and an Eternall cause of all things; which is that which men mean by the name of God: And all this without thought of their fortune; the solicitude whereof, both enclines to fear, and hinders them from the search of the causes of other things; and thereby gives occasion of feigning of as many Gods, as there be men than feigne them. (XII/6, 52–3)

On Hobbes's account, then, this curiosity about causes, this desire to know why and how, takes two radically different forms, being pursued for radically different purposes.

In the vast majority of individuals, curiosity is primarily practical in scope and orientation; its satisfaction is but a means to a further end: that of their own personal well-being. True, virtually everyone has some degree of so-called idle curiosity about the why and how of things that come to their attention, but most people are preoccupied with 'the causes of their own good and evill fortune.' Somehow sure that everything has a cause, but foiled by the complexity and obscurity of the world, and by want of a sound method whereby might be determined the true causes of what each person most cares about (procuration of goods desired, but especially security against evils feared), people are perpetually anxious about their future. In such a condition, they prefer the illusion of understanding what they ought to fear, and attempt to propitiate – invisible, supernatural powers that ultimately rule the world, causing whatever happens – to their living in the state of objectless, helpless, hopeless fear such as attends ignorance about natural causation. However illusory their beliefs, they provide psychic comfort.

So it is that *fear*, stimulating countless people's diverse imaginations, has *naturally* led to the creation of countless gods, but ones with consciousnesses sufficiently akin to that of humans as to allow their being intelligible to their anxiety-ridden creators. Thus, the substance of these gods is conceived as being 'the same with that of the Soule of man.' They are thought of as spirits, or ghosts, who cause their effects by whatever antecedent events people happen to notice; as spirits, moreover, whose causal powers people may influence by worship, using the same 'expressions of their reverence, as they would use towards men,' and who prophesy the future to people – 'especially concerning their good or evil fortune in generall, or good or ill successe in any particular undertaking' – by coincidental conjunctions of events that those people choose to interpret as 'Prognostiques' (often after but 'one or two encounters'; XII/7–10, 53–4). On this basis, Hobbes summarizes:

And in these foure things, Opinion of Ghosts, Ignorance of second causes, Devotion towards what men fear, and Taking of things Casuall for Prognostiques, consisteth the Naturall seed of *Religion*; which by reason of the different Fancies, Judgements, and Passions of severall men, hath grown up into ceremonies so different, that those that are used by one man, are for the most part ridiculous to another. (XII/11, 54)[9]

Notice, Hobbes makes no allowance here for the possibility of there being any sort of kinship between the Human and the Divine, much less of Man's being made in God's Image (an incoherent notion, given the utter incomprehensibility of God). Nor does he allow for even a germ of something *distinctive* in human nature deserving of the name 'piety,' whence might come reverence when amalgamated with modesty and gratitude, wonder and awe.[10]

Notice, also, no consideration is given here to the possibility of a natural seed of religion planted by God Himself. But the very problem of religion as Hobbes is addressing it, especially bearing in mind the sheer multiplicity of beliefs and conceptions, argues against this possibility. For if God planted the seed of Religion, why not that of *True* Religion – in which case it would grow into basically the same religious 'plant' in everyone, everywhere, albeit perhaps of differing size and vigour according to variations in local growing conditions? Unless, that is, God, for some mysterious reason, has singled out one particular group of people for special treatment, which raises two further, very different possibilities: one, His planting in His chosen people a *natural* seed of true religion. In that case, however, such people would be significantly different from all the rest; there would not in fact be a common human nature (as by all the other natural, or at least bodily, evidence there is).[11] The other possibility is that God might choose to plant true religion in a particular people by *super*natural means; and this Hobbes explicitly allows for: 'where God himselfe, by supernaturall Revelation, planted Religion; there he also made to himselfe a peculiar Kingdome' (XII/22, 57). But to outsiders not vouchsafed this revelation, the religious beliefs and practices of His chosen people appear as but one more of the countless religions mankind displays, all the rest still in need of explanation.

Hobbes is at pains to emphasize the wonderful variety of things that humans have deified, everything from Primordial Chaos to 'their own ignorance, by the name of *Fortune*,' from all sorts of plants and animals to abstract qualities and conditions. Indeed, as his entire pages of examples attest, 'concerning the nature of Powers Invisible, there is almost nothing that has a name, that has not been esteemed amongst the Gentiles, in one place or another, a God, or Divell; or by their Poets feigned to be inanimated, inhabited, or possessed by some Spirit or other' (XII/13, 54–5). Reflecting on his reminders, one is led to suspect that *polytheism*, or even *pantheism*, not monotheism, is natural to mankind in general (as is the tendency to anthropophuize), and that the ancient Greeks – who not only regarded the heavenly bodies, the four winds, the ocean, and the Earth itself as Gods, but deified their own virtues and desires, and 'filled almost all places, with spirits called *Daemons*' – were the most natural of people in the promiscuity with which they ascribed divinity. That the Romans were imbued with a similar attitude is perhaps indicated by the ease with which, having 'conquered the greatest part of the then known World, made no scruple of tollerating any Religion whatsoever in the City of *Rome* it selfe; unlesse it had something in it, that could not consist with their Civill Government' (XII/21, 57).[12]

By way of concluding his chapter devoted to explaining scientifically, by means of natural causes, the origin of the countless religions so far – and the fact that they all share the same *origin*, springing causally from the same sort of seeds, is the real basis of their commonality, making them all *religions* – Hobbes suggests that one can ratify his account by causally reasoning backwards from a different point of departure, namely, from how a religion is successfully propagated, or alternatively, how destroyed: 'From the propagation of Religion, it is not hard to understand the causes of the resolution of the same into its first seeds, or principles; which are only an opinion of a Deity, and Powers invisible, and supernatural' (XII/23, 58). Surely, however, we are meant to recall here the *relevance* of such Powers: that they are ultimately the cause of men's good and evil fortune.

Be that as it may, given this propensity of people to believe in the existence of supernatural agents who rule the natural world, Hobbes explains that 'all *formed* Religion, is founded at first, upon the faith which a multitude hath in some one person, whom they believe not only to be a wise man, and to labour to procure their happiness, but also to be a holy man, to whom God himselfe vouchsafeth to declare his will supernaturally' (XII/24, 58; my emphasis). Consequently, when the ordinary believers come to suspect that 'they that have the Government of Religion' are not in fact either wise, or sincere, or caring, or graced by God, the religion itself becomes suspect. Hence, clerics espousing contradictions endanger religion, for that discredits their wisdom. And their sincerity is compromised by such things as 'Injustice, Cruelty, Prophanesse, Avarice, and

Luxury. For who can believe, that he that doth ordinarily such actions, as proceed from any of these rootes, believeth there is any such Invisible Power to be feared, as he affrighteth other men withall, for lesser faults?' (XII/26, 58). Thus Hobbes concludes, 'I may attribute all the *changes* of Religion in the world, to one and the same *cause*; and that is, unpleasing Priests' (XII/32, 60; my emphases).

But as for the causes of Religion itself, those 'first seeds,' they remain ever the same: people's presumption that everything that happens has a cause, coupled with a curiosity about causes, especially about 'the causes of their own good and evill fortune'; and, an inability to determine what those natural causes really are, resulting in anxiety and fear of imaginary causes, associated with invisible supernatural Powers. Moreover, these seeds (Hobbes assures us) 'can never be so abolished out of humane nature, but that new Religions may againe be made to spring out of them, by the culture of such men, as for such purpose are in reputation' (XII/23, 58). Being ignorant of the natural processes of causation, and suffering the fear that naturally attends such ignorance, people are credulous, not to say gullible: 'So easie are men to be drawn to believe any thing, from such men as have gotten credit with them; and can with gentlenesse, and dexterity, take hold of their fear, and ignorance' (XII/19, 56). And so, six chapters after the chapter on the *passions* in which, seemingly so strangely, 'Religion' was first defined, Hobbes has provided an account of the phenomenon that would seem to justify his definition: '*Feare* of power invisible, feigned by the mind, or imagined from tales publicly allowed, RELIGION.' Thus it is that one form of curiosity about causes, a narrow curiosity dominated by the practical concern for one's own well-being, is itself a contributing cause of Religion.

The broader, more catholic form of curiosity – what might be called 'theoretical curiosity,' being the 'love of the knowledge of causes' per se, hence sought for the sheer enjoyment of knowing the Why and How of things[13] – is *not* a cause of Religion, though it may well lead some few individuals motivated by it to a belief in 'one God Eternall.' For as Hobbes explains, a person who is ruled by this peculiar 'Lust of the mind,' who experiences a persisting 'delight in the continuall and indefatigable generation of Knowledge,' does not rest content with having discovered the cause of this or that thing, but instead treats its cause as yet another effect to be causally explained. Being thus naturally drawn to attempt to discover the entire chain of causation, 'of necessity he must come to this thought at last, that there is some cause, whereof there is no former cause, but is eternall; which is it men call God ... though they cannot have any Idea of him in their mind, answerable to his nature' (XI/25, 51). Here it is pertinent to recall that Hobbes earlier cited the greater or lesser desire for Knowledge as one of the passions responsible for 'the differences of Wit' (VIII/15, 35).

As previously noted, Hobbes endorses what 'the old Poets said, that the Gods were at first created by humane Feare' (mark the latter plural). And indeed, the old Poets ought to know, for according to Hobbes, they played upon this normal human propensity to believe in imaginary beings, 'insomuch as there was nothing, which a Poet could introduce as a person in his Poem, which they did not make either a *God*, or a *Divel*' (XII/16, 55). But as for 'the acknowledging of *one* God Eternall, Infinite, and Omnipotent,' that, Hobbes argues, 'may more easily be derived, from the desire men have to know the causes of naturall bodies, and their severall vertues, and operations; than from the feare of what was to befall them in time to come.' The desire *some* men have, that is, for as Hobbes had observed at the outset, the strength of a *general* desire to enquire 'into the Causes of the Events they see' is *variable* among people ('some more, some lesse'). It is only the 'indefatigably' inquisitive sort of person who will proceed from cause to cause, 'and plonge himselfe profoundly into the pursuit of causes' – this being for Hobbes the practical definition, *not* of a religious believer, but of a *philosopher* (cf. IX/1, 40; XLVI/1, 367). The relentless pursuit of causes leads at last to the conclusion that there 'must be (as even the Heathen *Philosophers* confessed) one First Mover; that is, a First, and an Eternall cause of all things; which is that which men mean by the name of God' (XII/6, 53; emphasis added). If it were strictly necessary that causal analysis leads at last to this Deist conclusion, there could in a sense, then, be a True Religion, but it would be confined to philosophers.

In sketching his position in the previous chapter, however, Hobbes did not seem quite so definite: 'profound enquiry into naturall causes' merely '*enclined*' a thinker 'to believe there is one God Eternall' (unimaginable though Its nature might be; XI/25, 51). And here in chapter 12, providing a nice example of his rhetorical subtlety, Hobbes has not actually said what he seems to have said. It is surely true that *rationally deriving* the existence of 'one God Eternall, Infinite, and Omnipotent' is more *easily* done from rigorous causal analysis than from endless worrying about what the future has in store for oneself (infinitely more easily, I should think). But this is not to say that such a derivation is unproblematic, nor that it is the only reasonable conclusion one might reach. It presumes, of

course, strict determinism, and that every cause has an antecedent cause –
and short of supernatural revelation, there is no conceivable way that one
could *know* either of these presumptions to be true, both being implicated as they are in any investigation of the issues, rendering it circular.
Whereas there are grounds for suspecting neither is universally valid.[14]
But in any case, the idea of a First Cause contradicts the premise upon
which is based the entire causal sequence supposedly leading to it: that an
uncaused cause is as impossible, as rationally unintelligible, as creation
from nothing. On the other hand, if one must ultimately acknowledge the
possibility of an uncaused cause, however mysterious and baffling the
human mind finds that notion to be, why not accept it closer to home, as
it were, in so-called free will – something we would seem to experience
every day – rather than in a remote, abstract, altogether incomprehensible conception of a divine power, about which there is nothing positive to
analyse (cf. XXXI/28, 191)?

However, as is well known, Hobbes claims to find the very idea of free
will absurd, the name itself an example of speech every bit as nonsensical
as 'round square.' His fullest discussion of the matter comes in chapter 21
('*Of the* Liberty of Subjects'), where he argues that '*Liberty*, and *Necessity* are Consistent':

[I]n the Actions which men voluntarily doe: which, because they proceed from
their will, proceed from *liberty*; and yet, because every act of mans will, and
every desire, and inclination proceedeth from some cause, and that from
another cause, in a continuall chaine, (whose first link is in the hand of God the
first of all causes,) proceed from *necessity*. So that to him that could see the connexion of those causes, the *necessity* of all mens voluntary actions, would
appear manifest. And therefore God, that seeth, and disposeth all things, seeth
also that the *liberty* of man in doing what he will, is accompanied with the
necessity of doing that which God will, & no more, nor lesse. For though men
may do many things, which God does not command, nor is therefore Author of
them; yet they can have no passion, nor appetite to any thing, of which appetite
Gods will is not the cause. And did not his will assure the *necessity* of mans will,
and consequently of all that on mans will dependeth, the *liberty* of men would
be a contradiction, and impediment to the omnipotence and *liberty* of God.
(XXI/4, 108)

I shall here ignore the problems this view raises with respect to morality
and sin, predestination and salvation.[15] Also, whether Hobbes means to
imply that the 'liberty of God' is similarly subject to a certain necessity

(such as that manifested in geometrical truths). But it is of some interest to the matters at issue that Hobbes's references to God's *seeing* all things, of His having *hand* and *will*, are rhetorical exploitations of 'Metaphoricall' speech, as he later makes explicit in discussing the logical implications of God's infinitude; for example, 'Nor to ascribe to him (unless Metaphorically, meaning not the Passion, but the Effect) Passions that partake of Griefe; as *Repentance, Anger, Mercy*: or of Want; as *Appetite, Hope, Desire*'; 'Likewise when we attribute to him *Sight*, and other acts of Sense; as also *Knowledge*, and *Understanding*' (XXXI/19–27, 190). However, to use words metaphorically is, according to Hobbes, an 'Abuse' of speech apt to 'deceive others' (IV/4, 13), and is one of seven causes of 'Absurd conclusions' (V/14, 20), and thus is to be 'utterly excluded' from 'all rigourous search of Truth' (VIII/8, 34). So much, then, for 'the *hand* of God [being] the first of all causes,' for His 'seeing' and 'willing' whatever. Similar remarks pertain equally to the idea of God's having 'liberty' if one accepts Hobbes's assurance that 'properly' this word means 'the absence of Opposition [by] external Impediments of *motion*' (XXI/1, 107; cf. XIV/2, 64), for He neither 'is *Moved*, or *Resteth*' (XXXI/23, 190). However, the main point to be noted about Hobbes's Liberty-Necessity contention is that the linchpin of his argument – indeed, all there is to his argument, the rest being but so many assertions – is that the idea of human Free Will is 'a contradiction, and an impediment to the omnipotence and *liberty* of God.' Needless to say, that argument falls apart if there is no such God.

But has His existence not been logically assured by rigorous causal analysis that explains each cause by an antecedent cause? As noted before, the necessary existence of a First Cause in a *temporal* sense is *not* the only rational possibility. And here one feels acutely the absence of any explicit analysis in *Leviathan* of causation; that is, an analysis explicating the various *kinds* of Cause – or senses of the word, as Hobbes would have it – such as those provided by Aristotle or Francis Bacon (both to be examined in later chapters). For there is no need to posit an originating First Cause, or First Mover (the presumption of which squarely contradicts the premise of the reasoning supposedly leading to it), if the Universe is Eternal. Hobbes is perfectly aware of this possibility, of course, and so provides arguments against it – rhetorically effective with those who already believe in an omniscient, omnipotent, eternal God; utterly question-begging for those that regard His existence as questionable; and beautifully ironic to those who, such as myself, suspect that Hobbes is not even a Deist, much less a sincere Christian:

That we may know what worship of God is taught us by the light of Nature, I will begin with his Attributes. Where, First, it is manifest, we ought to attribute to him *Existence*: For no man can have the will to honour that, which he thinks not to have any Beeing.

Secondly, that those Philosophers, who sayd the World, or the Soule of the World was God, spake unworthily of him; and denyed his Existence: For by God, is understood the cause of the World; and to say the World is God, is to say there is no cause of it, that is, no God.

Thirdly, to say the World was not Created, but Eternall, (seeing that which is Eternall has no cause,) is to deny there is a God.

Fourthly, that they who attributing (as they think) Ease to God, take from him the care of Man-kind; take from him his Honour: for it takes away mens love, and fear of him; which is the root of Honour. (XXXI/14–17, 190)

It is worth noting that nowhere does Hobbes indicate that the 'worship of God' is mandated by Natural Law. For he is explicit that while the Commandments of the Decalogue's Second Table are 'indeed the Laws of Nature ... and therefore to be acknowledged for God's Laws; not to the Israelites alone, but to all people,' those of the *First* Table are 'peculiar to the Israelites' (XLII/37, 282). Moreover, since Hobbes insists, 'Hee that will attribute to God, nothing but what is warranted by naturall reason' can say nothing positive about His 'Nature' other than 'I AM' – and, in particular, that on such a basis one cannot ascribe to Him either mercy or anger (XXXI/25 & 28, 190–1; cf. XXXIV/4, 208) – it would seem that a thoughtful reader must, at the least, count Hobbes among those who deny the existence of a divine power that cares for men, thus whose anger they ought to fear or whose aid they might seek. And if one credits Hobbes with being fully aware of the complete irrelevance of the above arguments for God's existence (as I believe is both fair and prudent); and if one presumes that he has none better to offer (since he would have presented them if he did); and that, as a philosopher, Hobbes himself believes 'nothing but what is warranted by naturall Reason,' then one can scarce avoid suspecting that he is to be included among those who 'deny there is a God,' period.[16]

In summary, analysis of chapters 11 and 12 suggests that, while Hobbes is ostensibly concentrating here on presenting a scientific account of Religion in terms of its natural causes, he is at the same time – inconspicuously, but just as surely – providing a contrasting account of *Philosophy*. Both spring from curiosity about causes, but they are the very different 'produce' of divergent motives for pursuing knowledge of causes: a narrow, focused concern for procuring one's own good and security from evil, *versus* a broad search for intellectual satisfaction. Moreover, these motives, while by no means logically exclusive, nonetheless do not fit well together psychically. As Hobbes troubles to point out in regards to people's (typically excessive, and futile) 'solicitude' for their own fortune, it 'both enclines to fear, and hinders them from the search of the causes of other things.' Each pursuit, then, is energized by a radically different passion: fear in the case of religion, philosophy by love – fear of imaginary invisible powers and agents, *versus* love of knowledge for its own sake. One leads naturally to polytheism and pantheism; the other to a single ultimate ruling power or principle, 'which men *call* God,' or 'which men *mean* by the name of God,' but insofar as it naturally commands love and obedience, is perhaps more aptly called The Good.[17] True, 'Felicity of this life, consisteth not in the repose of a mind satisfied,' but is rather 'a continuall progresse of the desire, from one object to another; the attaining of the former, being still but the way to the later' (XI/1, 47). This, however, fairly describes the felicity of someone who is ruled by a 'Lust of the mind,' and who thus experiences a persisting 'delight in the continuall and indefatigable generation of Knowledge,' each provisional conclusion being but a springboard to further inquiry.[18] Moreover, a life so lived – a philosophical life – may in its own way alleviate, even entirely eliminate, the principal source of human anxiety: fear of death.

As should be evident, an adequate analysis of *Cause* – what is meant by the term, whether it refers to more than one kind and, if so, how each is determined, how they relate, and what causal reasoning requires of (and reveals about) the human mind – is needed if one is to have a clear understanding of Science, Philosophy, and Religion. And, consequently, of Politics as Hobbes would have us see it. For all three of those world-shaping forms of activity are inextricably interwoven with Hobbes's political prescription – as his entire treatise attests, albeit the concern to tame religion is the most obvious. He observes in the chapter devoted to the topic, the natural seeds of religion 'have received culture from two sorts of men':

One sort have been they, that have nourished, and ordered them, according to their own invention. The other, have done it, by Gods commandement, and direction: but both sorts have done it, with a purpose to make those men that relyed on them, the more apt to Obedience, Lawes, Peace, Charity, and civill Society. So that the Religion of the former sort, is a part of humane Politiques; and teacheth part of the duty which Earthly Kings require of their Subjects. And the Religion of the later sort is Divine Politiques. (XII/12, 54)

A warning note about the pernicious political influence of irrational religious beliefs is sounded as early as chapter 2 ('*Of* IMAGINATION'), conjoined with a tacit indication of the remedy: science. Having argued that 'dreames are caused by the distemper of some of the inward parts of the Body,'[19] Hobbes cites people's 'ignorance of how to distinguish Dreams, and other strong Fancies, from Vision and Sense' as the source whence arose 'the greatest part of the Religion of the Gentiles in times past.' He then goes on to speak of the power of Witches:

For as for Witches, I think not that their witchcraft is any reall power; but yet that they are justly punished, for the false beliefe they have, that they can do such mischiefe, joyned with their purpose to do it if they can: their trade being neerer to a new Religion, than to a Craft or Science. And for Fayries, and walking Ghosts, the opinion of them has I think been on purpose, either taught, or not confuted, to keep in credit the use of Exorcisme, of Crosses, of holy Water, and other such inventions of Ghostly men ... But evill men under pretext that God can do any thing, are so bold as to say any thing when it serves their turn, though they think it untrue; It is the part of a wise man, to believe them no further, than right reason makes that which they say, appear credible. If this superstitious fear of Spirits were taken away, and with it, Prognostiques from Dreams, false Prophecies, and many other things depending thereon, by which, crafty ambitious persons abuse the simple people, men would be much more fitted than they are for civill Obedience. (II/8, 7–8)

The key to doing away with superstition, and disenchanting the world generally, is the advancement of science: explaining by natural causes what people are otherwise apt to regard as white or black magic, or attribute to supernatural agents and forces. In so doing, science also undermines the power of religion and thereby mitigates the potential political danger posed by that power being appropriated by private men pretending to be prophets, who in God's name purport to declare what people must do to achieve everlasting happiness. 'For he that pretends to teach men the way of so great felicity, pretends to govern them; that is to say, to rule, and reign over them; which is a thing, that all men naturally desire, and is therefore worthy to be suspected of Ambition and Imposture' (XXXVI/19, 230). All the more reason, then, that such power as religion retains be kept in politically responsible hands, such as will not endanger civil peace: 'The maintenance of Civill Society, depending on Justice; and Justice on the power of Life and Death ... it is impossible a Common-wealth should stand, where any other than the Soveraign, hath a power of giving greater rewards than Life; and of inflicting greater punishments, than Death ... seeing that *Eternall life* is a greater reward, than the *life present*; and *Eternall torment* a greater punishment than the *death of Nature*' (XXXVIII/1, 238).[20]

Thus, one can appreciate Hobbes's insistence on the overriding importance of integrating the power of religion within that of the civil authority. Doing so *securely*, however, is not possible so long as people remain susceptible to believing in all sorts of supernatural forces and phenomena: 'For such is the ignorance, and aptitude to error generally of all men, but especially of them that have not much knowledge of naturall causes, and of the nature, and interests of men; as by innumerable and easie tricks to be abused' (XXXVII/12, 236). Hence, the role of the supernatural within religion, and of irrational beliefs in general, must be reduced to manageable proportions if a rational political science is to prevail.

This is partly a matter of reinterpreting religious doctrines, the 'Propheticall' words of God as enunciated in Scripture, so that they both square with natural reason and endorse the authority of natural reason as being itself indicative of God's Will. That almost the entire second half of *Leviathan* is devoted to this task indicates its importance. For although it treats explicitly only Christianity and its Bible, it may nonetheless have a universal significance. First, it provides a paradigm for dealing with prophetical writings and teachings generally. Second, in that Christianity is quasi-monotheistic (and if Hobbes had his way, would be interpreted as strictly so), it more readily harmonizes with a philosophically sound theology. And third, because so-called Christian civilization, suitably reformed and rationalized in accordance with Hobbes's political prescription, could conceivably come to dominate the world.

However, the principal means of domesticating religion, curtailing its power within the narrow limits of political utility, is Science: 'The Light of humane minds is Perspicuous Words, but by exact definitions first snuffed, and purged from ambiguity; *Reason* is the *pace*, Encrease of *Science*, the *way*, and the Benefit of man-kind, the *end*' (V/20, 22). Jesus is not 'the way.' Science is.[21]

Given its prominence in all the foregoing, the 'Perspicuous Word' that would seem most in need of exact defining is 'cause.' But, as noted at the outset, that is one definition Hobbes never provides.[22] He does, however, provide clear advice as to what one must do in such a situation. Given 'how necessary it is for any man that aspires to true Knowledge, to examine the Definitions of former Authors; and either to correct them, where they are negligently set down; *or to make them himselfe*' (IV/13, 15; emphasis added), we are implicitly invited to frame a definition of 'cause' that would be adequate for Hobbes's and our purposes, taking into account both his actual uses of the term and any explicit indications of his conception. So, what *is* Hobbes's understanding of Cause?

To determine that, one might (first of all) assemble his scattered remarks about Cause, beginning with the provocative statement made in the chapter '*Of Religion*' concerning the way people imagine 'Invisible Agents wrought their effects; that is to say, what immediate causes they used, in bringing things to passe':

[M]en that know not what it is that we call *causing*, (that is, almost all men) have no other rule to guesse by, but by observing, and remembring what they have seen to precede the like effect at some other time, or times before, without seeing between the antecedent and subsequent Event, any dependence or connexion at all: And therefore from the like things past, they expect the like things to come; and hope for good or evill luck, superstitiously, from things that have no part at all in the causing of it. (XII/8, 53)

Here, Hobbes seems to equate one kind of cause, *Efficient* cause, with Cause simply (to employ Aristotle's typology, as will be reviewed in a subsequent chapter; for the moment, let it suffice that an efficient cause is whatever precipitates an event). And Hobbes's claim about all chains of causation converging in the necessary recognition of a First Cause would seem to pertain solely to sequences of Efficient causes, each event having been precipitated by a preceding event. At the same time, however, he shows his awareness of the basic empirical problem with determining Efficient cause – namely, how to distinguish between coincidental correlations and valid causal connections. Yet he gives no indication of a reliable way this might be done.[23]

Be that as it may, Hobbes begins Part Two of *Leviathan*, 'OF COMMON-WEALTH,' with reference to a very different kind of cause: 'The finall Cause, End, or Designe of men, (who naturally love Liberty, and Dominion over others,) in the introduction of that restraint upon themselves, (in which wee see them live in Common-wealths,) is the foresight of their own preservation, and of a more contented life thereby.'

Here, as Hobbes himself makes explicit, the explanation of the phenomenon – people living in political associations – is in terms of a *Final* cause, that is, as fulfilment of a purpose, a goal, an end, a *telos*. This deserves emphasizing: Hobbes begins this chapter '*Of the Causes, Generation, and Definition of a* Common-Wealth' with a *teleological* explanation of polities: they are the *means* to an *end*, namely, self-preservation and a more contented life than would be lived in a State of Nature. He effectively concludes the scientific portion of Part Two likewise, commencing chapter 30 thus: 'The OFFICE of the Sovereign, (be it a Monarch, or an Assembly,) consisteth in the end, for which he was trusted with the Soveraign Power, namely the procuration of *the safety of the people*' (XXX/1, 175). In between, we are told, 'no written Law, delivered in few, or many words, can be well understood, without a perfect understanding of the finall causes, for which the Law was made; the knowledge of which finall causes is in the Legislator' (XXVI/21, 143). Hobbes's usage in such instances is a matter of no small consequence for an understanding of his conception of Science, if we presume that he believes himself to be presenting a science of politics in *Leviathan*. For on this reading, political science is necessarily Teleological. This, in turn, lends a different coloration to his original discussion of what 'men call SCIENCE': 'And whereas Sense and Memory are but knowledge of Fact, which is a thing past, and irrevocable; *Science* is the knowledge of Consequences, and dependence of one fact upon another: by which, out of that we can presently do, we know how to do something else when we will, or the like, another time' (V/17, 21). There are grounds for being ever cautious in conflating Hobbes's own definition with what 'men call' something. Here, however, he seems to speak also in his own name. And while what Hobbes says 'Science *is*' readily lends itself to a strictly technological interpretation, with its natural focus on Efficient causation, careful consideration of his words reveals their compatibility with causes of whatever kind. And as will be shown (chapter 5), explanation of a Commonwealth in terms of its Final cause, or even of a conjunction of Final and Efficient causes, is inadequate, because incomplete.

Indeed, the 'Generation' of a Commonwealth as Hobbes expounds it provides the perfect exemplification of why all four of the kinds of Causes Aristotle identifies (Material, Formal, Efficient, and Final) are necessary for a complete understanding of anything purposive, be it natural, artificial, conventional, or some combination thereof (as Aristotle regards language and polities, and as Plato treats money and music).[24] Admittedly, whether a given thing, such as a nightmare or a rainbow[25] or the life of a man, does in fact have a purpose is not always immediately apparent. Nor, by the same token, is something's true purpose necessarily that which it first seems to be. When it comes to judging purposes, especially those motivating what an obviously clever man says and does, one best not jump to conclusions.

Suffice it to say for now, all that is revealed by Hobbes's scattered remarks about causation, or by his own usage of causal language, is that he does employ all four of the forms of Cause recognized by Aristotle. He does not indicate much of any substance about them, however, nor of how they relate to each other or to the phenomena they explain. So, for that one has little choice but to return to Aristotle's original analyses. Prior to doing so, however, it will prove useful to address the issues raised by Materialism, both in order to make clear Aristotle's analysis of Material Cause, and because Hobbes is usually understood as subscribing a metaphysical position that reduces all genuine understanding of reality to Matter and its motions.

2

Reality and the
Problem of *Materialism*

Following the lead of Aristotle, one must first attempt to clarify what it means for something to be 'natural,' or to have 'a nature,' as doing so not only facilitates understanding causation, it also prepares the way for assessing Hobbes's apparent Materialism – which, though repeatedly invoked throughout the first half of *Leviathan*, is expounded (strangely enough) only in part 3, 'OF A CHRISTIAN COMMONWEALTH,' specifically in chapter 34, '*Of the Signification of* SPIRIT, ANGEL, *and* INSPIRATION *in the Books of Holy Scripture*':

The Word *Body*, in the most generall acceptation, signifieth that which filleth, or occupyeth some certain room, or imagined place; and dependeth not on the imagination, but is a reall part of what we call the *Universe*. For the *Universe*, being the Aggregate of all Bodies, there is no reall part thereof that is not also *Body*; nor anything properly a *Body*, that is not also part of (that Aggregate of all *Bodies*) the *Universe*.[1] The same also, because Bodies are subject to change, that is to say, to variety of apparence to the sense of living creatures, is called *Substance*, that is to say, *Subject*, to various accidents; as sometimes to be Moved, sometimes to stand Still; and to seem to our senses sometimes Hot, sometimes Cold, sometimes of one Colour, Smel, Tast, or Sound, sometimes of another. And this diversity of Seeming, (produced by the diversity of the operation of bodies, on the organs of our sense) we attribute to the alterations of the Bodies that operate, & call them *Accidents* of those Bodies. And according to this acceptation of the word, *Substance* and *Body*, signifie the same thing; and therefore *Substance incorporeall* are words, which when they are joined together, destroy one another, as if a man should say, an *Incorporeall Body*.

But in the sense of common people, not all the Universe is called Body, but only such parts thereof as they can discern by the sense of Feeling, to resist their force, or by the sense of their Eyes, to hinder them from a farther prospect. Therefore in the common language of men, *Aire*, and *aeriall substances*, use not to be taken for *Bodies*, but (as often as men are sensible of their effects) are called *Wind*, or *Breath*, or (because the same are called in the Latine *Spiritus*) *Spirits*; as when they call that aeriall substance, which in the body of any living creature, gives it life and motion, *Vitall*, and *Animall spirits*. But for those Idols of the brain, which represent Bodies to us, where they are not, as in a Looking-glasse, in a Dream, or to a Distempered brain waking, they are (as the Apostle saith generally of all Idols) nothing; Nothing at all, I say, there where they seem to bee; and in the brain it self, nothing but tumult, proceeding either from the action of the objects, or from the disorderly agitation of the Organs of our Sense.[2] (XXXIV/2–3, 207–8)

In the balance of this chapter, Hobbes expands on certain of these claims, for instance: 'But if Corporeall be taken in the most vulgar manner, for such Substances as are perceptible by our external Senses; then is Substance Incorporeall, a thing not Imaginary, but Reall; namely, a thin Substance Invisible, but that have the same dimensions that are in grosser Bodies'. And he claims that nothing said in the Old Testament would warrant concluding that 'there is, or hath been created, any permanent thing (understood by the name *Spirit* or *Angel*,) that hath not quantity ... and, in summe, which is not (taking Body for that, which is some what, or some where) Corporeall' (XXXIV/15, 211; /23, 213).

Hobbes returns to these themes in his chapter on 'Vain Philosophy' (46), where he offers the reader who has laboured this far a half-apology for bothering in a work on politics to criticize the *'Jargon'* of the Schools. With respect to the criticisms he offers, however, he gives fair warning that 'there is need of somewhat more than ordinary attention' – a pertinent caution, bearing in mind the book's penultimate sentence (whose implications I shall address further in Part Two):

I ask pardon of those that are not used to this kind of Discourse, for applying my selfe to those that are. The World, (I mean not the Earth onely, that denominates the Lovers of it *Worldly men*, but the *Universe*, that is, the whole masse of all things that are) is Corporeall, that is to say, Body; and hath the dimensions of Magnitude, namely, Length, Bredth, and Depth: also every part of Body, is likewise Body, and hath the like dimensions; and consequently every part of the Universe, is Body; and that which is not Body, is no part of the Universe: and because the Universe is All, that which is no part of it, is *Nothing*; and consequently *no where*. Nor does it follow from hence, that Spirits are *nothing*: for they have dimensions, and are therefore really *Bodies*; though that name in common Speech be given to such Bodies onely, as are visible, or palpable; that is, have some degree of Opacity.' (XLVI/15, 371)

By consistently referring here to 'Body' rather than 'Matter' or 'Material' (terms that do occur frequently enough in the book),[3] it would seem that Hobbes intends thereby to endorse a materialistic conception of Reality without having to resolve the profound paradoxes that necessarily inhere in any outright Materialism (i.e., that regards Matter as both the fundamental reality and causally efficacious). Since 'body' includes both matter and form – the latter manifested in the dimensions of a body, the outer envelope of that body's composing matter, but also its inner structure; thus, no matter, no form – Hobbes apparently believes he can evade having to declare either form or matter to have metaphysical priority, or even having to provide explanatory definitions of either.[4] In order to see why this strategy will not work, with the result that the metaphysical position established thereupon is hopelessly inadequate, one need only review Aristotle's analysis of how Nature as a Whole, as well as the countless 'natures' comprised by it, must be understood.

Aristotle begins by observing, 'Of things that exist, some exist by nature, some from other causes. By nature the animals and their parts exist, and the plants and simple bodies [i.e., the material 'elements' out of which all physical objects are composed; for Aristotle, 'earth, fire, air, and water'; for us, protons, neutrons, and electrons] – we say that these and the like exist by nature. All these things plainly differ from things that are not constituted by nature.'[5]

So, 'Nature' is, first of all, a term of *distinction*: not everything that exists is natural. But what, then, is distinctive about natural things; how do things that come to be 'by nature' so 'plainly differ' from non-natural things, such as the products of human art and convention, or chance happenings? Is it merely by the mode of their production? No, for each natural thing, be it animate or inanimate, has within itself principles both of motion or change and of stability or rest. This is what is meant by something's having 'a nature': an inherent principle of movement insofar as it changes (e.g., moves about in space, grows, transforms itself, decays, etc.) and of maintaining itself insofar as it resists change and the impact of outside forces. Obviously this applies to all living things: their innate principles of growth, behaviour, aging, reproduction, ingesting nourishment (for self-maintenance), etc. – the specifics unique to each species. But it applies equally to non-living things: each of the various naturally occurring materials has its specific characteristics of stability and decay. Granite is practically impervious to the rain that will dissolve salt and the heat that will evaporate water or the cold that will transform it to ice; still, granite will eventually deteriorate in accordance with its nature. In sum, 'things which have a principle of this kind [are rightly said to] have a "nature"'; and the phrase 'according to nature' is applicable to all such things and their properties (e.g., it is 'natural' that smoke rise and that water flow downhill).

By contrast, artificial things do not have an *inherent* governing principle of either stability or change. They have only whatever principles of movement or stability their makers build into them, along with whatever is innate in the natures of the materials out of which they are made. So, in addition to the fact that an artefact (such as a pruning knife, a bed, or a coat) is not produced spontaneously, it also neither grows nor restores itself (a nicked and dull knife will not sharpen itself, nor a slept-in bed reorder itself, nor a torn coat mend itself), nor does it have its own innate trajectory of decay beyond what is inherent in the design and materials out of which it is made: an unused pruning knife safely stored away will remain as it is indefinitely, whereas the one that quickly wears out from daily use does so because of properties of its metal blade (*not* because knives per se only last so long). Nor, of course, do artefacts reproduce themselves: big coats do not make little coats that grow up to be big coats; and in the unlikely event that one were to bury a wooden bedstead and something were to grow from it, it would be (as Aristotle troubles to remind us) a tree, not a bed. It may be noticed, however, that artefacts, in their lack of generative and regenerative powers, have more in common with inanimate natures (i.e., natural materials) than animate ones; this turns out to be revealing about 'matter' generally.

In analysing any perceptible 'object' – meaning, roughly, whatever can be regarded as a detachable whole unto itself, whether natural or artificial – we recognize that it has two basic components: its shape or *form*, and its *matter* upon which the form is imposed (or, alternatively expressed, whereby the form is made manifest). And so we may ask, in which of these components does a natural thing's nature inhere: in the form, or in the matter, or in both? As Aristotle reports, 'Some identify the nature or substance of a natural object with the immediate constituent [of which it is made]' and so contend that all of that thing's natural characteristics are due to its composing matter. Thus, the explanation of why the tree burned: because trees are made of wood, and it is in the nature of wood to be flammable; were trees made of granite, they would not burn; therefore, Nature is in the matter. Also, presuming Nature to be eternal – and this would seem to be the only rationally intelligible possibility (difficult, or even impossible as it may be to grasp the idea of Eternity) – matter would clearly qualify, as it must be indestructible and have always existed. Whence could it come? Where could it go?[6]

However, since typically the material of a thing – such as the wood of a tree or the flesh and blood, bone and hooves of a horse – is itself composed of still simpler, hence more basic, matter (as bone is of calcium, phosphorus, etc.), and *that* matter, in turn, composed of matter even simpler (for us, protons, neutrons, and electrons), one is faced with the prospect of having to account for the various specific natures of things, all the species of plants and animals and kinds of naturally occurring materials – and they number in the many millions, we are told – in terms of a very few kinds of elementary matter (Aristotle's four, our three). How can one account for the millions of distinctive 'natures' and their specific properties by what they all have in common: composed ultimately of the same three or four kinds of matter? that wood is flammable because it is composed of protons, neutrons, and electrons; and granite is *not* flammable because it is composed of protons, neutrons, and electrons?

While this would be sufficient reason to conclude that specific natures cannot inhere simply in matter, there are other important considerations that support Aristotle's concluding, 'The form [*eidos*] indeed is nature rather than the matter.'[7] First of all, 'A thing is more properly said to be what it is when it has attained to fulfilment than when it exists [merely] potentially.' The point being, the matter out of which something is made is potentially that thing, but potentially many other things as well. In Nature, as in Art, the identity of something is determined by its completed form; a block of marble is potentially a statue of the biblical David, but equally so an engraved lintel over the entrance to a library, some plutocrat's bathtub, or slabs of flooring in a bank. Likewise, the matter out of which grew a wildebeest (i.e., the grass it ate, the water it drank, the air it breathed, the salt it licked) could as readily have composed a zebra or an antelope or a buffalo. Similarly, one can grow dozens of different vegetables from the same air, soil, water, and sunshine. Whereas, once the matter is formed into this rather than that – taken on a specific form, become *informed* matter – only then is it *actually* something in particular, having a distinct nature, with a unique set of properties. For unlike the matter, which is potentially many things (and thus may be thought of simply as *potentia*), each thing's form is unique to that kind of thing: the form of swan is exclusive to swans.

Secondly, form governs orderly change. Things that grow do so according to a natural *pattern* of change that is not simply homogeneous movement (as, roughly, is that of the planets, endlessly orbiting about the Sun), but is made up of qualitatively different motions: a more-or-less eager growth towards a mature *prime* (*acmë*), and a reluctant decline away from its prime into senescence. This *pattern* of growth, manifested in the orderly trans-*form*ing of the growing thing towards its complete form, is itself a form (it certainly is not matter). And insofar as inanimate nature also exhibits orderly change (e.g., the changing lengths of days and nights with the cycles of the Seasons, the behaviour of falling stones in a gravitational field, or the decay of radioactive materials), it too con-*forms* with patterns that are themselves not material (many being essentially mathematical in character, hence their expressibility in mathematical 'formulas').

Thirdly, Nature as a whole is not adequately characterized as simply the 'Aggregate of all Bodies' or the 'whole masse of all things that are,' but is itself an *ordered* arrangement: a Cosmos, not a jumble, much less a Chaos. Indeed, the order itself is 'admirable' according to Hobbes (XI/25, 51). So, while one may refer summarily to the countless parts of nature – the millions of relatively stable specific natures, and the always-changing billions of particular instances of those natures – as an 'aggregate' or 'mass,' such expressions leave out their being ordered in a coherent whole (as partially acknowledged in such expressions as 'food chain,' 'balance of Nature,' 'the higher animals,' 'ecological niche'). This answers the question that Aristotle treats as primary: 'In what sense is it asserted that all things are one?'[8] But neither the order itself nor the ordering principles, such as those upon which are based biological taxonomies, or those that determine our table of the chemical elements, is material. These are *forms* of order, comprising the hierarchical order of Nature as a whole.

Finally, and absolutely decisive, is the fact that matter itself, in all the modes we actually encounter it or can even imagine encountering it, is intelligible only as form: as a *form* of matter. Thus, the distinction between Form and Matter, while indispensable for purposes of analysis and understanding, is not quite the radical distinction it first seems to be. In all actual analyses of particular things, 'form' refers to something absolute, whereas 'matter' is always relative to the compositional level of the thing being analysed.

So, to adapt an example from Aristotle, steel can be either form or matter, depending on the focus of analysis. Steel is matter in relation to a

sword-maker; it is the material out of which he fashions swords, imposing onto the steel the form of a particular kind of sword. But steel is a
form to a steelmaker, whose defining task is to impose the form of steel,
or of a particular kind of steel, on the various more basic kinds of matter
out of which steel is made (iron, carbon, chromium, whatever, in their
proper *proportions*, as determined, not by the ingredients, but by the
form of steel he aims to make). And since the end product, steel, has characteristics different from those of its composing materials, those characteristics must be attributable to the form, not the matter. Similarly, as
brick is matter to the house builder, it is a form to the brickmaker imposing it on clay and straw; and the water he mixes with the other materials
is itself a form composed of two atoms of hydrogen and one atom of
oxygen, but having properties utterly different from its two gaseous constituents. And thus it is with everything that men make using materials,
whether those materials are themselves man-made (such as steel and
brick), or naturally occurring (such as clay and water): what counts as
matter is *relative* to what it composes. Likewise with things that come to
be by nature. Bone is matter vis-à-vis a horse, being one of the materials
essential to its form; or, more precisely stated, bone is an ingredient of all
of the *formed* parts that make up the semi-rigid skeletal *structure* (the
arrangement of 'bones') that is unique to the form of the horse. But bone
is itself form at the level of analysis to which one addresses the question
'what is bone?': it is a certain molecular form naturally compounded of
more elementary materials (carbon, calcium, phosphorus, whatever) – not
simply a mix of those materials, but formed in a unique molecular structure – and having its own properties which are a consequence of that
structure, much as are the structural properties of the arch or the I-beam.[9]

Moreover, this reductive analysis can be continued, reducing each form
of matter, be it carbon or iron, calcium or phosphorus, to its more basic
constituents – whereupon the properties distinctive of the unreduced
material are lost. For all of the hundred-odd chemical 'elements' have
turned out not to be truly *elementary*. An 'atom' of any one of them (the
smallest identifiable quantity of that particular form of matter) is not
truly *a-tomos* ('uncuttable'), but can be 'split' because it is composed of
still more basic forms of matter: protons, neutrons, electrons – each particle of whichever kind being identical to every other one of its kind:
there is nothing distinctive about the protons in a carbon atom; they are
completely interchangeable with the protons in a uranium atom.[10] And
these 'subatomic' part(icle)s, in turn, are formed from even more basic
stuff, or so our physicists speculate – a reductive analytical sequence that

necessarily terminates in a single substance that can never be perceived, only intellected, which Aristotle calls 'prime matter.' It is an idea at which Hobbes sometimes seems to scoff,[11] using it as analogy for the pro-nouncements of ancient oracles, such as those of the Pythia at Delphi: 'of whose loose words a sense might be made to fit any event, in such sort, as all bodies are said to be made of *Materia prima*' (XXXVI/8, 226). Or is Hobbes, while seeming to ridicule the idea, actually conceding the point: that reduced to its ultimate homogeneous stuff, matter per se explains nothing? For as pure *potentia*, capable of becoming anything, it must itself be both devoid of properties (what Hobbes calls 'accidents'), and *inert*, incapable in itself of becoming any more particular kind of thing (i.e., some higher form of matter). Thus, something besides matter must be invoked to explain *why* there are different forms of matter, at whatever level of analysis: subatomic, atomic, molecular, and so on.

Clearly, then, matter as such cannot be the *cause* of anything. Nor, consequently, is it the ultimate basis of Reality; something else must be causally efficacious, creating and governing the world we directly expe-rience. For that world is the furthest thing from one great homogeneous, featureless, unchanging blob. It is a stupefyingly complex ordering of practically countless heterogeneous kinds of things (forms of matter, forms of life, structured groupings and hierarchies of those forms, etc.), all in motion, endlessly coming into being and passing away. Nor, then, can anything be *explained* by reference to matter pure and simple. Insofar as Matter 'matters,' it is always *formed* matter, and as such only *matter* relative to a given analytical context, with all its properties and effects a consequence of that particular form. This includes the particu-lar effects of any kind of *motion* upon a given body: the effect of wind on water differs mightily from its effect on stone. As for Motion per se, it can no more explain particular change than can undifferentiated Matter. The forms of motion and their actual effects depend decisively on the forms of the matter being moved: the effects on the human eye of wind-borne ocean spray are quite different from those of a sandstorm. Hence, there is no possibility of a coherent Materialism, if by that one means a metaphysical doctrine wherein Matter (or Matter-in-Motion) is regarded as the ultimate reality, and the ultimate cause of all that is and happens.[12] The most that could be claimed for *unformed* matter is that it might be the basis for that mysterious force we call 'gravity,' apparently a power of attraction of matter for matter regardless of form, which perhaps holds the entire universe together. But, as is easily seen, such an undiscriminating power cannot conceivably be the cause of any of the countless differentiated forms manifest in the heterogeneous world we wish to understand.

What, then, of Hobbes's 'bodyism'? Does it provide credible criteria for distinguishing what is real from what is not, thus ensuring that all imaginary causes and effects are excluded while leaving open for investigation all real possibilities? And has Hobbes thereby laid the metaphysical basis for – whatever else – a rationally coherent Science of Politics? Specifically, does his strategy of regarding Bodies as the ultimate reality ('every one of them Individuall and Singular'; IV/6, 13)[13] – and as such, the primary *cause* of all perception, imagination, and thought – amount to an implicit endorsement of Materialism while evading responsibility for defending it against the objections, seemingly decisive, that any journeyman Aristotelian would raise? Because with respect to part of his account Hobbes claims to be but 'briefly' summarizing in *Leviathan* 'the same' as that which he has 'else-where written of ... at large' (I/3, 3),[14] the reader may not feel altogether confident that an assessment of his doctrine can justly be made on the basis of its presentation here. Still, Hobbes's inclusion of his ostensible metaphysical principles, however abbreviated their exposition, tacitly suggests that they can withstand inspection. So, can they?

The first difficulty arises from the fact that Hobbes provides no explicit definition of the crucial term 'body.' Judging from what is implicit in the analyses in which it figures, 'body' invariably refers to: something perceptible, albeit not necessarily to immediate sight or touch, but ultimately to one or more senses, so as to cause a sensation or 'Fancy'; occupying space, hence a 'solid' having three definite dimensions, hence a certain shape, albeit subject to change; located in a particular place at any given instant of time. Along with weight or 'heaviness,' these are the characteristics usually associated with Matter (at least at the perceptible level). But inasmuch as Hobbes is explicit that both air and water qualify as bodies (as of course they must, being undeniably real), one readily sees that all of the problems attending the relativity of matter once again arise. For in what sense does a wind, for example, have a shape or a place? Presumably not as some vague sort of whole, but as individual particles – bodies – of air, each with its definitive shape, and at any given instant occupying a particular place. But is not this the same with all bodies subject to change in shape and matter (as Hobbes says, 'every part of Body, is likewise Body, and hath the like dimensions'; XLVI/15, 371)? Thus, perceptible bodies must necessarily be composites, since for matter to be added or subtracted, that matter must itself be a body subject to change in both form and matter, which in turn means its matter must be a body subject to change, and so on down to homogeneous, propertiless, inert (i.e., strictly *passive*) prime matter. Thus, one again reaches Aristotle's conclusion: at any level of composition, the properties of bodies (*formed* matter) must be due to their respective forms.

The conception of Form implicit in Hobbes's Bodyism, however, is wholly inadequate, being merely the outer and inner boundaries of the composing matter – the shape of occupied space – which cannot account for the diverse structural and behavioural properties of the countless kinds of Body. Whereas, any sort of conception that plausibly *can* account for the observable phenomena must grant that all effective forms (of matter) have, first of all, some sort of independent existence and, secondly, some sort of active or passive power. To take the simplest example, consider the arch. This form and the properties it imparts to solid matter so arranged was not invented by the Romans (or whomever), much less created by them; they merely *discovered* a natural form already existing quite independently of material embodiment in artificial structures, quite as *real* and permanent 'as the Lawes of Nature.' In order to put the discovery to use, they went on to invent practical techniques whereby to erect structures of properly shaped stones and bricks that exploit the natural properties of the arch,[15] and so to build countless such structures, many of which are still standing after two millennia. And when these arch-shaped bodies – the bridges, doorways, domes, aqueducts, whatever – do collapse, it is not because of a failure in the form of the arch (that it has somehow lost its power, its structural properties), but from other causes.

For anyone who can think, it is impossible to believe that 'the *Universe*, being the Aggregate of all Bodies, there is no reall part thereof that is not also *Body*.' Forms, too, are real, with a mode of being independent of material embodiment. Nor does this apply only to the forms that structure the innumerable kinds of inanimate matter and in which inhere each kind's identity and respective properties.[16] For, according to the modern theory of evolution, there are also countless viable forms of *life* that once enjoyed material embodiment but are now extinct.[17] Whereas all of the life forms now materially actualized on earth once existed only in potential, so one must presume that whatever *forms* of life are viable in a given environment must have always been so, be so now, and for all future time.[18] But there are also forms that are real, yet not capable of embodiment strictly speaking, though they pertain to the perceptible realm and relations among the embodied things within it (e.g., numbers, figures of geometry, and generally all of the things expressed in mathematical formulas are not material; as one scholar commented, 'There is nothing less solid than a geometrical "solid"').[19] In this category would belong the human virtues, according to Plato and Aristotle; for though embodied people may be virtuous, the forms of the virtue whereby they are judged to be so are not themselves material.[20]

And what about the *form* of the Hobbesian Commonwealth, and the 'Principles of Reason' upon which it is supposedly based?

As the art of well building, is derived from the Principles of Reason, observed by industrious men, that had long studied the nature of materials, and the divers effects of figure, and proportion, long after mankind began (though poorly) to build: So, long time after men have begun to constitute Common-wealths, imperfect, and apt to relapse into disorder, there may Principles of Reason be found out, by industrious meditation, to make their constitution (except by externall violence) everlasting. And such are those which I have in this discourse set forth. (XXX/5, 176)

There have been many actual commonwealths, but not one such as Hobbes has 'derived from the Principles of Reason.' So, is this *form* of regime, though neither then nor yet embodied precisely as 'set forth' by its architect, something *real*, in light of which actual regimes can be judged, their defects detected, understood, and perhaps corrected? Or is it a mere 'Idol' of Hobbes's brain, and as such signifying 'nothing'? Hobbes expresses 'some hope' it may eventually be properly actualized. What is the existential status of his hope? And what about those 'Principles of Reason' – are *they* real? Could anything be validly derived from what is not real? And do they or do they not 'really' have the *power* to dictate the form of regime that suits Hobbes's political purposes? So much, then, for the covert Materialism residing within Hobbes's claim that 'there is no reall part [of the Universe] that is not also *Body*.' As an ontology, it is – to repeat my initial assessment – hopelessly inadequate.

However, the clarity with respect to Matter, Form, and Nature that one gains by working through the inadequacies in Hobbes's Bodyism leaves one the better prepared to address what he treats as the key idea of philosophy and science: Cause. And because it is just possible that Hobbes means his silence about this basic concept to be interpreted as approval of Aristotle's quadriformal analysis – that 'having examined the Definitions' of this former author respecting causation, he saw nothing with which to take issue, and accordingly relied upon them himself (for so he apparently did) – Aristotle's account is worth a brief review.

3

The Aristotelian Analysis
of Cause

For Aristotle, just as for Hobbes and for us, Science (from *scientia*, Latin for 'knowledge,' equivalent to the Greek *epistēmē*) is essentially involved with the discovery of causes. We naturally expect a science worthy of its name to explain 'what causes what.' As Aristotle observes, 'humans do not think they know a thing until they have grasped the "why" of it, which is to grasp its primary cause.'[1] Whereas Metaphysics is exclusively knowledge of the intelligible realm of Being (of whatever is unchanging, or eternal), Physics – i.e., all of what we today think of as Natural Science – focuses on the perceptible realm of Becoming, the realm of form and matter mixed. That is, *Physica* ('Nature') comprises the countless particular physical objects that populate our everyday sensual world and which are perpetually in all kinds of motion, changing, from the time they come into being until they pass away. Thus Nature is the realm of causation, for causing involves change, either to *effect* change (of form, position, motion, quality, quantity, whatever) or to prevent change (as bracing a building prevents its collapse, or as freezing meat prevents decay). To be sure, change, and thus causation, is not confined to Nature, but applies as well to the Artificial and the Conventional, the two sorts of things that exist through human making. However, while the distinction between what exists by nature and what in some other way is important (requiring, as previously noted, clarification of what it means for something to have 'a nature'), because humans themselves exist by nature, and whatever they make by art is through the manipulation of that which exists by nature, there is a sense in which Nature encompasses the entire realm of causation. In any case, Aristotle's analysis of cause applies to all change, whether due to so-called natural causes or human making.

Aristotle presents essentially the same account of Cause in both his *Physics* and his *Metaphysics*;[2] this in itself indicates both its pervasive importance and the absence of a firm boundary between the two subjects. For certain issues of *ta physika* ('the natural things') shade directly into those of *hë meta ta physika* ('the things beyond, or above, the natural things').[3] Traditionally, Aristotle's exposition of cause was regarded as a philosophical tour de force, revealing so much about the world that we are otherwise apt to overlook, since often a person is practically interested in but one or two aspects of a *complete* causal analysis – that is, of an analysis adequate for the theoretical purpose of a full understanding. Thus, anyone wishing to mount either a challenge to, or a defence of, the Aristotelian view of the world is obliged to provide a convincing critique of his treatment of causation. However, a fair appreciation of its strengths and weaknesses requires a fuller exposition of his conception of Nature, and of how and why it is properly investigated, than is practical to undertake here. Still, enough can be sketched to allow for a clearer understanding of the causal basis of Hobbes's political science, as well as of the problems that attend his ostensible metaphysical views, his treatment of Reason, and his mechanistic Psychology.

The prevalence with which people think 'causally' is implicit in how they speak, employing a broad range of locutions in which this predisposition is present, some explanatory (e.g., because, so that, owing to, since, in order that, on account of, due to, inasmuch as, thanks to, by reason of), others interrogative (e.g., why, how, what for). One must suppose such modes of speaking to be revealing about human nature or, more precisely, about the human mind: the extent to which our normal posture towards the world presumes that everything is bound together by a tight net of causal connections. Why *do* we believe so strongly in causation as such, so sure (as Hobbes notes) that things do not 'just happen' but are *caused*? An adequate psychology must address, and plausibly answer, this question. As a practical matter, one is more apt to *seek* after the cause when something unexpected happens or something expected does not happen, or when for whatever reason routine occurrences arouse one's interest. But this unevenness of curiosity is irrelevant to an understanding of Causation per se, as multiple causes are operative all the time with respect to all things of the sensible realm. Selective curiosity is, however, *highly* relevant to an understanding of the related ideas of Chance and Fortune.

Beneath the endless references to causation that pervade people's everyday speech, Aristotle discerns four primary senses of the word 'cause,' reflective of four distinct kinds of causes that collectively account for both the persisting properties and relations of things, and the changes they undergo.

First is *Material* cause: 'that from which' – that from which a thing is made or composed, out of which it comes to be and endures (so long as it does). For example, the bronze of a statue; the flesh, blood, feather, and bone of a chicken; the stone, wood, and glass of a house. That the properties of each particular form of matter involved are due to its form, and that it is 'matter' only in relation to the sort of thing it composes (i.e., that level of composition, as previously discussed), in no way affects its particular causal role in determining the properties of whatever is made from it. Thus, the statue turned green because it is made of bronze, which oxidizes in the open air, leaving a green film called (appropriately enough) 'verdigris.' Thus, the walls and roof of the house burned (because made of wood, and wood is 'by nature' flammable), whereas the foundation remained (because made of stone, impervious to fire). Thus, the flesh of the corpse promptly decayed, whereas its skeleton did not, because of the different natures of the respective materials. However, in discussing the Material cause of things, Aristotle includes the syllables of a word, the notes of a song, the premises of an argument; and generally speaking, any parts that make up a recognizable whole can be thought of as constituting its matter.[4] Everything that actually exists in the perceptible realm – which need not mean that it is itself perceptible: the rationale of a particular argument is not itself perceptible, but its place is in the perceptible realm – is made of something; and that material out of which it is made, having its own properties, imparts those properties to whatever is made from it. Thus, the chord is harmonious because the frequencies of its composing notes are whole mathematical ratios of each other. And one argument is explanatory because its premises are true, whereas another is fallacious because its premises are false.

Second, *Formal* cause: the shape, sequence, design, arrangement, or 'formula' that orders, shapes, directs, or structures the matter or parts into the distinct kind of whole thing it happens to be, including the pattern of its changes and transformations and the trajectories of its natural motions. Formal cause pertains not only to explanations in terms of immediately perceptible shapes, movements, and structures, but also of organizational forms such as the structure of a wolf pack, or of a patriarchal family – forms that can only be intellected, not seen or heard (though, of course, the intellecting involves discerning a pattern in the perceptible evidence). Aristotle also includes as formal causes all logical entailments, hence all geometrical and other mathematical relations. When one is asked why the sum of the squares of the two legs of a right triangle is equal to the square of its hypotenuse, the explanation is purely formal, the explanandum being the logical implication of initial definitions and the propositions derived therefrom. However, while mathematicians deal with forms, they do not do so 'as the limits of natural bodies,' but instead as purely formal objects; whereas the study of Nature is of form and matter combined, each constituent of which enters into explaining a thing's properties.[5] Thus, a wine goblet is easily shattered *because* of its delicate shape (obviously, the brittleness of glass is also a factor – were it made of acrylic or rubber, it would not shatter; still, that the same brittle matter cast in the form of a marble, or even a shot glass, would be far more sturdy points to the causal significance of form). Thus, one auto goes faster (or burns less fuel) than another with the same engine and of equal weight (equal matter) because of its more aerodynamic form (though here, too, material cause enters; the speed or fuel efficiency of either car might be increased by reducing its weight, making it of lighter material). Thus birds and airplanes can fly because of the shape of their wings. Thus a particular poem is not only 'moving,' but first of all intelligible because of the *order* of its composing words. And, thus, a certain song pleases because of its beautiful melody, which is a particular sequential *arrangement* of notes; the collection of notes or tones (the song's 'matter') is one thing, the tuneful form imposed on them a different kind of thing entirely. If music were just quantities of notes, everyone – and no one – would be a master composer. And while most of us can appreciate the forms of music only when hearing them, it is important to understand that these forms exist independently of their audibility (thus the peculiar poignancy of one of the greatest composers being famously deaf).

Third is *Efficient* cause: the agency which immediately brings about some change, setting in motion something at rest, or affecting the motion of something already in motion (stopping, slowing, deflecting, accelerating, reversing, or sustaining it) – briefly put, that which is credited with 'precipitating' a *change*. This is the only type of cause to which Hume's famous analysis applies;[6] and generally when anyone speaks of a 'chain' of causation (as does Hobbes), they mean a sequence of efficient causes. Thus, the forest fire was caused by a bolt of lightning – though there would have been an efficient cause of the lightning, and before that efficient causes of those atmospheric conditions, and so forth. To be sure, both the matter and the form of the individual trees, as well as the pattern of forestation, were also causal factors; yet the fact remains that the trees did not spontaneously combust, but were set ablaze by the lightning, or careless campers, or an arsonist – some discrete event that started a fire in flammable material that was not previously burning, some initiating cause essential to explaining what happened precisely *when* it did. Thus, the sculptor is the efficient cause of the statue, as is generally the maker of anything made (the beaver of its dam, the composer of his song, the architect of the design or model, the builder of the actual structure based thereon, the general of the victory, the pilot of the voyage). Thus, the adviser (or commander) is the cause of action undertaken on his advice (or command). And, thus, the father is the efficient cause of the child (for a woman's latent potential for conceiving a child is not actualized without a particular precipitating event).

Fourth, there is *Final* cause: the purpose, end, aim, function, use (the *telos*) 'that for the sake of which' something exists or is done, the goal towards which change is directed, or for which efforts to prevent change are expended. However – and this deserves all the emphasis that one can give it – not everything that exists or happens serves a particular purpose. The waves beating endlessly on the shore do so of mechanical necessity as determined by the other three kinds of cause (or, as we are more apt to say, in accordance with the natural laws of physics), but not for any particular purpose. So with falling meteors, erupting volcanoes, flowing rivers, all weather, the particular rock one stumbles upon – indeed, so it is with most non-living matter not presently incorporated in the life-world. But where there *is* purpose, citing it is explanatory. Thus, the athlete trains in order to be victorious in competition. Thus, the owner of the house repairs his roof to prevent its leaking (i.e., for the sake of keeping dry the interior of his house). Thus, the potter makes his pottery for the purpose of selling it, and the buyer acquires it for the sake of its uses (a sequence of final causes that explains the existence of the pottery, though it is important to notice that the logical priority of *utility* explains the temporal priority of making artefacts; generally speaking, we *make* in order to *use*, not vice versa). Thus, one studies Hobbes's *Leviathan* for the sake of better understanding political life (which is presumably also one of the purposes for which he wrote it). And, thus, the lover sings with the aim of wooing his beloved (perhaps having composed, or commissioned – and, of course, learned – the song in order to sing it). Whereas birds may sing in order to claim territory, as well as to attract a mate; and they build nests for the sake of having a secure place in which to raise their young – not out of conscious purpose, but instinctively. Similarly, various birds and animals migrate in order to escape the rigours of winter and/or to procure more readily available food. The protective coloration of many animals serves an obvious purpose, and that same purpose explains seasonal *changes* in colour. The placement, form, and matter of the heart are determined by its purpose: to circulate the blood, which in turn serves further vital purposes. In order to explain (i.e., serve the purpose of explaining) *why* any bodily part exists, such as the eye, one must recognize the purpose it serves; and to explain *how* it accomplishes that purpose, one must understand the purpose of each of the subordinate parts of the eye, why those various components exist.

This illustrates a general principle: the same overall purpose can serve as the final cause of many distinct things, activities, processes, behaviours, and qualities. For example, the concern for Health is the final cause of much of what has to do with nutrition and diet and exercise, with rest and clothing, with refraining from certain practices (e.g., smoking, sun-bathing), with personal and public and occupational safety, with protecting the quality of air and water, with undergoing medical treatment, with support for medical research, and the entire existence of our enormous medical establishment.[7] Indeed, most of what humans do has ultimately the same final cause: the good life (or 'happiness') – that is, what they believe to be the good life. For 'all things by nature seek their good.'[8] This is the single most important conclusion to be drawn from the study of Nature, the First Principle of both Knowing and Being.[9] And as this purposeful disposition is innate in the natures of all living things, Nature is the ultimate final cause of all that is and happens in life.

To repeat an earlier point: while typically we are interested in only one or two causal dimensions of whatever we wish to understand – usually either what precipitated some change (the efficient cause), or why something exists or was or was not done (for what purpose, the final cause) – nonetheless, a complete analysis would specify all four causes (presuming final cause to be pertinent). In practical matters, there are instances where people differently situated have different causal interests. For example, in a murder case, 'the cause of death' according to the forensic pathologist might be several blows to the head with a blunt instrument (mortally disrupting the functional form of the victim's matter), whereas the detectives working the case concentrate on efficient and final causes – that is to say, on Who and Why, perpetrator and motive. So, in practice Aristotle's analysis can be and is used selectively, with the purpose of the inquiry implicitly focusing attention on one kind of cause rather than another. In seeking after 'the cause' of a bridge's collapse, investigation would normally concentrate on material and formal causes (was it inferior-quality concrete or poor design?), though efficient cause might be the issue if the collapse was caused by a truck exceeding the weight limit, or by an unprecedented earthquake, or by sabotage (and even final cause in the event of a saboteur).

As Aristotle is at pains to point out, this analysis is intended to clarify one's thinking about cause (that is *its* final cause), especially the complex ways things causally interact. For two things can be the cause of each other, but in different senses of the word, reflective of different kinds of causes. So – to cite the classic example – exercise is an efficient cause of health and strength and beauty, whereas being healthy, or strong, or beautiful may each or all be the final cause of the exercise.[10] Similarly, the rocket is the efficient cause of the satellite being placed in orbit, whereas the satellite being in orbit is the final cause of the rocket (and the satellite, in turn, may be the efficient cause of gaining meteorological data, whereas gathering the data would then be the final cause of the satellite). Alcohol in the blood is the material cause of intoxication, whereas the intention of getting intoxicated (in search of solace, or liberation, or fellowship, whatever) is the final cause of the alcohol's alien presence in the blood. And the thrilling plots of his novels is a formal cause of the author's being rich and acclaimed, while being rich and acclaimed is the final cause of his endeavour to form thrilling plots.

The same factor can be *spoken* of as the cause of contrary results, according to its presence or absence – as the presence of a skilled player was the (efficient) cause of his team's victory, whereas his absence would have meant sure defeat; and the presence of rebar steel in the concrete would have been a (material) cause of the bridge's withstanding the earthquake, whereas its absence caused the bridge to collapse (though, more *strictly* speaking, the material cause was the weakness of the matter out of which it was actually composed). And it is especially important to be clear on how the same thing can be more than one kind of cause, serving in different causal capacities, since this figures so prominently in political life. Humans are frequently at once the formal, efficient, and final causes of the artefacts they invent or design and then make: the design being the source of the thing's form, the making its efficient cause, its final cause being the human purpose for its making. The pioneer who builds his own log cabin is at once its formal, efficient, and final cause, as Michelangelo is the formal, efficient, and (in an immediate sense, at least) the final cause of his David. Moreover, in explaining such conventional things as manners and ceremonies, debating clubs and sports teams, people figure in all four causes. In legislative assemblies, people are its matter, the designers of its formal procedures, the initiators of its actions, and the source of its purpose.

4

The Human Psyche
and the Problem of *Chance*

With this much clarified about causation, one is rationally prepared to understand what is meant by Chance or Accident (*to automaton*), and the special kind of chance called Fortune or Luck (*hē tychē*) – topics that bulk huge in human affairs, as no less an authority than Machiavelli observes:

It is not unknown to me that many have held and hold the opinion that worldly things are so governed by fortune and by God, that men cannot correct them with their prudence, indeed that they have no remedy at all; and on account of this they might judge that one need not sweat much over things but let oneself be governed by chance. This opinion has been believed more in our times because of the great variability of things which have been seen and are seen every day, beyond every human conjecture. When I have thought about this sometimes, I have been in some part inclined to their opinion. Nonetheless, so that our free will not be eliminated, I judge that it might be true that fortune is the arbiter of half of our actions, but also that she leaves the other half, or close to it, for us to govern.[1]

Hobbes, as noted earlier, singles out people's curiosity about 'the causes of their own good and evill *fortune*' as itself a primary natural cause of their belief in Gods. And like Machiavelli, Hobbes subtly, and repeatedly, assimilates God with Chance and Fortune. For example, in defining and discussing Power, he includes among the 'Instrumental' kinds of power, 'the secret working of God, which men call Good Luck'; X/2, 41). As such, 'Good fortune (if lasting,) [is] Honourable; as a signe of the favour of God' (X/40, 44). And generally, 'men that know not what it is that we call *causing*, (that is, almost all men) ... attribute their fortune to a stander by, to a lucky or unlucky place, to words spoken, especially if the name of God be amongst them' (XII/8, 53–4).

References to Chance under one or another of its various names ('fortune,' 'luck,' 'accident')[2] figure often enough in *Leviathan* – as one would expect in any book about political life. For example, he warns of the difficulty of distinguishing 'a mans dream, from his waking thoughts' that can arise 'when by some accident we observe not that we have slept.' This is his explanation of Brutus's reportedly being visited by 'a fearfull apparition' in the night before the battle of Philippi. He goes on to assure us that 'this is no very rare Accident' (II/7, 7; cf. XXVII/20, 155–6). And because a man entrusted with Sovereign Power still remains a man, 'if the publique interest *chance* to crosse the private, he prefers the private' – this being an argument for the superiority of monarchy, wherein (Hobbes contends) the private and public interests most often congrue (XIX/4, 96). 'Common-wealths can endure no Diet' of revenues and expenditures, he warns, 'For seeing their expense is not limited by their own appetite, but by externall Accidents, and the appetites of their neighbours, the Publique Riches cannot be limited by other limits, than those which the emergent occasions shall require' (XXIV/8, 129). And since 'Law [is] onely to those, that have the means to take notice of it,' so all 'those from whom Nature, or Accident hath taken away the notice of all Lawes' are 'excused' from obedience and are incapable of 'the title of just, or unjust' (XXVI/12, 140). In short, as these and other passages show, Hobbes clearly acknowledges the pervasive influence in human life, including the political consequences, of what men call 'Accident' or 'Chance,' 'Luck' or 'Fortune.'

This said, it is fair to add that the aspiration to *master* Fortune, that the desire to minimize if not entirely eliminate the role of Chance in human life, is the founding and continuing purpose – the overall Final cause – of Modern Science.[3] Moreover, Hobbes's political science is meant to be seen as of a piece with this ambition, offering a universally applicable political prescription to replace all previous depictions of the good regime, which by their creators' own admissions are applicable only in fortunate circumstances, and even then remain vulnerable to chance happenings.[4] Whereas, we moderns have come to expect a truly *scientific* account to be universally valid, hence universally applicable irrespective of time and place – and to that extent, not subject to the vagaries of Chance. Still, one must be clear as to what this means. That a valid science of medicine is universally applicable offers no guarantee that a trained doctor will always be immediately available whenever and wherever one happens to be needed. Similarly, even if one grants Hobbes to have produced a science of politics in this modern sense, it remains subject to chance in this crucial respect, as he himself concedes: *When (if ever)* it will be fully and properly put into practice (XXX/5, 176).

Despite its prominence in their writings, however – as in all political life heretofore – neither Machiavelli nor Hobbes, nor Bacon, nor Descartes attempts to explain what Chance *is*, or what people are referring to when they speak of Fortune, or Luck.[5] Perhaps this is because Aristotle left nothing more that needed to be said on the subject.

As Aristotle observes, people often speak as if Chance were itself a cause or, alternatively, an unpredictable force that sometimes interferes with or supersedes natural causation: 'some believe that chance is a cause, but an inscrutable one to human intelligence, as being a divine thing and full of mystery.'[6] Now, as then, there are those who regard all life on earth, and even the entire Cosmos as due to Chance, 'as if there was no necessity of things being the way they are.' This suggests that an analysis of Chance involves an analysis of Necessity also.[7]

Aristotle begins his exposition with a review of common opinions about the subject, which (not untypically) are inconsistent. On the one hand, people will attribute a certain outcome to chance, or accident, and (as we say) 'accidents will happen' – seeming to imply that accidents just happen, spontaneously. For example, 'by chance' one is involved in a minor automobile 'accident' on the way to the airport, 'causing' one to miss one's plane. 'Bad luck,' we are apt to call it. If, however, something disastrous should 'happen' to the flight one missed, one then regards oneself as extremely 'lucky,' and the auto accident turns out to be 'most fortunate.' But on the other hand, we are also disposed to believe that there are definite causes of everything: that however practically difficult it may be to determine, there *is* in principle a complete causal explanation to be had of what caused the minor auto mishap, and another of the major airplane catastrophe. How are these apparently conflicting views, each quite sensible, to be reconciled?

On Aristotle's analysis, Chance is not really a cause of anything; or as he sometimes says, it is only 'incidentally' (or 'concurrently,' or 'contingently') a cause in the sense that the sculptor who was the formal, efficient, and final causes of the statue of David just happened to be named Michelangelo. But the name had nothing whatsoever to do with causing the statue.[8] It is merely a contingency, concurrent with the existence of the man so named. In any event, 'Chance' does not refer to some mysterious, unpredictable force at large in the Universe. Rather, it is a name for a class of events that stand out to humans as outcomes that could conceivably have been intentional, purposeful – done 'for the sake of' – but presumably were in fact *not* the result of any such final cause, but instead were due to other causes. That is, we are antecedently aware that some things do occur 'for the sake of' some end or purpose, be it conscious or innate; whereas, there is another class of happenings that are not purposive (the wind blowing the dust, a solar eclipse, the gentle rain that falls indifferently on the fields of the righteous and the wicked). Thus, whenever an outcome appears as if it could be of the former kind, but we believe it to be in fact of the latter kind, we *notice* it, single it out, and call it 'an accident,' or a 'chance happening.'[9]

So, accidents are unforeseen, because unusual, conjunctions of chains of natural causes (for, as Aristotle rightly notes, we do not attribute to Chance what always or usually happens). Accidents are results that stand out *for us* because of our natural disposition for seeing things in purposeful terms – for recognizing purpose – even when we presume the purpose is merely apparent, not real. For example, were a chair to fall off a passing truck and land upright precisely where one wished to sit, one would regard that as a chance happening: it ends up just as if someone had intentionally placed it. But having seen it fall off, one knows that it was actually an unusual result of natural mechanical forces. However, these abnormal conjunctions of natural causes can also include *other* purposes, as is typically the case in collisions between automobiles; the drivers were intentionally going somewhere when they happened to collide – an accidental event that could have been, but presumably was not, intentional (for there *are* reasons why someone might ram into another's car 'on purpose'; but were one to believe that such was the case, one would no longer regard it as 'an accident').

This last example can serve to introduce the sub-class of events or outcomes called Fortune, or Luck, names we reserve for certain chance happenings that involve human beings capable of rational deliberation, hence of acting with conscious intention, 'deliberately.' We do not normally call inanimate things either 'fortunate' or 'unlucky'; and if we do sometimes so refer to animals, we are guilty of anthropomorphizing (an intellectual fault to which humans are naturally, and revealingly, prone). So, the house that burned to the ground because it chanced to be struck by lightning was not unlucky, though its owner was. Similarly, the block of marble out of which Michelangelo carved his David was not fortunate to be transformed into something so generally admired, whereas the people of Florence were fortunate – as are we all – to be the beneficiaries of the sculptor's genius (and the Medicis's largesse). What accounts for the difference? Simply that the house owner and the Florentines, as self-conscious, rational beings, were capable of appreciating what chanced to happen to or for them – capable, that is, of *regarding* themselves as lucky or unlucky, according to whether what happened either contributed to or detracted from their own good as they saw it (a capability small children, like animals, do not have, as we acknowledge whenever we might say, 'they don't know how lucky they are').

Thus, the man who goes to the market for the purpose of buying bread, and there by chance encounters someone buying wine who owes him money (and is then willing and able to pay it), has had a piece of good luck; had it been someone the man had reason to avoid, he would have regarded their meeting as bad luck. Aristotle provides an endlessly fascinating example in his *Physics*.[10] Noting that both 'the end, and the means towards it, may come about by chance,' he continues: 'We say, for example, that a stranger [or, foreigner] has come *by luck*, paid the ransom, and gone away, when he does so *as if* he had come for that purpose, though it was not for that that he came.' This rather curious example is apparently inspired by an episode in the life of Plato, whom Dionysios, the tyrant of Syracuse, conspired to have sold into slavery.[11] One can scarce imagine what would have been the subsequent course of history had not an acquaintance of Plato been most fortunately present, *and* possessed of sufficient means, to foil the scheme – nor can one readily conceive a more powerful illustration of 'the role of Fortune in human affairs'; that is, of the effects of chance happenings on the fates of individuals, nations, and the whole human race.

So, 'Chance' and 'Fortune' are not names of a mysterious, inscrutable power at large in the universe, capriciously, randomly causing things to happen. One might try to imagine what that would presuppose: a disjointedness in Nature, a lack of consistency and continuity in natural causation – in effect, something supernatural, like a passionate and wilful God, who intrudes at His pleasure. As Aristotle observes, 'if chance were real, it would seem strange indeed'; this succinctly expresses the judgment about the natural world that Hobbes himself labours so assiduously to persuade his readers to accept. Rightly understood, 'chance,' 'accident,' 'fortune,' 'luck' (and synonymous terms) are the names of concepts that we need for rational analysis of the world as we experience it, and only to that extent do these terms have *real* referents: there *really are* unusual conjunctions that stand out *for us*, given our own purposive mode of being and consequent disposition to recognize purposiveness, including an ability to distinguish between 'genuine' and 'apparent but false' instances of it. It is in this sense that Aristotle can say, 'Chance and Luck are posterior to Intelligence and Nature.'[12] Both the various forms of natural causation (which are the real causes of all things caused), and intelligent minds capable of recognizing and analysing those forms (especially that of purpose, or final cause), are the logical prerequisites of there being classes of happenings of which it makes sense to say they are (incidentally, contingently) 'due to chance,' 'fortune,' or 'dumb luck.'

In short, the Human Psyche being teleologically disposed by nature, we conceive of the idea of Chance for the same reason we are confident that there is such a thing as *causing*: namely, our immediate psychic experience of causing effects ourselves, some of which we intend, but also some that are incidental or even counter to what we intend, others inadvertent or accidental. David Hume's abstract logical analysis to the contrary notwithstanding, when I strike the cue ball with my cue and send it careening into other balls on the table, I am absolutely sure that I am the efficient cause of the sequence of events that my action initiated.[13] When I walk barefooted on damp sand and leave behind me rows of clear impressions of the forms of my two feet, I have not the slightest doubt that I am the efficient cause of those tracks. When I slap a mosquito, I know not only that it is I who killed it, but how and why. Whereas, when I trip and fall against the china cabinet, feel the impact, see and hear the plates and glasses breaking, I am equally sure that it is I that caused the damage, but only 'by accident,' not 'on purpose' (as one might in a fit of anger). And when I speak aloud, and hear my own voice say the very words that I intend, I am certain that it is I who formed those sounds.

On the basis of these and ten thousand similar 'internal' experiences, I naturally believe in such a thing as *causing*, whether efficiently or purposefully or both. Neither my nor anyone else's understanding of causation as such is *based* on externally observing correlations and regularities – as it seems Hobbes, like Hume, would have us believe. Correlations of themselves could not provide any more understanding of *causing* than could the statistical frequencies of word usage provide apprehension of what is being said; to the contrary, our treatment of correlations as possible *signs* of causal relationships presumes a *prior* insight into cause. And through reasoning, I readily extend my belief in my own causal efficacy to what I see about me, not only to other human beings that I observe causing effects not unlike those I cause, but to other forms of life, and inanimate things as well. Watching a dog bark, I am certain that it is the cause of the sounds emanating from its mouth. And having hungrily observed a deer trotting across damp ground, I am sure that it is the efficient cause of the tracks I am now following (just as I am aware that my hunger played its part in moving me to 'track' it). And I can see ponds and streams being formed, being *caused*, by a steady rain, though I cannot see what causes the rain, and so may wonder about it.

This capacity for causal understanding, pervading our entire conscious life, is thus an all-important constituent of human nature. And it is profoundly revealing about the structure and powers of, not just the human mind, but the human *soul* – the *rational* soul – whose form we share (but which Hobbes has so inadequately described in the first twelve chapters of *Leviathan*). For one's curiosity about what causes everything that oneself does not cause – as Hobbes rightly observes, 'it is peculiar to the nature of Man, to be inquisitive into the Causes of the Events they see, some more, some lesse' – this theoretical interest in causation per se involves more than just curiosity, the rational desire to know. Equally important is the spiritual strength that sustains inquiry, and the spiritual satisfaction that attends each success.[14] Our intuitive recognition of causing, working in conjunction with our intuitive recognition of *learning* – for obviously one's initial recognition of having learned cannot itself have been learned – along with certain principles of reason whose validity we intuitively recognize,[15] results in knowing and its surrogates (believing, supposing, suspecting, doubting) being the basis of distinctly human life. In the case of all other animals, by contrast, their lives are based almost entirely on 'feeling.'

Thus, the *common* human essence is the set of rational faculties and their relationships with the lower parts of the soul. The *individual* essence, on the other hand, the 'identity' of each person, is first and foremost what he or she believes, for that ultimately governs a person's feelings towards everything else, including his or her own self. As Hobbes rightly argues, 'the Actions of men proceed from their Opinions' (which has a clear political implication: 'in the wel governing of Opinions, consisteth the well governing of mens Actions'; XVIII/9, 91). Imagine taking away everything that one believes, which includes everything that one remembers, and is the basis of whatever one thinks about the past or the future, all one's hopes and fears. What, then, would be left of one's personal identity? There would be the respective strengths of one's instinctive drives, presumably; but lacking the guidance of thought, these would be as undiscriminating as those of beasts. Given, then, that the core of each person's own psyche is whatever he or she believes, what most importantly *differentiates* people is how much they *care* that what they believe be *true*. For this will largely govern how inquisitive each one is – about causes, for instance, 'some more, some lesse.' And to the extent these qualities of the human soul: care and curiosity about the truth, are consequences of antecedent factors (e.g., genetic makeup, the family into which a person happens to have been born, similarly the political environment, the educators happened upon, the whole 'lottery of life'), to that extent – and how much *is* that, exactly? – human beings are inescapably subject to Chance, lucky or unlucky as the case may be.

Does Hobbes disagree with any of this? One cannot say with certainty, since he does not deign to define or discuss any of the Chance-relevant terms. Nor, as I noted earlier, does he expressly include either 'Cause' or 'Chance' among the eighteen examples of 'Names' relevant to *Philosophia prima*, though he does allow for the existence of 'divers others' (XLVI/14, 371). But from the various things he *does* say that would seem pertinent, one gathers nothing that would conflict with Aristotle's account and some indications of basic agreement with it. For example, in condemning certain doctrines that weaken a commonwealth, he includes the view '*That Faith and Sanctity, are not to be attained by Study and Reason, but by super-naturall Inspiration, or Infusion.*' Against this notion, Hobbes contends:

Faith comes by hearing, and hearing by those accidents, which guide us into the presence of them that speak to us; which accidents are all contrived by God Almighty; and yet are not supernaturall, but onely, for the great number of them that concurre to every effect, unobservable. Faith, and Sanctity, are indeed not very frequent; but yet they are not Miracles, but brought to passe by education, discipline, correction, and other naturall wayes, by which God worketh them in his elect, at such times as he thinketh fit. (XXIX/8, 169)

The outcomes of most interest to people typically result from the concurrent interactions of a great number of factors, but all of them (including human actions) constrained by natural laws. The problem is not some loose cannon called Chance, but the sheer complexity of the world: 'There is no action of man in this life, that is not the beginning of so long a chayn of Consequences, as no humane Providence, is high enough, to give a man a prospect to the end' (XXXI/40, 193). If one thinks of the Laws of Nature as ordained by God, then there is no conflict between Fortune and the Necessity that results from the interweaving strands of natural causation: Luck, then, simply *is* 'the secret working of God.' Observation and experience are of limited value, since 'the causes of good and evill fortune for the most part are invisible' (XII/4, 52). Thus the Promethean futility of 'that man, which looks too far before him, in the care of future time, [and who] hath his heart all the day long, gnawed on by feare of death, poverty, or other calamity; and has no repose, nor pause of his anxiety, but in sleep' (XII/5, 52).

5

The Causes of a Commonwealth

As I presume the previously quoted portions of *Leviathan* have amply shown, Hobbes is emphatic in his insistence that a scientific explanation of anything is one given in terms of natural causes. What, then, is – or ought to be – his own account of the natural causes of the political association? He gives some indication in the second paragraph of his Introduction. Having in the first paragraph developed a detailed analogy between the *artificial* 'body politic' (for so Hobbes would have us regard it) and the *natural* body of a human, he follows this with a brief description of the four parts of his treatise:

To describe the Nature of this Artificiall man,[1] I will consider

First, the *Matter* thereof, and the *Artificer*, both which is *Man*.
Secondly, *How*, and by what *Covenants* it is made; what are the *Rights* and *just Power* or *Authority* of a *Soveraigne*; and what it is that *preserveth* and *dissolveth* it.
Thirdly, what is a *Christian Common-wealth*.
Lastly, what is the *Kingdome of Darkness*.

In that only the first two parts figure in Hobbes's scientific account of the origin and resulting character of polities (based solely on rational analysis of natural phenomena), the latter half of *Leviathan* is largely irrelevant to the causal explanation of a commonwealth (though far from irrelevant to a causal explanation of *Leviathan*).

In the portion of the Introduction just quoted, Hobbes clearly indicates that humans – whose common nature is the subject of Part One – are both the Material and the Efficient causes of commonwealths (being both the Matter thereof, *and* the Makers).[2] And while the other two causes are alluded to in the second point above, only at the beginning of Part Two ('Of Commonwealth') are they made fully explicit. Its first sentence, partially quoted earlier, identifies the Final cause:

The finall Cause, End, or Designe of men, (who naturally love Liberty, and Dominion over others,) in the introduction of that restraint upon themselves, (in which wee see them live in Common-wealths,) is the foresight of their own preservation, and of a more contented life thereby; that is to say, of getting themselves out from that miserable condition of Warre, which is necessarily consequent (as hath been shewn) to the naturall Passions of men, when there is no visible Power to keep them in awe, and tye them by feare of punishment to the performance of their Covenants, and observation of those Lawes of Nature set down in the fourteenth and fifteenth Chapters. (XVII/1, 85)

As for the Formal cause of a commonwealth, it is spelled out in the balance of chapter 17, which describes in detail the formal requirements of making and maintaining the Founding Covenant – or Foundational Covenant, one should perhaps call it, for it is primarily a logical, not an historical, idea.

On the face of it, then, Hobbes needs, and thus should forthrightly endorse, Aristotle's analysis of causation.[3] That he does not do so, that he instead leaves it tacitly attainted in the penumbra of his scathing dismissal of Aristotle's *Physics* and *Metaphysics*, may be for ulterior reasons. Certainly all four kinds of cause figure in his explanation of what polities *are*, and why and how they come to be. Or should one say, what *true* polities are; and how they come to be, *if properly constituted*? Definitely not, for that is a second respect, related but separate, in which Hobbes's political science is teleological. Not only is Hobbes's own description of Leviathan that of a polity which (in his view) perfectly fulfils the true or proper *telos* of a commonwealth, but the existence of polities as such – *all* polities, all the various types of actual commonwealths 'in which wee see men live' – is explicable in terms of men's efforts, variously inadequate, to extricate themselves from the misery of quasi-anarchy so as to secure 'their own preservation, and a more contented life thereby.'

Still, it would seem that Hobbes's political science must not be teleological in quite the same way as is Aristotle's. For Aristotle is famously associated with the claim that Man is 'by *nature* a *political* animal,' that is, a being naturally suited (or adapted) to live in a *polis*. Given, then, that a political association is man's natural habitat, polities as such are natural. And that being the case, it is not *man's* purpose but *Nature's* purpose that is the Final cause of polities. To be sure, polities are made by human beings (particular individuals are the efficient causes); and various people, having their reasons, may choose to make many different kinds. But, on Aristotle's view, men do not choose to be political any more than they choose to be articulate: that is intrinsic to human nature.

Whereas, Hobbes is just as famously associated with a contrary view: that man is *not* naturally political, that at most his nature includes some pro-political tendencies but is marbled throughout with strong streaks of the anti-political (implicit in the passions that incline him to war). The natural human environment or true State of Nature is basically the same as that of all other animals: the jungle. Accordingly, the political association is profoundly artificial, for it not only has to be constructed by men, the very possibility of living together 'politically' has first to be conceived, invented, designed by men as a means of achieving the conscious human purpose of a safe and comfortable life. As with all other artefacts, human utility, not a purposeful Nature, is the Final cause of the commonwealth. Ultimately, Nature (or God, if one wishes to add another link to the causal chain) deserves at least some of the credit for the *efficient* causation of polities, being the cause of the passions. For it is certain of the passions, Hobbes contends – namely, the fear of violent death, the desire for commodious living, and hopefulness – that motivate men to exercise the self-restraint required to extricate themselves from their natural state of war in favour of an artificial state of civil peace. The truth is, the Final cause of every political association is human through and through – from start to finish, as it were. Ironically, this partly explains why 'the first Founders, and Legislators of Common-wealths amongst the Gentiles, whose ends were only to keep the people in obedience, and peace, have in all places taken care' to appeal for ratification – not to Nature, not to the requirements of man's supposed political nature – but to some divine authority (XII/20, 57).

However, this disagreement over whether the polity is natural or artificial does not lay bare the root of the difference between Aristotle and Hobbes. For Aristotle might not (I believe almost surely does not) disagree with Hobbes that the *polis* emerged from some pre-political, more brutish condition. The traditional mythologies, the poets' genealogies, and the histories of the Greeks are replete with such suggestions; and there was a general awareness among Aristotle's contemporaries of peoples still living in comparatively primitive, even savage, conditions. Moreover, Aristotle's own account of the natural evolution from family to village to town to *polis* shows clearly enough his awareness that humans have not always lived in *poleis*, and that in his own time many still did not. Hence, this is *not* what he means in claiming that man is political by nature, and that a polity is man's natural environment. Rather, his point is that human nature is such that it can be perfectly fulfilled by living the kind of life, a fully civilized life, such as only a self-sufficient *polis* makes possible (being large and complex enough to meet all human needs and call forth all human virtues and talents, but no larger). In short, Aristotle contends that man – like all natural forms of life, like all of Nature – has a *telos*, a naturally given purpose, a fulfilled condition, a completion, hence, a natural standard of perfection. Indeed, on his view, one approaches *full* humanity only insofar as one acknowledges, pursues, and substantially approximates that perfect completion.

Hobbes is aware, of course, of all that civil life makes possible, and thus of how much human potential, especially of the mind and spirit, could never conceivably be actualized in the State of Nature as he describes it, lacking agriculture, navigation, large-scale construction, geographical knowledge, a rational account of time and seasons, all the arts and literature, and much else – lacking everything that is entailed in the word 'Society.' He emphasizes how comparatively isolated, poor, nasty, brutish, and short human life would necessarily be in that State. But measured by the description 'Of Man' that Hobbes himself provides in the first twelve chapters of *Leviathan*, those living in the State of Nature nonetheless *are* human, equally human, as fully human as anyone can be. For Hobbes does not credit man with having a natural *telos*, which actual people fulfil to varying degrees. On the contrary, he assures us 'there is no such *Finis ultimus*, (utmost ayme,) nor *Summum Bonum*, (greatest Good,) as is spoken of in the Books of the old Morall Philosophers' (XI/1, 47). This includes the 'ayme' and 'Good' of becoming fully human. There is a plenitude of purposes *within* human life – in fact, that is all human life is, an endless succession of purposes: 'a continuall progresse of the desire, from one object to another; the attaining of the former, being still but the way to the later' – but there is no overall governing purpose *to* human life, by light of which one might objectively judge what is good and bad, right and wrong, noble and debased.

On the surface, at least, Hobbes does not acknowledge a natural human *telos* because he does not conceive Nature per se as Teleological. In this, he seems distinctly modern and scientific. According to standard accounts of the Scientific Revolution, jettisoning the teleological view of Nature in favour of a strictly mechanistic-materialistic conception was the key to its success. Teleology, largely misunderstood, has come to be regarded by leading acolytes of the natural sciences as an anti-empirical, even quasi-mystical notion, and as such seen as ridiculous, its long tenure in the Western philosophic-scientific tradition something of a scandal. This view, for the most part thoughtlessly adopted and propagated, betrays an ignorance not only about teleology but about the actual character of modern science. As a corrective – in this case, as in so many – it is helpful to review the considerations that led Aristotle to reach conclusions that commanded the respect of sensible people for the following two thousand years. Might his teleological view of Nature, rightly understood, still be credible today? If so, this alone would render suspect Hobbes's brusque dismissal of Aristotle's '*Metaphysiques*, and *Physiques*' as but so much '*Vain Philosophy*' (XLVI/30, 376).

6

Nature and
the Problem of *Teleology*

Aristotle regards Nature as an order of necessity, determined by causes of all four kinds. What is controversial about this view, as Aristotle is the first to insist, is whether Final cause is inherent in Nature.[1] Do natural things exist and natural events happen 'for the sake of' some goal, end, purpose, fulfilment, some *telos* – do they aim at the Good (at some good result), as human purposive actions aim at some apparent good? To describe the natural world, the realm of change, as more precisely the realm of Becoming (of things 'coming into being') is implicitly to acknowledge that it is filled with *goal-directed* change: for such things are not simply 'becoming' in the abstract; each is becoming something in particular. Similarly, to speak of both generation and degeneration (or decay) implicitly acknowledges qualitatively different kinds of change, each of which is intelligible only in light of a particular thing's *prime* (*acmë*): a mature, fulfilled condition towards which it eagerly grows, then endeavours to maintain, and from which it reluctantly declines. But might all this apparent purposiveness be illusory, only so much evidence, not of purposiveness in Nature, but of the anthropomorphizing propensity in human nature?

Thus, Aristotle asks, 'Why should we suppose that Nature acts *for* something, and because it is better?' Why not regard it simply as a realm of mechanical necessity in which everything happens as does rain, which simply falls of necessity; a particular shower does not fall for the sake of making the corn grow (if it happens to be growing), nor for the sake of making it decay (if it happens to be lying on the threshing floor):

Why then should it not be the same with the parts in nature, e.g., that our teeth should grow up of [mechanical] necessity – the front teeth sharp, fit for tearing, the molars broad and useful for grinding down the food – that they did not arise *for* this end, but it was merely a coincidental result; and so with all the other parts in which we suppose there is purpose. Wherever, then, all the parts came to be just what they would have been *had* they come to be for a [particular] end, such things survived, being organized accidentally in a fitting way. Whereas those that grew otherwise perished, and continue to perish, as Empedocles says his 'man-faced ox-progeny' did.[2]

Moreover, Aristotle's own analysis of chance presumes that things can appear purposeful despite not actually being so. Aristotle nonetheless concludes that it is practically impossible to credit the Empedoclean view if one bears in mind all of the empirical evidence: how, species by species, virtually every morphic and behavioural detail of their make-up – and these must number in the hundreds if not thousands in the case of each of the higher animals – seems purposive. What is the likelihood of such a *conjunction* of purposive parts occurring simply by chance?

But irrespective of *how* such a vast panoply of purposively organized species came to be (whether designed and created by an omniscient, omnipotent God; or, as the net result of a billion-year-long evolutionary process; or, simply having somehow existed forever), the essential fact remains: one cannot give a complete account of any plant or animal, or of the parts that compose it, or of anything it does, without reference to its purpose or 'function.' To explain the 'why' of anything's existence – of hearts, lungs, livers, or kidneys; of antlers, hooves, claws, or beaks; of stalks, stamen, petals, leaves, or roots – one must discern its function. So, likewise, to explain processes, activities, behaviour – why blood circulates in the body, but quickly clots when exposed to air; why birds migrate to wherever, whenever; why certain plants turn to face the sun; why bears hibernate; why squirrels bury nuts – to understand such things, one must see what purpose is thereby served.

And notice, the 'why' question often has a practical priority vis-à-vis the 'how' question, in that typically one has to know something's purpose, its function, its proper work (its Final cause) in order to investigate *how* it does whatever it does (through Efficient, Formal, and Material causes). Only by first knowing the purpose of the Eye can one judge whether a particular eye is functioning properly. This exemplifies a most important general principle, equally applicable to both Nature and Art:

knowing something's purpose provides the standard for judging good and bad, better and worse instances of it (e.g., knowing that the purpose of a mirror is to reflect, clearly and without distortion, the image of what is put before it allows one to assess the comparative 'virtues' of actual mirrors). And, secondly, being able to recognize a properly functioning eye is a prerequisite of investigating *how* it works – that is, how it is *supposed* to work, providing 'perfect,' '20-20' vision. Only in light of knowing *that* can the causes of *defective* vision be investigated – which, unlike perfect vision, is not a single thing, but a vast plurality of kinds and degrees (near-sightedness, astigmatism, colour-blindness, total blindness, etc.).[3] Only by recognizing that the behaviour of migrating geese is purposive, that they are not just flying about, but are travelling somewhere definite, can one then inquire into the mechanisms whereby they navigate over the great distances they must journey. And could one ever understand an acorn – what it *is* – in complete ignorance of its final purpose: to produce an oak tree? Only in awareness of an acorn's *telos* can one then inquire after the various mechanisms whereby it endeavours to fulfil that *telos* (e.g., how it orients itself in space and time; how as its cells divide they differentiate, some to become roots that go down, some trunk that goes up, some leaves that bud in the spring, etc.). This illustrates another natural principle of first importance: one can understand the immature in light of the mature, but not vice versa.[4]

However, to lay to rest the suspicion that in conceiving Nature teleologically, one is tacitly anthropomorphizing it, attributing purposiveness where it is merely apparent but not real, more needs to be said about Purpose per se. There is no serious doubt as to whether teleological explanations are appropriate within the human sphere; almost all human activity would be incomprehensible without reference to the motives, designs, intentions, objectives – the various purposes – of the actors. We are all intimately familiar with *conscious* purpose. And, as Aristotle notes, there are those who argue that this is the only kind of purpose there is; and that, accordingly, teleological explanations of natural phenomena which are admittedly not the result of conscious choice are illegitimate (and no one suggests that the snowshoe rabbit's change of coat colour is intentional on the rabbit's or anyone else's part; or that geese deliberate before deciding en masse to leave the Arctic to spend the winter in Texas).

On this point – that Purpose presupposes conscious intention, if not actual deliberation – Aristotle argues that it is simply *not true*, attacking the contention from two directions. First, he reminds us that much of our own activity that is unquestionably purposeful is nonetheless done without each step being consciously intended – including walking. To be sure, there is almost always an overall purpose determining where, when, and how one walks (which is why it is rightly regarded as purposeful); but the actual actions are for the most part done unconsciously. Indeed, one's mind may be, as we say, 'a thousand miles away.' The unconsciousness of most walking is clearly revealed in situations where one becomes aware of some reason to be careful where one steps. Thus it is with much of what we do routinely, including that most human of purposeful activities, talking: those occasions when we carefully consider our words, and perhaps have to search for the right ones, are the exception, not the rule.

Secondly, most of what humans *make* have purpose 'built in' to them; that is why they are called 'useful': they have an intended use, a purpose that determines their design, and their existence is inexplicable apart from that inherent purpose. Our artefacts prove conclusively that purposiveness need not be conscious purpose in order to be real; it can be innate, built in. And if it can be built into the things that humans make, why not in the things that Nature makes? The kidney dialysis machine has the same purpose as the kidney of a human body; the purpose of eyeglasses is to correct and enhance the functioning of eyes so that they better achieve their natural purpose: to see clearly. Lacking knowledge of its purpose, one's understanding of an artefact is radically incomplete. This is shown whenever archaeologists dig up something that is clearly man-made, but are unsure what it is *for*, hence do not know what it *is*. And the same is true of any natural morphic or behavioural feature of a life form; we acknowledge that it is not understood unless we can see *why* it exists, a question that is satisfactorily answered only by seeing the purpose it serves. The assumption is that Nature is purposive throughout – that, as Aristotle famously put it, 'Nature makes nothing in vain.'[5] The fact that this assumption seems 'perfectly natural' to us need not be interpreted as evidence of a misplaced anthropomorphism; to the contrary, it is far more plausibly explained as a natural propensity well-suited for rational beings capable of understanding the world as it naturally is, the better to live in it (perhaps having been 'selected' – not *consciously*, but effectively – by evolutionary pressure for this very advantage).

So, there is no reason to conclude that only conscious purpose is real, and a multitude of reasons to conclude the contrary. The natural order teems with examples of purposiveness: all functioning body parts, the overall configurations of bodies, all instinctive behaviour; goal-directed change in the growth of life forms; the fact that living things are not indifferently healthy or sick but include mechanisms to maintain and restore health (the very idea of which bespeaks a naturally best condition, with the individual at the peak of its natural powers). Naturalists generalize that animals tend to be 'programmed' for either 'fight or flight,' whichever best serves their survival and/or reproductive prospects. Is not the survival instinct pre-eminent evidence that purpose pervades Nature? There is nothing unscientific, much less wildly speculative about any of this. Based simply on empirical observation of what the countless life forms do to survive and reproduce, what they make and build, how they treat their young – were one to attribute a human-like consciousness to them (as Aristotle most assuredly does not), one would conclude without question that it is all purposeful; it appears so in all other respects, and indeed is unintelligible on any other basis.

Thus, one must agree with Aristotle that Purpose can be *either* conscious *or* 'built in' (i.e., innate: as inherent in design or instinctive in behaviour). In fact, it fair to suggest that it is precisely those who recognize only conscious purpose who are guilty of anthropomorphizing, that it is they who have got it backwards: *most* purposiveness in Nature is innate; conscious purpose is the *exception*, not the rule. And that so much of human purposive behaviour is consciously such (or embraced within behaviour that is, as when one takes a walk) is precisely because our instincts are so attenuated, compared with those of other animals. For Reason itself to have a purpose – for there to be any point to inquiring, learning, assessing, deliberating, choosing, planning, scheming – there must be some significant latitude of action, which requires that behaviour *not* be ruled by instinct. Reason supplants brutish instinct; or alternatively conceived, the distinctly *human* instinct is to reason, so as to learn, know, and on that basis choose how to live.

Given what has been argued thus far, one might respond that it has only been shown that there is *some* purposiveness in Nature, but not that everything natural has a purpose, nor that the natural order as a whole must be understood teleologically. More precisely, the analysis is far more persuasive with respect to forms of life than with inanimate things. More precisely still: it is most immediately compelling with respect to the human form of being (since we are all intimately familiar with conscious purpose); to see its applicability to animals or to our body parts is harder (as it requires overcoming the consciousness prejudice derived from personal psychical experience); to extend it to plants perhaps a bit harder still; and highly implausible when applied to rocks and dirt and all inanimate matter. One might notice that this corresponds to the commonsense ranking of things. We readily speak of higher and lower forms of life, ranking humans higher than brutes, brutes higher than plants, and plants higher than dead matter.[6] We naturally, and quite rightly, care more about endangered whales and condors than about threatened snail darters and grasshoppers, to say nothing of thistles and bacteria. As for inanimate nature, its primary if not exclusive importance is as an environment for living things. Our hierarchical ordering of things (in which we rank humans higher than other primates, primates higher than other mammals, mammals higher than other animals, animals higher than plants, and plants higher than the dirt they grow in) reflects a natural standard of decreasing awareness and self-control, terminating in all the forms of inanimate matter, which have none. And it is precisely this total lack of all capability to *do* anything that makes the invocation of purpose, of Final cause, with respect to the inanimate realm so suspect, hence a teleological conception of the whole of Nature equally so.

Still, it *is* one World, a Uni-verse. Without knowing quite how it all fits together, we confidently intuit that it somehow does. Should this one World really require two kinds of Science – the teleological approach invoking all four kinds of cause being mandatory for making sense of the life world, whereas a purely mechanistic approach (confined to Efficient, Material, and Formal causes) being equally mandatory for explaining inanimate Nature? And yet, with every breath one takes, every glass of water one drinks, every grilled beefsteak or stewed soy bean one eats, one reaffirms that 'dead' matter is in constant communication between the two realms, the Animate and the Inanimate, integrating the two. And therein lies the key.

In claiming that Nature as a whole must be understood teleologically, Aristotle is manifestly *not* contending that everything that exists has a particular purpose, or everything that occurs does so in fulfilment of some Final cause. First of all, accidents happen – those unusual conjunctions of chains of causation. A storm blows a tree over, killing the deer that had bedded down near it. A volcano erupts, killing the fit and the unfit indiscriminately. Neither the storm nor the volcano occurred for the sake of killing the creatures that happened to be killed, favouring their competitors that happened to escape. There are explanations of all such natural happenings – of weather, tides, astral phenomena, avalanches – be they regular or abnormal; but these explanations would be given solely in terms of Efficient, Formal, and Material causes. Nor is there a purpose to the shape of any particular granite boulder (as there is to the shape of every swan, giraffe, shark, bison, falcon, snake, anteater, every tortoise and hare, every ant and grasshopper, every sequoia and sunflower; as there is to the upright posture of Man). A boulder's shape, like that of most chunks of inanimate matter, is accidental, and – to repeat – explicable solely in terms of Efficient, Formal, and Material causation. Moreover, in Nature, as in Art, mistakes happen. A clumsy sow inadvertently smothers one of her numerous shoats. Or the composing matter of an individual creature is defective, or insufficient, or obstacles interfere with its normal growth. Sometimes the result is a monstrosity, an almost complete perversion of nature, rather than an approximation of a fulfilled *telos*.[7] As for inanimate natural things – particular batches of rocks and minerals, soil and sand, water and air – they simply are; they have distinctive natures, inner necessities determined by the distinctive forms of their composing matter, and that is all there is to be said about them: they have no final cause, no particular purpose. Considered in isolation, that is.

But such is far from the case when considered from a more synoptic perspective. For, on Aristotle's view, the inanimate natural things lacking specific *telei* (all the 'raw materials') are encompassed within a teleologically ordered system and are essential to it. Inanimate nature provides the material basis for the entire hierarchy of animate natures. Matter (at whatever level of formation) being mere *potentia*, and as such capable of being the material cause of many different things, is thus not 'for the sake of' any one thing *in particular*. But it *is useful*, and available to be used by whatever life form has a use for and access to it. So, while a particular molecule of oxygen in the air, or gulp of water in some stream, or patch of dirt on the ground, does not have a specific final cause, they are there for the sake of whatever needs to breathe oxygen, or drink water, or grow in the soil – or simply needs a place to stand (for land animals need land to live on: to stand on, lie on, run around on, fight on, procreate on, and generally do whatever is specific to their respective natures, just as all the things that live in the oceans require that immense amount of liquid matter that makes up the oceans). When we carefully analyse any 'ecosystem,' we discover that the amount of non-living matter directly involved in supporting a particular 'food chain' is greater by whole orders of magnitude than the amount of matter that is at any moment actually embodied in the life forms the system comprises. And of course, that matter is all at or near the surface of the earth, and the surface requires an interior. Moreover, many life processes require the directionality provided by the gravitational field that only massive amounts of matter can generate.

In short, for all of its quantity and variety, life on earth (and it remains the only life we know of) requires an enormous material base; the ratio of non-living to living matter must be at least several million to one. And on Aristotle's perfectly sensible view, if something is ordered by a Final cause, then whatever is necessary to the fulfilment of that *telos* is also encompassed by it – a principle that Hobbes certainly agrees with, as he repeatedly affirms that a commitment to the End, the Purpose, necessarily includes the Means (XIV/21, 68; XVIII/8, 90; XXX/3, 175; XLII/125, 316). Consequently, with the various forms of matter being conditionally necessary for the actualization of the forms of life, the natural order as a whole is purposive.[8] For through each individual of a species striving to sustain and reproduce itself, each species is thereby sustained (unless and until supplanted by another), and thereby the entire dynamic hierarchy of life forms is sustained, and so the comprehensive *telos* of Nature is fulfilled, namely: To Be. The 'survival instinct' of animals is merely the most obvious manifestation of Nature's ruling purpose: To Be, rather than Not Be. Thus, Being exists in space and time through this self-perpetuating stream of Becoming that is Nature: the realm of Change – of things coming into being, existing as the distinct kinds they happen to be, then passing away – an endless flux of Matter through Form.

The dynamism of Nature is worth emphasizing, though it does not take much thought to see why the sorts of life forms as presently exist, each one's morphic and behavioural qualities organized for purposes of survival and reproduction, cannot remain forever in their prime. Reproduction would be pointless (being unnecessary), and nourishment non-existent. Whereas, speaking succinctly about the world as presently constituted, 'All these living things are tied together in a great web of eating and being eaten.'[9] One can perhaps imagine a world of perpetually peaceful co-existence – where lion look-a-likes lie down with lamb look-a-likes, and nothing untoward ever happens – but it is certainly not the world we live in. Animals could not *be* the heterogeneous kinds of beings they are (carnivores, omnivores, herbivores, whatever) were they not fitted for the competitive rigours of natural existence – Hobbes's State of Nature – fighting when they fight (some being victors, others losers and victims), pursuing or fleeing as appropriate to their respective natures, coping with every contingency that arises, on pain of death if they are not up to the challenge, as sooner or later will be the case for one and all. The net result of this whole array of purposeful striving by the individuals of various species is a natural order that is a self-regulating, self-sustaining teleological system, purposeful and purpose-filled. So, for example, predation serves a *higher* purpose than merely feeding the predator: it keeps the prey species fit; this is not the intention of the predator, of course, but it is a natural consequence of predation. As Aristotle puts it, Nature is like a doctor doctoring himself; that is, it has the purposiveness of Art built into it.[10]

The natural telei, the Final causes inherent in the natures of the various species, are timeless, and in that sense always exist. Misunderstanding this point has led to the mistaken criticism that to 'believe in' teleology – expressed as if it were some quasi-religious precept, rather than a principle supported by masses of empirical evidence – presumes that something which does not yet exist (a future prime condition) can cause effects in something which does exist (surely a logical impossibility). But this misconceives the being of a species' *telos*; it pre-exists the effects it causes in the same timeless way as do all the laws of physics and chemistry. Its mode of being is not that of existence in space and time – unlike the ever-changing things of Nature, the motions of whose formed matter is constantly subject to these unchanging *telei*.[11] The physical principles that determine, that cause, the trajectory of a projectile fired from a cannon to be parabolic in *form* are timeless. So, too, is the *telos* guiding the growth of a chicken from fertilized egg to that of mature adult, capable of making or fertilizing more eggs. Moreover, we are pretty sure that we know the mechanism (the Efficient, Formal, and Material causes) whereby this *telos* makes its presence effective: DNA – strands of formed matter in which is encoded all the relevant in*form*ation guiding the growth process (and much else). But just as the design of a building precedes the building itself, and is not to be confused with the mechanism whereby that design is made manifest (e.g., the paper and ink of the blueprint), the genetic information is something distinct from its carrier.

Thus, Aristotle provides a unified view of the World, and a unified approach to understanding it. He sees the Universe as a teleologically organized Whole, explicable in terms of four distinct but complementary kinds of causes. This much *cannot* be said for the account provided by the Modern sciences, which present a deeply bifurcated understanding of this one world. The portions of Reality that come within the purview of the so-called hard sciences (mathematics, physics, chemistry, geology, astronomy, and such) are studied non-teleologically. But the part that falls to the so-called Social sciences – the various dimensions of the Human world (economics, sociology, psychology, politics, linguistics, and such) – of necessity continue to employ teleological explanations that appeal to purposes and functions. And Biology is deeply divided between the two approaches, since it is the locus of the bifurcation. Biologists working at the macro-level (e.g., naturalists, ecologists, ethologists, evolutionary theorists) necessarily seek to understand the phenomena they study in purposive, functional terms; whereas, their colleagues engaged with the study of certain basic life processes (micro-biologists, organic chemists, most geneticists, etc.) do their work on a non-teleological, mainly mechanistic basis.[12] Awareness of the resulting incoherence implicit in the Modern Scientific World view is muted, however, by scientific specialization: the rational division of intellectual labour that unintentionally, but quite effectively, discourages attempts to understand the whole of things as a Whole.

Specialization, however, is at the very core of Modern Science, being the means of its technological successes.[13] And as I noted before, ever-increasing technological power is the Final cause, the *telos*, governing the entire modern scientific project.[14] But setting it in motion required a radical revision in the understanding of causation – a revision that directed attention away from the intellectually satisfying but technologically impotent knowledge of Final causes, in favour of focusing exclusively on the effective knowledge of Material and Efficient causes, and especially on a radically reconceived Formal cause, these being the key to utility. And the utility of this new kind of science, promising 'the Relief of Man's Estate,' was meant to be, as it has most emphatically proven to be, the basis for a complete reordering of the relationship between the pursuit of knowledge and the rest of political life. Once upon a time, a man might be exiled, imprisoned, or even hemlocked for too assiduously prying into the secrets of things in the heavens and beneath the earth.[15] Now such people win Nobel prizes, are seen as public benefactors, enjoy great prestige and financial reward, and are generally regarded as the highest intellectual authorities. Clearly there has been a sea change. But for that altogether new relationship to become established, it was not sufficient that the conception of science be transformed. Equally important was the design of a polity perfectly suited to promote and profit from the new kind of science Bacon envisioned. Enter Hobbes. For him to have undertaken the task, however, means that he was a firm believer in this revolutionary modern project – which need not imply that he accepted at face value the public justification for it, as opposed to his seeing other reasons instead, or in addition.[16]

To understand what Hobbes is committed to and why, the logical place to begin is with Bacon's criticism of Aristotelian science, and in particular with his radical reinterpretation of the four kinds of causes, which effectively displaced teleology from its central role in natural science. Bacon thereby transformed profoundly the very idea of Nature, and in so doing, effected the most momentous change of all: destruction of the only credible ground upon which objective evaluation might be based – short of Revelation, that is. According to the teleological view, as I noted before, things can be assessed in light of how closely they approximate the natural perfection of their kind, as implicit in each kind's *telos* (which the human mind can envision on the basis of analysing and synthesizing the perceptual evidence gathered from a suitable sampling of individual instances). Whereas, in the modern non-teleological conception of Nature, everything is 'equally natural,' being equally a consequence of mechanistic natural laws. Hence, Nature cannot be a source of criteria whereby the various instances of a given kind may be *ranked*. It is practically impossible to exaggerate the significance for human life of the change in perspective that has attended the supplanting of Aristotle's view of Nature and Science by that of Francis Bacon.

7

The Essentials of Baconian Science

The scope of the revolution Francis Bacon sought to bring about is indicated in the 'Proem' that fronts the prefatory material he provided for his *New Organon*:

[T]he entire fabric of human reason which we employ in the inquisition of nature is badly put together and built up, and like some magnificent structure without any foundation. For while men are occupied in admiring and applauding the false powers of the mind, they pass by and throw away those true powers, which, if it be supplied with the proper aids and can itself be content to wait upon nature instead of vainly affecting to overrule her, are within its reach. There was but one course left, therefore – to try the whole thing anew upon a better plan, and to commence a total reconstruction of sciences, arts, and all human knowledge, raised upon the proper foundations. And this, though in the project and undertaking it may seem a thing infinite and beyond all the powers of man, yet when it comes to be dealt with it will be found sound and sober, more so than what has been done hitherto. For of this there is some issue; whereas in what is now done in the matter of science there is only a whirling round about, and perpetual agitation, ending where it began. (3–4)[1]

Ostensibly, Bacon's main complaint with the (then) extant body of knowledge was that it was 'fruitful of controversies but barren of works' (8) – that it led to nothing truly useful to the life of man. And while he cites mankind's misplaced admiration for this sterile, static edifice bequeathed by the ancients as 'the cause and root of nearly all evils in the sciences' (40), his diagnosis of why previous investigators went wrong and what is required to get it right focuses on four main aspects.

First, he emphasizes the importance of a rigorous, thorough, complete empiricism that patiently gleans and winnows all of the relevant observable facts of Nature – gathered not only when she is 'free and at large' and so acting naturally, but including especially whatever can be revealed from seeing Nature artificially 'under constraint and vexed' in cleverly designed experiments (for 'the nature of things betrays itself more readily under the vexations of art than in its natural freedom'; 25).[2] This strategy bespeaks both what has become the modern conception of Nature: non-teleological, in which everything is natural in the sense of being subject to, hence revelatory of, universal natural laws; and the modern conception of Science: utilitarian, hence aimed at the discovery of technologically exploitable knowledge. So understood, the distinction of such profound importance for classical philosophy – between the natural and the artificial, or between 'nature acting naturally' and 'nature vexed' – is of little or no ontological significance. Thus Hobbes can begin his book by characterizing 'Nature' as 'the Art whereby God hath made and governes the World,' and go on to speak of 'the Nature of this Artificiall man [i.e., a commonwealth].'

Only Natural Histories that are complete in the modern Baconian sense – fully representative accumulations of all phenomena relevant to a given subject, patiently gathered from whatever sources (free nature, arts, experiments) – provide a sound basis for inducing explanatory principles or 'axioms':

For all those who before me have applied themselves to the invention of arts have but cast a glance or two upon facts and examples and experience, and straightway proceeded, as if invention were nothing more than an exercise of thought, to invoke their own spirits to give them oracles. I, on the contrary, dwelling purely and constantly among the facts of nature, withdraw my intellect from them no further than may suffice to let the images and rays of natural objects meet in a point, as they do in the sense of vision. (13–14)

By the various ways that he would have us screen the amassing and presenting of 'instances' (what would today be called 'data'), Bacon hopes to have 'established forever a true and lawful marriage between the empirical and the rational faculty, the unkind and ill-starred divorce and separation of which has thrown into confusion all the affairs of the human family' (14).

The second main concern is that of establishing the correct logico-scientific *method* for analysing all the data. Because 'the universe to the eye of the human understanding is framed like a labyrinth, presenting as it does on every side so many ambiguities of way, such deceitful resemblances of objects and signs, natures so irregular in their lines and so knotted and entangled' (12), the unaided human faculties are no match for the subtle complexities of Nature. Perception needs to be artificially enhanced, but especially intellection must be artificially directed by a sure method if we are to enjoy success in prying Nature's secrets from their hiding places: 'the mind itself [must] be from the very outset not left to take its own course, but guided at every step; and the business be done as if by machinery' (34). Providing this logical 'machine' to replace the six logical treatises of Aristotle (known collectively as the 'Organon,' i.e., 'Instrument') is – to judge by its title – the primary purpose of Bacon's *Novum Organum*, though that task is not actually taken up until Book Two. Induction is the key. He avers, 'in dealing with the nature of things I use induction throughout ... For I consider induction to be that form of demonstration which upholds the sense, and closes with nature, and comes to the very brink of operation, if it does not actually deal with it' (20). The problem, however, with basing general conclusions on inductive reasoning, at least as traditionally understood, is that (unlike deduction) it does not yield certainty. For in arguing on the basis of a finite number of instances that something is true in all possible such instances, hence expanding knowledge by reaching a conclusion that extends beyond the evidence upon with is based, one sacrifices logical certainty. Bacon is fully aware of the problem:

But the greatest change I introduce is in the form itself of induction and the judgment made thereby. For the induction of which the logicians speak, which proceeds by simple enumeration, is a puerile thing, concludes at hazard, is always liable to be upset by a contradictory instance, takes into account only what is known and ordinary, and leads to no result.

Now what the sciences stand in need of is a form of induction which shall analyze experience and take it to pieces, and by a due process of exclusion and rejection lead to an inevitable conclusion. (20)

What Bacon here calls for he half promises to deliver himself: a new kind of induction that combines the virtues of the existing forms of both deduction and induction, yielding certainty while expanding knowledge. But neither he nor anyone subsequently has been able to provide this; for while Bacon's various tables and procedures are useful paradigms for ordering and analysing data, they do not ensure the certainty of one's conclusions, as he well knew. Perhaps that is why Hobbes sides with Aristotle (though without acknowledging it, of course) in continuing to stress the importance of *deduction* for the generation of knowledge; this he makes clear in the paragraph marginally labelled '*Science*':

[F]irst in apt imposing of Names; and secondly by getting a good and orderly Method in proceeding from the Elements, which are Names, to Assertions made by Connexion of one of them to another; and so to Syllogisms, which are the Connexions of one Assertion to another, till we come to a knowledge of all the Consequences of names appertaining to the subject in hand; and that is it, men call SCIENCE. (V/17, 21; cf. VII/4, 30–1)

What Hobbes does *not* make clear, however, is whether he fully appreciates the importance of induction for the 'apt imposing of Names,' or for ensuring the validity of the assertions in which the various names are connected.[3] But in any event, while Hobbes remains committed to the deduction of knowledge by means of the syllogisms so disparaged by Bacon, he nonetheless seems wholly in agreement as to the utilitarian purpose of science rightly conceived.

This being the third and arguably the most radical respect in which Bacon transforms the conception and practice of Science: that of the End, the *telos*, for which it is sought – 'not either for pleasure of the mind, or for contention, or for superiority to others, or for profit, or fame, or [personal] power, or any of these inferior things, but for the benefit and use of life.' Concerning his own role, we may all 'be well assured that [he is] laboring to lay the foundation, not of any sect or doctrine, but of human utility and power' (15–16). On the face of it, this appears to be pure altruism, or Christian benevolence on Bacon's part, setting the example for a like philanthropy and charity on our part: that we pursue truly useful knowledge, and then employ it – not for any of the narrow, selfish reasons people might entertain – but for the common good. However, the first selfish reason that Bacon expressly decries, 'pleasure of the mind,' has a significance that many of his readers might not immediately recognize. Indeed, it would be difficult to exaggerate the importance of the change in perspective that this represents. In castigating knowing for its own sake as a mere self-indulgence, Bacon apparently repudiates the entire conception of philosophy or science previously held (these two, philosophy and science, becoming distinguished only much later, and as a consequence of the proven success of his project).

It would seem, then, that Bacon rejects as well the human *telos* whence that original conception of philosophy was derived; as expressed by Aristotle in the first line of his *Metaphysics*, 'All humans by nature reach out [*oregeis*] to know.' Thus our name for our species: *Homo sapiens*. The established view was that theoretical knowledge, sought simply for its own sake, is the highest kind of knowledge, reflecting the very essence of distinctly human nature. Accordingly, the person whose entire life is dedicated to pursuing such knowledge, the Philosopher, is the highest kind of human being, the natural aristocrat; and his way of life, the contemplative life (on the unlikely chance that one is suited for it), the best life. For it manifests the formal characteristics of the kind of good life virtually all people implicitly aspire to: secure, coherent, self-sufficient. It therefore provides the standard whereby all lives are to be judged. Being a life of self-cultivation and self-knowing, hence self-rule, it is a life of true freedom, even a sort of mortal approximation of divinity. All this Bacon is apparently repudiating insofar as he rejects the legitimacy of seeking knowledge purely for the sake of knowing, to satisfy the natural hunger of one's soul.[4] Established in its place is the primacy of seeking useful knowledge – meaning, first and foremost, useful to the needs and wants of the body, relieving pain, toil, sickness, hunger, and promoting those 'other Contentments of life' that Hobbes belatedly includes under the rubric 'Safety of the people' (XXX/1, 175). And until all useful knowledge has been found, this implies seeking *only* useful knowledge, such as will contribute to 'the relief of man's *natural* estate' – one extreme version of which is captured in Hobbes's pithy formula: 'solitary, poore, nasty, brutish, and short.'

A fourth change is necessary, however, if Bacon's ambition for a new form of science, one productive of works that can improve human life, is to be realized: namely, a profound transformation in the very conception of Cause. Bacon repeatedly emphasizes the importance of understanding causes; as one of his most famous aphorisms has it, 'Human knowledge and human power meet in one; for where the cause is not known the effect cannot be produced. Nature to be commanded must be obeyed; and that which in contemplation is as the cause is in operation as the rule.'[5] Speaking at greater length in the intended Preface (which provides the only overview of the entire project that was to constitute *The Great Instauration*), Bacon observes:

I have made a beginning of the work – a beginning, as I hope, not unimportant: the fortune of the human race will give the issue, such an issue, it may be, as in the present condition of things and men's minds cannot easily be conceived or imagined. For the matter in hand is no mere felicity of speculation, but the real business and fortunes of the human race, and all power of operation. For man is but the servant and interpreter of nature: what he does and what he knows is only what he has observed of nature's order in fact or in thought; beyond this he knows nothing and can do nothing. For the *chain of causes* cannot by any force be loosed or broken, nor can nature be commanded except by being obeyed. And so those twin objects, human knowledge and human power, do really meet in one; and it is from *ignorance of causes* that operation fails. (28–9; my emphasis)

This statement nicely encapsulates Hobbes's view as well. That said, I doubt that even Bacon, unsurpassed visionary though he was, could himself have 'conceived or imagined' anything like the amounts and kinds of technological power that have since devolved upon the human race as a consequence of his reorientation of scientific inquiry. Essential to his doing so was his radical revision of Aristotle's four kinds of cause.

This is the task with which Book Two of Bacon's *New Organon* begins – a set of thirteen 'Aphorisms' (for so he calls them)[6] that together constitute the most densely metaphysical portion of the book. The very first sentences announce the complementary ambitions that are to rule Baconian Science:

On a given body, to generate and superinduce a new nature or new natures is the work and aim of human power. Of a given nature to discover the form, or true specific difference, or nature-engendering nature, or source of emanation (for these are the terms that come nearest to a description of the thing), is the work and aim of human knowledge. (121)

To each of these primary aims – one of power, the other of knowledge – there are immediate corollaries. With respect to actualizing human power, we are to seek the ability to transform 'concrete bodies, so far as this is possible.' As for 'the work and aim' of knowledge, it is 'the discovery, in every case of generation and motion, of the *latent process* carried on from the manifest efficient and the manifest material to the form which is engendered; and in like manner the discovery of the *latent configuration* of bodies at rest and not in motion.'

While insisting upon the 'ill condition' of human knowledge then current, Bacon endorses the traditional view that knowledge of causes is what constitutes genuine knowledge of Nature. And, moreover, that causes 'are not improperly distributed' into the four kinds that Aristotle identified. Agreement ends there, however; for Bacon challenges both the conception and the applicability of each kind:

> But of these the final cause rather corrupts than advances the sciences, except such as have to do with human action. The discovery of the formal is despaired of. The efficient and the material (as they are investigated and received, that is, as remote causes, without reference to the latent process leading to the form) are but slight and superficial, and contribute little, if anything, to true and active science ... For though in nature nothing really exists besides individual bodies, performing pure individual acts according to a fixed law, yet in philosophy this very law, and the investigation, discovery, and explanation of it, is the foundation as well of knowledge as of operation. And it is this law with its clauses that I mean when I speak of *forms*, a name which I the rather adopt because it has grown into use and become familiar.[7] (121–2; cf. *Leviathan* XV/41, 80)

Fully explicating the implications of this brief statement would require a lengthy commentary; however, the following observations may suffice for the present more limited purpose of seeing its bearing on Hobbes's political project.

First, in confining Final cause to human actions, Bacon rejects the teleological conception of Nature, including human nature. For although he acknowledges *conscious* purposes *in* human life, human actions being unintelligible otherwise – including pre-eminently those involved in pursuing knowledge (after all, this is the basis of his own criticism of all science heretofore: it has been guided by the wrong purpose) – he has precluded there being a naturally given purpose *to* human life. Consequently, man is radically free, being free to conceive his own *telos*. In addition, this insistence that Final cause is legitimately sought only within human life directly implies that Man is the sole source of purpose in the Universe. As such, it tacitly encourages Humanism and the Protagorean view that Man is the Measure of all things – the perspective that has come to dominate contemporary science-saturated Hobbesian societies. But what about all of the innate purpose to be observed in Nature? Surely Bacon does not mean to deny what is virtually self-evident (e.g., the functions of bodily organs, the purposes served by the distinctive morphic features and behavioural instincts of plants and animals). Not necessarily. But he does wish it understood that none of this counts as proper scientific knowledge (for one cannot *do* anything with it; knowing 'why' is not in itself *useful*).[8] Moreover, in providing the illusion of an adequate understanding, discerning purposes and functions diverts attention away from investigating 'how' (the mechanisms whereby) these 'whys' are accomplished, and so 'corrupts' rather than 'advances' the sciences.

Secondly, while Bacon sees Form and Formal cause to be the key to both understanding and manipulating Nature ('the foundation as well of knowledge as of operation') – even, like Aristotle, identifying 'natures' with forms – it is a very different conception of Form (and 'nature'), being what we, following Bacon, have come to regard as a 'fixed law' of nature, to which the generations and configurations and motions of bodies conform. As for the primary 'natures' *caused* by the forms, they are not the naturally occurring animate and inanimate species of things. Rather, Bacon's forms are each responsible for a particular natural property (or quality, what Hobbes usually refers to as an 'accident'), and these in their various conjunctions make up all the complex individual 'bodies' (so, seemingly like Hobbes, Bacon contends that 'in nature nothing really exists besides individual bodies').[9] Moreover, manipulation of such forms is the means whereby one body can be transformed into another. For this is the first 'rule or axiom for the transformation of bodies': a body is to be regarded 'as a troop or collection of simple natures,' a 'compound' that is in principle transformable into something else. Thus, Gold (Bacon's enticing example) is to be understood as a conjunction of 'the forms' responsible for its yellowness, ductility, specific weight, malleability, conductivity, etc. And whoever knows how to superinduce those forms upon a suitable body can accomplish 'the transformation of that body into gold' (124) – the Alchemist's dream become real.

This generally, then, is the key to a useful kind of science: knowledge of forms (or laws) whereby the various natures (or properties) can be superinduced upon bodies. As Bacon puts it, 'the form of a thing is the very thing itself [i.e., the nature as it manifests itself in some property], and the thing differs from the form no otherwise than as the apparent differs from the real, or the external from the internal, or the thing in reference to man from the thing in reference to the universe' (142). On Bacon's view, these nature-causing forms are analogous to 'the letters of the alphabet and the notes of music' (129); as from a manageable number of letters and notes an infinitude of words and tunes can be compounded, so too can countless kinds of bodies be made from the conjoining of a limited number of simple, primary natures.

However, application of this knowledge requires, in turn, knowledge of both the *'latent configurations'* ultimately responsible for the compound structure of a given body (that is, the structures or configurations of each of its 'parts' or constituent natures, such as can be discovered only 'by reasoning and true induction, with experiments to aid; and by a comparison with other bodies, and a reduction to simple natures and their forms, which meet and mix in the compound'; 128); and of the *'latent processes'* of 'compound bodies, as they are found in nature' (for example, how the digestive process works in a given kind of animal, or how its 'voluntary motion' is initiated and carried through; or the process governing all the motions involved in a person's 'utterance of articulate sounds'). Summarily speaking:

> [W]hosoever is acquainted with forms embraces the unity of nature in substances the most unlike, and is able therefore to detect and bring to light things never yet done, and such as neither the vicissitudes of nature, nor industry in experimenting, nor accident itself, would ever have brought into act, and which would never have occurred to the thought of man. From the discovery of forms therefore results truth in speculation and freedom in operation. (122)

Of the countless exemplifications of this truth that have since been brought forth, proving Bacon's incomparable prescience, perhaps the best is provided by the forms or laws of electromagnetism. Who, simply on the basis of natural observation, would have suspected that the same laws account for things so 'unlike' as lightning, a compass needle's pointing North, the chemistry of a living cell, the attractive powers of an amber rod rubbed with cat's fur, and the workings of the human brain and nervous system? Or who could have imagined any of the thousands upon thousands of tools and appliances powered by an electrical grid serving tens of millions of factories, shops, and ordinary households – so much testimony to the limitless technological potential inherent in man's coming to understand those laws?

The priority of Formal cause is further confirmed by Bacon's disparaging remarks about both Material and Efficient causes as being 'slight and superficial,' and not only as they were then 'investigated and received … without reference to the latent processes leading to the form.' For even when properly conceived, they are 'unstable causes, and merely vehicles, or causes which convey the form in certain cases' (122). To see what Bacon means, one might ask 'What is *the* Efficient cause of fire?' There is no single, universal answer; it varies with the particular case: sometimes matches, other times lightning, or friction, electrical spark, chemical combustion, whatever. Hence, this is no important part of scientific knowledge itself (though the multitude of efficient causes play a major role in humans *using* that knowledge). What is scientifically important is the 'latent process' of *burning*, of understanding *fire*, or more generally what causes heat (hence, *ignition*) – that is, the forms or laws governing these processes. Similarly, Material cause in itself is no significant part of 'true and active science.' The properties of matter (whether it does or does not burn, for example) are all due the particular conjunction of forms that compose it. Nor is there just one kind of matter that transmits heat; they all do so to varying degrees, and explaining *why* this is so depends on understanding, not matter as such, but the various latent configurations and processes manifesting what is of permanent scientific interest: the forms or laws.[10]

Based on his new way of understanding the four kinds of causes, Bacon proposes 'a just division' between what had heretofore been seen as conceptually inseparable: Philosophy and Science. On the ancient view, the latter, consisting of knowledge universally valid and permanently true (hence worthy of the name 'wisdom'), is simply the objective of the former, 'love of wisdom.' Whereas, Bacon proposes that they be differently conceived:

Thus, let the investigation of forms, which are (in the eye of reason at least, and in their essential law) eternal and immutable, constitute *Metaphysics*; and let the investigation of the efficient cause, and of matter, and of the latent process, and the latent configuration (all of which have reference to the common and ordinary course of nature, not to her eternal and fundamental laws) constitute *Physics*. And to these let there be subordinate two practical divisions: to Physics, *Mechanics*; to Metaphysics, what (in a purer sense of the word) I call *Magic*, on account of the broadness of the ways it moves in, and its greater command over nature. (129)

The separation between Philosophy and Science that has since become established – and which was inevitable, in that the ever narrower specialization which technology requires runs counter to Philosophy's traditional objective: knowledge of the Whole – is not along the line Bacon delineated. Still, his thinking prepared the way for it.

Similarly, Bacon's distinction between the pursuit of 'pure and uncorrupted' knowledge of Nature (symbolized by Adam's naming of the animals) and 'the ambitious and proud desire of Moral knowledge to judge of Good and Evil' (responsible for his and Eve's – and all posterity's – fall from grace; 15) precursed the altogether misleading and pernicious distinction between 'facts' and 'values,' the former supposedly objective and the latter incorrigibly subjective.[11] This fallacious fact-value distinction has given rise, in turn, to the false view that Science is exclusively concerned with and confined to 'the facts,' and that it alone provides 'objective knowledge.'[12] Non-teleological Science having thus become the highest intellectual authority for most people – seemingly validated beyond doubt by the technological wonderworks it makes possible – the practical result is that people have come to believe that there is no genuine knowledge about so-called values, no truth to be had about standards of right and wrong, good and bad, noble and debased. The belief that these are all mere 'matters of opinion' resting ultimately on nothing more substantial than subjective 'value judgments,' has become part and parcel of modern scientism. Although this is neither Bacon's nor Hobbes's view – indeed, its supposed justification is utterly at odds with their views – in *practice* there is little difference between contemporary 'value relativism' and the hedonism licensed in Hobbes's political prescription.

8

The Baconian Character
of Hobbes's Political Project

There are two sets of reasons why this much background on the form of science which Bacon fathered is necessary for an understanding of Hobbes's political project. First of all, one must appreciate the extent to which the revolutionary Baconian project requires a public, polity-wide commitment if it is to be successful. The vast amount of fact-gathering, sorting, and winnowing needed to provide the 'solid foundation of experience of every kind' for Bacon's new conception of science requires the contributions of thousands upon thousands of people:

[T]he third part of the work embraces the 'phenomena of the universe'; that is to say, experience of every kind, and such a natural history as may serve for a foundation to build philosophy upon. For a good method of demonstration or form of interpreting nature may keep the mind from going astray or stumbling, but it is not any excellence of method that can supply it with the material of knowledge. Those, however, who aspire not to guess and divine, but to discover and know, who propose not to devise mimic and fabulous worlds of their own, but to examine and dissect the nature of this very world itself, must go to the facts themselves for everything. Nor can the place of this labor and search and world-wide perambulation be supplied by any genius or meditation or argumentation; no, not if all men's wits could meet in one. This, therefore, we must have or the business must be forever abandoned.[1]

Some partial sense of the scale of this merely preliminary task is indicated by the Catalogue of 130 'Particular Histories' that Bacon included as an appendix to his *New Organon*. Hobbes selected variations on four of these to illustrate 'The Register of *Knowledge of Fact* ... called '*Natural History*' (i.e., 'Facts, or Effects of Nature, as have no Dependance on

Mans *Will*; Such as are the Histories of *Metalls, Plants, Animals, Regions*'). As his schematic table of the Sciences clearly implies, these precede 'the Registers of Science ... called *Books of Philosophy*' (IX/2–3, 40). Equal in importance to all this fact-gathering, however, there must be some means of organizing the efforts of the requisite army of under-labourers and of their communicating their findings – first of all among themselves; then, as useful knowledge accumulates, to the broader society. And, of course, there must be sufficient financial backing to fund the enterprise. Thus Bacon concluded his Dedicatory Letter by propos-ing that King James, who had previously set a small army of scholars the task of producing an authoritative English translation of the Bible, further display his Solomon-like qualities by using the great resources of the Crown to sponsor this enormous task of 'taking order for the col-lecting and perfecting of a natural and experimental history, true and severe ... such as philosophy may be built upon.'[2]

All of this Hobbes is implicitly endorsing with his formula, '*Reason* is the *pace*; Encrease of *Science*, the *way*; and the Benefit of man-kind, the *end*' (V/20, 36).[3] His chapter '*Of* Systemes *Subject, Politicall, and Private*' (XXII), dealing with the formalities of the Sovereign's relationships with 'Systemes subordinate' (meaning 'any numbers of men joyned in one Interest, or one Business'), is readily applicable to authorizing Societies for the Advancement of Science and other forms of Royal patronage. More fundamental, however, Hobbes sees clearly the importance of the regime's promoting social equality and personal liberty if it is to realize fully the scientific, hence technological, hence economic, hence political potential of Baconian science. There is an enormous amount of work to be done which only the talented minority can do. Thus, if one wishes to muster all those who are capable of contributing, there should be no arti-ficial barriers to natural talent asserting itself, however humble its social origins. And who better than Hobbes could appreciate that genius – whether for analysis and inquiry, or invention and creation, or organiza-tion and marketing – is no respecter of social convention? After all, he is 'Thomas Hobbes of Malmesbury': born in a small cottage on the out-skirts of an insignificant country town, to a barely literate, choleric, and alcoholic clergyman who abandoned his family when Hobbes was but a boy. Were it not for his (and our) good fortune, to wit, his having received an excellent grammar school education, courtesy of an excellent tutor and a prosperous, dutiful uncle – and the further good fortune this made pos-sible (attending Oxford, Cavendish family patronage, etc.) – there would have been no *Leviathan*, with who knows what historical consequences.

However, a (if not *the*) major obstacle to furthering this revolution in Science – requiring as it does a corresponding alteration in the character of political life, both to accommodate its requirements and to exploit its potential benefits – is the established Religion. Accordingly, both Bacon and Hobbes are at pains to ward off clerical interference from scientific research. As Bacon warns in the 89th aphorism of his *New Organon*:

Neither is it to be forgotten that in every age natural philosophy has had a troublesome and hard to deal with adversary – namely, superstition, and the blind and immoderate zeal of religion. For we see among the Greeks that those who first proposed to men's then uninitiated ears the natural causes for thunder and for storms were thereupon found guilty of impiety. Nor was much more forbearance shown by some of the ancient fathers of the Christian church to those who on most convincing grounds (such as no one in his senses would now think of contradicting) maintained that the earth was round, and of consequence asserted the existence of the antipodes.

Moreover, as things now are, to discourse of nature is made harder and more perilous by the summaries and systems of the schoolmen who, having reduced theology into regular order as well as they were able, and fashioned it into the shape of an art, ended in incorporating the contentious and thorny philosophy of Aristotle, more than was fit, with the body of religion.

...

Lastly, you will find that by the simpleness of certain divines, access to any philosophy, however pure, is well-nigh closed. Some are weakly afraid lest a deeper search into nature should transgress the permitted limits of sober-mindedness, wrongfully wresting and transferring what is said in Holy Writ against those who pry into sacred mysteries, to hidden things of nature, which are barred by no prohibition ... Others fear from past example that movements and changes in philosophy will end in assaults on religion. And others again appear apprehensive that in the investigation of nature something may be found to subvert or at least shake the authority of religion, especially with the unlearned ... [Thus] it is not surprising if the growth of natural philosophy is checked when religion, the thing which has most power over men's minds, has by the simpleness and incautious zeal of certain persons been drawn to take part against her. (87–9)

No one familiar with *Leviathan* could fail to recognize in the above passages views which Hobbes also repeatedly expressed. To cite only one, but especially telling, example:

With the Introduction of False, we may joyn also the suppression of True Philosophy, by such men, as neither by lawfull authority, nor by sufficient study, are competent Judges of the truth. Our own Navigations make manifest, and all men learned in humane Sciences, now acknowledge there are Antipodes: And every day it appeareth more and more, that Years, and Dayes are determined by Motions of the Earth. Neverthelesse, men that have in their Writings but supposed such Doctrine, as an occasion to lay open the reasons for, and against it, have been punished for it by Authority Ecclesiasticall. But what reason is there for it? Is it because such opinions are contrary to true Religion? that cannot be, if they be true. Let therefore the truth be first examined by competent Judges, or confuted by them that pretend to know the contrary. (XLVI/42, 380)

In the Latin version of this same chapter, Hobbes claims that 'formerly it was a sufficient reason to prevent someone from achieving the honour of a bishopric that he had learned the mathematical arts, or that he believed the earth to be round, or believed those parts of the earth we call antipodes to be inhabited' (XLVI/15 OL).[4] Hobbes advises Teachers of Religion not 'to be displeased with this losse of their antient Authority: For there is none should know better than they, that power is preserved by the same Vertues by which it is acquired; that is to say, by Wisdome, Humility, Clearnesse of Doctrine, and sincerity of Conversation; and not by suppression of the Naturall Sciences, and of the Morality of Naturall Reason' (XLVII/20, 385).

Bacon not only warns against the danger to Science of meddling zealots and dogmatic schoolmen, however; he also attempts to reassure sensible believers (while perhaps amusing irony-attuned sceptics) that neither is there anything impious in scientific inquiry, nor are its findings any danger to the true Faith – indeed, quite the contrary. Having 'humbly' prayed 'that things human may not interfere with things divine, and that from the opening of the ways of sense and the increase of natural light there may arise in our minds no incredulity or darkness with regard to the divine mysteries' – nice use of the power of suggestion – so may people 'give to faith that which is faith's.' Just how much or how little truly 'belongs' to faith is not clear, but people are exhorted to give no more than that lest they fall 'into the opposite error' of thinking 'that the inquisition of nature is in any part interdicted or forbidden. For it was not that pure and uncorrupted natural knowledge' that occasioned Adam's and all mankind's Fall from Grace, but rather 'the ambitious and proud desire of moral knowledge to judge of good and evil, to the end that man may revolt from God and give laws to himself.' Whereas, 'of the sciences which regard nature, the divine philosopher [Solomon, supposedly] declares that "it is the glory of God to conceal a thing, but it is the glory of the King to find a thing out"' (14–15). Hobbes more than once advances what is essentially the same rationale:

But why then does our Saviour proceed in the curing of [certain insane men], as if they were possest; and not as if they were mad? To which I can give no other kind of answer, but that which is given to those who urge the Scripture in like manner against the opinion of the motion of the Earth. The Scripture was written to shew unto men the kingdome of God, and to prepare their mindes to become his obedient subjects; leaving the world, and the Philosophy thereof, to the disputation of men, for the exercising of their naturall Reason. (VIII/26, 38–9)

Men may ... aske, why Christ that could have given to all men Faith, Piety, and all manner of morall Vertues, gave it to some onely, and not to all: and why he left the search of naturall Causes, and Sciences, to the naturall Reason and Industry of men, and did not reveal it to all, or any man supernaturally; and many other such questions: Of which neverthelesse there may be alledged probable and pious reasons ... [O]ur Saviour, in conducting us toward his heavenly Kingdome, did not destroy all the difficulties of Naturall Questions; but left them to exercise our Industry, and Reason ... If wee require of the Scripture an account of all questions, which may be raised to trouble us in the performance of Gods commands; we may as well complaine of Moses for not having set downe the time ... of the Creation of the Earth, and Sea, and of Men, and Beasts. (XLV/8, 355)

Of course, Hobbes knows full well that it is not really the exact *time* of the various 'creations' that had by then begun to 'exercise' thoughtful men's 'Industry, and Reason' – though Bishop Ussher (among others) had already risen to the challenge, having published in 1650 his calculation that creation commenced at night on 22 October 4004 B.C.[5] Rather, it was the whole Creation story itself, taken literally, that was being called into question.

Bacon contends that scientific inquiry, far from undermining true religion, is actually a servitor of it:

But if the matter be truly considered, natural philosophy is, after the word of God, at once the surest medicine against superstition and the most approved nourishment for faith, and therefore she is rightly given to religion as her most faithful handmaid, since the one displays the will of God, the other his power. For he did not err who said, 'Ye err in that ye know not the Scriptures and the power of God,' thus coupling and blending in an indissoluble bond information concerning his will and mediation concerning his power. (88–9)

Of course, this is the posture Hobbes also adopts, insisting that the Laws of Nature discovered by Science – including his new Science of Politics – indubitably reflect God's Power (Who by virtue of His power also 'by right commandeth all things'; XV/41, 80; XXXI/5, 187); and that valid science perfectly harmonizes with God's Revealed Word in Scripture (if properly interpreted). Indeed, God practically mandates scientific inquiry, especially the pursuit of a sound political science: 'we are not to renounce our Senses, and Experience; nor (that which is the undoubted Word of God) our naturall Reason. For they are the talents which he hath put into our hands to negotiate, till the coming again of our blessed Saviour; and therefore not to folded up in the Napkin of an Implicite Faith, but employed in the purchase of Justice, Peace, and true Religion' (XXXII/2, 195).[6] Even 'Soveraigns are all subject to the Lawes of Nature; because such lawes be Divine' (XXIX/9, 169).

The second major respect in which the Baconian revolution in natural science is germane to Hobbes's political project derives from its repudiation of the teleological understanding of Nature. As I noted in a previous chapter, it would be hard to exaggerate the importance of this change in mental architecture. For in rejecting the idea of naturally ordained *telei*, one eradicates the only credible ground – other than Revelation – upon which objective evaluation might be based. According to the teleological view, a natural being can be evaluated in light of how closely it approximates the natural perfection of its kind (implicit in each kind's *telos*). By contrast, the Baconian non-teleological conception of Nature treats everything as equally natural, being equally a consequence of mechanistic natural laws. Hence, Nature cannot be a source of criteria whereby the various instances of a given kind – humans and their arrangements included – may be *ranked* as better or worse, assessed as right or wrong, beautiful or ugly, noble or debased. Having rejected the possibility of a pre- or trans-human order of valuation, man may indeed indulge 'the ambitious and proud desire of moral knowledge to judge of good and evil, to the end that man may revolt from God and give laws to himself.'

Thus, in denying any scientific significance to the idea of natural *telei*, the door is opened to a new *kind* of political science. Politics can take its bearings from another direction if it is not constrained by an a priori commitment to actualizing a human *telos*, the substance of which people will never agree upon. For example, even those who would appear to agree that the end of human life is to live piously would not necessarily agree as to what this substantially consists of; there will always be some holier than thou puritans conflicting with their more easy-going fellows whom they regard as not holy enough. Similarly, those who might seem to agree that the ruling *telos* of political life should be the promotion of human virtue do not necessarily agree in practical terms what virtue *is* ('For one man calleth *Wisdome*, what another calleth *feare*; and one *cruelty*, what another *justice*, [etc.]' IV/24, 17). As for the Aristotelian view of the natural human *telos*: to become knowledgeable, even wise – a life dedicated to this end appeals to very few people. Nor should it, as they are little suited for it, and so it would not be a good life, a fulfilling life, for them. Aristotle is doubtless right that most people are primarily lovers of sensual pleasures, hence of wealth; whereas the better few hold the life of sensual pleasure-seeking in contempt. But this, then – the profound disagreements among people concerning what is or ought to be the ruling purpose of life – is the political reality that must somehow be peacefully accommodated. Whereas overtly committing a regime to only one conception of the Good Life is to sow within it seeds of recurring civil strife, and ultimately of its own destruction (cf. *Republic* 562a–c).

Given that there is no single way of life that is best for everyone, much less agreement on what it might be, a universal *science* of politics (the core of which must be – or at least seem to be – a universally applicable prescription for a well-ordered polity) cannot take its bearing from a particular conception of the Good Life at which the well-ordered polity ought to aim. But it can be guided by the situation that any and every rational person does, or at least should, most want to *avoid*: 'that miserable condition of warre' that is the State of Nature. This, then, can be the fundamental axiom of a science of politics, derived not from people's cooperative effort to realize the non-existent single greatest good, but from their common desire to escape the very real single greatest bad. The key thing is not the fulfilment of some natural End (*telos*) of life, but securing an escape from the common natural Origin (*archë*) of life. A return to that State of Nature – always a possibility – is to be avoided at all costs. Anything that risks such a return is evil. This being axiomatic, it figures in the justifying rationale for every one of Hobbes's 'natural laws' (explicitly mentioned in the discussions of more than half of them).

In sum, Hobbes's political science is teleological, but not in the manner of Aristotle – that is, guided by a naturally given *telos* or purpose to human life. Rather, it is teleological in the sense permitted by Baconian science, wherein the appeal to Final cause is restricted to actions that arise from *within* human life. The escape from the State of Nature into Civil society, 'that is to say, of [people's] getting themselves out from that miserable condition of Warre,' is certainly a purposive activity of the sort that qualifies. Moreover, were men purposefully to order their civil societies into 'Common-wealths' along the lines Hobbes prescribes, thereby creating the environment in which Baconian natural science can flourish, they would eventually become *collectively* knowledgeable and so realize of their own volition something like the *telos* that Aristotle ascribed to Nature. What is of much more interest to most people, however, is that the resulting, ever-multiplying technological power would generate the material prosperity that they themselves attest – by their actions, if not in so many words – is the natural *telos* of their own lives.

9

Philosophy and
the Problem of *Determinism*

Judging by *Leviathan*, Hobbes, like Aristotle, regards the World as an order of necessity, determined by causes of all four kinds. But like Bacon, Hobbes restricts the role of Final cause to purposive human activity. Beyond that, however, it seems he would have us regard conscious purpose as strictly determined by antecedent causes, thereby endorsing the universal Determinism that was the basic metaphysical premise of all modern Natural Science from its founding to the dawn of the twentieth century and for the most part still is. It is a perspective that was famously encapsulated by the French scientist-mathematician the Marquis Pierre Simon de Laplace, writing in 1814:

We may regard the present state of the universe as the effect of its past and the cause of its future. An intelligence which at any given moment knew all the forces that animate nature, and the respective positions of the beings that compose it, and further possessing the means to analyze the data, could condense into a single formula the movement of the greatest bodies of the universe and that of the least atom: for such an intelligence, nothing could be uncertain, and past and future alike would be before its eyes.[1]

This is to contend that, were there a demon (say) who had complete understanding of Nature's 'laws' governing causation, and perfect information as to the state of the Universe at any one instant, and a sufficiently powerful mind (or computer), it could perfectly predict or retrodict the entire state of the Universe down to the least detail at any other time (as at present we but partially do with respect to planetary astronomy – an almost ridiculously simple 'system' compared with, say, a beaver pond). One might think of Laplace's statement as the ultimate intellectual ideal implicit in the modern scientific project: an anemic kind of God-like omniscience, fantastic (and pointless) though it might be.[2]

To the extent that intelligent people have had reservations about universal determinism, they have centred almost exclusively on human 'free will.' As noted earlier, Hobbes seems to reject the idea categorically; '*A free Subject*; *A free-will*' are presented as paradigmatic instances of absurd, nonsensical speech (V/5, 19). To a certain extent, he attempts simply to define free will out of existence: 'LIBERTY, or FREEDOME, signifieth (properly) the absence of Opposition; (by Opposition, I mean externall Impediments of motion;) and may be applyed no lesse to Irrational, and Inanimate creatures, than to Rational' (XXI/1, 107; cf. XIV/2, 64). And since he declares that 'every part of the Universe, is Body; and that which is not Body, is no part of the Universe' (XLVI/15, 371), he also contends, 'when the words *Free*, and *Liberty*, are applyed to any thing but *Bodies*, they are abused; for that which is not subject to Motion, is not subject to Impediment.' In particular, then, 'from the use of the word *Free-will*, no Liberty can be inferred of the will, desire, or inclination, but the Liberty of the man; which consisteth in this, that he finds no stop, in doing what he has the will, desire, or inclination to doe' (XXI/2, 108). The inadequacies of Hobbes's Bodyism, upon which these crucial claims are based, have already been addressed – insofar, that is, as it is understood to be his stand-in for a strict Materialism. So, too, the inconclusiveness of his Theological argument ('And did not [God's] will assure the *necessity* of mans will, and consequently of all that on mans will dependeth, the *liberty* of men would be a contradiction, and an impediment to the omnipotence and *liberty* of God'; XXI/4, 108). Apart from this problematic invocation of a caring, willing God – to Whom the word 'liberty' ought not be 'applyed' since He is 'not subject to Motion' (or so Hobbes elsewhere assures us; XXXI/23, 190) – Hobbes offers no *reason* to reject Free Will and subscribe instead to a strict Determinism.

Nor could he, for upon assuming determinism, there is no conceivable justification for believing it – or anything else. The instant one assumes it, all 'reasoning,' all 'evidence,' all 'experience,' all 'intuitive recognition' become utterly irrelevant because one must presume them to be predetermined irrespective of the truth. Indeed, the very idea of *truth* as we intuitively understand it becomes meaningless, for (per the determinist hypothesis) we have no access to it, merely the predetermined illusion that we do, which some people (in turn) have been predetermined to detect, and to persuade others of, who (in turn) have been predetermined to agree or not, and so on. Whereas, on the other hand, the belief in something like free will, while profoundly perplexing and perhaps incorrigibly mysterious, is certainly *not* the self-evident *contradictio in adjecto* that Hobbes professes to regard it (no less oxymoronic than round quadrangle). As for its mysteriousness, even incomprehensibility, it is no more so than Space and Time: for it seems the former must be either infinite or finite, and neither alternative is comprehensible;[3] similarly, the latter must either be eternal or have a beginning, and both possibilities surpass human understanding.[4] But practically no one treats the fact that these matters are 'above reason' (to appropriate Hobbes's happy phrase) as sufficient justification for denying the reality of Space and Time.

Or, to take an example that is more closely connected to 'free will,' there is an equally profound mysteriousness of the relation between Body and Soul (or Mind, or Consciousness). It is indisputable that one *is* conscious of bodily experience, be it the conscious discomforts called 'hunger' and 'thirst' that accompany the body's deprivation of certain kinds of material replenishment; or the 'tastes' of various kinds of matter mixing with the saliva touching specialized nodules in one's mouth; or the beauty of a 'sight' conveyed by electromagnetic radiation entering through the lens and striking the retinas of one's eyes; or the recognition of a 'voice' aroused by the effects on one's inner ear of a particular pattern of changes in pneumatic pressure; or the 'pain' caused by a kick in the shins. It is most doubtful that anyone will ever truly understand this communication between radically different modes of being: moved matter, and consciousness – for even those who argue, as do most determinists, that the latter is merely epiphenomena caused by the former cannot deny the *existence* of the very consciousness to which their claims are addressed. Hence, treating it as epiphenomenal in no way dispels the mystery of how anything involving matter could generate a conscious experience (though we are nonetheless sure that somehow it does).

Contrary to the determinist's presumption, however, the causal relationship between body and mind is certainly a two-way street: only upon one's consciously *understanding* the joke does one's face 'maketh those *Grimaces* called LAUGHTER.' For even according to Hobbes's laughably incomplete account of why humans laugh (that laughing is a '*Sudden Glory* ... caused either by some sudden act of their own, that pleaseth them; or by the apprehension of some deformed thing in another, by comparison whereof they suddenly applaud themselves'; VI/42, 27), this 'being pleased' requires the conscious *recognition* of something pleasing *prior* to the body's being moved to laughter. A joke, or an insult, conveyed in a language one does not understand will not itself cause the bodily reaction that it otherwise would, though the aural sensations caused by the pneumatic waves striking one's eardrums would be the same in either case. Hobbes, notice, presumes to evade the Body-Soul (or Body-Mind) problem the same way as he disposed of free will: by declaring that reality consists of bodies and nothing but bodies. Ergo, no problem.

That Hobbes wishes to be seen as endorsing the distinction between the 'Primary' and the 'Secondary' qualities of perceived things, intrinsic to the materialistic determinism of modern science,[5] is indicated in the discussion with which he begins his book:

Concerning the Thoughts of man ... *Singly* they are every one a *Representation* or *Apparence*, of some quality, or other Accident of a body without us; which is commonly called an *Object*. Which Object worketh on the Eyes, Eares, and other parts of mans body; and by diversity of working, produceth diversity of Apparences.

...

The cause of Sense, is the Externall Body, or Object, which presseth the organ proper to each Sense, either immediately, as in Tast and Touch; or mediately, as in Seeing, Hearing, and Smelling ... And this *seeming*, or *fancy*, is that which men call *Sense*; and consisteth, as to the Eye, in a *Light*, or *Colour figured*; To the Eare, in a *Sound*; To the Nostrill, in an *Odour*; To the Tongue and Palat, in a *Savour*; And to the rest of the body, in *Heat, Cold, Hardnesse, Softnesse*, and other such qualities, as we discern by *Feeling*. All which qualities called *Sensible*, are in the object which causeth them, but so many several motions of the matter, by which it presseth our organs diversly. Neither in us that are pressed, are they any thing else but divers motions; (for motion, produceth nothing but motion.) But their apparence to us is Fancy. (I/1–4, 3; cf. VI/9, 25; XXXIV/2, 207).

Accordingly, in his schematic Table of the various Sciences that accompanies chapter 9, the basic division in 'Natural Philosophy' is between those sciences which deal with primary qualities of 'Bodies Natural, which are *Quantity*, and *Motion*,' and those that analyse natural phenomena in terms of secondary qualities.

On this view, then, the 'real' qualities of a thing are the various motions of its matter, while the sensory experience of these primary qualities (as colour, sound, smell, taste, texture, etc.) is due to the perceiver's bodily make-up, specifically the conscious 'fancy' produced by the various motions of his sense organs as stimulated by the motions of the object perceived. Confusing these conscious effects with actual qualities of the things themselves is one 'cause of Absurd conclusions': 'giving of the names of the *accidents* of *bodies without us*, to the *accidents* of our *own bodies*; as they do that say, the *colour is in the body*; *the sound is in the ayre*, &c' (V/11, 20). Objects are not in themselves actually coloured; they simply reflect light of various frequencies, which have a specific effect on that light-sensitive apparatus known as the Eye, the effect being consciously experienced as 'seeing' a certain coloured shape. Hence, the 'colour' of something is a derivative, 'secondary' quality.[6] And so to the question, 'When a tree falls in the forest and there is no one there to hear it, does it make a sound?' the answer is 'No.' The fall of a tree does, of course, produce a disturbance in the air that would be heard as sound were there anything in the vicinity equipped with an apparatus sensitive to such slight fluctuations in air pressure, and of registering them as 'sound' in the consciousness. But the colourful panoramas we see, the music and noise we hear, the delicious and noxious things we taste and smell, the pleasant and painful things we touch – this world of immediate experience – is 'in reality,' i.e., from this modern scientific point of view, illusory, epiphenomenal (though, of course, we have no choice but to experience it as we do).[7]

Needless to say, this is a profoundly unnatural posture to adopt. Its plausibility rests entirely on one's tacit acceptance of Materialism and Determinism: that Matter and its Motions are the fundamental, indeed exclusive, Reality, causally determining everything else; and that the richer heterogeneous world one observes and feels, and attempts to understand by thinking about it, is wholly a product of one's mind, which in turn is a mysterious consequence of the mechanical workings of one's material brain and nervous system. And so, however inexplicable the causal process whereby conscious experience is generated, one's body is the agent, one's mind the patient. Supposedly.

There are, however, reasons to doubt the adequacy of this view of things. Begin with the fact that this entire materialistic analysis rests on conscious experience and thinking, which in a strictly logical sense must be regarded as primary – both as one's necessary point of departure and as the final ratification of this or any account's adequacy: it must square with the evidence of which one is conscious. Thus, an analysis which somehow concludes that conscious experience is strictly derivative, illusory, epiphenomenal, 'unreal,' undercuts its own basis. There is no way to evade this self-denying effect: the analysis is no more plausible as an hypothesis, a suspicion, an 'article of faith,' whatever – they all inescapably presume what they purport to deny: the authenticity of conscious experience. The experiencing of the blueness of the sky or the greenness of the grass must be granted a reality – some genuine mode of being – if there is to be anything for physiology to explain. And the physiological explanation can (at best) provide a consistent pattern of physical manifestations correlated with the psychic experiences, which remain the essential validating evidence for the adequacy of the physiological account. Moreover, regardless of how precisely and extensively this correlation is mapped, the communication between these two radically different modes of being would remain as mysterious as ever.

The necessarily separate and distinct ontological status of conscious experience, or 'thought,' is easily seen by re-enacting Descartes's experiment of radical doubt: imagine that the existence of everything outside of one's own consciousness is illusory – and it is impossible to prove otherwise: this is a logical possibility, however difficult to take seriously. As the experiment shows, the only mode of being that one cannot logically doubt is that of conscious experience (in this case, of doubting). Moreover, the qualitatively loaded interpretation of the distinction between primary and secondary qualities – wherein the former is accorded the status of 'true reality,' being the cause of the latter, mere 'illusory reality' – and the materialistic-deterministic analysis that supposedly justifies this interpretation, trivializes the distinctly human experiences that in the natural way of living are so important. It does so, moreover, despite its inability to provide convincing explanations of them. For example, the mathematics of harmonious tones do not in themselves account for why one finds some music surpassingly beautiful, and other equally harmonious music banal, boring, or insipid. Similar remarks pertain to all experiences of visual beauty and ugliness, whether of places or people, whether by art or accident – analysis in terms of various frequencies of electromagnetic radiation throws no 'light' at all on anything that 'matters.'

The question of 'free will' is the metaphysical issue of greatest importance to human beings, however, since (as noted before) it is bears directly upon the issues of theology, psychology, and morality, consequently a fortiori on any putative science of politics. As such, it warrants the most careful exploration.[8] To be sure, there are circumstances in which one would insist that one had 'no real choice' but to do as one did. Thoroughly analysed, however, these virtually always turn out to be situations of *con-*

ditional necessity: that is, *if* one wished for a certain outcome (e.g., to save one's reputation, say, or one's job, or one's life, or the lives of others), *then* one had no choice but to do (whatever). And insofar as the 'if' is not *strictly* necessary – whereas plummeting to the ground *is*, should one fall off a tall building – such situations do not actually call into question one's freedom of choice; for there are people who have chosen to sacrifice riches, reputation, career, even their own lives and the lives of others they care about, rather than do what was required to save them.

Still, any thoughtful person, reflecting on his own experience in light of his deterministic presumptions about the rest of the natural world, has questioned the reality of free will. How much of one's behaviour seems thoughtless, almost 'automatic,' hence 'predetermined' in some sense? And even in those cases where one consciously deliberates over what to do, one is virtually always aware of antecedent factors not of one's own choosing that bear on whatever decision one takes. Might not these, perhaps conjoined with other factors one is not aware of, actually *determine* what one decides and does in every case? As Hobbes would have it, 'Sense, Memory, Understanding, Reason, and Opinion are not in our power to change; but alwaies, and necessarily such, as the things we see, hear, and consider suggest unto us; and therefore are not the effects of our Will, but our Will of them' (XXXII/4, 196) – the result being, apparently, that one's freedom to choose is illusory, the belief in self-determination actually an unchosen form of self-deception. And approached from the other side, as it were, the belief in free will seems equivalent to believing in an uncaused cause, the very idea of which is difficult if not impossible to conceive, and utterly at odds with what one believes regarding everything else in Nature. Adding it all together, then, one may become persuaded that the presumption implicit in one's natural psychic posture, that humans are uniquely endowed with 'free will,' is a naivety, and so in the name of rational consistency resolve to adopt instead a strictly deterministic view of human life.

But if one does so, it will surely be in ignorance of the far greater perplexities that attend Determinism.[9] The notion that everything one does, no matter how trivial or momentous – this sip of tea, that choice of mate – was determined from the Beginning of Time (if it had a beginning; or 'from forever' if it did not), while not logically impossible, is at least mind-boggling. Yet such is necessarily the case according to determinism, since there can be no flexibility in such a view; if one regards an uncaused cause as a logical absurdity, it is equally so in matters micro and macro. Any apparent exceptions and aberrations must be just that: merely apparent, but in truth equally the fated result of antecedent causes stretching back into the mists of Beyond. For if one does one's sums correctly (as Hobbes would have us understand reason), one sees there is no rational middle ground between Freedom and the most rigorous, meticulous Fatalism. Of course, one must apply the view reflexively to one's own considerations of it, seeing every least detail as having been determined before one even existed, or anyone else existed, before there was life on Earth, indeed before there was an Earth.

And here it is easy to see that 'free *will*' is a misleading characterization of what is really at issue, namely, whether or not the human *mind* is free to conclude whatever it will. On the determinist view, it is not; what (if anything) one concludes is predetermined, even though it may differ from what one is predetermined to conclude tomorrow (perhaps having been predetermined then to notice, or forget, something one was predetermined to overlook, or remember, today) – everything eternally fated, as is one's observing that this is so, and observing that one observes, and so on, reflections endlessly compounding, but none of it a free activity of the mind, all of it preordained in the Big Bang that supposedly initiated this latest shuffling of the cosmic deck.

The bewilderment that may result simply from attempting to unravel the endlessly multiplying reflexivities of this view (taxing the mind's power of comprehension, to say the least) is by no means the most telling objection to it, however – indeed, strictly speaking it is irrelevant. The essential point is this: once one entertains the determinist's contention that one's sense of mental freedom is a determined *illusion*, the floodgates open. For there is no way to confine the implications of this prospect: that though whatever one thinks is strictly determined, it is not necessarily *true* (as might seem freshly confirmed every time one's mind changed about anything – presuming that one's awareness of having changed one's mind could be trusted as true, which it could not, being just one more predetermined mental event).

Hence, Determinism as a *positive doctrine* is self-refuting, since it renders access to the truth, on this or any other question, impossible. Should it happen to be true, there would be no way to *know* it (or to know anything else), nor rational grounds for even suspecting it (or anything else), thus absolutely no reason to believe it, much less have perfect confidence that it is the truth. For upon presuming it to be so, every assessment of evidence, every distinction one might draw, every argument for or against opposing views, every evaluation of those arguments, all so-called reasoning – indeed, the very rules of logic, of grammar, all positing of alternative views, or of Hobbes's all-important definitions, the form and substance of all conceptions, every ingredient of one's consciousness, must be regarded as determined *irrespective* of the *truth*, to which no one has credible access. Consequently, the very idea of Truth becomes practically meaningless.[10] We could (or is it, we must?) still use all the same words – reason and reality, knowledge and opinion, true and false, probable and improbable, objective and subjective, factual, coherent, consistent, contradictory, valid, illusory, absurd, perceive, suppose, hypothesize, know, speculate, imagine, prove, refute, and myriad others related to them – but they would no longer have their ordinary, 'natural' meaning. This is readily confirmed by comparing one's antecedent understanding of these ideas with the view which results from presuming that whatever one thinks is not something oneself freely *decides*, but is strictly predetermined. Not that the results of this comparing are exempt from the bizarre dualism of interpretation that it entails, nor is this observation about it, and so on.

On the determinist's view, then, every word one speaks is duplicitous – not in the ordinary sense of insincere or ambiguous, but in the far more radical sense of one's language being both allegedly referential to, yet irremediably isolated from, 'reality,' the very conception of which is equally equivocal. One could (must?) still exert oneself investigating, discussing, arguing, assessing, evaluating, and so reach whatever conclusions one in fact reaches. But if we presume a person is not really *free* to conclude whatever he will from all of this activity, do we not 'necessarily' regard both the activity and the status of such 'conclusions' – and thus ourselves – in a radically different light? If a person could *consistently* believe that *all* thought is epiphenomenal (and I am most dubious whether anyone really can), would it not undercut all intellectual and moral *seriousness*, thereby vitiating practical commitment and resolve? Yet, the most pertinent consequence would be that, immediately upon acceding to the deterministic premise, one could no longer take Determinism seriously. Is not this very fact itself revealing about the human soul, that it will not be dictated to in this way? That in the very attempt to accept a claim that is radically inconsistent with one's self-conscious, rational nature, one can no longer take it seriously? For anyone who could surrender himself to a strictly determined view of human nature – that is, do so fully cognizant of its implications – there could be no philosophy or science in the ordinary, natural sense, merely a kind of mock-philosophy or mock-science, which is taken seriously only so long as one forgets that everything one notices, analyses, concludes (or forgets) is in fact determined irrespective of the truth. For the moment one remembers that one is not free to pursue the truth, or to see the world as it is – oneself included – everything suddenly becomes but the shadows of a puppet play. No amount of pinching could prove that one is not dreaming.

Moreover, if one succumbs to the determinist view (whereupon such succumbing must, of course, be seen as itself determined), this mock-philosophizing must be regarded, not as something one *does* (in the natural sense), but as something that happens to, or in, oneself. Surely there is some question whether anyone can really live like that, becoming accustomed to, even comfortable with, the resulting intellectual schizophrenia: the liability to radical flip-flops in self-understanding, regarding oneself one moment as philosophizing, and the next as being mock-philosophized upon (or within). Liable, that is, to sudden gestalt switches from autonomous self to automaton, and back again, switching 'purposefully' when one 'chooses' (to lapse into a mode of expression that comes naturally to us, as in discussing these matters one can scarce avoid doing, time and again), but subject to spontaneous switches as well – though in every case actually determined, presumedly. Thus, one is left with a duplicitous view of oneself: that of the natural consciousness with which one begins, and never entirely surrenders; and this endlessly convoluting, artificial view of one's being a determined mechanism, complete with a determined consciousness (whose very ambivalence, along with all else, has been forever predetermined).

The decisive point, however, is not that the determinist view, strictly adhered to, is apt to be psychically uncomfortable (to put it mildly), but that upon reflexive application, it collapses. For upon assuming it, one obviates any and all reasons for believing it. To be sure, the alternative view – that we are in some sense free, and first of all free to think whatever seems true (which entails acknowledging the formal idea of Truth) – is also perplexing, perhaps incorrigibly so. But it does not carry the same liabilities as does determinism. Applied reflexively, it is not self-refuting, but remains a coherent view, however puzzling.[11] And in squaring with our natural, immediate experience of ourselves, it provokes no chronic psychical tension, such as I presume would attend the interminable effort of managing radically irreconcilable views of oneself. Also, mental freedom is compatible with a number of vitally important human concerns: with ascribing personal responsibility, as is implicit in the ordinary meaning of morality, and of justice in particular; with the existence of genuine nobility and magnanimity, rightly deserving of admiration; and perhaps most importantly, with self-respect – for we can genuinely, and do naturally, respect a free rational being, as we cannot an automaton (more so than any other machine).

A full understanding of ourselves as free rational beings – free because rational – may remain ever elusive. The interaction of reason and non-rational factors may ever remain mysterious to us, much as does the interaction between mind and matter, consciousness and body. But if we consult our actual experience, we do not *feel* 'unfree' in having our thoughts determined by reason. Quite the contrary: in assenting to reason, we feel we do so freely, even when we are acceding to a conclusion we regret that we 'must' accept; for in such cases, it is not the *acceding* we regret, but whatever we feel reason obliges us to accept, regretting that it should be so. We feel free when accepting the dictates of reason, for we are aware that not everyone does, nor do we ourselves all the time. Many people many times reject conclusions, not because they can fault the reasoning that leads to them (nor do they even trouble to try), but simply because they do not *like* the conclusion at issue; they have opinions they prefer to hold, irrespective of the truth.

Aware of these facts, however dimly, we tacitly recognize that the acceptance of whatever reason determines is itself a manifestation of our 'free will.' Reason alone cannot make us *heed* reason, since all reason can do is provide rational arguments for heeding reason. But if we are deaf to reason, choose to ignore reason, such arguments are impotent. In the final analysis, the only power any philosopher (qua philosopher) has – Hobbes included – is the power of reason (for even sophistry is parasitic upon this power, sophistry *being* a false appearance of valid reasoning). What Hobbes himself notes with respect to interpretation of Scripture is a truth every bit as pertinent to *Leviathan*: 'And generally in all cases of the world, hee that pretendeth any proofe, maketh Judge of his proofe him to whom he addresseth his speech' (XLII/32, 280). So, Hobbes may threaten us with death if we fail to heed his arguments (and thereby risk a return to the malevolent anarchy of the State of Nature), but the force of the threat is only as great as the influence of his reasoning upon us.[12] However, this is the single most significant variable among people: the extent to which they freely submit to reason.

The natural relationship between freedom and reason presumably explains why, generally speaking, we are prouder of ourselves when we choose to be rational: then we regard ourselves as at our best, fulfilling our true nature, thus most fully human. We *choose* to be rational, so far as we are. Or more to the point, we *will* ourselves to be rational, for we abide by what we rationally choose only so far as we have sufficient 'will power.' If we attend to our actual, natural experience of ourselves, we notice that we do not ordinarily feel that our will is either free or unfree. Rather, as Nietzsche observes, 'in real life it is solely a question of *strong* and *weak* wills.'[13]

So, admittedly, *how* human freedom works is perplexing, and probably always will remain so: how, within one's psychic crucible – in which rational considerations meet and mix with sub-rational drives and desires, passions and prejudices – a definite decision is congealed. But determinism is not merely perplexing; in attempting to take it seriously, in full awareness of its implications (presuming that to be possible), it is intellectually disintegrating, since it destroys the significance of thought. Thus, it is utterly alien to one's natural experience of oneself. For it is not even like feeling oneself 'possessed' by a demon, insofar as this still allows for distinguishing one's natural self from the demon. Whereas, determinism obliterates all meaningful sense of self. By contrast, the view that acknowledges some degree of freedom within the embracing constraints of Nature (the material demands of life and health, the somewhat variable cycles of life, the invariable ones of celestial and terrestrial motions, the inflexible rigour of natural forces, and so on) squares with our psychic experience. And this *is* the criterion that Hobbes himself so rightly insists must be the final authority: 'For this kind of Doctrine, admitteth no other Demonstration' (concluding sentence of his Introduction). Right he is. Self-awareness, then, however hazy and poorly understood, is a legitimate basis for people's believing that they enjoy some freedom of choice and action, and that they are mostly free to think what they will. And, similarly, it is the basis for their distinguishing situations in terms of the degree of freedom each offers, seeing some as comparatively open, whereas other situations practically dictate a single course of action. Every time a person says, 'I had no choice,' he implicitly means to contrast that situation with the many others in which he felt that he did – as would we in his place.

None of these considerations are acknowledged by Hobbes, of course, much less refuted. But as was noted at the outset of this discussion, no rational justification of Determinism is conceivable, since it renders all reasoning irrelevant by its implication that, whatever one's view, it is not something one freely decides on the merits of the case. One can still go through the motions, but given how the human psyche is constituted, one simply cannot simultaneously take seriously *both* Determinism *and* whatever arguments supposedly imply it. Thus, it is not 'free will' that is self-contradictory, but the denial of it. Rationally speaking, that is.

Could Hobbes really have supposed otherwise? That is hard to believe. And a careful consideration of what he actually says raises more doubt than validation that he himself subscribed to what is generally taken to be his teaching:

> *A* FREE-MAN, *is he, that in those things, which by his strength and wit he is able to do, is not hindred to doe what he has a will to.* But when the words *Free,* and *Liberty,* are applyed to anything but *Bodies,* they are abused; for that which is not subject to Motion, is not subject to Impediment. And therefore, when 'tis said (for example) *The way is Free,* no Liberty of the way is signified, but of those that walk in it without stop. And when we say *a Guift is Free,* there is not meant any Liberty of the Guift, but of the Giver, that was not bound by any law, or Covenant to give it. So when we *speak Freely,* it is not the Liberty of voice, or pronunciation, but of the man, whom no law hath obliged to speak otherwise than he did. Lastly, from the use of the word *Free-will,* no Liberty can be inferred of the will, desire, or inclination, but the Liberty of the man: which consisteth in this, that he finds no stop, in doing what he has the will, desire, or inclination to doe. (XXI/2, 108)

First, as I observed earlier, 'free will' is a misleading name for what is really at issue here: mental freedom. No one who has thought much about it would likely argue that our desires and inclinations are themselves freely chosen; he would agree they are determined by antecedent causes. The question concerns our having any choice whether or not to *accede* to this desire or that inclination, and, conversely, whether sometimes we may act despite having no desire for what we nonetheless choose to do (often this is true of the fulfilment of one's duty – that is why it must be a *duty*). So, strictly speaking, Hobbes is quite correct to insist that 'from the use of the word *Free-will,* no Liberty can be inferred of the will, desire, or inclination.' But notice that he is silent here about *thought.* Moreover, antecedent thoughts may figure among those antecedent causes of particular desires (as the desire to quit smoking may result from learning of its harmful effects).

Secondly, it would seem that 'impediments' to the motion of bodies are *not* exclusively what we are first led to believe: material obstacles and constraints ('For whatsoever is so tyed, or environed, as it cannot move, but within a certain space, which space is determined by the opposition of some externall body, we say it hath not Liberty to go further. And so of all living creatures, whilest they are imprisoned, or restrained, with walls, or chayns'; XXI/1, 107). This fits well enough the example of 'the way being free,' meaning that it is clear of obstacles so that a person may 'walk in it without stop.' However, if freedom is simply a matter of bodily motion, one is freely bestowing a 'Guift' in surrendering one's wallet to an armed robber, provided only that in passing it to the thief one's hand is not physically constrained. And any person who is not bound and gagged can 'speak Freely,' irrespective of what the law commands. For laws and covenants themselves cannot be readily assimilated to 'externall Impediments' of *bodily* motion, since here pretty clearly the 'impediment' in the first instance is something *internal* (e.g., fear of punishment, or sense of honour, or wish not to offend – all manifested in thought). So, if we are to acknowledge, as Hobbes clearly implies and as we ordinarily would, that the *law* can 'impede' freedom of speech, it is because a person may be *unwilling* to speak otherwise than the law allows (for whatever reason; e.g., regarding oneself as morally obliged to obey the law, or in the belief that doing so would be prejudicial to one's own good; cf. III/7, 10).[14] In this case, the issue is *not* whether the body is free of physical trammels, but (once again) whether the human *mind* may freely choose to speak regardless of obligations and risks – as over the centuries many people have for various reasons (religious convictions being not the least of these). Or whether, instead, one's decision is predetermined in every case.

To be sure, one's mind is embodied, and the matter in one's brain 'subject to Motion'; but are the *mind's* motions – as, for example, when I, or you, think through this problem – strictly determined by antecedent factors? For so Hobbes might seem to be claiming in his discussion of 'the Captivity of our Understanding': 'Sense, Memory, Understanding, Reason, and Opinion are not in our power to change; but alwaies, and necessarily such, as the things we see, hear, and consider suggest unto us; and therefore are not the effects of our Will, but our Will of them.' Thoughtfully considered, one sees this is essentially correct. For example, one might *wish* to forget a painful remembrance, but one's memory is no more subject to one's will than is what one sees when one opens one's eyes. But – to repeat – it is not actually freedom of the *will*, but of the mind (or thought) that is at issue. Thus, what one wills is indeed the 'effect' of the thought that results from *considering*, from *reasoning* about, whatever sensory evidence, memories, opinions, and prior understanding are recognized as germane to a problem at hand. Such being the case, one can agree with Hobbes that a person, having his reasons, may or may not 'wilfully' submit 'the Will to Obedience, where obedience is due,' even to the point that he would 'forbear contradiction' (XXXII/4, 196). In short, appearance to the contrary, Hobbes has been careful here not to rule out the freedom of mind to which his book is necessarily addressed. Moreover, he has scattered throughout his text several *positive* indications that he recognizes the mind of man to be 'free' – if that is quite the right word for one's thinking not being predetermined, but open to considering evidence and argument, along with feelings and beliefs (to the extent one so wishes, that is, and has the ability), and thereupon reaching one's own conclusions.

For example, in speaking of the early converts to Christianity by the Apostles, 'whom the people [having been] converted, obeyed, out of Reverence, not by Obligation,' Hobbes goes on to say, 'Their Consciences were free, and their Words and Actions subject to none but the Civill Power' (XLVII/19, 384). Are 'consciences' *bodies*, then? To appreciate the larger significance of this claim, one must bear in mind Hobbes's insistence that 'a mans Conscience, and his Judgement is the same thing'; XXIX/7, 168). And in his sceptical discussion of miracles, Hobbes is quite explicit in declaring that the human mind enjoys a domain of freedom: 'A private man has alwaies the liberty, (because thought is free,) to beleeve, or not beleeve in his heart, those acts that have been given out for Miracles' (XXXVII/13, 238). And, of course, if 'thought is free' with respect to what one concludes about miracles, it must be so as well with respect to any other judgment that is generated from one's rational assessment of relevant evidence and arguments.[15]

In discussing what someone alleges is a commandment unto men that God has revealed to him, Hobbes notes that this raises two questions. First, as to how anyone else can know for sure that it is genuine, he concludes 'it is evidently impossible' short of oneself being the recipient of the same revelation. But answering the second question, how can one be bound to *obey* such a commandment, is not difficult: 'For if the Law declared, be not against the Law of Nature (which is undoubtedly Gods law) and he undertake to obey it, he is bound by his own act; bound I say to obey it, but not bound to believe it: for mens belief, and interior cogitations, are not subject to the commands, but only to the operation of God, ordinary, or extraordinary' (XXVI/40, 149). Presumably by 'the ordinary *operation* of God' (as distinct from His commands), Hobbes means 'as God intended the human mind to operate' – that is, in its natural mode (cf., e.g., XXXVII/5, 234); whereas 'extraordinary' refers to the possibility of revelations. Later, arguing along the same lines about someone who pretends 'that God hath spoken to him supernaturally': if 'I make doubt of it, I cannot easily perceive what argument he can produce, to oblige me to beleeve it. It is true, that if he be my Soveraign, he may oblige me to obedience, so, as not by act or word to declare I beleeve him not; but not to think any otherwise then my reason perswades me' (XXXII/5, 196). Still later, Hobbes discusses 'the Office of Christs Minister,' namely: 'to make men Beleeve, and have Faith in Christ. But Faith hath no relation to, nor dependence at all upon Compulsion, or Commandement; but only upon certainty, or probability of Argument drawn from Reason, or from something men beleeve already' (XLII/9, 270).

Notice that, while affirming the independence of the human mind, Hobbes challenges the propriety of any and all forms of Inquisition. But notice especially *how* he does so – or, rather, how he does *not* do so, namely, *not* by arguing that a person should not be persecuted for his beliefs because they are strictly determined by antecedent causes over which he has no control. Rather, a man 'may without blame beleeve his private Teachers ... For internall Faith is in its own nature invisible, and consequently exempted from all humane jurisdiction' (XLII/43, 285). His most explicit statement to this purpose, however, comes not in any of the sixteen chapters ostensibly dealing with religion, but in the one chapter promising to expose 'Vain Philosophy':

There is another Errour in [Churchmen's and Schoolmen's] Civill Philosophy (which they never learned of Aristotle, nor Cicero, nor any other of the Heathen,) to extend the power of the Law, which is the Rule of Actions onely, to the very Thoughts, and Consciences of men, by Examination, and *Inquisition* of what they Hold, notwithstanding the Conformity of their Speech and Actions: By which, men are either punished for answering the truth of their thoughts, or constrained to answer an untruth for fear of punishment. It is true, that the Civill Magistrate, intending to employ a Minister in charge of Teaching, may enquire of him, if hee bee content to Preach such, and such Doctrines; and in case of refusall, may deny him the employment; But to force him to accuse himselfe of Opinions, when his Actions are not by Law forbidden, is against the Law of Nature; and especially in them, who teach, that a man shall bee damned to Eternall and extream torments, if he die in a false opinion concerning an Article of the Christian Faith. For who is there, that knowing there is so great danger in an error, whom the naturall care of himself, compelleth not to hazard his Soule upon his own judgement, rather than that of any other man that is unconcerned in his damnation? (XLVI/37, 378)

Admittedly, since these and most of the few other statements bearing on the matter have to do with religion, it is possible they are meant to serve an ulterior purpose. In that connection, consider once more Hobbes's sole argument against 'free will,' to wit: 'And did not [God's] will assure the *necessity* of mans will, and consequently of all that on mans will dependeth, the *liberty* of men would be a contradiction, and an impediment to the omnipotence and *liberty* of God' (XXI/4, 108). It in effect confronts the reader with a stark choice. What do you really believe in: Your mental freedom? Or, an omnipotent God? Needless to say, all this complicates the problem of deciding with absolute certainty just what Hobbes's view about freedom of thought actually is.

But there is no such difficulty in deciding what it *ought* to be; and if we credit him with generally knowing his own business, he deserves the benefit of the doubt on this all-important point. Otherwise, it is exceedingly difficult – I would say, psychologically impossible – to take seriously the idea that any sort of moral *obligation* could arise from promises and covenants (such that, e.g., having once transferred one's 'right' to something, one is 'OBLIGED, or BOUND, not to hinder those, to whom such Right is granted'; XIV/7, 65); or that the *legitimacy* of sovereign power could derive from the *consent* of the governed; or that one is 'obliged' to be *grateful* to the Giver of a 'Free Guift' (as *per* Hobbes's fourth natural law, XV/16, 75). To repeat, it is practically impossible to take *any* moral obligation seriously if all such promising and consenting, giving and receiving are regarded, not as acts of free agents, but of beings whose behaviour is as strictly determined as that of Ants and Bees and Cicadas – indeed, as that of a falling stone.

And lest there be confusion on this matter, the issue of Determinism is altogether separate from that of how, if at all, various passions bear on the moral status of one's undertakings – for example, whether (as Hobbes claims) 'Covenants entred into by fear, in the condition of meer Nature, are obligatory' (XIV/27, 69). Generally speaking, passions of one sort or another are ingredients in all of life's decisions, and not infrequently are dominant factors; but virtually never do they strictly and precisely *determine* what one does. Even terror can sometimes be successfully resisted, as courageous individuals have proven. Extreme pain, however, may (as Aristotle concedes) 'destroy the soul' – that is, nullify its natural capacity for self-rule.[16]

The paramount consideration, however, is whether Hobbes's reasoning and rhetoric, upon which he lavished such care in crafting his *Leviathan*, can be taken seriously on any basis other than the presumption that he was free to pursue the truth about political life to the best of his ability, and then to write about it in whatever manner he judged would most effectively serve his purpose or purposes for doing so. And that, correlatively, the reader of what Hobbes has 'set down [so] orderly, and perspicuously' about Mankind, is mentally free 'to consider, if he also find not the same in himself.' I suspect that Hobbes knew full well that he could count on his readers tacitly presuming this mental freedom, regardless of its violating the strict and universal determinism integral to the metaphysical basis of the natural sciences, with which he wished his political science to seem affiliated. After all, the presumption of mental freedom is the natural human posture, while there is not one person in a dozen myriads who is or ever will be fully cognizant of the paradoxical implications of determinism, including its radical incompatibility with the natural perspective.

The question that remains is *why* Hobbes would wish to cultivate an erroneous impression of the metaphysical basis of his new understanding of politics. That is, what rhetorical purpose is it intended to serve? One can only speculate, of course, but the most obvious explanation is that Hobbes means thereby to enhance the 'scientific' status of his political prescription. By seeming to employ the same metaphysical postulates as that of the modern Baconian-Cartesian science his regime is designed to promote and exploit, especially its Materialism and Determinism and non-teleological conception of Nature; and by grounding his account of politics in a State of Nature so conceived, including a 'realistic' conception of human nature, his new Political Science is the more readily, albeit spuriously, assimilated to this new form of Natural Science. Moreover, insofar as Hobbes shared Bacon's and Descartes's confidence in the wonder-working potential of its technological orientation – given a political environment in which to flourish – he anticipated the status of Natural Science would steadily rise, from the 'small Power; because not eminent' of his day, to that of being the supreme intellectual authority of ours. And that the credibility of his political doctrine would be strengthened commensurately.

I suspect there is more to his rhetorical rationale than this, however. In particular, that he wishes to provide a metaphysical validation – false, but nonetheless plausible – for the *Hedonism* essential to the functioning of the Hobbesian regime. Regarding Pleasure as the Good (with Hobbes's blessing), people need not be embarrassed to pursue 'such things as are necessary to commodious living,' since they are free to regard themselves as strictly determined by Nature to do so – and by God as well, ascetic religious teachings to the contrary notwithstanding, given that Nature simply *is* (Hobbes assures us) 'the Art whereby God hath made and governes the World.' For the majority of people, the practical effect of Hobbes's arguing for determinism probably does not go much beyond this: it liberates their acquisitiveness and pleasure seeking, thereby further motivating their 'Industry,' while enhancing their appreciation for a peaceful environment in which to enjoy the fruits of their labours.[17] In most other respects, they will retain the natural human posture that all morality and honour presumes – including that preached by Hobbes.

As a comprehensive assessment of political life readily reveals, however, strict and universal Hedonism is incompatible with the very survival of any polity, much less its decency. Hobbes's Commonwealth is no exception. Nor does almost anyone in practice faithfully adhere to the hedonistic credo, whatever they might think or say. But these and related issues will be more conveniently explored after an examination of Hobbes's treatment of what he himself regards as matters of first importance, namely, the topics of Reason and Language – so intimately related that (as he notes) the Greeks had but one word for both: *logos*. *Logos* is the key. The rest of the world we encounter may be strictly determined, but humans by virtue of *logos* enjoy a freedom unique to the species.

10

Reason and the Problem of *Revelation*

As I have argued, freedom of the mind (hence 'freely willed' action) – however perplexing – is not self-contradictory, whereas the denial of it is virtually incoherent insofar as the presumption of such freedom is the prerequisite of taking seriously *anything* thought or said on this or any other subject. Rationally considered, that is. For there remains the possibility of one's subscribing to Determinism on the basis of Divine Revelation. And judging from the dogmatic tenacity with which some people today espouse it (including, oddly enough, many who supposedly think for a living), one would presume they were the beneficiaries of just such a privileged communication. To be sure, sufficiently thought about, the doctrine would still remain every bit as confusing (and psychically unsettling) as ever – for they must regard their adherence to it, like everything else they believe, as determined, rendering nugatory all possible evidence or argument for or against it, whether from natural sources or divinely supplied. As evidence or argument, that is. For words, whether spoken or written, will still *affect* people exposed to them, but those effects will have been predetermined, and their relationship to any meaningful idea of Truth radically indeterminable. But if the dogmatic determinist can forget the epistemic irrelevance of what anyone says, God included, he might find reassurance, if not exactly comfort, in Hobbes's droll principles of Scriptural hermeneutics:

For though there be many things in Gods Word above Reason; that is to say, which cannot by naturall reason be either demonstrated, or confuted; yet there is nothing contrary to it; but when it seemeth so, the fault is either in our unskilfull Interpretation, or erroneous Ratiocination.

Therefore, when any thing therein written is too hard for our examination, wee are bidden to captivate our understanding to the Words; and not to labour in sifting out a Philosophicall truth by Logick, of such mysteries as are not comprehensible, nor fall under any rule of naturall science. For it is with the mysteries of our Religion, as with wholsome pills for the sick, which swallowed whole, have the vertue to cure; but chewed, are for the most part cast up again without effect. But by the Captivity of our Understanding, is not meant a Submission of the Intellectuall faculty, to the Opinion of any other man; but of the Will to Obedience, where obedience is due ... We then Captivate our Understanding and Reason, when we forbear contradiction; when we so speak, as (by lawfull Authority) we are commanded; and when we live accordingly; which in sum, is Trust, and Faith reposed in him that speaketh, though the mind be incapable of any Notion at all from the words spoken. (XXXII/2–4, 195–6)

Now, one might wonder, first of all, how Hobbes (or anyone else) could *know* – short of divine Revelation – that there is nothing in 'Gods Word' that is contrary to what humans would rightly regard as 'naturall reason.' For that matter, is the crucial distinction between 'above Reason' and 'contrary to it' sufficiently clear for practical application? Is the Christian doctrine of the Trinity, for example (that God is both One and Three, a single Godhead yet comprising a distinct Father, Son, and Holy Spirit), *contrary* to Reason (as it would seem to be), or is it one of those incomprehensible 'mysteries' that are simply 'above reason'?[1]

For what it is worth, Hobbes would seem to have left open the possibility of Revelations, whether they be fully intelligible or not, having been careful to acknowledge the orthodox view as to the various media whereby God might communicate with man. Thus, he assures his reader:

God declareth his Lawes three ways; by the Dictates of *Naturall Reason*, by *Revelation*, and by the *Voyce* of some *man*, to whom by the operation of Miracles, he procureth credit with the rest. From hence there ariseth a triple Word of God, *Rational*, *Sensible*, and *Prophetique*: to which Correspondeth a triple Hearing; *Right Reason*, *Sense Supernaturall*, and *Faith*. (XXXI/3, 187)[2]

And if God can declare his Will in all three such ways, obviously He could communicate likewise whatever else He might wish Man to know (such as a correct understanding of the principles 'whereby [He] hath made and governes the World'). Needless to add, however, Hobbes does *not* allege divine revelation as the basis for his claim that everything is strictly determined; as with his related assertion that the entire universe consists of nothing but bodies and their motions, he simply proclaims it to be so, swallowed whole, without any attempt either to demonstrate its truth – not surprisingly, as one cannot conceive how that could be done – or to rebut objections to such a view. Moreover, though Hobbes may himself speak in a prophet's declarative mode, he provides grounds for doubting that he, or anyone else, does so by divine authority. Putting together all that he says on the subject, it seems that what he giveth with one hand, he taketh away with the other.

Consider, first of all, Miracles, which Hobbes assures us with his first mention are the exclusive means of identifying someone whom God has author-ized to speak for Him, i.e., a genuine prophet (the truth of whose words we then accept on 'Faith,' as opposed to 'arguments taken ... from the thing it selfe, or from the principals of naturall Reason'; cf. VII/7, 32):

[T]he testimony that men can render of divine Calling, can be no other, than the operation of Miracles; or true Prophecy, (which also is a Miracle;) or extraor-dinary Felicity.[3] [Notice, this last is not expressly denominated miraculous.] ... For as in naturall things, men of judgement require naturall signes, and arguments; so in supernaturall things, they require signes supernaturall, (which are Miracles,) before they consent inwardly, and from their hearts. (XII/28, 59)

Fair enough. But what, then, actually *counts* as a 'miracle' or 'supernatu-rall signe' such as can win men's inward consent? Despite the obvious pertinence of this question to his account of Religion, and tacitly conced-ing the need for its being addressed (by subsequently addressing it), Hobbes does not do so until well into Part Three, 'Of a Christian Common-wealth.' Its sixth chapter, '*Of* Miracles, *and their Use*,' begins with the explanation that 'By *Miracles* are signified the Admirable works of God: & therefore they are also called *Wonders*.' Consequently:

To understand therefore what is a Miracle, we must first understand what works they are, which men wonder at, and call Admirable. And there be but two things which make men wonder at any event: The one is, if it be strange, that is to say, such, as the like of it hath never, or very rarely been produced: The other is, if when it is produced, we can not imagine it to have been done by naturall means, but onely by the immediate hand of God. But when wee see some possible, nat-urall cause of it, how rarely soever the like has been done; or if the like have been often done, how impossible soever it be to imagine a naturall means thereof, we no more wonder, nor esteem it for a Miracle. (XXXVII/2, 233)

Given Hobbes's glosses on these 'two things which make men wonder,' it is clear that they are a *pair* of criteria, each necessary but not in itself sufficient: the event must be *both* rare and seemingly impossible to account for naturally.

Hobbes leaves the impression – though he does not actually say – that such events would be almost universally acknowledged as miraculous. And we can readily imagine ones that would be so regarded (some person twelve days dead being revived, say; or – taking a hint from Hobbes – someone being turned into a pillar of salt). However, he had earlier noted without further comment, 'Miracles are Marvellous workes: but that which is marvellous to one, may not be so to another' (XXVI/39, 148). And as his later discussion continues, it becomes clear not only that a susceptibility to believe in miracles is variable among people, but that the reason why so is readily explicable:

[S]eeing Admiration and Wonder, is consequent to the knowledge and experience, wherewith men are endued, some more, some lesse; it followeth, that the same thing, may be a Miracle to one, and not to another. And thence it is, that ignorant, and superstitious men make great Wonders of those works, which other men, knowing to proceed from Nature, (which is not the immediate, but the ordinary work of God,) admire not at all: As when Ecclipses of the Sun and Moon have been taken for supernaturall works, by the common people; when neverthelesse there were others, could from their naturall causes, have foretold the very hour they should arrive. (XXXVII/5, 234)

One implication of this is so obvious as hardly bears mentioning: belief in the very possibility of miracles will generally wither, and the domain of the possibly miraculous shrink, with the advancement of science – presuming, that is, the popular diffusion of a view of reality based on the findings of natural science. And such diffusion is almost certain to attend exposure to the wonderworks of the resulting technology, even if not otherwise actively promulgated.

Ignorance of natural causation, however, does not merely leave people credulous, inclined to superstition, and thus to treating as miraculous unusual natural happenings. Their gullibility also invites exploitation by skilled and unscrupulous fellows, who are able by clever trickery to pass themselves off as possessing supernatural powers. So, the reliability of miracles as evidence of divine favour is compromised not only by ignorance about Nature, but also (Hobbes warns) by the possibility of clever frauds perpetrated for selfish gain – not infrequently in order to establish a spurious religio-political power:

If therefore Enchantment be not, as many think it, a working of strange effects by spells, and words; but Imposture, and delusion, wrought by ordinary means; and so far from supernaturall, as the Imposters need not the study so much as of nat- urall causes, but the ordinary ignorance, stupidity, and superstition of mankind, to doe them.

...

So that all the Miracle consisteth in this, that the Enchanter has deceived a man; which is no Miracle, but a very easie matter to doe.

For such is the ignorance, and aptitude to error generally of all men, but espe- cially of them that have not much knowledge of naturall causes, and of the nature, and interests of men; as by innumerable and easie tricks to be abused. What opinion of miraculous power, before it was known there was a Science of the course of the Stars, might a man have gained, that should have told the people, This hour, or day the Sun should be darkned? (XXXVII/10–12, 236)

Indeed, the challenge of distinguishing true from false prophets is some- times so difficult that even a genuine prophet may be deceived – for the Old Testament includes at least one such case (I Kings 13), as Hobbes pointedly reminds his reader. Faced with this perplexing possibility, 'what certainty is there of knowing the will of God, by other way than that of Reason?' Hobbes answers: 'out of the Holy Scripture, that there be two marks, by which together, not asunder, a true prophet is to be known. One is the doing of miracles; the other is the not teaching any other Religion than that which is already established. Asunder (I say) neither of these is sufficient.' Then, quoting Deuteronomy (13:1–5) as his authority, Hobbes further emphasizes his point: 'that God wil not have miracles alone serve for arguments, to approve the Prophets calling' (XXXII/7, 197).

Subsequently, however, Hobbes nudges miracles out of the picture almost entirely:

In this aptitude of mankind, to give too hasty beleefe to pretended Miracles, there can be no better, nor I think any other caution, then that which God hath pre- scribed, first by Moses [again citing the Deuteronomy verses]; That we take not any for Prophets, that teach any other Religion, then that which Gods Lieutenant, (which at that time was Moses,) hath established ... [Thus,] the Head of the Church in all times, are to be consulted, what doctrine he hath established, before wee give credit to a pretended Miracle, or Prophet. And when that is done, the thing they pretend to be a Miracle, we must both see it done, and use all means possible to consider, whether it be really done; and not onely so, but whether it be such, as no man can do the like by his own naturall power, but that it requires the immediate hand of God ... So also if wee see not, but onely hear tell of a Miracle, we are to consult the Lawful Church; that is to say, the lawful Head thereof, how far we are to give credit to the relators of it. And this is chiefly the case of men, that in these days live under Christian Soveraigns. For in these times, I do not know one man, that ever saw any such wondrous work, done by the charm, or at the word, or prayer of a man, that a man endued but with a mediocrity of reason, would think supernaturall. (XXXVII/13, 237)

Suffice it to say, as one proceeds through Hobbes's book, the possibility of divine authorization being established by miracles diminishes, while the case for the sovereignty of natural reason is steadily strengthened. For example, in discussing 'Divine Positive Laws,' which would necessarily have to be proclaimed by someone 'whom God hath authorized' for the purpose, Hobbes asks:

But this Authority of man to declare what be these Positive Lawes of God, how can it be known? God may command a man by a supernaturall way, to deliver Lawes to other men. But because it is of the essence of Law, that he who is to be obliged, be assured of the Authority of him that declareth it, which we cannot naturally take notice to be from God, *How can a man without supernaturall Revelation be assured of the Revelation received by the declarer?* and *how can he be bound to obey them?* For the first question, how a man can be assured of the Revelation of another, without a Revelation particularly to himselfe, it is evidently impossible: For though a man may be induced to believe such a Revelation, from the Miracles they see him doe, or from seeing the Extraordinary sanctity of his life, or from seeing the Extraordinary wisedome, or the Extraordinary felicity of his Actions, all of which are marks of Gods extraordinary favour; yet they are not assured evidences of speciall Revelation. Miracles are Marvellous workes: but that which is marvelous to one, may not be so to another. Sanctity may be feigned; and the visible felicities of this world, are most often the work of God by Naturall and ordinary causes. And therefore no man can infallibly know by naturall reason, that another has had a supernaturall revelation of Gods will; but only a beliefe; every one (as the signes thereof shall appear greater, or lesser) a firmer, or a weaker belief. (XXVI/39, 148–9)[4]

In a later chapter, however, Hobbes effectively undercuts the credibility also of any means of 'Revelation particular to oneself,' at least in the mind of a thoughtful reader. Initially, he implies that there is nothing especially problematic about it: 'How God speaketh to a man immediately, may be understood by those well enough, to whom he hath so spoken.' Seemingly, he confines rational scepticism to revelations claimed by someone else: 'For if a man pretend to me, that God hath spoken to him supernaturally, and immediately, and I make doubt of it, I cannot easily perceive what argument he can produce, to oblige me to beleeve it' (XXXII/5, 196). But the objections he marshals against crediting the other person's claim should sow doubt in a thoughtful reader about the possibility of revelation in his *own* case as well:

To say [God] hath spoken to him in a Dream, is no more then to say he hath dreamed that God spake to him; which is not of force to win beleef from any man, that knows that dreams are for the most part naturall, and may proceed from former thoughts ... To say he hath seen a Vision, or heard a Voice, is to say, that he hath dreamed between sleeping and waking: for in such manner a man doth many times naturally take his dreams for a vision, as not having well observed his own slumbering. To say he speaks by supernaturall Inspiration, is to say he finds an ardent desire to speak, or some strong opinion of himself, for which hee can alledge no naturall and sufficient reason. [The Latin edition is more derisively dismissive here: 'If someone says that some new doctrine has been breathed into him supernaturally by God, the wise will understand that he is raving, out of admiration for his own mind.'] So that though God Almighty can speak to a man, by Dreams, Visions, Voice, and Inspiration; yet he obliges no man to beleeve he hath so done to him that pretends it; who (being a man) may erre, and (which is more) may lie. (XXXII/6, 196; cf. XXXIII/24, 205)

At the risk of belabouring the obvious, surely Hobbes intends a cumulative effect by his repeatedly voicing and thereby encouraging the greatest scepticism towards alleged miracles and revelations. Complementing this is his repeated insistence on the limited intellectual competence of most people: 'the ordinary ignorance, stupidity, and superstition of mankind'; 'this aptitude of mankind, to give too hasty beleefe to pretended Miracles'; 'ignorant, and superstitious men make great Wonders of those works, which other men, knowing to proceed from Nature ... admire not at all'; 'the ignorance, and aptitude to error generally of all men, but especially of them that have not much knowledge of naturall causes'; 'by innumerable and easie tricks ... abused.' Whatever respect for the mental abilities of people in general Hobbes may have raised by his earlier claim to find 'a greater equality amongst men' in 'faculties of mind' than of bodily strength, it is surely dissipated by the time one reaches his comments on their proven capacity to ascribe divinity to man-made idols:

And though some man may think it impossible for people to be so stupid, as to think the Image to be God, or a Saint; or to worship it in that notion; yet it is manifest in Scripture to the contrary ... And wee see daily by experience in all sorts of People, that such men that study nothing but their food and ease, are content to beleeve any absurdity, rather than trouble themselves to examine it. (XLV/30, 363)

In short, by casting doubt, first, on miracles, then in a similarly suggestive manner on revelations – while at the same time insinuating that anyone who believes in such things is a gullible ignoramus, if not an outright idiot – Hobbes works indirectly to enhance respect for what he proclaims is 'the undoubted Word of God': 'our naturall reason' (XXXII/2, 195; cf. XXXVI/5–6, 224). He thereby, and not at all incidentally, elevates the status and authority of those who, such as himself, manifestly command a greater share of this power.[5]

Besides arousing scepticism about miracles and revelations per se, Hobbes expressly contends that all claims regarding these and other matters supernatural are necessarily *subordinate* to natural human reason inasmuch as one is reliant upon it to judge between possibly conflicting revelations (for example) and to assess the validity of alleged miracles. His book practically begins with one example (previously quoted). Having opined that witchcraft is not 'any reall power,' and derided the existence of 'Fayries, and walking Ghosts' as beliefs propagated by those who profit in 'the use of Exorcisme, of Crosses, of holy Water, and other such inventions,' he continues: 'But evil men under pretext that God can do any thing, are so bold as to say any thing when it serves their turn, though they think it untrue; It is the part of a *wise* man to *believe* them no further, than *right reason* makes that which they say, appear credible' (II/8, 7; emphasis added). The balance of this early paragraph enucleates the political rationale that underlies Hobbes's pervasive concern with religion: 'If this superstitious feare of Spirits were taken away, and with it, Prognostiques from Dreams, false Prophecies, and many other things depending thereon, by which, crafty ambitious persons abuse the simple people, men would be much more fitted than they are for civill Obedience.'

To exemplify the problem posed by false prophecies, Hobbes cites the biblical account of King Ahab (I Kings 16:29–22:40), of whom Scripture says, 'Ahab did more to provoke the LORD, the God of Israel, to anger than all the kings of Israel who were before him' (16:30, 33). As I noted previously in discussing Melville's Ahab, Hobbes refers directly to only one episode in Ahab's story, but he does so no less than three times. And that this might prompt a thoughtful reader to recall other notable features of King Ahab and his disastrous reign, including the pernicious influence of Jezebel, his idolatrous Queen. Ostensibly, however, Hobbes first invokes the example of Ahab to support his contention that the Bible tacitly acknowledges the difficulty of distinguishing true from false prophets as revealers of God's Will. Here, Ahab is not identified by name: 'How then can he, to whom God hath never revealed his Wil immediately (saving by the way of natural reason) know when he is to obey, or not to obey his Word, delivered by him, that sayes he is a Prophet. Of 400 Prophets, of whom the K. of *Israel* asked counsel, concerning the warre he made against *Ramoth Gilead*, only *Micaiah* was a true one' (XXXII/7, 196–7). Subsequently, Hobbes refers to the same episode as offering Scriptural confirmation that a visitation from '*the Spirit of the Lord*' does not mean by a ghost, but simply a vision (XXXIV/8, 209). His final citation of this episode serves to instantiate a warning about the general prevalence of false over true prophets – thus underlining the 'need of Reason and Judgment to discern between naturall, and supernaturall Gifts, and between naturall, and supernaturall Visions, or Dreams':

[A]nd seeing there is so much Prophecying in the Old Testament; and so much Preaching in the New Testament against Prophets; and so much a greater number ordinarily of false Prophets, then of true; every one is to beware of obeying their directions, at their own perill. And first, that there were many more false then true Prophets, appears by this, that when Ahab [I Kings 22.] consulted four hundred Prophets, they were all false Imposters, but onely one Michaiah. (XXXVI/19; 231)

Hobbes's construal of this episode is misleading, at least to judge by the account Micaiah gives of *why* the prophesying of the four hundred was false (I Kings 22:19–23): not because all four hundred were false prophets, but because God Himself arranged that they all be given *false inspiration* in order that Ahab be led to his doom.[6] This opens up a far more disturbing prospect. Sufficiently thought about, the idea of a god who not only actively intervenes in human affairs, but who may choose to deceive men by imbuing them with a false understanding – a god who is a Deceiver – raises great, seemingly insurmountable, objections, not merely to relying on the revelations allegedly vouchsafed to other men, but to any reliance on Revelation per se. Might this be why Hobbes repeatedly directs attention to this episode in the reign of King Ahab? Confronted with the implications of Micaiah's Vision, one must choose what sort of god to believe in: a Deceiver, or one whose Will is reliably revealed by judgments based on natural reason.[7]

Having referred repeatedly to Ahab's preference for the advice of four hundred 'false' prophets, while rejecting that of the one true prophet, it is curious that Hobbes does not refer at all to another episode involving a showdown between rival prophets during the reign of King Ahab: that of Elijah's defeat – and slaughter! – of 450 false prophets (in this case, surely false, being servitors of the false god Ba'al). Perhaps Hobbes shies away from the Elijah episode because the matter at issue in that case was not who were the true and who the false prophets, but that of determining the True God (I Kings 18:17–40) – a question which Hobbes has his own preferred way of settling. Be that as it may, in the very chapter devoted to considering Prophets as conveyers of 'the Word of God,' Hobbes insists on the decisive role of Reason:

Seeing then all Prophecy supposeth Vision, or Dream, (which two, when they be naturall, are the same,) or some especiall gift of God, so rarely observed in mankind, as to be admired where observed; And seeing as well such gifts, as the most extraordinary Dreams, and Visions, may proceed from God, not onely by his supernaturall, and immediate, but also by his naturall operation, and by mediation of second causes; there is need of Reason and Judgment to discern between naturall, and supernaturall Gifts, and between naturall, and supernaturall Visions, or Dreams. (XXXVI/19, 230)

Having cited an assortment of passages from Scripture to buttress his claims, Hobbes argues:

Seeing then there was in the time of the Old Testament, such quarrels amongst the Visionary Prophets, one contesting with another, and asking, *When departed the Spirit from me, to go to thee?* ... and such controversies in the New Testament at this day, amongst the Spirituall Prophets: Every man then was, and now is bound to make use of his Naturall Reason, to apply to all Prophecy those Rules which God hath given to us, to discern the true from the false. (XXXVI/20, 231)

Even in the course of seemingly endorsing the supreme authority of Scripture, Hobbes tacitly gives the nod to the power of natural reasoning:

Seeing therefore Miracles now cease, we have no sign left, whereby to acknowledge the pretended Revelations, or Inspirations of any private man; nor obligation to give ear to any Doctrine, farther than it is conformable to the Holy Scriptures, which since the time of our Saviour, supply the place, and sufficiently recompense the want of all other Prophecy; and from which, by wise and learned interpretation, and careful ratiocination, all rules and precepts necessary to the knowledge of our duty both to God and man, without Enthusiasme, or supernaturall Inspiration, may easily be deduced. (XXXII/9, 198)

Needless to add, the requisite 'wise and learned interpretation, and careful ratiocination' is that which Hobbes himself purports to provide in the second half of *Leviathan*, devoted to showing that the 'ground of [his] Discourse' is compatible with a distinctly *Christian* commonwealth, and so is 'not only the Naturall Word of God, but also the Propheticall' (XXXII/1, 195).[8]

It would not be lost on a thoughtful reader that subjecting the possibility of miracles and supernatural Revelation to a critique solely in terms of natural reasoning and causation necessarily begs the essential question. For, by definition, the *super*natural is 'above Reason' (to adopt Hobbes's felicitous formula). And it is impossible to *prove* that miracles are impossible. Moreover, the rational attack on faith in revelation presumes a perhaps equally problematic faith in the adequacy of natural reason. Thus Hobbes does not, directly and openly (and foolishly), challenge the possibility of revelation or miracles. Instead, he treats all allegedly supernatural phenomena as posing perplexing issues of epistemology, not metaphysics. And by ingeniously combining logical analysis with insinuating rhetoric in addressing those issues, he cultivates a wholesale scepticism towards the supernatural, and to that extent undermines the credibility of anything that smacks of it.

However, this practical subordination of Revelation to Reason – as is necessary if there is to be a thoroughly rational, universally valid *science* of Politics, including a prescription for the well-ordered regime that is capable of fulfilling the *natural* purpose for which people willingly gather into political associations ('their own preservation, and a more contented life thereby') – this subordination of Revelation throws into high relief the supreme importance of correctly understanding Reason. Not surprisingly, the reflexivity inherent in reasoning about Reason imparts a peculiar complexity to the problem. In particular, can Reason, in the course of explicating itself, somehow establish its own adequacy?[9] As will become clear in what follows, Hobbes's *explicit* conception surely cannot; but it will also become clear that this is a singularly inadequate account of human reasoning, as is confirmed by reflection on the form and substance of his masterpiece. But emasculated though it be, it is an account that roughly corresponds to what most people have in mind when they think of 'reasoning.'[10] Might this have something to do with why Hobbes employs it?

11

Rationality
and the Problem of *Reason*

If one troubles to think about it, Hobbes's treatment of Reason – this topic so crucial to every aspect of his teaching – is profoundly puzzling. He never so much as *mentions* what Bacon stresses is of paramount importance for any science that would come to grips with empirical reality: Induction. And he separates Reason entirely from Prudence, Deliberation, Belief, Judgment, Imagination, Intelligence, Invention, Supposing, and Trust (or Faith). Not surprisingly, then, his explications of these in turn are equally curious, contrasting radically with traditional philosophical accounts endorsed since antiquity, as well as with everyday psychic experience. One's puzzlement is further compounded if one presumes, as surely one must, that Hobbes is quite familiar with the traditional accounts, hence with the 'work' attributed to these other facets or powers of human reason, and so must be aware of his own failure to explain how such work *is* done. That is, his explicit treatment does not acknowledge the existence of human powers adequate to account for what the human mind clearly is capable of.

Oddest of all, however, he would have his reader distinguish what would ordinarily be called 'reasoning' about 'Particulars' (things, situations, proposals, whatever) from Reason proper, which (supposedly) involves only general terms, and as such exists primarily if not exclusively for the sake of producing and utilizing scientific knowledge. This is not simply a terminological issue. For the reader is left with a profoundly fragmented conception of the human mind – of human rationality – with no understanding of what integrates the 'parts' into a single coherent consciousness (as could be capable of creating, e.g., *Leviathan*). One can hardly help wondering what purpose is served by Hobbes's leaving this all-important matter in such disarray.

Hobbes's chapter entitled 'Of REASON, and SCIENCE' follows his chapter 'Of SPEECH' (which I, reversing his order, shall examine in my next chapter). For he contends, there is 'no Reasoning without Speech,' and alleges (rather curiously) the fact that 'the Greeks have but one word λόγος, for both *Speech* and *Reason*' as attesting to the logical priority of language to reason (IV/14, 16). According to Hobbes, that priority is implicit in what Reason *is*: simply calculation on the basis of the meaning of 'names,' as exemplified by arithmetic.

When a man *Reasoneth*, hee does nothing else but conceive a summe totall, from *Addition* of parcels; or conceive a Remainder, from *Substraction* of one summe from another: which (if it be done by Words,) is conceiving of the consequence of the names of all the parts, to the name of the whole; or from the names of the whole and one part, to the name of the other part ... These operations are not incident to Numbers onely, but to all manner of things that can be added together, and taken one out of another. For as Arithmeticians teach to adde and substract in *numbers*; so the Geometricians teach the same in *lines, figures* (solid and super-ficiall,) *angles, proportions, times,* degrees of *swiftnesse, force, power,* and the like; The Logicians teach the same in *Consequences of words;* adding together *two Names,* to make an *Affirmation;* and *two Affirmations,* to make a *Syllogisme;* and *many Syllogismes* to make a *Demonstration;* and from the *summe,* or *Conclusion* of a *Syllogisme,* they subtract one *Proposition,* to finde the other. Writers of Poli-tiques, adde together *Pactions,* to find mens *duties;* and Lawyers, *Lawes,* and *facts,* to find what is *right* and *wrong* in the actions of private men. In summe, in what matter soever there is place for *addition* and *substraction,* there also is place for *Reason;* and where these have no place, there *Reason* has nothing at all to do.
   Out of all which we may define, (that is to say determine,) what that is, which is meant by this word *Reason,* when wee reckon it amongst the Faculties of the mind. For REASON, in this sense, is nothing but *Reckoning* (that is, Adding and Substracting) of the Consequences of generall names agreed upon, for the *marking* and *signifying* of our thoughts; I say *marking* them, when we reckon by our selves; and *signifying,* when we demonstrate, or approve our reckonings to other men. (V/1–2, 18)

Regarding these claims, one may object that the mental operations involved in the various 'addings' and 'subtractings' of the latter four examples are *not* actually arithmetical, such terms being accurately descriptive only of – no surprise – the Arithmetician's defining activity (who deals with perfectly homogeneous 'parts' and 'wholes' composed of featureless 'units'). But when a Lawyer 'adds' heterogeneous 'parts' –

such as an alleged Fact ('Mr. Fawkes attempted to murder the King') to an established Law ('Attempted assaults on the King shall be punished by Death') – to argue for a particular 'whole' ('Mr. Fawkes deserves to die'), this 'summary' conclusion bears scant resemblance to that of adding two identical 'ones' together with two more to get four.[1] Consequently, it would seem that Hobbes is guilty here of what he earlier condemned: using words metaphorically (IV/4, 13). Alternatively (and more usefully), having reflected on the entire set of five exemplars with an eye towards seeing what is common to their respective reasoning operations, one may conclude that what Hobbes actually *means* by 'adding' and 'subtracting' is more familiarly known as deductive reasoning (epitomized by the defining activity of the Geometrician). This squares with Hobbes's own use of 'deduce' as synonymous with 'reckon' and 'infer' (e.g., XXVI/4, 137; XXXII/9, 198).

That said, however, the mental operation whereby one recognizes and abstracts this underlying commonality from Hobbes's examples is itself *inductive*, not deductive, much less arithmetical (despite Hobbes's – deliberately ironical? – summation: 'In summe ...'). Similarly, the mental operation whereby Hobbes (or anyone else) could cast an adequate *definition* of Reason (or of anything else) bears scant resemblance to 'reckoning'; nor could anyone '*reckon* it amongst the Faculties of the mind' simply by deductive, much less arithmetical 'reckoning.' So, one must conclude either that these activities – recognizing commonalities and differences, framing accurate definitions – are not rational (what, then, is their status?), or that Hobbes's definition of Reason as 'nothing but *Reckoning* (that is, Adding and Substracting) of the Consequences of generall names agreed upon' is grossly inadequate.[2]

Consider the provocative analogy with which Hobbes begins his book: between the *body* of 'that Rationall and most excellent worke of Nature, *Man*,' and the pre-eminent product of human 'Art': 'that great LEVIATHAN called a COMMON-WEALTH, or STATE, (in Latine CIVITAS) which is but an Artificiall Man.' Can one imagine any way such an analogy could arise, or its appropriateness be assessed, using only calculation? Whatever one might deduce from analogies once established, analogical reasoning itself requires intuiting some formal similarities in substantially different kinds of things. Thinking about the human body, for example, how might one go about establishing analogues between it and the 'body politic'? Would one *deduce*, for example, that '*Magistrates*, and other *Officers* of Judicature and Execution' are the 'artificiall *Joynts*' of a commonwealth? Notably, the first use of 'reason' in the text occurs in

Hobbes's elaboration of this very analogy ('*Equity* and *Lawes*, an artificiall *Reason* and *Will*').[3] As it turns out, this association of Equity with Reason figures vitally in Hobbes's political prescription. Thinking concretely, however, about the practical difficulties of *judging* what in various instances *is* equitable (as required by Hobbes's eleventh Natural Law) – the *synoptic* perspective that is required in order to judge what is fair and equitable to all concerned – suggests that there must be more to the powers of reason than simply calculation. And in that connection, Hobbes's purely formal, practically vacuous definition of 'Equity' is hardly helpful, though it is not therefore without interest: 'the equall distribution to each man, of that which in reason belongeth to him, is called EQUITY' (XV/24, 77).[4]

According to a philosophical tradition maintained since antiquity, judging what is equitable in a particular case – or what is right, beneficial, proper, or decent in any given circumstance – requires 'practical wisdom' or 'prudence' (*phronësis*).[5] Thus understood, exercising Prudence is the rational activity of greatest importance for living a good life, being the intellectual virtue whereby one recognizes what general principle (or principles) is (or are) pertinent to a particular case or situation, and judges the proper means whereby correctly to apply it (or them) so as most likely to realize a good result. That is, by means of prudential judgment one establishes a rational *bridge* between the general and the particular. It would be involved, for example, in each and every compliance with Hobbes's Laws of Nature. As such, Prudence is learnable, but – strictly speaking – not teachable. For while one may be instructed in sound general principles, it requires a considerable amount and variety of practical experience to develop, strengthen, and refine the necessary powers of recognition and judgment whereby one may best cope with the particularities of all conceivable situations. Thus, even the most prudent person's judgment remains fallible. Given the sheer variety of circumstances, the number of factors frequently involved, the difficulties in accurately assessing them, the incompleteness or inaccuracy of information, the pressure of time – for these and other reasons, one's rational powers can never be so perfected that errors of prudential judgment are precluded. However, allowing appropriately for the possibility of such mistakes, and being prepared to cope with them so as to minimize their damage, also falls within the purview of Prudence.

By contrast, Hobbes's account of Prudence is a trivialization, equating it to the guesswork of mere empirics. For he contends that Prudence is simply foresight derived from 'much Experience' (V/21, 22), being a presumption about the future based on the memory of observed regularities in the past.[6] He acknowledges that it is sometimes called '*Wisdome*,' but not deservedly, since 'such conjecture, through the difficulty of observing all circumstances, be very fallacious':

> But this is certain; by how much one man has more experience of things past, than another; by so much also is he more Prudent, and his expectations the seldomer faile him. The *Present* onely has a being in Nature; things *Past* have a being in the Memory onely, but things *to come* have no being at all; the *Future* being but a fiction of the mind, applying the sequels of actions Past, to the actions that are Present;[7] which with most certainty is done by him that has most Experience; but not with certainty enough. And though it be called Prudence, when the Event answereth our Expectation; yet in its own nature, it is but Presumption. For the foresight of things to come [i.e., genuine foresight], which is Providence, belongs onely to him by whose will they are to come. From him onely, and supernaturally, proceeds Prophecy. The best Prophet naturally [as opposed to *super*naturally] is the best guesser; and the best guesser, he that is the most versed and studied in the matters he guesses at: for he hath most *Signes* to guesse by.
>
> A *Signe*, is the Event Antecedent, of the Consequent; and contrarily, the Consequent of the Antecedent, when the like Consequences have been observed, before: And the oftener they have been observed, the lesse uncertain is the Signe. And therefore he that has most experience in any kind of businesse, has most Signes, whereby to guesse at the Future time; and consequently is the most prudent …
>
> Neverthelesse it is not Prudence that distinguisheth man from beast. There be beasts, that at a year old observe more, and pursue that which is for their good, more prudently, than a child can do at ten. (III/7–9, 10–11)[8]

Needless to say, a provocative claim. However, Hobbes himself subsequently renders suspect this notion of bestial prudence by observing that beasts have 'little, or no foresight of the time to come, for want of observation, and memory of the order, consequence, and dependance of the things they see' (XII/4, 52). While this seems plainly to contradict the passages previously quoted, strictly speaking it does not. For if one conceives of prudence in the manner Hobbes has defined it, beasts may not have *much* prudence, but if they have *any* 'foresight' based on past experience, they qualify as prudent. That said, however, it hardly explains why Hobbes has made a point of first endowing certain unspecified beasts with what would seem a generous measure of prudence, only later, in the context of a discussion relating religion to curiosity about causes, to retract almost all of it. Prudence as Hobbes has defined it may not be that which 'distinguisheth man from beast,' but religion and philosophy certainly do – though not in children. And to be sure, judged by adult standards, most ten-year-olds are notoriously *imprudent* with respect to knowing and pursuing their own good, not least because they are too much ruled by the immediate prospects of pleasure and pain – as are beasts, which suffices well enough for pursuing bestial goods. That children may not be as 'prudent' as some beasts in pursuing their own good has less to do with their being children than it does with the nature of the human good, any credible conception of which requires at least some cultivation of man's rational faculties.

Nonetheless, meditating on animal behaviour provides a useful entry point for this very thing: considering human rationality. For even if we concede that the higher animals show, as Hobbes claims, some rudimentary ability to calculate means to their ends (III/5, 9), as well as to remember certain observable sequences of events, we are apt to resist the idea that this amounts to prudence. But why so? We might say that animals act on a recognition of 'signes' simply out of instinct, or habit, or through 'being conditioned' to respond 'automatically' to some cue (e.g., go to a food trough upon hearing a bell ring) – implying that the human case is *essentially* different. But if human prudence involved nothing but remembering various sequences of immediately perceptible events, albeit many more sequences than any beast can, would that be true?

To begin to see the profound difference in the significance of 'empirical regularities' for human beings (versus habituated beasts), one can scarce do better than ponder the very example that Hobbes provides by way of introducing his 'brute correlation' view of prudence: 'supposing like events will follow like actions. As he that foresees what wil become of a Criminal, re-cons what he has seen follow on the like Crime before; having this order of thoughts, The Crime, the Officer, the Prison, the Judge, and the Gallowes.' Presuming this sobering example to have been carefully chosen, Hobbes's own conception of Prudence cannot be anything like what it first seems. Simply consider all that is involved in *recognizing* a particular event to be a *crime* (of theft, say – which is not just any 'taking' of things). And the sense in which this will be 'followed' – sooner or later – by someone recognizable as an 'Arresting Officer' doing his duty. Perhaps the (alleged) criminal is then hauled off to something called a 'prison,' eventually put on trial before a person authorized to 'judge' the case, duly sentenced to hang by the neck until dead, and accordingly executed at a time and place so specified. Most or none of this is apt to be witnessed first-hand; and even if it were, it would be a meaningless concatenation of sensations apart from some *understanding* of what one is observing. Of course, to establish the reliability of such a sequential correlation, one would have to 'experience' a *series* of 'similar' event sequences – but they would almost surely *not* be *perceptually* similar. Rather, once again, only by virtue of understanding various formal criteria could they be recognized as 'the same kind of business' (e.g., theft, crime, arrest, trial, punishment, etc.). Having accumulated sufficient experience of the consequences of a broad assortment of criminal activity, one may then *induce* the prudential generalization 'Crime does not pay.' Now, is there anything even remotely comparable to this in the observable behaviour of beasts? And if it is not through a power of Reason that one obtains the requisite understanding of what one perceives (or, more likely, learns all or part of *by report*), and concludes what to make of it, then what does allow for this? Reflecting on one's own psychic experience, it is virtually impossible to believe that understanding simply arises automatically out of any given 'TRAYNE of Thoughts' (that which Hobbes calls '*Mentall Discourse*'; III/1, 8). If, instead, it also presupposes a kind of 'reckoning,' how as a mental activity is it *distinct* from reckoning exclusively in general terms? But if it is not distinct, why, then, does Hobbes reserve the name 'Reason' exclusively for the latter employment? Must we not presume an ulterior purpose?

Hobbes returns to the subject of Prudence in his chapter '*Of the* VERTUES *commonly called* INTELLECTUALL; *and their contrary* DEFECTS.' He first defines intellectual virtues as 'such abilityes of the mind, as men praise, value, and desire should be in themselves; and go commonly under the name of a *good wit*' (VIII/1, 32). He then distinguishes 'two sorts' of such abilities: '*Naturall*, and *Acquired*.' The sole form of the latter – excellence of 'Wit' that is 'acquired by method and instruction' – is 'Reason; which is grounded on the right use of Speech; and produceth the Sciences' (VIII/13, 35). The former sort is goodness of mind or wit 'gotten by Use onely, and Experience; without Method, Culture, or Instruction,' and it consists primarily 'in two things; *Celerity of Imagining*, (that is, swift succession of one thought to another;) and *steddy direction* to some approved end.' By contrast, 'a slow Imagination,' meaning a slow succession of thoughts, accounts for what people call 'DULNESSE, Stupidity' (VIII/2, 32). One may observe in passing that this account bears little resemblance to what we ordinarily mean by an active, or fertile, or vivid, or 'creative' imagination – such as that manifested by the plays of Shakespeare's invention, or by the frontispiece of *Leviathan*. Hobbes further claims that the *cause* behind people's differing speeds of 'imagining' lies in their differing passions. One might presume that he means their differing intensity, great passion 'driving' thoughts more quickly; yet what he chooses to *say* seems aimed at the *substance* of a person's imagining, rather than the *speed* at which he does so ('that love and dislike, some one thing, some another: and therefore some mens thoughts run one way, some another'). But on this basis, he reduces mental operations to the following:

And whereas in this succession of mens thoughts, there is nothing to observe in the things they think on, but either in what they be *like one another*, or in what they be *unlike*, or *what they serve for*, or *how they serve to such a purpose*; Those that observe their similitudes, in case they be such as are but rarely observed by others, are sayd to have a *Good Wit*; by which, in this occasion, is meant a *Good Fancy*. But they that observe their difference and dissimilitudes; which is called *Distinguishing*, and *Discerning*, and *Judging* between thing and thing; in case, such discerning be not easie, are said to have a *good Judgement*. (VIII/3, 33)

One may be right dubious that merely having a sharp eye for differences and distinctions suffices for good *judgment*. But what is especially note-worthy is that here Hobbes in effect endorses what the Platonic Sokrates identifies as the mental activity fundamental to dialectical reasoning, *diairesis kai synagögë*, 'division and collection': dividing, distinguishing, differentiating things (in thought) according to their natural 'forms' or 'classes' (*eidë*), this being the basis of *analysis*; and collecting, integrating, summarizing many dispersed particulars in a single *idea*, the basis of *syn-thesis*, hence of all generalizing and 'making of clear definitions.'[9] As can be readily seen, both tasks are performed by a single rational power and are distinguished only by *conscious focus*; for to recognize all the respects in which two things *differ* is simultaneously, albeit tacitly, to acknowl-edge the respects in which they do *not* differ, i.e., are the *same*. Thus, this single rational power makes possible in principle the attainment of a clear *synoptic* view of a whole composed of heterogeneous parts, seeing how it is at once a unity and a plurality. And the capability to achieve such a view in practice is, according to Plato's Sokrates, 'the greatest test of whether a nature is dialectical, or not.'[10]

In noting that people differ in the skill with which they perform these two intellectual tasks – some having a more ready eye for 'similitudes,' hence for synthesizing disparate parts into wholes; others for the differences among things, hence for analysis, dissolving wholes into their constituent parts – Hobbes signals his agreement with his erstwhile employer, Francis Bacon. For in discussing the various '*Idols of the Cave* [that] take their rise in the peculiar constitution, mental or bodily, of each individual,' the Lord Chancellor observes:

There is one principal and as it were radical distinction between different minds, in respect of philosophy and the sciences, which is this: that some minds are stronger and apter to mark the differences of things, others to mark their resemblances. The steady and acute mind can fix its contemplations and dwell and fasten on the subtlest distinctions; the lofty and discursive mind recognizes and puts together the finest and most general resemblances. Both kinds, however, easily err in excess, by catching the one at gradations, the other at shadows.[11]

As Hobbes continues his own discussion of these intellectual virtues, 'good Fancy' and 'good Judgement,' his comparison of them takes a political turn: 'particularly in matters of conversation and businesse; wherein, times, places, and persons are to be discerned, this Vertue is called DISCRETION. The former, that is, Fancy, without the help of Judgement, is not commended as a Vertue: but the later which is Judgement, and Discretion, is commended for it selfe, without the help of Fancy.' There is no need to quarrel with these claims, provided one employs a more substantial understanding of 'judgment' than that which Hobbes supplies. For important as is the power of distinguishing (differentiating, discriminating) to sound judging, its use is pointless if one lacks pertinent criteria whereby to *evaluate* what is *appropriate* regarding (for example) 'the times, places, and persons.' It is not sufficient to distinguish friends from enemies in order to judge how each kind ought to be treated.[12]

Moreover, anyone acquainted with the traditional view of Reason would argue that every particular attempt to carry Hobbes's general maxims into practice would involve, not just distinguishing, but the exercise of prudential judgment in the full (i.e., Aristotelian) sense. Chapter 30, for example, is chock full of Hobbes's advice to the Prince; but it can be acted upon only case by case, each requiring recognition as to *what* maxim applies and *how* to apply it most effectively. Prudence thus understood is a cardinal intellectual virtue – indeed, among practically minded men, it is regarded as the consummate intellectual virtue, and as such the sine qua non of a Statesman. Perhaps in anticipation of this likely reaction, Hobbes restates his novel view of the matter:

When the thoughts of a man, that has a designe in hand, running over a multitude of things, observes how they conduce to that designe; or what designe they may conduce unto; if his observations be such as are not easie, or usuall, This wit of his is called PRUDENCE; and dependeth on much Experience, and Memory of the like things, and their consequences heretofore. In which there is not so much difference of Men, as there is in their Fancies and Judgements; Because the Experience of men equall in age, is not much unequall, as to quantity; but lyes in different occasions; every one having his private designes. To govern well a family, and a kingdome, are not different degrees of Prudence; but different sorts of businesse; no more then to draw a picture in little, or as great, or greater then the life, are different degrees of Art. A plain husband-man is more Prudent in affaires of his own house, then a Privy Counsellor in the affaires of another man. (VIII/11, 34)

This doubly qualified, seemingly egalitarian conception of Prudence figures prominently in Hobbes's contention that men in the State of Nature would be sufficiently equal 'in the faculties of body, and mind' for each to pose a mortal threat to every other: 'For Prudence, is but Experience; which equall time, equally bestowes on all men, in those things they equally apply themselves unto' (XIII/2, 60–1).

Upon but little reflection, however, one readily sees that, since most people are *not* 'equall in age,' there actually would be very little equality of prudence in the State of Nature (or anywhere else). And even allowing for the likelihood that the *kinds* of experiences most people would have in that State are apt to be more similar than in Civil Society – all being preoccupied with survival under nasty, brutish conditions – surely the admitted differences of imagination and judgment among men would matter greatly in determining what each is able to make of his respective experiences. As a result, some robust thirty-year-olds could actually be twice as prudent as other men twice their age (rather than vice versa), and so would prosper accordingly. Bearing in mind that Hobbes's State of Nature is that of War, might not then some men emerge as chieftains for the very reason Hobbes gives: 'Reputation of Prudence in the conduct of Peace or War, is Power; because to prudent men, we commit the government of our selves, more willingly than to others' (X/10, 41)?[13]

This possibility points back, however, to Hobbes's provocative claim that 'To govern well a family, and a kingdome, are not different degrees of Prudence; but different sorts of businesse; no more than to draw a picture in little, or as great, or greater then the life, are different degrees of Art.' Is Hobbes's curious analogy between Prudence and the Art of

Drawing (or Painting) *sound* – given that he himself implies that the issue is *not* simply one of *quantitative* scale, but of *qualitatively* 'different sorts of businesse'?[14] True, there is a sense in which all painting is painting, just as Prudence pertains to all sorts of matters, both great and small. But do not the challenges of prudently governing a family compared with those of governing a kingdom differ at least as much as miniaturist Portraiture compared with painting Land, Sea, and City scapes? Or might this be what Hobbes means to suggest?

In any case, the claim that 'a plain husband-man is more Prudent in affaires of his own house, then a Privy Counsellor in the affaires of another man' clearly makes a quite separate point. For the *essential* difference is in the respective motivation, hence care, with which each would exercise whatever prudence he commands. As Hobbes would be the first to insist, self-interest tends to ensure that the husbandman will do his best in managing his affairs; whereas, the Privy Counsellor, if his own welfare is not at stake, cannot be relied upon to be quite so keen. And does not this difference reflect back on the distinction between governing a household versus a kingdom? For governors, as well as those who counsel them, are 'by definition' attending to the 'affairs of other men,' as well as to their own. Are they apt to be as carefully prudent about the one as the other? If one agrees this cannot always be counted upon, Hobbes will have established his first argument in favour of absolute Monarchy ('where the publique and private interest are most closely united'; XIX/4, 96).

So much for Hobbes's peculiar treatment of the pre-eminent *political* virtue, Prudence. For thus it has been regarded virtually throughout the tradition of political philosophy, as Practical Wisdom, involving several distinguishable powers of Reason: of recognition, of memory, of induction (whereby generalizations are abstracted from experience), of hypothesizing, of imagination (upon which foresight is dependant), as well as of deduction (in practical syllogisms consisting of generalizations and statements of facts that together imply what ought to be done in a particular case). But as noted, Hobbes's explicit account of 'Reason' reserves this term exclusively for deduction of generalizations from other generalizations, ultimately from general definitions. And though, as also noted, he speaks of other mental activities that would seem to be reason-related, he does not expressly tie them together in a single coherent account of man's rational powers. This has the ironic consequence that *Leviathan*, taken as a whole, is not itself a work of Reason, judged according to the standard articulated therein. Whereas, it is surely a supreme example of synthetic reasoning, manifesting both exquisite fineness of Discretion and rare greatness of Fancy.

Admittedly, *Leviathan* includes some impressive examples of Hobbes's deducing substantial implications from his basic definitions (e.g., of 'Counsell,' XXV/7–15, 133–6; of 'Civill Law,' XXVI/3–12, 137–40; of 'Punishment,' XXVIII/1–13, 161–3). But for all of his use of deductive reasoning *within* the book, his conceiving its overall design, as well as its interior articulation and many of its most memorable features and definitions, required much more in the way of rational powers than just calculation, however broadly construed. Surely the most famous line in *Leviathan* is Hobbes's summary assessment of what (he contends) would be 'the life of man' in a State of Nature: 'solitary, poore, nasty, brutish, and short' (XIII/9, 62). Now, Hobbes does precede this claim with effective reminders of factors that would figure in his and our reaching this sobering judgment: 'every man is Enemy to every man ... no place for Industry ... no Culture of the Earth; no Navigation ... no commodious Building ... no Knowledge of the face of the Earth; no account of time; no Arts, no Letters; no Society; and which is worst of all, continuall feare, and danger of violent death.'

Sounds pretty grim, all right. But does all of this, even if supplemented by other general claims of a similar kind, simply 'add up' to Hobbes's famous claim? Such that one could *deduce* it – it, and nothing *contrary* to it?[15] Or is there much more involved in generating such a conclusion (or in a reader's agreeing to it)? Obviously, there must be generalizations about human nature that serve as implicit premises; and whether or not one accepts those that Hobbes has presented in the preceding chapters, *any* valid generalizations could only be *induced* from a sufficient plenitude of observations of actual people. Moreover, does not an appeal to one's *Imagination* figure crucially here – that we are bidden to imagine what life would be like were there 'no common Power to keep [men] all in awe' – which in turn highlights the inadequacy of Hobbes's account of Imagination (a matter I will address in the following chapter on language)?

Similarly, one might question what series of 'additions and subtractions' could have led Hobbes to *analogize* between the slow, laborious acquisition of rational principles underlying 'the art of well building' houses, and whatever is involved in mastering the principles of well-ordering polities (with Hobbes tacitly likening himself to a 'very able architect'; XXIX/1, 167): 'So, long time after men have begun to constitute Common-wealths, imperfect, and apt to relapse into disorder, there may Principles of Reason be found out, by industrous meditation, to make their constitution (excepting by externall violence) everlasting. And such are those which I have in this discourse set forth' (XXX/5, 176; cf. XX/19, 107; XXVI/11, 140). By industrous *meditation*! What does Hobbes mean by this? Simply checking and rechecking one's sums? Or has he reflected thoroughly and repeatedly on the disparate considerations – on both the commonalities and the diversities of human nature, and on the variety of material circumstances and historical experiences – that bear on the problem of establishing and maintaining stable, decent political life? And having done so, somehow discerned what is most basic to a universal solution; figured out a practical framework wherein that solution could be approximately realized; and imagined a persuasive form in which to present it? Was all this accomplished solely by musical inspiration, or some other equally mysterious means? Or is everything that Hobbes did – not merely his overt deductions – explicable in terms of the various powers comprised by human Rationality, rightly conceived, perhaps including even his *motive* for doing it?

In explaining why justice 'is perpetually disputed, both by the Pen and the Sword,' Hobbes treats people's refusal to give strict priority to reason as 'the cause' of these endless disputes. Provided custom or precedent as alternatives, men readily 'appeale from custome to reason, and from reason to custome, as it serves their turn; receding from custome when their interest requires it, and setting themselves against reason, as oft as reason is against them' (XI/21, 50). Most readers of even modest experience with life would probably concede a large measure of truth in Hobbes's assessment of people's fickle allegiance to supposed principles (whether of custom, reason, religion, or whatever). But would many readers notice how puzzling is Hobbes's use of 'reason' here? For what can it mean as the *basis* of one's appeal, supposedly in contrast to an appeal to the authority of custom, since in either case the appellant is *calculating*? One person argues deductively from the premise that (in the present instance) custom is authoritative – for he calculates that doing so best serves his interest. But if Reason simply *is* calculation (albeit exclusively in general terms), how can it serve as the premise from which the other person (or the same person on another occasion) deduces an outcome that he calculates best 'serves his turn'? Can one calculate on the basis of an appeal to calculation? Deduce from the premise of deduction? So stated, the spectre of an infinite regress immediately arises. In order to make practical sense of the contrast to which Hobbes points, one necessarily, and unthinkingly, substitutes some fuller conception of Reason. What is 'reasonable' in the sense of 'equitable,' perhaps? But in this context, Hobbes's definition of *Equity* – 'the equall distribution to each man, of that which *in reason* belongeth to him' – merely leads one in a circle, lacking that fuller conception.

Or consider what actual 'addings and subtractings,' or any other line of strictly deductive calculations, could have 'contracted' all the Laws of Nature 'into one easie sum, intelligible, even to the meanest capacity; and that is, *Do not that to another, which thou wouldst not have done to thy selfe*' (XV/35, 79). Note, the issue is not whether one can rationally 'see' that each of the nineteen or twenty 'Lawes of Nature dictating Peace'[16] are *consistent* with the so-called Golden Rule (and that all possible counter-claims are not) – it is not whether there is some rational power or other whereby one *recognizes* that this is so – but whether all these laws simply 'add up' to this general principle. And whether they each and all are, in turn, strictly deducible ('subtractible') from it. Or, rather, 'to' and 'from' *this version* of the Golden Rule, for Hobbes employs some seven or eight variations of it – which in itself ought to give one pause! The plurality of versions, in turn, invites the question, Can anything of consequence be gained from *comparing* them;[17] and if so, what does doing so involve? Is it a rational activity?

One would normally think so, since comparing is intrinsic to all sorts of judging and evaluating, and as such to virtually all deliberation about alternatives. Human life abounds with occasions to make comparisons, many of which involve heterogeneous factors, the relative importance of which must somehow be assessed and a composite judgment reached. Indeed, the most comprehensive judgment of all – and the most important – concerns the potential scope of Reason in human life, hence, what leading a rational life would mean. The value of any such judgment necessarily depends, of course, upon the adequacy of one's understanding of Reason, as well as of Passions, Desires, and Willing. And for some appreciation of how strangely limited is Hobbes's explicit account of Reason's role in life, one need merely consider his bizarre treatment of Deliberation:

When in the mind of man, Appetites, and Aversions, Hopes, and Feares, concerning one and the same thing, arise alternately; and divers good and evil consequences of the doing, or omitting the thing propounded, come successively into our thoughts; so that sometimes we have an Appetite to it; sometimes an Aversion from it; sometimes Hope to be able to do it, sometimes Despaire, or Feare to attempt it; the whole summe of Desires, Aversions, Hopes, and Feares, continued till the thing be either done, or thought impossible, is that we call DELIBERATION. (VI/49, 28)

I submit this is *not* what *we* call 'deliberation.' To be sure, desires, aversion, hopes and/or fears, as well as other passions, figure prominently in deliberating, whether on one's own or with others. And necessarily so, for they are representative of why one cares about whatever is being deliberated upon. Elsewhere we are told, there are 'Passions that encline men to Peace,' including 'Feare of Death; Desire of such things as are necessary to commodious living; and a Hope by their Industry to obtain them' (XIII/14, 63). However, there Hobbes is explicit that these passions alone are not sufficient for actually avoiding death and securing commodious living, as he adds: 'And Reason suggesteth convenient Articles of Peace, upon which men may be drawn to agreement.' Yet this is what is conspicuously absent from Hobbes's descriptive definition of 'deliberation': any mention of actual 'reasoning' or 'reckoning' about 'the thing propounded,' such as would be necessary if 'a *Multitude* of men' were to be '*drawn*' to 'Agree, and *Covenant*' with each other as required to 'Institute a Common-wealth' (XVIII/1, 88). Hobbes is explicit on this point himself: 'The matter, or subject of a Covenant, is alwayes something that falleth under deliberation' (XIV/24, 69). There is no indication in the defining paragraph, however, of what accounts for the diverse assessments of possible consequences, raising or allaying hopes or fears accordingly. The 'whole summe' Hobbes speaks of is no *arithmetical* result.

A reader who proceeded no further would be left with the impression that the deliberative *outcome* is determined not by any objective calculation of the person's long-term self-interest (much less of some common good, or compromise over private goods, involving other people), but solely by whichever passion turns out to be strongest at the relevant time. Indeed, this conclusion is implicit in Hobbes's reductionist (and misleading, if not simply impertinent) account of Willing: 'In Deliberation, the last Appetite, or Aversion, immediately adhaering to the action, or to the omission thereof, is what wee call the WILL.' The same irrelevance of Reason to deliberation is indicated by Hobbes's further contention that 'Beasts also Deliberate' ('This alternate Succession of Appetites, Aversions, Hopes and Fears, is no lesse in other living Creatures then in Man: and therefore Beasts also Deliberate'; hence 'must necessarily also have

Will'; VI/51–3, 28). Notice, then, that – according to Hobbes – *delibera-tion does not require language!*[18]

This brutish conception perhaps accounts for a second conspicuous feature of Hobbes's definition: the simple bifurcation of outcomes that can bring a stop to deliberating – 'till the thing be either done, or thought impossible' – as if 'the thing' *will* be attempted unless it is believed impossible to do. There is no acknowledgment that a person, having deliberated, may conclude not to do something because it is seen to be unjust, or otherwise immoral; or because seen to be ignoble, or otherwise dishonourable; or because seen to be sacrilegious, or otherwise impious. And, I hasten to add, reach these conclusions out of a genuine concern for justice, nobility, or piety – *not*, that is, out of fear of punishment or hope of reward. The omission of such possibilities is not surprising, however, since they are outcomes that presume reasoning about considerations *other* than the deliberator's own immediate desires and aversions, hopes and fears.

However, this whole understanding of deliberation is thrown into doubt, if not into utter confusion, by what Hobbes says subsequently about 'The formes of Speech by which the Passions are expressed,' that they are 'partly the same, and partly different from those, by which wee expresse our Thoughts.' For in this connection, we are told that deliberation does indeed require speech, and of a particular kind:

Deliberation is expressed *Subjunctively*; which is a speech proper to signifie suppositions, with their consequences; as, *If this be done, then this will follow*; and differs not from the language of Reasoning, save that Reasoning is in generall words; but Deliberation for the most part is of Particulars. (VI/55, 29)

Moreover:

[B]ecause in Deliberation, the Appetites, and Aversions are raised by foresight of the good and evill consequences, and sequels of the action whereof we Deliberate; the good or evill effect thereof dependeth on the foresight of a long chain of consequences, of which very seldome any man is able to see to the end ... so that he who hath by Experience, or Reason, the greatest and surest prospect of Consequences, Deliberates best himselfe; and is able when he will, to give the best counsel unto others. (VI/57, 29)

In light of the foregoing, if 'Beasts also Deliberate,' they cannot be very good at it, having no language (much less one with a subjunctive mood), and 'little, or no foresight of the time to come, for want of observation, and memory of the order, consequence, and dependance of the things they see' (XII/4, 52).

The more serious issue these passages raise, however, concerns the mental activity that 'differs not' from that involved in Reasoning, except that the terms employed refer mainly to 'Particulars.' According to the traditional understanding of deductive reasoning, the mental activity involved differs *not at all*, being equally applicable to deducing both general and particular conclusions. Thus its role in prudential judgment as traditionally understood, the intellectual virtue whereby general principles are applied to particular situations in practical syllogisms. And surely this squares with our psychic experiences: whether the terms be general or particular, there is no detectable difference in the syllogistic reasoning whereby one derives a valid conclusion. In short, Hobbes's defining the mental faculty of Reason as 'nothing but *Reckoning* ... of the Consequences of generall names agreed upon,' insisting that Reason per se 'is in generall words' exclusively, seems quite arbitrary. Hence, as I previously suggested, a thoughtful reader must suspect it serves an ulterior purpose.[19]

Be that as it may, the mere mention of *human* hopes and fears, as distinct from any similar-seeming passions in lower animals, provides some purchase for rational calculation (of probabilities, say, in light of a person's beliefs about the world). But to what point, exactly? Hobbes expressly warns that 'the Passions of men, are commonly more potent than their Reason' (XIX/4, 96). Indeed, so far as *doing* anything (all '*Animall motion*, otherwise called *Voluntary motion*'), the power of passion would seem to be all that motivates and energizes either man or beast, at least according to Hobbes's explicit account. For though he tells us that 'the Imagination [meaning, some 'precedent thought' ultimately traceable to sensation] is the first internall beginning of all Voluntary Motion,' which is 'called ENDEAVOUR,' it activates only as either 'APPETITE, or DESIRE' (motion towards) or 'AVERSION' (motion away; VI/1–2, 23). Still, he does acknowledge that there is *some* 'potency' inherent in Reason as such, albeit less than that inherent in strong passions with respect to ruling the minds and so the actions of most people.

Accordingly, one may wish to know more about the *power* of Reason. Is it the same *kind* of power as is inherent in the passions, originating perhaps in a 'desire to be rational' (if there is such a thing)? Can it be amplified, as the dominating power of anger is amplified by the person becoming angrier? Or is the power of reason in one's consciousness something altogether different from that of the passions, including a passion for Reason (if there is such a thing). Hobbes never directly addresses questions of this sort, leaving the reader to reflect on his own experience of Reason's power as *felt* in performing arithmetical calculations, working through geometrical proofs, and such. These are the most readily recognizable, hence most familiar, manifestations of something distinctive called 'reasoning,' since it requires a peculiar kind of exertion that people are necessarily aware of when they are doing it. Calculations are purposeful (even if merely 'to find the answer,' or 'for practice'); they take time; require conscious effort; and produce a result which, if deemed correct, 'determines the mind.' But – as I have been at pains to demonstrate – a comprehensive analysis of our mental experience will show that there is much more to man's rational powers than is revealed in arithmetic and geometry.

Most competent adults know from experience that one can rid oneself of certain hopes and fears – not only by supplanting them with others, but simply by coming to regard them as 'irrational.' After all, we were children once, with childish hopes and fears. Can one *solely* through deductive reasoning, however, show a certain hope to be foolish, and thereby eliminate that hope? Or can rational calculations *alone* reveal certain fears to be irrational, and thereby dissipate the fear (not merely overrule it in the name of a still more powerful passion)? Or is it not rather the case that all such reasoning presumes premises that deduction alone cannot supply?

For most everyday reasoning, the premises employed are embedded in the general understanding of Reality that at any given time and place passes for 'common sense' (the regnant world-view of this or that 'Cave,' to employ an old image). Historically, at least, much of the form and substance of a people's commonsensical conception of reality comes from the teachings of one or another religion. With this being so in Hobbes's own time and place, clearly the ambient view of reality would *not* serve his efforts to dispel credence in ghosts, demons, fairies, witches, spells, charms, exorcisms, incantations, curses, potions, prayers – his efforts to, in effect, undermine the entire fabric of belief in magic, invisible spirits, and miraculous happenings, thereby eliminating a fecund source of both foolish hopes and groundless fears. To accomplish this, he must persuade his readers to accept a new view of reality as a basic framework for his new political science – a world-view radically at odds with that which most of his contemporaries would have regarded as orthodox. Can he possibly have believed that this could be done through deductive reasoning alone, even granted its being supplemented with emphatic assurances, subtle insinuations, and open ridicule? Did he not appreciate that the overall *coherence* of his presentation would determine its acceptance or rejection by a reader amenable primarily to *rational* persuasion, and that recognition of such coherence requires some rational power besides deduction? I presume that he did. Moreover, as I shall endeavour to show in a later chapter, the reader who will settle for nothing less than a rationally convincing account is, necessarily, the reader Hobbes most truly cares to persuade – on pain of his writing this book being a futile exercise. Hence the comprehensive puzzle. Is there a coherent interpretation of *Leviathan* – presumably as held by Hobbes himself – that somehow explains or otherwise accounts for what (I contend) are clearly 'problematic' treatments of issues which he acknowledges are of fundamental importance?

By insisting that Reason is the 'Naturall Word of God,' Hobbes clearly intends that this will be understood primarily as the account of the world revealed by Science: 'Reason; which ... produceth the Sciences.' God 'speaks' exclusively in generalities. And, as I argued in the first chapter and have alluded to several times since, the promotion of modern, essentially Baconian-Cartesian, Science is the ruling purpose of the regime Hobbes prescribes. The 'foresight of their own preservation, and of a more contented life' through Civil Peace may be 'the finall Cause, End, or Designe of men' dictating their acceptance of the restraints upon natural liberty which political life requires. However, *that* is *not* the 'finall Cause' of the Commonwealth *Hobbes* has 'Designed,' though it both exploits and caters to these dominant human desires – indeed, is dressed in that garb. But its actual ruling rationale has been conveniently 'contracted into one easie sum,' even if not fully intelligible to the meanest capacity: '*Reason* is the *pace*; Encrease of *Science*, the *way*; and the Benefit of man-kind, the *end*' (V/21, 22). This Baconian mantra implicitly defines the political mission, which, in turn, determines both the regime's design and its intended mode of functioning (a way of life that is now taken for granted).

Most of what I have said about the form and matter of *Leviathan* – and of what capabilities Hobbes's mind must be credited with in order to have conceived his new political science, and to have presented it as he has – applies to Science generally. And inasmuch as Hobbes's explicit account of Reason is patently inadequate for explaining his book, it is not surprising that his explicit account of Science – 'a knowledge of all the Consequences of names appertaining to the subject at hand' (V/17, 21) – is similarly questionable (as I shall endeavour to show in the following chapter on Language). But if the view of Reason as nothing but Calculation, exemplified by Arithmetic, or Deduction in the manner of Geometry, cannot possibly account for Hobbes's crafting of his masterpiece, or the various readers' understandings of it, or a statesman's determination to put it into practice, is it plausible that Hobbes truly believed otherwise? Bearing in mind Hobbes's own use of 'Reason' and related terms, but especially how self-conscious we must credit him with being in order to write a book of such ingenuity – launching what has proven to be the most successful political doctrine in mankind's history – I most strongly suspect not. So, what conception of Man's rational powers, then, *is* sufficient to account for normal mental experience, for the human capacity for language and rational inquiry, as well as for Hobbes's own practice? Only in light of an adequate explication of the whole of Reason, of its manifold functions and capacities, can one readily appreciate how extremely limited is the explicit account Hobbes chose to provide.

To my mind, one can scarce make better its deficiencies than by consulting one of the first systematic analyses of the human soul's rational part, that laid out in the famous 'Divided Line' of Plato's *Republic*. Much about that surprisingly rich image, and Sokrates's discussion of it – especially as it relates to the rest of the dialogue – is not of present concern. The most relevant points are these.

We are asked to divide a line into unequal parts, and then subdivide each part by the same proportion (509d ff.). Sokrates does not specify the exact ratio, later claiming it would involve one in over-long arguments (534a); but however one divides it, the laws of Geometry dictate that the two middle segments will be of equal length.

The segments of the Line are used, first of all, to represent four distinct modes of Being; the proportional lengths of the segments represent each exemplar's respective 'degree of reality,' hence represent degrees of reality per se. With the exception of the shortest segment, representing the 'least real' mode of Being (*eikones*, 'images,' such as shadows and reflections in mirrors), the categories of Being are not named but rather described. The segment immediately adjacent to that representing Images is longer, and represents perceptible things that cast shadows and reflections; we might call them 'empirical objects' or just 'empiricals,' though there is some indication in the dialogue that they could be labelled perceptible 'phantoms' (*eidōla*), implying they are derivatives of something 'more real.'

Both of these modes (that of images, and of empiricals) belong to the 'Visible Region,' or the Realm of *Becoming* – for they are ever changing, coming into being and passing away, each according to its nature. The remaining two modes belong to the 'Intelligible Realm,' the Realm of *Being* proper, as they cannot be perceived by the senses, but only grasped by the mind (intellected). The first, represented by the line segment equal in length to that of the empiricals, hence of somehow different but equivalent degree of reality and truth, are the sorts of things that mathematicians and physicists conceive hypothetically and then reason about (e.g., geometrical objects, subatomic particles, receding galaxies, evolutionary precursors of man). Since their existence is hypothetical, they might be called that: 'hypotheticals.' Finally, the longest segment represents that which is most Real, whatever 'powers' of Being rule – that is, *cause* – the Realm of Becoming; they are referred to as *archai* ('beginnings,' 'sources,' 'rulers'), but modern scholars commonly presume these are what in other contexts are spoken of as 'Forms' (*eidë*).

These four modes of Being are relevant to an understanding of human Reason in that Plato has Sokrates explain the four distinct faculties inherent in the rational part of the soul as each *corresponding* to one of these modes, in effect affirming that the structure of the human mind congrues with Reality (511d–e). Thus, the love, hence pursuit, of Wisdom – philosophy – is an activity that, in principle, makes sense; even if in practice it is humanly impossible to succeed in finally becoming wise, the attempt is not utter madness. For on this understanding of Mind and World, man's access to Reality provides an objective criterion of Truth: thought that faithfully imitates reality (cf. 500c).

Corresponding to the *archai* is what Sokrates first calls 'Intellection' or 'Intuition' (*noësis*), as this is our power of immediate recognition, whereby we might affirm valid first principles (necessary for there to be genuine – i.e., unconditional – knowledge, *epistëmë*, of anything). But it is also by virtue of rational intuition that we can grasp self-evident truths (e.g., that the shortest distance between two points is a straight line); affirm the validity of the basic rules of logic;[20] recognize what is the same (and what different) in a plurality of things, hence make the distinctions and recognize the commonalities that Hobbes speaks of as the basis of 'good Judgement' and 'Good Fancy' (VIII/3, 33); and identify objects according to the kind of thing each is (one immediately recognizes a chair, say, in light of one's idea of chairness; similarly, a dog, a city, a science – generally, anything for which one has a name is recognized immediately in light of one's implicit criteria for that kind of thing). Our noetic reason

– this rational 'seeing' – operates for the most part effortlessly, as typically does the visual seeing with which it is so closely linked in everyday life.

Not so *dianoia*: 'thinking,' 'reasoning' in either direction, whether from particulars to generalities or vice versa – hence inducing and generalizing, as well as deducing and calculating – requires purposeful effort. This is the mode or power of Reason that corresponds to the hypotheticals, about which one thinks or reasons – both to conceive them ('B, C, D, etc. would be explicable if one hypothesizes A'), and to make explicit their consequences ('if A, then B, C D, etc.'). It is by inductive reasoning that one makes universal claims on the basis of a finite number of instances, the same means whereby one may ascend from the less general to the more general, perhaps even to first principles that noetic reason may recognize to be *archai*. It is *dianoia* in the form of deduction – whereby one moves from the more to the less general – that Hobbes treats as the whole of Reason, epitomized in what he defines as Science ('knowledge of Consequences, and dependence of one fact upon another'; V/17, 21; 'and is Conditionall'; IX/1, 40). Since 'reasoning' is an activity of the mind requiring effort and conscious attention, it is (as previously noted) the rational faculty people are most conscious of, hence are apt to regard as Reason simpliciter.

The third part of Reason, corresponding to empiricals, is 'Trust' (or, 'Faith'; *pistis*). Inasmuch as all awareness of a reality external to the mind is dependent upon perception, one necessarily trusts what perception discloses. Not that the senses are perfectly reliable, such that appearances never deceive – every child soon learns otherwise – but one must trust that one actually 'sees what one sees' in order to analyse and explain appearances, including those that are deceptive. For example: a stick placed in a bucket of water appears to bend at whatever point it enters the water; when felt with the hand, however, it still seems straight; we conclude that 'bending' is an illusion and expect a valid science of optics to explain it; but any purported explanation must account for what we trust we do see (the apparent bending). Thus it is with the entire world disclosed by perception: we trust in its existence, and in our reason's capacity to understand it (cf. *Republic* 603a). Indeed, a reliance upon Trust pervades human life, and not only with respect to perception (such that, as a rule, seeing is believing). For *most* of what a person believes is *not* based on what he himself observes, discovers, or experiences, but rather on what he is told by others: parents, teachers, clerics, public officials, various kinds of experts and authorities, friends, and others that he trusts. Moreover, human life is virtually inconceivable otherwise, so reliant are we on *logos* ('rational speech') simply for *information*. One can scarcely imagine how impoverished one's life would be if one were dependent solely on one's own mental resources for an understanding of the world. Similarly, trust is implicit in the division of labour, whereby the various economic specialists serve each other's needs and wants – this being the very foundation of political life, binding a political community together by virtue of the members' resulting interdependency.[21] Most (by no means all) of people's commercial transactions presume that everyone involved trusts the other(s) and is trustworthy himself; however, prudential maxims such as *caveat emptor* remind us of the danger of misplaced or 'excessive' trust – and not only in buying and selling. For trust is inherently a variable in two respects. First, it is bestowed in proportion to a person's judgment (or presumption) of the degree of reliability of a source, of a person, of a means to an end, whatever. Second, people vary as to their competence in making such judgments – some being generally sound, others overly trusting (even downright gullible), still others unduly suspicious. Both kinds of variations attest to the fact that trust *is* a rational faculty: one rightfully expects reasons for the degree of trust (or distrust) a person expresses or exhibits; and the justifications that people provide vary greatly in quality, in proportion to their rational abilities.[22]

The fourth rational faculty, Imagination (*eikasia*) – corresponding to the shortest ontic section of the Divided Line (that representing Images, *eikones*) – is not fourth in importance. For, as is obvious enough, it is by virtue of their imaginations that certain gifted people can invent new devices and techniques, others create the fine art and literature that beautify and enrich human life, still others hypothesize scenarios in light of which one might explain present outcomes of either natural or human history. And surely of at least equal significance are those works of the philosophical imagination whereby political life can be understood and improved, beginning with the 'City in *logos*' of Plato's *Republic* (369c ff.). Reflection on these and other fruits of the imagination readily confirms that it is an integral part of Reason, working on rational principles. Moreover, imagination is of pervasive everyday importance, for it is the means whereby one envisions the future (here, too, constrained by what is rationally conceivable); and, equally important, the means whereby one understands other people (e.g., how a person likely feels in a certain situation, or is likely to react, by imagining oneself in his or her place – as confirmed when we find someone's behaviour utterly perplexing, and so admit, 'I can't imagine what he was thinking of'). In these cases, imagination operates so automatically, so effortlessly, that most people remain unaware of how profoundly dependent upon it they are. Even more automatic, hence inconspicuous, is its work in constituting a three-dimensional perceptual world – a world with *depth* – out of the endless stream of two-dimensional tableaux revealed through vision. Thus the correspondence of *eikasia* with *eikones*. For what we actually *see* with each eye is a two-dimensional image – every bit as lacking in depth as a reflection in a mirror, or a shadow on a wall – and on the basis of experiencing countless sequences of these images as seen from various perspectives, conjoined with evidence supplied by the other senses, the rational imagination effortlessly 'creates' a three-dimensional world that corresponds with material reality.

Equipped with *this* understanding of man's rational faculties – rather than reliant on Hobbes's grossly incomplete and otherwise suspect treatment of these matters – one can recognize Hobbes's *Leviathan* to be in all respects a work of Reason. Thus, one can not only account for his producing it, but also reformulate and thereby transcend the philosophical limitations of his explicit treatment of Reason and much else, including – most importantly – of Language.

12

Science
and the Problem of *Language*

There are two separate, albeit related, aspects to Hobbes's problematic treatment of language in *Leviathan*. The first concerns the glaring inadequacy of his account of how language works as a means of ordinary communication among native speakers. The second concerns his reliance on a precisely formulated language as a means of philosophizing and generating knowledge ('in the right Definition of Names, lyes the first use of Speech; which is the Acquisition of Science'; IV/13, 15).

As the first problem leads into the second, it is best to begin by examining Hobbes's explicit treatment of what he acknowledges to be 'the most noble and profitable invention of all other,' namely, 'SPEECH, consisting of *Names* or *Appellations*, and their Connexion ... without which there had been amongst men, neither Common-wealth, nor Society, nor Contract, nor Peace, no more than amongst Lyons, Bears, and Wolves' (IV/1, 12). Interesting examples, for surely Hobbes knows that lions live in 'prides' and wolves (notoriously) in 'packs' – they co-exist naturally in *groups*, that is, *not* as 'atomic individuals.' And doubtless they use sounds and gestures to communicate 'what they desire, feare, or have any other passion for.' The male lion's roar, sounding a warning heard literally for miles, is as famous as the soulful howl of the wolf that can add so eerie a note of menace to the night. But all such growls and snarls, squawks and squeals, purrs and chirps, bleats and barks, cries and whimpers, clucks and crows are to be distinguished from the human use of language whereby people may deliberate about justice and the common good – which, as I noted previously, Aristotle points to as the most important indication that Man is by nature a political animal.[1]

Hobbes begins his fourth chapter, '*Of* Speech,' with a brief mytho-historical account of the origin of language. He dutifully credits God with being 'the first author of Speech,' citing the same biblical episode that Bacon uses to indicate the 'innocence' of pursuing scientific knowledge of Nature: Adam's naming of the animals under the direct tutelage of '*God* himself.' On that basis, we may surmise that Adam could on his own see how to 'adde more names ... and to joyn them in such manner by degrees, as to make himself understood,' thereby generating 'so much language ... as he had found use for.' Hobbes immediately assures us, however, that the resulting amount would be 'not so copious, as an Orator or Philosopher has need of,' mentioning seven terms pertinent to analysis of language itself, as well as seven classes of things there is no indication in Scripture that Adam was taught 'all' the names of: 'Figures, Numbers, Measures, Colours, Sounds, Fancies, Relations.' The list is interesting in that *no one* knows *all* the names thereof, though for different reasons in each case (e.g., the higher numbers trailing off towards infinity have no agreed-upon names, whereas the spectrum of distinguishable colours can be differently parsed and named, and conventional measures come and go). Indeed, one can learn some important truths about Naming per se from reflecting on these different categories – which may be Hobbes's real purpose in presenting them, since this divine origin of language turns out to be largely irrelevant to the origins of present languages: 'But all this language gotten, and augmented by *Adam* and his posterity, was again lost at the tower of *Babel*.' Hence, the various peoples, dispersed over the face of the Earth, had to reinvent a plurality of languages on their own, 'as need (the mother of all inventions) taught them.'

This leads to Hobbes's account of what people need language *for*. Notice, then, his scientific account of language, like that of polities, is teleological. Speaking most generally, the purpose of language is 'to transferre our Mentall Discourse, into Verbal,' and that in turn for two still quite general purposes: one for 'the Registring of the Consequences of our Thoughts' so as to facilitate remembering them; the other to communicate our thoughts, desires, fears, and other passions to those who 'use the same words.' All sorts of problems begin here, most of which I shall ignore (being more concerned with the political and philosophical implications of those that come later). But to give one example, the first general purpose seems to point towards what was a staple of controversy in much of the previous century, the logical and/or practical possibility of a 'private language.'[2] On this topic, I shall confine myself to a couple of observations. Despite all of our ordinary dependence on language as the medium of thought – that we think almost exclusively in the linguistic terms we are already familiar with – Hobbes must be correct in his granting logical priority to thought over language.[3] In order to account for the *origin*, and to a considerable extent, the *growth* of language, someone must first recognize some phenomenon 'needing a name' (some distinguishable object, quality, formation, process, relation, whatever) for a new word to be coined (or an old word adapted to a new use). One's universe of thought is not hermetically sealed by one's extant body of language. However, the notion that names help one to remember one's thoughts seems quite puzzling, since one still has to remember what the name refers to.[4] To be sure, Hobbes specifies 'the *Consequences* of our Thoughts,' but he seems to include the names of particular things as well. For example, in discussing Scriptural references to particular angels, he (mischievously?) exempts God from any reliance on language: 'God needeth not, to distinguish his Celestiall servants by names, which are usefull onely to the short memories of Mortalls' (XXXIV/23, 213).

As for the second general purpose (to communicate with those who 'use the same words'), therein lurks the real problem with the origin of language, given the radical isolation Hobbes seems to ascribe to men in the State of Nature: how could language ever arise were people as naturally asocial, even antisocial – '*solitary ... nasty, brutish*' – as he would have us believe? Rousseau neatly encapsulates the conundrum: 'I leave to anyone who wishes to undertake it the discussion of this difficult Problem: which is the more necessary, an already united Society for the institution of languages, or already invented Languages for the establishment of Society.'[5] While at first blush this may seem analogous to the 'Chicken-Egg' dilemma, reflection readily resolves it; the only credible answer is 'an already united society.' That is, the problem of the origin of language validates Aristotle's view: man *must* be by nature, not a solitary, but a social animal, hence proto-political, living in stable groups, if the composing individuals are ever to learn to 'use the same words.' And is it conceivable that Hobbes failed to see this? I think not. In which case, his conception of the State of Nature as peopled by solitary individuals is not primarily intended to serve as historical anthropology; hence one must reconsider what its purpose truly is.[6]

To my mind, however, the most curious problem with Hobbes's account of language arises from his discussion of the four 'Speciall uses of Speech' to which 'there are also foure correspondent Abuses' (IV/3–4, 13). With respect to the first, third, and fourth special uses, the respective abuses 'correspond' straightforwardly. For example, to the first special use ('to Register, what by cogitation, wee find to be the cause of any thing, present or past; and what we find things present or past may produce, or effect; which in summe, is acquiring of Arts') corresponds the abuse resulting 'when men register their thoughts wrong, by the inconstancy of the signification of their words ... and so deceive themselves.' Similarly, to the third special use of expressing one's will and purposes corresponds the abuse of lying about these things, and to the fourth of using language to amuse oneself and others corresponds the abuse of using it to grieve others.[7] The curiosity pertains to the second special use: 'to shew to others that knowledge which we have attained; which is, to Counsell, and Teach one another.' Left to one's own devising, what might one say would be a corresponding abuse of language? Perhaps something about using language to mis-advise, mis-instruct, or somehow to conceal what one knows? But I would go through a long list of possibilities before arriving at anything resembling Hobbes's choice: using words 'metaphorically; that is, in other sense than that they are ordained for; and thereby deceive others' (my emphasis).

This prohibition of metaphoric speech is echoed elsewhere in the text. For example, 'the use of Metaphors, Tropes, and other Rhetoricall figures, in stead of words proper' is the sixth of seven 'causes' of 'Absurd assertions'; hence, though 'lawfull ... in common speech ... yet in reckoning, and seeking of truth, such speeches are not to be admitted' (V/14, 20; cf. VIII/8, 34). Similarly, 'metaphoricall Speeches' have no place in the discourse of Counselors (XXV/12, 134). In his own sometimes eccentric interpretation of Scripture, Hobbes repeatedly argues that certain claims in the Bible are not properly understood precisely because they are metaphorically expressed (e.g., that the word 'spirit' is 'used in the Scripture metaphorically onely,' XXXIV/25, 214; and, 'that which is thus said concerning Hell Fire, is spoken metaphorically,' XXXVIII/11, 243; cf. also XXXI/2, 186; XXXIV/14, 210; XXXIX/1, 247). And inasmuch as the doctrine of Transubstantiation is a metaphysical abomination to Hobbes, it is hardly surprising that he insists, 'The words, *This is my Body*, are aequivalent to these, *This signifies, or represents my Body*; and it is an ordinary figure of Speech: but to take it literally, is an abuse' (XLIV/11, 338). Notice, here the *abuse* consists of taking literally something that Hobbes argues must have been intended metaphorically. On the other hand, he assures us that 'The Kingdome therefore of God, is a reall, not a metaphoricall Kingdome' (XXXV/11, 219). Speaking summarily, 'The *Word of God*, as it is taken for that which he hath spoken, is understood sometimes *Properly*, sometimes *Metaphorically*' (XXXVI/3, 223). The flexibility this introduces into Scriptural interpretation, while convenient for harmonizing Scripture with Hobbes's ostensible metaphysics, indirectly supports his disallowing the use of metaphorical language in science.

Still, his exclusion of metaphors from 'all rigourous search of truth' is an odd and dubious dictum for several reasons. First of all, Hobbes violates it repeatedly himself.[8] To recur to an example that figured prominently in the chapter with which this first Part began, Hobbes speaks of four things as each a 'Naturall seed of *Religion*,' and notes that 'these seeds have received culture from two sorts of men' (XII/11–12, 54). He continues to employ this agricultural imagery to the very end, arguing that 'there ought to be no Power over the Consciences of men, but of the Word it selfe, working Faith in every one, not always according to the purpose of them that Plant and Water, but of God himself, that giveth the Increase' (XLVII/20, 385). Indeed, one need not range beyond the very chapter proscribing metaphors to find evidence of Hobbes's 'good Fancy.' He speaks of the man who becomes 'entangled in words, as a bird in lime-twiggs; the more he struggles, the more belimed,' and of those who 'spend time in fluttering over their bookes.' And here is a nice set: 'For words are wise mens counters, they do but reckon by them: but they are the mony of fooles, that value them by the authority of an *Aristotle*, a *Cicero*, or a *Thomas*, or of any other Doctor whatsoever, if but a man' (IV/12–13, 15). If these and dozens if not hundreds of others are all to be explained (i.e., explained away) by Hobbes's once conceding that 'sometimes the understanding have need to be opened by some apt similitude' (VIII/8, 34), understanding politics must differ mightily from geometry and physics. He seems to hint as much at the end of his book: 'Reason, and Eloquence, (though not perhaps in the Naturall Sciences, yet in the Morall) may stand very well together' (R&C/4, 389).

Secondly, metaphorical usage is a principal way language grows, as words are adapted to new uses, hence take on new meanings, which may become the dominant meaning (e.g., 'concentrate,' 'delineate,' 'revolutionary,' 'eccentricity,' 'ruminate,' 'circumvene,' 'glean') – even to the point of supplanting the original meaning completely (e.g., 'captivate,' 'inkling,' 'vacillate,' 'gorgeous'). And this adaptability of existing vocabulary has proven useful in scientific and technical discourse as well as in everyday speech, despite Hobbes's claim that metaphoric usage risks defiling the linguistic clarity and precision requisite to capturing and communicating knowledge. For example, contemporary physicists refer to the *charm* of quarks, chemists to *families* of elements, geologists to tectonic *plates*, astronomers to asteroid *belts* and meteor *showers*. Were we to heed Hobbes's proscription against using words metaphorically (even if applied only in counselling and teaching), the result would be a stultification of language, gravely restricting both its growth and its flexibility. And given how readily we resort to such usage, hence how natural it evidently is, and how indeterminate and unstable can be the boundary between literal and metaphoric usage, it is doubtful whether such a ban could ever be practical.

Thirdly, using words metaphorically seems the only way to develop a language whereby one may speak of inner psychic experiences not directly perceptible to others, or of intelligible but wholly imperceptible phenomena. A word whose meaning originates in a realm open to public perception (and which is thus in principle amenable to ostensive definition, at least partially) is appropriated, and applied to a quite different phenomenon that nonetheless seems in some sense analogous.[9] That this process *works* is the amazing thing, and further reveals the inadequacy of the psychology Hobbes provides in the early chapters of *Leviathan*, especially with respect to the soul's rational powers. For we quite naturally liken various states of consciousness to something physical – that puzzling mind-body relation again – and speak, for example: of *burning* with indignation, of feeling *embittered*, or *agitated*, or *tense* (as opposed to *cool*, *calm*, and *collected*), of *bubbling* with enthusiasm (which no one could confuse with being *boiling* mad), of being *stung* by criticism, or *stricken* with fear, *hard*-hearted (or -headed), having a *dirty* mind, or a *burden* of guilt, of being *filled* with joy. Virtually any adult would understand what is meant by such expressions and acknowledge their appropriateness. Similarly, we speak of all sorts of intelligible but not actually perceptible political phenomena in physical terms – social *stratification*, *dissolving* Parliament, *forging* an alliance, *sparking* a debate, fiscal *restraint*, the *separation* of Church and State, a policy *in shambles*, a campaign *in tatters*, a *leak* to the news media, a *buoyant* economy (contrasting with both an economic *depression* and a *boom*) – physical, usually visual images that naturally seem to fit the mental phenomena (which almost always involve a synthesis of various sorts of perceptible evidence and rational analyses). These expressions come to us so naturally, intelligible the first time heard (which, after all, is their point), that one easily forgets, if one ever noticed, their metaphoric origin. Indeed, that we resort to physical images in speaking about philosophy itself – beginning with the *thirst* (or *hunger*) for knowledge, and employing the whole language of vision to speak of understanding – attests both to the fact that language, in order to provide a basis for communication, originates with reference to the realm of common perception; but also, that once having come into being, it can readily be adapted to talk about matters far remote from those original referents.

Fourthly, then, far from metaphoric speech being deceptive to others, the sense in which it is meant is usually understood at once (indeed, this is so typically the case that overly literal-minded people have been staples of comedy since the days of Aristophanes). This, in turn, as noted earlier, is profoundly revealing about the power of the human mind to recognize some sort of formal similarity (or whatever) in things radically heterogeneous – of the mind's capability *to* do so, that is, not of *how* it actually does so. This latter remains deeply mysterious, like 'free will' and so much else about the functioning of the rational soul. No surprise, then, that several eminent philosophers who focus on the larger mystery of how language works as a means of communicating about the world treat metaphoric speech as at the centre of the problem.[10]

Not that there are no other puzzling complications affecting language as people actually employ it. For example, there is the use of euphemisms, part of the more general question of the How and Why of *politeness* in language. Hobbes is perfectly aware of the fact: 'The secret thoughts of a man run over all things, holy, prophane, clean, obscene, grave, and light, without shame, or blame; which verball discourse cannot do, farther than the Judgment shall approve of the Time, Place, and Persons' (VIII/10, 34). But while this observation is pertinent, it throws no light on what is most curious about euphemisms. For while they may originate as purposefully ambiguous expressions, this would seem an inadequate explanation for their continued use once their ambiguity has dissipated, or in contexts where there would seem no need for them, nor any possibility of their meaning being variously construed. However, despite the importance of these and other forms of linguistic politeness for both the practice and the understanding of political life, Hobbes does not explicitly address the issues involved, though one would presume that his strictures against metaphors would pertain to euphemisms as well. And, as noted earlier, he does single out as a special 'abuse' of speech that of using it 'to grieve one another'; thus, his eighth natural law forbids expressing hatred or contempt of one's fellows '*by deed, word, countenance, or gesture*' (XV/20, 76). But for the most part, he leaves it to the reader to think for himself what are the conventions regarding appropriate language for a given time, place, and kind of person, and why they are what they are. In practice, it requires that form of 'good Judgement ... in matter of conversation and

businesse; wherein times, places and persons are to be discerned ... called
DISCRETION' (VIII/3, 33).

Having indicated four special purposes of speech, it is noteworthy that
Hobbes conspicuously ignores the special *religious* uses of speech in ceremony, exhortation, prayer, or glorification, such as 'To *Consecrate* ... in
pious and decent language'. This omission is the more curious in that he
does cite what he would have his reader regard as clear abuses of religious
speech in such practices as Exorcism (II/8, 7; XLV/9, 356; XLVII/25, 386)
and Transubstantiation ('For example; if a man pretend, that after certain
words spoken over a peece of bread, that presently God hath made it not
bread, but a God, or a man, or both, and neverthelesse it looketh still as
like bread as ever it did; there is no reason for any man to think it really
done'; XXXVII/13, 237). The authority for such practices, he argues,
involves a 'generall abuse of Scripture,' namely, 'the turning of Consecra-
tion into Conjuration, or Enchantment' (XLIV/11, 337; cf. XXXI/28–34,
191–2). Hobbes's failure to acknowledge as 'special' the uses of speech in
connection with things divine is still the more curious, given what he says
in connection with Oaths, that '*Swearing*, or OATH, is a *Forme of Speech*,
added to a Promise; by which he that promiseth, signifieth, that unless he
performe, he renounceth the mercy of his God* [etc.]' (XIV/31–2, 71).[11]

Both the uses and abuses of speech having been thus catalogued, Hobbes turns
to explaining what language is and how it works, for 'the remembrance of
the consequence of causes and effects.' According to him, it is simply a
matter of 'the imposing of *Names*, and the *Connexion* of them.' There are
two basic kinds: Proper names, which apply 'to one onely thing' (he
includes here phrases using demonstrative pronouns such as '*This man,
this tree*'); and Common names, so-called because they are applied in
common 'to many things ... every of which though but one Name, is
nevertheless the name of divers particular things; in respect of all which
together, it is called an *Universall*; there being nothing in the world Universall but Names;[12] for the things named, are every one of them Individuall and Singular' (IV/5–6, 13).

Since in philosophy and science we mostly 'Reason in Words of generall signification,' hence are occupied primarily with Universals, Hobbes
focuses the balance of this chapter on them. He tells us, 'One Universall
name is imposed on many things, for their similitude in some quality, or
other accident; And whereas a Proper Name bringeth to mind one thing
onely; Universals recall any one of those many.' And that Universals vary
in scope, or 'extent,' some larger, some smaller, 'the larger comprehend-

ing the lesse large.' Here Hobbes's example is rather peculiar: 'the Name *Body* is of larger signification than the word *Man*, and comprehendeth it.' That goes without saying, one is tempted to respond, if the term 'body' is practically equivalent to 'Reality,' the universe supposedly comprising nothing but bodies; hence, *any* real thing might serve equally well to illustrate the principle. But it would not have the rhetorical effect of encouraging the reader to regard man as body and nothing but body.

While there exist many Universals that are of various extent, others are of 'equall extent, comprehending each other reciprocally.' Here again Hobbes's examples are especially interesting: 'the names *Man* and *Rationall*, are of equall extent, comprehending mutually one another.' This being so, the name 'rational' is rightly applied to nothing other than 'humans.' And yet 'our naturall Reason,' Hobbes assures us, 'is the undoubted Word of God.' But if nonetheless *only man* is rational, then it would seem that 'man is indeed a god to man' (an ancient view that Hobbes elsewhere endorses),[13] in that '*our* naturall Reason' is the ultimate 'divine' authority. For even if one thinks only of Reason itself as Divine (being in principle 'always Right Reason'), access to it is nonetheless all too human. This being so, people must accept as an artificial substitute 'for right Reason, the Reason of some Arbitrator or Judge.' For a peaceful civil society, this means, ultimately, the reasoning of one's Sovereign (V/3, 18–19; XXVI/11, 139-40; cf. XXXI/3–4, 187).

There are serious, not to say comprehensive, inadequacies with Hobbes's account 'Of Speech' as an explanation of what ordinary language is and how it works (crudely commonsensical though it may strike an overtrustful reader). First of all, language is not made up simply of common and proper 'names' of things. One might grant that many verbs, adjectives, and adverbs could have originated as names (e.g., verbs as gerunds: names of activities, such as 'fighting,' 'escaping,' 'dancing,' 'kissing,' and of processes, such as 'flowing,' 'boiling,' 'melting,' 'digesting'; adjectives derived from names of qualities, such as 'blackness,' 'heaviness,' 'ugliness,' 'slowness'). Hobbes, however, argues the reverse: that the nouns ('names') originate as abstractions 'of the accidents and properties, by which one Matter, and Body is distinguished from another,' or of their effects on the perceiver's own body (as when we speak of the colours, sounds, smells, etc. of things – their so-called 'secondary qualities'; IV/16–17, 16). Whatever the case, there remain countless words that cannot plausibly be construed as names whereby one refers to actions, things, or their properties, and yet are essential to the communicative power of language – for example, most prepositions (from, to, through), conjunctions (and, or, except), modal auxiliaries (if, would, shall, will), interrogatives (how, what, why, when). But not only is Hobbes's implicit reliance on the referential function of language defective as an explication of language per se – as if all words derived their meaning entirely from what they *referred* to – it is inadequate even for words that *do* have a referent (both 'that Broker' and 'that Swindler' may *refer* to the same man, but they do not have the same meaning).

Furthermore, Hobbes virtually ignores the significance of *grammar* in determining what a given assertion actually expresses, and whether it is true or false – as if all the 'joyning together' of names 'into a Consequence, or Affirmation' was simply a matter of using 'is' as a copula ('thus, *A man is a living creature* ... If the latter name *Living creature*, signifie all that the former name *Man* signifieth, then the affirmation, or consequence is *true*; otherwise false'; IV/11, 14–15). Hobbes later asserts that even this logico-grammatical signifier could be dispensed with:

For the placing of two names in order may serve to signifie their Consequence, if it were the custome, (for Custome is it, that gives words their force,) as well as the words *is*, or *Bee*, or *Are*, and the like.[14]

And if it were so, that there were a Language without any Verb answerable to *Est*, or *Is*, or *Bee*; yet the men that used it would bee not a jot the lesse capable of Inferring, Concluding, and of all kind of Reasoning, than were the Greeks, and Latines. (XLVI/16–17, 372)

This is simply false. The variety of logical operators in a language (e.g., conjunctions, prepositions, modal auxiliaries) – which are essential to making language work, whether in scientific discourse or everyday speech – cannot conceivably be all reduced to various word orders. Much less can the other linguistic complexities expressed by grammar (including mood and voice, as well as tense and case) – whether of a primarily syntactical language such as English, or of inflected languages such as Greek and Latin. For not only does 'Francis taught Thomas' say something very different from 'Thomas taught Francis,' the former is logically equivalent to 'Thomas was taught by Francis,' but not to 'Francis might have taught Thomas,' or 'would have,' or 'could have,' or 'should have,' or 'will have,' or 'might still,' or 'maybe did teach,' or 'is teaching,' etc.

Moreover, there are profound problems with the radical Nominalism implicit in Hobbes's treatment of Universals. It is fair enough to say, 'One Universall name is imposed on many things, for their similitude in some quality, or other accident.' But recognition of 'similitude' presumes not merely sensory faculties, but rational powers beyond anything Hobbes expressly acknowledged in the three chapters preceding the one on Speech. For it is certainly not the case that the visual sense data of all the 'Individuall and Singular' things to which one applies the name 'tree' roughly congrue, such that they all *look* similar (regardless of one's perspective, no less), and so match up with a previously named 'fancy' still vibrating in one's memory.[15] There are *many* 'similitudes' – rather, many *kinds* of similitudes – synthesized into a single coherent idea of 'tree' (or 'treeness,' applicable to things as diverse as palms and oaks, cedars and sequoia, weeping willows and lodge pole pines), but none of them are similarities of sense data; all the 'likenesses' that readily come to mind as being common to trees – e.g., their having leaves, bark, trunk, roots, etc. – depend upon an *intellectual* recognition of their similarity, not on sheer congruence of sense data. But in concluding his survey of the faculties 'of mans mind ... naturally planted in him, so, as to need no other thing, to the exercise of it, but to be born a man, and live with the use of his five Senses,' Hobbes went on to say:

Those other Faculties, of which I shall speak by and by, and which seem proper to man onely, are acquired, and encreased by study and industry; and of most men learned by instruction, and discipline; and proceed all from the invention of Words, and Speech. For besides Sense, and Thoughts, and the Trayne of thoughts, the mind of man has no other motion; though by help of Speech, and Method, the same Facultyes may be improved to such a height, as to distinguish men from all other living Creatures. (III/11, 11)

And yet, the capacity to invent, learn, and use speech – the means of acquiring and enhancing those 'other Faculties' – itself presumes the faculties whereby one recognize all kinds of 'similitudes.' However, as considering Hobbes's example of 'tree' reveals, this recognition typically involves the mind's capacity for analysis as well as of synthesis, hence those mental powers Hobbes further discusses (but still far from adequately) only in his later chapter on '*Vertues* INTELLECTUALL' (VIII/2–3, 32–3). Simply asserting that all thought is made up of prior sensations or 'fancies,' that there is *some* sort of relationship linking successive thoughts in any given 'trayne of thoughts,' that universal terms are imposed on things having *some* sort of similitude – this might be adequate for readers whose main interest is in understanding politics, and are satisfied with being reminded that we somehow manage to see, think, and talk. But as a philosophical account, it is next to vacuous. Whereas a rigorous analysis of the human capacity for inventing, learning, and using language is deeply revealing about the rational workings of the human soul (as I would hope the preceding pages have at least partly shown).[16] And the clarity one thereby gains about imagination, perception,[17] reasoning, and intellection contributes to understanding much more about the world than just language.

Beyond this, however, a philosophically adequate theory of language – as distinct from what might suffice for techno-scientific purposes – must account for the similarity that one recognizes in correctly using some universal term. For surely no one the least bit competent can believe that the various kinds of similarities acknowledged in speech by our countless Universals (such that the set of things to which a given term is applied are regarded as of the *same kind*) are purely arbitrary conventions – that just any assortment of things could be referred to by the term 'dog,' say. There would be no point to having such terms were there not common specific features whereby a person could judge to which things a given Universal rightly applied and to which it did not. Nor is it satisfactory to leave it at saying merely that various sets of things *seem* similar *to us*, since something independent of us still must account for the seeming. At least as regards Nature, we must generally presume that, in the final analysis, Appearance is due to Reality: things seem similar to us (in whatever respect) because they *really are* similar (in that respect). In continuing the work of Adam, we endeavour to name the various species of plants and animals and types of materials on the basis of each kind's specific differences – that is, to do as Plato advises, 'carve Nature at its joints,'[18] such that the resulting panoply of Universals matches the natural divisions in Reality itself. But these natural divisions remain to be accounted for.

And so one is carried back to Aristotle's analysis showing why one must conclude that 'natures' inhere in Forms. That its respective batch of Matter is what makes each thing 'Individuall and Singular,' but that its *Form* is what makes it the *kind* of thing it is. All the individuals of a certain species of animal partake of a common form, which involves much more than simply a similar visible shape, suitably differentiated between males and females; it includes everything distinctive about the species: life span, behaviour, diet, breeding, etc.[19] And it is the apperception of this shared form that provides a basis for correctly casting and using Universals. Surprisingly, then, there is a sense in which Hobbes is right to insist that there is 'nothing in the world Universall but Names;

for the things named, are every one of them Individuall and Singular'; this is true of every Form, the ultimate referent for the Universal, being the 'thing' actually named: each Form is indeed individual and singular, and nothing at all like its name (which is, after all, merely a word).

Still more problems arise, however, in connection with Hobbes's further claim that 'whereas a Proper Name bringeth to mind one thing onely; Universals recall any one of those many.' With this he is generally understood to be advancing the most extreme form of Nominalism, denying the existence of even general 'ideas' (i.e., mental correlates of Forms) to which in the first instance universal terms could refer. This is necessarily so, since general ideas would be precluded by Hobbes's failure to acknowledge the existence of rational powers whereby such ideas could be composed from the recognized similarities one abstracts from individual instances.[20] Apparently, then, he would have us believe that whenever one mentions the name 'dog,' one necessarily has in mind the image or 'fancy' of a particular dog (perhaps the family pet, Lucifer). Doubtful generally, I should think, though certainly possible in some cases. But Hobbes is explicit that 'of Names Universall, some are of more, and some of lesse extent; the larger comprehending the lesse large' (the 'most Universall' being those of *philosophia prima*, or *Metaphysiques*; XLVI/14, 371). So, what happens as one ascends the hierarchy of Universals that comprehend 'dog'? Say, 'canine' (also comprehending 'wolf,' 'coyote,' 'fox,' etc.); is one still thinking of Lucifer? Or 'land carnivore' (add in all the kinds of cats, bears, etc.); still Lucifer, or some other particular carnivorous *individual*? Or 'mammal'; does this call to mind, not a particular *kind* of mammal, but some individual member of some mammalian species? 'Animal'? 'Living thing'? 'Thing'? As one moves to ever 'larger, more comprehensive' Universals, this view loses whatever plausibility it might originally have had. And what about the term 'Universal' itself (this 'name of Names'; IV/18, 16; XLVI/16, 372) – is one necessarily thinking of a *particular* Universal to which the name 'Universal' would apply? Indeed, is not this paradoxical, in that whichever such term one invoked ('dog,' say) would supposedly arouse only the image of a single individual to which that Universal applies? Back to Lucifer, are we?

In sum, one sees that providing a fully adequate explication of the human use of language involves metaphysical questions about the nature of Reality, as well as psychological questions about the human mind's ability to comprehend it – issues Hobbes never expressly addresses, much less resolves.

Despite arousing expectations to the contrary, however, perhaps Hobbes does not actually intend to provide a complete analysis of language in his chapter 'Of SPEECH.' He certainly has primed his reader for such an account, having noted its 'generall use' as a means of people communicating about 'what they conceive, or think of each matter; and also what they desire, feare, or have any other passion for,' as well its 'Speciall uses' of soliciting assistance, and of entertainment. But even so, perhaps he has a more limited purpose in mind for the account he gives, namely, that of showing how language must be established and used if it is to serve as a reliable means of pursuing as well as communicating Knowledge – to present, that is, a philosophical *method* for generating Scientific Knowledge. There can be little doubt but that this *is* a principal concern in Hobbes's treatment of language; he identifies 'the *first* use of Speech' to be 'the Acquisition of Science' (IV/13, 15; which must mean 'first in importance'). The question is whether – despite appearances – it is actually his *sole* concern: to show only 'how Speech serveth to the remembrance of the consequence of causes and effects.' This is just possible, given his peculiarly restricted conception of Reason ('*Reckoning* ... of the Consequences of generall names'), coupled with his having noted that 'the Greeks have but one word λόγος for both *Speech* and *Reason*.'

If so, his approach to language bears some similarity to that of Logical Positivists in the first half of the twentieth century, who endeavoured to establish the requirements of a 'purified language' that (to their mind) would best serve the interests of Science, and indirectly that of a scientific approach to life in general.[21] It would be a language that was clear and precise, free of the semantic confusions that can arise from the various sources of ambiguity inherent in the ordinary use of language – a concern Hobbes also voices: 'How fallacious it is to judge of the nature of things, by the ordinary and inconstant use of words' (XXV/1, 131).[22] But the imagined language would also be greatly simplified in that there is no need for a multiplicity of moods, voices, tenses, or of exclamations, imperatives, pleas, requests, exhortations, etc., in order to express scientific laws and theories (cf. VI/55, 29). Thus, the focus could be almost exclusively on clearly defining Names (hence, 'Concepts'), on establishing the valid connections between Names so as to make true Assertions or Affirmations (hence, 'Empirical Laws,' and other 'Generalizations'), and on deducing the logical connections between Affirmations to produce Syllogisms (hence, 'Predictions,' 'Explanations,' and 'Theories') – 'till we come to a knowledge of all the Consequences of names appertaining to the subject in hand; and that is it, men call SCIENCE' (V/17, 21).

Beyond this, however, Hobbes's linguistic method of philosophizing differs profoundly from the doctrine of the Positivists. For they draw a radical distinction between Philosophy and Science, insisting that the former is a strictly logico-linguistic affair having nothing to say about the World, inasmuch as matters of fact (apart from those having to do with language and logic) play no part in legitimate philosophizing. On their view, all knowledge of the world, the human mind included, requires empirical investigation, and as such belongs exclusively to the domain of one or another of the specialized Sciences. Philosophy ends where Science begins. Obviously, this is not Hobbes's view. He, like Francis Bacon, regards the goal of Philosophy, rightly conceived, to be Scientific Knowledge, rightly conceived. As Hobbes explains:

There are of KNOWLEDGE two kinds; whereof one is *Knowledge of Fact*: the other *Knowledge of the Consequence of one Affirmation to another*. The former is nothing else, but Sense and Memory, and is *Absolute Knowledge*; as when we see a Fact doing, or remember it done: And this is the Knowledge required in a Witnesse. The later is called *Science*; and is *Conditionall*; as when we know, that, *If the figure showne be a circle, then any straight line through the Center shall divide it into two equall parts*. And this is the Knowledge required in a Philosopher; that is to say, of him that pretends to Reasoning. (IX/1, 40)[23]

Moreover, as noted before, Hobbes – good Baconian – explicitly endorses the utilitarian character of the requisite knowledge:

Science is the knowledge of Consequences, and dependance of one fact upon another: by which, out of that we can presently do, we know how to do something else when we will, or the like, another time: Because when we see how any thing comes about, upon what causes, and by what manner; when the like causes come into our power, wee see how to make it produce the like effects.' (V/17, 21)[24]

But if science is a guide to action as well as understanding, then obviously 'Names and their Connexions' must somehow mirror 'Things and their Relations.'

The conception of scientific philosophizing that Hobbes explicates in these early chapters relies on the empirical accuracy and completeness of one's definitions as the basis of analysing the world *via* language: 'Reason is ... attayned by Industry; first in apt imposing of Names; and secondly by getting a good and orderly Method in proceeding from the Elements, which are Names, to Assertions made by Connexion of one of them to another; and so to Syllogismes, which are the Connexions of one Assertion to another,' whereby 'we come to a knowledge of all the Consequences of names [called] SCIENCE' (V/17, 21). The Logical Positivists treat the defining of terms (hence 'concept formation') as a purely conventional affair, being part of the Context of Discovery for which there are no logical rules or criteria. On this view, one is free to *stipulate* the meaning of one's terms however one likes, there being no such thing, strictly speaking, as a true or correct (or false, wrong, incorrect) definition. Or alternatively construed, since a definition simply stipulates a verbal equivalence ($X = YZ$), its statement is a logical tautology, and thus it is necessarily 'true by definition.' The only relevant test of a 'good,' that is, well-defined, concept is whether or not it proves useful for investigating Nature and expressing the resulting knowledge (i.e., that it figures in significant scientific generalizations and theories).[25]

But Hobbes does not subscribe to this conventionalist view of definitions as nothing more than stipulations of how the definer intends to use his terms.[26] Time and again Hobbes emphasizes the importance, not only of remembering exactly 'what every name [one] uses stands for' so as to use it consistently, but of definitions being *rightly* cast in the first place. Thus, 'how necessary it is for any man that aspires to true Knowledge, to examine the Definitions of former Authors; and either to *correct* them, where they are negligently set down; or to make them himself ... So that in the *right* Definition of Names, lyes the first use of Speech; which is the Acquisition of Science: And in *wrong*, or no Definitions, lyes the first abuse'[27] (IV/13, 15; my emphases). In order to 'correct' a definition, or 'rightly' make it oneself, there must be some objective non-linguistic standards whereby to distinguish right from wrong, correct from incorrect definitions. And insofar as the governing purpose behind getting one's language right is to make possible gaining thereby useful knowledge about the World, the phenomena to be referred to by language must themselves constitute the objective standards.

The model might seem to be the Life World, as it is for Aristotle and the Bible – after all, there *really are* distinct species of plants and animals, each deserving of a Name. Conventionalists who profess to believe that how humans linguistically carve up the world is essentially arbitrary, or determined exclusively by human preferences, ought to give Biology a lot more thought. But apparently the natural species do not serve as Hobbes's model, despite his citing the biblical account as exemplary of the origin of language. He never explicitly addresses the crucial issue here:

precisely how one *does* go about generating *correct* definitions[28] – or to put the point more generally, how we are to understand the relationship between language and the things about which we speak. One may agree that '*True* and *False* are attributes of Speech, not of Things'; but surely speaking truly (or falsely) *about* things depends on how things *really are* and how (then) that reality is accurately captured in speech. As discussed earlier regarding the many elements of language that have no referent, the notion of a one-to-one correspondence between words and things (objects, qualities, actions, relations, processes, whatever) is a naivety. Thus, one may wonder whether it is really true that '*truth* consisteth of the right ordering of names in our affirmations' (IV/12, 15) – whether this is a *correct* definition of 'Truth,' not merely stipulated as such (a reflexive paradox if there ever was one). If, however, one is willing to accept it 'for the sake of the argument,' then obviously the prerequisite of truthful assertions is correct definitions. So, once again, how are these generated?

To the extent Hobbes's *Leviathan* provides any guidance, it is only whatever is implicit in his own use of language, and particularly in what can be gleaned from his presentation of the definitions he employs in his political science. Consider, for example, the set of definitions so important to the rationale of Hobbes's political prescription, those of the human passions. First of all, in order for Hobbes to refer to them, it is practically necessary that these passions already have names. As a consequence, Hobbes's scientific language cannot be entirely independent of ordinary language whereby the phenomena are first identified, prior to more precise and accurate, 'technical' definitions being determined.[29] And the explanatory definitions that he provides in chapter 6 have to fit with tolerable accuracy the named passions as people actually manifest and experience them, or those definitions are simply *wrong*, and the whole understanding of politics in which they figure compromised accordingly. Once alerted to this view of definitions and Names, one finds that Hobbes consistently adheres to it from beginning to end in *Leviathan*. Thus, speaking of First Philosophy in the penultimate chapter – that 'on which all other Philosophy ought to depend' – we are told that it 'consisteth principally, in *right* limiting of the signification of such Appellations, or Names, as are of all others the most Universall: Which Limitations serve to avoid ambiguity, and aequivocation in Reasoning; and are commonly called Definitions' (XLVI/14, 371; my emphasis).

So, for Hobbes the initial step of sound philosophizing is the 'apt imposing of Names'; or as he puts it in the chapter expressly devoted to 'Reason and Science,' 'The Light of humane minds is Perspicuous

Words, but by exact definitions first snuffed, and purged from ambiguity' (V/20, 22).[30]

The second step is that of 'getting a good and orderly Method in proceeding from the Elements, which are Names, to Assertions made by Connexion of one of them to another' (V/17, 21). Again, this emphasis on a proper *method* runs from one end of the book to the other. 'Want of method' is singled out as 'the first cause of Absurd conclusions' (V/8, 20). And speaking about ancient times and savage peoples in his penultimate chapter, Hobbes allows, 'there have been divers true, generall, and profitable Speculations from the beginning; as being the naturall plants of humane Reason: But they were at first but few in number; men lived upon grosse Experience; there was no Method; that is to say, no Sowing, nor Planting of Knowledge by it self, apart from the Weeds, and common Plants of Error and Conjecture' (XLVI/6, 368). However, it bears emphasizing again that Hobbes's scientific Method does not specify any protocols of *inquiry*.

A sure method is of particular importance for sound political thinking: 'The skill of making, and maintaining Common-wealths, consisteth in certain Rules, as doth Arithmetique and Geometry; not (as Tennis-play) on Practise onely: which Rules, neither poor men have the leisure, nor men that have had the leisure, have hitherto had the curiosity, or the method to find out' (XX/19, 107). As one all-important consequence, Sovereign rulers must be especially wary in choosing counsellors, and not defer to spurious qualifications:

Good Counsell comes not by Lot, nor by Inheritance; and therefore there is no more reason to expect good Advice from the rich, or noble, in matter of State, than in delineating the dimensions of a fortresse; unless we shall think there needs no method in the study of the Politiques, (as there does in the study of Geometry,) but onely to be lookers on; which is not so. For the Politiques is the harder study of the two. (XXX/25, 184)

These pointed analogies with Geometry are not arbitrary, for Hobbes would have his readers regard it as 'the onely Science that it hath pleased God hitherto to bestow on mankind' (IV/12, 15), providing the very paradigm of methodical reasoning.[31] Supposedly it is the failure to appreciate this general applicability of the geometric method that explains why what Cicero says 'somewhere'[32] is 'most true': 'that there can be nothing so absurd, but may be found in the books of Philosophers. And the reason is manifest. For there is not one of them that begins his ratiocinations from the Definitions, or Explications of the names they are to use; which is a method that hath been used onely in Geometry; whose Conclusions thereby have been made indisputable' (V/7, 20). Hobbes, again referencing Cicero, pursues this theme further in castigating the 'vain philosophy' of almost all the Ancient Schools: 'The naturall Philosophy of those Schools, was rather a Dream than Science, and set forth in senselesse and insignificant Language; which cannot be avoided by those that will teach Philosophy, without first having attained great knowledge in Geometry' (XLVI/11, 369). Geometry proves that 'all men by nature reason alike, and well, when they have good principles. For who is so stupid, as both to mistake in Geometry, and also to persist in it, when another detects his error to him?' (V/16, 21).[33] But it also shows that the full use of Reason is not like puberty, arriving automatically; rather, it is only 'attayned by Industry.' As a consequence, 'the most part of men, though they have the use of Reasoning a little way, as in numbring to some degree; yet it serves them to little use in common life' (V/18, 21).

Granted its being exemplary in both the precision of its language and the logical rigour of its method, there are nonetheless two sorts of questions raised by Hobbes's emphasis on Geometry. First of all, *is* it, as he claims, appropriately regarded as 'the Mother of all Naturall Science' (XLVI/11, 369)? Second, is it truly – indeed, could it possibly be – the model for Hobbes's own *Political* Science? With respect to the latter question, Hobbes himself (in a passage previously noted) raises doubts about that, given people's very different psychical posture towards the things of Politics and those of Geometry:

Ignorance of the causes, and originall constitution of Right, Equity, Law, and Justice, disposeth a man to make Custome and Example the rule of his actions.... [However, men are not] constant to their rule, ... because grown old, and stubborn, they appeale from custome to reason, and from reason to custome, as it serves their turn; receding from custome when their interest requires it, and setting themselves against reason, as oft as reason is against them: Which is the cause, that the doctrine of Right and Wrong, is perpetually disputed, both by the Pen and the Sword: Whereas the doctrine of Lines, and Figures, is not so; because men care not, in that subject what be truth, as a thing that crosses no mans ambition, profit, or lust. For I doubt not, but if it had been a thing contrary to any mans right of dominion, or to the interest of men that have dominion, *That the three Angles of a Triangle, should be equall to two Angles of a Square*; that doctrine should have been, if not disputed, yet by the burning of all books of Geometry, suppressed, as farre as he whom it concerned was able. (XI/21, 50)

Of special importance here is Hobbes's explicit recognition of Reason's limited influence with most people – a limitation burdening any political doctrine that has nothing but cold, dry geometrical reasoning to recommend it. Men may not persist in a mistake in Geometry, where 'men care not ... what be truth' insofar as it has no bearing on their vital interests. But where 'ambition, profit, or lust' *is* involved, it is a different story entirely; there people do not so readily bow to the authority of Reason, given any alternative.

Add to this what Hobbes says about words of '*inconstant* signification' – for instance, 'The names of such things as affect us, that is, which please, and displease us,' and 'the names of Vertues, and Vices' – that they 'can never be true grounds of any ratiocination' (IV/24, 17). What prospect can there possibly be, then, for a *science* of politics, much less one modelled on Geometry? Is not politics almost entirely about the things that please and displease people? Would not any conceivable political teaching be filled with references to such things, on pain of irrelevancy otherwise? Hobbes's certainly is, complete with 'authoritative' definitions of 'Right, Equity, Law, and Justice' and of all sorts of other pleasing and displeasing things, including the moral virtues and vices. Further add the fact that Hobbes does not strictly adhere to his stated principle of always using words in the same way, but instead tailors his usage to the matter at hand, and one must doubt that the geometrical method is truly the basis of his Political Science – that it is actually but one more rhetorical device, meant to create the illusion of deductive certainty for his conclusions.

As for his regarding Geometry to be 'the Mother of all *Natural* Science,' Hobbes seems to have two quite separate factors in mind. First, its method of reasoning, resulting in the certainty of its conclusions, given true premises (as discussed above, and to be discussed further below). But, second, its being intrinsic to an understanding of Nature itself: 'For Nature worketh by Motion; the Wayes, and Degrees whereof cannot be known, without the knowledge of the Proportions and Properties of Lines, and Figures' (XLVI/11, 369). This sounds as if the only kind of observable motion relevant to science is that which proceeds along geometric lines and curves. But even were one to suppose that all perceptible change is ultimately explicable in terms of matter moving in space – much of it, as Hobbes supposes, at the sub-microscopic level (VI/1, 23;

XXXIV/3, 207; /15, 211; XLV/5, 353) – it is not clear how the 'Properties of Lines, and Figures' would be relevant to explaining the motions underlying such ordinary phenomena as ice melting, flowers opening, meat decaying, eggs hatching, colours fading, wood burning, hearts pumping, fruit ripening, iron rusting, bread rising, ink drying, milk souring, water boiling, or countless other kinds of motions one may observe in various forms of matter, the *causes* of which are no more obvious than the bearing of geometry in explaining them.

Returning to the first factor, Geometry would seem a problematic model for the natural sciences for at least one obvious reason: the minimal empirical content of its basic definitions. One need not subscribe to the modern Analytic-Synthetic distinction – whereby geometry (along with the rest of mathematics and logic) is consigned to the former category, and all factual knowledge about the world to the latter[34] – to see that there is a problem here. One may agree with the premise that a straight line *really is* the shortest distance between two points (that this is *not* an arbitrary assumption, but an intuitively obvious truth about Reality as such), but mathematics and logic pretty much have a monopoly on this sort of elementary, self-evident truth whence such an amazing body of other truths can be deduced. And it remains the case that whatever is so deduced must be implicit in one's original definitions.

Hence, if one is to deduce *empirical* knowledge from one's definitions, and not from further investigation of the things defined (including their relationships with other things), those Universals must somehow incorporate everything 'essential' that is true about the kind of thing defined. This means that much, if not the entirety, of pertinent empirical inquiry must *precede* the casting of a definition, with the casting itself being the work of *inductive* reasoning (which Hobbes never mentions, though his own account of Prudence as simply generalizing from experience presupposes it). Moreover, as I noted before, this research cannot be undertaken unless one already has a working definition whereby to identify which 'Individuall and Singular' things one intends to study. Thus one comes to appreciate the rationale underlying Aristotle's natural order of questions, each leading logically to the next: first, what a name means or refers to; second, whether that named thing actually exists ('Whether it is.'); third, what essentially defines it, all sine quae non distinguishing it from everything else ('When we ascertain a thing exists, we inquire as to its nature.'); fourth, what its properties are, including its relations with other things; fifth, why it has those properties ('When we know the fact, we ask the reason' – the locus of causal analysis). Answering the fifth question terminates inquiry; having completely answered it, one knows everything knowable about the kind of thing being investigated.[35] The first question does not involve purposeful inquiry; it arises unintentionally (for example, upon seeing or hearing an unfamiliar word). Often in practice, the first and second questions arise (and are answered) simultaneously, as when a child points at a swan, or the picture of a unicorn, and asks, 'What is that?' If the answer to Aristotle's second question is 'No,' obviously nothing further can be truthfully said.

With such considerations in mind, one sees that Hobbes's geometrical method works the better the more the content of a defined Universal is formal rather than factual. Thus, having defined the simplest of all geometric figures, the Triangle, perhaps one *can* readily 'turn the reckoning of the consequences of things imagined in the mind, into a reckoning of the consequences of Appellations,' allowing one to 'boldly conclude Universally ... *Every triangle hath its three angles equall to two right angles*' (IV/9, 14). Similarly, having provided this largely formal definition of 'Punishment' as '*an Evill inflicted by publique Authority, on him that hath done, or omitted that which is Judged by the same Authority to be a Transgression of the Law; to the end that the will of men may thereby the better be disposed to obedience*,' Hobbes can plausibly deduce the eleven consequences he does, beginning with 'neither private revenges, nor injuries of private men, can properly be stiled Punishments' (XXVIII/1–13, 161–3). But even in this case, logic alone will not suffice, for it presumes the 'commonsense awareness' that people do seek and exact revenge (the deduction being meaningless otherwise). Thus, Hobbes's deductions are typically more like Aristotelian enthymemes – those practical syllogisms of rhetoric in which certain premises are unstated, being simply presumed – than they are geometric proofs.

Moreover, when the Universal pertains to something far more complex – a natural form of being, say, such as Lion, Bear, or Wolf – the prospects of deducing true and certain knowledge from the definition would rest on its comprehensiveness, and that in turn on an exhaustive empirical investigation. For example, the definition of 'Arctic Wolf' would have to include – among hundreds of other general truths – that its diet includes caribou (or at least that it is carnivorous, and inhabits a region frequented by caribou). But even knowing this would not allow one to deduce whether these wolves do or do not follow the migrating herds (both being logical possibilities).[36] So that information, too, would have to be (somehow) embodied in the definition. Or to focus upon the example of greatest importance in *Leviathan*: 'Man.' Hobbes's use of it to exemplify his method is strangely inept: 'When two Names are joyned together into a Consequence, or Affirmation; as thus, *A man is a living creature ...* If the later name *Living creature*, signifie all that the former name *Man* signifieth, then the affirmation, or consequence is *true*, otherwise false' (IV/11, 14). First of all, Hobbes seems to have stated it backwards: the latter name most certainly does *not* signify *all* that the former does – far from it; rather vice versa: whatever is implied by 'living creature' pertains to 'man.'[37] But this raises the more basic point to be made here; to do the work that Hobbes ascribes to it, the Universal 'Man' would have to support myriad such 'affirmations.' And it is *very* hard to believe that Hobbes does not appreciate this fact. After all, Part One of his book, comprising eighty-three pages, is entitled 'OF MAN.' Presumably everything in at least the first twelve, if not all sixteen, of its chapters is germane. For example, the definition of 'Man' would include that humans are animated by certain 'simple Passions' (e.g., Appetite, Aversion, Joy, Grief) that 'have their names for divers considerations diversified' into some forty-odd distinguishable passions (VI/13, 25), such as:

> For *Appetite* with an opinion of attaining, is called HOPE.
> The same, without such opinion, DESPAIRE.
> *Aversion*, with opinion of *Hurt* from the object, FEARE.
> The same, with hope of avoyding that Hurt by resistance, COURAGE.

But even including only these sorts of subordinate definitions in the definition of 'Man' would be insufficient, as is evident from Hobbes's subsequent uses of the name 'Courage.' For example, could one simply *deduce* from the definition given here that 'the ground of Courage is alwayes Strength or Skill' (X/49, 45) – and not, say, a belief in divine protection ('Yea, though I walk through the valley of the shadow of death, I will fear no evil, for Thou art with me')? Or, 'That which gives to humane Actions the relish of Justice, is a certain Noblenesse or Gallantnesse of courage, (rarely found,) by which a man scorns to be beholding for the contentment of his life, to fraud, or breach of promise' (XV/10, 74)? Or what is meant by a man being 'of feminine courage' (XXI/16, 112)? Or, 'the effects of Courage' are among 'things Honorable by Nature' (XXVIII/19, 164)?

Bearing in mind the foregoing problems, and giving Hobbes sufficient credit for being the thinker he doubtless is, one must conclude – as I earlier suggested – that the Geometrical appearance of *Leviathan* is just that: a carefully cultivated appearance, adopted for the rhetorical effect of attributing to his new Political Science the same character and rational certitude he ascribes to the Natural Science his political prescription is designed to promote. In this respect, his endorsement and show of Geometrical Method, whereby a great body of conclusions can be deduced from a small number of clearly defined terms, is of a piece with his professed Materialism and Determinism.

However, this simply highlights the more difficult question to answer, namely, what is one to make of Hobbes's *general* account of what Science *is* and of how it 'works'? True enough, the geometrical model is plausible when applied to planetary Astronomy, which in Hobbes's day amounted to little more than applied Geometry (*after*, that is, accumulating centuries of painstaking observations, along with centuries of ingenious efforts to fit the data to more-or-less simple geometric trajectories); and perhaps equally plausible to the original branches of Physics (i.e., Statics, and Kinetics). But geometry is highly *implausible* as a model for the 'Life Sciences,' as I hope my simple examples of 'wolf' and 'man' suffice to show.

Hobbes might seem to gloss the problem with terminology, at least to judge from the schematic of SCIENCE ('that is, knowledge of Consequences; which is called also PHILOSOPHY') accompanying chapter 9. The vast Botanical realm is represented by 'Consequences from the qualities of *Vegetables*,' and the equally vast Zoological kingdom by 'Consequences from the qualities of *Animals*,' which Hobbes subdivides into those 'of *Animals in generall*' and those 'of *Men in special*.' The former, in turn, is subdivided into 'Consequences from *Vision*' (resulting in 'OPTIQUES'), and 'from *Sounds*' (hence, 'MUSIQUE'!), and 'from the rest of the *Senses*.' The latter Hobbes subdivides into 'Consequences from the Passions of Men' (yielding 'ETHIQUES') and 'Consequences from *Speech*' (whence 'POETRY, RHETORIQUE, LOGIQUE,' and 'The *Science* of JUST and UNJUST'). Hobbes's liberal use of the term 'Consequences' simply conceals beneath a veneer of uniformity the enormous empirical disparity between deductions possible in Astronomy and all the constituents of what is now known as Biology. And although Hobbes was well acquainted with William Harvey, perhaps having even shared with him some anatomical research,[38] there is no acknowledged science of medicine or physiology (whereas no less than twenty-seven of Bacon's one hundred and thirty called-for 'Natural and Experimental Histories' – the 'primary material' upon which the Sciences are to be based – pertain to these two fields).

Is Hobbes's conception of Science, and in particular its supposed geometrical character, defensible? What can be said in its favour? Quite a lot, actually. But, first of all, we must be clear about his conception, as it is much narrower than what is included under that rubric today. Hobbes's use of the term remains close to its Latin source, *scientia,* meaning simply (genuine) 'Knowledge.' That is, he does *not* include the *search* for knowledge – all the various modes of scientific inquiry and research, the observations, fieldwork, experiments, and general fact-gathering and classifying, much less the formal academic courses and degrees, the specialized institutes, laboratories, journals, conferences – all of which we have come to think of as part of Science, or the Scientific Enterprise. Science, as Hobbes uses the term, is confined to the solid *results* of all this activity – that is, to the more or less well-confirmed *generalizations.* This does not mean, of course, that he is insufficiently aware of the massive amount of empirical work these generalizations presuppose; his chapter describing '*the Several* SUBJECTS *of* KNOWLEDGE' includes recognition of '*Natural History*' as (genuine) knowledge 'of such Facts, or Effects of Nature, as have no Dependence on Mans *Will*' (IX/2, 40). And with Bacon having laid out the entire scientific program in his *New Organon* and elsewhere, stressing in particular the collection of exhaustive natural histories as supplying the 'food' of science (whence to induce 'axioms'), Hobbes need not repeat that. All that he need make explicit is the model of knowledge whereby the reader may recognize the scientific character of his political prescription.

Second, the geometrical character of this knowledge pertains in the first instance only to its logical form. For not only are scientific claims exclusively of a *universal* kind, they are, as Hobbes emphasizes, only *conditionally* true, like those of Geometry (VII/3–4, 30–1; IX/1, 40). That is, they are logically valid deductions based on hypotheses, or suppositions, such that they are true only *if* these initial suppositions are true (cf. *Republic* 510c–511b). Thus, if one were challenged to demonstrate the truth of a given scientific claim, a complete argument would be strictly analogous to a series of geometrical proofs that traced the claim all the way back to first principles that could not themselves be deductively proven. Indeed, the ability to provide such a demonstration is the sole 'certain and infallible' sign that one commands a science: that one 'can teach the same; that is to say, demonstrate the truth thereof' (V/22, 22; cf. *Republic* 531e). Hobbes does not expressly allow for the apperception of first principles by rational intuition (*noësis*), as does Aristotle,[39] nor by dialectical reasoning, as does Plato,[40] nor by an inductive assent, as does

Bacon.[41] But neither does he expressly preclude some such thing. Still, the fact remains, nowhere in *Leviathan* does Hobbes indicate that scientific knowledge could ever be anything other than conditional.

Beyond its form, however, Hobbes seems to suggest that Natural Science in general is like Geometry in that some or even most of its *substance* can be generated simply by *deductive disclosure*. And it is in this respect that his conception seems clearly mistaken, in that (as noted earlier) this is plausible for only a small set of sciences, and just barely for them. Here again, however, one must in fairness be careful not to apply anachronistic ideas. The purview of Science has expanded enormously in the three and a half centuries since Hobbes wrote *Leviathan*, with specialized sciences proliferating accordingly. And while his formal schema allows for this happening, it is most unlikely that he or anyone else anticipated – indeed, could imagine even in his wildest dreams – anything like the scale of our present scientific establishment, with sophisticated sciences dominating everything from advertising to zookeeping. There is now scarcely a sector or facet of human life that has not been profoundly affected by science (or pseudo-science). As for the emerging sciences of Hobbes's day – such as astronomy, physics, chemistry, optics, physiology – they have been transformed beyond anything he would recognize.

The pioneers of these sciences, however, would readily have acknowledged the pertinence to their own work of Hobbes's geometrical model. For example, William Gilbert, whose treatise on Magnetism (*De Magnete Magneticisque Corporibus et de Magno Magnete Tellure Physiologia Nova*) was the first major scientific treatise published in England (1600), writes in his Preface:

And even as geometry rises from certain slight and readily understood foundations to the highest and most difficult demonstrations, whereby the ingenious mind ascends above the æther: so does our magnetic doctrine and science in due order first show forth certain facts of less rare occurrence; from these proceed facts of more extraordinary kind; at length, in a sort of series, are revealed things most secret and privy in the earth, and the causes are recognized of things that, in the ignorance of those of old or through the heedlessness of the moderns, were unnoticed or disregarded.[42]

The text of Isaac Newton's famous *Principia* (*Mathematical Principles of Natural Philosophy*, 1687 – which became virtually the template for scientific treatises), is clearly fashioned on the geometrical model, complete with dozens upon dozens of diagrams, proofs, and derivations. As he explains in the Preface to the first edition:

The ancients considered mechanics in a two-fold respect; as rational, which proceeds accurately by demonstration, and practical ... But as artificers do not work with perfect accuracy, it comes to pass that mechanics is so distinguished from geometry that what is perfectly accurate is called geometrical; what is less so, is called mechanical. However, the errors are not in the art, but in the artificers. He that works with less accuracy is an imperfect mechanic; and if any could work with perfect accuracy, he would be the most perfect mechanic of all, for the description of right lines and circles, upon which geometry is founded, belongs to mechanics. Geometry does not teach us to draw these lines ... To describe right lines and circle are problems, but not geometrical problems. The solutions of these problems is required from mechanics, and by geometry the use of them, when so solved, is shown; and it is the glory of geometry that from those few principles, *brought from without*, is able to produce so many things.[43] (emphasis added)

Geometrical arguments and diagrams figure prominently throughout Galileo's *Dialogues Concerning the Two New Sciences* (1638), as they do in Christiaan Huygens's *Treatise on Light* (written in 1678, though not published until 1690). Huygens, however, relates his work to Geometry – of which he was one of the leading authorities in the Europe of his day – somewhat differently:

There will be seen in [the treatise] demonstrations of those kinds which do not produce as great a certitude as those of geometry, and which even differ much therefrom, since, whereas the geometers prove their propositions by fixed and incontestable principles, here the principles are verified by conclusions to be drawn from them; the nature of these things not allowing of this being done otherwise. It is always possible to attain thereby a degree of probability which very often is scarcely less than complete proof. To wit, when things which have been demonstrated by the principles that have been assumed correspond perfectly to the phenomena which experiment has brought under observation.[44]

The importance of geometry to Descartes's scientific work is sufficiently well known as to require no documentation here. In short, among the leading men of science in Hobbes's day, there was a keen interest in Geometry, both for its own sake and for its role in investigating and explaining various natural phenomena.

That said, the geometric model nonetheless would seem of very limited utility for either studying or explaining the realm of living things. The term 'Biology' did not become established until the early nineteenth century, though the names of its two main branches, Zoology and Botany, came into use during Hobbes's lifetime. Judging from his schematic of the Sciences, however, he (oddly) did not regard them as subdivisions of the same life world per se; for 'Consequences of the qualities of *Vegetables*' is paired – not with those of '*Animals*' – but with 'Consequences of the qualities of *Minerals*' under the rubric 'Consequences of the parts of the Earth that are *without sense.*'

The material points are these. First, much of what we today accept as legitimate scientific knowledge pertaining to the biological realm would not qualify as Science according to Hobbes's definition. Acquainted as he was with Aristotle's treatises on Animals (cf. XVII/6, 86) and Pliny the Elder's *Natural History* and other such classic texts, Hobbes was aware that compiling accounts of the flora and fauna of nature has been a respectable intellectual activity since antiquity. But then, as now, the most basic work in these fields was taxonomic. Moreover, the pertinent generalizations were and are mainly descriptive, often teleological in character, and arrived at inductively from multitudes of observations (including those of anatomical research) – *not*, that is, deduced from 'the Qualities of Bodies *Terrestriall*'! And while all of this would count as Science according to the Aristotelian view of *Physica* as primarily *theoretical* knowledge (i.e., sought simply for the sake of knowing), that is the very conception which Bacon intends his revolution in Science to overthrow. This leads to the second point: few in Hobbes's day would have imagined that these sorts of natural histories would lead to much in the way of technologically useful knowledge. What little research there then was into, for example, 'Consequences of the qualities of *Vegetables*' was carried out mainly by doctors seeking effective medicines and remedies (ignoring, that is, the activities of alchemists). Whereas the selective breeding of animals had been carried out since earliest history without the benefit of Science, ancient or modern (cf. *Republic* 459a–d). There would have to be three centuries of scientific progress before the idea of cloning livestock, or of genetically modifying fruits and grains, would even be intelligible.

So much, then, for (and against) the validity of Geometry as a model for Natural Science. But as I will explore in chapter 22, Hobbes may have another entirely different reason for the emphasis he places on Geometry, one more in keeping with a comparable emphasis in Plato's *Republic* – which is also to say, a reason more truly reflective of the relation between Geometry, Philosophy, and Reality. Hobbes exempts Plato, notice, from his general dismissal of ancient philosophic schools: '*Plato* that was the best Philosopher of the Greeks, forbad entrance into his Schoole, to all that were not already in some measure Geometricians' (XLVI/11, 369). To judge from Plato's dialogues, however, the mode of philosophizing he exemplifies is *not* itself modelled on Geometry. But neither, for that matter, is much of what Hobbes wrote. Instead, he also often employed the dialogical form of writing – a simple fact worth pondering.

13

Honour
and the Problem of *Natural Law*

Arguably, Hobbes's most impressive show of deductive reasoning is that which is central to the secular political teaching laid out in the first half of *Leviathan*: his deriving those nineteen or twenty 'Lawes of Nature dictating Peace' from what he would have us regard as 'a' – surely, for his purposes, *the* – 'generall rule of Reason.' To be sure, these derivations fall short of geometrical rigour; nor do they constitute a 'chain' of reasoning (such that one could backtrack from the nineteenth through the rest to the first). But the paramount question is, how does Hobbes establish the basic claim whence the rest are deduced: '*That every man, ought to endeavour Peace, as farre as he has hope of obtaining it; and when he cannot obtain it, that he may seek, and use, all helps, and advantages of Warre*'? This 'precept' is a consequence of Hobbes's definitions of 'the Right of Nature,' of 'Liberty,' and of 'a Law of Nature,' applied to the human condition in the State of Nature as he has described it:

The RIGHT OF NATURE ... is the Liberty each man hath, to use his own power, as he will himselfe, for the preservation of his own Nature; that is to say, of his own Life; and consequently, of doing any thing, which in his own Judgement, and Reason, hee shall conceive to be the aptest means thereunto.

By LIBERTY, is understood ... the absence of externall Impediments: which Impediments, may oft take away part of a mans power to do what hee would; but cannot hinder him from using the power left him, according as his judgement, and reason shall dictate to him.

A LAW OF NATURE ... is a Precept, or generall Rule, found out by Reason, by which a man is forbidden to do, that, which is destructive of his life, or taketh away the means of preserving the same; and to omit, that, by which he thinketh it may be best preserved. For though they that speak of this subject, use to confound *Jus*, and *Lex*, *Right* and *Law*; yet they ought to be distinguished; because RIGHT, consisteth in the liberty to do, or to forbeare; Whereas LAW, determineth, and bindeth to one of them: so that Law, and Right, differ as much, as Obligation, and Liberty; which in one and the same matter are inconsistent. (XIV/1–3, 64)

Now, why should (or would, or might) we accept these definitions as a basis for deducing further propositions, such as that all-important 'generall rule of Reason' ('*That every man, ought to endeavour Peace,*' etc)? They are *not* universally accepted by all who deal with these matters (as Hobbes's discussion expressly notes). To be sure, his definitions do not strike us as arbitrary – quite the contrary – but neither are they self-evident truths in the geometrical sense. If we say his definitions seem 'reasonable,' what do we *mean*, and *why* do they seem so? Is it (at least partly) because they are in keeping with how we suppose people (ourselves included) would most likely behave in extremis, and (moreover) that there is no good reason why they would not or should not – that it is 'only natural,' even a practical necessity, for a human being, like any animal, to do 'whatever it takes' to survive? Hence, anyone's doing so *must* be right and proper, and should be conceded as such. Thus what we acknowledge is a natural fact becomes a 'Natural *Right*' – which if it means anything *beyond* the brute fact that creatures (humans included) 'will do what they do,' is a moral idea *legitimating* whatever one chooses to do (or not do) in the interest, or at least the name, of survival. Moreover, if we believe this natural impulsion to survive is, or can be, too strong to resist, we may even recognize it as a 'Natural Law,' in the sense of being descriptive of a pre-eminent disposition inherent in animate life. Notice, incidentally, this latter is *not* a deduction. It is a generalization *induced* from a vast array of evidence – introspection, experience, history, ethological data – to the effect that 'all natures, man and beast alike, are powerfully inclined to behave thus.'

Hobbes's generic Law of Nature, however, is *not* simply a descriptive generalization about animal behaviour, but a *prescriptive* maxim: a person is *positively forbidden* 'to do, that, which is destructive of his life, or taketh away the means of preserving the same; and to omit that, by which he thinketh it may be best preserved.' Needless to say, this prohibition has no pertinence whatsoever for any creature whose behaviour is strictly determined by a survival instinct, without any capacity to choose otherwise; thus it is addressed to 'a man,' and seems to presume what people mean by free will, as does the liberty inherent in a Right of Nature ('to do, or forbeare'). But where did this forbiddance, this 'thou shalt not,' come from? *Given* this general prohibition against a person doing anything destructive of his or her own life, one may then use Reason to derive various more specific Natural Laws consistent with it, as Hobbes has done (confining his attention mainly to those 'dictating [civil] Peace'). But he has provided no rational justification for the general principle itself. Is he simply relying on its intuitive appeal to readers, its apparent reasonableness, confident that most will accept it more or less gladly, but without pausing to trace out its practical implications – which are many, including some that pose grave, not to say insuperable, obstacles to the maintenance of political life. Or, is Hobbes surreptitiously relying on religious indoctrination prohibiting suicide and despair (although the principle's implications go well beyond these concerns)?

Certainly the ingenuity of Hobbes's rhetoric plays its part. For immediately preceding the chapter introducing his novel conception of Natural Law, the reader is confronted with Hobbes's hellish portrait of life in the State of Nature. It is a condition of universal and perpetual war, where every man must regard every other man as potentially his enemy, each and all 'without other security than what their own strength, and their own invention shall furnish them withall.' Consequently 'men have no pleasure, (but on the contrary a great deale of griefe) in keeping company' with each other (XIII/5–9, 61):

In such condition, there is no place for Industry; because the fruit thereof is uncertain: and consequently no Culture of the Earth; no Navigation, nor use of the commodities that may be imported by Sea; no commodious Building; no Instruments of moving, and removing such things as require much force; no Knowledge of the face of the Earth; no account of Time; no Arts; no Letters; no Society; and which is worst of all continuall feare, and danger of violent death; And the life of man, solitary, poore, nasty, brutish, and short. (XIII/9, 62)

However, Hobbes reserves revealing the full magnitude of mankind's misfortune for the thirteenth paragraph of this thirteenth chapter: there is no *Justice* in the State of Nature – meaning, not merely no administered justice, no appropriate punishing and rewarding, human or divine – but no relevant *idea* of Justice: *everything is permitted.* As Hobbes would have us see it, the implication of mankind's *natural* State being a condition of universal war is that 'nothing can be Unjust. The notions of Right and Wrong, Justice and Injustice have there no place.' Rather, 'Force, and Fraud' are 'the two Cardinall vertues.' There is no recognition of Property, 'no *Mine* and *Thine* distinct; but onely that to be every mans, that he can get; and for so long, as he can keep it' (XIII/13, 63). Indeed, 'every man has a Right to every thing; even to one anothers body [one shudders to guess for what purpose]. And therefore ... there can be no security to any man, (how strong or wise soever he be,) of living out the time, which Nature ordinarily alloweth men to live' (XIV/4, 64). Suffice it to say, Hobbes's rhetoric is crafted to predispose the reader to accept almost any proposal that promises protection from having to live under those conditions.[1]

So, against this background – of what is meant by a 'Right of Nature' and a 'Law of Nature'; and that the Natural State is 'a condition of Warre of every one against every one; in which case every one is governed by his own Reason; and there is nothing he can make use of, that may not be a help unto him, in preserving his life against his enemyes' (XIV/4, 64) – Hobbes advances the supposed 'precept, or generall rule of Reason' previously quoted: '*That every man, ought to endeavour Peace, as farre as he has hope of obtaining it; and when he cannot obtain it, that he may seek, and use, all helps, and advantages of Warre.*' From this he immediately abstracts both the 'Fundamentall law of Nature' ('*to seek Peace, and follow it*') and 'the summe of the Right of Nature,' which one never surrenders and can never be abrogated ('*By all means we can, to defend ourselves*' – somewhat curiously, it is expressed in the plural). As Hobbes makes explicit in introducing his 'second Law' of Nature, it and all the rest of the Natural Laws he specifies are to be understood as 'derived' (either directly or indirectly) from the first and 'Fundamentall Law.'[2]

However, if one pauses to think about this first step – upon which all the rest depend – it is quite puzzling. How can one derive from this single precept *both* a comprehensive fundamental Natural Law that positively 'determineth, and bindeth' a person to certain courses of action (as per the subordinate Laws derived therefrom), all being consonant with the defining feature of any such Law: that a person is *forbidden* 'to do, that, which is destructive of his life, or taketh away the means of preserving the same; and to omit that, by which he thinketh it may be best preserved'; derive that, *and* the summary Natural Right, which is a *liberty* 'to do, or forbeare'? How can one branch of this precept *oblige* a person to do everything in his power that may contribute to his survival, whereas the other branch *permits* the person to do, *or not do*, as he chooses (to use his own power 'according as his judgement, and reason shall dictate to him')? If the first branch is operative, the second branch must be null and void.

It is not as though the one branch applies to conditions of Peace, the other to 'Warre' – though Hobbes's rhetoric may contribute to that illusion. For both branches apply to the State of Nature (else there would be no requirement to leave it, and thereafter avoid it, if one safely can – no rational necessity 'to seek Peace, and follow it'). And both apply equally to the Civil State, wherein one retains one's Natural Right to defend oneself by any means available (as Hobbes makes explicit):

[T]here be some Rights, which no man can be understood by any words, or other signes, to have abandoned, or transferred. As first a man cannot lay down the right of resisting them, that assault him by force, to take away his life; because he cannot be understood to ayme thereby at any Good to himselfe. The same may be sayd of Wounds, and Chaynes, and Imprisonment … And therefore if a man by words or other signes, seems to despoyle himselfe of the End, for which those signes were intended; he is not to be understood as if he meant it, or that it was his will. (XIV/8, 66)

Thus, regardless of any covenant he may have entered into, a man has a *right* to resist arrest, a *right* to go kicking and screaming to the gallows – he is not obliged to go peacefully (XIV/29, 69–70). But since this is a right, a 'liberty to do, or forbeare,' neither is he *obliged* to resist: he may choose to go peacefully, having his own reasons for doing so. Hobbes, however, is careful not to call attention to this implication, expressly pointing here and elsewhere only to actions *permitted* by Natural Right that would be fully *consistent* with those *required* by his construal of Natural Law.[3] Thus, his reader is never directly confronted with the potential conflict between the two notions. For a man's 'forbearing' to resist arrest, or his submitting peacefully to just punishment, would violate the essential premise of every valid Law of Nature, according to Hobbes: that one is *forbidden*, not merely to risk self-destruction, but equally to *omit* doing anything that might further self-preservation. After all, resistance and escape attempts are sometimes successful, but only if one tries. Which is it to be, then, the rule of Natural Right, or of Natural Law? For they are not consistent.

Did Hobbes not realize this? That in allowing for an inalienable Natural Right, this 'liberty to do, or forbeare,' permitting *but not requiring* that one use all means one can to defend oneself, he undermined the foundation for his entire structure of Natural Laws, every one of which is premised on a strict *obligation* to do whatever maximizes survival? Of course he did. Moreover, he himself – exemplifying the kind of brazen irony of which he is the master – pointed straight to the contradiction. For he insists upon the crucial distinction between '*Right* and *Law*,' warning that other writers have 'confounded *Jus*, and *Lex*': whereas, properly understood, 'Law, and Right, differ as much, as Obligation, and Liberty; *which in one and the same manner are inconsistent.*'[4] But Hobbes well appreciated that no reader is apt to attribute any special significance to these words unless he has first recognized the contradiction that can arise between what Natural Right permits and what Natural Law requires.

Still, the question remains, *why* has Hobbes incorporated this contradiction at the very base of his political prescription? For on the face of it, there is no need to include a permissive Natural Right that is inconsistent with his conception of Natural Law. Why not simply stick to this Natural Law, with its absolute requirement that a person do everything he can to preserve his life? One must presume that here, as elsewhere, 'the face of it' is misleading: there must indeed be some need for both of his conceptions, of Natural Law and of Natural Right, if his Leviathan is to work in practice. And the fact that it results in a logical inconsistency is hardly fatal, for *very* few people are apt to notice it, and just as few of the few are apt to care much about it were it pointed out to them. Most people are blithely unaware of the many contradictions and inconsistencies in their own lives, and take in stride those of which they are made aware. Moreover, as I shall argue below, the contradiction in Hobbes's political theory is reflective of – one might even say, 'caused' by – a contradiction, or at least a profound ambiguity of disposition, in human nature. Hobbes, consummate political realist, well appreciates that it is not so much logic that rules political life, as it is '*psycho*-logic.' Thus, the reasoning he employs appeals to what people prefer to believe and how they typically act, mostly without special regard for the scruples of logic so long as 'things work out in practice.' He can get away with inconspicuous contradictions if they are needed to make things to work out in practice, people being people, not logicians. So, why does Hobbes need this one?

To be sure, the idea of founding a Commonwealth on a principle that, rightly understood, positively *obliges* any citizen who commits a felony to resist arrest and imprisonment – such that 'going peacefully' or 'accepting one's punishment' are not even options insofar as one is rational – is suspect, to say the least. Were everyone to take such a principle to heart, this might well aggravate the problem of policing beyond all practicality. Whereas, providing effective, reliable policing, ensuring that law-abiding citizens can be confident of the security of their persons and property, is *the* fundamental, everyday responsibility of the Sovereign, half of the very raison d'être of a Commonwealth (paired with protection from external enemies). As for those who are willing to resort to violent criminal behaviour, they hardly need Hobbes's legitimization of resisting lawful authority for their pursuit, capture, and guarding to be risky business. So, who is to do it? Or for that matter, who that is ruled by Hobbesian Natural Law would willingly perform *any* of the socially useful tasks that may be the least bit dangerous, from firefighter and bush pilot to coal miner and taxi driver? Only ignorant or irrational people? Only those who either do not *know* that reason forbids risking one's life – that its preservation outweighs all other concerns (including any amount of salary) – or who do not *care*? But to the extent they are thus ignorant or irrational, they would be indifferent to the entire rationale for 'Leviathan,' unmoved by any and every reason for structuring a Commonwealth according to the collection of Natural Laws Hobbes specifies. Clearly there is a problem here.

The larger problem is conveniently explored through examining its most obvious and pressing manifestation, hence the one that Hobbes cannot avoid addressing: the polity's need for soldiers. If Leviathan is not to be a toothless crocodile, incapable of defending its subjects not only from internal malefactors, but even more urgently, from external enemies – meaning mainly neighbouring polities capable of visiting wholesale destruction and enslavement on the populace (cf. XIII/12, 63) – some men must be willing to risk a not insignificant probability of dying in defence of the Commonwealth. But is not such willingness the very height of irrationality, judged by a standard of Reason that takes its bearings from Hobbes's conception of Natural Law (which *forbids* a man 'to do, that, which is destructive of his life,' and instead requires him to do everything 'by which he thinketh it may be best preserved')? Would Hobbes have Leviathan be defended only by the most reckless of men? Would they not be as great a threat to their fellow citizens – indeed, to each other – as to the enemy?

The obvious way to begin is by examining the adequacy of Hobbes's explicit resolution of this problem. It is prefaced with this general statement:

No man is bound by the word themselves, either to kill himselfe, or any other man; And consequently, that the Obligation a man may sometimes have, upon the Command of the Soveraign to execute any dangerous, or dishonourable Office, dependeth not on the Words of our Submission; but on the Intention; which is to be understood by the End thereof. When therefore our refusall to obey frustrates the End for which Soveraignty was ordained; then there is no Liberty to refuse: otherwise there is. (XXI/15, 112)

But surely, leaving this judgment to each self-interested citizen violates the entire rationale for establishing a single supreme Sovereign ('therein to submit their Wills, every one to his Will, and their Judgements, to his Judgement'; XVII/13, 87), and is expressly contrary to the sovereign's ninth Right (XVIII/12, 92). In any case, this supposed disposal of the problem simply straddles it. On the one hand, it is consonant with the obligation of citizens 'to assist him that hath the Soveraignty, in the Punishing of another' (XXVIII/2, 161), since it is obviously necessary that *someone* do it if there is to be law and order ('the End for which Soveraignty was ordained'). And by the Commonwealth-creating Covenant, all citizen-subjects supposedly confer 'all their power and strength upon one Man, or upon one Assembly of men,' in order that 'he [or they, presumably] hath the use of so much Power and Strength conferred on him, that by terror thereof, he is inabled to conforme the wills of them all, to Peace at home, and mutuall ayd against their enemies abroad' (XVII/13, 87–8).[5] Still (on the other hand), when it comes down to cases, providing assistance in the 'Punishing of another' could prove dangerous, since that 'other' retains the right to resist to the utmost whoever attempts 'to lay violent hands upon his person.' Might not – indeed, *should not* – each man, though favouring the principle in general, when actually called upon to help implement it, say to himself, 'But why me?' and invoke his Natural Right to opt out in the interest of self-protection?[6]

Having provided the general prefatory statement quoted above, Hobbes begins his response to the most conspicuous and important objection to his Natural Law doctrine – 'What about soldiers?' – in a somewhat equivocal vein:

Upon this ground [i.e., that no man is bound by the words themselves either to kill himself or any other man], a man that is commanded as a Souldier to fight against the enemy, though his Soveraign have Right enough to punish his refusall with death, may neverthelesse in many cases refuse, without Injustice; as when he substituteth a sufficient Souldier in his place: for in this case he deserteth not the service of the Common-wealth. And there is allowance to be made for naturall timorousnesse, not onely to women, (of whom no such dangerous duty is expected,) but also to men of feminine courage. (XXI/16, 112)

Though the implications of this statement trail off in several directions, let two comments suffice. Surely the notion that someone called upon for military duty may instead provide a substitute must carry the proviso '*if the law so allows.*' And there are some potent reasons militating against such an allowance. To mention only the most obvious: permitting the Rich to hire the Poor to do their fighting for them, while common enough in human history, is not a recipe for social harmony, and hardly squares with the 'equality before the law' that Hobbes calls for. Secondly, given the rationale supporting the entire body of Hobbes's Natural Laws, should not *everyone* be 'of feminine courage,' on pain of being deemed irrational otherwise? Thus, even to argue the legitimacy in principle of substituting a 'sufficient Souldier' presumes that one might be available, and so begs the very question at issue here. Confronted by an invading army bent on conquest, why not promptly surrender or run away, if either course seems more likely to preserve one's life? Hobbes concedes that this often happens; and moreover, that doing so may not even be unjust: 'When Armies fight, there is on one side, or both, a running away; yet when they do it not out of trechery, but fear, they are not esteemed to do it unjustly, but dishonourably. For the same reason, to avoyd battell is not Injustice, but Cowardice.'

Who, then, that is rational (in the special sense that Hobbes's Natural Laws require) is left to do the fighting? Hobbes answers:

But he that inrowleth himselfe a Souldier, or taketh imprest mony, taketh away the excuse of a timorous nature; and is obliged, not onely to go to the battell, but also not to run from it, without his Captaines leave. And when the Defense of the Commonwealth, requireth at once the help of all that are able to bear Arms, every one is obliged; because otherwise the Institution of the Commonwealth, which they have not the purpose, or courage to preserve, was in vain. (XXI/16, 112)

Commonsensical as these claims may be, they do not square with certain explicit provisions of Hobbes's political theory. Consider the volunteer soldier who accepts a signing bonus during peacetime, entering into a contractual requirement that, should the need arise, he would serve in the manner Hobbes describes. However, Hobbes also assures him and us, 'of the voluntary acts of every man, the object is some *Good to himselfe*' (XIV/8, 66). The man wanted the money and needed a job, but he did not intend to risk getting killed. Later, confronted with the prospect of going into battle, he fears he might be. Does that not render his contract invalid ('the cause of feare, which maketh such a Covenant invalid, must be alwayes something arising after the Covenant made'; XIV/20, 68)? Or, perhaps he did not *know* he had a 'timorous nature' until put to the test. Anyway, so what? The fact that reneging on one's contractual obligation is against the law is irrelevant when one's own life is on the line, according to Hobbes's express words:

> If a man by the terrour of present death, be compelled to doe a fact against the Law, he is totally Excused; because no Law can oblige a man to abandon his own preservation. And supposing such a Law were obligatory; yet a man would reason thus, *If I doe it not, I die presently; if I do it, I die afterwards; therefore by doing it, there is time of life gained*; Nature therefore compells him to the fact. (XXVII/25, 157)

This would apply whether one was bound by a single contract or a dozen. Thus, what Hobbes later argues – 'But if a man, besides the obligation of a Subject, hath taken upon him the new obligation of a Souldier, then he hath not the liberty to submit to a new Power, as long as the old one keeps the field, [etc]' (R&C/6, 390) – fails to meet the objection.

Hobbes acknowledges that there are readers who will fasten on what they see as a major contradiction in his theory. Consequently, in his 'Review and Conclusion' he resorts to declamatory rhetoric by way of rebuttal:

> From the contrariety of some of the Naturall Faculties of the Mind, one to another, as also of one Passion to another, and from their reference to Conversation, there has been an argument taken to inferre an impossibility that any one man should be sufficiently disposed to all sorts of Civill duty ...
>
> And amongst the Passions, *Courage*, (by which I mean the Contempt of Wounds, and violent Death) enclineth men to private Revenges, and sometimes to endeavour the unsetling of the Publique Peace: And *Timorousnesse*, many times disposeth to the desertion of the Publique Defence. Both these, they say, cannot stand together in the same person. (R&C/1–2, 389)

Hobbes's proof to the contrary is that he once knew a man who eminently manifested both 'a Courage for the Warre, and a Fear for the Laws' (among other sets of seemingly contradictory qualities), namely, his 'most noble and honored friend Mr. *Sidney Godolphin*,' referred to in the first line of the book's Dedication. However, this evidence is hardly decisive, for the issue that remains is whether Mr. Godolphin was rationally consistent in his doing so. Hobbes concedes that the need for opposing qualities and dispositions to abide in a single soul poses 'indeed great difficulties, but' – he assures us – 'not Impossibilities.' His solution to the problem: 'For by Education, and Discipline, they may bee, and are sometimes reconciled' (R&C/4, 389), points to what is arguably the single greatest lacuna in his political prescription: the absence of any substantial discussion of the education system requisite to a Hobbesian Commonwealth.[7] Might he be tacitly relying upon the pedagogical principles described by one of his predecessors, requiring a regimen that combines athletics with the right sort of 'music'?

Not at all incidentally, one must note that the characterization of 'Courage' quoted above does *not* square with how Hobbes originally defined it. Nor is it any mystery why not: the admission that there are those who are simply *contemptuous* of death, and moreover that it is necessary some men be so, would immediately call into question the rationale underlying all of Hobbes's Natural Laws. Thus his very different treatment of courage in the early chapters. Having defined 'Fear' as '*Aversion, with opinion of Hurt from the object,*' he follows with 'The same, with hope of avoyding that Hurt by resistence, COURAGE' (VI/16–17, 25). There could hardly be two construals more divergent than '*contempt* of wounds and violent death,' versus 'hope of *avoiding* that Hurt'! The latter version accords well with Hobbes's claim that 'the ground of Courage is always Strength or Skill, which are Power' (X/49, 45) – whereas the former fits the classical view that the ground of Courage, along with a 'Love of Victory and Love of Honour' (*philonikia kai philotimia*), is the strength of the soul's spirited part (*thumos*).[8]

In any event, so that there be no confusion as to what Hobbes would have the reader understand, he uses his 'Review and Conclusion' to state the following:

To the Laws of Nature, declared in the 15. Chapter, I would have this added, *That every man is bound by Nature, as much as in him lieth, to protect in Warre, the Authority, by which he is himself protected in time of Peace.* For he that pretendeth a Right of Nature to preserve his owne body, cannot pretend a Right of Nature to destroy him, by whose strength he is preserved: It is a manifest contradiction of himselfe. And though this law may bee drawn by consequence, from some of those that are there already mentioned; yet the Times require to have it inculcated, and remembred. (R&C/5, 390)

In light of my previous several pages, I presume there is no need to belabour the obvious. Hobbes's doctrine presents the citizen of a Commonwealth with a dilemma; and the above passage, far from resolving it, amounts to no more than an exhortation to choose one horn rather than the other.

As for the general obligation on *everyone* capable of bearing arms – timorous nature or not – to defend the Commonwealth should the need arise, the fact that otherwise the need will go unmet and people's banding together in a Commonwealth 'was in vain,' while obviously true, does not meet the objection. It merely points to the contradiction inherent in basing the Commonwealth on a set of Natural Laws, rational acceptance of which presumes that each person's dominant passion is (or ought to be) fear of death – since anyone whose *paramount* concern *is* his or her *own* survival must regard the survival of others, and of the Commonwealth as a whole, as necessarily subordinate. For such a person, the line of thought implicit in the following passage would pertain to *any* looming confrontation of armies where one's own side is not self-evidently of such overwhelming superiority as virtually to guarantee victory without a shot being fired, or at least with only negligible casualties (in which case, paradoxically, the regime would not in fact *militarily* require 'all that are able to bear Arms'):

For where a number of men are manifestly too weak to defend themselves united, every one may use his own reason in time of danger, to save his own life, either by flight, or by submission to the enemy, as hee shall think best; in the same manner as a very small company of souldiers, surprised by an army, may cast down their armes, and demand quarter, or run away, rather than be put to the sword. (XX/15, 105)

However, for the person who is ruled by Natural Law reasoning, the point in *any* engagement is *not* whether one's own *side* is likely, or even surely, to be victorious, but whether *oneself* is surely going to be alive to boast of it. Yet notice Hobbes's precise language here: 'every one *may* use his own reason in time of danger, *to save his own life*' – that is, he is not *obliged* to do so. The implication would seem to be that, in such a situation, Natural *Right* rules, *not* Natural Law. That being so, one is at 'liberty to do, or to forbeare' – one *may* choose to do whatever seems most likely to save one's own skin, in which case one behaves just as Natural Law requires; *or*, one may choose to stand by one's comrades and take one's chances, even choose to prevail or die trying. But *why* would anyone choose to do *that*?

To begin to see why – and see as well the *necessity* for Natural Right as well as Natural Law if Hobbes's political doctrine is to work in practice, inconsistent though they be in theory – we must return to a passage quoted earlier, for it includes a puzzling feature easily overlooked:

[T]he Obligation a man may sometimes have, upon the Command of the Soveraign to execute any dangerous, or dishonourable Office, dependeth not on the Words of our Submission; but on the Intention; which is to be understood by the End thereof. When therefore our refusall to obey frustrates the End for which Soveraignty was ordained; then there is no Liberty to refuse: otherwise there is. (XXI/15, 112)

Whence came this exemption from executing any '*dishonourable* Office' that the Sovereign might command (unless one's refusal would 'frustrate the End for which Soveraignty was ordained')? Whereas we have had multiple indications that one's inalienable Natural Right to defend one's *life* can trump certain Sovereign commands, there had been no prior hint of a right to refuse obedience on grounds of *honour*. What might Hobbes have in mind here? Perhaps those 'lusts, and other irregular passions of him, or them that have so unlimited a Power in their hands' (XVIII/20, 94)? Does one, then, also have a Natural Right to defend one's honour? Hobbes, ever the realist, knows that men, or at least some if not most men, *act* as if they do. Thus his Eighth Natural Law prohibiting any showing of hatred *or contempt* of one's fellows: 'because all signes of hatred, or contempt, provoke to fight; insomuch as most men choose rather to hazard their life, than not to be revenged' (XV/20, 76). This acknowledgment would seem to pose, at the least, a vexing complication for Hobbes's entire edifice of Natural Laws. For the appeal of the reasoning supporting each Law presumes that everyone's overriding concern is self-preservation – *not* revenge, or any other life-threatening action – such that any person the least bit rational would be determined to avoid at all costs the hazard-filled universal war that is the anarchic State of Nature.

The problem here was first broached by Hobbes in his Chapter 'Of POWER, WORTH, DIGNITY, HONOUR, *and* WORTHINESSE': 'private Duels are, and alwayes will be Honourable, though unlawfull, till such time as there shall be Honour ordained for them that refuse, and Ignominy for them that make the Challenge. For Duels ... for the most part [are] the effects of rash speaking, and of the fear of Dishonour, in one, or both the Combatants; who engaged by rashnesse, are driven into the Lists to avoyd disgrace' (X/49, 45). Men behave thus because doing so is 'Honourable, *though unlawfull*'! To be sure, hardly anyone is indifferent to social status. Indeed, Hobbes contends that 'men are continually in competition for Honour and Dignity,' such that it is a principal cause of quarrel in both the Natural and the Civil state (XVII/7, 86; XIII/5–6, 61). But Honour matters so much to *some* men that they will defy the law and risk death 'to avoyd disgrace.'⁹ The strength of a desire for honour – especially that accorded 'the manly virtue': Courage – is ironically confirmed by the 'Vain-glorious' man, in whom this desire can expose him to ridicule instead:

Vain-glorious men, such as estimate their sufficiency by the flattery of other men, or the fortune of some precedent action, without assured ground of hope from the true knowledge of themselves, are enclined to rash engaging; and in the approach of danger, or difficulty, to retire if they can: because not seeing the way of safety, they will rather hazard their honour, which may be salved with an excuse; than their lives, for which no salve is sufficient. (XI/12, 49)

Yet 'Vain-glorious men' attest to the existence of the real article; as Hobbes several times acknowledges, there are people who genuinely subscribe to a 'death before dishonour' ethos, rather than to 'survival at all costs.' Such men (and women like Lucretia) would not find fully compelling the rationale supporting Hobbes's structure of Natural Laws.¹⁰ Hence, their willing subjection to the rule of Civil Law cannot always be counted upon if death is the severest sanction available to the Sovereign. But the general tenor of Hobbes's book leaves precisely that impression: that since virtually everyone's foremost concern is (supposedly) 'their own preservation' (this being 'The finall Cause' of their willingness to abandon most of their natural liberty in subjecting themselves to a Commonwealth), the Sovereign's power to enforce obedience rests ultimately on everyone's fear of death.¹¹

However, in the chapter expressly devoted to discussing the rewards and punishments available to the Sovereign – these being 'the Nerves and Tendons, that move the limbes and joints of a Common-wealth'¹² – Hobbes specifies *five* categories of punishments: Corporal ('inflicted on the body directly,' including death); Pecuniary; Ignominy; imprisonment; and Exile, or Banishment (XXVIII/13–21, /26, 163–6). The central category, Ignominy, 'is the infliction of such Evill, as is made Dishonourable; or the deprivation of such Good, as is made Honourable by the Common-wealth.' But this latter, the Honours at the disposal of the Sovereign, are hardly mentioned in this chapter, presumably because discussed at some length in chapter 10 ('*Of* POWER [etc.]'):

A Soveraigne doth Honour a Subject, with whatsoever Title, or Office, or Employment, or Action, that he himselfe will have taken for a signe of his will to Honour him.

... So that of Civill Honour, the Fountain is in the person of the Common-wealth, and dependeth on the Will of the Soveraigne, and is therefore temporary, and called *Civill Honour*; such as are Magistracy, Offices, Titles; and in some places Coats, and Scutchions painted: and men Honour such as have them, as having so many signes of favour in the Common-wealth; which favour is Power. (X/35–6, 43–4; cf. /50–2, 45–6)

In short, the Sovereign *does* have some effective means of ruling those so fastidious of their honour that they would risk death rather than disgrace. He can reward them with honour, punish with dishonour (hence with promises and threats of same – including, perhaps, a *dishonourable* death).

But a problem still remains. For though 'the Soveraignty is the fountain of Honour,' it is so only of the public honours within its power to ordain, 'Civill Honour' (e.g., Ranks of conventional nobility; XVIII/19, 93). However, as Hobbes notes in his discussion of Ignominy as punishment:

For there be some things Honorable by Nature; as the effects of Courage, Magnanimity, Strength, Wisdome, and other abilities of body and mind: Others made Honourable by the Common-wealth; as Badges, Titles, Offices, or any other singular marke of the Sovereign's favour. The former, (though they may faile by nature, or accident,) cannot be taken away by a Law; and therefore the losse of them is not a Punishment. But the later may be taken away by the publique authority that made them Honourable, and are properly Punishments: Such are degrading men condemned, of their Badges, Titles, and Offices; or declaring them uncapable of the like in time to come. (XXVIII/19, 164)

Some things are 'Honourable *by Nature*,' meaning that human nature is so constituted that there are qualities and deeds which naturally command people's admiration, including 'the effects' of strength and the traditional virtues of courage, wisdom, and magnanimity. This is especially true of the most visible of the virtues, courage, doubtless because most people are deeply aware of their own fear of death and pain, and so both admire and envy those who give clear evidence that they have mastered that fear. Also, by implication, some things are naturally dishonourable, such as cowardice, pettiness, stupidity, slavishness, and other weaknesses of body or mind. Thus, in discussing the need for the Sovereign to ordain what 'signes of Honour' are to be employed in the public worship of God, Hobbes warns:

But because not all Actions are signes by Constitution; but some are Naturally signes of Honour, others of Contumely, these later (which are those that men are ashamed to do in the sight of them they reverence) cannot be made by humane power a part of Divine worship; nor the former (such as are decent, modest, humble Behaviour) ever be separated from it. (XXXI/39, 192)

However, this recognition that certain things are honourable by Nature, and certain other things naturally dishonourable, raises difficulties for Hobbes's analysis of Honour exclusively in terms of Power.

Hobbes's explicit treatment of Honour and the Honourable takes up fully three-fourths of his chapter on Power (X/16–52, 42–6). It is questionable from the beginning:

The *Value*, or WORTH of a man, is as of all other things, his Price; that is to say, so much as would be given for the use of his Power: and therefore is not absolute; but a thing dependant on the need and judgement of another. An able conductor of Souldiers, is of great Price in time of War present, or imminent; but in Peace not so. A learned and uncorrupt Judge, is much Worth in time of Peace; but not so much in War. And as in other things, so in men, not the seller, but the buyer determines the Price. For let men (as most men do,) rate themselves at the highest Value they can; yet their true Value is no more than it is esteemed by others.

The manifestation of the Value we set on one another, is that which is commonly called Honouring, and Dishonouring. To Value a man at a high rate, is to *Honour* him; at a low rate, is to *Dishonour* him. But high, and low, in this case, is to be understood by comparison to the rate each man setteth on himselfe. (X/16–17, 42)

One may well wonder whether Hobbes really believed his own '*true* Value' to be established thus. Or whether he regarded this mercenary standard of public valuations as valid for a political philosopher at any time, given how rare – yet how vital – is a genuine understanding of political fundamentals (cf. XX/19, 107; XXV/13, 134–5; XXIX/1, 167; XXX/5, 176). Or whether he would unblushingly argue that the 'Price' paid our contemporary sports and film stars, our litigation lawyers and talk show hostesses, does indeed accurately measure their true value – rather than make a mockery of the very idea. Or agree that a cup of hemlock was a fair assessment of Sokrates's value to Athens.

Be all that as it may, on this basis – that the worth of a person is established by the current market value of his apparent relative power, and that this is manifested in the honour (or dishonour) accorded him – Hobbes proceeds to list over a dozen 'naturall wayes of Honouring' (e.g., 'To shew any signe of love, or fear of another, is to Honour'; 'To praise, magnifie, or call happy, is to Honour'; 'To agree with in opinion, is to Honour'; whereas to dissent is to Dishonour). Speaking summarily, he contends that '*Honourable* is whatsoever possession, action, or quality, is an argument and signe of Power' – as if the *only* thing that commands people's admiration is Power, and that it does so unfailingly, irrespective of how power is obtained or used. And lest there be any mistake about this, Hobbes provocatively insists, 'Nor does it alter the case of Honour, whether an action (so it be great and difficult, and consequently a signe of much power,) be just or unjust: for Honour consisteth onely in the opinion of Power.' Consequently, not only grand glory-seeking, but limitless greed is honourable: 'Covetousnesse of great Riches, and ambition of great Honours, are Honourable; as signes of power to obtain them' (X/47–8, 44–5). Surely such claims are meant to give one pause. The peasants of medieval Transylvania doubtless feared the power of Vlad the Impaler; but one suspects they hated rather than honoured him. When one reflects on other vicious tyrants or unscrupulous robber barons, one can scarce resist protesting that we must distinguish genuine honour, respect, and admiration from sycophancy, envy, and flattery born of fear. As it turns out, Hobbes agrees.

So, rhetorically useful as this simplistic analysis of Honour may be for initially establishing a certain perspective on politics ('for political purposes, reduce everything to how it bears on power' – much as Hobbes explicitly reduces the 'more or lesse Desire of ... Riches, of Knowledge, [as well as] of Honour' to the common denominator of a desire for power; VIII/15, 35), this does not square with experience. Nor, not surprisingly then, does it square with Hobbes's own usage. Among his some 250 uses of 'honour' and its cognates in *Leviathan*, there are many that reflect some facet of people's ordinary understanding of the word, e.g., 'And therefore when the Soveraign of a Common-wealth appointeth a Salary to any publique Office, he that receiveth it, is bound in Justice to performe his office; otherwise, he is bound onely in honour, to acknowledgement, and an endeavour of requitall' (XXVIII/24, 166). Here clearly Hobbes uses 'honour' as reflective of an internal sense of moral integrity. And in attacking certain claims of a Scriptural basis for Purgatory, Hobbes insists, 'it is manifest, that the ceremonies of Mourning, and Fasting, when they are used for the death of men, whose life was not profitable to the Mourners, they are used for honours sake to their persons' (XLIV/30, 347). But it is also 'manifest,' I should think, that such honouring of *dead* men, who moreover were 'unprofitable' in life, cannot be out of regard for their *power*. Nor is it otherwise in most cases of honouring the dead. Especially revealing is Hobbes's acknowledgment of honour being rightly due in the *absence* of power, such as his insistence that 'the Fathers of families, when by instituting a Common-wealth, they resigned that absolute Power, yet it was never intended, they should lose the honour due unto them for their [children's] education' (XXX/11, 178). Similarly, he argues that colonies, even though fully independent and self-sufficient, nonetheless owe their Mother country 'Honour, and Friendship' (XXIV/14, 131).

On the other hand, many of the supposed examples Hobbes gives of 'naturall wayes of Honouring' do not necessarily reflect sincere admiration or gratitude at all, but instead may be no more than mercenary flattery and sycophancy, all of which are parasitic on sincere admiration or honouring (e.g., 'To give great gifts to a man'; 'To hearken to a mans counsell, or discourse of what kind soever'; 'To speak to another with consideration, to appear before him with decency, and humility'). All of these work as *signs* of Honour only because there is real admiration and honour (not to mention real affection and gratitude, real caring and good will), which must be analytically distinguished from the mere mercenary appearance of such things. Late in the book, Hobbes himself makes this very point:

And thus Honor is properly of its own nature, secret, and internall in the heart. But the inward thoughts of men, which appear outwardly in their words and actions, are the signes of our Honoring, and these goe by the name of WORSHIP, in Latine CULTUS. Therefore, to Pray to, to Swear by, to Obey, to bee Diligent, and Officious in Serving: in summe, all words and actions that betoken Fear to Offend, or Desire to Please, is *Worship*, whether those words and actions be sincere, or feigned: and because they appear as signes of Honoring, are ordinarily also called *Honor*. (XLV/12, 357; as per Tuck and Facsimile)

To pray to a King for such things, as hee is able to doe for us, though we prostrate our selves before him, is but Civill Worship; because we acknowledge no other power in him, but humane: But voluntarily to pray unto him for fair weather, or for any thing which God onely can doe for us, is Divine Worship, and Idolatry. On the other side, if a King compell a man to it by the terrour of Death, or other great corporall punishment, it is not Idolatry: For the Worship which the Soveraign commandeth to bee done unto himself by the terrour of his Laws, is not a sign that he that obeyeth him, does inwardly honour him as a God, but that he is desirous to save himselfe from death, or from a miserable life; and that which is not a sign of internall honour, is no Worship; and therefore no Idolotry. (XLV/22, 360)

With this in mind – and in the interest of theoretical adequacy – one might amend Hobbes's earlier account: that 'signes of Honouring,' *when insincere*, are explicable only as means of courting the Power of those so honoured. And, doubtless, there is much of that. Whereas, sincere honour is not confined to the honouring of Power – much less of Power simply, regardless of what kind, how acquired, or how used. In the centre of his book, some twenty-one chapters after his initial treatment of Honour and Power, Hobbes subtly acknowledges the *qualified* relationship between the two: 'Honour consisteth of the inward thought, and opinion of the Power, *and Goodnesse* of another' (XXXI/8, 188; emphasis added). Of course, people being the skilled deceivers that Hobbes warns we are, the distinction between sincere and insincere honouring is of limited utility in practical politics – which may be justification enough for his reductionist analysis: stick to what is politically relevant, which means the appearance of honouring, whether sincere or not. Still, genuine Lovers of Honour are lovers of genuine honour, hence of doing and being that which naturally commands sincere admiration and respect.

This being so – that some things are honourable by Nature, others dishonourable – the Sovereign's ability to rule prideful, honour-loving men through controlling the Commonwealth's Economy of Honour must respect the limits set by Nature. Not for nothing does Hobbes call his prescribed regime 'Leviathan' – choosing the name from the Book of Job (as he pointedly tells us), 'where God having set forth the great power of *Leviathan*, calleth him King of the Proud' (XXVIII/27, 166). For the Proud are at the heart of the political problem. Governing proud, honour-loving, death-defying men poses far greater dangers and difficulties than does ruling people whose foremost concern is physical security and comfort. The Sovereign is tacitly advised to avoid, so far as possible, making laws and policies – and especially appointments – that conflict with what is naturally honourable, and instead to align conventional signs and offices of honour so far as practical with what is honourable by nature. Simple prudence dictates that these potentially dangerous honour-lovers be recruited into occupations and practices that serve, rather than subvert, the Commonwealth. Thus they may become the solution to the Commonwealth's most pressing need: for soldiers and police.

The concern to harmonize natural and conventional honour is especially evident in the background of the final three 'Rights of Soveraignes.' For though Hobbes is careful to affirm in the foreground that Sovereigns have the *right* to do as they please in these matters, he makes it clear enough that they *ought* to 'do what's right':

Tenthly, is annexed to the Soveraignty, the choosing of all Counsellours, Ministers, Magistrates, and Officers, both in Peace, and War. For seeing the Soveraign is charged with the End, which is the common Peace and Defence; he is understood to have Power to use such Means, as he shall think most fit for his discharge.

Eleventhly, to the Sovereign is committed the Power of Rewarding with riches, or honour; and of Punishing with corporall, or pecuniary punishment, or with ignominy every Subject according to the Law he hath formerly made; or if there be no Law made, according as he shall judge most to conduce to the encouraging of men to serve the Common-wealth, or deterring of them from doing dis-service to the same.

Lastly, considering what values men are naturally apt to set upon themselves; what respect they look for from others; and how little they value other men; from whence continually arise amongst them, Emulation, Quarrells, Factions, and at last Warre, to the destroying of one another, and diminution of their strength against a Common Enemy; It is necessary that there be Lawes of Honour,[13] and a publique rate of the worth of such men as have deserved, or are able to deserve well of the Common-wealth ... To the Soveraign therefore it belongeth also to give titles of Honour; and to appoint what Order of place, and dignity, each man shall hold; and what signes of respect, in publique or private meetings, they shall give to one another. (XVIII/13–15, 92)

In effect, Hobbes tacitly advises Sovereigns to ensure that 'The publique worth of a man, which is the Value set on him by the Common-wealth ... which men commonly call DIGNITY,' corresponds to that man's 'WORTHINESSE.' This latter 'consisteth in a particular power, or ability for that, whereof he is said to be worthy ... usually named FITNESSE, or *Aptitude.*' So, while Hobbes expressly warns ambitious Subjects that being '*Worthy* of Riches, Office, and Employment' conveys no *right* to them, he at the same time reminds the Sovereign of what sensible people believe is proper in making appointments: that 'he is Worthiest to be a Commander, to be a Judge, or to have any other charge, that is best fitted, with the qualities required to the well discharging of it' (X/18, 42; /53–4, 46–7).

With these considerations in mind, one may understand Hobbes's actual resolution of the contradiction between the individual subject's Natural Law obligation to do whatever he can to survive, and the Commonwealth's need to be stoutly defended if attacked by external enemies. And one thereby also understands why Hobbes's doctrine requires *both* the 'Fundamentall Law of Nature' *and* the summary 'Right of Nature.' For the latter, being a 'liberty to do, or forbeare' allows an individual to *ignore* whenever he so chooses the self-preservation ethos upon which Hobbes has based the rational appeal of adhering to Natural Law. Hence, an individual for whom acting honourably greatly matters – whose self-respect depends upon it, and who places special value on the respect and admiration of fellows he himself respects – may on occasion choose to risk limb and even life should honour and duty require it. For him, it would be cold comfort that 'running away' is not *unjust* by the standards of the Social Covenant; the fact that it would be *dishonourable*, that 'to avoyd battell is not Injustice, but *Cowardice*,' would weigh far more heavily. Such men are a minority, but they must exist in sufficient numbers for any polity to be viable. Hobbes is confident that his prescribed Commonwealth can count on this, provided the Sovereign properly manages the Economy of Honour in the way Hobbes has tacitly indicated.

Of course, when one thinks concretely about everyday life, one readily sees that the relation between Liberty and Mortality is far more complex and varying than the 'either/or' dichotomy would suggest (i.e., either 'maximize your survival prospects,' or 'pay no heed whatsoever to risk of death'). After all, the first alternative – sensible though it may seem at first blush – implies that one would do *anything*, no matter how debased or destructive of others, in order to stay alive. And while most decent people are never themselves moved to imagine the extreme enormities physically possible, they would recoil in horror were they, in fiction or fact, actually confronted with them. Whereupon they would realize, perhaps to their surprise, that they do *not* subscribe to a 'survival above all' ethos. Of course, everyday life confirms this as well. For maximizing one's prospect of survival dictates that one never take any unnecessary risks, however slight: arrange one's home for maximum security from all conceivable hazards, never leave it for any unnecessary purpose (certainly not for anything as frivolous as entertainment), avoid all unnecessary travel, avoid direct exposure to the sun, avoid strangers – indeed, avoid unnecessary contact with other people in general (they may be carrying an infectious disease) – avoid fatty foods. The list is endless.

When one troubles to reason out the way of life implied by a strict and thorough adherence to minimizing danger and maximizing one's safety, one realizes that a life so lived would lose most of its savour. And, consequently, one becomes aware that an *enjoyable* life entails accepting a multiplicity of risks, day in and day out, mostly modest ones but occasionally more threatening ones. Thus the necessity of *some* courage, that strength of soul required to face and abide the unavoidable or otherwise acceptable hazards – and the occasional emergency – that living any sort of respectable human life demands. For Courage is the virtue whereby one copes with Chance. Clearly, people differ as to the degree of risk they are willing to accept in their work and in their play, just as they differ as to how important honour is in the hierarchy of life's satisfactions. Fortunately, it is sufficiently important to a sufficient number of people to make political life possible.

Still, a major question remains. Why is Hobbes not explicit about all this? Why does he not frankly admit that the vital but dangerous tasks of policing and defending the Commonwealth devolve primarily on a special minority: prideful, honour-loving men, who take special satisfaction in being willing and able to do what the majority of people are not? Answering this question adequately leads one to a radically different understanding of Hobbes's intention and prescription than that usually attributed to him. As such, I shall address it fully in Part Two. For now, one might consider whether the open acknowledgment of a reliance on a special class of men would not put the lie to the supposed egalitarian character of Hobbes's Leviathan – with profound reverberations for his entire political project.

14

Nobility
and the Problem of *Hedonism*

Hobbes is famously the originator of a doctrine called 'political hedonism.' The name is apt, for it is *primarily* a *political* doctrine, and in more than one sense. As rightly notes a scholar who has traced out its development, 'the founders of modern political philosophy consciously appropriated the principles of ancient hedonism and transformed them into political principles, making hedonism the major motive force in the rise of the modern liberal-democratic state.'[1] Whatever their other differences, both strands of modern Liberal thought, the Contractarian and the Utilitarian, have historically shared this view: that the Good, at least as humans experience it, is pleasure; and that pain (i.e., distress of any kind) is the Bad. True, the word 'hedonism' – derived from the Greek word for 'pleasure' or 'delight,' *hëdonë*, roughly equivalent to the Latin *voluptas* – is of recent vintage (i.e., nineteenth century). Thus, the term is never used by Hobbes. But it is a fair characterization of the desire for 'commodious living' that he argues is naturally people's principal motivation, accounting – most importantly – for their willing subjection to political authority.

The hedonistic conception of the Good certainly has 'mass appeal.' This fact has long been recognized. Plato's Sokrates warns that acquiring *knowledge* of the Good, in light of which the value and benefit of anything else can be rightly judged, is a long and arduous task. But that, nonetheless, 'seeing' the Good – with the mind, that is – is the ultimate goal of philosophy, for it is the ultimate cause of all things: all Being and Existence, all Truth and Knowledge and Power of Knowing. To most people, however, the matter could hardly be simpler: 'to the Many, it seems that pleasure is the Good.'[2] The view is not unreasonable, for surely pleasure per se is good, and pain likewise bad. But this is practi-

cally irrelevant in as much as it divorces such experiences from their consequences, which are never negligible: even supposedly 'harmless' pleasures may intensify the natural attractiveness of pleasure-seeking, making
rational self-rule that much more difficult; whereas enduring pain may
cultivate endurance per se, to the benefit of self-rule. Still, a life devoid of
pleasure would seem hardly worth living, much less be a good, happy, or
blessed life. And death would be preferable to living with intense,
unremitting pain.

However, granting that pleasure is good need not imply that the Good
is pleasure – a logical error many people are prone to make (though
assuredly not Hobbes). Hence, there may be other, even higher goods
than pleasure; one would surely want to consider, for example, Truth,
Knowledge, Virtue, Freedom, Mastery, Creativity, or even mere Existence. Moreover, whatever the good life, it may have its fair share of
pleasures despite not being a life consciously dedicated to pursuing pleasure. But given most people's simplistic view of happiness, equating it with
the pleasure-filled life, any political teaching that apparently endorses
their view – hence, licenses pleasure-seeking – is naturally apt to be more
attractive than one which rejects what most people feel, and so prefer to
believe, is true.

The doctrine is 'politic' in another distinct but related sense. It is useful
in generating popular support for a polity's promotion of the modern
Baconian conception of science, with its perpetual commitment to 'the
relief of man's estate' through scientific progress. The 'relief' in question,
at least as ordinarily understood, is from fear, pain, toil, and suffering of
all kinds, while providing in their place, comfort and security, 'ease and
sensual delight.' Thus the ruling maxim of public policy in *Leviathan*:
'*Reason* is the *pace*; Encrease of *Science*, the *way*; and the Benefit of mankind, the *end*.' But the knowledge and technological powers gained
through scientific progress further ends other than just those that cater to
popular hedonism. To mention only that which Hobbes is most obviously concerned with: science works to eliminate superstition, thereby
taming religion in the interest of civil obedience, domestic peace, political
unity, and rational rule. At the same time, scientific discoveries provide
'food' for philosophy as originally understood: the pursuit of knowledge
simply for the sake of knowing, or contemplating (*theoria*).

The account of the Good for which Hobbes is so deservedly famous is introduced, appropriately enough, in his chapter on 'The Passions.' For he
would have his reader acknowledge that the true ground of Good and

Evil is not some 'objective' reality discernible by Reason – much less, Revelation – but rather the subjective experience of one's own Passions, specifically, Desires and Aversions: the desire for pleasure and joy, and aversion to pain and grief, from which are derived Love and Hate.

That which men Desire, they are also sayd to LOVE: and to HATE those things, for which they have Aversion. So that Desire, and Love, are the same thing; save that by Desire, we always signifie the Absence of the Object; by Love, most commonly the Presence of the same. So also by Aversion, we signifie the Absence; and by Hate, the Presence of the Object.

Of Appetites, and Aversions, some are born with men; as Appetite of food, Appetite of excretion, and exoneration, (which may also and more properly be called Aversions, from somewhat they feele in their Bodies,) and some other Appetites, not many. The rest, which are Appetites of particular things, proceed from Experience, and triall of their effects upon themselves, or other men ...

Those things which we neither Desire, nor Hate, we are said to *contemne*: CONTEMPT being nothing else but an immobility, or contumacy of the Heart, in resisting the action of certain things; and proceeding from that the Heart is already moved otherwise, by other more potent objects; or from want of experience of them.

And because the constitution of a mans Body, is in continuall mutation; it is impossible that all the same things should always cause in him the same Appetites, and Aversions: much lesse can all men consent, in the Desire of almost any one and the same Object.

But whatsoever is the object of any mans Appetite or Desire; that is it, which he for his part calleth *Good*; and the object of his Hate, and Aversion, *Evill*; and of his Contempt, *Vile* and *Inconsiderable*. For these words of Good, Evill, and Contemptible, are ever used with relation to the person that useth them: There being nothing simply and absolutely so; nor any common Rule of Good and Evill, to be taken from the nature of the objects themselves; but from the Person of the man (where there is no Common-wealth;) or, (in a Common-wealth,) from the Person that representeth it; or from an Arbitrator or Judge, whom men disagreeing shall by consent set up, and make his sentence the Rule thereof.[3] (VI/3–7, 23–4)

Ostensibly, Hobbes is first of all describing how these evaluative words – 'good,' 'evil,' 'contemptible,' and their synonyms and analogues – 'are ever *used*,' to wit, *relativistically*, here meaning 'relative to the evaluator.' But beyond that, he suggests that this is necessarily the case, since there is in truth 'nothing simply and absolutely' good or evil. Hobbes thereby expresses a version of what would today be called 'Value Relativism.' Subsequent recurrences to the doctrine[4] give no indication that this relativism is simply the result of an incorrigible ambiguity in the human use of language – the sort of thing he warned of by way of concluding his chapter '*Of* SPEECH':

The names of such things as affect us, that is, which please, and displease us, because all men be not alike affected with the same thing, nor the same man at all times, are in the common discourses of men, of *inconstant* signification ... For though the nature of that we conceive, be the same; yet the diversity of our reception of it, in respect of different constitutions of body, and prejudices of opinion, gives every thing a tincture of our different passions. And therefore in reasoning, a man must take heed of words; which besides the signification of what we imagine of their nature, have a signification also of the nature, disposition, and interest of the speaker; such are the names of Vertues, and Vices; For one man calleth *Wisdome*, what another calleth *feare*; and one *cruelty*, what another *justice* ... And therefore such names can never be true grounds of any ratiocination. (IV/24, 17)

Inasmuch as politics consists almost entirely of 'such things as affect us, that is, which please and displease us,' one might conclude (as I previously noted) that there is no prospect of a true *science* of politics, not even of one grounded on what men variously 'feare.' But Hobbes has risen to the challenge posed by what he treats as the practical reality of value relativism. Indeed, it is the special virtue of his political prescription that it can not only accommodate this potential source of perpetual disruption – people's wide-ranging disagreements about what is good and evil, hence about the common good – but make it a source of strength and support for the Hobbesian regime. Provided, that is, Hobbes can persuade virtually everyone that the beginning of Wisdom is knowing what one ought *most* to fear.

That possibility itself suggests, however, that some caution is in order here. The fact that practically everyone is apt to *call* 'good' whatever *he* happens to desire, and 'evil' that to which he has an aversion, does not preclude the possibility that some people are *right* about their desires and aversions, and others not. Consequently, what the majority of people 'calleth *Good*' (whatever brings them pleasure; and 'bad' that which threatens pain) may not be identical with Hobbes's own view as to what in reality *is* good or bad.

Moreover, this doctrine of Value Relativism is obviously to be distinguished from a politically innocuous relativism that is inherent in the use of such terms, namely, that they implicitly mean 'relative to the *kind* of thing evaluated': a 'good poem,' for example, means 'good' relative to other poems – not, that is, relative to the goodness of foods, buildings, tools, intentions, actions, outcomes, questions, explanations, hunting, fishing, tests, ideas, jokes, disguises, songs, dances, drugs, trials, skills, governments, policies, weather, or ways of life. The relative goodness of things is implicit in our comparative vocabulary: 'better,' 'best'; worse,' worst'; 'more,' 'most'; 'less,' 'least.' Everyone's use of evaluative terms is with tacit reference to the appropriate *class* of the thing evaluated, whether or not one accepts the now-popular Value Relativism which Hobbes describes.

However, as noted, he not only explicates but apparently *endorses* this relativism – and the de facto hedonism which it legitimates – as *true*. For though he *begins* as if merely describing ordinary usage of these key words, he immediately blurs the distinction between people's language and the phenomena to which they refer, stating flatly that with respect to such evaluations, there is 'nothing simply and absolutely' good, or evil, or contemptible, 'nor any common Rule of Good and Evil, to be taken from the nature of the objects themselves.' This statement would seem to explain *why* 'these words of Good, Evil, and Contemptible, are ever used with relation to the person that useth them.' And there can be no doubt but that endorsement *is* its intended rhetorical effect. However – bearing in mind Hobbes's fondness for irony, and his skill in misdirection – it is *not* the only reasonable interpretation of the statement in question, since it would be equally pertinent to the 'relativity of kind or class' discussed in the preceding paragraph.[5] Moreover, a few moments' reflection on the practical infinitude of things that might be denominated as 'good' (similarly, as 'evil' or 'bad') is sufficient to show why it is most unlikely 'any common Rule of Good and Evil' is to be abstracted 'from the nature of the objects themselves.' Whatever the truth about the Good, it must be sought in some way other than as the least common denominator of everything to which the term might be legitimately applied.

However that may be, if Hobbes's claim is accepted at face value – that 'these words of Good, Evill, and Contemptible, are ever used with relation to the person that useth them' – a serious reader must examine with special care Hobbes's *own* use of such terms. Does his usage suggest that he himself regards good and evil as radically relativistic, inherently subjective and inconstant? It does not. Moreover, it would be most surprising if it did. After all, is not a governing premise of *Leviathan* that most people heretofore have not known what is objectively, permanently, hence truly good for them, namely, understanding political life in the terms that Hobbes sets forth in this treatise? Some textual evidence implying Hobbes's non-relativistic understanding of the Good will be adduced in what follows. But one might begin with the warning in his Introduction about the hazard of presuming to understand all human behaviour on the basis of one's own, thus being 'for the most part deceived, by too much trust, or too much diffidence; as he that reads [other men], is himself a good or evil man.'[6] Can one make any sense of this warning if 'a good or evil man' means nothing more than Hobbes's subjective preference for men who please him (being, whatever else, the 'too-trusting type'), and his dislike of those who annoy him? Even if, as is probable, he likes certain kinds of people and dislikes (perhaps even hates) others, might not this be *because* the former truly are *good* – that as a matter of both taste and principle, he likes good people, as decent people generally do – whereas the latter *are* bad or evil?

We are provided an indication of Hobbes's own view in the very course of citing Scriptural support for his claim that 'It belongeth therefore to the Soveraigne to bee *Judge*, and to praescribe the Rules of *discerning Good* and *Evill*: which Rules are Lawes.' Along with a dozen other examples, he invokes the disobedience of Adam and 'the Woman,' as told in *Genesis*:

For the Cognisance or Judicature of *Good* and *Evill*, being forbidden by the name of the fruit of the tree of Knowledge, as a triall of *Adams* obedience; The Divell to enflame the Ambition of the Woman, to whom that fruit already seemed beautifull, told her that by tasting it, they should be as Gods, knowing *Good* and *Evill*. Whereupon having both eaten, they did indeed take upon them Gods office, which is Judicature of Good and Evill; but acquired no new ability to distinguish between them aright. And whereas it is sayd, that having eaten, they saw they were naked; no man hath so interpreted that place, as if they had been formerly blind, and saw not their own skins: the meaning is plain, that it was then they first judged their nakednesse (wherein it was Gods will to create them) to be uncomely; and by being ashamed, did tacitely censure God himselfe. (XX/17, 106)

Notice, it is *Hobbes* who assures us that they had 'no new ability' to distinguish Good and Evil '*aright*.' But just as they retained their previous eyesight, we may presume they still experienced Pleasure and Pain as they always had. Apparently, then, *that* is *not* sufficient for *rightly* judging what is Good or Evil. In light of passages such as these, it is exceedingly hard – I think impossible – to believe that Hobbes himself subscribes to the political hedonism he preaches.

And careful consideration of his careful words confirms that, strictly speaking, Hobbes himself is *not* a hedonist: '*Pleasure* therefore, (or *Delight*,) is the apparence, or sense of Good; and *Molestation* or *Displeasure*, the apparence, or sense of Evill' (VI/11, 25). That is, Pleasure is *not* itself the Good; rather, Pleasure is an *appearance* of the Good, or sensory evidence of what is good (likewise Displeasure vis-à-vis Evil, or Bad).[7] Thus, pleasure and pain are merely the usual *signs* or *attendants* of what is good and bad, as one might regard the pleasing taste and aroma of 'good,' i.e., nutritious food, and the pain of fire. The difference is conveniently illustrated with the example of Health. Is it desired *because* it is naturally good, that is, an objective condition in which a person's 'Faculties of Body and Mind' function at the peak of his or her 'Naturall Power' – hence, desired because such a condition is rightly and truly *desirable* (much as Hobbes acknowledges some qualities are honoured because honourable by nature)? Or, is Health good simply because it is in fact desired, and desired because feeling healthy is pleasant, whereas feeling sick is unpleasant and injuries are painful? Regarding pleasure itself as the Good, and pain as the Bad or Evil obscures the question of *why* people are constituted to experience pleasure and pain in the manner and from the things as they do – as if a mother's milk just happens to be desired by her baby, and is *good* for the baby merely because it takes pleasure in satisfying its hunger therewith.

Although Hobbes generally treats what *appears* as evidence of what *is*, he does several times remind his reader that appearances can be deceiving. For example, some men adopt a pose of preoccupation simply in order to generate a false appearance of 'gravity' (X/43, 44).[8] And the images 'which appeareth in a Dream ... or in a Looking-glasse ... are nothing else but creatures of the Fancy,' though some men mistakenly 'think [them] to be real, and externall Substances' (XII/7, 53). For people, being fallible, are liable to regard as 'reall Substances' apparitions that are actually but 'Accidents of the brain' (XXXIV/17, 211). The senses themselves can be fooled, 'as pressing, rubbing, or striking the Eye, makes us fancy a light; and pressing the Eare, produceth a dinne' (I/4, 3; cf. XLV/1–2, 352). Moreover, 'Passions and Selfe-love' can distort both perception and judgment, such that 'every little payment' the Sovereign requires in order to fulfil his responsibilities 'appeareth a great grievance' (XVIII/20, 94). What is true of Appearances in general, then – that they are not invariably indicative of Reality – may apply to '*Pleasure* therefore, (or *Delight*,) [as] the apparence, or sense of Good; and *Molestation* or *Displeasure*, the apparence, or sense of Evill.' Hence, the goodness and badness associated with some pleasures and pains may be as illusory as images in dreams and nightmares. Indeed, if things can sometimes appear the very opposite of what they truly are, some pleasureful things may be downright bad. Hobbes's carefully chosen words leave open this possibility.

The fact remains, however, that Hobbes has gone to some trouble to appear a proponent of political hedonism. Necessarily so, as it is the conception of the Good whence the rationale for his political prescription takes its bearings. If one regards it in that light for the sake of further examination, there are several preliminary points worth noting about Hobbes's presentation of the doctrine.

First and foremost, one must bear in mind that Hobbes himself remains free to use all these 'value' terms *non*-relativistically, as if they referred to objective reality – not, that is, as mere indications of subjective assessments grounded in nothing more substantial than his own variable passions. He may have sought, and found, what is truly Good by Nature.

Second, though for all *practical* purposes Hobbes's Political Hedonism treats the Good as profoundly relativistic and subjective – being whatever a given person finds pleasing – in a certain analytical sense goodness remains absolute and objective.

Of Pleasures, or Delights, some arise from the sense of an object present; and those may be called *Pleasures of Sense*, (The word *sensuall*, as it is used by those onely that condemn them, having no place till there be Lawes.) Of this kind are all Onerations and Exonerations of the body; as also all that is pleasant, in the *Sight, Hearing, Smell, Tast, or Touch*; Others arise from the Expectation, that proceeds from foresight of the End, or Consequence of things; whether those things in the Sense Please or Displease: And these are *Pleasures of the Mind* of him that draweth those consequences; and are generally called JOY. In the like manner, Displeasures, are some in the Sense, and called PAYNE; others, in the Expectation of consequences, and are called GRIEFE. (VI/12, 25)

There is an objective, knowable truth about the Good that is grounded in the nature of things: the Good is experienced as pleasure, pleasure is real, and the experience of it cannot be gainsaid. Thus, the Good is not *radically* subjective, such that it is *whatever* a given person chooses to regard as good. This has consequences.

While acceptance of the doctrine precludes arguing that something which a person finds pleasing is not 'really' (to that extent) sensed as *good*, one can propose (e.g.) that something else would be *better* (i.e., provide still more pleasure), or, insist that certain activities are positively bad (e.g., self-abasement, self-mutilation, perhaps all 'mortification of the flesh' in the name of piety). For if one responds that someone might take pleasure in causing himself pain – not for some ulterior purpose, but simply to experience the pain – the doctrine of hedonism becomes incoherent. Whereas, if causing oneself pain is in pursuit of an ulterior purpose, it must *per hedonism* be one that pays off in greater pleasure (and not in greater sanctity, say – as that would imply something besides pleasure is good, e.g., God's grace – hence that the Good itself is still higher, in light of which one can understand the goodness of both pleasure and grace). The practical point, however, is this: hedonism does allow for advising other people, and even for evaluating whole ways of life, insofar as one is confident as to what provides pleasure or causes useless, unnecessary pain. Thus, there is nothing contradictory in Hobbes's advising us all to support our Sovereign, whatever the cost.

Third, the doctrine is profoundly Humanistic in the ancient, Protagorean sense: 'man is the measure.' Just as the tree falling in the forest makes no sound unless someone is there to hear it, so nothing is either good or evil unless someone is either pleased or pained by it, or by the thought of it. This, too, has consequences worth considering. For example, a man with the perverse taste of a vandal – that is, who positively enjoys destroying things – might cause great damage in some remote wilderness, yet do thereby no evil provided no one else is aware of it. Indeed, in pleasing himself, he will have done that much good. Whereas, the person who unwittingly saves some unseen beauty from destruction will not have done anything good (unless and until someone sees it).

Fourth, Hobbes's treatment of Pleasures and Displeasures of the Mind seems peculiarly inapt, or at least misleading in being grossly incomplete – as if these were simply and exclusively imagined expectations of sensual pleasure and pains. Thus, it neglects, if not excludes, pleasures truly *of the mind*, most notably that which attends the 'singular Passion' of man called Curiosity: the '*Desire* to know why, and how ... which is a Lust of the mind, that by the perseverance of delight in the continuall and indefatigable generation of Knowledge, exceedeth the short vehemence of any carnall Pleasure' (VI/35, 26). But it also leaves out of account the pleasures and pains that ancient thinkers associated with the part of the human soul that (as noted before) Hobbes chooses to ignore, the Spirit (*thumos*) – such as the pleasing beauty of poetry and other fine art and music, and not least 'that exultation of the mind which is called GLORYING,' which arises 'from imagination of a mans own power and ability' (VI/39, 26–7).

Fifth, there is a curious asymmetry in how Hobbes has expressed himself: 'But whatsoever is the object of any mans Appetite or Desire; that is it, which he for his part calleth *Good*; and the object of his Hate and Aversion, *Evill*' (VI/7, 24). Notice, 'Hate and Aversion' is *not* contrastingly paired, as one would expect, with 'Love and Desire,' but instead with 'Appetite and (redundantly) Desire.' Is Hobbes subtly acknowledging what anyone well acquainted with life knows to be true: that a person may love what he or she suspects, or even knows, to be *not* good, whether not good for his or her self, or not good simply, however pleasing or otherwise attractive?

Sixth, the plausibility of Hedonism rests on a conflation of pleasure with satisfaction and happiness. Typically, pleasures are discrete experiences that arise from readily identifiable causes, whereas the feelings of satisfaction and happiness are quite different, typically more general, even comprehensive in the case of happiness. One's general satisfaction with an outcome, a policy, a job, an education, a marriage, a residence, or the state of public services is not a matter of a quantity or sequence of whatever pleasures (or pains) may (or may not) be involved. But such satisfactions can certainly affect one's overall happiness. On the other hand, endless pleasure-seeking can be a symptom of deep dissatisfaction with one's life, of seeking to escape profound unhappiness through the transient distraction various pleasures provide. Hobbes only once uses 'happy' in the moral sense: 'To praise, magnifie, or call happy, is to Honour; because nothing but goodnesse, power, and felicity is valued' (X/25, 43). As in the line quoted, Hobbes prefers to speak of 'felicity,'[9] about which he assures his reader:

[T]he Felicity of this life, consisteth not in the repose of a mind satisfied. For there is no such *Finis ultimus*, (utmost ayme,) nor *Summum Bonum*, (greatest Good,) as is spoken of in the Books of the old Morall Philosophers. Nor can a man any more live, whose Desires are at an end, than he, whose Senses and Imaginations are at a stand. Felicity is a continuall progresse of the desire, from one object to another; the attaining of the former, being still but the way to the later. The cause whereof is, That the object of mans desire, is not to enjoy once onely, and for one instant of time; but to assure for ever, the way of his future desire. And therefore the voluntary actions, and inclinations of all men, tend, not onely to the procuring, but also to the assuring of a contented life; and differ onely in the way: which ariseth partly from the diversity of passions, in diverse men; and partly from the difference of the knowledge, or opinion each one has of the causes, which produce the effect desired. (XI/1, 47)

If this characterization of human life is understood as that of endless pleasure-seeking, with no prospect of attaining some stable ground of overall contentment and satisfaction with one's life, it would seem man is condemned to a base and futile existence. However, Hobbes need not be so understood. True enough, to be alive is to experience desires 'endlessly,' beginning with those most necessary to sustaining life itself: for food and drink. And there are sensual pleasures that naturally attend the gratification of one's discrete desires. But, as Hobbes knows, a contented life does not simply reduce to the assurance of future such gratifications. Were he to be believed, 'every man is contented with his share' of wisdom already and so does not likely strive for more (XIII/2, 61); and everyone *should* 'be content with so much liberty against other men, as he would allow other men against himselfe' (XIV/5, 65). Moreover, Hobbes expressly acknowledges that people do desire things other than their own pleasure, especially happiness, and even the happiness of others – for so one can interpret '*Desire* of good to another, BENEVOLENCE, GOOD WILL, CHARITY. If to man generally, GOOD NATURE' (VI/22, 26).

Seventh, then, is the problem within Political Hedonism of how to conceive the 'common good,' a 'name' that occurs only thrice in Hobbes's *Leviathan*, although a few uses of synonymous terms also figure ('common benefit'; 'common businesse'; 'publique interest'; 'publique good'). Curiously, the most concentrated occurrence of such terms is in the context of Hobbes's contrasting human beings with 'Bees, and Ants' – e.g., 'amongst these creatures, the Common good differeth not from the Private; and being by nature enclined to their private, they procureth thereby the common benefit'; 'having not (as man) the use of reason, do not see, nor think they see any fault, in the administration of their common businesse' (XVII/8–9, 86–7). With one largely irrelevant exception,[10] the only explicit mention of the Common Good in connection with human affairs has to do with the distribution of land: 'wherein the Soveraign assigneth to every man a portion, according as he, and not according as any Subject, or any number of them, shall judge agreeable to Equity, and the Common Good' (XXIV/6, 128). This single reference is augmented, however, by three mentions of 'the publique good,' and by three references to 'the Good of the People.' For example, Hobbes's list of the Rights of Sovereign includes that 'of Judging when [making war and peace] is for the publique good' (XVIII/12, 92; cf. XXVI/42, 150; XLII/70, 296).[11]

As the various lines quoted above clearly imply, there *is* a common or public good to be realized in a well-ordered commonwealth, and it is the Sovereign's responsibility to see to it. This means that he, at least, must have a clear idea of what that *is*. So how, then, is the *common* good rightly conceived, given that each of the composing individuals is presumed to be primarily, if not exclusively, self-interested? Indeed, is not this the main intellectual appeal of Political Hedonism: its apparent 'realism' about human behaviour? That it offers a seemingly realistic psychology of human motivation in terms of pleasure-seeking and pain-avoiding, as well as a simple, straightforward epistemology and ontology of the Good? On this view, each person has at most only an instrumental interest in the good of his fellow covenanters. There is no suggestion, for instance, of an obligation for anyone to concern himself with promoting 'the greatest happiness of the greatest number' of his fellows, much less doing so irrespective of its bearing on his own pleasures and pains. Such a doctrine would be more akin to the utopianism of Christ Jesus's Sermon on the Mount than to Hobbes's earthy practicality.

But if a hedonistic conception of the common good is *not* simply a maximization of the total quantity of pleasure (while minimizing total pain), then what is it? Prompted by Hobbes's mention of 'Equity' in the Sovereign's apportioning land, one might generalize from this: the common good is the maximization of so much pleasure and the minimization of so much pain as the Sovereign judges to be compatible with the *equitable distribution* of both. Is Equity per se, then, *also good*? But whether it is or not, why should we regard whoever is endowed with all the rights and powers of Sovereignty, be it one man or many, as exempt from the self-interested hedonism that supposedly dominates everyone else – such that he, or they, take a sincere interest in Equity and the Common Good?

Hobbes expressly claims the contrary, invoking it as an argument for the superior 'Convenience' of Monarchy:

First, that whosoever beareth the Person of the people, or is one of that Assembly that bears it, beareth also his own naturall Person. And though he be carefull in his politique Person to procure the common interest; yet he is more, or no lesse, carefull to procure the private good of himselfe, his family, kindred and friends; and for the most part, if the publique interest chance to crosse the private, he preferrs the private: for the Passions of men, are commonly more potent than their Reason. From whence it follows, that where the publique and private interest are most closely united, there is the publique most advanced. Now in Monarchy, the private interest is the same with the publique. The riches, power, and honour of a Monarch arise onely from the riches, strength and reputation of his Subjects. For no King can be rich, nor glorious, nor secure; whose Subjects are either poore, or contemptible, or too weak through want, or dissension, to maintain a war against their enemies. (XIX/4, 96)

Better still, one wants to add, would be having as Monarch the *un*common kind of man whose passions are *not* more potent than his reason. In any case, true though Hobbes's conclusion may be, the argument as a whole is inadequate – and from both directions, as it were. For example, the honour that might accrue to a king from his personal valour, temperance, wisdom, justness, or strategic acumen would not be attributable to the qualities of his subjects. Indeed, his greatest honour might derive from his employing those virtues to transform a weak, poor, dispersed, and despised populous into a unified people who are strong, prosperous, and admired for their strong sense of civic pride. Is it credible that a natural Prince – a 'Moses, Cyrus, Romulus, or Theseus', say – would undertake such a challenge simply for the *pleasure* it might bring?[12] On the other hand, a typical Subject witnessing the lavish lifestyle of his Sovereign would not likely concede that the Monarch's 'private interest is the same' as that of the 'publique.' Be all this as it may, there is no indication here that the public interest is anything other than the sum of individual or 'private' interests – presumably construed in terms of pleasures and pains – with every citizen-subject sharing a vital interest in maintaining a strong sovereign, whatever that entails.

One may wonder, however, whether a strictly hedonistic conception of the Good, hence of the Common Good, could inspire *anyone* to make personal sacrifices on its behalf, to forgo his own pleasure and perhaps endure pain – to say nothing of risk death – simply in the interest of promoting and protecting other people's pleasures.

The more one thinks about it, however, the most perplexing feature of Hobbes's presentation of Political Hedonism is his inclusion of a separate paragraph on *contempt*:

Those things which we neither Desire, nor Hate, we are said to *contemne*: CON-TEMPT being nothing else but an immobility or contumacy of the Heart, in resisting the action of certain things; and proceeding from that the Heart is already moved otherwise, by other more potent objects: or from want of experience of them.' (VI/5, 24)

As everyone would acknowledge, valid analysis of human experience requires other categories of things besides the two sets most pertinent to hedonism (Desire-Love-Pleasure *versus* Aversion-Hate-Pain). For no one simply bifurcates the world in those terms. There are indeed things for which one does feel positive contempt. But about the vast, *vast* majority of things of which people are aware, they feel – neither desire, nor aversion, nor contempt – but (instead) *indifference*, or *neutrality*.[13] Nor is this because their 'hearts' are so preoccupied with 'more potent objects' that these many other things simply make no impression. A person may be fully conscious of them – even admire some or otherwise acknowledge their value, while ignoring many things as personally irrelevant – but neither desire, detest, nor despise them.

Consider a commonplace experience: strolling through a shopping mall. One will see things (including other people) for which one feels at least a tinge of desire (but hardly love); other things one dislikes (sushi, perhaps), even a few one positively loathes; and still other things one despises or contemns (including some people's behaviour, or choice of dress). But one will be indifferent to most of what one sees. Being well past my athletic prime, I care little about what is on sale in the huge sports emporia. I am not in the market for any furniture. Modern so-called drug stores abound with products, both pharmaceutical and cosmetic, which I cannot imagine my ever having any use for. As a man, I have no interest in women's clothing or shoes, regardless of price, quality, colour, or style. Video games and their players hold no appeal for me. Never having taken to cooking, I feel at most bemusement about various gadgets on display in a Kitchen and Bath Boutique. Owning only one particular kind of car, most of what is available in the auto parts store is of no use to me, though I presume it is to someone or other. But I do not regard as '*Vile* and *Inconsiderable*' all these and countless other things about which I am indifferent.

Hobbes's implying that a person contemns whatever he neither desires nor detests is so implausible, so obviously contrary to ordinary human experience, that one can only wonder why he bothers to claim it. Might it be meant to encourage thoughtful readers to consider the larger implications of this distinctly human response called 'feeling contempt' – especially as it enters into human relations? For if there is one category of things with respect to which the distinction between indifference and contempt can be fuzzy, it is people. Virtually everyone is to some extent sensitive to how they are regarded by others, and thus liable to interpret certain manifestations of indifference as contempt (e.g., one's words, or mere presence being ignored). Because 'every man looketh that his companion should value him, at the same rate he sets upon himself ... all signes of contempt, or undervaluing' are potent sources of quarrel (XIII/5, 61). Indeed, Hobbes hints that not just contempt for, but indifference to, 'the calamity of others' may be regarded as outright 'cruelty' (VI/47, 28). Moreover, there are individuals who are conspicuously proud, or vain, or insecure, hence hypersensitive to anything they interpret as disrespect, and accordingly prone to 'seek satisfaction' – and there are many forms of revenge-seeking besides duels, almost all of which are prejudicial to civil harmony. Doubtless Hobbes is right that a rational man, fully confident of his worth, would ignore 'words of disgrace or some little injuries' which a lesser man fears that 'unlesse he revenge it, he shall fall into contempt, and consequently be obnoxious to the like injuries from others' (XXVII/20, 155). But since some, if not 'most men choose rather to hazard their life, than not to be revenged,' Hobbes prescribes his Eighth Law of Nature: '*That no man by deed, word, countenance, or gesture, declare Hatred, or Contempt of another*' (XV/20, 76). Hence, be careful in showing indifference, also.

However, there is a more important reason for thinking about contempt. Just as the counterpart of Desire is Aversion, and likewise Hate of Love, so is there a feeling directly *contrary* to Contempt, namely, *Admiration*. It is not a term that Hobbes uses a lot, though he does so often enough to remind us of the phenomenon. But here one encounters an immediate complication: the definition he asserts in the chapter on the passions is strangely partial, if not downright strange ('*Joy*, from apprehension of novelty, ADMIRATION; proper to Man, because it excites the appetite of knowing the cause'; VI/38, 26). This squares with neither the ordinary meaning of the term, nor with most (if any) of Hobbes's own uses – which do partake of the ordinary meaning.[14] He speaks, for example, of some men's desire for 'admiration, or being flattered for excellence in some art, or other ability of the mind' (XI/2, 47); he argues that whatever qualities we 'attribute to God' are not descriptive, but merely indicate 'how much wee admire him, and how ready we would be to obey him'

(XXXI/28, 191); and he warns the Sovereign that his people 'are to be taught, that they ought not to be led with admiration of the vertue of any of their fellow Subjects, how high soever he stand, nor how conspicuously soever he shine in the Common-wealth' (XXX/8, 177). Suffice it to say, Hobbes clearly acknowledges the existence of this particular reaction of the human spirit to certain conspicuous displays or accounts of virtue, valour, service, skill, strength, benevolence, stamina, dedication, creativity, and other kinds of human eminence, as well as of conspicuous beauty.

The Greeks had a word for that which we naturally admire: *To Kalon*, a term that originally meant 'The Beautiful' but evolved to include whatever commands admiration, notably 'The Noble' and 'The Moral.' The possible existence of things 'admirable by nature' challenges the adequacy of the hedonistic conception of the Good – that is, the simple, unqualified view that Pleasure is *the* Good, hence all pleasures of whatever kind are equally good *as pleasure*, and differ only in amount and 'purity' (i.e., degree of admixture with prior or subsequent pain). For anyone holding this view, the only rational consideration with respect to living the best life available is *quantitative*. But if *To Kalon* is *real* – such that one can assess things as to whether they are more or less *kalos*, and thus *qualitatively* assess pleasures as to which are the higher, more beautiful or nobler, and which the lower, base pleasures – then Hedonism, in regarding base pleasures as equal to the noble, is itself *base*. For baseness, or vulgarity, would essentially *be* a comparative insensitivity, thus indifference to the distinction between beautiful and ugly, noble and base, high and low.[15] Moreover, if *To Kalon* is not only real, but *good*, then Hedonism is *false*. For goodness is not, then, reducible to Pleasure. And to be clear about this, there is no possibility of a 'refined hedonism' that does not concede the Good to be something other, and higher, than pleasure. For he who rejects 'vulgar hedonism,' wishing to endorse instead the Epicurean conception of the Good Life (that only the 'finer pleasures,' the 'higher pleasures,' the 'pleasures worthy of a human being' – especially the pleasures of beauty and friendship – are good),[16] thereby tacitly acknowledges that the Good is higher than Pleasure per se: that it is something sovereign in light of which one may *discriminate* among pleasures, not with respect to whether they are more or less pleasing, but whether they are higher or lower, noble or base, wholesome or degenerative, human or bestial, ... good or bad.

The question of the Noble is of paramount importance, both politically and personally. How one answers it determines (for example) whether various forms of self-denial and self-sacrifice in the interest of one's fellows may be good, even if unpleasant. In addressing this question, it is helpful to begin one's consideration of *To Kalon* with Beauty. For the fact that humans recognize, appreciate, and are attracted by Beauty, and are offended and repulsed by what they find ugly, is undeniable. Moreover, this aesthetic sensitivity is as unique to human beings as Perplexity, Wonder, Reason, and Comedy. Despite the cliché that Beauty is 'all in the eyes of the beholder' – that is, something utterly and entirely subjective – this is surely not true. There is a vast amount of 'inter-subjective' and 'cross-cultural' *agreement* on what is beautiful that cannot be accounted for apart from the qualities of the *object* beheld. While people may argue endlessly over who is the very most beautiful man or woman in the world, everyone would concede this much: most of us are not in the running. Now, why is that? Mustn't it have a lot to do with how we *look* – the perceptible properties of *us* as 'objects'? The world has countless places so renowned for their natural beauty that people of all colours, races, religions, and traditions travel great distances to view them. Like-wise, the acknowledged masterpieces of architecture, and the famous col-lections of painting and sculpture, pottery and textiles, jewellery and glassworks.

The infinitude of effort that humans have invested in creating things of beauty for beauty's sake, but also in decorating utilitarian objects – including weapons and other accoutrements of war – and not least of all in beautifying themselves, attests to both the importance and the reality of Beauty: there *really are* distinct perceptible and intelligible configura-tions of phenomena to which human souls react with the special delight we experience as something beautiful. And likewise phenomena we call 'ugly' because of the special repugnance that they arouse; virtually every-one feels some revulsion at the sight of grossly deformed or mutilated bodies, or squalid slums, or even certain forms of life (such as croco-diles).[17] Any plausible analysis of aesthetics must accept the *experience* of Beauty and Ugliness as 'the given.' And at least *some* analysis of Beauty is possible, particularly of concrete instances, even if the terms used (e.g., symmetry, balance, harmony, grace, unity, warmth, repose, and such) often seem hardly less abstract than what they purport to explain. This is equally so of the account of '*Beautifull*' that Hobbes himself postulates – 'the *Mine*, or Countenance, that promiseth Good' (VI/8, 24) – with its intriguing correlate, 'Forme is Power; because being a promise of Good, it recommendeth men to the favour of women and strangers' (X/13, 41–2). Nice examples, incidentally, of Hobbes's non-hedonistic use of the word, as it is no more likely that we are to understand this 'promise of Good' as the 'promise of *Pleasure*' than in the case of 'Honour [as] the inward thought, and opinion of the Power, and Goodnesse of another' (XXXI/8, 188).

While it is surely true that most people's aesthetic appreciation is prejudiced in favour of whatever modes and styles of beauty are familiar to them, this does not render them incapable of appreciating what is foreign. Some foreign artefacts strike us as beautiful the first time we see them. And this is typical of visible Beauty: one's reaction to it is practically instantaneous. Nonetheless, a person's aesthetic sense, which the Classical philosophers associate primarily with the spirited part of the human soul, is educable; taste can be both broadened and narrowed, both liberalized and refined, through experience and rational analysis. Even apart from differences of aesthetic education, however, not everyone's soul is affected the same way or to the same extent by the forms of sights and sounds; some strictly personal element remains, presumably grounded in differences of nature as well as of nurture. Thus, while the time-worn cliché grossly exaggerates the degree of disagreement about Beauty and quite mistakes its implication, its being partially true accounts for its persistence as a cliché. Similarly, the view that beauty is 'all a matter of taste,' with the implication that 'naturally' people's tastes differ. But this common opinion is matched with a broad acceptance of another: that there is such a thing as *good* taste (in whatever), and that some people conspicuously have it, and so can advise others (be it about clothes or decor, manners or music). Granted, who does and does not have 'really' good taste can generate heated (and irresolvable) controversy; but that we readily eliminate from consideration whole swaths of mankind without any controversy whatsoever is equally significant for reaching a sound judgment about the nature of Beauty.

With these facts in mind, consider now The Noble. And one might start by pondering the Greeks' conflation of it with The Beautiful, both being comprised by *To Kalon* – much as the meaning of its opposite, *To Aischron*, ranges from 'The Ugly or Deformed' to 'The Base or Shameful.' In this latter case, as in the former, Greeks regarded as somehow the *same* what we would usually, but not always, distinguish. For occasionally we, too, might describe some conspicuous act of courage or generosity or thoughtfulness as 'a beautiful thing to do,' and, on the other hand, characterize an especially shameful outcome as 'an ugly business' – thus attesting to our own souls' tendency to assimilate beauty and nobility, and likewise shameful with ugly. What does this imply? First of all, a similar kind of reality: just as some things but not others strike us as beautiful, there *really are* traits and dispositions, actions and outcomes that naturally command our admiration. We recognize them as exceptional in some good sense: the passerby who risks his life to rescue children from a burning building, or an icy river; the woman who donates a healthy kidney to someone who would otherwise be reliant upon a dialysis machine; the person who finds a large sum of money and searches out its rightful owner; the man who intervenes to prevent a mugging. And just as the psychic reaction to Beauty is the fundamental datum, so too our natural response to what we recognize as a noble act.

The other side of this coin – recognition of the shameful or base – is equally important, and equally revealing. Any decent person feels disgust as well as indignation upon hearing of a fraudster who preys on elderly retirees, bilking them of their life savings. And would we not rightly despise a person who witnessed a serious auto accident, but found it too bothersome or expensive to use his cell phone to call for emergency assistance? Or a lazy man who prostituted his daughter to support his indolence? Is not such behaviour shameful, irrespective of whether the offender himself feels shame? Indeed, he is all the more debased if he does not, for as Nietzsche observes, 'Whoever despises himself still nonetheless respects himself as one who despises.'[18] Moreover, are not certain *pleasures* inherently ignoble, shameful, perverse, even monstrous – and for that very reason, far from good, but downright *bad*, regardless of how pleasureful?

Consider an extreme example: the man who tortures dogs and cats to observe their agony, taking pleasure in causing pain – and we must face the fact that he really does enjoy it, going to some trouble to acquire the animals for this purpose. Do we condemn such behaviour on the basis of some 'hedonistic calculus,' in which we suppose that the animals suffer more pain than the pleasure enjoyed by the man (as if it would matter whether we might 'greatly underestimate' his pleasure)? Or is this form of pleasure-seeking shameful regardless? The example may seem unclear, yet notice: we do no such calculation, nor is it likely we could if we wanted to. But if one were ruled solely by hedonistic principles (which preclude any qualitative distinction between human and bestial pleasure and pain), this would be the only rational ground for condemnation.[19]

Still, where one person's 'perverse' pleasure is at the expense of some other sentient creature's pain, one may not be confident as to the precise nature of one's psychic reaction. Is one experiencing primarily revulsion at the ignobility of the pleasure, or indignation aroused by injustice?[20] Consider, then, whether there are 'harmless' yet ignoble pleasures. Consider gluttony. True, it is not really harmless in that it typically results in obesity and other deleterious effects on the glutton's health, but why should that matter to anyone otherwise unaffected by his indulgence? If nonetheless one cannot help despising gluttons, or dirty and unkempt people, or habitually slothful people, or those who are rude and careless, or who delight in public obscenity – why not? In analysing one's feelings in such cases, it may still be difficult to decide whether one's aversion is aesthetic, or moral. Is one objecting to ugliness or to ignobility? But such ambiguity is itself revealing of why the Greeks regarded these as species of the same genus, denominated *To Aischron*.

Finally, consider the man who declines to speak in defence of an accused person he knows to be innocent merely because he fears public scorn, since the accused is of a widely despised group. To be sure, the feeling of being scorned can be unpleasant. Nonetheless, his behaviour is unjust; but it is also cowardly (which, not incidentally, illustrates the unity of the virtues: standing up for justice often requires courage, much as being just oneself often requires moderation). Thus, while we feel indignation on behalf of the falsely accused, we also feel contempt for this moral coward, who lacked sufficient strength of soul to endure scorn in a righteous cause. And are not both feelings equally justified? That much as acceding to the punishment of a person known to be innocent is by nature unjust (cf. XXVIII/22, 165), so is such cowardly timidity *really* ignoble, base, shameful.

Admittedly, most of us are not apt to experience any such feelings apart from a civilizing nurture. But this need not imply that their activation is always and entirely according to 'socially constructed' standards – as if virtually anything could be treated as just or unjust, noble or shameful, and people socialized to respond likewise. The effects of Courage, Magnanimity, Strength, and Wisdom are, as Hobbes affirms, 'things Honourable *by Nature*' (XXVIII/19, 164). Thus they naturally command the admiration of people practically everywhere; moreover, explaining why so is not all that difficult. Still, there is no doubt that people can and do hold differing views as to what in particular is (most) just, moral, noble, and decent – somewhat as they do with respect to beauty in various things. Moreover, in the vast majority of cases, these differences are traceable in large part to the respective social environments in which people are nurtured. But it is a fact of some importance that no known society is without broadly accepted criteria for making some such evaluations. Similarly important is the amount of *agreement* among societies regarding these matters.

The fact remains, however, that there are well-attested differences in moral evaluations, both within and between societies. This points to the main respect in which things we call 'beautiful' differ from those we speak of as 'noble' or 'admirable.'[21] There is generally more rational content implicit in judgments of the latter; challenged, most people can give *some* sort of reasoning, however partial or prejudice-laden, as to why they regard a particular action, policy, or person as noble or morally admirable. So, whereas people's reactions to the perceptible beauty of something is typically immediate (for which no one expects reasons), a person's admiring response to a particular action may be equally immediate, but nonetheless depend upon a certain understanding of *what* was actually done, and *why* (and sometimes even by *whom*). These elements would likely figure in any subsequent explanation of why in that case one was 'filled with admiration,' and the feeling itself be altered upon learning that one's assumptions were mistaken. For example, admiration of a person who attempts to save a drowning child is apt to be diminished or enhanced upon learning whether the person was or was not related to the child, was or was not himself a strong swimmer, did or did not have a duty to go to the child's aid (as does a professional lifeguard).

What is true of particular instances is true generally: our ideas of what is (most) just, or noble, or moral are subject to revision, even radical revision, in light of rational argument and of a more profound understanding of political life. Thus, if study and reflection lead one to conclude that the ultimate political desideratum is *not* peace, but *freedom*, one will evaluate many things differently, beginning with the importance of cultivating virtue and nobility.

However, even if one is convinced of the *reality* of Nobility, that it is every bit as real as Beauty, one may still have grave doubts about the inherent *goodness* of always acting nobly – as few would about being beautiful. It does not require a deep understanding of political reality to recognize the political *utility* of people, especially young men, being persuaded that 'noble self-sacrifice' is good, and (accordingly) that it be highly honoured by everyone. We have an imperative need for stalwart soldiers, policemen, firemen, and such; they certainly further the good of the people they protect. One might go further, arguing people's psychic 'need' for heroes, whose willing subordination of their own selfish good in the interest of some higher purpose proves that humans as such are higher than beasts (whose lives *are* determined by the selfish concerns of 'mere life').[22] But is noble service – even to the point of death – really good *for them that so serve*? Or is the inherent goodness of The Noble itself a 'noble lie,' and those who believe in it so many useful dupes? Even if one lives to enjoy the honour, is honour worth the price, the risk – indeed, is it really worth anything at all? Or does that depend on the quality of the people who bestow it (with the consequence that 'popularity' per se is worth little or nothing)? Whatever one's view about the value of honour, one must avoid confusing the *gratification* it provides (which is as real as any other pleasure for whoever enjoys it) with any supposed goodness inherent in *being* noble, which presumably would obtain quite apart from its acknowledgment by others through the gratuity of honour (which might be enjoyed on false pretences).

In reaching one's own conclusion about this all-important matter, it is helpful to recall the truth about Beauty: there is no possibility of proving either its reality or its goodness apart from human psychic experience. So, consider again the passing stranger who risks himself to rescue some children from a burning building or other mortal danger. Virtually everyone would feel admiration for his doing so, regarding it as a noble act; it would ennoble, or even beautify him in our eyes. And we can say why. Aware of our own fears of painful injury and death, we know it would be a hard thing to do: to master these powerful, self-centred passions in an effort to aid someone who otherwise would perish. And if that stranger were himself to perish in his attempt, he will be – that is, felt to be – no less noble in our judgment (indeed, perhaps even more so in that there can be no doubt as to the extremity of the danger). What we naturally *admire* in such cases is not the success or failure of such an attempt (that involves different feelings), but the self-mastery required to make it in the interests of something other than self, difficult as we appreciate that to be; and for the same reason, we are apt to excuse – but not congratulate – anyone who declined to so risk himself.[23]

Now, consider yourself to be this stranger, confronting his situation. You can either make the attempt, and so *be* this noble person for having the strength of soul to risk life and limb – and be so not merely in other people's eyes, but first of all in your own – or you can shrink from doing so. In the event, there is no wishing yourself out of the situation, such that there is no necessity to choose. Much as you cannot both have your cake and eat it, so you cannot *be* noble and yet decline to *do* the noble thing when actually confronted with a situation that calls for it. Of course, a person may be tempted to try to rescue the children, but nonetheless resist the temptation, having good reasons for declining (e.g., that he would be risking not only his own life, but the welfare of other people, or something else of great importance). If he can be sure about that, he should think no less of himself, and *feel* accordingly. However, if he declined out of all-too-human *weakness*, he remains safe and alive (for now), but aware that he is not as noble – and so not as *good*? – as the stranger. If you were he, would you wish that you were – that you were made of the stuff of heroes, equal to whatever challenges rightly define heroes? Is it, then, inherently *good* to be noble? How one *feels* about that must not be ignored in reaching a judgment: as in the case of Beauty, it is the fundamental datum. But if one answers affirmatively, then the hedonistic conception of The Good is simply wrong.

Major questions remain, of course. For example, is there any valid way to *rank* the nobility (or ignobility) of various actions, or of the people who perform them?[24] We may all agree that the stranger who attempts to save the children is noble. But is he *as* noble as Achilles, or as 'wily' Odysseus? Or as a physician who remains to tend the sick in the midst of a plague? Or as a missionary who devotes his whole life to saving souls? How does Sokrates, popularly understood – courtesy of Plato – to be a willing 'martyr to philosophy' (at age seventy), compare in nobility with Hobbes, who boasted he was 'the first that fled' the looming Civil War (at age fifty-two, and still in his philosophical prime), and so was able to compose *Leviathan* in the safety of exile (and other works thereafter)? Hard to say. But whether or not such questions of rank lack clear, incontrovertible answers in no way affects the fact that a courageous person steadfastly defending justice is more noble than a coward determined to avoid pain, whatever the cost.

Looming over all other questions, however, is the following: is there not an enormous difference between *risking* death, and accepting the *certainty* of it? Can the latter, even if granted to be noble (such that it would command the admiration of any fair-minded person), possibly be *good* for the person who so chooses? It's one thing, we might say, to have 'a fighting chance' of survival, but quite something else to willingly, knowingly, undertake an action that entails certain death – as did the Spartans and their allies who gained 'immortal fame' for holding the pass at Thermopylae (with incalculable consequences for subsequent world history). Indeed, is it not the presumed badness of death, and the goodness of living, that makes a willingness to *risk* death on behalf of others something admirable? But if actually dying in such a case is not good for the risk-taker, how can even *risking* it be good *for him*?

Of course, one might invoke a religious faith in arguing for the goodness of a noble death, believing (for example) that sacrifices in this life a just God will repay several times over in some other realm of existence. This, however, tacitly concedes that noble self-sacrifice is *not* inherently good for the sacrificer, but only insofar as it is redeemed by something that is. Not surprisingly, history is replete with polities that have relied upon some variation of this view to encourage a willingness to undertake dangerous activity in the name of the common good, tasks that too many men would not otherwise perform. This shows some of the political utility – hence, the value – of a shared religion, but not the goodness of a noble death. And as alluded to earlier, persons who do not accept any such beliefs are apt to regard them as, at best, so many 'noble lies.' For such people, doubtless including a fair portion of those who nonetheless admire the self-mastery that noble self-sacrifice requires, a profound scepticism remains concerning the inherent goodness of such sacrifice. Is their scepticism justified?

The Platonic Sokrates, in discussing with his young companions the musical training of those who would be Guardians of their 'City in *logos*,' asks whether they must not be told 'that which will make them fear death least,' thus nurtured to be sufficiently 'fearless of death' so as to 'choose death in battles over defeat and slavery.' Moments later, he speaks of what should *not* 'be heard by boys and men who must be free and more fearful of slavery than of death.'[25] The effect is to remind us that the fear of death – this minotaur dwelling at the centre of one's labyrinthine soul – is itself a kind of slavery. And that he who would be free to choose what is best in every situation must slay the minotaur, and so liberate himself from this natural animal fear.[26] This does not mean, of course, that as a result one becomes indifferent to the goodness of living; love of life is not to be confused with fear of death, though both serve to attach a person to life. However, for anyone sceptical about post-mortem existence, hence of divine rewards and punishments, Death – every person's eventual fate – cannot be a positive bad; it is bad only insofar as it puts an end to something good: living, which is not invariably good. But so long as one fears death as if it were the evil of evils, one is not free to choose it in situations where it might be rationally preferable, hence not free to choose an heroic death in preference to a slavish life.

This, I believe, is the only way one can usefully consider the possible goodness of dying nobly: as the *better* alternative in a concrete context –

not, that is, in the abstract, as if one could unqualifiedly either endorse or condemn Death per se. Or Life per se, for that matter. While a certain individual may have his reasons for actively *seeking* a noble death (and given that one is fated to die regardless, would not one prefer to do so nobly?), most situations that might confront one with that prospect arise unsought. Thus, to pose the question unqualifiedly of whether dying (hence, risking) a noble death is good for he who would (or may) die is profoundly misleading, ignoring as it does both the *purpose* served or sought by the death (or risk thereof), and the *consequences of alternatives* – as if a man's risking death merely to impress people as foolish as himself with his courage or 'death-defying skills' were as admirable as someone's doing so to rescue an endangered child or defend his nation. True, one may still admire the self-mastery of the normal fear of death manifested in the former case, but the triviality of the purpose for proving it detracts greatly from – perhaps entirely cancels – one's admiration for the man. On the other hand, if confronted with a situation where one is obliged to choose between dying in the course of noble action, and doing something profoundly ignoble in order to extricate oneself from that situation, the consequences of choosing the latter – most importantly, the inevasible psychic consequences – could be such as to undermine all value to the life thus saved. Unpleasant though it may be to make the effort, one can readily imagine behaviour that, were one to resort to it in a moment of weakness, it would be practically impossible to go on living thereafter.

I am aware that this line of reasoning would not be convincing to everyone. Much less would it necessarily dictate their conduct in extremis, since (as Hobbes well appreciated) 'the Passions of men, are commonly more potent than their Reason.' But even insofar as reason matters, many would not be fully persuaded by my analysis. Perhaps they discern some respect in which it is faulty. At the risk of seeming impertinent, however, I feel obliged to make explicit the implication of what I argue is of fundamental importance in understanding and assessing both the reality and the goodness of The Noble: that a person's capacity to recognize the beauty – hence the value – of nobility is itself a measure of the nobility of his own soul. That much as the beauty of fine music is as lost on some people as it is on dogs and sheep, so too is the nobility of heroism. But their obtuseness is as irrelevant in the one case as in the other.

Would Hobbes agree with the foregoing analysis? That is hard to determine. He does not say much about The Noble, at least under that name. Nor is this surprising, given the ostensible premise of his prescribed regime: that 'Nature hath made men' sufficiently equal 'in the faculties of body, and mind' as to preclude anyone's claiming special political status by virtue of any self-evident superiority of his own nature. It is clear, however, that Hobbes does recognize the existence of a natural nobility, and not only distinguishes it from the conventional kind (such as referred to, e.g., at X/11, 41 and XXX/25, 184), but exalts it. For among Hobbes's few mentions of nobility are two that acknowledge both its reality and its exemplars' superiority to 'the greatest part of Mankind.' The first has to do with the distinction between the genuinely *just* man ('that taketh all the care he can, that his Actions may be all Just'), and the merely 'guiltless' man: 'That which gives humane Actions the relish of Justice, is a certain Noblesse or Gallantnesse of courage, (rarely found,) by which a man scorns to be beholding for the contentment of his life, to fraud, or breach of promise' (XV/10, 74; cf. XIV/31, 70; XXVII/19, 155). Thus, the Noble Man is also the Magnanimous Man inasmuch as 'Magnanimity is contempt of unjust, or dishonest helps' (VIII/ 12, 35; but cf. VI/26–8, 26). The second example is more personal: Hobbes's singular proof that there is not invariably an 'Inconsistence of Humane Nature, with Civill Duties, as some think.' For his 'most noble and honored friend Mr. *Sidney Godolphin*' – in contrast to the vast majority of men – combined in his person 'cleernesse of Judgement, and largenesse of Fancy; strength of Reason, and gracefull Elocution; a Courage for the Warre, and a Fear for the Laws.' He paid the price that noble and honourable men are liable to pay for their probity, however, having been 'unfortunately slain in the beginning of the late Civill warre' (R&C/4, 390).

15

Justice
and the Problem of *Regimes*

As distinctive as the supposed Materialism, Determinism, and Hedonism of Hobbes's political science is its Legal Positivism: the view that, for all practical purposes, Justice is whatever is established by Law, which to be really and truly Law, must be enforced by sufficient coercive power such as only a 'Leviathan' can provide. Thus conceived, Justice is purely Conventional – unlike the Good, which has some basis in Nature, namely in the natural reality of Pleasure. Hence, even if originally the life of man were 'solitary, poore, nasty [etc.],' the Good would have as much pertinence then and there as in Civil Society. Whereas, in man's natural condition, given it to be a 'warre of every man against every man ... nothing can be Unjust':

The notions of Right and Wrong, Justice and Injustice have there no place. Where there is no common Power, there is no Law: where no Law, no Injustice. Force, and Fraud, are in warre the two Cardinall vertues. Justice, and Injustice are none of the Faculties neither of the Body, nor Mind. If they were, they might be in a man that were alone in the world, as well as his Senses, and Passions. They are Qualities, that relate to men in Society, not in Solitude. (XIII/13, 63)

Hobbes's rhetoric here, gliding so deftly from 'solitary' to 'solitude,' subtly misdirects the reader. If one presumes, not unreasonably, that the sole purview of justice is the regulation of one's relations with other people, then obviously it would have no scope in a condition of strict and perpetual *solitude*, and it is reasonable to suppose that human nature would be constituted accordingly. However, even if one were to accept the claim that man is by nature *solitary* – as is the fox, the cougar, and the porcupine – he clearly is not 'alone in the world,' hence must deal with others when they are met, and thus the question of the 'right' way of doing so would be pertinent.

Of course, if man is *not* by nature solitary, but social, it is conceivable that inherent in his nature would be some rudimentary sense or 'faculty' related to justice, not necessarily located in either his body or his mind, strictly speaking, but rather in the spirited part of his soul (perhaps manifested in Compassion, as Rousseau famously argued;[1] or in that distinct species of anger we call 'indignation,' as was the classical view). Be that as it may, if man is naturally a social being – as many species of animals are, including most other primates – there would seem to be a need for *something* to moderate relations among associates, even in the pre-political condition we have become accustomed to calling 'The State of Nature.'[2]

Presumably no one would contend that a comprehensive conception of justice, fully adequate for practical life, is complete in the breast of every man. Whither comes it, then? Hobbes argues that the whole of justice in its requisite specificity is established by a (more or less coherent) body of law, which it is the first responsibility of any functional polity to enforce within its claimed jurisdiction. But since what is legal varies from polity to polity, so too what people are to regard as just or unjust. Thus Justice is relative to these 'Artificial men' called 'Leviathans' or 'Common-wealths' or 'States,' much as the Good is relative to natural men. And while the different regimes that inform these various commonwealths may be assessed as to their relative strength, prosperity, and 'Convenience, or Aptitude to produce the Peace, and Security of the people' (XIX/4, 95), they cannot be judged as to their *justness*, being themselves the sources of justice for their respective subjects, while existing in something akin to man's natural condition with respect to each other. Or so Hobbes would be understood by the generality of his readership. But in this, as in so many respects, the matter is not as simple as it might appear.

There is a hint of this in Hobbes's first reference to Justice. It occurs in the second paragraph of his Introduction, where in describing his four-part treatment of the 'The Nature of this Artificiall man,' he promises to consider 'what are the *Rights* and *just Power* or *Authority* of a *Soveraigne*.' His reference to *just* power and authority would seem to carry two important implications: first, that it is to be distinguished from *unjust* power and authority which a Sovereign might claim to exercise; second, that there are (then) criteria or principles of Justice which are prior to and independent of any and every body of positive law.

Some indication that this is indeed Hobbes's own view can be gleaned from his use of the word 'just' and its cognates – for his usage does not always conform to the legal positivist paradigm he ostensibly endorses in *Leviathan*. To mention but a few, perhaps trivial, instances:

For if I should not believe all that is written by Historians, of the glorious acts of *Alexander*, or *Caesar*; I do not think the Ghost of *Alexander*, or *Caesar*, had any just cause to be offended; or any body else but the Historian. (VII/7, 32) [And if the Historian *does* have 'just cause,' it is not because Hobbes's private disbelief is illegal.]

Therefore the ancient Heathen did not thinke they Dishonoured, but greatly Honoured the Gods, when they introduced them in their Poems, committing Rapes, Thefts, and other great, but unjust, or unclean acts. (X/48, 45) [By what laws might acts of the *gods* be judged 'unjust'?]

It is a hard matter to know who expecteth benefit from publique troubles; but the signes that guide to a just suspicion, is the soothing of the people in their unreasonable, or irremediable grievances, by men whose estates are not sufficient to discharge their accustomed expenses. (XXX/25, 184) [The justness of one's suspicions in this or any other matter has to do with rational grounds, and ultimately truth, not laws.]

And for their *Faith*, it is internall, and invisible; They have the license that Naaman had, and need not put themselves into danger for it. But if they do, they ought to expect their reward in Heaven, and not complain of their Lawfull Soveraign; much lesse make warre upon him. For he that is not glad of any just occasion of Martyrdome, has not the faith he professeth, but pretends it onely, to set some colour upon his own contumacy. (XLIII/23, 331) [If there is such a thing as a 'just occasion for Martyrdome,' its having been legally specified is most unlikely.]

Of course, one could conclude that there is some trans- or pre-political justice grounded in the nature of things from the simple fact that Hobbes himself specifies some nineteen or twenty 'Lawes of Nature, dictating Peace' which he insists are 'Immutable and Eternall: For Injustice, Ingratitude, Arrogance, Pride, Iniquity, Acception of persons, and the rest, can never be made lawfull' (XV/38, 79). One would presume, then, that this body of Natural law provides at least a partial template whereby one can judge the justness of positive laws and the governments that enact them.

However, Hobbes has introduced two kinds of ambiguity into the status of these so-called Natural Laws.

In the first place, he does not refer to them as requisites of natural *justice*; he maintains they are not even properly called 'laws,' but rather 'dictates of Reason,' being simply 'Conclusions, or Theoremes concerning what conduceth to [men's] conservation and defence; ... wheras Law, properly is the word of him, that by right hath command over others. But yet if we consider the same Theoremes, as delivered in the word of God, that by right commandeth all things; then they are properly called Lawes' (XV/41, 80). It is not clear that Hobbes himself always grants this 'if.' In certain contexts he seems to insist upon it: 'Princes succeed one another; and one Judge passeth, another commeth; nay, Heaven and Earth shall passe; but not one tittle of the Law of Nature shall passe; for it is the Eternall Law of God' (XXVI/24, 144; cf. /40, 150; XLIII/5, 322; /23, 330. But elsewhere, Hobbes is silent as to their enjoying divine sanction. For example, in his chapter '*Of* CIVILL LAWES,' we are told:

The Law of Nature, and the Civill Law, contain each other, and are of equall extent. For the Lawes of Nature, which consist in Equity, Justice, Gratitude, and other morall Vertues on these depending, in the condition of meer Nature ... are not properly Lawes, but qualities that dispose men to peace, and to obedience. When a Common-wealth is once settled, then are they actually Lawes, and not before; as being then the commands of the Common-wealth; and therefore also Civill Lawes: For it is the Soveraign Power that obliges men to obey them. (XXVI/8, 138)

There would seem to be a practical problem here insofar as some of these natural laws *cannot* be effectively translated into positive laws (e.g., the Fourth, requiring 'Gratitude'; the Fifth, requiring 'Compleasance' or Sociability). The main analytical point apparently bears emphasizing, however, for later in that same chapter, he says:

The Interpretation of the Lawes of Nature, in a Common-wealth, dependeth not on the books of Morall Philosophy. The Authority of writers, without the Authority of the Common-wealth, maketh not their opinions Law, be they never so true. That which I have written in this Treatise, concerning the Morall Vertues, and of their necessity, for the procuring, and maintaining peace, though it bee evident Truth, is not therefore presently Law; but because in all Common-wealths in the world, it is part of the Civill Law: For though it be naturally reasonable; yet it is by the Soveraigne Power that it is Law. (XXVI/22, 143)

Now, if it were *true* that 'all Common-wealths in the world' incorporated Hobbes's natural laws (whatever else) into their bodies of positive law, then they would be part of what defines justice universally, and there would be no question as to their being obligatory wherever people live in political societies – as Hobbes sometimes seems to insist:

Ignorance of the Law of Nature Excuseth no man; because every man that hath attained to the use of Reason, is supposed to know, he ought not to do to another, what he would not have done to himselfe. Therefore into what place soever a man shall come, if he do any thing contrary to that Law, it is a Crime. (XXVII/4, 152; cf. /23, 156, XV/35, 79)

[I]f it be a Law that obliges all the Subjects without exception, and is not written, nor otherwise published in such places as they may take notice thereof, it is a Law of Nature. For whatsoever men are to take knowledge of for Law, not upon other mens words, but every one from his own reason, must be such as is agreeable to the reason of all men; which no Law can be, but the Law of Nature. The Lawes of Nature therefore need not any publishing, nor Proclamation; as being contained in this one Sentence, approved by all the world, *Do not that to another, which thou thinkest unreasonable to be done by another to thy selfe.* (XXVI/13, 140)

'Reasonable' as one might wish to regard these statements, Hobbes himself warns against any such blithe assumptions:

All Laws, written, and unwritten, have need of Interpretation. The unwritten Law of Nature, though it be easy to such, as without partiality, and passion, make use of their naturall reason, and therefore leaves the violators thereof without excuse; yet considering there be very few, perhaps none, that in some cases are not blinded by self-love, or some other passion, it is now become of all Laws the most obscure; and has consequently the greatest need of able Interpreters. (XXVI/21, 143)[3]

This problem would be ameliorated if the whole body of Natural Law could indeed be 'contracted into one easie sum, intelligible, even to the meanest capacity; and that is, *Do not that to another, which thou wouldest not have done to thy selfe*' (XV/35, 79). But some of Hobbes's Laws or Theorems are *not* obvious implications of the Golden Rule (e.g., acceptance of either 'Primogeniture' or 'First Seizure,' as required by the Fourteenth). Nor are all of them incorporated into the positive laws of every regime (most notably, the Ninth, outlawing Pride by dictating '*That every man acknowledge other for his Equall by Nature,*' and following upon that, the Tenth, requiring Equality of Rights).

The second ambiguity regarding Hobbes's Natural Laws stems from their conditional character, such that they can be at once 'Immutable and Eternall,' and yet inoperative. As he explains:

The Lawes of Nature oblige *in foro interno*; that is to say, they bind to a desire they should take place: but *in foro externo*; that is, to the putting them in act, not alwayes. For he that should be modest, and tractable, and performe all he promises, in such time, and place, where no man els should do so, should but make himselfe a prey to others, and procure his own certain ruine, contrary to the ground of all Lawes of Nature, which tend to Natures preservation. And again, he that having sufficient Security, that others shall observe the same Lawes towards him, observes them not himselfe, seeketh not Peace, but War; & consequently the destruction of his Nature by Violence.

   And whatsoever Lawes bind *in foro interno*, may be broken, not onely by a fact contrary to the Law, but also by a fact according to it, in case a man think it contrary. For though his Action in this case, be according to the Law; yet his Purpose was against the Law; which, where the Obligation is *in foro interno*, is a breach. (XV/36–7, 79)

Thus, the Laws of Nature determine a moral code that seems eminently practical; being well within virtually anyone's capabilities, it makes no excessive demands on a person. For, first of all, its fulfilment requires only a will to fulfil it; in other words, good intentions: 'because they oblige onely to a desire, and endeavour, I mean an unfeigned and constant endeavour, are easie to be observed. For in that they require nothing but endeavour; he that endeavoureth their performance, fulfilleth them; and he that fulfilleth the Law, is Just' (XV/39, 79; cf. XXVII/3, 152; XLIII/4, 322). Secondly, a person is obliged by this code only when it is safe to comply with it.

   But Hobbes himself has somewhat blurred this *interno/externo* distinction. On the one hand, it is consistent with another distinction he had made earlier in the same chapter:

The names of Just, and Injust, when they are attributed to Men, signifie one thing; and when they are attributed to Actions, another. When they are attributed to Men, they signifie Conformity, or Inconformity of Manners, to Reason. But when they are attributed to Actions, they signify the Conformity, or Inconformity to Reason, not of Manners, or manner of life, but of particular Actions. A Just man therefore, is he that taketh all the care he can that his Actions may be all Just; and an Unjust man is he that neglecteth it … That which gives to humane Actions the relish of Justice, is a certain Noblenesse or Gallantnesse of courage, (rarely found,) by which a man scorns to be beholding for the contentment of his life, to fraud, or breach of promise. This Justice of the Manners, is that which is meant, where Justice is called a Vertue; and Injustice, a Vice.

But the Justice of Actions denominates men, not Just, but *Guiltlesse*: and the Injustice of the same, (which is also called injury,) gives them but the name of *Guilty*. (XV/10–11, 74)

On the other hand, neither of these distinctions is consistent with the – doubtless well-chosen – illustration he earlier provided in clarifying his account of language as 'consisting of *Names* … and their Connexion': 'But here wee must take notice, that by a name is not always understood, as in Grammar, one onely Word; but sometimes by circumlocution many words together. For all these words, *Hee that in his actions observeth the Lawes of his Country*, make but one Name, equivalent to this one word, *Just*' (IV/8, 13–14). So, which is it? Is the man whose actions conform to the letter of the Law properly 'denominated' *Just*? Or is he merely 'Guiltlesse'; and only he who has internalized the rationale underlying the Laws of Nature – hence feels true gratitude, genuinely wishes to accommodate himself to his fellows, sincerely pardon offenses against him, always deals equitably, and so on – only he who feels obliged *in foro interno* is *truly* just? Or is there some reason Hobbes wishes to have it both ways? Does his new science of politics tacitly require two related but significantly different conceptions of the Just Man?

The one, presumably, is pertinent to the vast majority of people, from whom law-abidingness – hence, 'guiltlessness' – is as much as can reasonably be expected; after all, Hobbes himself teaches that most people are civilly obedient, not primarily out of a will to be just and otherwise moral, but out of a fear of punishment and a desire for good reputation. So, while it may in principle be easy for virtually anyone to comply with Hobbes's Natural Law morality, requiring as it does only good will and honest endeavour, this is precisely what cannot be counted upon insofar as a person is dominated by the concern for his or her own good, narrowly conceived.

The other, higher conception of a just individual pertains to the naturally 'noble' or 'gallant' Few who not only take to heart the spirit of the

Laws but who can be counted upon to manifest the courage of their convictions – a kind of person 'rarely found.' Their existence, however, raises a far more challenging question about justice. Why would they, or anyone intelligent and rationally committed to living the best life available to him, *choose* to be conscientiously just *unless* being so is naturally *good* for the just individual? Put another way, does Hobbes have a convincing response to the radical challenge posed to Sokrates by Glaukon and Adeimantos in Plato's *Republic*?[4] This question: 'Why *be* just?' – rather than merely *appear* just, that is, and thus reap the benefits both of that appearance and of selective injustices that go undetected – is one that any adequate 'theory of justice' must satisfactorily answer. Accordingly, I shall return to it in a subsequent chapter (21), examining what is in effect Hobbes's response to the challenge of these two 'Sons of *Ariston* ['Best'].' I believe that Hobbes does have in mind significantly different but related ideas of 'the just citizen,' and I will consider this possibility further in that later chapter. For now, let it suffice to observe that he would not be the first political philosopher to design a regime that not only allows for, but actually requires, different but related conceptions of the virtue of justice, each pertinent to a different category of citizen making a different kind of contribution to a prosperous and well-ordered polity.

Given that there are some trans-political standards of justice grounded in the nature of things – which Hobbes tacitly acknowledges, and which surely accords with most people's actual belief, regardless what some might say, or even think they believe – then it is possible that justice applies to regimes themselves. There are two distinct respects in which it may do so.

The first concerns relations among independent polities. Hobbes would have his reader see each commonwealth as existing in a State of Nature with respect to the others, which is 'a condition of warre one against the other.' He is explicit that by this he does not mean continual fighting, but rather such 'tract of time, wherein the Will to contend by Battell is sufficiently known' (XIII/8, 62). However doubtful historically there was ever a situation in which every human *individual* was in such 'a condition of warre' with all others, one may concede more credence to Hobbes's claim that 'in all times, Kings, and Persons of Soveraigne authority, because of their Independency, are in continuall jealousies, and in the state and posture of Gladiators; having their weapons pointing, and their eyes fixed on one another … which is a posture of War' (XIII/12, 63). Again, 'every Common-wealth … has an absolute Libertie, to doe what it shall judge … most conducing to their benefit. But withall, they live in the condition of a perpetuall war' (XXI/8, 110). Thus, States are ever in that situation where the Laws of Nature *pertain*, being 'Immutable and Eternall,' but are nonetheless largely *inoperative*:

Concerning the Offices of one Soveraign to another, which are comprehended in that Law, which is commonly called the *Law of Nations*, I need not say any thing in this place because the Law of Nations, and the Law of Nature, is the same thing. And every Soveraign hath the same Right, in procuring the safety of his People, that any particular man can have, in procuring the safety of his own Body. And the same Law, that dictateth to men that have no Civil Government, what they ought to do, and what to avoyd in regard of one another, dictateth the same to Common-wealths; that is, to the Consciences of Soveraign Princes, and Soveraign Assemblies; there being no Court of Naturall Justice, but in the Conscience onely; where not Man, but God raigneth. (XXX/30, 185)

The references to 'Consciences' are not irrelevant here, since the option as to which a given man in a given situation may choose to be ruled by – obligatory Natural *Law*, or permissive Natural *Right* – pertains to Sovereigns as well as Subjects. Thus, parallel to his view that 'Nature gave a Right to every man to secure himselfe by his own strength, and to invade a suspected neighbour, by way of prevention,' (XXVI/43, 150), so Hobbes notes that States also, 'to the good of their own Subjects let slip few occasions to *weaken* the estate of their Neighbours' (XXIX/3, 168; 'few,' notice, not 'no').[5] Accordingly:

[A]s small Familyes did then; so now do Cities and Kingdomes, which are but greater Families (for their own security) enlarge their Dominions, upon all pretences of danger, and fear of Invasion, or assistance that may be given to Invaders, endeavour as much as they can, to subdue, or weaken their neighbours, by open force, and secret arts, for want of other Caution, justly; and are remembred for it in after ages with honour. (XVII/2, 185)

Justly? Recall that in this 'condition of meer Nature, (which is a condition of Warre),' Hobbes argues, 'The notions of Right and Wrong, Justice and Injustice *have no place*' (XIII/13, 63; emphasis added). It is somewhat puzzling, then, that Hobbes later speaks as if they do. For instance, when discussing the 'nutrition' of a commonwealth, he observes that 'the superfluous commodities to be had within, become no more superfluous, but supply these wants at home, by importation of that which may be had abroad, either by Exchange, or by just Warre, or by Labour' (XXIV/4,

127). A '*just* Warre'? Given the line quoted above, one would have supposed that qualifier to be meaningless. Or does Hobbes mean for his reader to recognize a distinction between 'just' and 'unjust' war, after all? Consider also his insistence that 'if a weaker Prince, make a disadvantageous peace with a stronger, for feare; he is bound to keep it; unless (as hath been sayd before) there ariseth some new, and just cause of feare, to renew the war' (XIV/27, 69). Might this be the required criterion for a 'just war': that in light of a *natural* standard of justice, one has a '*just* cause of fear'? As to what the natural ground of justice might be, in this case at least it would appear to be Truth, and by extension honesty, sincerity, and respect for the truth, manifested in the concern to know it.

Be that as it may, it seems that Hobbes flatly contradicts himself with respect to the relevance of Justice to the State of Nature. For although having explicitly declared 'notions of Right and Wrong, Justice and Injustice' to be impertinent therein, he nonetheless (as noted) speaks several times of States, or their Sovereigns, possibly having 'just cause' for what they do, including that of waging war for wanted resources. How is this apparent contradiction to be explained? In one sense, rather easily. For immediately preceding the line quoted above, he argues as a consequence of the universal war that characterizes the natural state – 'the ill condition, which man by meer nature is actually placed in' – that 'nothing can be Unjust' (XIII/13, 63). One might agree with this, and immediately add, 'nor Just either' – much as Hobbes does ('Justice and Injustice have no place').

However, having subsequently defined Justice in terms of the Third Law of Nature ('*That men performe their Covenants made*'), and Injustice likewise ('*the not Performance of Covenant*'), he adds, 'And whatsoever is not Unjust, is *Just*' (XV/1–2, 71). By *that* token, in the State of Nature (wherein there is no reliable enforcement, hence no valid covenants, hence no possibility of non-performance), *any* action by either man or commonwealth – not merely those which fulfil contractual obligations – is positively Just. Any war, for whatever reason, or any other action by polities 'to subdue, or weaken their neighbours, by open force, and secret arts,' is justified ('for want of other Caution'). True, Hobbes has 'technically' equivocated here, first telling his reader that these terms 'justice' and 'injustice' simply *do not apply* in 'the condition of meer Nature,' while nonetheless applying them himself. Perhaps he is confident that a practically minded reader will overlook this equivocation, seeing no practical difference between regarding every action as equally just (on the one hand) and regarding justice as simply irrelevant (on the other).

There certainly is a major theoretical difference, however, between a view that simply *bifurcates* all activities and arrangements into those that are positively *unjust* (due to non-performance of contracted obligations), with everything else being denominated *just*; and the view that positively establishes *both* what is *just* and what is *unjust* in reference to some contract, leaving a vast *third* category – any and every thing not related to any contract – as *neither*.

To clarify the difference in the two views, consider Hobbes's brief definition of '*Plantations*, or *Colonies*': 'numbers of men sent out from the Common-wealth, under a Conductor, or Governour, to inhabit a Forraign Country, either formerly voyd of Inhabitants, or made voyd then, by warre' (XXIV/14, 131). On the former view, it makes no difference whether the territory to be colonized is uninhabited, or is instead 'made fit' for colonization by exterminating any indigenous peoples. Far from the first case (land uninhabited) being neither just nor unjust, and the second (already inhabited) being positively unjust (according to a natural standard), both kinds of colonial projects are equally *just*, there being no valid covenant pertaining to either case (since whatever is not positively unjust is just). Similarly, on this view it would be *just* for a Sovereign to order the slaughter of harmless pilgrims traversing his territory en route to some holy site, or sentence to slow death by painful torture all captured enemy combatants – 'Golden Rule' to the contrary notwithstanding.

On the latter view, however, in which justice is keyed to the fulfilment of contractual duties, one is not entitled to affix the honorific label of 'just' to the foregoing actions, nor to all wars between States. And if it *matters politically* whether people do or do not believe certain actions, policies, and arrangements to be (positively) just, even a practically minded reader may be unhappy with the ambiguity in which Hobbes has left this important point. What should one rightly think (he may wonder) about the alternatives Hobbes mentions in passing: 'And though a People coming into possession of a Land by warre, do not alwaies exterminate the antient Inhabitants, (as did the Jewes,) but leave to many, or most, or all of them their Estates [etc.]' (XXIV/06, 128)?[6] Moreover, if there *is* some pre- or trans-political form of Justice grounded in Nature (which includes natural reason, of course), then certain actions – including wars – may well be recognizable as just or unjust, irrespective of whether they fulfil specific contractual obligations.

The second respect in which Natural principles of Justice, as opposed to merely Conventional ones, may bear on States is equally obvious: actual polities and their governments may be compared, judged, and ranked as to their justness. The very archetypes of regimes may likewise be assessed, and so the respective justness of various types of kingships compared with that of various kinds of aristocracies, oligarchies, theocracies, democracies, martial dictatorships, and tyrannies. On the surface, however, there is no place for this sort of assessment in Hobbes's explication '*Of the severall Kinds of* COMMON-WEALTH,' which is simplicity itself:

> The difference of Common-wealths, consisteth in the difference of the Soveraign, or the Person representative of all and every one of the Multitude. And because the Soveraignty is either in one Man, or in an Assembly of more than one; and into that Assembly either Every man hath right to enter, or not every one, but Certain men distinguished from the rest; it is manifest, there can be but Three kinds of Common-wealth. For the Representative must needs be One man, or More: and if more, then it is the Assembly of All, or but of a Part. When the Representative is One man, then is the Common-wealth a MONARCHY: when an Assembly of All that will come together, then it is a DEMOCRACY, or Popular Common-wealth: when an Assembly of a Part onely, then it is called an ARISTOCRACY. Other kind of Common-wealth there can be none: for either One, or More, or All, must have the Soveraign Power (which I have shewn to be indivisible) entire.
>
> There be other names of Government, in the Histories, and books of Policy; as *Tyranny*, and *Oligarchy*; But they are not the names of other Formes of Government, but of the same Formes misliked. For they that are discontented under *Monarchy*, call it *Tyranny*; and they that are displeased with *Aristocracy*, call it *Oligarchy*: So also, they which find themselves grieved under a *Democracy*, call it *Anarchy*, (which signifies want of Government;) and yet I think no man believes, that want of Government, is any new kind of Government: nor by the same reason ought they to believe, that the Government is of one kind, when they like it, and another, when they mislike it, or are oppressed by the Governours. (XIX/1–2, 94–5)

Perhaps they *ought* not believe 'that the Government is of one kind, when they like it, and another, when they mislike it,' but this is precisely what Hobbes warned is typical 'of such things as affect us, that is, which please and displease us, because all men be not alike affected with the same thing, nor the same man at all times' (IV/24, 17).

According to what Hobbes goes on to say, and not say, the three basic kinds of Commonwealths themselves cannot differ in their overall justness, nor do they differ as to their essential power, but only in the 'Convenience, or Aptitude to produce the Peace, and Security of the people; for which end they were instituted' (XIX/4, 95). This claim underpins the usual understanding of Hobbes's legal positivism: that the laws in each polity define, insofar as its power enforces, what is just and unjust for its subjects. Such laws include, most importantly, those which determine how the various regimes themselves operate. As one of an earlier generation of legal positivists puts it, 'each [type of] Rulership establishes laws for its own advantage; a democracy [establishes] democratic ones, a tyranny tyrannical ones, and all others the same. And they declare what they have established – their own advantage – is "just" for the Ruled, and whoever deviates from this they punish as a lawbreaker and doer of injustices.'[7] Hobbes, too, insists that power is all-important, that rules are 'but vain words' – not merely ineffective, but practically meaningless – lacking sufficient power to sanction them. Thus, for the Sovereign, maintaining the particular form of his (or its) power is the first priority of legislation (cf. XXX/3, 175; /21, 182; XXXI/5, 187).

If one presumes all this to be so, there would be no valid trans-political standard whereby the justness of regimes and their laws may themselves be judged. But as the passages quoted earlier show, this strictly conventional view of justice does not square with all of Hobbes's own uses of justice-related terms. Moreover, the easily overlooked reference to *oppression* in the conclusion of the passage quoted above ('or are oppressed by the Governours') suggests he is well aware that, practically speaking at least, the question of regimes is not as simple as his merely quantitative typology would have it – as if, from a purely rational, scientific standpoint, the distinction between kingship and tyranny were merely a matter of subjective semantics, since all that counts objectively is that both are polities in which the sovereign representative is one man rather than a plurality of some or all. As if, that is, oppression – and therefore *concern* about oppression – were no part of political reality.

Without mentioning the name, the 'book of Policy' Hobbes clearly intends his discussion of regimes to be directly contrasted with is Aristotle's *Politics*. And the contrast could hardly be greater. For it is not merely with respect to their differing typologies, but most of all in the degree of importance each author attaches to differences among regimes. That which occupies well over three-quarters of Aristotle's treatise – analysing the strengths and weaknesses, advantages and disadvantages of various regimes under various circumstances, culminating naturally in an analysis of the best regime simply – warrants but one of forty-seven chapters, barely ten out of the nearly 400 pages that make up *Leviathan*. By the brevity of his treatment, Hobbes would persuade his readers, or at least those who are thus persuadable, that the various differences among regimes pale almost to insignificance compared with the one difference of truly great importance: that between life in virtually any functioning Civil Society, and life in the State of Nature:

[T]he estate of Man can never be without some incommodity or other; and that the greatest, that in any forme of Government can possibly happen to the people in generall, is scarce sensible, in respect of the miseries, and horrible calamities, that accompany a Civill Warre; or that dissolute condition of masterlesse men, without subjection to Lawes, and a coërcive Power to tye their hands from rapine, and revenge. (XVIII/20, 94)

Aristotle also categorizes regimes using the quantitative distinction in numbers of rulers, but subordinates that to another whereby one distinguishes legitimate kingships from tyrannies, true aristocracies from wealth-based oligarchies, and mixed polities from vulgar democracies.[8] And his criterion for doing so is not some subjective liking or 'misliking' of a government, but the objective reality of whether or not the regime is *oppressive*. That is, whether the rulers rule in the interest of all, in pursuit of the common good, hence rule justly; or whether instead they rule primarily in their own interest, hence unjustly, oppressing and exploiting those they rule in furtherance of their own private good. This being the most important distinction among regimes, right *versus* wrong rule, each legitimate form has a perverse, unjust counterpart. To the very best regime, true Kingship (rule by the single best man), corresponds the worst, most oppressive regime, Tyranny. To the second best type of regime, Aristocracy (rule by a minority of men notable for their virtue, both civic and personal), corresponds the unjust form of minority rule, Oligarchy (for though the term literally means 'rule of the few,' in practice it is the rule of the few Rich oppressing the many Poor). And to the compromise form of regime in which all the various plausible claims to share in rule – military service, free birth, wealth contribution, conspicuous prudence and other virtue – are recognized and blended so far as practical in what Aristotle calls 'Polity,' corresponds the least defective of the unjust forms, Democracy (which in practice is rule by the Poor in what they believe to be their own interest, namely, exploiting and oppressing the Rich).

Why does Hobbes apparently reject Aristotle's major, qualitative distinction among regimes, retaining only the minor, quantitative one (or wish to seem to, at least)? First of all, he challenges Aristotle's conception of political life. Aristotle, regarding men as political by nature, contends that they live together not merely for mutual utility, but out of preference, enjoying various kinds of friendship and communal activities with their fellows (*Politics* 1280a31–6). Moreover, he argues, doing so is essential to their living well, that is, nobly or finely, hence happily. And that providing an environment for living *well*, not for 'merely living,' is what they rightly regard as the purpose of their politically associating. Aristotle expressly rejects the view that the *polis* is no more but 'an alliance to prevent [men's] suffering injustice from anyone' (1280a33–4; cf. 1280a24–6). He further contends that the ground of living a good, thus happy, life is virtue; hence, the laws of legitimate regimes aim at cultivating the virtues of their citizens. It is against the background of this understanding of political life that Aristotle declares 'those regimes which look to the common advantage happen to be correct, according to what is unqualifiedly just, while those which look only to the advantage of the rulers are faulty, and are all deviations from the correct regimes; for they are despotic, but the *polis* is a partnership of the free people' (1279a17–22).

Hobbes, of course, takes issue with all of these claims. He contends that Man is *not* by nature political; his natural environment is the jungle, not the city; and that 'men have no pleasure, (but on the contrary a great deale of griefe) in keeping company, where there is no power able to over-awe them all' (XIII/5, 61). To be sure, man does have passions that incline him to live peacefully with his fellows, but these are matched with others that incline him to war; and the latter will prevail unless the former are artificially strengthened by hope, and the latter artificially suppressed by fear (XIII/14, 63). And because there is such a diversity of notions of the good life, traceable to the diversity of what men find pleasureful, the true purpose of the political association must be limited to the least common denominator of this plurality of good lives, namely, protecting mere life. It remains the responsibility of each individual to find his own happiness within the safety provided by a regime of law and order. Since this applies as much to the Rulers as to the Ruled, any functioning commonwealth necessarily serves the only 'advantage' that is truly 'common,' namely preserving and protecting mere life. Accordingly, Aristotle's major distinction is otiose. And just as people do not agree about what constitutes the Good Life, neither do they agree about the importance of virtue to living well, or even what virtue substantively is: 'For one man calleth *Wisdome*, what another calleth *feare*; and one *cruelty*, what another *justice*; one *prodigality*, what another *magnanimity*; and one *gravity*, what another *stupidity*, &c' (IV/24, 17).

Moreover, to teach that one can and should distinguish between right and wrong, just and unjust regimes, risks the inherently precarious existence of any and every regime, as does the idea that commonwealths are responsible for more than securing mere life. Such 'pernicious errors' are invitations to sedition and made to order for demagogues: 'for they induce men, as oft as they like not their Governours, to adhaere to those that call them Tyrants, and to think it lawfull to raise war against them' (XLVI/36, 378). After all, it is not as if the Ruled are fair and impartial judges, unbiased by self interest – indeed, the contrary's being true is basic to the rationale for the necessity of establishing a Sovereign whose judgments everyone must acknowledge to be authoritative (XVII/13, 87).

Thus, Hobbes would have the generality of people be persuaded that any functioning government, willing and able to enforce its laws, is as legitimate as a government can be, and that whatever its inconveniences, they are infinitely to be preferred to a return to the State of Nature *via* a civil war precipitated by rebellion. Hobbes lets pass no opportunity to warn of the danger inherent in what he would have his reader see as a fallacious distinction between just and unjust, legitimate and illegitimate regimes and governments. His admonitions, however, betray a marked preoccupation with the vulnerability of Monarchy's being cast as Tyranny:

And as to Rebellion in particular against Monarchy; one of the most frequent causes of it, is the Reading of the books of Policy, and Histories of the antient Greeks, and Romans ... From the reading, I say, of such books, men have undertaken to kill their Kings, because the Greek and Latine writers, in their books, and discourses of Policy, make it lawfull, and laudable, for any man so to do; provided before he do it, he call him Tyrant. For they say not *Regicide*, that is, killing of a King, but *Tyrannicide*, that is, killing of a Tyrant, is lawfull. (XXIX/14, 170–1)

And in reviewing 'Opinions, contrary to the peace of Man-kind,' taught chiefly by 'Divines in the Pulpit,' Hobbes specifies the view: 'That it is lawfull for Subjects to kill such, as they call Tyrants' (XXX/14, 179).

Hobbes expressly implicates Aristotle in the purveying of this particular poison, though he has to grossly misrepresent Aristotle's political science in order to make his point: 'From Aristotles Civill Philosophy, they have learned, to call all manner of Common-wealths but the Popular, (such as was at that time the state of Athens,) *Tyranny*. All Kings they called Tyrants; ... As also to call the condition of the people under the Democracy, *Liberty*. A *Tyrant* originally signified no more simply, but a *Monarch*' (XLVI/35, 377). While Hobbes also speaks of discontented subjects resorting to the 'disgraceful names' of 'Anarchy' and 'Oligarchy' in order to impugn the government of a Democracy or an Aristocracy, he here and elsewhere repeatedly evinces especial concern for the readiness with which a Monarchy can be libelled a Tyranny – a term which had long since become the strongest epithet of political denunciation available in the English language. To the very end, Hobbes sounds a warning against trusting its use: 'And because the name of Tyranny, signifieth nothing more, nor lesse, than the name of Soveraignty, be it in one, or many men, saving that they that use the former word, are understood to bee angry with them they call Tyrants; I think the toleration of a professed hatred of Tyranny, is a Toleration of hatred to Common-wealth in generall' (R&C/9, 392). Disgruntled subjects of Kingships are particularly susceptible to the political disease of '*Tyrannophobia*,' which Hobbes likens to being bitten by a rabid dog (XXIX/14, 171). Perhaps his emphasis reflects nothing more than a concern to provide his preferred form of commonwealth extra insulation against pernicious rhetoric. Then again, maybe there is more to it. I believe so, and shall endeavour to make clear what and why in a subsequent chapter.

However, the fact that any strong but scrupulous government can be unjustly denounced as 'tyrannical' does not alter the fact that there are genuinely oppressive governments, and that describing them as such is not simply a matter of inflammatory propaganda. If their oppressive modes of ruling – using the coercive machinery of the State to enforce laws and decrees and judgments that manifestly and routinely favour the interests of the Rulers at the expense of the Ruled – are not grounds for regarding them as *unjust*, hence illegitimate, what then is their status? Hobbes, for his part, does not deny the objective reality of oppression. For example, in the chapter devoted to cataloguing 'Those things that Weaken a Commonwealth,' Hobbes recurs to the danger of irresponsible clerics:

[I]n the Body Politique, when the Spirituall power, moveth the Members of a Common-wealth, by the terrour of punishments, and hope of rewards (which are the Nerves of it,) otherwise than by the Civill Power (which is the Soule of the Common-wealth) they ought to be moved; and by strange, and hard words suffocates their understanding, it must needs thereby Distract the people, and either Overwhelm the Common-wealth with Oppression, or cast it into the Fire of a Civill warre. (XXIX/15, 172)

Though by the logic of the human predicament (as Hobbes has analysed it), the former alternative (oppression) is preferable to the latter (civil war), there can be no doubt that Hobbes regards both alternatives as evil. What is more, the evil of oppression may ultimately lead – logic be damned – to a return to the State of Nature *via* 'the Fire of a Civill warre.' Whether or not it is rational to do so, severely oppressed people may rebel. And strange as it seems, one cannot be altogether sure that Hobbes would necessarily disapprove. Notice what he chooses to reveal in the penultimate paragraph of the first half – the Civil or Human or Natural half – of *Leviathan*. He speaks of seven 'Naturall Punishments' that attend violations of certain 'Lawes of Nature':

There is no action of man in this life, that is not the beginning of so long a chayn of Consequences, as no humane Providence, is high enough, to give a man a prospect to the end. And in this Chayn, there are linked together both pleasing and unpleasing events; in such manner, as he that will do any thing for his pleasure, must engage himselfe to suffer all the pains annexed to it; and these pains, are the Naturall Punishments of those actions, which are the beginning of more Harme than Good. And hereby it comes to passe, that Intemperance, is naturally punished with Diseases; Rashnesse, with Mischances; Injustice, with the Violence of Enemies; Pride, with Ruine; Cowardice, with Oppression; Negligent government of Princes, with Rebellion; and Rebellion, with Slaughter. For seeing Punishments are consequent to the breach of Lawes; Naturall Punishments must be naturally consequent to the breach of the Lawes of Nature; and therfore follow them as their naturall, not arbitrary effects. (XXXI/40, 193)

Nature itself punishes 'Cowardice, with Oppression,' and 'Negligent government of Princes, with Rebellion'! Even a careful reader is apt to be surprised by this belated pronouncement of a Natural Law against Cowardice, and that Natural Justice dictates its being punished with oppression[9] – much as the oppression of negligent Princes is apt to be punished by the Rebellion of Natural-Law-abiding Subjects who are not cowardly.[10]

There is a curious footnote, however, to this matter of oppression – which 'is indeed a great inconvenience' – for so Hobbes acknowledges it in the course of addressing the problem that he warns is most acute in monarchies, namely, 'the right of Succession.' Along with the more obvious hazards and objections requiring response, he raises one that seems rather remote, not to say unrealistic:

But if it be lawfull for a Monarch to dispose of the Succession by words of Contract, or Testament, men may perhaps object a great inconvenience: for he may
sell, or give his Right of governing to a stranger; which, because strangers (that is,
men not used to live under the same government, nor speaking the same language)
do commonly undervalue one another, may turn to the oppression of his Subjects;
which is indeed a great inconvenience: but it proceedeth not necessarily from the
subjection to a strangers government, but from the unskilfulnesse of the Governours, ignorant of the true rules of Politiques. (XIX/23, 101)

Actually, it is difficult to decide which is more curious: Hobbes's choosing to pose this particular objection, or the impertinence of his reply to it.
For notice, first of all, he utterly ignores the stated possibility that is sure
to be condemned by almost anyone: that of *selling* the Sovereignty to the
highest bidder, whether domestic or alien. Instead, he focuses exclusively
on the possibility of the buyer, or beneficiary, being a 'stranger' – which
he suggests (on rather unconvincing grounds) is more apt to be an
oppressive ruler. But instead of rejoining 'So what?' – as would be justified by his doctrine that Subjects owe virtually unqualified obedience to
any functioning government – he addresses a different point entirely, and
one that would pertain no more to government by 'strangers' than by
anyone else: namely, the 'great inconvenience' of *oppression*, arguing that
it is due to the political ignorance, hence unskilfulness of those who
govern. This carries the clear implication that governing in accordance
with 'the true rules of Politiques' – and Hobbes certainly means to
include those laid out in *Leviathan* – would *not* be genuinely oppressive
(whatever might be said about it by demagogues exploiting easily aroused
'Tyrannophobia'). Thus, there is no legitimate objection to 'Government
by Strangers' per se, only to a Stranger – or anyone else? – who is politically ignorant, consequently inept. And thus, the possibility of sovereign
power passing into the hands of a Stranger, far from invalidating
Hobbes's teaching, obliquely confirms it. The solution to the age-old
problem of providing stable, secure, enduring, prosperous, and *non-
oppressive* government is immediately available: the unprejudiced study
of *Leviathan*.

But for all of the importance embedded in this curious discussion of a
Stranger assuming Sovereign Power – and I shall argue in a later chapter
that it is of paramount importance – one must not lose sight of what is
ostensibly at issue: not the legitimacy of strangers governing, but the
danger of their doing so *oppressively*. And the fact that this would be due

to their incompetence, rather than (say) to greed or malice, would be cold comfort to those they oppressed. And even if, on balance, their subjects would be well-advised to grin and bear it – after all, Aristotle might advise them likewise – are they *mistaken* in regarding such a regime as *unjust*?

In light of the suspicions I have raised as to Hobbes's real views about a wide range of matters, but most lately about regimes, this seems an opportune point at which to direct attention towards what might be called 'The Grand Paradox' of his *Leviathan* – a paradox so comprehensive that it almost escapes notice – and further, to suggest that it may well explain his many ambiguities and equivocations, apparent inconsistencies and outright contradictions. Consider.

He argues strenuously that the Subjects of any functioning polity owe it their unquestioning obedience, denying them any grounds for challenging a Sovereign who is maintaining law and order, at least so long as their own lives are not directly jeopardized. They cannot claim he is guilty of illegality, or breech of contract, nor allege some sanctity of one's own conscience, nor claim invasion of private property, nothing. Hobbes insists that the logic of the Social Contract precludes their judging the quality of a Sovereign's governance or any of his decisions; those subject to him must understand themselves as obliged 'to submit their Wills, every one to his Will, and their Judgements, to his Judgement' (XVII/13, 87). All that, while he at the same time provides a detailed template for doing this very thing: for judging whether one's Sovereign is governing rightly, namely, in accordance not only with all the Natural Laws, but also with Hobbes's recommendations regarding property distribution, commerce, appointment of counselors, regulating private corporations, taxation, censorship, management of religion, crime and punishment, public awards and offices, and almost every other matter of importance to political life.

So skilful is his use of rhetoric that this paradox passes unnoticed by most readers, who are manoeuvred into viewing the political problem exclusively from the perspective of one of the Ruled. But as Hobbes states plainly by way of concluding the first half of his great treatise, he has written it so 'that men may learn thereby, *both* how to *govern, and* how to *obey*' (XXXI/41, 193; emphasis added). And while any Ruler would approve the teaching of unqualified civil obedience to the Ruled – that it is irrational for his Subjects to presume to judge the quality of his

Rule, and the height of irrationality even to contemplate rebellion – he would have to be a natural fool not to appreciate the political effect of embedding that teaching in a blueprint for *rational* rule, by which he will be judged, regardless of any prohibiting rationale to the contrary. Not for nothing has Hobbes several times reminded him that reason is less potent with most people than is passion.

16

Equity
and the Problem of *Egoism*

In the preceding chapter, I raised various objections to the legal positivist's conception of justice-as-convention. But I also expressed doubts
about Hobbes's own subscription to the version he advances in
Leviathan. In support of those doubts, I cited several instances of his use
of the term 'just' that would seem to suggest his recognition of some
natural principle(s) of justice, while conceding these instances might be
dismissed as trivial, or mere figures of careless speech. There are,
however, other examples that cannot be so blithely dismissed:

It is also against Law, to say that no Proofe shall be admitted against a Presumption of Law. For all Judges, Sovereign and subordinate, if they refuse to hear
Proofe, refuse to do Justice: for though the Sentence be Just, yet the Judges that
condemn without hearing the Proofes offered, are Unjust Judges; and their Presumption is but Prejudice; which no man ought to bring with him to the Seat of
Justice, whatsoever precedent judgements, or examples he shall pretend to follow.
(XXVI/24, 145)

[W]hen the sons of *Samuel*, being constituted by their father Judges in *Bersabee*,
received bribes, and judged unjustly, the people of Israel refused any more to have
God to be their King, in other manner than he was King of other people ... So
that Justice fayling, Faith also fayled: Insomuch, as they deposed their God, from
reigning over them. (XII/30, 59)

Distributive Justice [is] the Justice of an Arbitrator; that is to say, the act of defining what is Just. Wherein, (being trusted by them that make him Arbitrator,) if he
performe his Trust, he is said to distribute to every man his own: and this is indeed

Just Distribution, and may be called (though improperly) Distributive Justice, but more properly Equity. (XV/15, 75)

And therefore if the Soveraign shall have a question of Right grounded, not upon his present Will, but upon the Lawes formerly made; the Length of Time shal bring no prejudice to his Right; but the question shal be judged by Equity. For many unjust Actions, and unjust Sentences, go uncontrolled a longer time, than any man can remember. And our lawyers account no Customes Law, but such as are reasonable, and that evill Customes are to be abolished: But the Judgement of what is reasonable, and of what is to be abolished, belonged to him that maketh the Law. (XXVI/7, 138)

As is readily seen, these matters touch the very heart of Hobbes's political prescription, having profound implications for correctly understanding his view of justice and its administration. For it is the idea of Justice actually manifested that establishes the practical foundation of political life. But these same matters involving judges and other officials challenge the adequacy of the radically egoistic conception of human nature upon which Hobbes's entire political science apparently rests.

Moreover, as is clearest in the latter two passages quoted, the issues of both Justice (explicitly) and Egoism (implicitly) are inseparable from what Hobbes calls 'Equity.' Indeed, it is no exaggeration to say that substantial answers to many if not most of the questions involving justice and its practical application – questions left in obscurity by the formalistic view that justice is whatever the law, as interpreted and applied, establishes as such – Hobbes simply transfers to an equally formal idea of Equity. But it is exceedingly difficult (I think impossible) to make sense of this idea apart from some recognition of *natural* justice. Indeed, how else is one to understand Hobbes's own final reference to Equity than as an acknowledgment that a natural sense of justice is intrinsic to human nature: 'The *Word of God*, is then also to be taken for the Dictates of reason, and equity, when the same is said in the Scriptures to bee written in mans heart' (XXXVI/6, 224)? But even granting there to be natural justice, equitable outcomes rely upon notions of judicial impartiality and disinterestedness that are directly contrary to the 'selfish individualism' that Hobbes would have his general readership believe is the universal motivation of human behaviour. Needless to add, this egoism bears on other matters vital to political life besides that of administering justice, such as giving counsel and advice to others (including governors) and having a genuine concern for the common good. It is also at odds with a broad range of phenomena ordinarily associated with humane feelings.

It is useful to address first the problems posed for Hobbes's own political prescription by his apparent insistence on viewing human nature as radically egoistic: that every person is to be understood as profoundly selfish, concerned not just primarily, but exclusively, with his or her own good. There is no shortage of textual evidence expressing this egoism.[1] Speaking of the action which makes possible the (hypothetical) creation of a commonwealth, Hobbes contends: 'Whensoever a man Transferreth his Right, or Renounceth it; it is either in consideration of some Right reciprocally transferred to himselfe; or for some other good he hopeth for thereby. For it is a voluntary act: and of the voluntary acts of every man, the object is some *Good to himselfe*' (XIV/8, 65–6). And in his argument for the vitally important *'fourth Law of Nature, Gratitude,'* we are assured that 'no man giveth, but with intention of Good to himselfe; because Gift is Voluntary; and of all Voluntary Acts, the object is to every man his own Good' (XV/16, 75). Consider also the reasoning that leads to Hobbes's seventeenth Law: 'And seeing every man is presumed to do all things in order to his own benefit, no man is fit Arbitrator in his own cause'; also the eighteenth 'For the same reason' (XV/31–2, 78). And, as I have had occasion to note more than once, this Machiavellian realism about human nature figures importantly in Hobbes's argument for the superior 'Convenience' of the monarchical form of commonwealth.

[W]hosoever beareth the Person of the people, or is one of that Assembly that bears it, beareth also his own naturall Person. And though he be carefull in his politique Person to procure the common interest; yet he is more, or no lesse carefull to procure the private good of himselfe, his family, kindred and friends; and for the most part, if the publique interest chance to crosse the private, he preferrs the private: for the Passions of men, are commonly more potent than their Reason. From whence it follows, that where the publique and private interest are most closely united, there is the publique most advanced. Now in Monarchy, the private interest is the same with the publique. (XIX/4, 95–6)

And in addressing the problem peculiar to hereditary monarchies – the need for a regent when the crown devolves upon a child – Hobbes assures us:

[T]he Law of Nature hath provided this sufficient rule, that the Tuition shall be in him, that hath by Nature most interest in the preservation of the Authority of the infant, and to whom least benefit can accrue by his death, or diminution. For seeing every man by nature seeketh his own benefit, and promotion; to put an Infant into the power of those, that can promote themselves by his destruction, or dammage, is not Tuition, but Trechery. (XIX/9, 97)[2]

In light of these and numerous other passages, there can be little question but that Hobbes means to encourage his reader to view human nature as essentially egoistic: to regard every person as concerned exclusively with his or her own good, understood as the enjoyment of whatever brings pleasure and the avoidance of whatever causes pain (as per VI/7 & 11, 24–5).

The strictness of this egoism deserves all the emphasis Hobbes himself gives it: '*every* man *by nature* seeketh his own benefit'; 'of *all* Voluntary Acts, the object is to *every* man his own good'; '*every* man is presumed to do *all* things in order to his own benefit.' Hobbes is *not* merely asserting what almost any experienced adult would concede – that most people are for the most part primarily self-interested – though it is this virtual truism that lends immediate plausibility to Hobbes's unqualified claim. Nor, on the other hand, does the claim have any descriptive or explanatory power (hence any real point) if interpreted as a tautology, such that *whatever* anyone does is declared to serve his own good simply because he chooses to do it. To be sure, Hobbes allows that each person's good includes other people (family, friends, colleagues, servants, whatever), but – per hedonism – only insofar as whatever happens to them bears ultimately upon his own desire for more pleasure and less displeasure, whether of body or soul.

However, like all else presented in Part One of *Leviathan* ('Of Man'), the reader must ratify this 'reading' of 'Mankind' in light of his own experience and introspection; it is up to him 'to consider, if he also find not the same in himself. For this kind of Doctrine, admitteth of no other Demonstration' (Introd/4, 2). One might begin this verification exercise by reflecting upon Hobbes's defining discussions of certain passions, asking whether he has accurately captured in words the phenomena as experienced by oneself, and in particular whether they are amenable to a strictly egoistic interpretation – or even intelligible on that basis. Consider, for example, the passion so closely associated with Justice, *Indignation*. Hobbes defines it thus: '*Anger* for great hurt done to another, when we conceive the same to be done by Injury' (VI/21, 26). As a comprehensive definition, this is doubly strange. For it excludes what would seem the more obvious egoistic manifestation of indignation: the anger one feels upon believing *oneself* to have been treated unjustly;[3] and instead it directs attention to expressions of the passion seemingly most at odds with egoism. For doubtless we often *do* feel this special anger on behalf of others that we believe to have been unjustly treated, even strangers a half a world away. But why would such injury bother an egoist the least bit? Does not Hobbes's definition instead suggest the classical view, that some sense of justice as well as that of self-regard is intrinsic to human nature, such that one is naturally offended – that one's own spirit is irritated – by other people's suffering what one deems a wanton act of injustice?[4]

Or consider Hobbes's definitions of so-called altruistic feelings, which also seem puzzlingly 'unegoistic': '*Desire* of good to another, BENEVO-LENCE, GOOD WILL, CHARITY. If to man generally, GOOD NATURE' (VI/22, 26). He offers no explanation of why or how, in actions *motivated* by such feelings, a person's primary if not exclusive objective in every case 'is some *Good to himselfe*,'[5] or, to move the problem back a step, *why* a strictly egoistic creature would have such a desire. And in those cases where we suspect that the benefactor's true objective is indeed 'some *Good to himselfe*,' do we really regard it as charity or benevolence? Do we not – quite properly, even necessarily – distinguish mercenary actions from those motivated by genuine 'good will' towards others? And if Hobbes were to reply, 'In the latter cases, the deeper objective is still selfish: one wishes to feel good about oneself,' his response would clearly be question-begging. Why would charitable actions make one 'feel good' in a way that mercenary actions do not unless there is an important difference between the two – reflected, ironically, in one's taking a special pride in rising above the all-too-common selfishness which Hobbes would have us regard as universal and irrepressible? Moreover, if he means to allow for a person's getting pleasure from the sheer act of helping others, and/or from a sense of their being made better off, and/or of being pained by awareness of others' suffering – which surely is true for many people – would he not have to concede this is evidence of humans being naturally *political*, rather than egocentric individuals whose natural state is one by 'of Warre, where every man is Enemy to every man' (XIII/9, 62)?

Equally suspect, then, is Hobbes's overtly egoistic analysis of the '*Sudden Dejection* ... that causeth WEEPING' – that it is a consequence of 'such accidents, as suddenly taketh away some vehement hope, or some prop of their power: And they are most subject to it, that rely principally on helps externall, such as are Women, and Children. Therefore some

Weep for the losse of Friends; Others for their unkindnesse' (VI/43, 27). Is this really true: that a person weeps only for *himself*, and that what *saddens* him is the diminution of his own *power* upon the death of a beloved spouse, mother, daughter, or close friend? Hobbes speaks as if no one ever wept at the death of a child, dejected simply at the thought of its dying before having a fair chance to live. Or was never similarly moved to tears out of pity for the suffering of some decent person who was in no way involved in one's own life. Or, carrying such thinking further, as if no one wept at the tragic spectacle of *King Lear*.[6]

Hobbes acknowledges, of course, that humans feel pity, but his analysis of what it is and why we are susceptible to it is radically trimmed, not to say truncated, to fit the procrustean bed of an egoistic psychology: '*Grief*, for the Calamity of another, is PITTY; and ariseth from the imagination that the like calamity may befall himselfe; and therefore is called also COMPASSION' (VI/46, 27). Admittedly, pity (or compassion, commiseration, sympathy) relies upon imagining oneself in another's place, and how one would feel were one subjected to a similar adversity. And it is doubtless true, as Hobbes observes, 'for Calamity arriving from great wickedness, the best men have the least Pitty.' But one cannot as readily agree with what he adds: 'and for the same Calamity, those have least Pitty, that think themselves least obnoxious to the same.' For surely pity is not so narrowly restricted as that. It can be felt irrespective of any real possibility that a 'like Calamity' might actually befall oneself. I may pity an orphaned child, an abandoned wife, a hard-labouring peasant whose crops were devoured by locusts – I may pity an abused dog, for that matter. In order to sympathize or feel pity, there is no necessity that one be, in effect, subconsciously – and quite irrationally – feeling sorry for one's own imagined self (as per the egoistic view). And what would be the consequences were everyone to regard expressions of sympathy in that light: not as moved by genuine care for the suffering of others, but by the pain of self-pity? Would anyone then derive comfort from such expressions? Still less if one were persuaded by Hobbes that 'To revile, mock, or pitty is to *Dishonour*' (X/25, 43; emphasis added).[7] Pity may be a painful feeling, but humans' unique susceptibility to it is far more plausibly interpreted as evidence of their being political by nature, than of their being animated solely by self-regard.

Or consider Honour and Praise in this egoistic framework. In the chapter devoted to these topics, Hobbes makes a sequence of claims that seem intentionally designed to elicit objections. We are told, for example, that 'To obey, is to Honour; because no man obeyes them, whom they think have no power to help, or hurt them' (X/20, 42). Has no one ever obeyed another simply out of gratitude? or love? or admiration? or duty? Moreover, as I noted before, obedience rendered out of *these* feelings would be *genuine* expressions of honour – as distinct from the mere *appearance* of honour. Whereas obedience wholly out of self-regard might be accorded someone for whom one privately had the utmost contempt. We may be sure that Hobbes is aware of radical discrepancies between Appearance and Reality in human relations, as he warns in a different context that a 'counterfeit love' can mask a 'secret hatred' (XI/7, 48).

Similarly suspect is his contention that 'To give way, or place to another, in any Commodity, is to Honour; being a confession of greater power' (X/23, 42). Honour it may be, but often it is nothing more than ordinary politeness or graciousness, or proffered in respect, not of greater power, but of age, virtue, learnedness, public service, sanctity – indeed, of whatever one deems worthy of respect (which for some people includes mere celebrity). And must we not entertain comparable reservations about Hobbes's unqualified claim that 'To give great gifts to a man, is to Honour him; because 'tis buying of Protection, and acknowledging of Power' – just as, according to him, 'To be sedulous in promoting anothers good [is] a signe we seek his protection or ayde' (X/21–2, 64)? Doubtless this fits those many cases where the giver or promoter hopes to curry favour with someone whose power he solicits, or fears.[8] But taking into account the *entirety* of one's experience, here too one can insist that much gift-giving, whether great or small, is neither so selfishly motivated nor reflective of the recipient's relative power. Sometimes it is simply adherence to custom; other times the gift-giver wishes only to please people he likes (including those inferior in power), or to contribute to a ceremonial occasion (e.g., weddings), or to succour those in need, or to practise philanthropy on moral principle (perhaps even doing so anonymously).[9]

With such reservations in mind, it is worth revisiting various of Hobbes's Laws of Nature, beginning with the Fourth (partially quoted earlier):

As Justice dependeth on Antecedent Covenant; so does GRATITUDE depend on Antecedent Grace; that is to say, Antecedent Free-gift: and is the fourth Law of Nature; which may be conceived in this Forme, *That a man which receiveth Benefit from another of meer Grace, Endeavour that he which giveth it, have no reasonable cause to repent him of his good will.* For no man giveth, but with intention of Good to himselfe; because Gift is Voluntary; and of all Voluntary Acts, the

Object is to every man his own Good; of which if men see they shall be frustrated, there will be no beginning of benevolence, or trust; nor consequently of mutuall help; nor of reconciliation of one man to another. (XV/16, 75)

Doubtless, a person who gives freely of his time, skills, strength, money, or whatever does not intend as a consequence to suffer harm at the hands of his beneficiary. And sincere gratitude to one's benefactors is but an elementary form of natural justice, indeed, the minimum recompense for benefits received out of sheer graciousness. One must wonder, however, whether viewing benefactions in the mercenary light of Hobbes's rationale would not tend rather to compromise than to promote genuine feelings of gratitude, and wonder, further, whether he could possibly have thought otherwise. One's reservations are compounded by his earlier warning that – human nature being what it is – a return of bad for good is a real possibility to be guarded against:

To have received from one, to whom we think our selves equall, greater benefits than there is hope to Requite, disposeth to counterfeit love; but really to secret hatred; and puts a man into the estate of a desperate debtor, that in declining the sight of his creditor, tacitely wishes him there, where he might never see him more. For benefits oblige; and obligation is thralldome; and unrequitable obligation, perpetuall thralldome; which is to ones equall, hatefull. But to have received benefits from one, whom we acknowledge for superiour, enclines to love; because the obligation is no new depression: and cheerfull acceptation, (which men call *Gratitude*,) is such an honour done to the obliger, as is taken generally for retribution. Also to receive benefits, though from an equall, or inferiour, as long as there is hope of requitall, disposeth to love: for in the intention of the receiver, the obligation is of ayd, and service mutuall; from whence proceedeth an Emulation of who shall exceed in benefiting; the most noble and profitable contention possible; wherein the victor is pleased with his victory, and the other revenged by confessing it. (XI/7, 48)

'Revenged by confessing it.' Droll. But putting all this together, one may wonder whether Hobbes, sceptical of the natural justness of the vast majority of mainly egocentric people, is more concerned with dampening the resentment he warns of than with nurturing a general benevolence or trust, upon which one can never safely rely. Thus he encourages – on the part of both giver and receiver, notice – a strictly utilitarian, calculative understanding of 'benefits.' Insofar as this interpretation of 'ayd' dissipates ill-will born of feelings of inferiority, it may actually be more effective in nurturing civic friendship in most people than would endless lip-service to an unrealistic altruism. At the same time, licensing this self-serving attitude does not preclude more noble-souled people feeling – and exemplifying – genuine gratitude uncontaminated by either merce-nary calculations or vulgar resentment. As is typical of Hobbes's explicit reasoning, if people are better than he gives them credit for being, so much the better will be the functioning of the polity he prescribes.

Speaking of Revenge, however, the Seventh Law governing it – '*That in Revenges*, (that is, retribution of Evil for Evil,) *Men look not at the great-nesse of the evill past, but the greatnesse of the good to follow*' – conflicts with the egocentric hedonism Hobbes would apparently have his general readership adopt. In expounding the rationale for this being a Law of Nature, Hobbes argues, 'Revenge without respect to the Example, and profit to come, is a triumph, or glorying in the hurt of another, tending to no end; ... and glorying to no end, is vain-glory, and contrary to reason' (XV/19, 76). Ah, but is this so? The claim echoes Hobbes's rather inap-posite definition of 'Cruelty,' dismissing it as merely a manifestation of '*Contempt*, or little sense of the calamity of others ... proceeding from Security of their own fortune.' This is immediately followed by what, taken seriously, would stand out as arguably the most naive, *un*realistic statement in the book: 'For, that any man should take pleasure in other mens great harmes, without other end of his own, I do not conceive it possible' (VI/47, 27–8). But no '*other* end' is needed if every person's own pleasure is the good whence he takes his bearings – and that humans do derive pleasure from exacting revenge, sometimes the greatest pleasure, is proverbial[10] (to say nothing of those misbegotten individuals, not all that rare, who positively delight in cruelty). Why else would Hobbes bother to pronounce a Natural Law against 'pure' revenge, or use man's propen-sity for it as the rationale for his Eighth Law ('because all signes of hatred, or contempt, provoke to fight; insomuch as most men choose to hazard their life, than not to be revenged'; XV/20, 76)? Hobbes is decidely *not* naïve. He acknowledges that the desire for revenge can be so '*excessive*' as to be a form of madness (VIII/19, 35–6),[11] whereas having to *surrender* 'thoughts of revenge' due to 'Reconciliation' can cause a grown man to weep (VI/43, 27)!

Suffice it to say, there are various objections to be raised against the strict egoism Hobbes repeatedly advances. Some are based on the contrast between the ordinary experience and understanding of human feelings and behaviour (on the one hand), and Hobbes's construal of these same things. Other objections pertain to what seem internal contradictions in his presentation. None is of greater consequence, however, than the problems with egoism which surface in chapters 25 and 26 – the former ('*Of* COUNSEL') pertaining to the pervasive human activity of counselling and advising others, the latter ('*Of* CIVILL LAWES') to the all-important practical issue of how Justice is actually manifested in a commonwealth.

Hobbes begins his analysis '*Of* COUNSEL' by insisting upon the importance of clearly distinguishing between 'Counsels, and Commands.' In fact, he alleges their often being confused is the best illustration of 'How fallacious it is to judge of the *nature* of *things*, by the ordinary and inconstant use of *words*' (my emphasis). There is a bit of ironic humour here, as the 'natural things' in question are themselves certain kinds of *speeches*. The cause of this (supposed) confusion is that both counsels and commands are spoken in the 'Imperative manner.' While this is not so much a problem when one can observe who is speaking, to whom, and in what context, the mix-up (Hobbes warns) arises in 'mens writings,' whence come mistaken understandings as to the status of various 'Precepts.' The pertinence of this latter claim is not immediately clear, nor for that matter is the importance of first distinguishing counsel from command, given that the principal concern of the chapter is to elucidate the conditions for the Sovereign being well counselled; the chapter contains virtually nothing about commands. But it does include, appropriately enough, some discussion of rhetoric under the rubric of '*Counsell vehemently pressed*' in the forms of 'exhortation' and 'dehortation.' Hobbes's treatment of these forms is decidely prejudicial, however, as though they had little if any practical legitimacy.

A pronounced imbalance characterizes his initial definitions and subsequent discussion. Almost as if purposeful, everything is distorted, rendered confused or counterfactual, by the premise of strict egoism. Granted, the chapter's implicit focus is on counselling the Sovereign. Still, Hobbes presents his definitions as *generally* valid. If instead they are generally *objectionable*, one must presume their flaws affect this special case as well.

COMMAND is, where a man saith, *Doe this*, or *Doe not this*, without expecting other reason than the Will of him that sayes it. From this it followeth manifestly, that he that Commandeth, pretendeth thereby his own Benefit: For the reason of his Command is his own Will onely, and the proper object of every mans Will, is some Good to himselfe.

COUNSELL, is where a man saith, *Doe*, or *Doe not this*, and deduceth his reasons from the benefit that arriveth by it to him to whom he saith it. And from this it is evident, that he that giveth Counsell, pretendeth onely (whatsoever he intendeth) the good of him, to whom he giveth it.

Therefore between Counsell and Command, one great difference is, that Command is directed to a mans own benefit; and Counsell to the benefit of another man.[12] And from this ariseth another difference, that a man may be obliged to do what he is Commanded; as when he hath covenanted to obey: But he cannot be obliged to do as he is Counselled, because the hurt of not following it, is his own; or if he should covenant to follow it, then is the Counsell turned into the nature of a Command. A third difference between them is, that no man can pretend a right to be of another mans Counsell; because he is not to pretend benefit by it to himselfe: but to demand right to Counsell another, argues a will to know his designes, or to gain some other Good to himselfe; which (as I said before) is of every mans will the proper object. (XXV/2–4, 131–2)

Egoism cuts against both definitions, but in opposite ways. On the one hand, Hobbes speaks here as if no parent ever commanded his child out of concern for the child's own benefit,[13] likewise no drill sergeant a recruit, no coach an athlete, no teacher his student, no fire marshal a negligent homeowner, no lifeguard a careless swimmer, no policeman an inebriated pedestrian – as if no one in any position of rule ever commanded anything other than what redounded to his own good. On the other hand, egoism precludes any *motive* for providing counsel or advice that truly aims at 'the benefit of another man' except insofar as the recommendation's acceptance somehow also benefits the adviser. Were this a valid conception of human nature, no one would ever offer his advice, much less offer it unsolicited, simply out of a concern for another's welfare. After all, doing so usually takes some thought, time, and effort – and there would be no motive for an egoist to waste the least bit without some quid pro quo. Nor, then, would there be much point in anyone seeking advice, or accepting it at face value. In short, the presumption that a consistent egoism requires: that all advice and counsel is selfishly motivated, profoundly compromises any reason for either seeking or giving it. This simply does not square with everyday experience.

Simply consider the manifold ways in which advice, counsel, warnings, urgings, admonitions, and recommendations *pervade* human life, many of which are so natural, so taken for granted, as to be scarcely noticed. Even in the busiest metropolis, visitors usually have little difficulty getting directions on how to get to wherever – or advice on what to see or where to eat – from passersby they are unlikely to encounter again. Most people are willing to be helpful in these ways, without thought of reward. (And how would we regard anyone who *did* demand payment?) Similarly, most people would voluntarily and without prompting caution anyone they suspect may be unaware of a particular danger, whether comparatively minor ('Watch those stairs; they're slippery'), or more consequential ('Avoid that part of town – muggings are common'). Friends and neighbours, workmates and classmates routinely provide each other advice and recommendations, warnings and cautions that are neither self-serving nor apportioned in strict exchange: about schools, churches, dentists, restaurants, films, techniques, products, scams, speed traps, vacation spots, auto insurance, cold remedies, gardening tips – the list is endless. True, such advice-giving is normally reciprocal, but most of it is provided in a spirit of good will towards those to whom it is addressed, with no expectation of any definite return. And it is received on that same assumption – not, that is, as motivated strictly by self-inter-est, hence somehow skewed by an exclusively egoistic regard. Ordinary social life is filled with 'counselling' of all kinds and would be bizarre to the point of unrecognizable were all this sort of thing to cease.

How a strictly egoistic perspective distorts the understanding of human relations is equally clear in Hobbes's treatment of certain uses of rhetoric: 'EXHORTATION, and DEHORTATION, is Counsell, accompanied with signes in him that giveth it, of vehement desire to have it followed.' The principal sign, apparently, is:

[H]e that Exhorteth, doth not deduce the consequences of what he adviseth to be done, and tye himselfe therein to the rigour of true reasoning; but encourages him he Counselleth, to Action: As he that Dehorteth, deterreth him from it. And therefore they have in their speeches, a regard to the common Passions, and opin-ions of men, in deducing their reasons; and make use of Similitudes, Metaphors, Examples, and other tooles of Oratory, to perswade their Hearers of the Utility, Honour, or Justice of following their advice. (XXV/6, 132)

Here, too, Hobbes presumes, or would persuade his reader to presume, that self-interest is the only possible motive for someone strenuously urging anything involving other people – as if, having foreseen a grave danger, even certain disaster, in the course of action that a friend, or a com-mander, or a king, were contemplating, one were indifferent whether or not he heeded one's counsel against it. What, then, would be the point of offering it? So that one could have the pleasure of saying, 'I told you so'?

And as if he forgot the many times he warns that 'the Passions of men, are commonly more potent than their Reason,' Hobbes speaks here as if *reason alone* were always sufficient to persuade a person to do, or forbear, something truly to his own benefit. Such that any appeal to a person's passions (e.g., affection or pride) and beliefs (e.g., what is shameful, unjust, or impious) warrants concluding that whatever is being urged 'is directed to the Good of him that giveth the Counsell, not of him that asketh it' (XXV/7, 133). Why in the world should *anyone*, Prince or Pauper, conclude *that*? In cases where one truly cares about the welfare of others – be it intimate friends, family members, or the multitude of one's fellow citizens – surely one's primary concern in advising them is to do so in the most effective way. Speaking to what seems the principal concern of the chapter – counselling a sovereign – it would be a very special incumbent who could always be relied upon to be persuaded solely by reason, such that under no circumstances would a counsellor ever be justified in attempting to arouse or dampen his passions. And the fact that rhetoric can be used for basely selfish purposes is no argument against its being used for noble ends.[14] Moreover, it should be needless to add, not all selfish purposes are base; it is perfectly legitimate for someone falsely accused of a crime to use forensic rhetoric to defend himself, 'vehemently' exhorting the judge and jury – or the King himself – to do the right thing.

In short, were Hobbes to be consistent, and thus provide a strictly egoistic treatment 'Of Counsel,' it necessarily would be so contrary to ordinary assumptions and everyday experience as to be literally incredible. This is tacitly shown upon his shifting to the egoistic perspective in advancing a decidedly prejudicial critique of rhetoric ('*Counsell vehemently pressed*'), as if there were no legitimate uses of rhetoric in either private or public life. Suffice it to say, Hobbes's treatment of these matters is so inapposite that one must wonder what deeper purpose his analysis is meant to serve.

One thing seems clear. It is tailored for the counselling, not of just any kind of sovereign, but of a monarch, for whom an appeal to 'Utility, Honour, or Justice' would be especially pertinent. And it is tacitly addressed *to* a monarch. As he later observes:

[T]here is no choyce of Counsell, neither in a Democracy, nor Aristocracy; because the persons Counselling are members of the person Counselled. The choyce of Counsellours therefore is proper to Monarchy; In which, the Soveraign that endeavoureth not to make choyce of those, that in every kind are the most able, dischargeth not his office as he ought to do. The most able Counsellours, are they that have least hope of benefit by giving evill Counsell, and most knowledge of those things that conduce to Peace, and Defence of the Common-wealth. (XXX/25, 184)

The choice of the right counsellors, then, would seem the first duty of a *conscientious* king, one who endeavoured to 'discharge his office as he *ought*.' The conclusion of the passage quoted above, which introduces a substantial discussion of desiderata in a monarch's privy counsellors, implicitly refers back to the five formal conditions that Hobbes specifies make 'a good Counsellour,' the first being dictated by a prudent acknowledgment of natural egoism: '*That his Ends, and Interest, be not inconsistent with the Ends and Interest of him he Counselleth*' (XXV/11, 134). Notice, while this rule sensibly excludes employing counsellors whose interests are known or suspected to be contrary to those of the person being counselled, but does allow for seeking counsel from 'disinterested' parties, it throws no light on why these latter – presuming them to be nonetheless self-interested – would willingly be bothered to provide it. Is Hobbes here, too, relying upon men of honour (cf. X/28; /33; /35, 43)? Each of the subsequent conditions obviously pertains primarily, if not exclusively, to counselling a king – and a conspicuously intelligent, logically rigorous king at that. Consider the second condition:

Because the office of a Counsellour, when an action comes into deliberation, is to make manifest the consequences of it, in such manner, as he that is Counselled may be truly and evidently informed; he ought to propound his advise, in such forme of speech, as may make the truth most evidently appear; that is to say, with as firme ratiocination, as significant and proper language, and as briefly, as the evidence will permit. (XXV/12, 134)

Only cold, rational analysis is acceptable, expressed 'as briefly' as is consistent with solid evidence for the recommendation. Any busy chief executive would endorse this proviso, and none more so than the chief of all chief executives, the King of a 'great Common-wealth.' That even the most competent king would need a plurality of counsellors is implicit in the third condition of acquiring good counsel: 'Because the ability of Counselling proceedeth from Experience, and long study; and no man is presumed to have experience in all those things that to the Administration of a great Common-wealth are necessary to be known, *No man is presumed to be a good Counsellour, but in such Businesse, as he hath not*

*onely been much versed in, but hath also much meditated on, and consid-
ered*' (XXV/13, 134). On the expectation, then, that a king will have a
plurality of counsellors, Hobbes provides several reasons for a fifth condition of obtaining good counsel from them: 'a man is better Counselled
by hearing them apart, then in an Assembly' (XXV/15, 135). And while
Hobbes concedes the 'tooles of Oratory' are useful in addressing multitudes, he argues that they are (meaning 'should be') ineffective when
addressed to a single person, such as a King, who may 'interrupt [the
Orator], and examine his reasons more rigorously,' entering 'into
Dispute, and Dialogue with him' (XXV/8, 133).

Reflecting on how curious is Hobbes's treatment '*Of* COUNSELL' in the
chapter so named – emphasizing the egocentric propensity inherent in
human nature, while at the same time seeming to disavow it by insisting
that it is 'the *duty* of a Counsellour ... to regard, *not* his *own* benefit, but
his whom he adviseth'; seeking to arouse suspicion towards counsel too
vehemently pressed; disallowing all use of rhetoric, stressing instead 'the
rigour of true reasoning,' and the advantages of engaging one's counsellors in one-on-one dialogue – reflecting on these features of Hobbes's
own counsel, must we not presume that he has especially in mind counselling a very particular sort of Sovereign, or more precisely, a very special
kind of *King*?

Why (then) is there no explicit exposition of the virtues and other personal characteristics of a suitable King – one who could be counted upon
to 'dischargeth ... his office as he ought to do' in all his roles: as supreme
Lawgiver, Decision-maker, and Judge; as 'Generallissimo' (XVIII/12, 92);
and, as Archpriest and Defender of the Faith? The short answer is the
obvious one: providing a checklist of the qualities that constitute The
Perfect Prince would be an open invitation to every shallow, ignorant,
short-sighted, passion-ruled, hence irrational, demagogue-incitable, egocentric Subject to judge his actual Sovereign, and find him wanting – contrary to the entire rationale for establishing an unchallengeable Sovereign
as the sine qua non of a stable, peaceful commonwealth. There is,
however, a longer answer, not inconsistent with the short one, but much
less suited for popular consumption. Showing this to be so is central to an
exposition of what I believe to be Hobbes's deeper political teaching, the
interpretation I have titled 'The Platonic *Leviathan*.'

The Sovereign's responsibility as Head of the Church is not to be minimized, for the political problem posed by the priesthood is apparently
what is behind Hobbes's beginning this chapter with his emphatic dis-

tinction between 'command' and 'counsel,' warning that failure to heed it can be a source of confusion, particularly concerning precepts conveyed 'in mens writings.' As noted before, however, the distinction turns out to be almost completely irrelevant to his analysis 'of counsel' in the chapter so titled. The distinction figures in only one paragraph, which ostensibly is included solely to illustrate the distinction!

Examples of the difference between Command and Counsell, we may take from the formes of Speech that express them in Holy Scripture. *Have no other Gods but me*; *Make to thy selfe no graven Image*; *Take not Gods name in vain*; *Sanctifie the Sabbath*; *Honour thy Parents*; *Kill not*; *Steale not*, &c. are Commands; because the reason for which we are to obey them, is drawn from the will of God our King, whom we are obliged to obey. But these words, *Sell all thou hast; give it to the poore; and follow me*, are Counsell; because the reason for which we are to do so, is drawn from our own benefit; which is this, that we shall have *Treasure in heaven* ... [T]hese words, *Repent, and be Baptized in the name of Jesus*, are Counsell; because the reason why we should so do, tendeth not to any benefit of God Almighty, who shall still be King in what manner soever we rebell; but of our selves, who have no other means of avoyding the punishment hanging over us for our sins. (XXV/10, 133)

Given that the purpose of this paragraph is to clarify the distinction – 'in *mens* writings,' recall – it is surely strange that its actual effect is only to confuse matters. How can the precept '*Repent, and be Baptized*' be merely counsel because it is not aimed at benefiting God, and yet the Decalogue be genuine commands? Are we to understand all ten Commandments as tending to some benefit of *God*? Is God also egocentric, such that invariably the 'proper object' of His expressed Will also 'is some Good to himselfe' (inscrutable though it might be)? That would explain *our* egocentricity, presuming we are made in His image. But it would also call into question the divine lineage of Jesus, whose words and deeds – including those which Hobbes himself cites – are not ordinarily understood as endorsements of the egoistic hedonism Hobbes propounds.

Still, despite the muddle affecting the above passage, I presume the general distinction between counsel and command (of which Law is a species; XXVI/8, 137) is clear enough. Hobbes's purpose in introducing it, however, remains to be surmised. And the Biblical illustration provides the essential clue: the distinction is crucial to Hobbes's interpretation of Scripture in 'Part 3' of *Leviathan*, 'OF A CHRISTIAN COMMON-WEALTH.'

There are many instances of his so using it. For example, in arguing against Cardinal Bellarmine's defence of 'the Ecclesiasticall Power' of the Popes:

If now it should appear, that there is no Coercive Power left them by our Saviour; but onely a Power to proclaim the Kingdom of Christ, and to perswade men to submit themselves thereunto; and by precepts and good counsell, to teach them that have submitted, what they are to do, that they may be received into the Kingdom of God when it comes; and that the Apostles, and other Ministers of the Gospel, are our Schoolmasters, and not our Commanders, and their Precepts not Laws, but wholesome Counsells; then were all that dispute in vain. (XLII/5, 269)

And arguing along the same lines later: 'the Power of the Pope, though hee were S. Peter, is neither Monarchy, nor hath any thing of *Archicall*, nor *Craticall*, but onely of *Didacticall*; For God accepteth not a forced, but a willing obedience' (XLII/115, 312). Hobbes concludes his extensive critique of the doctrine of Excommunication thus: 'In summe, the Power of Excommunication cannot be extended further than to the end for which the Apostles and Pastors of the Church have their Commission from our Saviour; which is not to rule by Command and Coaction, but by Teaching and Direction of men in way of Salvation in the world to come' (XLII/31, 279). And apparently ignoring the plain intent of Jesus's most famous sermon, in which He repeatedly contrasts His message with what we call Old Testament teachings ('Ye have heard that it hath been said ... But I say unto you'), Hobbes insists to the contrary that Jesus merely reaffirms those teachings:

For our Saviour Christ hath not given us new Laws, but Counsell to observe those wee are subject to; that is to say, the Laws of Nature, and the Laws of our severall Soveraigns: Nor did he make any new Law to the Jews in his Sermon on the Mount, but onely expounded the Law of Moses, to which they were subject before. The Laws of God therefore are none but the Laws of Nature, whereof the principall is, that we should not violate our Faith, that is, a commandement to obey our Civill Soveraigns. (XLIII/5, 322)

Suffice it to say, this view does scarce justice to what is 'new' about the New Testament. And it is also worth noting, there is no inclusion of the Decalogue as a whole in the Laws '*wee* are subject to' (unlike the Jews).[15] The main point, however, is that the purpose behind Hobbes's emphatic distinction between 'Command' and 'Counsel' is to negate the political pretensions of any and all Christian clergy, and by extension, of any supposedly autonomous religious authorities.

Given the scepticism, not to say deep suspicion, with which a convinced egoist would view all advice offered him – doubting whether anyone actually fulfils 'the duty of a Counsellour' that Hobbes (conveniently ignoring egoism) specifies: 'to regard, not his own benefit, but his whom he adviseth' – a prudent counsellor would be reluctant, if not simply unwilling, to offer any advice he supposes a powerful egoist would be unhappy to hear. For were he to do so, he not only would he be unlikely 'to gain some Good to *himselfe*; which [supposedly] is of every mans will the proper object,' but quite the contrary, he would risk loss. To cope with this problem, Hobbes appeals to natural justice: 'This also is incident to the nature of Counsell; that whatsoever it be, he that asketh it, cannot *in equity* accuse, or punish it: For to ask Counsell of another, is to permit him to give such Counsell as he shall think best' (XXV/5, 132; emphasis added). But is Egoism compatible with making decisions in accordance with Equity, disregarding self-interest so far as equity requires?

This problem comes to the fore in the longest chapter in the first half of *Leviathan*, the twenty-sixth, 'Of CIVILL LAWES,' wherein Hobbes addresses the practicalities of a Sovereign's most important internal responsibility: dispensing Justice. But as a logical prerequisite of determining whether Equity and Egoism are consonant, one needs a clear idea of what Hobbes means by 'equity.' Gaining that clarity, however, is not as straightforward as his profligate use of the term might lead one to suppose (it occurs some forty times, all but two in the first half of the book). He mentions it initially in the Introduction, suggesting that we think of '*Equity* and *Lawes*, [as] an artificial *Reason* and *Will*' of that 'Artificiall Man,' the Commonwealth (Introd/1, 1). But his first substantial treatment of the idea – and that, not much – comes in the course of discussing 'Distributive Justice' as required by the Third law of Nature. We are told that this is 'the Justice of an Arbitrator; that is to say, the act of defining what is Just. Wherein, ... if he performe his Trust, he is said to distribute to every man his own: and this is indeed Just Distribution, and may be called (though improperly) Distributive Justice, but more properly Equity; which also is a Law of Nature' (XV/14–15, 75). Specifically, it is the Eleventh Law in Hobbes's sequence:

Also, *if a man he trusted to judge between man and man*, it is a precept of the Law of Nature, *that he deale Equally between them*. For without that, the Controversies of men cannot be determined but by Warre. He therefore that is partiall in judgement, doth what in him lies, to deterre men from the use of Judges, and Arbitrators; and consequently, (against the fundamentall Lawe of Nature) is the cause of Warre.

The observance of this law, from the equall distribution to each man, of that which in reason belongeth to him, is called EQUITY, and (as I have sayd before) distributive Justice. (XV/23–4, 77)[16]

Thereafter, equity is expressly invoked in the rationale for three more natural laws (Twelfth, Thirteenth, and Seventeenth), and is clearly implicit in the rationale for two others (Fourteenth and Eighteenth).

Notice, first of all, Hobbes regularly affiliates Equity with Reason. Indeed, he more than merely affiliates them; he practically equates them. According to its first appearance in the text, Equity *is* an 'artificiall *Reason.*' And what is evident in the above-quoted passages is reinforced throughout the balance of the text:

[I]f the Soveraign employ a Publique Minister, without written Instructions what to doe; he is obliged to take for Instructions the Dictates of Reason; As if he make a Judge, The Judge is to take notice, that his Sentence ought to be according to the reason of his Soveraign, which being alwaies understood to be Equity, he is bound to it by the Law of Nature ...

For the will of another, cannot be understood, but by his own word, or act, or by conjecture taken from his scope and purpose; which in the person of the Common-wealth, is to be supposed alwaies consonant to Equity and Reason. (XXVI/14–15, 141)

The Interpretation of the Law of Nature, is the Sentence of the Judge constituted by the Soveraign Authority, to heare and determine such controversies, as depend thereon; and consisteth in the application of the Law to the present case. For in the act of Judicature, the Judge doth no more but consider, whither the demand of the party, be consonant to naturall reason, and Equity; and the Sentence he giveth, is therefore the Interpretation of the Law of Nature. (XXVI/23, 143)

Therefore all the Sentences of precedent Judges that have ever been, cannot all together make a Law contrary to naturall Equity: Nor any Examples of former Judges, can warrant an unreasonable Sentence, or discharge the present Judge of the trouble of studying what is Equity (in the case he is to Judge,) from the principles of his own naturall reason. (XXVI/24, 144)

Now the Intention of the Legislator is always supposed to be Equity: For it were a great contumely for a Judge to think otherwise of the Soveraigne. He ought therefore, if the Word of the Law doe not fully authorise a reasonable Sentence, to supply it with the Law of Nature; or if the case be difficult, to respit Judgement till he have received more ample authority. (XXVI/26, 145)

The things that make a good Judge, or good Interpreter of the Lawes, are, first, *A right understanding* of that principall Law of Nature called *Equity*; which, depending not on the reading of other mens Writings, but on the goodnesse of a mans own naturall Reason, and Meditation, is presumed to be in those most, that have had most leisure, and had the most inclination to meditate thereon. (XXVI/28, 146-7)

Hobbes's last two mentions of Equity – 'that *principall* Law of Nature' – are in the chapter explicating his interpretation of what is meant by 'the Word of God' in various passages of the Bible; and here as elsewhere it remains paired with Reason:

There are also places of the Scripture, where, by the *Word of God*, is signified such Words as are consonant to reason, and equity, though spoken sometimes neither by Prophet, nor by a holy man …

   The *Word of God*, is then also to be taken for the Dictates of reason, and equity, when the same is said in the Scriptures to bee written in mans heart; as *Psalm* 36.31. *Jerem.* 31.33. *Deut.* 30. 11,14. and many other like places. (XXXVI/5–6, 224)

So, what can be gleaned from Hobbes's use of 'equity' in these various contexts? Not as much as one might wish for, but perhaps enough for confirming certain suspicions concerning Hobbes's real views about justice.

   As I noted before, the utter formality of the positivist conception of Justice which Hobbes expressly advances in the earlier chapters (e.g., XIII/13, 63; XVIII/10, 91) – that Justice is *whatever* is required, forbidden, or otherwise prescribed by the Laws of a functioning commonwealth – in itself provides no guidance at all regarding what *substantially* the Law *ought* to be. But in the chapter 'Of CIVILL LAWES,' we learn that the will of a commonwealth's Sovereign Representative 'is to be supposed alwaies consonant to Equity and Reason,' that those authorized to render judgments in his name are to presume that 'the Intention of the Legislator is always supposed to be Equity' – indeed, that it would be a grave insult 'to think otherwise of the Soveraigne.' Thus, Hobbes tacitly enjoins judges to *interpret* the Laws, so far as possible, *as if* the Legislator's intention were the realization of equity. For that is what the Law *ought* to aim at. Far from being just any whim, caprice, prejudice, ill-considered wish, or preference of the Sovereign, the Law is supposed to be 'Rational' and 'Equitable,' whatever else. While these formal parameters are obviously important, knowing only this much still does not advance matters much in a substantial sense, insofar as we lack a clear idea of 'Rational Equity.'

As for the interpretation of a given (general) law and its practical application to the countless (particular) cases to which it pertains, here too equity is the key consideration: 'the Judge doth no more but consider, whither the demand of the party, be consonant to naturall reason, and Equity.' Parenthetically, it is worth noting here how inadequate for this task is Hobbes's 'official' accounts of both Prudence ('much Experience, and Memory of the like things, and their consequences heretofore') and Reason ('nothing but *reckoning* [i.e., 'Adding and Subtracting'] of the Consequences of generall names'); and, correspondingly, how essential are the classical conceptions of these rational faculties to any understanding of a person's ability to recognize *what* general principle is pertinent to a particular set of circumstances, and *how* it is best applied.

The Eleventh Natural law also mentions Equality (that a judge or arbitrator '*deale Equally*' between parties to a controversy, that Equity requires 'the equall distribution to each man, of that which in reason belongeth to him'). In this respect, Equity derives in part from the Ninth Law: '*That every man acknowledge other for his Equall by Nature.*' This translates into the recognition that all citizen-subjects are 'equal before the Law' – that Equity requires 'an equall distribution of Justice' (XXVIII/22, 165; cf. XXX/16, 180). This is certainly not nothing, but it too is almost purely formal. Thus, as I also noted before, all the really taxing questions about what *substantially* is Just, and how it is brought into political practice, Hobbes 'answers' by invoking Equity in conjunction with Reason – as if we already understood what is meant by that.

Perhaps we do, at least to some extent. Virtually everyone recognizes – to take the most obvious example – 'a Soveraign Prince, that [knowingly] putteth to death an Innocent Subject [violates] the law of Nature, as being contrary to Equitie' (XXI/7, 109; cf. XXVI/24, 144; XXVIII/22, 165).[17] But if this is the case, then some rudimentary sense of Natural Justice, of Fairness, of Desert, is inherent in human nature, some sensitivity as to what is just in things themselves (such that, as Hobbes here acknowledges, 'naturall Equity' exists as surely as does 'naturall Reason'). It is necessary that Equity be inherent *both* in men *and* in the things they make and do. For there must be something for reason to *discern*, thereby distinguishing arrangements and outcomes that are equitable from those that are not. But there must also be something in the human make-up that *cares* which is which, gratified by what a person judges to be equitable and annoyed by what is not. To be sure, this sense is stronger and finer in some people than in others insofar as they are better reasoners, and have the time and inclination to ponder with requisite seriousness those questions of Equity to which the answers are not at all obvious. But it is this *caring* about what is naturally equitable (about what is naturally *just*, that is, equity *being* 'Just Distribution') – shown most *clearly* in cases where a person's self-interest is *not* involved – that is difficult (I think impossible) to square with a strictly egoistic conception of human nature. This comes out unmistakably when one considers the four 'things that make a good Judge, or good Interpreter of the Lawes,' according to Hobbes (XXVI/28, 146–7).

The characteristic of first importance I quoted earlier: '*A right understanding* of that principall Law of Nature called *Equity*; which [depends] … on the goodnesse of a mans own naturall Reason, and Meditation … presumed to be in those most, that have had most leisure, and had the most inclination to meditate thereon.' The problems posed by egoism begin right here. Were it universally true about human nature, why would *anyone* waste his leisure and energy in attempting to deepen, broaden, and refine his understanding of *Equity* – rather than (say) invest in scheming how to get more for himself? For that matter, why would a strict egoist care the least bit about Equity – about a fair distribution of benefits and burdens among all citizens, for example – rather than being concerned exclusively with getting the best deal for himself (while presuming that everyone else is behaving likewise, and that the chips will fall accordingly)? Does the idea of Equity per se even make sense, given a conception of human nature wherein '*every* man is presumed to do *all* things in order to his own benefit'? Rather, that is, than presuming merely that *most* men do *most* things *most* of the time *primarily* for their own benefit? This latter view of human nature makes generous allowance for the self-interested tendency evident in virtually everyone (whence the plausibility of Egoism, which elevates a loose generality into a strict universality), but leaves open many more possibilities. After all, for an appeal to equity to have any effect, one must presume precisely what egoism denies: that other people (such as a Judge and Jurors) can be and are moved, not only by their own interests, but by what seems fair treatment of others – that they are *not* strict egoists, indifferent to what happens to others unless it should happen to affect their own prosperity.

The second characteristic of a good Judge, as specified by Hobbes, is '*Contempt of unnecessary Riches*, and Preferments.' But riches and offices are forms of 'Instrumental Power' (X/2, 41). And Hobbes is notorious for contending that will to power is the paramount constituent of human nature:[18]

[I]n the first place, I put for a generall inclination of all mankind, a perpetuall and restlesse desire of Power after power, that ceaseth onely in Death. And the cause of this, is not alwayes that a man hopes for a more intensive delight, than he has already attained to; or that he cannot be content with a moderate power: but because he cannot assure the power and means to live well, which he hath present, without the acquisition of more. (XI/2, 47).

On this view, there is no such thing as '*unnecessary* Riches' – one never knows how much might come in handy. Moreover, 'Riches [i.e., riches per se], are Honourable; for they are Power. Poverty, Dishonourable' (X/40, 44). And 'Preferments' are understood to be 'a signe of [the Sovereign's] will to Honour him' on whom they are bestowed (X/35, 43). Hobbes (ever the realist) expressly endorses greed: 'Covetousnesse of great Riches, and ambition of great Honours, are *Honourable*' (X/47, 44; emphasis added). Supposing that to be true, Hobbes's second proviso would seem to exclude not merely wealth-loving men as Judges, but honour-loving men as well. In any event, it is fairly obvious that such covetousness goes well with egoism – and, not so incidentally, with the ethos of a commercial republic which presumes that citizens' foremost everyday concern is 'commodious living' – whereas, it is equally clear that '*Contempt of unnecessary Riches*, and Preferments' does *not* harmonize well with universal egoism.

Similar remarks apply, I submit, to Hobbes's third requirement of a good Judge (i.e., a 'good Interpreter of the Lawes'): '*To be able in judgement to devest himselfe of all feare, anger, hatred, love, and compassion.*' But Hobbes assures us that all action, all 'Endeavour,' is passion-motivated, traceable ultimately to some 'Appetite, or Aversion' of the actor (VI/9, 25). This includes what he calls 'deliberation' (VI/49, 28). If that is so, one must ask in what passion, then, *does* a good Judge go about his business? A passion 'to do the right thing as disclosed by Reason'? It is not among those catalogued in chapter 6. In any event, the 'right thing' for a rational egoist is to do what is best for himself.

Virtually everyone – including most people who avow Egoism – would agree with Hobbes that, ideally, a judge should be dispassionate in considering a case and reach a judgment based strictly on a rational appraisal of the evidence, testimony, and arguments presented. And they would agree as well with Hobbes's fourth and last characteristic required in a good judge, although it would not likely occur to them unprompted: '*Patience to heare; diligent attention in hearing; and memory to retain, digest, and apply what he hath heard.*' Clearly, this is no more than a Judge's being conscientious in the performance of his duty. But if a Judge is the egoist Hobbes would have unquestioning readers believe all men are, he would be asking himself, 'What's in it for me?' That is, he would prefer to dispose of each case as quickly and effortlessly as he can, given that his judgment will be regarded as authoritative regardless: 'If therefore a man have a question of Injury, depending on the Law of Nature; that is to say, on common Equity; the Sentence of the Judge, that by Commission hath Authority to take cognizance of such causes, is a sufficient Verification of the Law of Nature in that individuall case' (XXVI/17, 142).

In sum, were a strict and universal Egoism the truth about human nature, political life, both as we know it and as Hobbes prescribes it, would be impossible. Obviously, there would be no acts of heroism, such as we admire precisely because they confirm the human capacity to rise above a brute attachment to self. Expressions of admiration, reverence, and honour would be largely without meaning, since they would necessarily be calculated to serve the self-interest of the expresser, and construed as such by everyone; likewise criticism, rejection, and condemnation. There would be no generosity, charity, benevolence, nor any other form of disinterested concern for the welfare of others, much less a willingness to make any sacrifices for them. Hence, there would be no so-called caring professions (whether of body or soul) in which practitioners genuinely *cared* for the health and flourishing of those they ostensibly serve. We can imagine that there might still be people called nurses, teachers, priests, counsellors, and such, but whatever benefits they conveyed would be a function, not just partly or primarily – as doubtless is true in most cases – but *exclusively* of whatever brought maximum rewards to them (e.g., in remuneration, status, and promotion).

However, this same lack of any intrinsic concern that others be well served by whatever work a person does would, to some extent, affect virtually *all* professions. The effect would be to eliminate a principal source of social adhesion insofar as a rational division of labour, with its resulting mutual interdependence, is fundamental to political life. For the division of labour has a unifying consequence only to the extent each person is generally confident that his fellow citizens, when called upon, will use their expertise to serve him *well* – ideally, to the best of their abilities.[19] And were egoism to prevail universally, there would be little reason for any person to seek advice or counsel from another, or trust it if given unsolicited; for there would be no possibility that the other would disregard his own good, and instead concentrate solely on what is best for the person to whom the advice is addressed. Indeed, there would be little of the ordinary helpfulness we take for granted in everyday life. As for Hobbes's reduction of the 'second Table' of his Ten Political Commandments 'to this one Commandement of mutuall Charity, *Thou shalt love thy neighbour as thy selfe*' (XXX/13, 179), the egoistic conception of human nature he expounded throughout the preceding chapters renders it an absurdity.

Most important of all, if strict egoism were universal, there would be no *Justice*. There could still be *laws*, of course, but there would be no Sovereign concerned that those laws be genuinely *equitable*, as opposed to merely enforceable. Unless, that is, equitable laws make the task of law enforcement, and thus the preservation of 'the King's Peace,' more easily accomplished – that people more readily accede to laws they believe to be fair and equitable, i.e., *naturally just*. For if that is the case, even a thoroughly egoistic Sovereign would have an instrumental interest in framing equitable laws. This presumes, however, that the idea of Equity has something like its familiar meaning – as it would not have in a whole world of egoists (being indistinguishable from arrangements and outcomes determined simply by a balance of power, and accepted as such). But even if by some miracle just laws came to be established, there would be no possibility of their being interpreted and applied by disinterested judges and other administrative officials who aimed first and always at Equity, hence no justice actually entering into the regulation of practical life.

It is most unlikely that this represents Hobbes's own view of human nature, or what he intends to result from his offering the world this unsolicited 'Counsel': his new Science of Politics. Nor is it what has actually resulted: quite the contrary. For despite its philosophical 'shortcomings' (to put it mildly), the political prescription outlined in *Leviathan* has proven a political success nonpareil. And this in itself argues for Hobbes's pre-eminence as a *political* philosopher, that is, politically *efficacious*. One must presume that he foresaw what would be the actual consequences of presenting his teaching in the form that he did – how it would actually work in practice. Accordingly, I propose to begin all over again. That is, to reconsider Hobbes's political prescription from a different perspective, seeking a more plausible interpretation of his *Leviathan* than that which takes at face value the metaphysical principles he professes (or seems to profess) – the Materialism, the Determinism, the Nominalism, the Hedonism, and all the rest – none of which will withstand rigorous scrutiny, as I presume Hobbes understood full well. Just as he understood how rarely such scrutiny will be brought to bear, and how politically irrelevant when it is.[20]

Beyond this, however, I suspect that Hobbes is attempting to provide a political science that simultaneously serves two quite different – indeed, seemingly incompatible – purposes. The more obvious intention is to present the architecture of a polity suited for the modern scientific age, and that in two distinct respects. First, it is implicitly designed to promote and fully exploit the modern, technology-oriented, technology-driven science of Bacon and Descartes, who pledged 'the relief of man's estate' through our becoming 'the masters and possessors of Nature.' Or as Hobbes so nicely summarizes what has become the reigning ethos of Modernity, '*Reason* is the *pace*; Encrease of *Science*, the *way*; and the Benefit of man-kind, the *end*' (V/20, 22). Second, the political prescription itself is meant to be seen as of a piece with this modern conception of science, vested with the same authority and partaking of the same certitude. Thus, it ostensibly presumes the same metaphysical principles as pertain to the rest of Nature; is strictly empirical, hence 'realistic' about *human* nature (taking men as they *are*, not as variously supposed they ought to be); is rigorously rational, according to the method exemplified in Geometry; and is universally valid, irrespective of time or place, hence universally *useful*. And insofar as Hobbes can on this basis present a persuasive science of *politics* – of all things – he confirms the soundness, hence furthers the general acceptance, of the modern scientific approach to the understanding and mastering of all things.

For there to be a science of politics that is universally valid and useful, however, it must be based on some universal truths about human nature that have clear political consequences – some bedrock upon which to build a structure that is low but solid, capacious, and adaptable. Accordingly, Hobbes attempts to persuade his readers that there are several such truths which, collectively, will suffice: that all men regard Pleasure as the Good, Pain as the Bad; that everyone's most powerful passion is Fear of Death, especially violent death at the hands of other men; that everyone is strictly egoistic, such that all voluntary actions aim at what the actor believes to be his or her own benefit; that 'a generall inclination of all mankind [is] a perpetuall and restlesse desire of Power after power, that ceaseth only in death.' As I have argued, none of these claims are in fact *universally* true of human beings as a species, nor invariably true of most actual individuals – albeit they point to strong tendencies in virtually everyone, whence is derived their plausibility as universal truths. Moreover, as I have also argued, Hobbes's own political design could not function as he intends if these claims *were* in fact universally true, for the very survival of a Hobbesian commonwealth is crucially dependent on various 'exceptions' to these 'rules,' especially on men of courage, honour, and integrity who can, and will when needed, rise above the selfish hedonism so evident in most people's everyday lives. But no matter these 'contradictions.' Hobbes, being himself a rarity – a philosopher – fully appreciates that logical scrupulousness is *not* a universal truth of human nature, and that the general acceptance of his claims about 'how we naturally are' licenses behaviour and attitudes which are, on balance, beneficial, in that they promote progress while maintaining civil peace among citizen-subjects freely pursuing their various 'bourgeios' conceptions of The Good Life.

The fact remains, however, that there are any number of regimes that would conform to the basic principles Hobbes has propounded. And although he himself speaks of only 'Three kinds of Common-wealth,' according to whether the Sovereign Power be exercised by 'One, or More, or All' of those it represents, we can readily imagine what history partially shows: that there are many significantly different versions of each of these archetypes. If, for example, an 'Aristocracy' is any regime ruled by a subset of its citizenry, the actual character of the regime would profoundly differ according to whether that subset were all wealthy Merchants, professional Soldiers, large-scale Landowners, or a hierarchy of Priests and monks. Similarly, the actual quality of life in a Democracy could vary from puritanical to libertarian according to differing institutional arrangements: what offices are established (e.g., whether there are public censors); how they are distributed (e.g., by election, or by lot); the length of their terms; and how legislation is proposed, debated, and approved. And even with respect to Hobbes's apparent preference for

Monarchies, the real-life possibilities range from wise and benevolent Kings to ruthless and capricious Tyrants – and no one believes that the distinction is merely semantic, solely a matter of subjective 'liking' *versus* 'misliking.' Thus, for Monarchy to be a defensible choice, there must be some means of favouring the promotion of kings who are wise and just – thus, rational and equitable – while precluding the ruthlessly tyrannical.

Reflection on these and other possibilities naturally, unavoidably raises the ultimate question of political philosophy: what is the simply *Best* Regime, the regime one would pray for if unconstrained by circumstances? Circumspectly addressing, and *answering*, this age-old question is Hobbes's less obvious, not to say hidden, purpose in crafting *Leviathan*. The greatest circumspection is required, because indicating the single best version of his prescription must be in such a manner as will not undermine the appeal of the universal version, the version independent of circumstances, since that is the *only* version most circumstances practically allow for. His single best version does have a demonstrable bearing on the universal version, however, as I shall attempt to show in Part Two, 'The Platonic *Leviathan*.'

Prior to my taking up this task directly, however, it will prove useful to think afresh about the State of Nature, as this is ostensibly mankind's, hence Hobbes's, point of departure; and the ever-present threat of returning to it is the ultimate Big Stick of his reasoning. But Hobbes's exceedingly brief account of the human condition in that State (a mere two or three pages) hardly suffices to 'bring it to life.' That takes the genius of a great prose poet, such as Joseph Conrad.

A Conradian Intermezzo:
Variations on the State of Nature

'The essentials of this affair lay deep under the surface.'

The present chapter on Conrad's *Heart of Darkness* may seem an over-long intrusion to readers interested only in a critical analysis of Hobbes's *Leviathan*. They are welcome, as I suggested in my Prelude, to skip it. But for those whose patience will permit, I shall try to show how this novella can – among other things – contribute to a deeper understanding of Hobbes's teaching. For Conrad possesses the artistry (uniquely, I believe) to help us see, vividly and concretely, the manner of life out of which mankind emerged, and something of what a return to the State of Nature entails. There is much more involved than most would guess from Hobbes's own terse, pithy, famously formulaic description of what is, in so many respects, the key to his *Leviathan*. In an effort to make the chapter intelligible to readers unfamiliar with Conrad's tale, I have quoted the author extensively, offering a taste of the sobering psychic experience it evokes. But my main purpose is to draw out the Hobbesian features and implications of the story that might otherwise go unnoticed; I do not pretend to have done justice to the rich tapestry Conrad has woven.[1] Perhaps what I have to say about it, however, will move readers to consult – or consult again – the original themselves, to see and feel for themselves the 'virtual reality' so powerfully created therein. They might be surprised, moreover, by how frequent are the echoes of Hobbes's doctrine.

Heart of Darkness may not be Conrad's best story, but it is probably his most widely known and almost surely has been subjected to the greatest amount of scholarly criticism.[2] I do believe that, for all of the attention that has been paid it, its quality is underrated, even by some of Conrad's warmest admirers.[3] However, it is not my purpose here to make a case for its pre-eminence except insofar as might be incidental to expositing a dimension of the work – and of Conrad's writing generally – that has not, to my mind, been sufficiently appreciated. In any case, one need not regard *Heart of Darkness* as Conrad at his very best in order to defend either its artistic excellence or philosophical profundity. Few would rank *Charmides*, for example, among the half-dozen of Plato's most important dialogues, but this is not to suggest that it deserves or requires any less intensive study. It is, after all, a polished masterpiece by arguably the greatest philosopher of all time, whose least offerings tower over the finest works of lesser minds.

What I believe is under-appreciated about Conrad's *Heart of Darkness* has to do with its philosophical significance as a sustained meditation on the State of Nature. For surely it is that. But what distinguishes the book is the ingenuity with which Conrad has brought together two quite distinct situations of 'man in the state of nature': pre-civil man in his original primitiveness, and post-civil man returning to a pre-civil environment, wherein certain deeper impulses of his own nature – repressed, restrained, or narrowly channelled in civil society – freely emerge and show themselves, but not simply as they do in pre-civil man (indeed, simplicity is precisely what is precluded). The mere fact that Conrad comprehends the very different implications of each situation, as few readers of Hobbes do, attests to the special insight, at once political and psychological, embedded in his story. The 'return' Conrad portrays is not, however, the precipitous projection of men into a calamitous all-out civil war, an anarchic chaos where every man is potentially the enemy of every other. Rather, he shows us a more gradual Return, by stages, as men proceed ever further from civilization and ever deeper into a primitive wilderness, coming face to face with people still living in the natural state – as historically was done by various intrepid individuals: explorers, missionaries, naturalists and other servitors of either faith or science or empire. This kind of Return is no longer a practical possibility – in contrast to the permanent threat of civil war upon the breakdown of stable political life. But for the purpose of more deeply understanding human nature, viewing the Return in slow motion, as it were, has its advantages. Moreover, it points to a natural condition that is beyond civility, a 'transcivility' embryonic in Conrad's and our interest in the subject itself.

Our narrator's story, in briefest outline, is as follows. He along with four other companions are resting aboard a pleasure craft lying at the mouth of the Thames River, awaiting the turn of the tide. Night descends.

Without prompting, one of our narrator's shipmates, a man called
Marlow, proceeds to recount his abbreviated employment as a riverboat
captain for what turns out to be an especially nasty colonial company that
extracts huge amounts of ivory from the interior of a primitive land – at
an enormous cost in the lives of its native inhabitants, whom it enslaves
or otherwise exploits. After being transported from Europe to the River
offering ingress to this barely known, untamed wilderness, Marlow must
first travel up it to the Company's Central Station, where is located the
boat he is to captain. This long trek offers him his first exposure to the
atrocities, and imbecilities, of the Company's administration of the territory it claims as its own. Once arrived at the Central Station, Marlow
finds that he must first re-float and repair the small steamer, and then take
it up river to the Inner Station in order to retrieve its ailing Agent, along
with the large store of ivory he has amassed. An extraordinary success in
extracting ivory is the first thing Marlow learns about this Agent, named
Kurtz. But there are indications that he is remarkable in other respects as
well, and that while he is openly lauded, he is secretly resented by other
employees. On the subsequent journey up river with the Manager and a
handful of Whites – and thirty black Cannibals as woodcutters to provide
fuel for the boat's steam engine – Marlow experiences a mounting sense
of unease as they penetrate ever deeper into the wilderness. Upon
approaching the Inner Station, the boat is halted by thick fog, during
which it is attacked by natives who (Marlow subsequently learns)
worship Kurtz as their quasi-divine chieftain. In the melee, Marlow's
native helmsman is killed. Once finally arrived, Marlow meets an eccentric young Russian acolyte of Kurtz, and he sees for himself some evidence of the extent to which Kurtz has 'gone native' – including his
having taken a regal native mistress. Despite being mortally ill, Kurtz is
ambiguous about being rescued and brought back to civilization, and so
crawls off the boat in the dead of night to rejoin his savage followers.
Marlow retrieves him, and the whole party leaves the next morning for
the journey back down river, but not without great protest from the
natives. Kurtz dies, however, on the way. Once safely back in Europe,
Marlow – who has been entrusted by Kurtz with his personal effects –
visit's Kurtz's fiancée, an unsettling finale to his story.

That *Heart of Darkness* is about the State of Nature is not difficult to
establish, since Conrad has Marlow repeatedly refer to his adventure in
just such terms.[4] First, however, one might note the special significance of
each of Marlow's immediate auditors, four sailing companions who in

lieu of personal names are identified by Occupations ('with a capital' – so
Marlow puts it when subsequently finding himself regarded as 'one of the
Workers'; 71).[5] These vocational identifications are more revealing, more
useful to us, than names usually are; as Marlow notes in reference to
Kurtz before he had laid eyes on him, 'He was just a word for me. I did
not see the man in the name any more than you do' (100).[6] Collectively,
Marlow's comrades are pre-eminent representatives, not of just any civil
society, but of the commercial republic first fully envisioned and articulated by Hobbes. Apart from our anonymous narrator, an ideal Every-
man, there is "The Lawyer" (who had "the only cushion on deck, and
was lying on the only rug"), "The Accountant" (complete with a fitting
means of amusement: dominoes), and "The Director of Companies,"
who was their "captain" as well as their "host." Poised in the bows of
their little Ship of State as they await both dawn and a favourable tide, this
Director of Companies so "resembled a pilot" that it was "difficult to
realize that his work was not out there in the luminous estuary, but
behind him, within the brooding gloom" (54).

As for the philosophic Marlow himself, teller of this cautionary tale –
and "the only man … who still 'followed the sea,'" a sailor for whom all
ships are pretty much the same, and whose true country, the sea, "is
always the same" – his peculiar status amid this group requires separate
consideration best undertaken later. But that the sociopolitical context in
which Marlow's saga unfolds may have a special significance is subtly
suggested by our narrator's observing, "The yarns of seaman have a direct
simplicity, the whole meaning of which lies within the shell of a cracked
nut. But Marlow was not typical […], and to him the meaning of an
episode was not inside like a kernel, but outside, enveloping the tale
which brought it out only as a glow brings out a haze" (57). Later, Marlow
himself hints that there is more to his story than first meets the eye: 'I had
to keep guessing at the channel; I had to discern, mostly by inspiration,
the signs of hidden banks; I watched for sunken stones […] When you
have to attend to things of that sort, to the mere incidents of the surface,
the reality – the reality, I tell you – fades. The inner truth is hidden –
luckily, luckily' (113–14). Upon his adding an ironic comparison with
commercial life, our narrator tells us a voice "growled" out of the darkness, "'Try to be civil, Marlow,' and I knew there was at least one listener
awake besides myself." 'Try to be civil' – arguably, the moral of the story.

Conrad has provided ample reminders of the characteristic features of
this commercially oriented society, including its dominant ethos, its inner
rationale, and its inherent tendency towards an ever-expanding network

of economic interests, culminating in empire (as Hobbes subtly indicates).[7] The world-wisened, tale-telling Marlow, consummate realist
about men and their affairs, offers something like a supra-historical perspective on this expansive impulse:

> The conquest of the earth, which mostly means the taking it away from those who
> have a different complexion or slightly flatter nose than ourselves, is not a pretty
> thing when you look into it too much. What redeems it is the idea only. An idea
> at the back of it; not a sentimental pretense but an idea; and an unselfish belief in
> the idea – something you can set up, and bow down before, and offer a sacrifice
> to. (60)

For promoters of the Roman Empire, this background idea was perhaps
the Pax Romana. What was it for modern Europeans? Spreading Christian decency and salvation would doubtless be alleged, and with some
justice, though this construal may have been more an idol for domestic
reverence than the governing idea of most of those who actually promoted and executed the various modern nations' imperial projects. Such
certainly seems to be the mature Marlow's view. Not that his younger self
was altogether naive. As he tells it, just prior to departing on his voyage
to the wilderness, he calls to say goodbye to the 'excellent aunt' whose
connections had secured him a remote riverboat captaincy with a colonial
trading company headquartered on the European continent. He 'found
her triumphant,' mainly because of how she regarded him:

> Something like an emissary of light, something like a lower sort of apostle. There
> had been a lot of such rot let loose in print and talk just about that time, and the
> excellent woman, living right in the rush of all that humbug, got carried off her
> feet. She talked about 'weaning those ignorant millions from their horrid ways,'
> till, upon my word, she made me quite uncomfortable. I ventured to hint that the
> Company was run for profit. (71)

Undoubtedly profit, the key to material prosperity, is a ubiquitous
motive for the citizen-subjects of a regime brought together, not only by
their common 'Feare of Death,' but by their common 'Desire of such
things as are necessary to commodious living; and a Hope by their Industry to obtain them' (*Leviathan* XIII/14, 63).

However, related to the mercantile rationale that pervades the Hobbesian regime is that other, far grander, even noble idea: the Advancement
of Science. But respect for this motivation, also, is trimmed by the ironi-

cal parody of it that Marlow weaves into his description of the perfunc-
tory medical examination he was obliged to undergo prior to setting forth
on the Company's business:

The old doctor felt my pulse, evidently thinking of something else the while.
'Good, good for there,' he mumbled, and then with a certain eagerness asked me
whether I would let him measure my head. Rather surprised, I said Yes, when he
produced a thing like callipers and got the dimensions back and front and every
way, taking notes carefully. [...] 'I always ask leave, in the interests of science, to
measure the crania of those going out there,' he said. 'And when they come back
too,' I asked. 'Oh, I never see them,' he remarked; 'and, moreover, the changes
take place inside, you know.' He smiled, as if at some quiet joke. 'So you are going
out there. Famous. Interesting too.' He gave me a searching glance, and made
another note. 'Ever any madness in your family,' he asked, in a matter-of-fact
tone. I felt very annoyed. 'Is that question in the interests of science too?' 'It
would be,' he said, without taking notice of my irritation, 'interesting for science
to watch the mental changes of individuals, on the spot, but ...' (69)

The portrayal of these 'inside' changes and their outside effects is the
special virtue of Conrad's story. When Marlow at last returns from his
imperial adventure, having along the way become custodian of Kurtz's
personal effects and guardian of his memory, he meets with one final
attempt to exploit the hallowed name of Science:

A clean-shaved man, with an official manner and wearing gold-rimmed spectacles,
called on me one day and made inquiries, at first circuitous, afterwards suavely
pressing, about what he was pleased to denominate certain 'documents.' [...] He
became darkly menacing at last, and with much heat argued that the Company had
the right to every bit of information about its 'territories.' And, said he, 'Mr
Kurtz's knowledge of unexplored regions must have been necessarily extensive
and peculiar – owing to his great abilities and to the deplorable circumstances in
which he had been placed: therefore – ' I assured him Mr Kurtz's knowledge,
however extensive, did not bear upon the problems of commerce or administration. He invoked then the name of science. 'It would be an incalculable loss if,' etc.,
etc. I offered him the report on the 'Suppression of Savage Customs,' with the
postscriptum torn off. He took it up eagerly, but ended by sniffing at it with an air
of contempt. 'This is not what we had a right to expect,' he remarked. (187–8)

After a two-hundred-mile trek Marlow finally arrived at the Company's
so-called Central Station, only to find that the boat he was sent to

command had been sunk and was resting partially submerged on the bottom of the river. 'I was thunderstruck. What, how, why? [...] I did not see the real significance of that wreck at once. I fancy I see it now, but I am not sure – not at all. Certainly the affair was too stupid – when I think of it – to be altogether natural' (87). What had happened, Marlow learned, is that the manager had suddenly decided to set off up river without him, the boat piloted by a 'volunteer skipper' who promptly tore out the boat's bottom on some rocks. Evidently, Marlow in hindsight suspects the manager of scheming to delay a timely rescue of Kurtz.

Patching and re-floating the little tin-pot steamer ('grimy fragment of another world, the forerunner of change, of conquest, of trade, of massacres, of blessings'; 181) became Marlow's first task, assisted by one of the mechanics at the station. There were some sixteen or twenty other whites at this Central Station whom Marlow, with an ironic nod to Bunyan, refers to as 'faithless pilgrims,' ostensibly because of their appearance, strolling aimlessly about the yard with 'absurd long staves in their hands' (91–2). They despised the few mechanics ('on account of their imperfect manners,' Marlow supposes; 104) and were preoccupied with such matters as seating precedence at meals. As for the manager of this Central Station on the river, he seems distinguished mainly by his lack of distinction, by his sheer averageness. Marlow presumes that he owed his position to little more than the fact that he, unlike most Europeans, 'was never ill.' His 'triumphant health,' Marlow implies, was at least partly a result of his mental limitations, his body being in no danger from a troubled mind. Whereas Marlow admits that he 'had often "a little fever," or a little touch of other things – the playful paw-strokes of the wilderness, the preliminary trifling before the more serious onslaught which came in due course' (128). As it did – mortally – to Kurtz.[8]

In dramatic contrast to the Company's various employees – characters who would fit snugly into a political society of basically Hobbesian design – is the young man who attends upon Kurtz as some bizarre combination of occasional factotum, frequent symposiast, and ever-worshipful disciple. Marlow emphasizes what a problematic being he would be for almost any form of society: 'His very existence was improbable, inexplicable, and altogether bewildering. He was an insoluble problem. It was inconceivable how he existed, how he succeeded in getting so far, how he had managed to remain – why he did not instantly disappear' (153–4). In appearance, speech, and manner, the young man might have passed for one of Shakespeare's clowns: wearing 'a hat like a cart-wheel'; his clothing covered with bright blue, red, and yellow patches, which in 'the sunshine made him look extremely gay'; with 'a beardless, boyish face, very fair, no features to speak of,' his expression oscillating between extremes of delight and gloom – 'He looked like a harlequin' (149–50). We subsequently learn that he is Russian, the son of an arch-priest, that he ran away to sea, and now 'had been wandering about that river for nearly two years alone, cut off from everybody and everything.' The wilderness had captured him, drawing him in deeper and deeper, both physically and psychically, ever more remote from a life in civil society for which he was never really suited. As he himself confesses: '"I went a little farther, [...] and then still a little farther – till I had gone so far that I don't know how I'll ever get back"' (154). Virtually everything in Marlow's description of him violates some premise of Hobbes's political prescription, some generalization about human nature:

There he was before me, in motley, as though he had absconded from a troupe of mimes, enthusiastic, fabulous. [...] The glamour of youth enveloped his particoloured rags, his destitution, his loneliness, the essential desolation of his futile wanderings. For months – for years – his life hadn't been worth a day's purchase; and there he was, gallantly, thoughtlessly alive, to all appearance indestructible solely by virtue of his few years and of his unreflecting audacity. I was seduced into something like admiration – like envy. Glamour urged him on, glamour kept him unscathed. He surely wanted nothing from the wilderness but space to breathe in and to push on through. His need was to exist, and to move onwards at the greatest possible risk, and with a maximum of privation. If the absolutely pure, uncalculating, unpractical spirit of adventure had ever ruled a human being, it ruled this be-patched youth. (153–4)

Perhaps as a consequence of his being the son of an priest, he carried an extra dose of religiosity in his genes or his veins. In any event, the slavish reverence he showed towards Kurtz, equalling that of the most awestruck native followers, attests to the potency of the religious impulse in human nature ('If it had come to crawling before Mr Kurtz, he crawled as much as the veriest savage of them all'; 161). That such pious devotion could devolve upon a mere mortal would hardly have surprised Hobbes, who endorses as 'surely true' the ancient aphorism, 'Man is a god to man.' The Harlequin himself understands his worship of Kurtz in purely intellectual terms: '"this man has enlarged my mind."' Between the lines of his account, however, we see clearly that Kurtz's charisma is in the power of his words, his extraordinary eloquence (again, much as Hobbes would suppose). Like some wilderness Sokrates, Kurtz would hold the youth transfixed for whole nights at a time: '"We talked of everything," he said, quite transported at the recollection. "I forgot there was such a thing as sleep. The night did not seem to last an hour. Everything! Everything! Of love too. [...] He made me see things – things."'9 Despite benign feelings for this young exile, Marlow is openly critical of his devotion to Kurtz: 'He had not meditated over it. It came to him, and he accepted it with a sort of eager fatalism. I must say that to me it appeared about the most dangerous thing in every way he had come upon so far' (155).

Marlow tells of returning to the place whence he departed on his imperial adventure, the European headquarters of the trading Company which dominated a city that (as he had noted earlier) always made him 'think of a whited sepulchre' (65).10 He finds his risky excursion beyond civilized notions of good and evil to have been both intellectually elevating and socially alienating, the one necessarily proportionate to the other:

I found myself back in the sepulchral city resenting the sight of people hurrying through the streets to filch a little money from each other, to devour their infamous cookery, to gulp their unwholesome beer, to dream their insignificant and silly dreams. They trespassed upon my thoughts. They were intruders whose knowledge of life was to me an irritating pretense, because I felt so sure they could not possibly know the things I knew. Their bearing, which was simply the bearing of commonplace individuals going about their business in the assurance of perfect safety, was offensive to me like the outrageous flauntings of folly in the face of a danger it is unable to comprehend. (186)

Between his two visits to this city of smug burghers, 'going about their business' completely oblivious to dangers lurking just beyond – really, just beneath – the superficial safety of civil life, Marlow's own perspective had changed profoundly. His superior sense of knowing was the profit he garnered from his ill-considered flirtation with commercial imperialism, entailing as it did a doubly dangerous incursion into the dark heart of primeval Nature. Thus positively repulsed upon returning by the pervasive moral and intellectual complaisance he found risible, Marlow chose to remain the man 'who still followed the sea.'

Describing his voyage to the mouth of the river that provided grudging access into an obscure, barely discovered country, Marlow speaks of travelling 'along the formless coast bordered by a dangerous surf, as if Nature herself had tried to ward off intruders' (74). As for his ingress to the interior of this guarded domain, 'Going up that river was like travelling back to the earliest beginnings of the world.' He describes himself as feeling 'bewitched and cut off for ever from everything [he] had known once – somewhere – far away – in another existence perhaps [...] remembered with wonder amongst the overwhelming realities of this strange world of plants, and water, and silence. Yet this stillness of life did not in the least resemble a peace' (112–13):

The reaches opened before us and closed behind, as if the forest had stepped leisurely across the water to bar the way for our return. We penetrated deeper and deeper into the heart of darkness. It was very quiet there. [...] We were wanderers on a prehistoric earth, on an earth that wore the aspect of an unknown planet. We could have fancied ourselves the first of men taking possession of an accursed inheritance, to be subdued at the cost of profound anguish and of excessive toil. (115–16)[11]

But silent and empty as sometimes seemed the land through which their paddle-wheeler laboured, Marlow and his companions were not in fact the first men to take possession of it. In having civilized Europeans come face to face with the native inhabitants, Conrad in effect contrives a means of directly comparing two versions of man in relation to the State of Nature: aboriginal, primitive man, unaware of living under any other conditions, and 're-primitivizing' post-civil man, regressing towards that original natural state while nonetheless retaining certain facilities and ideas acquired in civil society. The effect is illuminating with regards to both variants. This is obliquely illustrated by Marlow's description of the native who had been trained to tend the boiler powering their riverboat:

He was an improved specimen; he could fire up a vertical boiler. He was there below me, and, upon my word, to look at him was as edifying as seeing a dog in a parody of breeches and a feather hat, walking on his hind legs.[12] A few months training had done for that really fine chap. [...] He ought to have been clapping his hands and stamping his feet on the bank, instead of which he was hard at work, a thrall to strange witchcraft, full of improving knowledge. He was useful because he had been instructed; and what he knew was this – that should the water in that transparent thing disappear, the evil spirit inside the boiler would get angry through the greatness of his thirst, and take a terrible vengeance. So he sweated and fired up and watched the glass fearfully. (118–19)

As Marlow's (and our) amused reflections presuppose, his (and our) state and mode of understanding are not merely *different* from that of the aboriginal. The latter's is practically impossible for us; there is no way (short of brain damage) that we or Marlow can forget all we know and so regress to a view of the world's workings comparable to that of his domesticated helper. Whereas it is by no means inconceivable that the native might eventually be brought to share our mechanistic, materialistic, de-mythologized understanding of a steam engine – as whole nations of erstwhile barbarians have since proven. This points to the deeper truth which struck Marlow so forcefully on his river-borne anabasis:

But suddenly, as we struggled round a bend, there would be a glimpse of rush walls, of peaked grass-roofs, a burst of yells, a whirl of black limbs, a mass of hands clapping, of feet stamping, of bodies swaying, of eyes rolling, under the droop of heavy and motionless foliage. The steamer toiled along slowly on the edge of a black and incomprehensible frenzy. The prehistoric man was cursing us, praying to us, welcoming us – who could tell? We were cut off from the comprehension of our surroundings; we glided past like phantoms, wondering and secretly appalled, as sane men would be before an enthusiastic outbreak in a madhouse. We could not understand because we were too far and could not remember, because we were traveling in the night of the first ages, of those ages that are gone, leaving hardly a sign – and no memories.

The earth seemed unearthly. We are accustomed to look upon the shackled form of a conquered monster, but there – there you could look at a thing monstrous and free. (116–17)

We are accustomed, that is, to a Nature tamed and transformed, domesticated and harnessed by the vast array of Baconian sciences that have been so successfully promoted and exploited within Hobbesian political forms. Brought face to face with mankind's primitive origins, the spectacle initially seemed so alien as to be utterly incomprehensible. 'Prehistoric man' at first seemed like a different species. 'Slowly,' however, came the contrary realization, based not on reasoned belief but on passionate recognition.

It was unearthly, and the men were – No, they were not inhuman. Well, you know, that was the worst of it – this suspicion of their not being inhuman. It would come slowly to one. They howled and leaped, and spun, and made horrid faces; but what thrilled you was just the thought of their humanity – like yours – the thought of your remote kinship with this wild and passionate uproar. Ugly.

Yes, it was ugly enough; but if you were man enough you would admit to yourself that there was in you just the faintest trace of a response to the terrible frank-
ness of that noise, a dim suspicion of there being a meaning in it which you – you
so remote from the night of first ages – could comprehend. And why not? The
mind of man is capable of anything – because everything is in it, all the past as well
as all the future. What was there after all? Joy, fear, sorrow, devotion, valour, rage
– who can tell? – but truth – truth stripped of its cloak of time. (116–17)

True though a strong person must admit it to be: that a common humanity does indeed lie beneath such radically different behaviour – that of the
intensely reflective, morally fastidious Marlow, and that of the howling,
cavorting, grimacing, near-naked savage – that they share the same repertoire of passions as the basis of their common nature (cf. *Leviathan*
Introd/3; 2) – there nonetheless are vitally important differences between
a human being who has never experienced civilized life and one who has.
    Travelling down the coast towards the mouth of his fateful river, portal
to a natural world beyond the reach of civil law and order, Marlow notes
the native's relationship to it:

It was something natural, that had its reason, that had a meaning. Now and then
a boat from the shore gave one a momentary contact with reality. It was paddled
by black fellows. You could see from afar the white of their eyeballs glistening.
They shouted, sang; their bodies streamed with perspiration; they had faces like
grotesque masks – these chaps; but they had bone, muscle, a wild vitality, an
intense energy of movement, that was as natural and true as the surf along their
coast. They wanted no excuse for being there. They were a great comfort to look
at. For a time I would feel I belonged still to a world of straightforward facts; but
the feeling would not last long. (73)

    By contrast, any civilized European accompanying Marlow must travel
by stages from a physical environment that is safe, comfortable, convenient, and orderly, to one that is the very opposite. And at each stage, his
mind must adapt to the new reality in which he finds himself – to his own
understanding of it, rather, his passions and desires responding according
to that understanding. How long this psychic transformation takes would
seem to be a measure of the proportionate strength of one's civil nurture
relative to one's residual nature. Moreover, understanding these psychic
changes raises an additional question of first importance: is it mainly a
matter of relaxing restraints, liberating natural feelings and desires long
repressed but essentially mature; or must the psychic qualities, perhaps

even the passions, appropriate to this radically different condition grow from mere germs, as it were? Conrad's Marlow seems to agree with Hobbes that it is the former; speaking specifically about Kurtz, he ventures that it was simply 'the heavy, mute spell of the wilderness' that drew him 'to its pitiless breast by the awakening of forgotten and brutal instincts, by the memory of gratified and monstrous passions' (176). If such is the case, there would be enormous practical consequences, should civil society give way to civil war.

The complex narrative frame Conrad has fashioned for his story can itself be seen to represent stages in an individual's regression back to the State of Nature, indicating thereby degrees of separation from that state.[13]

Kurtz may be regarded as the terminal stage, having 'gone native' to an extent far beyond the ordinary meaning of that phrase. On the ascent upriver to retrieve Kurtz, and prior to his ever having set eyes on him, Marlow alludes to the standard set by Kurtz, presumably aware in hindsight of the equivocal meaning of his words: 'Sometimes I would pick out a tree a little way ahead to measure our progress towards Kurtz by' (122). It is, to be sure, a strange, ironic sort of 'progress' he thereby measures: progress in understanding man's potential for moral regression – the sort of knowledge that the returning Marlow feels elevated him so far above the oblivious denizens of the sepulchral city. If Kurtz does represent the last stage of fully civilized man's return to a pre-civil natural state, entailing a descent into the depths of his sub-civil soul, he also reveals the limits on that return. But there are complications in generalizing from his case, for he is in every important respect an uncommon man. Kurtz had gone native; that is, part of him had, most of him perhaps, but not all, leaving him a deeply divided, tortured being. For there remains that within him which could not forget his civilized heritage (manifested concretely in the tract 'Suppression of Savage Customs').

This becomes a recurrent source of inner torment. And if Marlow's assessment is to be trusted, it had driven him insane: 'Believe me or not, his intelligence was perfectly clear – concentrated, it is true, upon himself with horrible intensity, yet clear; [...] But his soul was mad. Being alone in the wilderness, it had looked within itself, and, by Heavens! I tell you it had gone mad' (177). This very capacity for introspection, for ruthless self-examination, and the standards whereby Kurtz condemns what it reveals, the felt obligation to those standards – all these are acquisitions made in a civilized culture, and apparently unforgettable for anyone who, with some fullness of understanding, has once taken them to heart. Also, it is worth noting that, despite acknowledging that Kurtz was regularly surrounded by native people, Marlow nonetheless speaks of him as 'being alone in the wilderness' – that his existence in this State of Nature was essentially 'solitary.' And as well as nasty and brutish, we know it to have been, true to his name, *short*.

Conrad has taken pains to establish a special kinship of character between this ostensible protagonist of his story and the man telling it. Just as Marlow speaks repeatedly of Kurtz as 'very little more than a voice,' so too is Marlow for his immediate auditors sitting in the "pitch dark." Persons within the Company also assimilate Marlow to Kurtz; for example, the indolent 'brickmaker' at the central station: '"You are of the new gang – the gang of virtue. The same people who sent him specially also recommended you"' (96). And the manager of the Central Station eventually affiliates them: 'I found myself lumped along with Kurtz as a partisan of methods for which the time was not ripe' (169). Marlow shared the experience of direct exposure to the State of Nature in a manner similar to that of Kurtz, but for a much shorter duration. It was long enough to gain a sympathetic understanding of Kurtz, given his being possessed of a nature similar in certain essential respects ('I had – for my sins, I suppose – to go through the ordeal of looking into [Kurtz's soul] myself'; 177), but not so long as to risk the same degree of corruption, the permanent damage. Marlow retraced the history of his human heritage to the point where he too glimpsed the 'appalling face' of truth about human nature; but unlike Kurtz, he had not crossed over the line – or, in his own words, he had but 'peeped over the edge' of the abyss.[14] Kurtz, however,

had made that last stride, he had stepped over the edge, while I had been permitted to draw back my hesitating foot. And perhaps in this is the whole difference; perhaps all the wisdom, and all truth, and all sincerity, are just compressed into that inappreciable moment of time in which we step over the threshold of the invisible. (185)

This, of course, is what Conrad means to allow us to glimpse as well, and what we wish to gain: an intellectual appreciation of primordial Nature, including ourselves as part and parcel of it (or that at the least, though preferably something psychically richer), but without endangering either body or soul. Yet Conrad has Marlow voice scepticism as to whether any merely verbal account, however vivid one's imaginative response to it, can do justice to the full spiritual impact of the actual experience: '... No, it is impossible; it is impossible to convey the life-sensation of any given epoch of one's existence – that which makes its truth, its meaning – its subtle and penetrating essence. It is impossible. We live, as we dream – alone ...' (100). Since this is Marlow's judgment, but not necessarily Conrad's, we may apply it reflexively to his reported 'ordeal' of peering into Kurtz's soul, and so conclude that he regards the insight thereby gained to be a form of self-understanding. Or as the Company's chief accountant informed Marlow, oblivious to the deeper significance we can attach to his words: "'In the interior you will no doubt meet Mr Kurtz'" (83).

As for our anonymous narrator (himself no fool, judging from his prefatory observations), he admits being fascinated by the tale Marlow tells, and the vicarious experience it provides. Even before Marlow's recounting is very far along, he confides, "The others might have been asleep, but I was awake. I listened, I listened on the watch for the sentence, for the word, that would give me the clue to the faint uneasiness inspired by this narrative that seemed to shape itself without human lips in the heavy night-air of the river" (101). His 'faint uneasiness' – both the unease and its faintness – help us to locate him relative to the State of Nature. Presumably the uneasiness is akin to that which Marlow felt much more intensely at this stage of his journey, having penetrated partway up the river, and so had that much direct exposure to the jungle and its primitive inhabitants, and having seen something of their effects on fellow Europeans.

Finally, there is ourselves as readers of this tale within a tale. Our narrator had his account of one man's journey back in time directly from the one who undertook it – a man whom our narrator knows well, and evidently trusts and respects, with whom he has long shared "the bond of the sea," a man who avows a mortal hatred of the Lie (99)[15] – all this adding a depth of personal involvement (one presumes) to our narrator's reception of the account. Whereas, we are ostensibly a further step removed from the primordial experience, and thus subject to that much more distortion and attenuation of it. Upon reflection, of course, we realize we are reliant upon the wisdom and artistry of the author for all the levels or degrees of exposure to that experience, validated so far as may be by whatever resonance we feel within ourselves. Thus, the knowledge that this story has a basis in Conrad's own personal experience doubtless enhances its authority. As he explains in the 'Author's Note' which prefaces the volume in which the tale was collected: '[I]t is well known that curious men go prying into all sorts of places (where they have no business) and come out of them with all kinds of spoil. This story, and one other [...], are all the spoil I brought out from the centre of Africa, where, really, I had no sort of business' (xi).

It is generally supposed, given the personal experience to which Conrad refers, that *Heart of Darkness* is set primarily in the centre of what was once commonly referred to as The Dark Continent: Africa. 'Dark' because so much of its interior was then unknown to denizens of the civilized world, though the fact that Africa is populated mainly by dark-skinned peoples added a special piquancy to the label, as did their benighted intellectual condition. From the perspective of post-Enlightenment Europeans knowing little about them, the peoples of sub-Sahara Africa – tribally balkanized and living by Stone Age techniques, with a mentality to match – would obviously provide ocular proof of just how poor, nasty, brutish, and short human existence would be in the State of Nature. And so, if one wished to return to that state and experience living 'according to nature' oneself, one could scarce do better than take up residence in central Africa, as some intrepid souls did.[16]

The fact is, however, that the locale of Marlow's story is never explicitly identified.[17] After Marlow begins his tale by explaining, 'Now when I was a little chap I had a passion for maps. I would look for hours at South America, or Africa, or Australia, and lose myself in all the glories of exploration' – after this, the name 'Africa' is never mentioned. Nor are any of the places that roughly correspond to those which figured in Conrad's own journey into the heart of darkness ever identified by name.[18] To be sure, there is a suggestive pattern of circumstantial evidence inviting the reader to locate the story concretely in the Belgian Congo – regarded then and now as the most egregious instance of colonial exploitation – yet the fact that Conrad has taken some trouble to imply this without actually saying it must be regarded as significant.

But even granting that the inference is unmistakable, Conrad has precluded the implications of his story being confined to this one portion of the globe. His account, like Hobbes's, is one of universal significance. This is signalled by Marlow's leading into his 'seaman's yarn' with reflections on another, earlier journey up a river, this one into the heart of Hobbes's own England ('And this also,' said Marlow suddenly, 'has been one of the dark places of the earth'; 57). So begins his tale: 'I was thinking of very old times, when the Romans first came here, nineteen hundred years ago – the other day. ... Light came out of this river since – [...] But darkness was here yesterday' (58).

The philosophical significance of Conrad's story, however, is not confined to its providing a persuasive ratification of Hobbes's general view of human nature as it would appear if stripped of the artificial acquisitions civil society makes possible – pertinent equally to antique Greeks or Romans, Elizabethans or Victorians, Russians or Africans of whatever tribe, then or now. Conrad offers an enormous deepening of Hobbes's scanty psychology (primarily through the souls of Kurtz and Marlow, still to be examined), while tacitly *rejecting* certain of Hobbes's claims about man in the natural state. As these claims are ordinarily understood, that is. The most important respects in which Conrad's State of Nature would seem to *differ* from that of Hobbes are three in number.

First, the men Conrad portrays in the State of Nature – whether aboriginal or recidivist – are social beings, and as such proto-political. Man's competitive desire for scarce goods, his vanity, and his fear of others does not make him so defensively aggressive as to drive him into a physically isolated existence. Quite the contrary. The savage peoples Marlow encountered were all members of tribes, and lived in villages with fellow tribesmen; likewise the Europeans, for all of their self-centred, competitive acquisitiveness, mostly stuck together. And Kurtz, in going native, or the part of him that goes native, simply changed tribes, abandoning a promising career in the Company's tribe to assume leadership among a group of natives abiding along the shores of some lake he discovered still further in the interior. This fact of man's sociopolitical nature (for it is a fact, consistent with all we know about palaeoanthropology and primate behaviour) in itself obviates several of the analytical difficulties with Hobbes's account regarded as pre-history – most notably, the origin of language, but also of morality, art, sport, love, and friendship. The wandering hermit is not the norm, but rather the rare exception, rarer even than the Harlequin, who repeatedly professed himself 'a simple man [who wants] nothing from anybody' (162, 170), and doubtless means it, but who eagerly solicits and accepts shoes, bullets, and tobacco from Marlow before once again setting off into the jungle night with three natives in a canoe (171).

Second, neither in faculties of body or in mind are men equal in the State of Nature, neither equally dangerous nor equally intelligent. The tribes Marlow speaks of have chiefs, such as the one attacked by Marlow's predecessor (the Dane named Freleven, the only other character in the book given a name, curiously).[19] And it would seem that at least some have established themselves by the eminence of their personal qualities, such as the head-man of the party of cannibals who served as woodcutters for Marlow's steamer. To be sure, the rigours of a condition in which there is no compromise between vigour and death would tend to cull out the weak. This truth suddenly struck home as Marlow noticed his cannibal head-man resting 'his heavy and glittering eyes' on the Harlequin: 'never, never before, did this land, this river, this jungle, the very arch of this blazing sky, appear to me so hopeless and so dark, so impenetrable to human thought, so pitiless to human weakness' (155). As a result, those who survive life in the state of nature are apt to be more nearly equal than are people who live within the security and assistance of civil society. But the very challenge of prospering in an environment in which each individual is so much more reliant upon his own natural faculties, and in which everyone's actual qualities are unobscured by the artificialities and conventions that dominate civil life, means that the natural differences among men (and women) – their natural rankings – are fairly obvious to one and all.

The position that Kurtz established for himself in the wilderness exemplifies the precedence of hierarchy over equality in the State of Nature. And, we are no doubt meant to notice, recognition of his natural superiority was 'cross-cultural,' that is, inter-tribal. His repute among Company men is attested by everyone Marlow tells of meeting. He first heard of Kurtz from the Company's chief accountant: 'On my asking who Mr Kurtz was, he said he was a first-class agent: "He is a very remarkable person. [...] Oh, he will go far, very far"' (83–4). The manager of the Central Station assured Marlow that 'Mr Kurtz was the best agent he had, an exceptional man, of the greatest importance to the Company' (91). The agent supposedly in charge of brick-making submits that Kurtz '"is a prodigy, [...] an emissary of pity, and science, and progress, and devil knows what else"' (96). As for his ascendance over the aboriginals, there is the testimony of the Harlequin:

'But he had no goods to trade with by that time,' I objected. 'There's a good lot of cartridges left even yet,' he answered, looking away. 'To speak plainly, he raided the country,' I said. He nodded. 'Not alone, surely!' He muttered something about the villages round that lake. 'Kurtz got the tribe to follow him, did he?' I suggested. He fidgeted a little. 'They adored him,' he said. [...] 'What can you expect?' he burst out; 'he came to them with thunder and lightning, you know – and they had never seen anything like it – and very terrible. He could be very terrible. You can't judge Mr Kurtz as you would an ordinary man.' (156–7)

Lest one misunderstand this as no more than the natives' tacit adoration of the power of modern technology, there were plenty of other Europeans bearing guns, men more 'ordinary,' who were not worshipped – as Marlow saw for himself that Kurtz was, attested by the strenuous efforts of the savages to prevent his being taken from them. Voicing his own assessment of Kurtz, Marlow insists, 'Whatever he was, he was not common. He had the power to charm or frighten rudimentary souls into an aggravated witch-dance in his honour; he could also fill the small souls of the pilgrims with bitter misgivings' (146).

A third respect in which Conrad's portrayal contrasts with that of Hobbes – most definitely, and most tellingly – is in its explicit attention to the differences between the sexes. Moreover, the differences between men and women are differently manifested in the State of Nature than in Civil Society – indeed, so differently that they serve as a measure of the cultural distance between civilization and barbarism. But beneath the disparate manifestations of each sex runs a deeper commonality of nature (and contrast to the opposing sex), exemplified by the absolute commitment to Kurtz of the two so very different women – as different, so to speak, as night and day – one a natural queen among savages, the other a very picture of civilized feminine refinement.[20]

It is doubtful that this ignoring of sex-specific differences in *Leviathan* – contrasting so dramatically with the political writings of, say, Plato or Aristotle, Rousseau or Nietzsche – is due to oversight, much less to ignorance on Hobbes's part. Thus, one must assume a rhetorical purpose to his relative neglect of something this important to most people's lives. Be that as it may, Marlow's comments on the two female votaries of Kurtz forcefully reminds us of certain matters that any lover of truth must address: not merely the differences between the sexes, but the various complexities of their relationship, and the competition within each sex for the favours of the other – the one cause of quarrel that Hobbes, translator of Euripides' *Medea* at age fourteen and of Homer's *Iliad* at age eighty-six, chose not to mention (cf. *Leviathan* XIII/6–7, 61–2).

Needless to say, each woman's devotion to Kurtz is to a very different idea of the man. Significantly, we never hear his aboriginal consort speak. Intelligibly, that is. Because neither Marlow nor the Harlequin understands the dialect of her tribe, their reports of her speaking (e.g., the Harlequin tells Marlow, '"she talked like a fury to Kurtz for an hour"'; 167) convey nothing meaningful to us. But her countenance and behaviour provide eloquent testimony of her visceral, savage attachment to the one who has acquired demi-god status among her people. Marlow first learns of her existence when the mortally ill Kurtz has been carried aboard the steamer, leaving his native followers prowling the edge of the forest in dismay.

And from right to left along the lighted shore moved a wild and gorgeous apparition of a woman.

  She walked with measured steps, draped in striped and fringed cloths, treading the earth proudly, with a slight jingle and flash of barbarous ornaments. She carried her head high; her hair was done in the shape of a helmet; [...] She must have had the value of several elephant tusks upon her. She was savage and superb, wild-eyed and magnificent; there was something ominous and stately in her deliberate progress. And in the hush that had fallen suddenly upon the whole sorrowful land, the immense wilderness, the colossal body of the fecund and mysterious life seemed to look at her, pensive, as though it had been looking at the image of its own tenebrous and passionate soul. (165–6)

As Marlow's description so pointedly suggests, this regal savage female is symbolic of the pervasive life force, the very soul, of Nature itself; thus her mute protest is an ominous sign.

The other woman in Kurtz's life, identified simply as The Intended (suggesting a contrast with – what exactly? – The *Un*intended? The Actual? The Adventitious? The Irresistible?), expresses an almost exclusively spiritual, if not ethereal, understanding of the man. Marlow's own generalizations about women and men's relationship to them is indicated mainly in the context of discussing her, though foreshadowed in connection with women introduced earlier in his tale. There are the two women knitting black wool in an outer office of the Company's headquarters: 'Often far away there I thought of these two, guarding the door of Darkness' (68; cf. 174). Notable also is his response to his 'excellent aunt' with her fanciful missionary interpretation of the job she had secured for him: 'It's queer how out of touch with truth women are. They live in a world of their own, and there had never been anything like it, and never can be. It is too beautiful altogether, and if they were to set it up it would go to pieces before the first sunset' (71).

  Marlow expands upon this view with his first reference to Kurtz's Intended: 'Did I mention a girl? Oh, she is out of it – completely. They – the women I mean – are out of it – should be out of it. We must help them to stay in that beautiful world of their own, lest ours gets worse' (141). Thus Marlow alludes to the gentling, softening, refining, beautifying, altogether civilizing effect that women have upon social life – insofar (that is) as they come to be regarded by men, and to regard themselves, as the weaker sex, as more idealistic, pious, and in need of protection from the harsher aspects of the world, hence remaining somewhat naive about it. [21] In attempting to understand mankind's historical evolution from a way of life that is poor, nasty, and brutish to a life that is not, one must not ignore – as Hobbes would seem to – the pervasive influence of women, of their needs and preferences, upon men desirous of pleasing them.[22]

Marlow first sets eyes on Kurtz's fair-haired lady only upon returning to the 'sepuchral city' whence he departed. Kurtz had, however, before dying, entrusted Marlow with his personal effects, including 'a slim packet of letters and the girl's portrait.' Judging from her picture, Marlow found this woman also beautiful, but in a way utterly different from that which struck him so powerfully when first beholding Kurtz's black consort striding boldly along the river bank. Speaking of the white woman upon initially meeting her: 'I mean she had a beautiful expression. I know the sunlight can be made to lie too, yet one felt that no manipulation of light and pose could have conveyed the delicate shade of truthfulness upon those features. She seemed ready to listen without mental reservation, without suspicion, without a thought of herself' (189–90).

Having decided to return the woman's portrait and letters in person, Marlow admits to a certain curiosity about her, 'and also some other feeling perhaps.' Face to face, she appeared almost angelic ('This fair hair, this pale visage, this pure brow, seemed surrounded by an ashy halo from which the dark eyes looked out at me. Their glance was guileless, profound, confident, trustful.') – a dramatic contrast to that other incarnation of Woman: complexion dark, hair a black helmet, 'wild-eyed and magnificent,' but also 'fierce' of aspect, 'brooding' and 'ominous,' even 'sinister' (almost diabolic?). Kurtz's Intended, who had patiently awaited his return to civilization, was no longer young and girlish; hence, she had a mature woman's 'capacity for fidelity, for belief, for suffering' (192). This also amounts to a capacity for profound falsification of reality, albeit often of an ennobling hence salutary kind, as in this woman for whom Kurtz was ever young and altogether beautiful ('For her he had died only yesterday'). A woman of this kind brings out a different side of a man, insofar as he is desirous of living up to her elevated expectations, her idealized conception of him. Marlow's conversation with her leaves the reader, privy like Marlow to the dark side of Kurtz's nature and cognizant of his last words – thus aware of the chasm between her civilized and civilizing Illusion and the natural Truth – feeling positively uncanny:

'But when you think that no one knew him so well as I! I had all his noble confidence. I knew him best.'

'You knew him best,' I repeated. And perhaps she did. But with every word spoken, the room was growing darker, and only her forehead, smooth and white, remained illumined by the unextinguishable light of belief and love. [...]

I listened. The darkness deepened. [...]

' ... Who was not his friend who had heard him speak once?' she was saying. 'He drew men towards him by what was best in them.' She looked at me with intensity. 'It is the gift of the great,' she went on [...] 'But you have heard him! You know!' she cried.

'Yes, I know,' I said with something like despair in my heart, but bowing my head before the faith that was in her, before that great and saving illusion that shone with an unearthly glow in the darkness, in the triumphant darkness from which I could not have defended her – from which I could not even defend myself.

'What a loss to me – to us!' – she corrected herself with beautiful generosity; then added in a murmur, 'To the world.' By the last gleams of twilight I could see the glitter of her eyes, full of tears – tears that would not fall. [...]

She stood up; her fair hair seemed to catch all the remaining light in a glimmer of gold. I rose too.

'And of all this,' she went on mournfully, 'of all his promise, and of all his greatness, of his generous mind, of his noble heart, nothing remains – nothing but a memory. You and I –'

'We shall always remember him,' I said hastily.

'No!' she cried. 'It is impossible that all this should be lost – [...] Something must remain. His words, at least, have not died.'

'His words will remain,' I said.

'And his example,' she whispered to herself. 'Men looked up to him – his goodness shown in every act. His example –'

'True,' I said; 'his example too. Yes, his example. I forgot that.'

Of course, the unforgettable 'example' that Kurtz serves for Marlow – and for us readers of Hobbes – could not be more opposed to what this fair lady has in mind.

'I cannot believe that I shall never see him again, that nobody will see him again, never, never, never.'

She put out her arms as if after a retreating figure. [...] Never see him! I saw him clearly enough then. I shall see this eloquent phantom as long as I live, and I shall see her too, a tragic and familiar Shade, resembling in this gesture another one, tragic also, and bedecked with powerless charms, stretching bare brown arms over the glitter of the infernal stream, the stream of darkness.

At this point, the queer Shakespearean quality of the scene is especially evident: a piece of suffering humanity, this pale and beautiful woman, bereft of the ruling love of her life, does indeed strike one as tragic. And yet there is at the same time something disturbingly comic about it as well. For unlike King Lear lamenting that his dear Cordelia shalt come no more ('Never, never, never, never, never!'), the Intended remained profoundly mistaken about the character of her lost beloved. If one conceives this to be the essence of philosophic irony – that it is at once true and false, tragic and comic – one must judge the finale of Marlow's tale accordingly, as doubtless Conrad intends:

She said suddenly very low, 'He died as he lived.'

'His end,' said I, with dull anger stirring within me, 'was in every way worthy of his life.'

'And I was not with him,' she murmured. My anger subsided before a feeling of infinite pity.

'Everything that could be done –' I mumbled.

'Ah, but I believed in him more than anyone on earth – more than his own mother, more than – himself. He needed me! Me! I would have treasured every sigh, every word, every sign, every glance.' [...] 'You were with him – to the last? I think of his loneliness. Nobody near to understand him as I would have understood. Perhaps no one to hear ...'

'To the very end,' I said shakily. 'I heard his very last words. ...' I stopped in a fright.

'Repeat them,' she murmured in a heart-broken tone. 'I want – I want – something – something – to – to live with.'

I was at the point of crying at her, 'Don't you hear them?' The dusk was repeating them in a persistent whisper all around us, in a whisper that seemed to swell menacingly like the first whisper of a rising wind. 'The horror! The horror!'

I pulled myself together and spoke slowly.

'The last word he pronounced was – your name.'

I heard a light sigh, and then my heart stood still, stopped short by an exulting and terrible cry, by the cry of inconceivable triumph and unspeakable pain. 'I knew it – I was sure!' ... She knew. She was sure. I heard her weeping; she had hidden her face in her hands. It seemed to me that the house would collapse before I could escape, that the heavens would fall upon my head. But nothing happened. The heavens do not fall for such a trifle. Would they have fallen, I wonder, if I had rendered Kurtz that justice which was his due. Hadn't he said he wanted only justice? But I couldn't. I could not tell her. It would have been too dark – too dark altogether. ... (194–9)

Suffice it to say, the presence of these two women in Marlow's story, situated at the opposite ends of mankind's historical trajectory – the one still existing in the very heart of a dark interior, the other so far removed therefrom as to be practically oblivious to darkness altogether – serve as reminders, not only of the pervasive significance of the sexual division in the life of humanity, but (equally consequential) of the importance of embellishment, illusion, myth, fiction, fantasy, deception, and outright falsehood for both cultural progress and maintaining civility.[23]

As Marlow's anabasis proceeded, penetrating a region effectively beyond the rule of law, the veneer of civilization affecting him and his companions became thinner, its restraints more tenuous. And for Conrad, as for Hobbes, Restraint *is* the primary issue: what other than a fearsome coercive power – if anything – does or can or might restrain men from acting on every wilful impulse. Marlow inadvertently overhears a conspiratorial conversation between the manager of the so-called trading Company and his recently arrived uncle, leader of a band of 'sordid buccaneers' calling itself The Eldorado Exploring Expedition. They were discussing what to do about a 'wandering trader' supposedly at large in Kurtz's area (as it turns out, they were referring to the Harlequin): '"We will not be free from unfair competition till one of these fellows is hanged for an example," he said. "Certainly," grunted the other; "get him hanged! Why not? Anything – anything can be done in this country"' (110). Marlow later learned from the same be-patched wanderer that Kurtz himself gave voice to a similar perspective: '"He could be very terrible. [...] He declared he would shoot me unless I gave him the ivory and then cleared out of the country, because he could do so, and had a fancy for it, and there was nothing on earth to prevent him from killing whom he jolly well pleased. And it was true too. I gave him the ivory"' (157).

Whatever else, Conrad means to show us the consequences of 'returning' to a pre-political condition that is essentially solitary, in that one becomes ever more mentally isolated the further one proceeds, or recedes rather; that is nasty and brutish, bereft as it is of all the conveniences, securities, graces, and niceties of civil life; that is poor, despite one's having a 'right' to claim *everything* as one's own; and, given the pervasive threats to the health of both body and soul, apt to be short:

You should have heard him say, 'My ivory.' Oh yes, I heard him. 'My Intended, my ivory, my station, my river, my –' everything belonged to him. It made me hold my breath in expectation of hearing the wilderness burst into prodigious peals of laughter that would shake the fixed stars in their places. Everything belonged to him – but that was a trifle. The thing was to know what he belonged to, how many powers of darkness claimed him for their own. [...] You can't understand. How could you? – with solid pavement under your feet, surrounded by kind neighbors ready to cheer you or to fall on you, stepping delicately between the butcher and the policeman, in the holy terror of scandal and gallows and lunatic asylums – how can you imagine what particular region of the first ages a man's untrammelled feet may take him into by way of *solitude – utter solitude*, without a policeman – by way of silence – utter silence, where no warning voice of a kind neighbor can be heard whispering of public opinion? These little things make all the great difference. When they are gone you must fall back upon your own innate strength, upon your own capacity for faithfulness. Of course, you may be too much of a fool to go wrong – too dull even to know you are being assaulted by the powers of darkness. (142–3, emphasis added)

'Your own capacity for faithfulness.' Hobbes, too, acknowledges in passing that there are men who naturally manifest 'a certain Noblenesse or Gallantnesse of courage' such that their word is their bond, men of honour that would keep faith with their fellows – or their own principles – simply as a consequence of their manliness. But as Hobbes warns, this sort is too 'rarely found' to be presumed upon (*Leviathan* XV/10, 74; XVII/2, 85).

Here again, however, it is important to distinguish the two sorts of existence within a State of Nature: pre- versus post-civil. Were men of the latter category to venture into a wilderness, many would likely retain within themselves a modicum of some sort of restraint, be it natural or acquired – and not necessarily to their own credit, though most times salutary in its effects. For as Marlow's reference to 'the whispering of public opinion' reminds us, some people out of ingrained habit would continue to imagine hearing such whispering. They, and others who as well or instead are simply 'too much of a fool to go wrong – too dull even to know [they] are being assaulted by the powers of darkness' – thus incapable of thinking sufficiently radical thoughts to liberate themselves altogether from conventional morality – would never of their own accord exploit to the full the natural freedom of their situation. Such people are not as revealing about either the heights or depths of human nature as a Kurtz would be, nor indicative of the range of possibilities inherent in the natural state.

Kurtz is the most interesting, the most illuminating example with respect to the problem of restraint, and not least because he is – for better or worse – so wholly representative of modern Western civilization. As Marlow explains, 'The original Kurtz had been educated partly in England, and – as he was good enough to say himself – his sympathies were in the right place. His mother was half-English, his father was half-French. All Europe contributed to the making of Kurtz' (144).[24] In his case, the result of this hybrid heritage is a large-souled man whose rational powers are fully developed; who is blessed with an array of artistic talents as well (for music, painting, and especially a poet's gift of powerful speech; as the Harlequin enthuses, '"You ought to have heard him recite poetry – his own too it was, he told me. Poetry!"' [171]); and who has sufficient comprehension of human nature and history and science to be capable of radical thought. But despite advantages so suited for prospering in the most refined echelons of civil society, he nonetheless willingly projects himself into what is in effect a political tabula rasa. It is mainly through him, along with Marlow's response to him, that Conrad conveys to his readers whatever psychological insight he has to offer concerning the effects of a return to the State of Nature on a man of surpassing potential for either good or evil,[25] providing thereby a deeper understanding of the human soul per se (far richer and more insightful than the narrow, simplistic psychology presented in the early chapters of Leviathan). And through Kurtz's ascendancy among savage natives, Conrad at the same time supplies a clue to the historical puzzle of how mankind moved beyond primitive tribal life – how it emerged from the State of Nature, that is, and began its long, halting journey towards civilized political life.

Because Conrad portrays Marlow as sufficiently akin to Kurtz for empathetic understanding, and yet sufficiently distinct from him to allow for the possibility of near-objective appraisal, he serves as our primary interpretive source. We see Kurtz almost entirely through Marlow's eyes. In this connection, however, two points should be borne in mind. First, Marlow never so much as implies that he thinks himself superior to Kurtz; if anything, he credits Kurtz with a certain moral superiority:

I was within a hair's-breadth of the last opportunity for pronouncement, and I found with humiliation that probably I would have nothing to say. This is the reason why I affirm that Kurtz was a remarkable man. He had something to say. He said it. Since I had peeped over the edge myself, I understand better the meaning of his stare, that could not see the flame of the candle, but was wide enough to embrace the whole universe, piercing enough to penetrate all of the hearts that beat in the darkness. He had summed up – he had judged. 'The horror!' He was a remarkable man. After all, this was the expression of some sort of belief; it had candour, it had conviction, it had a vibrating note of revolt in its whisper, it had the appalling face of a glimpsed truth – the strange commingling of desire and hate. (184–6)

'He had judged' – and, as Marlow recognizes, whatever Kurtz meant by 'The Horror,' it presupposes a *moral* standard beyond any that might originate in savagery.

Second, it seems that Marlow eventually comes to regard Kurtz as a revelation of the dark side of himself that he had heretofore evaded confronting, his preferred 'choice of nightmares.' An intimation of this first occurs to Marlow in conversation with the Company manager, who is expressing anxious concern to save the great amount of ivory Kurtz has gathered, while at the same castigating the 'unsound method' whereby it was collected. Marlow avows, 'It seemed to me I had never breathed an atmosphere so vile,' and rather than be associated with *that* nightmare, 'turned mentally to Kurtz for relief,' but 'turned to the wilderness really' (168–9). Later, with Kurtz back aboard the steamer but obviously near death, Marlow mused: 'I saw the time approaching when I would be left alone of the party of "unsound method." The pilgrims looked upon me with disfavour. I was, so to speak, numbered with the dead. It is strange how I accepted this unforeseen partnership, this choice of nightmares forced upon me in the tenebrous land invaded by these mean and greedy phantoms' (180). Shortly thereafter, the manager's insolent boy announced to those gathered in the vessel's mess room, '"Mistah Kurtz – he dead,"' whereupon the pilgrims eagerly rushed out to see for themselves. Marlow, however, simply went on eating his dinner:

I went no more near the remarkable man who had pronounced a judgment on the adventures of his soul on this earth. The voice was gone. [...] I remained to dream the nightmare out to the end, and to show my loyalty to Kurtz once more. Destiny. My destiny! Droll thing life is – that mysterious arrangement of merciless logic for a futile purpose. The most you can hope from it is some knowledge of yourself – that comes too late – a crop of unextinguishable regrets. (184)

The crucial question left for the reader to confront is whether Marlow's nightmare might not be his own as well – indeed, mankind's nightmare, as Hobbes contends, on strictly rational grounds, it ought to be. Still, that Marlow remains far from sure what to make of Kurtz, that he is still struggling 'to account' for him, may explain whatever puzzlement we ourselves experience about 'that man.'[26] And about ourselves?

What else may be garnered from Marlow's portrayal of Kurtz? Marlow stresses two things, intimately related. One, Kurtz's inner turmoil, how deeply divided his soul became as the result of his return to the State of Nature. For one part of him remained attached to the kind of high-minded ambitions that could be cultivated only by a beneficiary of civilization. This noble side of his spirit was ultimately overruled, however – overruled, but never obliterated – by the powerful, heretofore dormant brutish instincts that exposure to raw Nature had awakened. For 'the wilderness had found him out early, and had taken on him a terrible vengeance for the fantastic invasion. I think it had whispered to him things about himself which he did not know, things of which he had no conception till he took counsel with this great solitude – and the whisper had proved irresistibly fascinating' (160).

That is one discovery which this large-souled post-civil man made upon venturing deep into the State of Nature: a 'great *solitude*,' despite the wilderness being populated with countless natives living a pre-civil tribal existence. And in that solitary existence, isolated from the countless distractions that relentlessly occupy the minds of men in the civil state, but confronting instead novel possibilities, a naturally reflective man may turn his attention inward, asking radical questions of himself about himself. These questions honestly answered can have a liberating effect, but at the price of inner peace. For however powerful the appeal of gratifying one's passions, no one the least bit reflective can persuade himself that self-indulgence, which is easy, is more *admirable* than self-control, which is hard (requiring the strength of will to master one's emotions and desires, regardless of the temptation or provocation). Thus, whatever natural nobility remains within a person will continue to protest against passions and practices that he tacitly recognizes should be beneath him as a human being.

By way of accounting for Kurtz's ascendancy among the natives, he apparently exploited to the full the truth with which he began his report for 'the International Society for the Suppression of Savage Customs.' That, armed as he was not only with the destructive power of modern technology, but with a superior understanding of the world, he appeared to them 'in the nature of a supernatural being,' wielding 'the might of a deity.' So his worshipful acolyte in motley testifies, '"They adored him"' (156). Whether there was more prompting their adoration – personal courage; white skin and blue eyes; a commanding, aristocratic presence, 'charisma' – Marlow provides no clue. Still, regardless of how Kurtz acquired his quasi-divine status, we are to understand that the basis of his autocratic power amongst these pre-civil people was essentially *religious*. The practically important issue, of course, concerns the use to which he put such power.

In that ironic report (minus its doubly ironic postscript), one sees the continuing presence of his higher nature inspiring his words, the extraordinary eloquence whereby he appealed 'to every altruistic sentiment' – not of the savages, for whom the very *idea* of altruism would in all likelihood be incomprehensible – but of those piously intent on suppressing savagery. Kurtz's verbal facility reminds us, not merely of the pervasive importance of speech for distinctly human life, but that the effectiveness of great rhetoric, such as will transport men beyond their petty selfishness, depends crucially on the speaker's ability to invoke ideals that naturally appeal to what is noble in human nature (justice, virtue, love, 'a power for good,' hence for creation, progress, amelioration of needless suffering). Or so is the case, at least, among civilized peoples. According to Marlow, Kurtz was pre-eminently a person capable of doing just that:

The man presented himself as a voice. Not of course that I did not connect him with some sort of action. Hadn't I been told in all the tones of jealousy and admiration that he had collected, bartered, swindled, or stolen more ivory than all the other agents together. That was not the point. The point was in his being a gifted creature, and that of all his gifts the one that stood out pre-eminently, that carried with it a sense of real presence, was his ability to talk, his words, the gift of expression [...]. (139)

The Journalist who called upon Marlow after his return to the sepuchral city attests to the obvious political significance of Kurtz's remarkable skill, that 'his proper sphere ought to have been politics "on the popular side. [...] Heavens! how that man could talk! He electrified large meetings [...] He would have been a splendid leader of an extreme party"' (189; cf. *Leviathan* XIX/8, 97). Kurtz's rational ideals continued to be the subjects of his speeches; but his lower soul once liberated – a libidinous genie out of its bottle – the dark side of his nature dominated his deeds, his chosen actions. Doubtless in his honest moments, he was keenly aware of the dissonance.

The Kurtz-besotted Harlequin also attested to the deep division in his hero's soul: '"This man suffered too much. He hated all this, and somehow he couldn't get away. When I had a chance I begged him to try and leave while there was time; I offered to go back with him. And he would say yes, and then he would remain; go off on another ivory hunt; disappear for weeks; forget himself among these people – forget himself – you know." "Why! he's mad," I said. He protested indignantly. Mr Kurtz couldn't be mad. If I had heard him talk, only two days ago, I wouldn't dare hint at such a thing ...' (157–8). Marlow did hear him talk, and confirms Kurtz's love-hate relationship with existence in the State of Nature, and the chaos these conflicting sentiments made of his soul – part of him still attached to what he knows are the higher ideals that constitute civilization (and desirous as well of the rewards society sometimes confers on those who supposedly promote those ideals), but another part powerfully drawn down towards the barbarous freedom of sensual self-indulgence.

The other thing that Marlow emphasizes about Kurtz derives from this chaos of his soul, and points directly to Hobbes's teaching about the State of Nature: the problem of most people's inadequate self-restraint unless artificially reinforced. For the Ancients, genuine *self*-restraint is the ground of virtue, of Moderation (*söphrosunë*, literally 'sensibleness,' which presupposes the capacity to exert one's reason over one's emotions, desires, and revulsions). Whatever one calls it, put to the ultimate test, Kurtz lacked it. Once liberated from the impediments and encouragements of modern civilized life – the whole gamut of external demands and supports for moderate behaviour, from coercive law to social approval – he succumbed to his sub-rational drives and desires. However, it is significant that he continued to pay lip service to his rational ambitions and ideals. This should not be lightly dismissed as hypocrisy, pointless in his circumstances, but rather as an expression of his continuing, albeit lamed, recognition of what ought to govern him.

Marlow first voices his summary judgment of Kurtz upon the death of his native helmsman who had needlessly exposed himself to the attacking spears and arrows of Kurtz's jealous aboriginals: 'Poor fool! If he had only left that shutter alone. He had no restraint, no restraint – just like Kurtz – a tree swayed by the wind' (147). Marlow expands on this theme upon discovering that the round knobs adorning the poles fronting Kurtz's hut were 'not ornamental but symbolic,' being dried human heads ('food for thought and also for the vultures'):

I want you clearly to understand that there was nothing exactly profitable in these heads being there. They only showed that Mr Kurtz lacked restraint in the gratification of his various lusts, that there was something wanting in him – some small matter which, when the pressing need arose, could not be found under his magnificent eloquence. Whether he knew of this deficiency himself I can't say. I think the knowledge came to him at last – only at the very last. (160)

With respect to this belated self-knowledge, Marlow submits, 'No eloquence could have been so withering to one's belief in mankind as his final burst of sincerity [i.e., 'The horror! The horror!']. He struggled with it himself, too. I saw it – I heard it. I saw the inconceivable mystery of a soul that knew no restraint, no faith, and no fear, yet struggling blindly with itself.' (177)

Kurtz lacked restraint. But why? After all, lesser mortals have ventured into a wilderness populated only by primitive people living in the natural state – explorers and missionaries, naturalists and prospectors – yet not had their humanity so profoundly subverted as a result. Why did this happen to Kurtz? The bare explanation Marlow offers is: 'because he was hollow at the core ...' (160). So, what would account for *that*, for the core of his soul being, or having become, 'hollow' – again, bearing in mind those other, less-gifted but more morally stalwart persons who by implication retained something substantial in the cores of their souls? Or were they just too much fools to go wrong? Marlow finds it 'mysterious' that there could be a continuous 'blind struggle' in a soul that 'knew no restraint, no faith, and no fear.'

But perhaps another emissary from beyond ordinary human life, Shakespeare's Hecate, can provide some insight here. For do not Marlow's words recall those of Hecate plotting the ruin of great Macbeth? 'He shall spurn fate, scorn death, and bear / His hope 'bove wisdom, grace, and fear' (*Macbeth* 3.5.30–1). Kurtz – lacking a fear of anything, including death (the fear at the base of so many other fears, and upon which rests Hobbes's political psychology), and lacking faith in anything (such as the opinions and principles, duties and purposes that guide most people's souls), but especially lacking faith in any divine grace – Kurtz had no restraining power at the very core of his soul. For he also lacked wisdom. Intellectually and otherwise gifted as we are told Kurtz was, he apparently had only sufficient dialectical power to destroy all the variously ill-supported views he encountered, but not enough to reconstitute adequate replacements for himself. He exemplifies the great danger of dialectical reasoning that Plato's Socrates first warned of over twenty-three centuries ago.[27]

Thus Kurtz was left with the mind of a nihilist, believing nothing is forbidden, which for all practical purposes is a licence for radical hedonism. But the nobility inherent in the high side of his spirit longed for something in which a man may take pride, and a barbarous, brutish life of sensual self-indulgence does not qualify. Indeed, it is positively repugnant to the spirit's distinctly human capacity to recognize and admire nobility. Thus Kurtz's lingering attachment to the ideals he could no longer justify. And thus he struggled, blindly. For the spirited part of the soul is blind, utterly reliant upon the rational part to recognize the qualities of things, to which it then passionately responds as appropriate. But Kurtz's rational part was not equal on its own, in the solitude of a State of Nature, to meet the enormous challenge he took upon himself: to create a world in his own image, an intellectual and ethical architecture that could command the unqualified respect of his own soul. For anyone still capable of appreciating tragedy, Kurtz's fate must seem a tragic one – as tragic as Lear's. But like all true tragedies, it is revealing of human limitations.

In reconsidering Hobbes's State of Nature, and the political prescription based thereupon, it will prove useful to bear in mind the seaman Marlow's tale, and not least his assessment of Kurtz: 'Whatever he was, he was not common. He had the power to charm or frighten rudimentary souls into an aggravated witch-dance in his honour; he could also fill the small souls of the pilgrims with bitter misgivings' (146). For though the surface of Hobbes's teaching presumes that the common man is in fact the universality of men, the success of his project – as has been hinted, and will be further shown in the following chapters – depends crucially on harnessing the natural powers of uncommon men.

PART TWO

The Platonic *Leviathan*:
Ἁρμονία

A devotion to Church and Throne is not itself a criminal sentiment; to prefer the will of one to the will of many does not argue the possession of a black heart or prove congenital idiocy.

– Conrad, *Under Western Eyes*

Because of Hobbes's psychological peculiarity, it is possible that behind the image of the leviathan is hidden a deeper, symbolic meaning. Like all the great thinkers of his times, Hobbes had a taste for esoteric cover-ups. He said about himself that now and then he made 'overtures,' but that he revealed his thoughts only in part and that he acted as people do who open a window only for a moment and close it quickly for fear of a storm.

– Carl Schmitt, *The Leviathan in the State Theory of Thomas Hobbes*

And do you hear? take heed of speaking your mind so clearly in answering my *Leviathan*, as I have done in writing it.

– *Six Lessons* (*English Works*, vol. 7, 356)

For it is not the bare Words, but the Scope of the writer, that giveth the true light, by which any writing is to bee interpreted; and they that insist upon single Texts, without considering the main Designe, can derive no thing from them cleerly.

– *Leviathan* XLIII/24, 331

17

The Crucial Paragraph: Platonic Intimations

For someone whom Melville might accuse of having too often 'fallen into Plato's honey head,' the most intriguing feature of Hobbes's *Leviathan* is the forty-first paragraph of the thirty-first chapter. It is the concluding paragraph of Part Two, and as such of the first half of the book, separating the half that Hobbes tempts us to call 'humane Politiques' from the half that might then qualify as 'Divine' (cf. XII/12, 54). It reads:

And thus farre concerning the Constitution, Nature, and Right of Soveraigns; and concerning the Duty of Subjects, derived from the Principles of Naturall Reason. And now, considering how different this Doctrine is, from the Practise of the greatest part of the world, especially of these Western parts, that have received their Morall learning from *Rome*, and *Athens*; and how much depth of Morall Philosophy is required, in them that have the Administration of the Soveraign Power; I am at the point of believing this my labour, as uselesse, as the Commonwealth of *Plato*: For he also is of opinion that it is impossible for the disorders of State, and change of Governments by Civill Warre, ever to be taken away, till Soveraigns be Philosophers. But when I consider again, that the Science of Naturall Justice, is the onely Science necessary for Soveraigns, and their principall Ministers; and that they need not be charged with the Sciences Mathematicall, (as by *Plato* they are,) further, than by good Lawes to encourage men to the study of them; and that neither *Plato*, nor any other Philosopher hitherto, hath put into order, and sufficiently, or probably proved all the Theoremes of Morall Doctrine, that men may learn thereby, both how to govern, and how to obey; I recover some hope, that one time or other, this writing of mine, may fall into the hands of a Soveraign, who will consider it himselfe, (for it is short, and I think clear,) without the help of any interested, or envious Interpreter; and by the exercise of entire Soveraignty, in protecting the Publique teaching of it, convert this Truth of Speculation, into the Utility of Practice. (193)

Thus, the conclusion of a chapter with the ponderable title, '*Of the* KING-DOME OF GOD BY NATURE.' What are we to make of this strange paragraph, so strikingly dissimilar in tone from the 789 paragraphs that preceded it – half confessing a worry that all the labour he has invested in crafting *Leviathan* may come to naught, while nonetheless hoping otherwise? Not that many pages earlier, he left the impression that this was a matter of indifference to him. Having assured us that with respect to constructing commonwealths, 'there may Principles of Reason be found out, by industrious meditation, to make their constitution (excepting by externall violence) everlasting,' he adds, 'And such are those which I have in this discourse set forth: Which whether they come not into the sight of those that have Power to make use of them, or be neglected by them, or not, concerneth my particular interest, at this day, very little' (XXX/5, 176). Of course, this disclaimer need not be read as *absolute* indifference concerning whether his 'Truth of Speculation [be converted] into the Utility of Practice.' Hobbes may simply be stating here his acceptance of its not happening more or less *immediately* ('this day'), while still entertaining the hope that it shall 'one time or another.'[1]

The more one thinks about it, however, the stranger seems the way he chose to express his worry: that the political teaching he has presented may turn out to be 'as uselesse, as the Common-wealth of *Plato*.' On the face of it, the comparison is singularly inapt. Hobbes speaks as if the *polis* that Plato has his dialogical character Sokrates 'make in *logos*' were intended, like *Leviathan*, to provide a general blueprint for actual political life – rather than to serve its stated purpose: to see therein the form of justice writ large, the better to discern justice in the soul of an individual person. And that, in turn, so as to judge whether or not *being* just, as opposed to merely *appearing* just, is inherently good, hence desirable. The philosopher's 'city-making' in *Politeia*[2] is undertaken in response to the challenge of Glaukon and Adeimantos to show that the just life is invariably preferable to the most unjust life, not merely for the many mediocre people, but for the naturally superior, strong-souled few as well – those capable of leading the *most* unjust life (should they so choose): that in which one successfully poses as just while surreptitiously resorting to injustice. Seen in light of that challenge, how 'uselesse' has been Plato's 'labour'? Perhaps more to the point, how does it compare with Hobbes's own effort to meet what is essentially that same challenge: to refute 'The Foole [that] hath sayd in his heart, there is no such thing as Justice' (XV/4, 72)?[3]

But insofar as one cares to compare the status and substance of each regime as described, the two philosophers' creations could hardly appear more different (to say nothing of their respective metaphysical contexts). The one is premised on Man's being naturally a *political* animal by virtue of his being 'not self-sufficient' (*ouk autarkēs*) – that he instead has many needs which, practically speaking, can be adequately met only in a rule-governed association with his fellows that *is* self-sufficient, partly because founded on a rational division of labour. Insofar as such a polity is requisite to anyone's living a fully human life (i.e., fulfilling one's natural, distinctly *human* potential), the polity may itself be regarded as natural, being the natural environment of Man as *Man*. The other account depicts Man as a creature whose *natural* state is profoundly *non*-political, being a condition of absolute freedom such as that enjoyed – or suffered – by other animals (i.e., limited solely by each individual's own power). On that premise, all political associations are understood to be of strictly human invention, being convention-grounded arrangements contrived to serve ends envisioned by their constituting individuals (which, for most, means mainly comfort and security), and not only distinct from but superior to life in the natural state.

Regarding the substance of each regime as described: one depiction is primarily, indeed almost exclusively, focused on education and *erôs* – more precisely, on the basic musical and athletic education of the ruling warrior class, on the philosophical education of an elite carefully selected from that class, and on managing their erotic relationships. After a brief but exceedingly dense treatment of the foundation of political life, the discussion becomes focused almost entirely on the nurture of those suited by nature to be warriors, hence rulers, and their manner of life. There are virtually no institutions or laws specified; and apart from those having to do with education and *erôs*, the only policies discussed have to do with sickness (whether of body or soul), religious observances (very brief, amounting to 'stick with tradition'), and the conduct of warfare (in which the distinction between 'Greek' and 'Barbarian' is of paramount importance).

By contrast, it is no exaggeration to say that – with the massive exception of religion – attention to these matters is conspicuous by its virtual absence from Hobbes's blueprint for the well-ordered commonwealth. In particular, as previously noted, there is no discussion of the natural qualities most desirable in those who might serve as sovereigns, nor of their suitable nurture. Indeed, there is little discussion of education at all, and most of that little is focused on the Ruled, not the Rulers – on the 'how to obey' side of the 'Morall Doctrine' Hobbes purports to teach. One's sense of this lacuna is merely heightened by his belated assurance that, with respect to a host of apparently contradictory expectations regarding the individuals composing his prescribed commonwealth – of mental faculties, of passions, of opinions and manners, and especially of the tension between '*Courage*, (by which I mean the Contempt of Wounds, and violent Death)' and a necessary civil docility – that 'by Education, and Discipline, they may bee, and are sometimes reconciled' (R&C/2–4, 389). Where is one to find the essentials of such an education?[4]

As for *erōs*, Hobbes's treatise contains precious few reminders that we are erotic beings,[5] and next to nothing about the higher manifestations of *erōs* in art, literature, music, and not least of all in politics and philosophy. Instead, he provides extensive discussions of something called 'rights' (mainly of Sovereigns) and duties (mainly of Subjects), of civil liberties, of subordinate associations, of various ministers and officers and counsellors, of civil laws and judges, of property and taxation policies, of crimes and punishments, and other practical arrangements essential to a functioning polity. Almost all of these matters are scanted in Plato's most celebrated presentation of political philosophy, which focuses instead on 'how to govern,' especially on the sine qua non of the best government: wisdom. From a reflective comparison of these two regimes – the 'City in *logos*' of Plato's Sokrates and the Commonwealth of Hobbes's *Leviathan* – one might characterize their contrast as that of complementary parts.

In any event, it should be a matter of interest and surprise, not to say astonishment, that in the final paragraph of the first half of his treatise, Hobbes directly associates the two regimes – 'out of the blue,' as it were, and despite their appearing so radically different that almost all readers acquainted with both works regard them as polar opposites: one the very epitome of political 'idealism,' the other a cynic's idea of realism. Why ever would it occur to Hobbes to in *any* way associate his efforts with those of Plato, much less imply that, as political architects, they share an equally slight chance of their designs being fully realized, *for essentially the same reason*? Given the form and substance of the thirty-one chapters that lead up to it, who could have anticipated such an extraordinary conclusion? Having laboured through a two-hundred-page treatise in which, to all appearances, the management of stable, peaceful political life has been reduced to an exact science, universally valid irrespective of time or place, and requiring no rare or special talent to put into practice – is it not confounding to learn that this prescription actually requires 'much depth of Morall Philosophy' in whoever is entrusted with sovereign power? Indeed, so much depth that the regime's conjurer suspects his creation may turn out be a waste of effort unless 'Soveraigns be Philosophers.' The unlikelihood of this conjunction of Philosophy and Sovereignty ever coming to pass explains what one might call the 'melancholy' quality of Hobbes's slender hope for the full realization of what he has in mind.

But equally noteworthy – and, I believe, even more revealing – is the *location* Hobbes chose for his surprising pronouncement: precisely in the *centre* of his treatise (according to the original pagination, it occurs on page 193 of the 385 pages comprised by the text's forty-seven chapters).[6] This *placement* in the text of what would seem a most improbable, and certainly unanticipated, affiliation[7] amplifies immeasurably its importance. Why so? Because the specific 'opinion of Plato' to which Hobbes refers – the astonishing, apparently outrageous formula[8] that Sokrates advances as the very keystone of his imagined regime – occurs *precisely* in the *centre* of the *Republic*:

Unless philosophers exercise kingly rule, or those now said to be kings and lords genuinely and adequately philosophize, and political power and philosophy coalesce in the same place, while the many natures now pursuing either apart from the other are by necessity excluded, there can be no rest from evils for the polities, nor I believe for the human race. (473c–d)

It is this prescription, probably the most famous in the entire history of political philosophy, that Hobbes subtly but unmistakably associates himself with: 'For he [Plato] *also* is of opinion that it is impossible for the disorders of State ... ever to be taken away, till Soveraigns be Philosophers.' Many are acquainted with the formula (doubtless several times more than have actually read the whole dialogue in which it appears, much less studied it with any seriousness). But very, *very* few are aware of its exact placement in Plato's text. Clearly, however, Hobbes figures among those rare few, having expressed his agreement with this, literally central, teaching of Plato's *Republic* in the exact centre of his own *Leviathan*.

Must one not suppose this singular feature to be of some interpretive significance? For whatever else, it indicates, first of all, the fact that Hobbes has studied Plato's dialogue with exemplary care; presumably, then, he found doing so to be profitable. Secondly, that knowledge of his having done so is at least relevant – perhaps even essential – to a *complete* understanding of his treatise; that is, to the kind of understanding vouchsafed readers who recognise what Hobbes has indicated, and are willing to explore its possible implications. Thirdly, it implies that the importance of what Hobbes states here, including its immediate context, is strictly analogous to the importance of what occurs at exactly the same location in Plato's *Republic*.

To be sure, Hobbes no sooner identifies his efforts with those of Plato than he partially retracts the identification, or so it would seem. As Hobbes reminds us, the Platonic Sokrates would seem to require that kings actually be or become philosophers, whose preparatory education consists of a revolutionary curriculum of five mathematical disciplines (described as but a 'prelude' [or, 'overture'; *prooimion*], i.e., to dialectics; 531d). Whereas Hobbes's prescription requires merely the rule of 'a Soveraign' sufficiently intelligent and open-minded to understand and accept the advice of a philosopher (specifically, Hobbes) – with the proviso, however, that he would enact 'good Lawes' encouraging the study of Mathematics. And insofar as a certain kind of mathematical study is useful training for tackling more challenging philosophical problems (as Hobbes insists it is, speaking derisively of 'those that would teach Philosophy, without having first attained great knowledge in Geometry'),[9] his hoped-for Sovereign would through such legislation in effect promote philosophy, whatever its other effects.

Perhaps it is mere coincidence that the Platonic Sokrates had tacitly recommended something similar in explaining the virtual non-existence in his day of solid geometry, that is, of the mathematical representation of three-dimensional objects, which (unlike shadows) have 'depth,' hence 'weight,' as well as height and breadth (528b; cf. 602d). It is a discipline whose status, as Sokrates describes it, is analogous to his account of genuine philosophy in actual political life. 'There are two causes' for the underdeveloped state of solid geometry, he suggests. With 'no city honouring it, it is weakly sought after because of its difficulty. And those who do seek after it need a supervisor,' lacking which they seek in vain. Whereas, 'if a whole *polis* would jointly supervise it, and take the lead in honouring it,' the requisite knowledge would 'come to light' (528b–c). Hobbes also ascribes special significance to geometry ('the onely Science that it hath pleased God hitherto to bestow on mankind'; IV/12, 15), taking pains to appear to employ the geometrical method as the means of generating a science of politics. Whence came he by this – seemingly extravagant – respect for *geometry*, of all things? Was it really just that chance encounter with Euclid that both Hobbes and Aubrey (rather more dramatically) recount?[10]

Still, the main point remains, namely, the apparent difference between the one thing needed to fulfil Hobbes's prescription for putting an end to the ills of mankind, and that which Plato supposedly mandates: the former requiring merely the *indirect* rule of a philosophy via a Sovereign willing and able to be advised by a philosopher (that is, willing to read and able to understand Hobbes's book), the latter specifying the direct rule of one or more philosophers. While this is not the place to go into details,[11] suffice it to say that the Platonic prescription – insofar as it has a practical application to actual political life – is essentially the same as that of Hobbes. There is a constellation of obstacles, beginning with considerations of justice to philosophers and non-philosophers alike, that preclude the day-to-day administration of political affairs by men who are themselves ruled by their love of, hence endless pursuit of, wisdom.[12] For like the proverbial housewife, a philosopher's work is never done. But so, too, is governing a full-time occupation. Hobbes is explicit on this point:

There is no doubt but any King, in case he were skilfull in the Sciences, might by the same Right of his Office, read Lectures of them himself, by which he autho-rizeth others to read them in the Universities. Neverthelesse, because the care of the summe of the businesse of the Common-wealth taketh up his whole time, it were not convenient for him to apply himself in Person to that particular. A King may also if he please, sit in Judgment, to hear and determine all manner of Causes, as well as give others authority to doe it in his name; but that the charge that lyeth upon him of Command and Government, constrain him to bee continually at the Helm, and to commit the Ministeriall Offices to others under him. (XLII/73, 297)

In short, both philosophers agree that the best imaginable form of polity is that in which Philosophers are Kings, or Kings Philosophers, were that somehow workable. However, since it is not – mainly because philoso-phers are not willing to sacrifice philosophy for the sake of endlessly 'straightening out the troubles [or, 'bads,' 'evils'; *kaka*] of others' (*Republic* 346e; cf. 520d), but are, like Hobbes, ever eager to 'return to [his] inter-rupted Speculation of Bodies Naturall' R&C/17, 396) – they further agree upon the closest practical approximation of philosophical rule. Namely, some arrangement whereby philosophers discharge their obligation to their supporting polity through advising and educating the best of the non-philosophers (patriotic, honour-loving gentlemen, such as Adeiman-tos presumably represents, as too perhaps a Francis Godolphin), who in turn would serve in the polity's most important ruling offices, and be appropriately honoured for their virtuous efforts. This is the form of philosophical 'rule' which the dialogue actually portrays in the figure of

Sokrates – and which Hobbes himself exemplifies in having written *Leviathan*.

For his treatise provides, or so he clearly implies, 'the onely Science necessary' for managing political life in accordance with his prescription, namely, 'the Science of Naturall Justice.' *Natural* Justice? How could that be? Hobbes's explicit treatment of justice – that is, of the substance of justice – is radically (indeed, notoriously) *conventional* and *relative*, being determined by the positive laws of each polity. The only natural ground of Justice, again according to his explicit account, is the Third Law of Nature, '*That men performe their Covenants made*,' from which he derives 'the definition of INJUSTICE, [as] no other than *the not Performance of Covenant*. And whatsoever is not Unjust, is *Just*' (XV/2, 71). However, as I previously argued, this strictly formal account, licensing as 'just' virtually anything that could be written into law, is manifestly inadequate and (not surprisingly) does not square with Hobbes's own use of the term. More to the point, however, neither does it square with the rest of his political prescription, which presumes precisely what he here treats as the one thing needful: knowledge of what is Just *by Nature* – most evidently for the sake of legislating, governing, and judging 'equitably.'[13] To the extent *Leviathan* does provide such knowledge, then, it must be implicit in an understanding of the full prescription, meaning *as it would actually work in practice*. But that still leaves the essential question unanswered: why should we regard 'how it would actually work' as being naturally *just*? Might Hobbes be relying on *that* having been established by his most illustrious predecessor – the very one who first proposed as the best imaginable regime, a 'Commonwealth' in which the 'Soveraigns be Philosophers'?[14]

Hobbes distinguishes himself from Plato in another respect, however, by claiming 'that neither *Plato*, nor any other philosopher hitherto, hath put into order, and sufficiently, or probably proved all the Theoremes of Morall Doctrine, that men may learn thereby, both how to govern, and how to obey.' But this sentence, too, needs careful parsing. Apart from implying – but no more than implying – that Hobbes *has* done what no predecessor had accomplished: 'proved *all* the Theoremes of Morall Doctrine,' as well as put them into their proper order, he has not claimed that Plato failed 'sufficiently, or probably' to prove *any* of these so-called 'Theoremes' (what he more commonly calls 'Laws of Nature').[15] So, Hobbes may credit Plato with having 'sufficiently, or probably' proven *some* of those that Hobbes presents in their logical order. Indeed, Plato may have 'proved' the most important Theorem of them all: that which Hobbes endorses in his central paragraph. In any case, what is one to make of Hobbes's rather puzzling qualification of his having 'proved' the requisite Theorems '*sufficiently*, or *probably*'? For someone whose supposed model of *proof*, hence of *knowledge*, is Geometry, 'sufficiently' can only mean 'absolutely, unqualifiedly,' whereas 'probably proved' amounts to an oxymoron.[16] On the other hand, greater or lesser probability may be the appropriate rational expectation when dealing with matters moral and political – very much as Plato's most distinguished pupil argued.[17]

There are other, albeit less conspicuous, echoes of Plato's *Republic* in this remarkable paragraph that Hobbes crafted to conclude the civil half of his *Leviathan*. For example, in noting 'how different [his] Doctrine is, from the Practice of the greatest part of the world,' he echoes Sokrates's warning to Adeimantos that 'this is the very accusation' he is making against all the current regimes: that none are worthy of comparison with the one they have created; that it is 'really *divine*,' whereas the others are all too human (497a–c). And Hobbes's title for this chapter that concludes with his endorsement of Philosophical Kingship? 'The Kingdome of *God* by Nature.' It is also of interest that Hobbes, for all of his apparent emphasis on the strictly determined character of Reality, leaves the clear impression that converting his 'Truth of Speculation, into the Utility of Practice' is necessarily a matter of *Chance*: he has 'some *hope*, that one time or other, this writing of [his], *may* fall into the hands' of the right sort of Sovereign. Here a reader might be reminded of Sokrates assuring Adeimantos 'that neither city nor regime will ever become perfect [or complete, fulfilled; *teleos*] ... until some necessity [*anagkē*] somehow chances [*tychē*]' to bring about philosophical rule (499b).

The very fact that Hobbes can, but halfway through his treatise, pause to express a hope that someday, somewhere, a suitable Sovereign will chance upon the book, and put into practice the doctrine expounded therein, sufficiently indicates the rational *independence* of its first half. (So, too, does his speaking of it as '*short*, and I think clear' – a fair enough claim about a tract of less than 200 pages; less plausible of one just shy of 400). Moreover, there is nothing essentially *Christian* about Hobbes's political philosophy as expressed in this first half. Being a political teaching 'derived from the Principles of Naturall *Reason*,' it is accessible and – presuming it to be correct, and correctly interpreted – should be acceptable to any rational person regardless of race or religion. By contrast, the second half of the book has mainly a polemical purpose, dictated by, hence tailored to, the rhetorical requirements of the predominately Christian time and place in which Hobbes lived and wrote.[18] But the political teaching itself, manifesting the universality one rightly expects of a genuinely scientific account, is equally applicable to both Christian and non-Christian peoples. Strictly analogous observations can be made about the regime described in the *Republic*. For although Sokrates asks Glaukon, 'Will not the city you are founding be Greek?' (and Glaukon affirms, 'It must be' – after all, they are Greeks, living amid a plurality of Greek polities, all of whom purport to revere the same gods; 470e), Sokrates subsequently makes it clear that there is no reason why a philosophically ruled polity could arise only in Greece; that, indeed, it may already exist in some faraway 'barbaric place' of which they are unaware (499c).

Consider also the provision that, in order to convert Hobbes's Speculative Truth into Useful Practice, a suitable Sovereign must, 'by the exercise of *entire* Sovereignty,' *protect* 'the Publique teaching' of this doctrine. That is, essential to the successful implementation of Hobbes's political prescription is the necessity for a more or less strict supervision, not only of the positive conveyance to the general public of so much of its rationale as concerns their 'Duty [as] Subjects' (cf. XXX/3–13, 175–9), but also of limiting people's exposure to alternative doctrines. What else would *protecting* his own doctrine entail? In this, too, Hobbes apparently follows Plato, having recognized the importance of the scarcely noticed 'underside' of Sokrates's famous formula: that in addition to excluding those incapable of genuine philosophizing from political rule (the 'upperside' of the prescription, which naturally attracts almost everyone's entire attention), it is equally vital – perhaps even more so – that those incapable of behaving in a politically responsible, 'kingly' way must be prohibited from philosophizing (which, as a practical matter, can only mean prevented from 'Publiquely teaching' their views). The implication of this usually overlooked facet of the Platonic formula is that sophistry and the propounding of misbegotten doctrines are threats as great to wholesome political life as is the corrupt or incompetent wielding of political power. Hobbes expressly identifies six 'seditious doctrines' that are actually so much 'poyson' to a commonwealth (XXIX/6–12, 168–70).

Accordingly, Hobbes advises his hoped-for Monarch to exercise by all means the central Right of Sovereignty:

[T]o be Judge of what Opinions and Doctrines are averse, and what conducing to Peace; and consequently, on what occasions, how farre, and what men are to be trusted withall, in speaking to Multitudes of people; and who shall examine the Doctrines of all bookes before they be published. For the Actions of men proceed from their Opinions; and in the wel governing of Opinions, consisteth the well governing of mens Actions' (XVIII/9, 91).

In the centre of the book's longest chapter, '*Of* POWER ECCLESIASTICALL,' Hobbes reiterates a variation of this profoundly important political truth: 'For it is evident to the meanest capacity, that mens actions are derived from the opinions they have of the Good, or Evill, which from those actions redound unto themselves' (XLII/67, 295).[19]

There is a specification in Hobbes's expressed hope that bears emphasizing: that his book 'may fall into the hands of a Soveraign, who will consider it himselfe.' This suggests that an existing monarchy, with its potential for being transformed into a philosophical or philosophically counselled kingship, offers the most favourable prospect for the complete realization of his political teaching (remote as he concedes that possibility might be).[20] His reasoning here is obvious. One can scarce imagine a majority in a Democracy, much less an entire citizenry, understanding the whole doctrine well enough to put it into practice themselves, in the sense of acting the part of a philosophical Sovereign directly. On the other hand, one should not rule out the possibility that a charismatic ruler of philosophical inclinations might arise out of a Popular commonwealth and transform it into a de facto Monarchy. Hobbes, translator of Thucydides, was well aware of that ancient author's judgment of Pericles, sometimes King of Athens in all but name, who privately consorted with the philosopher Anaxagoras and with others reputedly wise.[21] Perhaps even more thought-provoking is the case of Alkibiades, ward of Pericles and longtime associate of Sokrates. The War *Commentaries* of Julius Caesar attest to his perceptivity and intelligence, as well as to his eloquence.[22] Of course, the most famous philosopher-king relationship in all of history is that of Aristotle and Alexander, whose history-shaping conquests introduced Greek culture and civilization to half the known world. Although Hobbes refers to Alexander four times, he never mentions this singular fact: that in his youth, Alexander was tutored by a philosopher (cf. *Republic* 499b–c).[23]

A final point: Hobbes characterizes his entire Reason-based political prescription as a 'Truth of *Speculation*.' Since this is a term he never defines, and could be subject to misinterpretation – especially as its meaning today would seem to differ from that of Hobbes's day – it is worth some effort to clarify. One can begin by considering his other three uses of the word. It first occurs in the chapter of greatest historical importance, namely, '*Common-wealth by Acquisition*' (meaning, 'where the Soveraign Power is acquired by Force'): 'And thus much shall suffice, concerning what I find by speculation, and deduction, of Soveraign Rights, from the nature, need, and designes of men, in erecting of Common-wealths' (XX/15, 105). Hence, Speculation can yield *Truth*; but it is not identical with whatever results simply from Deduction and the 'calculative' power of Reason. Much later, in distinguishing the methodical search for knowledge that leads to philosophy, from truths discovered in the course of the ordinary use of reason and language, he allows there to have been 'divers true, generall, and profitable Speculations from the beginning; as being the naturall plants of humane Reason,' but that they were indiscriminately mixed in with 'the Weeds, and common Plants of Errour and Conjecture' (XLVI/6, 368). Hence, Speculation is not to be confused with mere Conjecture. And in the penultimate sentence of his book, Hobbes speaks of his intention to 'return to my interrupted Speculation of Bodies Naturall' (R&C/17, 396). It would seem, then, that by 'speculation' Hobbes has in mind the older, original meanings of the word: 'the faculty or power of seeing, esp. with comprehension,' hence that comprehensive *mental* 'seeing' called 'Contemplation'[24] – an activity reliant upon the synoptic power of Reason that according to Sokrates distinguishes someone of the dialectical nature requisite for philosophy ('For he who is *synoptikos* is *dialektikos*, while he who isn't, is not'; 537c). As such, Hobbes's 'speculation' is the English equivalent of Plato's *theoria* (cf. *Republic* 327a, 486a, 517d, 556c). And his 'Truth of Speculation,' then, is 'theoretical' in the sense of its being the product of extensive Contemplation, which he hopes someday a suitable Sovereign will 'convert … into the Utility of Practice.'

In light of the Crucial Paragraph, certain other features of Hobbes's *Leviathan* take on added significance, further suggesting an underlying relationship with Plato's *Republic*. For example, the four mentions of Alexander,[25] the four uses of 'Speculation,' and the four references to Natural Justice exemplify a stylistic feature the two books share, namely, the pervasive presence of the number Four, which since antiquity has been symbolically associated with Justice. In directing attention to this, along with other 'numerological' features of Hobbes's text, I am aware that the significance I attribute to it is apt to be regarded with scepticism by many scholars today – as it most certainly would *not* have been by educated readers of Hobbes's own day.[26]

Whatever allusive significance it may or may not have, the prominence of Four in the organization of Hobbes's book is almost too obvious to overlook. Not only is the text divided into four main parts, three of those parts also manifest this quadratic character: 'Part 1' comprises sixteen chapters (i.e., 4 × 4), 'Part 3' twelve chapters (3 × 4), 'Part 4' four chapters (beginning with chapter 44). Four unpaginated items precede the 'Introduction' (Frontispiece, Title page, Epistle Dedicatory, tabulated 'Contents of the Chapters'). The 'Introduction' itself consists of four paragraphs; provides four names in block letters for the regime Hobbes prescribes ('the great LEVIATHAN called a COMMON-WEALTH, or STATE, [in latine CIVITAS]' – with a slightly different set of four names supplied later, 'STATE' being replaced by '*Mortall God*,' XVII/13, 87); employs four other 'latine' expressions, complete with their supposed English equivalents (*Automata, Salus Populi, Fiat, Nosce teipsum*); cites four factors that so obscure 'the characters of mans heart' that they are rendered 'legible onely to him that searcheth hearts' (namely, 'dissembling, lying, counterfeiting, and erroneous doctrines');[27] and describes 'the Nature of this Artificiall man' in terms of four headings. If one were to include the 'Review and Conclusion,' the book would consist of forty-eight 'chapters' (i.e., 3 × 4 × 4).[28] There are ostensibly 396 pages (i.e., 400 – 4), with four of these being blank (three separating the main Parts, and one between Part 4 and the 'Review and Conclusion').[29] But this total is misleading inasmuch as there are certain aberrations in the pagination. Four pages figure in duplicate numbering: two '247's, and two '248's. Whereas four other pages are simply 'missing,' in that the pagination skips from page 256 – i.e., 4^4 ! – to 261.[30] In light of the broader numerical pattern, it seems unlikely that these are merely the mistakes of a careless compositor, those 'Mischances of the Presse' Hobbes warns might prejudice an 'Elocution' he is confident is otherwise 'not obscure.'[31]

What is true of the book's structure is variously reflected in its contents as well. I would suggest that four chapters in the first Part, 'OF MAN,' have a special pertinence to philosophy; as listed in the table of contents, they are: '*Of Speech*' (ch. 4); '*Of the Vertues, commonly called Intellectuall, and their contrary Defects*' (ch. 8), '*Of Religion*' (ch. 12), and '*Of Persons, Authors, and things Personated*' (ch. 16, which deals with the fundamental conceptional problem of Hobbes's theory: how 'A multitude of men, are made one Person'; XVI/13, 114). In the twenty-four paragraphs of chapter 4, Hobbes highlights four 'Speciall uses of Speech' and 'foure correspondent Abuses,' 'foure generall' kinds of names (IV/15-18, 16), and gives four pairs of examples illustrating his claim that one man's idea of virtue is another man's vice (IV/24, 17). He gives four reasons why the 'simple Passions ... have their names for divers considerations diversified' (VI/13, 25). In the thirty-two paragraphs of chapter 12, Hobbes presents his scientific account of religions in terms of four natural causes, or 'seeds,' while at the same time subtly contrasting religion with philosophy (as I discussed in chapter 1). Moreover, the paragraph in which this all-important contrast is introduced (XII/6, 52) just happens to be the 256th (i.e., 4^4) paragraph of the entire text. Also, he cites by name four pagan gods whom 'the Gentiles' credited with specific causal responsibilities (Venus, Apollo, Mercury, Aelous; XII/17, 55). And he specifies four causes that weaken people's faith, causing changes in religious belief (XII/24, 58). Also, the sixteenth paragraph of the chapter contains one of Hobbes's best jokes; in listing some of the practically countless things that various peoples have deified, his fourth example is 'a Crocodile'! Chapter 16 cites four exemplary classes of things that may be 'represented by [the] Fiction' of Personation (XVI/9–12, 81–2). This is but a sampling of the 'sets of four' that occur in Part One.

The pattern continues in the Second Part, 'OF COMMON-WEALTH.' It begins with Hobbes's characterizing the 'Lawes of Nature' in but four terms: '*Justice, Equity, Modesty, Mercy*' (XVII/2, 85; cf. XV/40, 80; XXVI/36, 148). Chapter 23 describes four categories of Officials that 'have speciall Administration': those having to do with 'the Oeconomy'; with 'the Militia'; with Public education; and Judges (XXIII/4-7, 124–5). In Chapter 25, Hobbes gives four reasons why it is better for a Sovereign to hear each of his Counsellors separately than in an assembly (XXV/15, 135–6). And he concludes the chapter with the observation that 'no great Popular Common-wealth' endured unless it was sustained by at least one of four causes: 'either by a forraign Enemy that united them; or by the reputation of some one eminent Man amongst them; or by the secret Counsell of a few; or by the mutuall feare of equal factions' (XXV/16, 136). In the longest, and arguably most important chapter of the Part (26, comprising forty-four paragraphs), Hobbes's specifies four characteristics of 'a good Judge,' i.e., a 'good Interpreter of the Laws' (XXVI/28, 146) – the practical key to the Sovereign's fulfilling the primary purpose of the political association: civil peace through justice based on civil law. In chapter 27 he identifies four crime-producing passions (namely, 'Hate, Lust, Ambition, and Covetousnesse'), and distinguishes four 'Degrees of Crime' (XXVII/18, 155; /29, 157). In chapter 28, Hobbes speaks specifically of four classes of things that are 'Honorable by Nature,' namely, 'the effects of Courage, Magnanimity, Strength, Wisdome' (XXVIII/19,

164). And in chapter 30, he identifies four classes of crimes 'that are of most Danger to the Publique,' hence deserving of 'the severest Punishments': 'those which proceed from malice to the Government established; those that spring from contempt of Justice; those that provoke Indignation in the Multitude; and those, which unpunished, seem Authorized' (XXX/23, 182–3).

The list could be continued with examples from the remaining two Parts. Suffice it to note how Hobbes concludes his treatise: with a four-chapter Part Four, 'OF THE KINGDOME OF DARKNESSE,' addressing what he would persuade his readers are the four 'tares of Spirituall Errors' sown by 'The Enemy': 'First, by abusing ... the Scriptures'[!]; 'Secondly, by introducing the Daemonology of the Heathen Poets'; 'Thirdly, by mixing with the Scripture divers reliques of the Religion, and much of the vain and erroneous Philosophy of the Greeks, especially of Aristotle'; 'Fourthly, by mingling with both these, false, or uncertain Traditions, and fained, or uncertain History' (XLIV/3, 334).

Now, what does all this 'fourness' of Hobbes's *Leviathan* have to do with Plato's *Republic*? At first blush, it might seem to indicate – if anything – a *contrast* rather than a kinship. For Plato's famous dialogue on Justice and Philosophy seems dominated by practically countless trios and triads, not quartets and quadruplets. To mention but a few of the more obvious examples, Book One consists of three separable conversations about what Justice is, and each of these divide rather neatly into three parts. Constructing the 'City in *logos*' takes place in three stages (the simplified city that Glaukon calls a 'city of pigs'; a luxuriated, 'fevered' city – 372e; and a purified, moderate city – cf. 399e). It has a tripartite class structure; the 'musical' education of potential Rulers focuses on three aspects (*logos* component, style, and melodic mode); there are three criteria of eligibility for selection to the uppermost class of 'Guardian' (age, skill at guarding, love of the city); there are three sets of tests for this patriotic love; and the whole arrangement is ratified by a three-part 'noble' or 'well-born' Lie (cf. 415a and 416e). The human soul is found to consist of three distinct parts; there are three 'proofs' offered that the Spirit (*thumos*) is distinct from Desiring part, and likewise three proofs that it is distinct from the rational part. The discovery of Justice occurs in three stages: its form is discerned first in the City; then the same form is found to be applicable to the human soul; finally, it is compared with ordinary views, and found to account for their limited validity (cf. 442e–443b). Book Five is obviously structured by the 'Three Waves'

(Sexual Equality amongst the ruling class, Familial Communism likewise, Philosophers as Kings). Philosophy is explicated in terms of three famous images (Sun-Good analogy, Divided Line, Cave Allegory). Etc., etc., etc.

However, this threefold character is but a veneer, a triadic Appearance masking a more significant quadratic Reality. Book One, for example, actually comprises *four* distinct parts, having a brief but symbolically very important 'prologue': a philosopher and his young 'auxiliary' being arrested on their way to the Higher City, and made to return to a Lower City, where the philosopher will in effect become its ruler (cf. 519d). The three radical features introduced in Book Five amount to a fourth stage in constructing the City in *logos*, as they entail profound modifications in the city as described through Book Four (especially in the specification of the Rulers: elderly warriors, dogmatically attached to both their opinion-based virtues and their city, being replaced by philosophers). As for Book Five itself, although the Three Waves naturally attract the most attention, it has a fourth part of enormous importance: the discussion of warfare that immediately precedes the introduction of philosophical kingship, necessitating a revision in the distinction between 'Greeks' and 'Barbarians' that is every bit as radical as the other proposed innovations.[32]

Moreover, there are actually four distinguishable classes in the City in *logos*, for the Producing, Money-making class is made up of two very different components, farmers and craftsmen, dissimilar in several respects – not least in that those 'suited by nature' for farming and herding and country life generally, are apt to differ considerably from potters and cobblers, to say nothing of shopkeepers and other townfolk. This is subtly confirmed by the 'Myth of the Metals' part of Sokrates's Noble Lie, with the Producing class being represented by *two* metals, Iron and Bronze (one simple, the other complex; 415a–c). The 'musical' education likewise has *four* distinguishable aspects, not three, Sokrates lumping together two quite different features, harmonic mode and rhythm (cf. 399e). There are four virtues attributed to the City, with the last, Justice, being discovered in an unusually roundabout way ('Therefore, much as with any other four things, if in seeking any one of them in something or other ... we recognized the other three first, this would also serve for recognizing the thing sought. For plainly it couldn't be anything but the remainder'; 428a). And with the introduction of a new conception of suitable Ruler for what is in fact a second City in *logos*, a fourth criterion of selection is added: educability in dialectics (cf. 535a ff.). The Familial Communism of this second City requires that a fourth part be added to the Noble Lie (459c ff.). The 'longer and fuller' psychology Sokrates alludes to (435d) requires a recognition that the Spirit has two distinguishable halves, resulting in a quadriform rather than a tripartite conception of the soul.[33] The three-stage account of Justice discovered by the end of Book Four has an additional stage – one that, in effect, tests its adequacy by inquiring whether the same form of Justice is valid, both politically and psychically, for *women* (first half of Book Five). The formal explication of Philosophy involves a fourth component, set apart from the famous visual images (Sun, Line, Cave) by the mathematical curriculum; fittingly, it is expressed in geometrical reasoning, being a Proportion (*analogian*; 533e–534a).

But insofar as Philosophy is the central theme of Plato's *Republic*, the dialogue's most important quadratic feature is the unequally Divided Line (509d–511e), its four proportional parts representing, first of all, four distinct 'degrees' of Reality – two belonging to the Intelligible realm of Being, two to the Perceptual realm of Becoming. With the exception of the shortest segment, representing 'Images' (*eikones*) such as shadows (*skiai*) and reflections in smooth surfaces, the other, more substantial categories of this ontology are not identified by name. The most memorable 'shadows' spoken of in the dialogue are those projected on the inner wall of the Cave, representing the perceptual world that the shackled prisoners mistake for ultimate reality. (How important *is* it, then, that Hobbes – most curiously – includes in his schematic Table of 'Sciences, that is, knowledge of Consequences; which is called also Philosophy,' a discrete 'Science of Sciography,' radically separated from 'Optiques'; IX/3, 40?) As I discussed in a previous chapter, the Line's various segments also represent four distinct *pathēmata* that correspond to the ontological categories; that is, the four powers of Reason as experienced in the human soul: Intellection (*noēsis*), Thinking (*dianoia*), Trust (or 'Faith'; *pistis*), and Imagination (*eikasia*). Not incidentally, Sokrates suggests that the study of Numbers per se – the first of those 'Sciences Mathematicall' of the pre-dialectical curriculum – is compulsory precisely because it requires the soul to use the Intellect (*noēsei*) itself upon the Truth itself (526a–b).

To the extent that the *Republic* provides a philosophical understanding of actual *political* life, it does so in terms of a fourfold typology of variously defective, 'human' (*anthrōpina*; 497c) Regimes.[34] In the Platonic taxonomy, the character of each type of regime is determined – and eventually undermined – by its internal ruling principle: Timocracy (rule by a warrior class pre-occupied with war-making; 548c); Oligarchy (ruled by 'lovers of money-making,' hence 'greedy for wealth'; 551a, 562b); Democracy ('greediness for freedom'; 562b); and Tyranny (the lawless desires of the tyrant). As for the other 'names' that figure in Hobbes's explicit discussion of Regimes, 'Aristocracy' is reserved for the first City in *logos* (cf. 445d), an unlikely but nonetheless possible regime ruled by the *crème* of its elder warriors, whereas 'Kingship' would be the appropriate designation for the second City in *logos*, that problematical regime ruled directly by philosophers (of which 'perhaps a pattern is laid up in Heaven'; 592b).

According to Sokrates, to his four archetypical forms of polity correspond as many kinds of souls: the high-spirited Timocrat, so-named because ruled by his love of Honour (*timë*); the Oligarch, a lover of Wealth (*ploutos*) because ruled by the appetitive part of his soul, but nonetheless frugal out of concern for wealth accumulation; the Liberty-loving Democrat who lacks a single constant ruling desire, and so feels free to pursue whatever desire is uppermost at the time (cf. *Leviathan* VI/53, 28), hence is typically profligate and fashion-led; and the Tyrant, tyrannized by his own erotic drives.[35]

In short, despite their being of such different literary genre and apparently written to such different purposes, both Plato's *Republic* and Hobbes's *Leviathan* share a pervasive fourness that profoundly affects both the form and the substance of each work.[36] Perhaps this numerological similarity is due simply to Chance. Alternatively – and far more plausibly – each author may have consciously but independently crafted his text in this quadratic manner as being symbolically appropriate to his text, given the historical association of the number Four with *Justice*, the dominant theme of both works. Obviously, I believe there is more to it in Hobbes's case, given the broader pattern of Platonic associations in his text, signalled by the remarkable paragraph at the very centre of his book. I suspect the fourfold character of *Leviathan* to be one more indication whereby Hobbes means to suggest a genealogical relationship between the founding text of political philosophy and his own masterwork (albeit only to readers who might recognize the numerical similarity and ponder its possible significance).[37]

With respect to that relationship, consider finally certain peculiarities of the Dedicatory Letter Hobbes prefixed to his *Leviathan*. Most readers today pay it little or no heed. And considered as simply an isolated 'atom' of text, there is not a lot to be made of it. But in light of the other affinities between his treatise and Plato's *Republic* – what I have here suggested partakes of Hobbes's 'main Designe' – one might consider, first of all, his associating his 'discourse of Common-wealth' with a *pair* of *brothers,*

Sidney and Francis Godolphin. For what Hobbes in the Crucial Paragraph calls the 'Common-wealth of *Plato*' also exists to the lasting honour of a pair of brothers, those 'Sons of Ariston,' Glaukon and Adeimantos, who challenged Sokrates to show what Justice is, its inherent power, and how being Just profits a man. Might there be any larger significance to this common feature?

Strangely, perhaps, the possible importance of Hobbes's dedication is increased by the mercenary account of it that Edward Hyde, Earl of Clarendon, provides by way of introducing his damning critique of the book while nonetheless professing an intimacy with, and admiration for, its author: 'Mr *Hobbes* is one of the most antient acquaintance I have in the World, and of whom I have alwaies had a great esteem, as a Man who besides his eminent parts of Learning and knowledg, hath bin alwaies looked upon as a Man of Probity, and a life free from scandal.'[38] His account of Hobbes's dedication, while perhaps not intended to be prejudicial (nor would have been nearly as much so in his as in our day), does have that effect. But of more interest, it raises a slight puzzle. Hyde speaks of the time when most Royalists, like him, were living in exile, he in Jersey and Prince Charles in Paris:

I heard … that Mr *Hobbes* who was then at *Paris*, had Printed his Book *De Cive* there. I writ to Dr *Earles*, who was then the Princes Chaplain, and his Tutor, to remember me kindly to Mr *Hobbes* with whom I was well acquainted, and to desire him to send me his Book *De Cive*, by the same token that *Sid. Godolphin* (who had bin kill'd in the late Warr) had left him a Legacy of two hundred pounds. The Book was immediately sent to me by Mr *Hobbes*, with a desire that I would tell him, whether I was sure that there was such a Legacy, and how he might take notice of it to receive it. I sent him word that he might depend upon it for a truth, and that I believed that if he found some way secretly (to the end there might be no public notice of it in regard of the Parliament) to demand it of his Brother *Francis Godolphin*, (who in truth had told me of it) he would pay it. This information was the ground of the Dedication of this Book to him, whom Mr *Hobbes* had never seen.[39]

Apart from the personal acquaintance one would presume from Hobbes's heading of the Dedicatory Letter ('To My Most Honor'd *Friend* Mr Francis Godolphin'), Hyde's account squares with its first and last sentences. For it begins with what seems a veiled reference to the legacy Sidney left Hobbes ('and *otherwise* to oblige me, as you know, with reall testimonies of his good opinion');[40] and ends with a disclaimer Francis may use if he prefers to disassociate himself from a book that may be 'generally decryed' ('you may be pleased to excuse your selfe,' etc.). The fact that Hyde did not 'decry' Hobbes's *De Cive*, but found *Leviathan* pervaded by 'most mischievous Principles, and most destructive to the Peace both of Church and State,' suggests that what he found obnoxious about the latter book was precisely what Hobbes anticipated in the Letter: his interpretations of Scripture, along with their broader implications for religion in general and Christianity in particular.

For this is one of two concerns that dominate the substance of the Dedicatory Letter. After three sentences that constitute the actual dedication, Hobbes offers what amounts to an 'apology' in the old-fashioned sense of the word. And he begins it in the same manner as Plato's Sokrates began his: with a profession of ignorance ('I know not how ...') – in Hobbes's case, how his book will be received; in Sokrates's case, how his accusers' persuasive claims about him will be regarded, in particular that he is 'a clever speaker' (*deinos legein*; in that '*deinos*' originally, and more typically, meant 'terrible/terrifying,' the phrase here might be translated as 'a terrifying speaker,' or – combining the literal with the emphatic use – as 'a terribly clever speaker'). Hyde in effect warns that Hobbes is a *deinos* speaker, both dangerously clever and terrible.[41] And he does so with some justice, I would add, especially regarding what Hobbes himself acknowledges 'perhaps may most offend,' namely, his interpretation of various Biblical passages.

Prior to voicing this concern, however, Hobbes anticipates that his treatise faces a more general objection, and he invokes a rather peculiar image in defence of his purpose:

For in a way beset with those that contend, on one side for too great Liberty, and on the other side for too much Authority, 'tis hard to passe between the points of both unwounded. But yet, me thinks, the endeavour to advance the Civill Power, should not be by the Civill Power condemned; nor private men, by reprehending it, declare they think that Power too great. Besides, I speak not of the men, but (in the Abstract) of the Seat of Power, (like to those simple and unpartiall creatures in the Roman Capitol, that with their noyse defended those within it, not because they were they, but there,) offending none, I think, but those without, or such within (if there be any such) as favour them.

As is well attested, educated readers of Hobbes's time could be expected to recognize references to classical authors, and consequently to Greek and Roman history. Indeed, Hobbes half laments the fact: 'And by reading of these Greek, and Latine Authors, men from their childhood have gotten a habit (under a false shew of Liberty,) of favouring tumults [etc]; as I think I may truly say, there was never any thing so deerly bought, as ... the learning of the Greek and Latine tongues' (XXI/9, 111). He claims to have himself 'neglected the Ornament of quoting ancient Poets, Orators, and Philosophers, contrary to the custome of late time' (R&C/15, 394). True, he has not much *quoted* such authors, but there are allusions aplenty in his text, as in the passage above.

There may actually be *two* allusions intended, though only one is made explicit: that to the Capitoline geese. But Hobbes's description of the rhetorical problem he confronts – 'to passe between' different but equally dangerous options – rather obviously suggests the challenge Odysseus confronted in attempting to negotiate his way between the Monster Scylla and the violent Whirlpool Charybdis (this having become a familiar literary trope, Hobbes can count on it occurring to a thoughtful reader without so much as a hint from him). But it may have a more precise pertinence, in that these respective hazards can be interpreted so as to fit Hobbes's problem tolerably well: the danger of a monstrously over-powerful, voracious Sovereign, *versus* that of the destructive, anarchic Chaos resulting from excessive Liberty.[42]

Be that as it may, the explicit allusion is interesting enough. It is to a famous episode in the history of the Roman Republic recounted by Livy, Plutarch, and Diodorus Siculus, virtually a literary icon in the works of Lucretius, Virgil, and Dante (among others), and subsequently the subject of interpretive commentary by Machiavelli. The story involves the invasion of Italy in 390 B.C. by a massive army of Gauls (referred to as *barbaroi* by Plutarch). Near the city of Veii, they defeated the Roman army, which then fled in disarray, half into Veii, the other half back to Rome. Deciding that their city as a whole was indefensible, the remnants of the Roman army retreated into the fortified Capitol, along with their women, children, and Senators, leaving the elderly and the plebeians to fend for themselves (most of the latter fleeing into the countryside). The Gauls plundered and burned the city, but in a frontal assault on the Capitol were repulsed with heavy losses. So they laid the Capitol under siege, intending to starve out the defenders. However, having noticed that an undefended cliff face could be scaled, the barbarians attempted a surprise assault at night. They approached the summit undetected, so stealthily that even the Romans' dogs remained asleep. But the sacred geese of Juno inhabiting the temple area awoke, and, by their alarmed cackling and loud flapping about, awakened the citadel's defenders in time to beat back the Gauls. Thereafter, despite the privations suffered, the Romans held out until their assailants wearied of the siege and negotiated a ransom for withdrawing. Before they could leave, however, the half of the Roman army which had recuperated at Veii arrived, being led by Camillus, whom the Senate had approved as Dictator. In that capacity, he repudiated the ransom agreement, and in the course of two ensuing battles, the barbarians were annihilated. Rome's subsequent recovery was regarded as a second founding of the city. And the geese, treated as symbolic of Divine Providence, were ritually honoured in public ceremonies for centuries thereafter.

In likening himself to these Capitoline geese, sacred to pagan Juno, what does Hobbes intend to suggest? Merely that he defends 'in the Abstract' the necessity of allowing the Civil Power sufficient Authority to meet its vital responsibilities – being himself as 'unpartiall' as a goose with regards to whoever may exercise the Sovereign Authority, however well or ill, in whatever form of commonwealth? Or does he intend to suggest something more than that? Specifically, that there is an ever-imminent danger of an assault by barbarians under the cover of 'Darknesse'? Whoever, or whatever, he might mean by this, Hobbes the philosopher cannot by himself defend any Seat of Power from that which threatens it. He can only raise the kind of 'noyse' that should awaken politically capable and responsible men, thereby encouraging *them* to meet and defeat those assailing civil society's essential Seat of Power. His own civic role of honking goose, albeit divinely precious, seems a suitably modest one. But is it not curiously like that claimed by the notorious ironist, Sokrates, who characterized himself as a humble insect, a stinging gadfly, *also* divinely approved, *also* charged with the mission of awakening his fellows (those composing the sluggish horse of a city called Athens; *Apology* 30e)? Of course, mere-bug-slapped-dead is *not* the 'verdict of history' as to the effect of Sokrates. Nor, one suspects, does Hobbes regard the effort he has invested in his *Leviathan* as but so much noise whereby to awaken the gentlemen of mid-seventeenth-century England to a parochial danger. Indeed, might he see its ultimate consequence to be nothing less than a second founding of political life? And that he himself will be recognized for all subsequent centuries as the causal agent precipitating this revolution in human thought and practice?

Still, the image he has chosen for himself – that of a sacred goose warning of barbarians exploiting the dark of night to attack the political citadel – raises further questions. Who are these threatening barbarians? Must it not be those who insist upon 'too great Liberty,' opposing what they would regard as 'too great Authority' being granted the Sovereign? And who, then, are *they*? Presumably, Hobbes has in mind especially those he admits he 'may *most* offend' by his interpreting 'certain Texts of Holy Scripture ... to other purpose than ordinarily they use to be by others.' Interpretations that, for example, challenge the prerogatives of the professional clergy, that deny Scriptural authority for much established Christian doctrine, that question the historical accuracy of present Biblical texts, that license Sovereigns as the undisputed heads of their respective religious communions, that even grant Sovereigns the right to determine the canon of authentic Scripture. But, Hobbes insists, his extraordinary interpretations are necessary to his larger purpose, since the more familiar renderings serve as 'the Outworks of the Enemy' – of the barbarians – 'from whence they impugne the Civill Power.' These barbarians are, in effect, agents of 'the Kingdome of Darknesse,' which 'is nothing else but a *Confederacy of Deceivers, that to obtain dominion over men in this present world, endeavour by dark, and erroneous Doctrines, to extinguish in them the Light, both of Nature, and of the Gospell'* (XLIV/1, 333).

Hobbes's erstwhile friend, the Royalist Edward Hyde, amply proves Hobbes's prescience with respect to many readers – and not merely those whose vested interests he threatened – finding his Scriptural exegesis highly offensive:

And I am still of opinion, that even of those who have read his Book, and not frequented his Company, there are many, who being delighted with some new notions, and the pleasant and clear Style throughout the Book, have not taken notice of those down-right Conclusions, which overthrow or undermine all those Principles of Government, which have preserv'd the Peace of this Kingdom through so many ages ... much less of those odious insinuations, and perverting some texts of Scripture, which do dishonour, and would destroy the very Essence of the Religion of Christ.

Yet I hope nothing hath fallen from my Pen, which implies the least undervaluing of Mr *Hobbes* his Person, or his Parts. But if he, to advance his opinion in Policy, too imperiously reproaches all men who do not consent to his Doctrine, it can hardly be avoided, to reprehend so great presumption, and to make his Doctrines appear as odious as they ought to be esteemed: and when he shakes the Principles of Christian Religion, by his new and bold Interpretations of Scripture, a man can hardly avoid saying, He hath no Religion, or that He is no good Christian; and escape endeavouring to manifest, and expose the poison that lies hid and concealed.[43]

Sokrates was brought to trial, convicted, and executed for holding heterodox religious beliefs with which he corrupted the youth, while being widely suspected of outright atheism (*Apology of Sokrates* 26a–d) – the very event Hobbes alludes to in his one reference to Sokrates.[44] And as is generally known, Hobbes likewise stood in danger of a heresy trial, also being widely suspected of outright atheism (advocacy of which was criminal). According to Aubrey, 'There was a report, (and surely true) that in Parliament ... some of the Bishops made a motion to have the good old Gentleman burn't for a Heretique.' Some such possibility cannot have been far from Hobbes's mind when he attempted in his Dedication to pre-empt such attacks by defending the *necessity* of his Scriptural interpretations as integral to the coherence of his political prescription. For those who favour 'too great Liberty' – especially with regard to religious preaching and practice, including prophesying and proselytizing – threaten the Sovereign's ability to maintain civil peace, hence risk returning everyone to the barbarous anarchy of a State of Nature.

Moreover, in his chapter '*of* POWER ECCLESIASTICALL' (dauntingly, four times the length of the next longest chapter), Hobbes addresses the unavoidable necessity of Scripture being interpreted. Having contested the Scriptural basis for the doctrine of Excommunication (XLII/20-31, 276–9), Hobbes turns to the question 'Of the Interpreter of the Scriptures before Civil Soveraigns became Christians' (marginal gloss at XLII/32, 280). Invoking the Biblical account of St Paul's indifferent attempt to persuade the Jews of Thessalonica that Jesus was the Messiah foretold in the Old Testament (for while 'some of them beleeved ... some of them beleeved not'), Hobbes addresses the obvious question:

What was the reason, when they all beleeved the Scripture, that they did not all beleeve alike; but that some approved, others disapproved the Interpretation of St. Paul that cited them; and every one Interpreted them to himself? It was this; S. Paul came to them without any Legall Commission, and in the manner of one that would not Command, but Perswade; which he must needs do, either by Miracles, as Moses did to the Israelites in Egypt, that they might see his Authority in Gods works; or by Reasoning from the already received Scripture, that they might see the truth of his doctrine in Gods Word. But whosoever perswadeth by reasoning from principles written, maketh him to whom hee speaketh Judge, both of the meaning of those principles, and also of the force of his inferences upon them ... And generally in all cases of the world, hee that pretendeth any proofe, maketh Judge of his proofe him to whom he addresseth his speech. (XLII/32, 280)

Hobbes notes that originally 'Every of the Evangelists was the Interpreter of his own Gospel; and every Apostle of his own Epistle' – which, after all, is the only credible standard of *correct* interpretation: the author's own. Whereas 'of the Old Testament, our Saviour himselfe saith to the Jews (John 5.39) *Search the Scriptures*.' On that basis, Hobbes concludes 'If hee had not meant they should Interpret them, hee would not have bidden them take thence the proof of his being the Christ: he would either have Interpreted them himselfe, or referred them to the Interpretation of the Priests' (XLII/34, 281). So, according to Hobbes, the situation necessarily remained thus 'till such time as there should be Pastors, that could authorize an Interpreter, whose Interpretation should generally be stood to: But that could not be till Kings were Pastors, or Pastors Kings' (XLII/35, 281). The formula sounds familiar somehow.

We may be sure that Hobbes fully appreciated the reflexive implications of his stating that 'whosoever perswadeth by reasoning from principles written, maketh him to whom hee speaketh Judge, both of the meaning of those principles, and also of the force of his inferences upon them.' Thus the hope he expresses in the concluding sentence of the central paragraph of his book: 'that one time or another, this writing of mine, may fall into the hands of a Soveraign, who will consider it himselfe ... *without the help of any interested, or envious Interpreter*,' and on that basis, 'convert this Truth of Speculation, into the Utility of Practice.'

I earlier suggested that, for the purpose of interpreting the Dedicatory Letter, it may be pertinent to bear in mind that what Hobbes calls 'the Common-wealth of *Plato*' arises as a direct response to the challenge posed by a pair of brothers who are of similar nature, both being high-spirited, yet who differ significantly in how that spiritedness is expressed: Glaukon exemplifying a lover of *victory*, and Adeimantos a lover of *honour*. Moreover, Glaukon – his name means 'Shining' or 'Gleaming' – is accorded preferential treatment in that he is the philosopher's sole companion at the beginning of the dialogue, which ends with a moral tale addressed expressly to him. Having introduced the need for philosophical rulers, Sokrates warns a sceptical Adeimantos that philosophers such as he has in mind are rare because genuine philosophy requires a complex of apparently conflicting qualities of soul that 'do not grow together willingly' in a single person (503b–d, cf. 375b–c). But in the course of what must have been at least a twelve-hour conversation, Glaukon shows himself to have, or be capable of acquiring, that same rare complex of qualities which, according to Plato's Sokrates, constitute a philosophical nature.[45]

In light of this, we might notice a subtle difference in how Hobbes speaks of the brothers Godolphin. Although he declares his intention to do honour to both brothers, he expressly addresses Francis in terms of honour ('Honor'd Friend'; 'Honor'd Sir'), whereas he describes Sidney as 'most worthy' and refers 'to the worthinesse of his person' – a difference in descriptors the more significant in light of Hobbes's later discussions of 'honour' (X/17ff, 42–3) and 'worthiness' (X/53–4, 46–7). Hobbes also singles out the one brother for special praise: 'For there is not any vertue that disposeth a man, either to the service of God, or to the service of his Country, to Civill Society, or private Friendship, that did not manifestly appear in his conversation, not as acquired by necessity, or affected upon occasion, but inhaerent, and shining in a generous constitution of his nature.' A *shining* virtue, inherent in his *nature*, manifested in his *conversation*.[46]

Hobbes concludes his treatise with a 'Review' in which he responds to the objection that 'the contrariety of some of the Naturall Faculties of the Mind, one to another, as also of one Passion to another … inferre an impossibility that any one man should be sufficiently disposed to all sorts of Civill duty.' He admits 'that these are indeed great difficulties, but not Impossibilities: For by Education, and Discipline, they may bee, and are sometimes reconciled.' As evidence confirming this claim, Hobbes expressly invokes his 'most noble and honored friend Mr. *Sidney Godolphin*,' who united in his person, 'cleernesse of Judgment, and largenesse of Fancy; strength of Reason, and gracefull Elocution; a Courage for the Warre, and a Fear for the Laws' (R&C/1–4, 389–90). Like Glaukon, Sidney was living proof that the requisite complex of seemingly conflicting qualities is possible, given the right combination of nature and nurture. And though, also like Glaukon (368a), Sidney distinguished himself in battle, he did not survive to enjoy his eulogy, but like the warrior Er, was slain by an undiscerned, and undiscerning hand.[47]

A fair consideration of all such textual evidence, it seems to me, amplifies the significance of what I contend is *Leviathan's* 'crucial paragraph.' The following chapters will do so still further. A sceptic might object, however, that the commonality between Hobbes and Plato suggested by their both endorsing the necessity that 'Soveraigns be Philosophers' is superficial, more semantic than substantial, in that Hobbes's conceptions of 'philosophy' and 'philosopher' differ profoundly from Plato's. I do not believe so, but must reserve addressing this important – indeed, truly fundamental – matter until my penultimate chapter.

18

The Heartless Introduction: Hobbes's Disposable Physiology

According to Plato's Sokrates, 'The beginning [*archë*] of every work is most important [*megiston*].' This is certainly true of the beginning of the dialogue in which this observation appears (*Republic* 377a). But it is equally so of Hobbes's *Leviathan*. Its first two sentences imply radical departures from orthodox thought:

NATURE (the Art whereby God hath made and governes the World) is by the *Art* of man, as in many other things, so in this also imitated, that it can make an Artificial Animal. For seeing life is but a motion of Limbs, the begining whereof is in some principall part within; why may we not say, that all *Automata* (Engines that move themselves by springs and wheeles as doth a watch) have an artificiall life?

Nature. There could scarcely be a more suitable First Word for a political treatise whose most famous, or infamous, feature is its hellish portrait of human existence in the conditions of 'mere Nature.' That is, the conditions to which God, via Nature, consigned man upon expulsion from the Garden of Immortality.[1] Or so Believers would have to interpret Hobbes's account. And what *is* Nature? Nature is the Divine Art – the Art *itself*, notice, *not* the product of this Art (as a hasty reader might mistakenly presume). The *product* of Nature-as-Art is 'the World.' Nature, being an Art, is itself a set of principles, the assemblage of 'Natural Laws' (say) according to which all the natural things of the World are made and governed. Does it require the constant attention of an Artisan, i.e., God? Or has the whole World been fashioned as an *automata*, a grand watch-like mechanism created by a watch-maker God: an enormously complex self-propelling, self-regulating, self-replenishing machine, ruled 'automatically' by Nature, whose Laws are 'immutable' and 'Eternall' (cf. XXVI/24, 144)? In the latter case, the World may require a 'first cause,' but thereafter it does not require direct governance by God. Such that, if God could die, or were to desert his Creation, the World would go on working as it ever has. Whichever it is, insofar as man can learn what these Natural Laws are, and how to use them to manipulate things *in* the World – how to practise the Divine Art himself – he will to that extent wield Godlike power.

Not everything in the World, however, is the direct result of the Divine Art that is manifested in Nature acting naturally. Some things are the result of *human* Art, other things exist by virtue of human agreement: rules and conventions (e.g., table manners, various weights and measures), covenants and contracts (e.g., alliances and partnerships). As I have noted before, philosophy practically originates in the recognition of this fundamental distinction: between what is due to Nature (thus, is a permanent presence, exists spontaneously, and would be everywhere the same), and what is *not* due to Nature, but to Art or Agreement (thus, transient, man-made, and varying from time to time and place to place). Since only knowledge of the former could claim to be permanently true, the first seekers after Wisdom were philosophers of Nature, or 'physiologists,' ignoring if not despising as mere *ephëmera* the human things, including 'politics.' Indeed, Aristophanes portrays Sokrates in *Clouds* as just such a 'pre-Sokratic' philosopher himself. But Sokrates, in turning his attention from things in the Heavens and beneath the Earth to the study of Cities and Men, is credited with reorienting subsequent philosophy, such that understanding *human* nature in its natural setting became the first priority.[2] In Plato's portrayal of him, Sokrates preserves 'Nature' (*Physis*) as a term of distinction, while at the same time greatly refining the idea of it, such that – far from Nature being seen as radically contrasting with the human things – its fulfilment or perfection serves as man's standard for judging things, including human things, especially politics.

Hobbes, while seeming to honour the distinction between Nature and Art, blurs if not eradicates it. He would have us understand Nature itself as 'artful,' and human art as modelled upon it. Bearing in mind the range of mankind's arts, this is an implausible claim. It is true that Man does purposefully 'imitate' some of what nature does spontaneously. Grasses and other plants spontaneously produce their seeds, which drop to the ground, germinate, and grow into new plants. The arts of the farmer, the vintner, the orchardist, the forester, and the like are all based on imitating this natural process, though not reducible to it – quite the contrary: for while they incorporate the natural process in their arts, they employ techniques that greatly increase its productivity, and thereby its human utility. In this respect, the arts of cultivation are like philosophy, according to Hobbes:

For as there were Plants of Corn and Wine in small quantity dispersed in the Fields and Woods, before men knew their vertue, or made use of them for their nourishment, or planted them apart in Fields, and Vineyards; in which time they fed on Akorns, and drank Water: so also there have been divers true, generall, and profitable Speculations from the beginning; as being the naturall plants of humane Reason: But they were at first but few in number; men lived upon grosse Experience; there was no Method; that is to say, no Sowing, nor Planting of Knowledge by it selfe, apart from the Weeds, and common Plants of Errour and Conjecture. (XLVI/6, 368)

But as for most other elementary arts – such as that of the carpenter, the blacksmith, the potter, the wheelwright, the weaver, the mason, the cobbler – anything recognizable as *imitation* of natural processes is minimal. Hobbes, however, simplifies the issue to that of 'making': Nature makes things; and Man, imitating Nature, also makes things. But the most conspicuous things that Nature makes are *living* beings, the countless instances of the countless species of plants and animals. Whereas, everything that man makes by his various arts is *non*-living, is it not? Surely this reveals the limit of human art: Man cannot make *life* (from scratch, that is).

Of course, that depends on what is meant by 'life.' Is it the very breath of God, as recounted in Scripture? Hobbes directly confronts this ancient view, and in effect 'neutralizes' it:

Gen. 2.7. It is said, *God made man of the dust of the Earth, and breathed into his nostrills* (spiraculum vitae) *the breath of life, and man was made a living soul.* There the *breath of life* inspired by God, signifies no more, but that God gave him life; And *(Job 27.3.) as long as the spirit of God is in my nostrils*; is no more then to say, *as long as I live.* (XXXIV/10, 209)

That word therefore is used in the Scripture metaphorically onely: As (*Gen.* 2.7.) where it is said, that God *inspired* into man the breath of life, no more is meant, then that God gave unto him vitall motion. For we are not to think that God made first a living breath, and then blew it into Adam after he was made, whether that breath were reall, or seeming; but only as it is (*Acts* 17.25.) that *he gave him life, and breath*; that is, made him a living creature. (XXXIV/25, 214)

Now, the suggestion that taking these Scriptural passages *literally* would imply 'that God made first a living breath,' etc., is a red herring. The usual understanding would be that God breathed His *own* 'vitality' into man, who was thereby 'made a living soul.' But if we agree to treat 'the breath of God' and 'the breath of life' and all such expressions as merely *metaphors* that mean nothing more than life simply, which requires breathing, then what life actually *is* remains an open question.

So, *is* life merely 'a motion of Limbs, the beginning whereof is in some principall part within?' Why *wouldn't* we say that a watch – or a refrigerator, or a traffic light, or a lawn sprinkler system, or a compact disc player, or an ATM, or a washer and dryer, or a robotic auto assembly line, or any of ten thousand other fully or partially automated machines – are 'artificially' *alive*? Or, for that matter, that the sometimes placid, sometimes raging rivers, and erupting volcanoes, and the ever-changing clouds, and the trembling Earth itself – to say nothing of the Heavenly bodies – are similarly alive? After all, there have been people who have thought so, and not all of them inconsiderable. But in ascribing Life to such things (and, as Hobbes reminds us, even Divinity), they, like us, would have more in mind than matter-in-motion. By *our* definition of 'alive,' we include sentience, or even consciousness; some self-sustaining and self-restoring capacity; and – perhaps especially – a reproductive capability, hence a natural life cycle: *growth* from embryo to maturity, decline into senescence, and eventually death. That is, we *would* have an answer to Hobbes's thought-provoking question explaining '*why* we may *not*.'

However, Hobbes has prepared a response to our answer. And, ironically, it is not *essentially* different from that which now enjoys scientific status throughout much of today's Enlightened, or Post-Enlightened, world: that sensation, perception, ingestion and digestion, growth, sickness and health, all desire and passion, all thought – and, not least of all, reproduction – are 'in reality' totally explicable in terms of matter and its motions. Hobbes's physiology, as sketched in the early chapters of *Leviathan*, is exclusively mechanical, and hopelessly inadequate for explaining our common experience of sensation, perception, imagination, emotion, reasoning, etc. (as I argued in various chapters of Part One). Whereas, the orthodox physiology of today combines complex electro-chemical processes with mechanics; and there is no question but that it is a thousand times more plausible as an explanation of the physical correlates of many of our various psychic experiences. But, to repeat, it does not differ *fundamentally* – that is, in *kind* – from the account Hobbes provides.

In any case, the glaring inadequacies of Hobbes's physiology do not in themselves compromise his *political* science in the least. By some deft philosophical surgery he could replace his physiology with ours, and not have to change anything important in his political analysis and prescription. For none of that is actually *based* on his mechanical physiology *at all*, but rather upon what every profound political thinker has based his conclusions: history, personal observation, introspection, and dialogue with other thinkers, including long-since-departed predecessors. As such, the geometric appearance of Hobbes's book, as if it proceeds deductively from chapter 1 to 31, is illusory. His own beginning point is – *necessarily* – somewhere in what occupies the middle of Part One, whence he reasons 'backwards' to construct a physiology such as will suit his purpose, which is determined by the political understanding he has reached quite independently. In that sense, Hobbes's version of human physiology is *disposable*.[3] But for that matter, so is ours. Neither his nor ours does justice to Love, for example, nor to Creativity, Ambition, Courage, Hope, Joy, or Knowledge (to mention but some of the distinctly human things that work collectively to define political life). However, the widely accepted, but mistaken, impression that our version explains much more than it actually does – that physiology offers a truly *scientific* account of human nature – has profound political consequences, which is why Hobbes troubled to supply a version himself.

The Introduction to *Leviathan* provides a preview of his version in an elaborate analogy between a Man and a State. This sort of analogizing has been done before, most famously by Plato in his *Republic*. Hobbes, however, does not draw parallels between the proper order and virtues of the human soul and those of a polity, as does Plato's Sokrates, but rather between – primarily – the human *body* and various components of a commonwealth.

For what is the *Heart*, but a *Spring*; and the *Nerves*, but so many *Strings*; and the *Joynts*, but so many *Wheeles*, giving motion to the whole Body, such as was intended by the Artificer? *Art* goes yet further, imitating that Rationall and most excellent worke of Nature, *Man*. For by Art is created that great LEVIATHAN called a COMMON-WEALTH, or STATE, (in latine CIVITAS) which is but an Artificiall Man; though of greater stature and strength than the Naturall, for whose protection and defence it was intended; and in which, the *Soveraignty* is an Artificiall

Soul, as giving life and motion to the whole body; The *Magistrates*, and other *Officers* of Judicature and Execution, artificiall *Joynts*; *Reward* and *Punishment* (by which fastned to the seate of the Soveraignty, every joynt and member is moved to performe his duty) are the *Nerves*, that do the same in the Body Naturall; the *Wealth* and *Riches* of all the particular members, are the *Strength*; *Salus Populi* (the *peoples safety*) its *Businesse*; *Counsellors*, by whom all things needfull for it to know, are suggested unto it, are the *Memory*; *Equity* and *Lawes*, an artificiall *Reason* and *Will*: *Concord*, *Health*; *Sedition*, *Sicknesse*; and *Civill war*, *Death*. Lastly, the *Pacts* and *Covenants*, by which the parts of this Body Politique were at first made, set together, and united, resemble that *Fiat*, or the *Let us make man*, pronounced by God in the Creation.

Notice, Hobbes speaks first of animals in general, or at least of the higher ones having hearts, nerves, joints, and such. The self-powered, self-regulating machines that man makes are likened to animals such as these. Rhetorically, however, does not the alleged likeness necessarily suggest – 'and *vice versa*' – that the animals are to be understood simply as Nature-made machines, with all of their organs but so many mechanical components? Man, too, is an artwork attributed to Nature, at least in the immediate sense, albeit of the animals Man is the 'most excellent,' presumably because 'Rationall' (the only one, we later learn; IV/8, 13), and thus capable not merely of imitating the artfulness Man perceives in Nature, but of *surpassing* it. For while Man recognizes himself as the pinnacle of this Divine Art – and so, as his own highest achievement, models an artificial version upon himself – his 'Artificiall Man' is 'of *greater* stature and strength than the Naturall.' Moreover, it could be said to remedy the deficiencies of God's handiwork, for the life of Natural Man would otherwise be short (not to mention poor, nasty, and brutish – certainly nothing to brag about), lacking the protection and other benefits provided by the Artificial Man.

But this Artificial Man – which Hobbes names 'Leviathan,' but which all other English speakers call a 'Commonwealth' or 'State,' and Latin speakers (or at least readers) call a *Civitas* – is *not* a *mechanical* contrivance that moves by means of 'springs and wheeles as doth a watch.' It is something else entirely.[4] One can plausibly liken a wheel, hinge, or socket in some machine to the elbow of a human body; in fact, this and similar likenings have been resorted to many times. But the 'artificiall *Joynts*' of a Commonwealth are not *wheels*; they are 'The *Magistrates*, and other *Officers* of Judicature and Execution.' And the '*Nerves*' of a State are not 'but so many *Strings*'; rather, they are '*Reward* and *Punish-*

ment (by which fastned to the seate of the Soveraignty, every joynt and member is moved to performe his duty) ... that do the same in the Body Naturall.' ('the *same*'? do the 'joynts and members' of the human body have *duties*, and thus work properly only insofar as they are 'dutiful'?) An anatomist, having traced out the nerves 'strung' throughout a human body, might see some propriety in calling them 'strings.' But who other than Hobbes would imagine likening those nerves to the rewards bestowed and punishments inflicted by the Ruler of a Polity? And so with the rest of Hobbes's cunning analogy.[5] How, then, does it work – that is, accomplish his rhetorical purpose?

Obviously, it's a three-way analogy; that is, Hobbes stipulates various analogues among three ostensibly very different kinds of things: self-powered, self-regulated machines; animals, including humans; and polities. Why this complexity? If Hobbes wished simply to draw parallels between the 'Body Politique' and the Human body, why not do so directly and exclusively? Why include machines – which, even by his own strained comparison, share only a couple of analogues with that which the analogy is primarily supposed to explicate, namely, a commonwealth? Yet it is with so-called *automata* that he begins, apparently in order to establish – what exactly? – that natural life can be understood as simply mechanical activity ('a motion of limbs'), and that, consequently, man can through his artisanship make life *artificially* – the payoff being that the man-made *political* 'machine' called a commonwealth may be regarded as a living thing?[6] But why does Hobbes want his reader to think of his commonwealth as *alive*? Presumably he has something more important in mind than legitimizing his naming it after a monstrous animal. Perhaps he intends a careful consideration of the various elements of the Man-State analogy to suggest an answer.

Hobbes begins by proposing that with the establishment of 'Sovereignty' (properly conceived, that is, which turns out to be a – if not *the* – principal concern of his treatise to teach), one animates the State with 'an Artificiall *Soul*, as giving life and motion to the whole body.' There was no mention of 'soul' in connection with watches, which 'come to life' (as motion) with the winding of their main springs. Hobbes speaks next of the State's having 'Joynts' and 'Nerves'; doing so rhetorically obscures his *transition* from the initial Machine-Animal analogy – passing *through* without comment an implicit, but problematic, Animal-Man analogy – to that of the Man-State; for he continues with elements having no specified analogues for *automata*. Nor are any easily imagined; but what he says makes tolerable sense in the context of a Man-State analogy: people's

'Wealth and Riches' as the 'Strength' of a State; their 'Safety' as its 'Business' or purpose; 'Counsellors' as its 'Memory'; 'Equity' as its 'Reason,' 'Laws' as its 'Will,' etc. One analogue is conspicuously absent, however: namely, that which would correspond to the first bodily organ Hobbes mentioned: the Heart. Hobbes's Leviathan is Heartless. It is unlikely that this is an oversight.

There certainly is no shortage of times the heart is mentioned in the chapters that follow. But, interestingly, in only a few of the more than four dozen instances is Hobbes's usage literal. In speaking of 'The cause of Sense,' he contends that it results from pressure exerted by an 'Externall Body,' which 'by the mediation of Nerves, and other strings, and membranes of the body, continued inwards to the Brain, and Heart, causeth there a resistance or counter-pressure, or endeavour of the heart, to deliver itself' (I/4, 3; cf. VI/9, 25). And he explains Contempt as 'nothing else but an immobility, or contumacy of the Heart, in resisting the action of certain things [because] already moved otherwise' (VI/5, 24). And in discussing the 'Nutrition' of a commonwealth, he recurs to the 'Man's Body/Political Body' analogy with respect to taxation and expenditures: 'And in this also, the Artificiall Man maintains his resemblance with the Naturall; whose Veins receiving the Bloud from the severall Parts of the Body, carry it to the Heart; where being made Vitall, the Heart by the Arteries sends it out again, to enliven, and enable for motion all the Members of the same' (XXIV/13, 130–1; cf. XXIX/18, 173). This alleged 'resemblance,' however, is false – and, one must suppose, deliberately so – since an *artificial Heart* is precisely the one component that Hobbes neglected to provide his Artificial Man.

Moreover, it raises a puzzle. For this description of the heart does not fit at all well with Hobbes's initially likening it in his Introduction to a *spring*. Even with just so much understanding of the circulation of blood as indicated in the quote above, a *pump* would be the obvious mechanical analogue. And the fact that Hobbes was on familiar terms with William Harvey makes this all the more puzzling. According to one eminent scholar, Hobbes spent some of his free time 'in the stimulating company of the lawyers John Selden and John Vaughan, and the physicians William Harvey and Charles Scarborough,' and 'It also seems likely that he had dissected deer with William Harvey,' and 'it was probably through Harvey that Hobbes met John Aubrey.'[7] Hobbes lauds Harvey in the Dedicatory Letter of *De Corpore*: 'the science of *man's body*, the most profitable part of natural science, was first discovered with admirable sagacity by our countryman Doctor Harvey, principal Physician to King James and King Charles, in his books of the *Motion of the Blood,* and of the *Generation of Living Creatures.*' So, why did Hobbes liken the heart to the main spring of a watch – that is, to a component that is a mechanism's source of *energy* – rather than to one that merely moves matter? I shall return to this question shortly.

Apart from these few references to the heart as a bodily organ, all of Hobbes's other forty-odd mentions of the word use it in a figurative or metaphorical sense. True, several of these occurrences are in quotes from Scripture, such as: '*They made their hearts hard as Adamant*' (XXXVI/12, 228); '*Servants obey in all things your Masters according to the flesh, not with eye-service, as men-pleasers, but in singlenesse of heart, as fearing the Lord*' XLII/10, 270); and '*If thou beleevest with all thy heart*' XLIII/15, 326). But Hobbes himself uses the word in these same figurative senses. For example, in belatedly addressing who is to carry out the Sovereign's punishments, especially in Capital cases (a problem, given his earlier asserting, 'No man is bound by the words themselves, either to kill himselfe, or any other man'; XXI/15, 112), Hobbes argues that the job typically falls to those 'in whom want of means, contempt of honour, and hardnesse of heart, concurred, to make them sue for such an Office' (R&C/10, 392; if this 'hardnesse' were meant *literally*, such men – given Hobbes's mechanical theory of sensation – would be *equally* insensitive to *everything*). And in speaking of the difference between outer show and inner belief: 'Profession with the tongue is but an externall thing, and no more then any other gesture whereby we signifie our obedience; and wherein a Christian, holding firmely in his heart the Faith of Christ, hath the same liberty which the Prophet Elisha allowed to Naaman the Syrian. Naaman was converted in his heart to the God of Israel,' but was obliged by his Sovereign to bow 'before the Idol Rimmon.' Hobbes likens this case to that of a person required to participate in a Christian service though he 'be inwardly in his heart of the Mahometan Religion' (XLII/11, 271; cf. XLV/27, 362). And he assures us, 'A private man has alwaies the liberty, (because thought is free,) to beleeve, or not beleeve in his heart, those acts that have been given out for Miracles' (XXXVII/13, 238). Moreover, he is repeatedly on record that 'God onely knoweth the heart' (XXXI/32, 191; cf. XL/2, 249); hence only God, 'who knoweth the Heart of man, and truth of his Penitence and Conversion,' can forgive sins absolutely (XLII/19, 275; cf. /80, 300; /107, 310; XLIII/4, 322). In all of these passages, Hobbes speaks as if the heart were the locus of sincerity and conviction.

Lest one presume that Hobbes confines the figurative use of 'heart' to religious contexts, there are enough instances (besides his endorsing hard-hearted Executioners) to prove otherwise. Indeed, one need not range beyond this Introduction for evidence that Hobbes, like the rest of us, treats 'the heart' as symbolic of our very humanity. For in its third paragraph, he warns 'that the characters of mans heart, blotted and confounded as they are, with dissembling, lying, counterfeiting, and erroneous doctrines, are legible onely to him that searcheth hearts.' In another instance, its meaning is 'memorize,' Hobbes assuring us, 'A naturall foole ... could never learn by heart the order of numerall words' (IV/10, 14). And when he describes the excessively anxious man as one who 'hath his heart all the day long, gnawed on by feare of death, poverty, or other calamity' (XII/5, 52), neither the 'gnawing' nor the 'heart' are to be taken literally. Hobbes concedes the special importance, and difficulty, of refuting 'the Foole [who] hath sayd in his heart, there is no such thing as Justice,' since 'taking away the feare of God, (for the same Foole hath said in his heart there is no God,)' (XV/4, 72), he is apt to think that sometimes Injustice is 'rational' (meaning, 'in his own interest'). Such Fooles apart, presumably, Hobbes insists that 'the Law of Nature, that is to say, the Precepts of Naturall Reason [are] written in every mans own heart' (XLII/37, 282). And most men, exposed to the chaos of unstable government, can be counted upon to 'desire with all their hearts, to conforme themselves into one firme and lasting edifice,' but do not know how, lacking 'the help of a very able Architect' (XXIX/1, 167). And with respect to a King, his being recognized as the rightful holder of sovereign power 'is so popular a quality, as he that has it needs no more, for his own part, to turn the hearts of his Subjects to him, but that they see him able absolutely to govern his own Family' (XXX/29, 185). As for genuine Honour, it is 'properly of its own nature, secret, and internall in the heart' (XLV/12, 357).

In light of Hobbes's usage, both literal and figurative – that is, of everything he attributes to the heart – what is the significance of his 'Artificiall Man' being *heartless*? Apparently, 'It' would know neither sympathy nor mercy – indeed, know no desires, no passions, neither fear nor worry, neither joy nor hope. It would be incapable of either affection or admiration, of either loyalty or honouring. It could have neither sincerity of belief nor faith, and be without what men call a 'conscience.' It has nothing upon which is written the Laws of Nature, those 'Precepts of Naturall Reason.' Since a heartless Artificial Man has none of the attributes we ordinarily ascribe to a human soul, it is incapable of actions and reactions that presume those attributes (of showing mercy, e.g., or bestowing honours). How, then, can it function? How, for example, can it decide upon what to spend the taxes it collects? We are told that '*Soveraignty* is an Artificiall *Soul*, as giving life and motion to the whole body.' Sovereignty itself, however, is but an idea, more precisely, a complex idea comprising twelve essential Rights. What, then, makes it operative, what actually 'breathes life' into it? Pertinent here is the ridicule Hobbes pours over 'Aristotles Politiques' for (allegedly) propagating the view 'that in a wel ordered Common-wealth, not Men should govern, but the Laws. What man, that has his naturall Senses, though he can neither write nor read, does not find himself governed by them he fears, and beleeves can kill or hurt him when he obeyeth not? or that beleeves the Law can hurt him; that is, Words, and Paper, without the Hands, and Swords of men?' (XLVI/36, 377–8).

Necessarily, then, the collectivity of people composing the Artificial Man is brought to a single unified 'life' by the *Natural* man who serves as the Sovereign *Representative*: 'A Multitude of men, are made *One* Person, when they are by one man, or one Person, Represented; ... For it is the *Unity* of the Represener, not the *Unity* of the Represented, that maketh the Person *One* ... And *Unity*, cannot otherwise be understood in Multitude' (XVI/13, 82).

This done, the Multitude so united in one Person, is called a COMMON-WEALTH, in latine CIVITAS. This is the Generation of that great LEVIATHAN, or rather (to speake more reverently) of that *Mortall God*, to which wee owe under the *Immortall God*, our peace and defence. For by this Authoritie, given him by every particular man in the Common-wealth, he hath the use of so much Power and Strength conferred on him, that by the terror thereof, he is inabled to con-forme the wills of them all, to Peace at home, and mutuall ayd against their enemies abroad. And in him consisteth the Essence of the Common-wealth; which (to define it,) is *One Person, of whose Acts a great Multitude, by mutuall Covenants one with another, have made themselves every one the Author, to the end he may use the strength and means of them all, as he shall think expedient, for their Peace and Common Defence.*

And he that carryeth this Person, is called SOVERAIGNE, and said to have *Soveraigne Power*; and every one besides, his SUBJECT. (XVII/13–14, 87–8)

The artificial unity of the multitude of men who collectively compose the Artificial Man derives from the *natural* unity of a Natural Man: 'And in him consisteth the Essence of the Common-wealth.' But so too does its 'life' insofar as a Polity can be considered a *living* unity, capable of acting and reacting in a manner analogous to that of a human being – which is to say, as would a man with a heart. This is subtly confirmed by Hobbes's treating 'the Right of *Succession*' in a Monarchy – whereupon the death of a sitting King, his rightful Successor *immediately* ascends the Throne – as providing thereby the 'Artificiall Man ... an Artificiall Eternity of life' (XIX/14, 99). Thus: 'The King is dead. Long live the King!' In short, Hobbes has left his Artificial Man without an artificial Heart on the silent understanding that a Commonwealth will be animated by a stout-hearted Natural Man ruling as Sovereign. The Hobbesian State can act as if it had a heart because its *King* is its Heart.[8]

Some further confirmation that Hobbes has this in mind might be found in William Harvey's Dedication of his *Anatomical Disquisition on the Motion of the Heart and Blood in Animals*, first published in 1628, one year prior to Hobbes's translation of Thucydides. Indeed, one cannot rule out the possibility that this famous book by his famous friend was the source of Hobbes's inspiration. Addressing his dedicatee (Charles I), Harvey writes:

The heart of animals is the foundation of their life, the sovereign of everything within them, the sun of their microcosm, that upon which all growth depends, from which all power proceeds. The King, in like manner, is the foundation of his kingdom, the sun of the world around him, the heart of the republic, the fountain whence all power, all grace doth flow ... almost all things human are done after human examples, and many things in a King are after the pattern of the heart. The knowledge of the heart, therefore, will not be useless to a Prince, as embracing a kind of Divine example of his functions.... Here, at all events, best of Princes, placed as you are on the pinnacle of human affairs, you may at once contemplate the prime mover in the body of man, and the emblem of your own sovereign power. Accept therefore ... this, my new Treatise on the Heart; you, who are yourself the new light of this age, and indeed its very heart.[9]

But granted it fitting to name the resulting Commonwealth or State after some animal, why with a world to choose from, select 'Leviathan' – a name surely no one else would ever have thought to use?[10] In the Biblical context whence Hobbes chose it, the name refers to a notoriously dangerous beast – the Crocodile – epitome of what men call a 'heartless monster.' Although Hobbes's treatise bears it as its title, the name appears only four times in the book: once in its Introduction, once again in the passage quoted shortly before, and twice in Hobbes's own belated explanation for choosing the name:

Hitherto I have set forth the nature of Man, (whose Pride and other Passions have compelled him to submit himselfe to Government;) together with the great power of his Governour, whom I compared to *Leviathan*, taking that comparison out of the two last verses of the one and fortieth of *Job*; where God having set forth the great power of *Leviathan*, calling him King of the Proud. *There is nothing*, saith he, *on earth, to be compared with him. He is made so as not to be afraid. He seeth every high thing below him; and is King of all the children of Pride.* (XXVIII/27, 166–7)[11]

Throughout his book Hobbes does indeed treat Pride as the special Nemesis of political life: 'Pride, subjecteth a man to Anger, the excesse whereof, is the Madnesse called RAGE, and FURY' (VIII/19, 35). His Ninth Natural Law 'outlaws' Pride, requiring instead *'That every man acknowledge other for his Equall by Nature.* The breach of this Precept is *Pride'* (XV/21, 77). Proud men can be hard to govern insofar as they may value their honour higher than life itself. Thus, as I discussed earlier in chapter 13, a Sovereign's success in ruling depends more on his management of the Honour economy than the Money economy.

But Hobbes no doubt has in mind other features of the Biblical Leviathan as being appropriate descriptors for a commonwealth properly understood (having conveniently provided his reader with the chapter in Job where the whole portrait of Leviathan is to be found). These features are embedded in the form of rhetorical questions that God puts to long-suffering Job, features which emphasize Leviathan's fearsomeness and practical invulnerability to assaults from puny individuals; but they do more than that:

3 Will he make many supplications unto thee? will he speak soft words unto thee?
4 Will he make a covenant with thee? wilt thou take him for a servant for ever?
5 Wilt thou play with him as *with* a bird? or wilt thou bind him for thy maidens?
6 Shall the companions make a banquet of him? shall they part him among the merchants? (Job 41)

We are not to presume the Commonwealth is obliged to speak softly and politely to each of us, much less as requiring our permission for anything. No one is to regard this dangerous, powerful creature – who 'laugheth at the shaking of a spear' (41:29) – as leashed or otherwise restrained, or as existing for anyone's amusement. It is our master, not our servant, and is party to no contract with us (the founding and sustaining covenant – covenants, rather – are each singular, and made by 'every man with every man'; XVII/13, 87).[12] And in particular, the Commonwealth is not the tool of merely commercial interests, of 'traders' and 'merchants.'

However, to appreciate what is most significant in Hobbes's choosing to affix the name 'Leviathan' to his political prescription, one must bear in mind the larger context in which God's conversation with Job takes place. Hobbes himself elsewhere calls attention to this in the course of addressing the age-old question, '*Why Evill men often Prosper, and Good men suffer Adversity*' – Job being a case in point.

And *Job*, how earnestly does he expostulate with God, for the many Afflictions he suffered, notwithstanding his Righteousnesse? This question in the case of *Job*, is decided by God himselfe, not by arguments derived from *Job's* Sinne, but his own Power. For whereas the friends of *Job* drew their arguments from his Afflic-tion to his Sinne, and he defended himselfe by the conscience of his Innocence, God himselfe taketh up the matter, and having justified the Affliction by argu-ments drawn from his Power, such as this, *Where wast thou when I layd the foun-dations of the earth*, and the like, both approved *Job's* Innocence, and reproved the Erroneous doctrine of his friends. (XXXI/6, 188)

The fearsome description of the monstrous crocodile Leviathan, along with the equally forbidding portrait of the full-grown hippopotamus (Behemoth) – two of God's 'like arguments drawn from his Power' – are prefaced with this challenge to Job:

10 Deck thyself now *with* majesty and excellancy; and array thyself with glory and beauty.
11 Cast abroad the rage of thy wrath: and behold every one *that is* proud, and abase him.
12 Look on every one *that is* proud, *and* bring him low; and tread down the wicked in their place.
13 Hide them in the dust together; *and* bind their faces in secret.
14 Then will I also confess unto thee that thy own right hand can save thee. (Job 40)

God says to Job, in effect, 'If *you* could make a creature as awesome as Leviathan – one that could 'Look on every one that is proud, and bring him low; and tread down the wicked where they stand,' one that will be 'King over all the children of Pride' – *then* might you declare your inde-pendence from Me.'

And so, what has Hobbes done? Provided a blueprint for our making our own Artificial Leviathan.[13]

19

The Original State of Nature: Hobbes's Palaeoanthropology

'And which is worst of all, continuall feare, and danger of violent death; And the life of man, solitary, poore, nasty, brutish, and short.' These are surely the most famous words Hobbes ever penned – and among the most famous in the entire history of political philosophy. Hobbes is as renowned for this summation of mankind's condition in the State of Nature as is Sokrates for pronouncing the Unexamined Life as not worth living. Hobbes's oft-repeated phrase – the more memorable for its staccato, blank verse cadence – concludes a paragraph that *begins*, 'Whatsoever therefore is consequent to a time of Warre, where every man is Enemy to every man; the same is consequent to the time, wherein men live without other security, than what their own strength, and their own invention shall furnish them withall.' Any reader might be expected to agree that this would be a condition of great privation and danger. But hardly any reader notices that this description – which is actually a hypothetical conditional proposition – *does not fit* Hobbes's account of pre-civil man. In no statement about how humans lived before entering anything that might reasonably be called 'civil society' does Hobbes ever indicate that they lived in a solitary manner, each dependent solely on his or her own strength and invention, and enemy to *every* other person, or even every other *man*.[1] Life in the Original State of Nature would typically have been poor, perhaps even nasty and brutish by civil standards, but it was *not* solitary, nor necessarily always short.[2] If there is a condition to which the famous phrase fully applies, it is *not* that out of which human life first evolved – or in which human language ('the most noble and profitable invention of all'; IV/1, 12) could conceivably have originated.

Hobbes never discusses in a systematic, detailed way what human life would be like *prior* to the formation of sizeable, more or less stable societies; nor how historically the transition to such societies would likely come about; nor how people's consequent exposure to the manner of civil life therein might *alter* their thinking and behaviour. Even the most superficial comparison with Rousseau's *Discourse on Inequality* – wherein he expressly challenges Hobbes's conclusions[3] – reveals the scantiness of the latter's treatment of these issues. Hobbes does, however, provide enough observations en passant his treatment of other matters to give a reader some indication as to how he conceives pre-civil life, and of how man moved beyond it. What is particularly notable is the significance of *families*.

Curiously, perhaps, one of the most comprehensive indications of Hobbes's view is provided in the context of his discussing the origins of various signs of honour and conventional nobility that are found in many civil societies:

For *Germany*, being antiently, as all other Countries, in their beginnings, divided amongst an infinite number of little Lords, or Masters of Families, that continually had wars one with another … [had to devise means to identify] the Old Master, that is to say in Dutch, the *Here-alt* … But when many such Families, joyned together, made a greater Monarchy, this duty of the Herealt, to distinguish Scutchions, was made a private Office a part. And the issue of these Lords, is the great and antient Gentry; which for the most part bear living creatures, noted for courage, and rapine; or Castles, Battlements, Belts, Weapons, Bars, Palisadoes, and other notes of War; nothing being then in honour, but vertue military. Afterwards, not onely Kings, but popular Common-wealths, gave divers manners of Scutchions, to such as went forth to the War, or returned from it, for encouragement, or recompense to their service. All which, by an observing Reader, may be found in such antient Histories, Greek and Latine, as make mention of the German Nation, and Manners, in their times. (X/51, 45–6)

One might wonder what more 'an *observing* Reader' – as opposed to the other kind – is intended to find in Hobbes's book. Be that as it may, pre-civil Germany, 'as *all* other Countries,' was originally peopled by warring *families*; the 'universal war' was not quite the 'every man, against every man' that it *would* have been if families did not stick together. Hobbes concedes as much himself:

It may peradventure be thought, there was never such a time, nor condition of warre as this; and I believe it was never generally so, over all the world: but there are many places, where they live so now. For the savage people in many places of *America*, except the government of small Families, the concord whereof dependeth on naturall lust, have no government at all; and live at this day in that brutish manner, as I said before. (XIII/11, 63)

Still, they do not live simply as gregarious beasts, with their behaviour strictly determined by pleasure and pain. As Hobbes later acknowledges, they not only have language, but morality as well: 'The Savages of America, are not without some good Morall Sentences; also they have a little Arithmetick, to adde, and divide in Numbers not too great' (XLVI/6, 367).[4] And notice, families have a *natural* basis, with the result that people *are* governed to some extent. But whether 'naturall lust' as Hobbes has defined it ('*Love* of Persons for Pleasing the sense onely'; VI/31, 26) is an adequate explanation for *stable* family groupings is doubtful – a question I shall return to shortly.

First, however, it is important to recognize that Hobbes, still addressing a sceptical reader, shifts to a very different situation as he continues the above-quoted passage:

Howsoever, it may be perceived what manner of life there would be, where there were no common Power to feare [which, typically, there *is* in families]; by the manner of life, which men that have formerly lived under a peacefull government, use to degenerate into, in a civill Warre. (XIII/11, 63)

Surely *this* situation differs profoundly from that out of which mankind first emerged. Men who have experienced the benefits of living in a peaceful polity – freely enjoying the fruits of their own Industry, the advantages of Commercial exchange, the comfort and utility of commodious Buildings, various kinds of Knowledge, a rational understanding of Time, some awareness of the Earth's great expanse, both fine and practical Arts, humane Letters, and best of all, feeling safe from predation – such men could readily imagine all sorts of possibilities and incentives that would be inconceivable for people whose lives had always been confined to 'the condition of meer Nature.' Possibilities for both good and evil, it should be emphasized, such that the conditions of people trapped in a civil war could degenerate to a state far *worse* than that typical of the *original* State of Nature (as I shall endeavour to explain in the following chapter).

In any event, 'naturall lust' is not the whole of Hobbes's account of why, in the original State of Nature, the natural human environment was that of a Patriarchal family. For, first of all, there is normally the father's special regard for children he recognizes as his own, as well as a natural affection among family members in general. Hobbes invokes this in arguing for what should be the implicit Right of Succession in Monarchies 'where neither Custome, nor Testament' clearly indicate a particular Successor:

Secondly, that a Child of his own, Male, or Female, be preferred before any other; because men are presumed to be more enclined by nature, to advance their own children, than the children of other men; and of their own, rather a Male than a Female; because men, are naturally fitter than women, for actions of labour and danger. Thirdly, where his own Issue faileth, rather a Brother than a stranger; and so still the neerer in bloud, rather than the more remote; because it is alwayes presumed that the neerer of kin, is the neerer in affection; and 'tis evident that a man receives alwayes, by reflexion, the most honour from the greatnesse of his neerest kindred. (XIX/22, 101)

But important as lust and affection might be in maintaining the cohesiveness of family groupings in the original State of Nature, it would be augmented by two powerful supplements. One, 'Naturall force; as when a man maketh his children, to submit themselves, and their children to his government, as being able to destroy them if they refuse' (XVII/15, 88) – though we are to understand that the Father's exercise of Dominion rests ultimately on 'the Childs Consent, either expresse, or by other sufficient arguments declared' (XX/4, 102). That such consent is extorted by fear of the Father is irrelevant, just as 'Covenants entred into by fear, in the condition of meer Nature, are obligatory' (XIV/27, 69). The other support of familial cohesion would be everyone's chronic fear of isolation in perpetually dangerous circumstances: 'in a condition of Warre ... there is no man can hope by his own strength, or wit, to defend himselfe from destruction, without the help of Confederates'; for 'if he be left, or cast out of society, he perisheth' (XV/5, 73).

In all of Hobbes's references to pre-civil man, we find he normally lived in family-centred groups; solitary individuals would have been as uncommon, and as disadvantaged, as a lone wolf. Thus, anyone left family-less would be eager to attach himself to any family that would have him, whatever their terms: 'every man having equall right to submit himselfe to such as he thinks best able to protect him' (XIX/18, 100). Hobbes as much as admits 'there had never been any time, wherein *particular* [i.e., individual] men were in a condition of warre one against another' (XIII/12, 63; my emphasis; cf. IV/6, 13). To be sure, mankind's larger setting was one of chronic conflict, even a *kind* of universal war: 'in

Nations not thoroughly civilized, severall numerous Families have lived in continuall hostility, and invaded one another with private force' (XXII/31, 122). Necessarily, then, everyone would distinguish between 'us' and 'them,' between 'one's own' and 'the others,' 'insiders' and 'outsiders,' 'friends' and 'enemies.' And, consequently, there would have been a premium on whatever contributed to martial success: courage, of course, the most visible of the virtues; but also wiles and skills, and whatever else naturally marks a man as a natural leader, especially 'prudence in counsel,' hence rhetoric.

Reflecting upon such evidence as Hobbes provides, one may detect the proto-political germ of what may naturally grow into political associations to which familial commitments are subordinated.

And in all places, where men have lived by small Families, to robbe and spoyle one another has been a Trade, and so farre from being reputed against the Lawes of Nature, that the greater spoyles they gained, the greater was their honour; and men observed no other Lawes therein, but the Lawes of Honour; that is, to abstain from cruelty, leaving to men their lives, and instruments of husbandry. And as small Familyes did then; so now do Cities and Kingdomes which are but greater Families (for their own security) enlarge their Dominions, upon all pretences of danger, and fear of Invasion.' (XVII/2, 85)

[A] great Family if it be not part of some Common-wealth, is of it self, as to the Rights of Soveraignty, a little Monarchy; whether that Family consist of a man and his children; or of a man and his servants; or of a man, and his children, and servants together: wherein the Father or Master is the Soveraign. But yet a Family is not properly a Common-wealth; unless it be of that power by its own number, or by other opportunities, as not to be subdued without the hazard of war. (XX/15, 105)

One can only wonder what 'other opportunities' Hobbes might have in mind. And his conspicuous omission of 'Wife' and 'Mother' from all three of his conceptions of 'Family' is the more puzzling – I would say, provocative – given his earlier refutation of a standard justification for Patriarchy:

The right of Dominion by Generation, is that, which the Parent hath over his Children; and is called PATERNALL. And is not so derived from the Generation, as if therefore the Parent had Dominion over his Child because he begat him ... For as to the Generation, God hath ordained to man a helper; and there be always two that are equally Parents: the Dominion therefore over the Child, should belong equally to both; and he be equally subject to both, which is impossible; for no man can obey two Masters. (XX/4, 102)

Why then does it invariably devolve upon the Father? Because, as some have argued, the male is 'the more excellent Sex'? This, too, is a mistake, Hobbes responds: 'For there is not always that difference of strength, or prudence between the man and the woman, as that the right can be determined without War.' Recall, everyone in the State of Nature is both endangered and dangerous, even if not equally so, for 'the weakest has strength enough to kill the strongest, either by secret machinations' – after all, everyone has to sleep – 'or by confederacy with others' (XIII/1, 60).

Moreover, Hobbes argues, 'in the state of meer Nature,' the Mother has priority: 'If there be no Contract, the Dominion is in the Mother.' Why so? Because 'in the condition of meer Nature, where there are no Matrimonial lawes, it cannot be known who is the Father, unlesse it be declared by the Mother' (XX/5, 103). How, then, does it come about that the Original State of Nature is peopled, not by solitary individuals, but mainly by Patriarchal families? And a *Contract* in the State of Nature? Yes: 'In this condition of meer Nature, either the Parents between themselves dispose of the dominion over the Child by Contract; or do not dispose thereof at all' (XX/4, 103). For there *can* be valid contracts in this situation, a 'contract' being nothing but 'The mutuall transferring of Right' (and a 'covenant' a contract in which one or both parties take on trust the other's future performance: XIV/9 and 11, 66). Moreover, 'Signes of Contract, are either *Expresse*, or by *Inference*'; and signs of the latter may be either 'consequences of Words' or 'of Silence,' of Actions or Inactions – anything whatsoever which 'sufficiently argues the will of the Contractor' (XIV/13–14, 66–7). However, 'If a Covenant be made, wherein neither of the parties performe presently, but trust one another; in the condition of meer Nature … upon any reasonable suspition, it is Voyd' (XIV/18, 68). As should be obvious, this entire analysis is intended simply to lay bare an inner logic of people's living in such a situation; but it does so in terms that would make sense only to someone located in civil society, thus familiar with such ideas as 'dominion,' 'contract,' 'marriage laws.' It is *not*, that is, descriptive of how anyone 'in the condition of meer Nature' could, much less would, actually think, and thereupon act.

But if one continues in that vein, and so analyses what would be the specifics of an implicit contract between the man and the woman regarding children – given both 'the naturall inclination of the Sexes one to another, and to their children,' and the even more precarious situation of a woman alone than that of a man, to say nothing of her children – one can readily work out the further logic of family formation in these raw and dangerous circumstances (i.e., what the man tacitly 'covenants' to provide, and how the woman 'covenants' to behave so as to assure the man that any children she bears are his). Mothers implicitly ceding to the Father complete Dominion over both her and their children, this arrangement is typically carried over into Civil Law,[5] 'because for the most part Common-wealths have been erected by the Fathers, not by the Mothers of families.' The only exception Hobbes cites is mytho-historical: the Amazons (XX/4, 102–3).

Hobbes is at pains to emphasize the insecurity of *property* in the Original State of Nature: 'amongst men, till there were constituted great Common-wealths, it was thought no dishonour to be a Pyrate, or a Highway Theefe; but rather a lawfull Trade, not onely amongst the Greeks, but also amongst all other Nations' (X/49, 45). How so 'a *lawfull* Trade'? By the fundamental Law of Nature, which in the exposed condition of perpetual conflict permits everything, for 'there is nothing that [a man] can make use of, that may not be a help unto him, in preserving his life against his enemyes'; hence, 'every man has a Right to every thing; even to one anothers body' (XIV/4, 64; cf. XV/3, 72). Hobbes anticipates Locke in investing 'property' with an expanded meaning: 'Of things held in propriety, those that are dearest to a man are his own life, & limbs;[6] and in the next degree, (in most men,) those that concern conjugall affection; and after them riches and means of living' (XXX/12, 179). Expanding upon the 'principall causes of quarrel' that are grounded in human nature – Competition, Diffidence, Glory – resulting in the State of Nature being a condition of perpetual war (meaning, not constant fighting, 'but in the known disposition thereto'), Hobbes affirms both the human norm of familial existence and its proprietary character: 'The first, maketh men invade for Gain; the second, for Safety; and the third, for Reputation. The first use Violence, to make themselves Masters of other mens persons, wives, children and cattell; the second, to defend them; the third, for trifles, as a word, a smile, a different opinion, and any other signe of undervalue, either direct in their Persons, or by reflexion in their Kindred, [etc]' (XIII/7, 62).

How, then, are we to understand the first *arising* of Civil Society, presuming as it does the existence of a single dominant Power, able to enforce its Will irrespective of other wills? That is, how did 'Sovereignty' emerge out of Man's original primitive, savage, 'molecular' (versus 'atomic') circumstances? Hobbes tells us there are two quite different ways Commonwealths can become established:

> The attaining of this Soveraigne Power, is by two wayes. One, by Naturall force; as when a man maketh his children, to submit themselves, and their children to his government, as being able to destroy them if they refuse; or by Warre subdueth his enemies to his will, giving them their lives on that condition. The other, is when men agree amongst themselves, to submit to some Man, or Assembly of men, voluntarily, on confidence to be protected by him against all others. This later, may be called a Politicall Common-wealth, or Common-wealth by *Institution*; and the former, a Common-wealth by *Acquisition*. (XVII/15, 88)

The 'Institutional' alternative is irrelevant to the first emergence of Civil Society, as it would presume widespread knowledge that could be gained only through extensive experience within Civil Society. Rousseau – doubtless with Hobbes and Locke in mind – nicely captures the paradox in the discussion of Natural Law that prefaces his *Discourse on Inequality*:

> The Moderns, since they allow the name of Law only for a rule prescribed to a moral being, that is to say to a being that is intelligent, free, and considered in its relations with other beings, restrict the province of natural Law to the only animal endowed with reason, that is to say to man; but while each of them defines this Law in his own fashion, all of them base it on such metaphysical principles that even among us there are very few people capable of understanding these principles, let alone of discovering them on their own. So that all of the definitions of these learned men ... agree only in this, that it is impossible to understand the Law of Nature and hence to obey it without being a very great reasoner and profound Metaphysician. Which precisely means that in order to establish society men must have employed an enlightenment which develops only with much difficulty and among very few people within society itself.
>
> ...
>
> Indeed, all [the definitions of natural Law] that are found in Books, besides not being uniform, suffer from the further defect of being derived from a range of Knowledge which men do not naturally have, and from advantages the idea of which they can conceive of only once they have left the state of Nature. One begins by looking for the rules about which it would be appropriate for men to agree among themselves for the sake of the common utility; and then gives the name natural Law to the collection of these rules, with no further proof than the good which, in one's view, would result from universal compliance with them.[7]

Allowing for a certain flippancy, this fairly describes what Hobbes has done. However, Rousseau's critique poses no objection to the validity of those laws unless one insists – that is, has rational grounds for insisting – that natural laws, to be valid, must preside over the original foundings of civil societies. And this, most definitely, is *not* Hobbes's view.

Thus, in order to understand Man's extricating himself from the original State of Nature, one is left with Hobbes's first alternative: 'Naturall force' in some combination of its two manifestations – the growth of patriarchal families, and alliances of families (through intermarriage) who live together in villages, eventually becoming tribes; and tribal wars of conquest, ultimately resulting in the formation of nations that could seize and hold distinct geographic regions. Needless to add, the 'commonwealths' that were established on *this* basis did *not* conform to Hobbes's 'collection' of Natural Laws. That they were *defective* for just this reason is his very point: 'So, *long time after* men have begun to constitute Common-wealths, imperfect, and apt to relapse into disorder, there may Principles of Reason be found out, by industrious meditation, to make their constitution (excepting by externall violence) everlasting. And such are those which I have in this discourse set forth' (XXX/5, 176; emphasis added). But this is to get ahead of the story, for any such 'making' would necessarily have to be a *re*-making out of some commonwealth that came into existence the old-fashioned way: by conquest.

One can piece this together from observations Hobbes has scattered throughout his text. His discussion of '*Naturall Power,*' for example – those eminent 'Faculties of Body, or Mind' – tacitly indicates how Leaders and Chiefs of extended families and tribes would *naturally arise*. For apart from the personal value inherent in 'Strength, Forme, Prudence, Arts,' and such, these natural powers are the means of acquiring '*Instrumentall* Powers' as well, especially the collective powers of other men obedient to their leader's will: 'For the nature of Power, is in this point, like to Fame, increasing as it proceeds' (X/2, 41).

Reputation of power, is Power; because it draweth with it the adhaerence of those that need protection.

...

Also, what quality soever maketh a man beloved, or feared of many; or the reputation of such quality, is Power; because it is a means to have the assistance, and service of many.

Good success is Power; because it maketh reputation of Wisdome, or good fortune; which makes men either feare him, or rely on him.

Affability of men already in power, is encrease of Power; because it gaineth love.

Reputation of Prudence in the conduct of Peace or War, is Power; because to prudent men, we commit the government of our selves, more willingly than to others.

...

Eloquence is power; because it is seeming Prudence.

Forme is Power; because being a promise of Good, it recommendeth men to the favour of women and strangers. (X/5–13, 41–2)

And whereas all men *desire* to augment their own power – 'So that in the first place, I put for a generall inclination of all mankind, a perpetuall and restlesse desire of Power after power, that ceaseth onely in Death' (XI/2, 47) – the *strength* of this desire, as well as the means to satisfy it, distinguish a select subset of men. And their ambitions generate a defensive reaction, and perhaps even arouse in turn an offensive ambition, in others:

Also because there be some, that taking pleasure in contemplating their own power in acts of conquest, which they pursue farther than their security requires; if others, that otherwise would be glad to be at ease within modest bounds, should not by invasion increase their power, they would not be able, long time, by standing only on their defence, to subsist. And by consequence, such augmentation of dominion over men, being necessary to a mans conservation, it ought to be allowed him. (XIII/4, 61)

Perhaps with the Alexanders and Caesars in mind, Hobbes expresses this thought even more strongly in his later Latin version of *Leviathan*: 'there are those who, from spirit and glory [*qui animi et gloria*], would conquer the whole world.'

The crux of Hobbes's historical account, however, is chapter 20, '*Of Dominion* PATERNALL, *and* DESPOTICALL.' In the preceding three chapters, he dealt with 'Commonwealths by *Institution*,' presenting a logico-hypothetical way of establishing polities, including a descriptive evaluation of the basic kinds. This mode of establishment is without actual precedent in history. It would be, as I noted before, literally inconceivable in the *original* State of Nature. However, given men with sufficient experience in a post-civil political environment, one might deem the outcome of this revolution, or that war, or some successful confederation, to be a partial approximation of it. In any event, the *primary* aim of these chapters is to facilitate understanding the inner rationale of the requirements for *maintaining* stable, decent, prosperous political life – regardless of how it might *originate*. For, as Hobbes baldly states in the 'Conclusion' of his treatise: 'there is scarce a Common-wealth in the world, whose beginnings can in conscience be justified' (R&C/8, 392). But, practically speaking, that is irrelevant. What must be clearly understood is that the true foundation of an *enduring* commonwealth is a people's recognition of the inalienable and indivisible Rights of the Sovereign.[8] This rationale having been provided, Hobbes then applies it to polities as they have historically been established: 'by Naturall force.'[9]

A *Common-wealth by Acquisition*, is that, where the Soveraign Power is acquired by Force; And it is acquired by force, when men singly, or many together by plurality of voyces, for fear of death, or bonds, do authorise all the actions of that Man, or Assembly, that hath their lives and liberty in his Power.

And this kind of Dominion, or Soveraignty, differeth from Soveraignty by Institution, onely in this, That men who choose their Soveraign, do it for fear of one another, and not of him whom they Institute: But in this case, they subject themselves, to him they are afraid of. In both cases they do it for fear: which is to be noted by them, that hold all such Covenants, as proceed from fear of death, or violence, voyd: which if it were true, no man, in any kind of Common-wealth, could be obliged to Obedience. (XX/1–2, 101–2)

The fact that Sovereignty is of the same whole cloth regardless of how its dominion is originally established does not preclude, however, a Sovereign's ruling disparate parts of his realm differently (cf. XIX/13, 99).

The one difference between the two modes of establishment does have a further implication, however, at least at the theoretical level. On the 'Institutional' model, all the covenants are *among* those who subject themselves to the Sovereign Representative whom they establish; the Sovereign himself, as such, is not party to any covenant, hence can never be charged with 'breach of contract.' Hobbes is quite explicit on this point: 'Because the Right of bearing the Person of them all, is given to him they make Soveraigne, by Covenant onely of one to another, and not of him to any of them; there can happen no breach of Covenant on the part of the Soveraigne; and consequently none of his Subjects, by any pretense of forfeiture, can be freed from his Subjection' (XVIII/4, 89). But more than once Hobbes is equally explicit that in the case of Sovereignty established by Conquest, the Sovereign himself *is* in an individual contractual relationship with each and every person who submits to him:

Dominion acquired by Conquest, or Victory in war, is that which some Writers call DESPOTICALL, from Δεσπότης, which signifieth a *Lord*, or *Master*; and is the Dominion of the Master over his Servant. And this Dominion is then acquired to the Victor, when the Vanquished, to avoyd the present stroke of death, covenanteth either in expresse words, or by other sufficient signes of the Will, that so long as his life, and the liberty of his body is allowed him, the Victor shall have the use thereof, at his pleasure. And after such Covenant made, the Vanquished is a SERVANT, and not before [whereas those kept in bonds or prisons are Slaves, and have no obligation at all to their captors].

It is not therefore the Victory, that giveth the right of Dominion over the Vanquished, but his own Covenant. Nor is he obliged because he is Conquered; that is to say, beaten, and taken, or put to flight; but because he commeth in, and Submitteth to the Victor; Nor is the Victor obliged by an enemies rendring himselfe, (without promise of life,) to spare him for this his yeelding to discretion; which obliges not the Victor longer, than in his own discretion hee shall think fit. (XX/10–11, 103–4)

Later, Hobbes himself several times calls attention to the difference in the contractual relationships, depending upon the mode whereby a Commonwealth is established (or expanded): 'Soveraignty by Institution, is by Covenant of every one to every one; and Soveraignty by Acquisition, by Covenants of the Vanquished to the Victor, or Child to Parent' (XXI/11, 111); and 'every subject in a Common-wealth, hath covenanted to obey the Civill Law, (either one with another, as when they assemble to make a common Representative, or with the Representative it selfe one by one, when subdued by the Sword they promise obedience, that they may receive life;)' (XXVI/8, 138; cf., also, XLII/123, 314).

Thus, in the case of Sovereignty by Acquisition, it would seem that 'breach of contract' on the part of the Sovereign *is* theoretically possible, thereby providing the erstwhile Servant with legitimate grounds for absconding or rebelling, or even killing the defaulting Master. Obviously, as a practical matter, the Servant/Subject would have no *legal* recourse. But that a vanquished Nation, despite all those individual pledges of obedience, might attempt through violence to throw off the yoke of a foreign conqueror, *is* a practical possibility. Might Hobbes's own doctrine be invoked to legitimize it?

There are two pertinent responses to this question. The first is a 'theoretical' response in that it addresses what would seem a flaw in Hobbes's theory. In laying out the logic of 'Sovereignty by Institution,' he insists (as I noted) that the Sovereign himself is not properly thought of as a party to any covenant with his Subjects, either individually or collectively. The latter is impossible because the multitude of Subjects is not a unity except in the Person of the Sovereign, hence cannot themselves undertake *anything* 'collectively.' As for the former, even if (for the sake of argument) the Sovereign was presumed to 'make so many severall Covenants as there be men, those Covenants after he hath the Soveraignty are voyd, because what act soever can be pretended by any one of them for breach thereof, is the act both of himselfe, and of all the rest, because done in the Person, and by the Right of every one of them in particular' (XVIII/4, 89). While this argument is moot with respect to 'Sovereignty by Institution' – since (correctly understood) the resulting Sovereign is not party to any covenants with his Subjects – it bears directly on 'Sovereignty by Conquest.' And its effect is to dissipate the theoretical difference in the two modes of establishment.

The practical response, however, is more important. One should begin by noting that in the case of Sovereignty being established by Conquest, the problem raised by the *personal* covenants between Victor and Vanquished only lasts for the one generation of people involved. Thereafter, everyone is born into the same situation, namely, an established Commonwealth offering conditions of life preferable to the only alternative: life outside of it, which is ruled by the Law of the Jungle, and wherein one will be regarded by everyone else as an enemy, not least by the members of the Commonwealth one has (foolishly) rejected.[10] Hobbes several times insists that *any* Commonwealth offering the protection of one's life (and sufficient liberty to secure the means of preserving it; e.g., XIV/8, 66; XV/22, 77) deserves one's allegiance and support, being rationally preferable – in most case, infinitely so – to the Hell on Earth that is the State of Nature outside of Civil Society. In short, anyone born into a functioning Commonwealth should thank his lucky stars, regard himself as morally obliged to his fellows to do whatever is necessary to sustain their common good fortune, and otherwise just get on with his life.

For this is the primary purpose of working through the logic of 'Commonwealth by Institution' (or, 'Sovereignty by Institution' – the ideas are practically equivalent): to reconcile people to what is necessary for securing the one thing most needful for their own good, namely, a safe, orderly environment.[11]

But a man may here object, that the Condition of Subjects is very miserable; as being obnoxious to the lusts, and other irregular passions of him, or them that have so unlimited a Power in their hands ... not considering that the estate of Man can never be without some incommodity or other; and that the greatest, in any forme of Government can possibly happen to people in generall, is scarce sensible, in respect of the miseries, and horrible calamities, that accompany a Civill Warre; or that dissolute condition of masterlesse men, without subjection to Lawes, and a coërcive Power to tye their hands from rapine, and revenge ... For all men are by nature provided of notable multiplying glasses, (that is their Passions and Selfe-love,) through which, every little payment appeareth a great grievance; but are destitute of those prospective glasses, (namely Morall and Civill Science,) to see a farre off the miseries that hang over them, and cannot without such payments be avoided. (XVIII/20, 94)

And though of so unlimited a Power, men may fancy many evill consequences, yet the consequences of the want of it, which is perpetuall warre of every man against his neighbour, are much worse. The condition of man in this life shall never be without Inconveniences; but there happeneth in no Common-wealth any great Inconvenience, but what proceeds from the Subjects disobedience, and breach of those Covenants, from which the Common-wealth hath its being. (XX/18, 107)

However dubious this final claim might be, Hobbes defends the rational preferability of Subjects supporting Absolute Sovereignty even in what we would call the 'Worst-Case Scenario.' And though Hobbes does acknowledge the possibility of 'evill and cruell Governours' (XXXVIII/14, 244), 'worst cases' are rare, since even just moderately sensible Sovereigns can appreciate that 'the dammaging, or weakening of their Subjects' undermines 'their own strength and glory.' Moreover, if the principles of Hobbes's political science were widely circulated, such worst cases would become still rarer. Hence, the balance of Part Two (chapters 21 through 30) is primarily addressed, if only tacitly, to Sovereigns and their officials, providing advice which, if followed, would tend towards the 'Best-Case Scenario.'

It is not simply advice, however. For it also provides criteria of 'Good Government' to anyone who can read. Astute Sovereigns will understand that following Hobbes's advice is in their own interest, appreciating the implications of what he has repeatedly emphasized: the limited rationality of most people. It may be irrational for Subjects to risk the murderous chaos of civil war by rebelling, but that in itself offers little security to an indolent, careless, extravagant, or oppressive Sovereign. Hobbes expressly warns that breach of Natural Laws will be met with 'Naturall Punishments,' such as 'Cowardice with Oppression' and 'Negligent government of Princes, with Rebellion' (XXXI/40, 193). Chapter 30, '*Of the* OFFICE *of the Soveraign Representative*,' begins with a clear statement of the Sovereign's comprehensive responsibility: 'namely the procuration of *the safety of the people* ... But by Safety here, is not meant a bare Preservation, but also all other Contentments of life, which every man by lawfull Industry, without danger, or hurt to the Common-wealth, shall acquire to himselfe' (XXX/1, 175). Hobbes thus indicates clearly enough that 'Rule in the Common Good' entails more than mere protection of mere life.

Reflecting on Hobbes's account of the original State of Nature, and of how mankind moved beyond it, one cannot help but be struck by its surprising similarity to the sketch of political evolution one finds in Aristotle's *Politics* – and which in itself, Aristotle contends, implies that man is *political by nature*. The equally profound agreement of Hobbes's account with that to be gleaned from Plato's *Republic* is much less obvious, mainly because Plato's actual view is much less obvious. Showing this will be reserved for a later chapter.

Aristotle begins his account with an explicit endorsement of the genetic method for understanding political things: 'If one were to see how things develop naturally from the beginning (*ex archës*), one would in this matter (*pragmata*), as in others, get the finest view of them' (1252a24–6).[12] Thus he begins with the nuclear family: female and male partnering 'for the sake of generation (and this not from deliberate choice, but as do also the other animals, having a natural desire to leave behind that which is like themselves).' Along with the resulting children and any servants or slaves, households are thereby formed to meet everyday needs. 'But from the first joining together of several households in a community for [meeting] other than daily needs, comes a village' (1252b16–17). This is typically an extended family, being the households of the 'children and children of children' and of those they have married with.

Like Hobbes, Aristotle traces Monarchy to this patriarchal arrangement: 'And this is why the cities [*poleis*] at first were ruled by kings, and some nations [*ethnë*] are so even now, because those who came together were living under kings; for in every household, the eldest man is king.' Aristotle adds that this is also why everyone says the gods are ruled royally. For a variety of reasons, however – not the least being self-defence – a village is not self-sufficient. Whereas the community made up of several villages joining together to make a city (*polis*) *is* self-sufficient;

indeed, this is the defining criterion of a *polis*: the self-sufficient community. And while Aristotle agrees that the polity 'comes into being [*ginomenë*] for the sake of staying alive,' he argues that 'it *exists* [*ousa*; i.e., 'continues to *be*'] for the sake of living well' (1252b28–31; of course, Hobbes also allows that not only 'Fear of Death,' but the desire and hope for 'commodious living,' inclines people to civil society). Thus, on Aristotle's view, the political association having come into being by a natural process, it is itself natural: 'And that the *polis* is prior (*proteron*; i.e., logically prior) to the individual is plain; for if each individual apart is not self-sufficient, he is like all other parts in relation to the whole' (1253a25–8). Moreover, 'a human being is by nature more a political animal' than any merely herd animal, or any so-called 'political' insect (such as the bees and ants Hobbes discusses, citing Aristotle; XVII/6–12, 86–7). For humans possess *logos* ('reason/speech') whereby they can deliberate concerning what is advantageous and harmful, just and unjust, and it is these things – justice and the common good – that form the basis of their communal existence.

That, in a broad outline, is Aristotle's palaeoanthropology. Contrary to what one might gather from textbook accounts of 'Aristotle's political thought,' neither his claim that the political association is natural, nor that man is by nature a political animal implies that he believed polities have always existed. And contrary to textbook versions of 'Hobbes's political thought,' *he* does not hold that originally man lived as a solitary being – the (in)famous 'atomic individual.' Accordingly, these two philosophers' respective views of human nature in relation to politics is much closer than is generally recognized – or than Hobbes wished it to seem, having his own reasons for keeping his distance from Aristotle, darling of the Church and its Schoolmen. Presuming that these reasons are mainly political, they do not necessarily indicate how Hobbes stands with respect to the theoretical issue of whether or not Man is 'political by nature.'

Hobbes never directly addresses the question in *Leviathan*. Or, at least not in the way he does in a note added to *De Cive* some four years prior to the publication of *Leviathan*. For there he expressly examines the claim 'that Man is an animal born fit for Society, – in the Greek phrase, Ζῶον πολιτικόν':

Since we see that men have in fact formed societies, that no one lives outside society, and that all men seek to meet and talk with each other, it may seem a piece of weird foolishness to set a stumbling block in front of the reader on the very threshold of civil doctrine, by insisting that man is not born fit for society. *Something must be said in explanation. It is indeed true that perpetual solitude is hard for a man to bear by nature or as a man, i.e. as soon as he is born. For infants need the help of others to live, and adults to live well. I am not therefore denying that we seek each other's company at the prompting of nature. But civil societies are not mere gatherings; they are Alliances [Foedera], which essentially require good faith and agreement for their making. Infants and the uninstructed are ignorant of their Force, and those who do not know what would be lost by the absence of Society are unaware of their usefulness. Hence the former cannot enter Society because they do not know what it is, and the latter do not care to because they do not know the good it does. It is evident therefore that all men (since all men are born as infants) are born unfit for society; and very many (perhaps the majority) remain so throughout their lives, because of mental illness or lack of training* [disciplina]. *Yet as infants and as adults they do have a human nature. Therefore man is made fit for Society not by nature, but by training.*

Clearly, Hobbes's argument to this point rests on a quibble about the meaning of 'born fit,' he choosing to interpret it (absurdly) as 'fit at birth' to contract, contribute to, and otherwise participate in political life – though even in that sense it requires acknowledging (as he does) that humans are *social* beings, the helplessness of infants necessitating at a minimum the society of a family. But the issue that Hobbes's quibble actually raises concerns how human nature is rightly understood: teleologically, or non-teleologically. For on the former view, 'born fit' means 'informed by a nature that, *fully actualized,* is suited for – indeed requires – living in political association with others.' Whereas Hobbes, apparently rejecting the teleological understanding of Nature and natures (as per the Baconian prescription for modern science) here accords full humanity to infants and to anyone who was once an infant, regardless of the extent to which they have or have not reached the 'maturity' of which the best humans are capable. The balance of his argument, however, raises a quite different issue:

Furthermore, even if man were born in a condition to desire society, it does not follow that he was born suitably equipped to enter society. Wanting is one thing, ability another. For even those who arrogantly reject the equal conditions without which society is not possible, still want it.[13]

One readily grants that a desire for something is no reliable indicator of a capacity for it. Hobbes's illustration of this point, however – the political necessity of recognizing 'equality' – is quite problematic, and I shall address it in chapter 21. For now, suffice it to observe that almost all of those 'constituted societies' Hobbes acknowledged at the beginning of his note managed to exist, some quite successfully, despite manifestly, even expressly and emphatically, *rejecting* Hobbes's egalitarian dictum.

There are certain details of Aristotle's account that also are pertinent to a sorting of how it does and does not differ from Hobbes's. For example, in the context of discussing how a people's way of life is shaped by the means of sustaining life, Aristotle also includes *piracy* (or 'brigandage'; *lësteia*) among the five basic alternative ways of life available prior to the establishment of 'great Common-wealths' able to suppress the practice (1256a35–1256b2; cf. X/49, 45).[14] And while Aristotle does not expressly credit the threat of outside predation as a primary cause of people's gathering into larger associations, he is explicit that 'the political life' is divided between 'the needs of war and those of peace' (1254b31–4); that a polity unable to defend itself is naturally apt to be enslaved by whoever attacks it, indeed, does not even deserve to be called a *polis* (1291a6–10); and that 'war is for the sake of peace' (1333a35). And whereas Hobbes's affirmation of the political superiority of men over women is slightly qualified, Aristotle flatly declares that *by nature* the relation between the male and the female is that of superior to inferior, of ruler to ruled (1254b13–14); but he, too, acknowledges that things do not always turn out as nature intended (1259b2–4). On the other hand, Aristotle distinguishes three distinct forms of rule: Kingly or Royal rule, as that of a father over children, with an eye towards preparing them for the freedom of moral autonomy; Political rule, as over those one recognizes to be one's equal; and Despotic rule, as that of a Master over his servants or slaves. Furthermore, the husband's rule over his wife is properly of the Political kind (1259b1–2) – whereas Barbarians know only Despotic rule, and so treat their wives as slaves, rather than as free women, thereby proving themselves to be barbarians indeed (1252a7–b9).

Hobbes does not distinguish among kinds of rule, treating the father in the original State of Nature as the Sovereign of his family or household, and Sovereignty as being by nature Absolute and Arbitrary: 'In summe, the Rights and Consequences of both *Paternall* and *Despoticall* Dominion, are the very same with those of a Sovereign by Institution' (XX/14, 104). But we are not free to conclude that Hobbes sides with the Barbarians on this profoundly important matter. First of all, there is his 'ninth law of Nature … *That every man acknowledge other for his Equall by*

Nature' (XV/21, 77). Of course, this is inconclusive, for it depends on whether 'man' is to be understood in the *generic* sense (as it surely is throughout Hobbes's presentation of his materialist physiology), or whether, instead, it is *gendered*, as when he observes that 'there is not always that difference of strength, or prudence between the man and the woman, as that the right can be determined without War' (XX/4, 102).[15] Differently ambiguous is Hobbes's general statement about the status of Families within a well-ordered commonwealth:

Private Bodies Regular, and Lawfull, are those that are constituted without Letters, or other written Authority, saving the Lawes common to all other Subjects. And because they be united in one Person Representative, they are held for Regular; such as are all Families, in which the Father, or Master ordereth the whole Family. For he obligeth his Children, and Servants, as farre as the Law permitteth, though no further, because none of them are bound to obedience in those actions, which the Law hath forbidden to be done. In all other actions, during the time they are under domestique government, they are subject to their Fathers, and Masters, as to their immediate Soveraigns. For the Father, and Master being before the Institution of Common-wealth, absolute Soveraigns in their own Families, they lose afterwards no more of their Authority, than the Law of the Common-wealth taketh from them. (XXII/26, 121)

What, then, *ought* the Law to be; that is, how far should it permit the rule of the Father to extend? In keeping with the overall flexibility of his political prescription, it would seem that Hobbes has, quite intentionally, left this open to determination by each commonwealth's particular circumstances – geographical, historical, economic, religious, whatever might shape a people's beliefs and practices. But this openness does not preclude Hobbes having his own view of which familial arrangement is simply best, any more than the formality of his discussion of regimes precludes his having a clear idea of the simply best regime. Might both questions be connected?

Be that as it may, the burden of the present chapter and the one that follows is to expose what are two related but nonetheless importantly different versions of the State of Nature: the original condition out of which mankind first emerged, and to which there would seem practically no possibility of ever returning; and an even more savage condition that man can never with finality escape. If Hobbes's famous formula – 'And the life of man, solitary, poore, nasty, brutish, and short' – accurately summarizes a State of Nature, it is *not* that of the first version. Were the 'solitary' proviso descriptive of man's *original* condition, the acquisition of language and all dependent thereon – virtually everything human – would have been impossible (as Hobbes knows full well, and so has cleverly, inconspicuously indicated). However, upon recognizing that Hobbes is actually employing two distinct versions of a State of Nature, and yet has not only declined to make this as clear as he easily might have, but instead has intentionally allowed the vast majority of his readers to conflate them, one is tacitly challenged to explain to himself why so. What purpose, or purposes – political, or philosophical – is or are served by this, Hobbes's rhetorical tour de force?

20

The Ever-Present State of Nature: Greeks versus Barbarians

If there is a surprising affinity between the views of Hobbes and Aristotle with respect to the primitive conditions in which humans originally lived – a State of Nature out of which more or less stable civil societies first, haltingly, arose – the pertinence of Thucydides' *History* to understanding the even more barbarous condition to which humans can 'return' is not the least bit surprising. Hobbes, after all, was the first to translate that *History* into English directly from the original Greek. And in his preface 'To the Readers,' Hobbes declares Thucydides to be, quite simply, 'the most politic historiographer that ever writ': 'who, though he never digress to read a lecture, moral or political, upon his own text,' yet he 'filleth his narrations with that choice of matter, and ordereth them with that judgment, and with such perspicuity and efficacy expresseth himself, that, as Plutarch saith, he makes his auditor a spectator.'[1] And later in a like vein: 'Digressions for instructions cause, and other such open conveyances of precepts, (which is the philosopher's part), he never useth; as having so clearly set before men's eyes the ways and events of good and evil counsels, that the narration itself doth secretly instruct the reader, and more effectually than can possibly be done by precept.'[2] Hobbes does, however, include a note of caution pertaining to the complaint about the Historian's occasional obscurity. Some of it, he suggests, is due merely to the length of his sentences (!); as for the rest:

[It] proceedeth from the profoundness of the sentences; containing contemplations of those human passions, which either dissembled or not commonly discoursed of, do yet carry the greatest sway with men in their public conversation. If then one cannot penetrate into them without much meditation, we are not to expect a man should understand them at the first speaking. Marcellinus saith, he was obscure on purpose; that the common people might not understand him. And not unlikely: for a wise man should so write, (though in words understood by all men), that wise men only should be able to commend him.[3]

If we presume that Hobbes would have his readers regard him also as a wise man, the reflexive possibilities of this last sentence are intriguing, to say the least. And there may be forms of writing other than history whereby an author can 'secretly instruct the reader.'

Whether or not Hobbes agreed with Aristotle that, in general, 'Poetry is more philosophical and serious than is History, because Poetry speaks about the universals whereas History about individuals,'[4] he obviously does not regard Thucydides as merely an historian in this sense, but rather as one who tacitly presents universal truths by means of the individual events he chooses to narrate. Only in that light may we understand Thucydides' claim to have intended his work, though about events of his own time, to be a possession for all time. As for Hobbes – 'The greatest of Thucydides' English readers,' according to one eminent Thucydides scholar[5] – the common elements in the political perspective of the ancient historian whom he translated, and in the perspective which he himself manifested two decades later in his *Leviathan* (and elsewhere), allow one to attribute a common motive to both of these literary efforts. That motive is first and foremost *cautionary*:

Thucydides may thus appear to share with his great student Hobbes a 'negative' political orientation. We ought to take our political bearings not from what attracts us as best, but what repels us as worst. For Hobbes, that than which nothing is worse is the state of nature or of anarchy; in this he and Thucydides are at one. No reader of the two writers will fail to note the similarities of their accounts of anarchy, which is for both the definitive human evil. Stasis ['faction'] is a war of all against all, in which no one can trust anyone, the preemptive strike is de rigueur, and those who might seem superior to others fare, if anything even worse than they.[6]

The great superiority of Thucydides's History to the writings of all others, Hobbes's writings included, is his unrivalled ability to 'make his auditor a spectator' of this collapse of civil society into anarchy, and to 'so clearly set before men's eyes the ways and events of good and evil counsels' that any reader but half-awake cannot fail to draw the moral lesson. Thus it is that 'the narration itself doth secretly instruct the reader, and more effectually than can possibly be done by precept,' Hobbes's precepts included. In this respect, Thucydides' book is supplementary to that of Hobbes.

But it bears emphasizing that 'the definitive human evil' Thucydides so effectively portrays is that of a State of Nature which man never entirely escapes; it remains a permanent threat, lurking just over the horizon of even the most placid and prosperous of societies. For although he begins his history with a sketch of the *original* State of Nature – an age of pirates and brigands, prior to the establishment of polities strong enough to suppress them – it is not for *this* that his account is of permanent and incomparable value. Rather, it is for his so vividly documenting his contemporaries' descent into a Hell of fratricidal civil war that spiralled ever downward with each passing year: grievances accumulating, with a proportional increase in the lust for revenge, often indiscriminate; all traditional restraints on behaviour – the common religion, customs, norms of decency, the code of honour – ignored, if not openly repudiated; and any hope for a better future supplanted by despair, leaving people living only for the day.

The first harbinger of even worse things to come occurred at Corcyra in the fifth year of the war between the Athenian Empire and the Peloponnesian League led by Sparta. Factional strife broke out openly in Corcyra between 'The People' (*ho dēmos*: the many poor who favoured alliance with Athens), and the traditional elite, 'The Few' (*hoi oligoi*) and their supporters who wished to side with the Peloponnesians. The former got the upper hand and 'slew such of their enemies as they laid hands on':

Next they went to the sanctuary of Hera and persuaded about fifty men [who had sought refuge there] to take their trial, and condemned them all to death. The mass of the suppliants who had refused to [stand trial], on seeing what was taking place, slew each other there in the consecrated ground; while some hanged themselves upon the trees, and others destroyed themselves as they were severally able. During the seven days that [the Athenian general] Eurymedon stayed with his sixty ships, the Corcyraeans were engaged in butchering those of their fellow-citizens whom they regarded as enemies: and although the crime imputed was that of attempting to put down the democracy, some were slain also for private hatred, others by their debtors because of the money owed them. Death thus raged in every shape; and, as usually happens at such times, there was no length to which violence did not go; sons were killed by their fathers, and suppliants dragged from the altar or slain upon it; while some were even walled up in the temple of Dionysus and died there.

So bloody was the march of the revolution, and the impression which it made was the greater as it was one of the first to occur. Later on, one may say, the whole

Hellenic world was convulsed; struggles being everywhere made by the popular leaders to bring in the Athenians, and by the oligarchs to introduce the Spartans ... The sufferings which revolution entailed upon the cities were many and terrible, such as have occurred and always will occur as long as the nature of mankind remains the same ... In peace and prosperity states and individuals have better sentiments, because they do not find themselves suddenly confronted with imperious necessities; but war takes away the easy supply of daily wants and so proves a rough master that brings most men's characters to a level with their fortunes. Revolution thus ran its course from city to city, and places which it arrived at last, from having heard what had been done before, carried to a still greater excess the refinement of their inventions, as manifested in the cunning of their enterprises and the atrocity of their reprisals ... [E]ven blood became a weaker tie than party ... Revenge also was held of more account than self-preservation.[7] Oaths of reconciliation, being only offered on either side to meet an immediate difficulty, only held good so long as no other weapon was at hand; but when opportunity arose, he who first ventured to seize it and to take his enemy off his guard, thought this perfidious vengeance sweeter than an open one since, considerations of safety apart, success by treachery won him the prize for superior intelligence. Indeed it is generally the case that men are readier to call rogues clever than simpletons honest, and are as ashamed of being the second as they are proud of being the first. The cause of all these evils was the lust for power arising from greed and ambition; and from these passions proceeded the violence of parties once engaged in contention ... [R]eligion was in honor with neither party; but the use of fair phrases to arrive at guilty ends was in high reputation ...

Thus every form of iniquity took root in the Hellenic countries by reason of the troubles. The ancient simplicity into which honor so largely entered was laughed down and disappeared; and society became divided into camps in which no man trusted his fellow. To put an end to this, there was neither promise to be depended upon, nor oath that could command respect; but all parties dwelling rather in their calculation upon the hopelessness of a permanent state of things, were more intent upon self-defense than capable of confidence. In this contest the blunter wits were most successful. Apprehensive of their own deficiencies and of the cleverness of their antagonists, [they] at once boldly had recourse to action ...

... In the confusion into which life was now thrown in the cities, human nature, always rebelling against the law and now its master, gladly showed itself ungoverned in passion, above respect for justice, and the enemy of all superiority; since revenge would not have been set above religion, and gain above justice, had it not been for the fatal power of envy. (3.81–4)[8]

Here we are presented with a State of Nature in which the life of man is not only 'poore, nasty, brutish, and short,' but also '*solitary*' inasmuch as 'no man trusted his fellow.'[9] This kind of solitude, borne in the very midst of other men, is far more threatening than would be that experienced by a solitary wanderer in prehistoric times. For everyone was immersed in evidence that your ally and confidante of today may find it advantageous to betray you tomorrow. Accordingly, decent feelings, loyalties, senses of honour and justice, being vulnerabilities, perished with those who felt them. Not even one's family could be relied upon: as envious Cain had killed his brother Abel, here 'sons were killed by their fathers,' and vice versa.

The most important question that all this raises is 'why?' Why are men who have experienced a higher order of life than anything imaginable by people who know only primitive, pre-political conditions of existence, liable to sink to ways of behaving that might well scandalize many savages?[10]

In one sense, the answer could hardly be simpler: the worst men set the terms of existence for everyone. As Hobbes reminds us, this truth is manifest even within the comparative safety of a peaceful, well-policed civil society. We take precautions against our fellow men: most of us, but women especially, would prefer to be accompanied late at night retrieving our cars from an urban parking lot, or when walking in a strange, ill-lit neighbourhood; and we lock our doors when we leave our houses for any length of time (XIII/10, 62). This is not because we suspect *everyone* that might come along is a mugger or a thief – quite the contrary: we presume that such people are a small minority. But we know that they do exist, and that they may be indistinguishable in appearance from decent people. So, we take precautions, and lock our doors against one and all. Nor are our friends and neighbours, much less strangers, offended by our doing so; for they do likewise. The Worst set the conditions for All. Intuitively, moreover, it seems probable to most of us that these Worst would proliferate and prevail if the coercive apparatus prepared to maintain law and order were to disappear.

But the simple answer is simplistic, too superficial to be satisfying. For as the above examples make clear, it is *always* true that 'the worst set the terms of existence for everyone.' But the *extent* of their influence varies radically with circumstances. Their actual effect on the behaviour of law-abiding people in well-established, internally peaceful societies is minimal, limited mainly to prudent cautions against their predation. No decent person models his own treatment of his fellows on that of criminals. Hence, the simple answer raises only more questions. Why are these Worst what they are at any time, and why would they become even worse in conditions of malevolent anarchy? Yet more disturbing, why in that situation would ever more people descend to their level? The presumption that it is on pain of perishing themselves if they do *not* is inadequate as an explanation. First, because it would soon become clear enough to many people that they likely will perish even if they *do* (whereas 'keeping faith' with one's more decent fellows would seem to offer more security). But judging from history – whether ancient or modern – the ranks of the erstwhile decent majority always include a surprisingly large number who, circumstances permitting, are tempted to become barbarians themselves. Thus, placing the onus exclusively on 'necessity' ignores the possibility that something in human nature finds barbarity positively attractive, at least sufficiently attractive in chaotic conditions to overcome the normal repugnance to behaving savagely.

This is but a roundabout way of asking why the non-coercive restraints on people's deportment – religious doctrines, ethical norms, humane feelings, personal affections – generally *fail* to restrain those same people should their lawful government break down. After all, these ideas and sentiments are so effective in an adequately governed civil society that the state's coercive mechanisms rarely need be brought to bear on any but a disreputable few. It is exceedingly difficult (impossible, I suspect) to explain the rapid withering of these moral restraints without conceding Hobbes's basic point, which is *not* that fear of bodily harm and violent death overrules all else. Rather, it is a subtler truth of genuinely *political* psychology: that most people's voluntary compliance with a 'live and let live' ethos, to say nothing of more exacting moral rules, will be forthcoming only when each person is *confident* that everyone *else* will be *forced* to comply should they not do so willingly.[11] But why do most so-called civilized people, in their heart of hearts, not believe that they can count on most other people's sense of fairness, honour, and basic human decency – nor even on the piety of the Pious – in the absence of a Leviathan? Must not self-knowledge, however dim and inchoate, be the grounds of this doubt?

Naturally, in any setting the love of life as well as the fear of death enter on the 'To be' side of almost everyone's ledger. But so, too, does an awareness that, strong as these complementary passions may be, they do not always rule oneself to the exclusion of all other impulses – and that what is true of 'me' is equally true of 'them.' In an orderly, well-governed commonwealth, people presume that the various passions variously operative in every Subject's soul are 'centrally managed' by virtue of being habituated within a structure of coercion-backed rules, and that, consequently, each person can be reasonably confident he is not endangered by any of his fellows' pursuit of their own good and avoidance of their own harm. It is within the structure of those rules, which provide safety but establish only crude outer limits of 'admissible' behaviour, that the refining influences on social life of a common religion and morality, of humane arts and letters, and of the economy of honour and shame, can tame and channel ambition and love of gain in ways that elevate human existence far above anything possible in the original state of nature.

Granted, the refined way of life entails its own costs and hazards. A degree of sometimes irritating conformity is unavoidable (thus Hobbes's Fifth Natural Law mandating '*Mutuall accommodation, or Compleasance*'; XV/17, 76). And compared to the rude health of those fit enough to survive in pre-political conditions, civilized men may become more softened in both body and soul than is altogether good for them. Also, the artificial manners that define politeness may compromise people's simple honesty, creating a veneer of civility that in many cases merely conceals a person's true character. More worrisome are the possibilities for gross disparities of wealth and status to become established and protected by law, especially galling if those inequalities are wholly unconnected with personal merit or public service. Still, these consequences seem an acceptable price to pay for maintaining an environment in which ordinary people can lead tolerably decent lives, and in which the higher potentials of distinctly human nature can be cultivated and expressed by those who care to do so. Almost everyone could be counted upon to pay this price, quite willingly – indeed pay it countless times over – were they sufficiently cognizant of the basic alternative that threatens them. But there's the rub.

Most denizens of a society that, despite latent divisions of class or culture, has long been internally peaceful, take for granted the ambient civility that is due more directly to shared religious teachings, customs, conventional morality, kinship, and neighbourliness than to overt law enforcement. Thus, such people would be quite unpleasantly surprised by the *rapidity* with which civility erodes should sedition and revolution – which perhaps they themselves actively promoted or passively encouraged – result in a civil war that 'returned' them to conditions akin to the pre-political State of Nature, but actually worse. They would be shocked by how quickly things got out of hand, how quickly the behaviour of people can spiral downward, including that of people whom they thought they knew and always 'thought better of.' What happened to their piety, their morality, their sense of fairness and compassion, their basic human decency? Or so they would wonder after such things have been irretrievably lost. And it *is* a worthy question. Why might the normal restraints on people's baser passions so weaken – more or less overnight, seemingly – such that almost everyone would perceive everyone else (including former friends and even some family members) as *potential enemies*? And erstwhile decent people begin to behave like barbarians – or worse? After all, savage peoples maintain ties of family and tribe, and 'are not without some good Morall Sentences' regulative of their conduct among themselves. But if Thucydides is to be believed, the Corcyreans – precursing even worse to come – surpassed in savagery that of so-called savages.

To the extent a reader is not convinced that this is a real possibility – that it is the natural punishment which may, likely will, be visited upon people who fail to do, and to tolerate, all that is necessary to maintain Civil Society – to that same extent the rational force of Hobbes's political prescription is weakened. And as Hobbes allows, 'It may seem strange to some man, that has not well weighed these things; that Nature should thus dissociate, and render men apt to invade, and destroy one another: and he may therefore, not trusting to this inference, made from the Passions, desire perhaps to have the same confirmed by Experience' (XIII/10, 62). No one today need read Thucydides for empirical confirmation of the depths of depravity that human beings are capable of plumbing; the scale of atrocities committed around the world in the past half-century more than match those he chronicles.[12] However, the rational *explanation* for it – not only for the weakness of civilized restraints, but for the virility of barbaric urges – is not as self-evident as Hobbes seems to imply. And insofar as the behaviour of *other* peoples in faraway lands is not fully persuasive of what is *universally* true (people whose 'civilized' status, moreover, may be suspect, or who are seen as the products of peculiar historical circumstances), a convincing rational explanation is necessary. Since Hobbes does not choose to provide more than his bare-bones citing of passions that cause the State of Nature to be a State of War, his reader is left to seek a deeper understanding from whatever sources seem promising.

A suspicion that Reason is culpable, at least partly, is not easily allayed. Within civilized life, where men are forbidden to use open force in competing for life's good things – where most contesting is done with arguments and laws rather than fists and clubs, rapiers and pistols; and where a talent for 'wheeling and dealing' is apt to be more rewarding than is martial virtue or a personal sense of honour – a premium is placed on cleverness in calculating, in persuading and plotting, and in concealing one's aims insofar as this facilitates their realization. But one can *act* on the basis of one's calculations only insofar as one can suppress any feelings that might undermine one's resolve, or otherwise interfere with resolute action. Similarly, maintaining always a respectable facade (to say nothing of posing, 'dissembling, lying, counterfeiting': Introd/3, 2) requires exerting sufficient rational control over any feelings whose outward expression would compromise the desired appearance – not only manifestations of malevolence and aggression, but also of excessive complaisance, docility, or submissiveness.

Moreover, merely by inhabiting an environment in which reasoning is increasingly prominent – even if mainly of but the narrowest, most utilitarian kind – people become more aware of the extent to which the grounds of certain hopes and fears are questionable. For example, by the time of the Peloponnesian War, many Greeks were already mindful that various 'Sophists' ('Wise men') not only taught rhetorical techniques and sophistical argumentation, but also questioned the existence of the gods, and taught that '*man* is the measure of all things.'[13] And what could that mean in practice but that actual men are 'the measure,' and of good and bad in particular? As Hobbes himself reminds us with his allusion to 'the fate of Sokrates,' the philosopher was expressly charged with not believing in the gods officially recognized by the Athenians, while being widely suspected of not believing in any gods at all. In defending himself, Plato's Sokrates notes the ready availability of Anaxagoras's writings in which he advances the view that the Sun and the Moon, far from being deities, are stone and earth (*Apology*, 26c–d).[14] The point being, within the security and prosperity of internally peaceful civilized settings – offering some men the leisure that Hobbes affirms is the one thing needful – rational analysis is more apt to be brought to bear on any and every thing, including tenets of the popular religion. Indeed, questions may be pursued with such persistence and thoroughness that inquiries worthy of being called 'philosophy' may arise. Ancient Greece, and Athens in particular, is credited with being particularly fecund in this respect, but Hobbes implies that it was simply a natural consequence of 'the erecting of great Commonwealths' (XLVI/6, 368).

In short, civil societies provide an environment wherein people are tacitly encouraged to approach life in a more calculating spirit, while at the same time their faith in anything 'trans-human' is subtly eroded. As Rousseau bluntly declares:

It is reason that engenders amour propre, and reflection that reinforces it; reason that turns man back upon himself; reason that separates him from everything that troubles and afflicts him: It is Philosophy that isolates him; by means of Philosophy he secretly says, at the sight of a suffering man, perish if you wish, I am safe. Only dangers that threaten the entire society still disturb the Philosopher's tranquil slumber, and rouse him from his bed. One of his kind can with impunity be murdered beneath his window; he only has to put his hands over his ears and to argue with himself a little in order to prevent Nature, which rebels within him, from letting him identify with the man being assassinated. Savage man has not this admirable talent; and for want of wisdom and of reason he is always seen to yield impetuously to the first sentiment of Humanity. In Riots, in Street-brawls, the Populace gathers, the prudent man withdraws; it is the rabble, it is the Market-women who separate the combatants, and keeps honest folk from murdering one another.[15]

If one discounts the romantic hyperbole, I believe one must concede that here Rousseau has rightly identified certain problematic consequences of man's accepting the sovereignty of Reason. Vanity feeds on favourable comparisons that only reasoning can supply, whether valid or 'rationalized' – and not least of all concerning one's own reasoning abilities. Thus Hobbes's amusing rebuttal of whoever would challenge his ironic evidence for the equality of men's mental faculties ('that every man is contented with his share'): 'That which may perhaps make such equality incredible, is but a vain conceit of ones own wisdome, which almost all men think they have in a greater degree, than the Vulgar' (XIII/2, 61).

Furthermore, in turning reason upon one's own feelings, one may learn to distrust their promptings insofar as one sees that often they are at odds with one's own good. Genuine charity, generosity, care, and solicitude tend to be curtailed accordingly, while adeptness in their feigning is fostered. For that matter, why suffer even the slightest psychic discomfort over some else's troubles, especially if doing so in no way alleviates them? In a man's coming to regard himself as an individual whose own well-being is not invariably bound up with that of his fellows – and in habituating himself to accept what reason shows to be lamentably true: that oftimes one man's gain necessitates another man's loss – he hardens his heart. After all, from the strictly rational perspective, the Philosopher is *right*. Of course, most people never come close to attaining a strictly rational perspective, but some do become sufficiently rational to recognize the prudence of avoiding riots and street brawls. The Philosopher, however, shows where the relentless cultivation of Reason ultimately leads: to an aloof detachment from ordinary people and their transient, mainly petty, everyday concerns. (Ordinary people repay the compliment, regarding the Philosopher and his preoccupation with cosmic questions as exceedingly strange, surely useless, and possibly dangerous in that his radical questioning exerts an unhealthy charm over the young. Thus Philosophy isolates from both directions, as it were.)

But whereas a Philosopher attempts to reconstruct a coherent understanding of the world out of the rubble to which his dialectical reasoning has reduced the ordinary understanding of those around him (the views regnant in this or that 'Cave,' which invariably are flawed), most of the minority of people who bring their reason to bear on fundamental matters necessarily settle for having shown conventional opinions to be questionable. That is, they manage to partially expose the apparent or real shortcomings in various orthodoxies, and to that extent compromise their own confidence in them, along with that of anyone who defers to their views.[16] Most of these vain reasoners, however, are neither inclined nor able to replace what they have damaged with something better, and they presume no one else can do so either. Their net effect is the seeping into society of a kind of watery scepticism about traditional wisdom and anything that is not factually self-evident, which rather obviously includes the claims of religion and morality. The authority of these claims – their psychic grip – is thereby weakened, even if their regulatory effect on people's outward behaviour for the most part continues. So long as the society remains internally stable and peaceful, that is. But as a natural consequence of the increasing salience of reasoning in civil life, doubts will have been raised about that which, to be fully effective, should be accepted as 'beyond doubt': the validity of basic beliefs and norms upon which a people's common way of life is, quite literally, *founded*. Thus these restraining influences are more vulnerable than is readily apparent, and so may quickly crumble when the secure environment they presuppose is overturned.

The inherent weaknesses of moral restraints on barbarism, as revealed when the civil order breaks down, is but the negative half of the story, however. What remains to be explained are the agencies that actively *promote* barbaric behaviour. Having Thucydides in mind, one might pose the question in a concrete form: why would his contemporary Greeks – proud of their cultural superiority, of their refined powers of reasoning and speaking (exemplified in the speeches his *History* recreates), of their capacity for self-rule and consequent moral autonomy – why would, or how could, the most civilized people of antiquity so readily turn into Barbarians (or worse) towards each other?[17] Thucydides simply informs us of the fact; he does not attempt to explain it except in the same formal terms as does Hobbes (e.g., as the result of fear and greed, ambition and envy).[18] Thus, for insight into the psychodynamics of the perennial struggle between Greekness and Barbarism, one must look elsewhere. Who better to consult on such a subject than 'the finest growth of antiquity,' Plato?[19]

Plato's account begins near the very centre of his *Republic*. It immediately precedes Sokrates's paradoxical pronouncement about the necessity of Philosophers being Kings or Kings becoming Philosophers if mankind's political troubles are to be finally resolved. Moreover, this beginning has the advantage of being cast against the background of the Peloponnesian War. It may not be entirely a matter of chance that both works, Plato's *Republic* and Hobbes's *Leviathan*, were written in the wake of civil wars, profound political troubles giving birth to profound political thinking.

Sokrates seems ready to address the practicality of his City in *logos*, whether it is possible for such a polity to come into being, and if so, how most readily (with the advent of Philosopher-Kings, when he at last answers his own question). But instead of directly taking up that matter, he diverts attention with the seemingly dismissive observation about the City's Guardians: 'I presume it's plain how they'll make war' (466e). Predictably, this elicits a query from Glaukon ('How?'), whereupon the philosopher launches into a ten- or twelve-minute exposition outlining some quite unconventional war-waging policies for their City. The most controversial would seem to be his – admittedly risk-ladened – proposal that the children of the ruling warrior class accompany their parents on campaign, so that like 'those of other craftsmen' they might learn their future trade through first-hand observation.

That agreed upon, Sokrates turns to how their soldiers would behave towards each other, and how towards their enemies. As for the first matter, he suggests that any of theirs who displays cowardice would be demoted to the class of artisans and farmers; and – doubtless mindful of the paralysing effect on Sparta of the capture of some three hundred of its soldiers at Pylos[20] – he asks, 'And of one taken alive by the enemy we'll give as a gift to his captors to use their catch however they wish?' (468a–b). Whereas those soldiers 'who have proven best and most distinguished' will be honoured in all ways that serve the interests of the City (including, especially, enhanced breeding opportunities via the rigged marriage lottery, so that the most children might be begotten by such men; 468c).

But in addressing the second matter – 'How our soldiers will deal with their enemies' – Sokrates suggests that they first distinguish between Greeks and Barbarians (469b–471b). Not only are they never themselves to enslave Greeks, neither will they allow other Greeks to do so. Given the ever-present danger of enslavement by the always far more numerous Barbarians, Greeks cannot afford any depletion in their ranks. The plundering of corpses is strictly forbidden, being illiberal and greedy, 'both womanish and small-minded'; and in the interest of maintaining the goodwill of other Greeks, forbidden also is the raising of trophies made from the confiscated weapons of defeated Greeks. Indeed, paralleling the distinction between Greeks and Barbarians is a distinction between two kinds of conflicts: *war* (*polemos*) pertains to the hatred of and struggle against 'what is alien and foreign'; whereas conflicts between 'what is one's own and akin' is best thought of as *faction* (*stasis*). Thus, properly speaking, the term 'war' is reserved for conflicts between Greeks and Barbarians, who are 'enemies by nature' (470c). Whereas, all Greeks being 'by nature friends,' conflicts among them should be termed 'faction.' The philosopher is silent regarding conflicts among Barbarians.

At this point, however, Sokrates acknowledges that the usage he proposes is a departure from what is presently thought of as 'faction,' namely, that it pertains to political divisions within a given city. In light of the events at Corcyra, emblematic of how brutally vicious such internal strife can be, the *irony* of Sokrates's entire treatment of 'Greek factionalism' becomes clearer. Recalling the Athenians' slaughter of the men and enslavement of the women and children of Melos has a similar effect; likewise Plataea at the hands of the Spartans and Thebans, and hundreds of other such atrocities in the course of three decades of such 'factionalism.' It is only against this background that one can appreciate how radical – and how naive, an irony-deaf 'realist' would add – are the philosopher's proposals with respect to moderating the actual practices among Greek *poleis*. Indeed, it is almost comical the blithe manner in which Sokrates proposes that all conflicts among Greeks be prosecuted with an eye towards eventual reconciliation, that in dealing with their opponents they 'correct [*söphroniousi*; lit., 'make moderate'] in a kindly way, not punishing with a view to slavery or destruction, acting as correctors, not enemies.' Any reasonable person viewing the great Greek commotion from above the struggle would agree that this would be in everyone's long-term best interest. Outsiders easily condemn the senselessness of mutually destructive conflicts and tout the 'obvious necessity' of ending 'the cycle of violence.' But it is precisely the apparent impotence of such reasonableness in the midst of all-out civil war that must be addressed. For the *first* concern of people actually caught up in such a conflict is *not* future reconciliation, but present victory and thereby survival in the here and now, perhaps along with a spirit-satisfying measure of 'just revenge.' (Thus the imperative whence are derived the whole body of Natural Laws guiding Hobbes's political prescription: by all means *avoid* a return to the State of Nature via a civil war. For the simple truth is, there is *no sure way* to moderate such conflicts once they begin, no reliable means to prevent their degenerating into a total and most barbarous anarchy.)

Also, however, it is only against this same background of the Peloponnesian War that one can appreciate how sobering – not to say, chilling – is Glaukon's (presumably innocent) summary of Sokrates's policies: 'I for one agree that our citizens must behave this way towards their opponents; and towards the Barbarians as the Greeks do now towards one another' (471b). Sokrates, notice, does not object to this interpretation, whereas many a reasonable person would. Why should Greeks behave with restraint only towards other Greeks? Did not their own behaviour during this fratricidal conflict prove beyond all shadows of doubt that they are not one wit superior to those whom they arrogantly denigrate as 'Barbarians'? And is Plato himself, then, a captive of the narrow prejudice of his time and place, of the 'Cave' into which he happened to have been born? Or does the validity of the policies he has Sokrates articulate actually presume a quite *un*conventional idea of the distinction in question, though cloaked in conventional ideas and prejudices which it rhetorically exploits?

If that is the case, who then *are* the Greeks, and who the Barbarians? Or, alternatively stated, what makes a true Greek *Greek*, and a genuine Barbarian *barbarous*? If the distinction is neither racial nor linguistic, what then *is* its basis? The clues are few, subtle, and scattered; but they are sufficient.

Barbarians are first mentioned in the context of the dialogue's earlier discussion of war. Doubtless having in mind the initial advantage Athens enjoyed from control over the huge treasure collected from its Delian League-become-Empire, Adeimantos challenges Sokrates to explain 'how our City will make war, possessing no money, especially if compelled to make war against a great and wealthy one?' (422a) Along with outlining a Machiavellian foreign policy, the philosopher's reply includes an analysis of what constitutes true *greatness* in polities. It is an analysis with which Hobbes, to judge from his own political prescription, would most emphatically agree. Most polities are not truly 'one' but 'many' – that is, potentially if not actually riven by factions, particularly of the Rich and the Poor, 'enemies to each other,' but each class further factionalized, with many divisions within itself. Sokrates's proposed foreign policy rests on ruthlessly exploiting these divisions (cf. 422d, 423a). Whereas, so long as their City in *logos* is 'moderately governed in the way they've arranged,' it will be truly *unified*, thus truly the 'greatest,' and many times stronger than its mere numbers would suggest. And insofar as it is not factionalized itself, its own foreign policy strategy could not be used against it. In conclusion, Sokrates avers, 'You'll not easily find one city so great as this, either among the Greeks or the Barbarians, though many seem to be many times its size' (423a–b). Apparently, then, it would be as reasonable to search for a great polity among those of the various so-called Barbarians as among those that regard themselves as Greeks (cf. 544d).

The next reference to Barbarians is in connection with Sokrates's suggestion that, if some women are to be included among the Ruling class, they too must exercise naked with the male warriors, ridiculous though the idea might seem. He reminds the young men with whom he's conversing that not so long ago, 'it seemed shameful and ridiculous to the Greeks, as even now it does to The Many [*hoi polloi*] of the Barbarians,' to see men exercising together naked. But since Greeks have gotten used to the practice, they see its value (452c–d). Ignoring the obvious question of whether the two innovations in athletic practices are really analogous, notice: first, that Greeks, unlike Barbarians, do not allow themselves to be ruled by passions (in this case, shame) at the expense of doing what reason and experience confirm is best; second, that among those who are conventionally regarded as Barbarians, just as among the Greeks, there is actually a distinction to be drawn between the custom-bound Many and the presumably more free-thinking, hence more rational, Few.

And it is of some interest that, in defending the practical possibility of their City in *logos* being actualized, Sokrates reminds Adeimantos that, so far as they know, this may already have happened – 'if those on the heights of philosophy have been compelled to take charge of a city in the infinite time that has past or is still to come, or whether even now [such has happened] in some barbaric place far beyond our vision' (499c). Of course, this is a possibility only if philosophy of the highest level is a possibility within various nations that most Greeks would, rightly or wrongly, regard as barbarous.[21] Might Plato, like Hobbes, be willing to regard as philosophers some of 'The *Gymnosophists* of *India*, the *Magi* of *Persia*, and the *Priests* of *Chaldea* and *Egypt*' (XLVI/6, 368)?[22]

However, Sokrates's most telling reference to things 'barbaric' occurs in the context of his analysis of 'the power of dialectical reasoning' to reveal the truth about Being. He suggests that at least this much is beyond dispute: that it must be 'by way [*hodö*] of some *other* mode of inquiry [*methodos*]' than the usual ones if a person is ever to grasp what each several thing really *is*. For all the other arts are directed towards the opinions and desires of humans, or to the generation and composition of changeable things, or to the caring of what is grown and composed (in short, exclusively towards the realm of Becoming). As for the remainder, such as *do* grasp 'something of Being – geometry and that which follows it' (i.e., the other three studies of the 'pre-dialectical' curriculum; 526c–531d) – in actuality, they but dream about Being. For they are powerless (*adynaton*) to show it in full wakefulness so long as they rely upon suppositions (*hypothesesi*) of which they do not have the power to give a rational account (*logon*). For when the beginning (or foundation; *archë*) is not *known*, the end and that which comes in between being derivative of what is not known, all this too remains merely 'hypothetical'; and there is no means, then, of converting this entire fabric into genuine knowledge. Thus, 'only the dialectical mode of inquiry' (*hë dialektikë methodos monë*) is able to proceed in the opposite direction, doing away with hypotheses in order to arrive at a secure understanding of the foundation itself. For 'the eye of the soul really is buried deep in a barbaric mire [*borborö*[23] *barbarikö*]'; but dialectical inquiry can gently draw it out and lead it up, employing in an unconventional way those mathematical arts to assist in turning the soul's attention from Becoming to Being (533a–d).

A barbaric mire is in the soul of each of us, and most people remain more or less bogged down therein throughout their lives. Not being able to fully extricate themselves – that is, to fully empower their Reason and free themselves by gaining genuine knowledge, the only solid ground of moral confidence – they remain vulnerable to the welter of arational passions and desires that make up this 'mire.' Thus, should they ever find themselves deprived of the various suspended supports and 'lifelines' that keep them from sinking, and which they may use to draw themselves at least part-way up and out, they will be sucked under. To that extent they remain part-Barbarians, whatever they might call or think themselves.

For a more substantial understanding of the constituents of this 'bog,' however, one must attend to the scattered elaborations of Plato's psychology. The preliminary analysis of the human soul establishing its three basic parts is presented in the middle of Book Four. Sokrates warns at the time that it is a simplification, that it is lacking in precision, that the way to a full account is longer and more involved (435c–d). This longer 'way' is actually threaded throughout the dialogue; it requires, in particular, integrating various subsequent pieces of analysis that indicate important subdivisions in each of the basic parts. For example, central to the finer understanding of the soul's Rational part, as I have spoken of before, is Sokrates's image of the Divided Line, which matches four kinds of rational powers with four distinct categories of existence (509d–511e).

But of especially vital importance, about which I have also spoken before, is the division in the Spirited part of the soul. One side is exemplified by Love of Victory (*philonikia*), hence is the seat of ambition and competitive drive, but also of a sense of fairness, of freedom and order, of love of beauty and nobility and excellence, as well as other distinctly human traits, most of them good. The spirit's other side, however, is more problematic. Exemplified by Love of Honour (*philotimia*), hence concerned with status and respectful 'recognition,' here is seated the sense of shame and pride, and self-love along with love of one's own, hence patriotism – good things, both politically and personally, but only if properly nurtured and directed. For an excessive sensitivity to slights can make a man quarrelsome, quick-tempered, and generally irascible; love of one's own can profoundly distort one's assessments of all things, being stubbornly resistant to reason; and given the opportunity, this side of the spirit takes pleasure in sheer domination and forcing homage. Moreover, the spirit's Honour-loving side is also the seat of envy, spite, and resentment – ignoble inclinations best suppressed, for given free rein they corrupt souls and erode political harmony. Thus, the mores and morals of a decent society work to channel and otherwise manage the impulses and revulsions native to the human spirit, encouraging and directing those that are beneficial while suppressing or deflecting those that are pernicious.

These various rules and customs, teachings and codes attempt to do likewise with respect to the Desiring part of the human soul. For it, too, is not simple. Fittingly, Sokrates indicates its first major division – between the 'necessary' and the 'unnecessary' desires – in the context of discussing the soul of the natural Democrat, the person who pays no heed to this difference but instead regards all desires and the pleasures they yield as qualitatively 'equal' (561b). However, the very distinction Sokrates draws involves a further complexity, as the category of 'necessary' desires includes two quite different kinds. There are those that a person simply *cannot* suppress (e.g., the desire for food, water, and sleep); but there are also those whose satisfaction is truly beneficial. As he puts it, 'We are compelled by nature to long for both kinds, are we not?' (558d–e) Of course, some objects of desire, such as wholesome food, are 'necessary' on both counts; whereas spices and sweetmeats are unnecessary.

But it is of special significance, I presume, that in discussing how a Democratic soul *originates*, Sokrates resorts to language which might have been lifted straight from Thucydides. This type of soul is one of four presented in parallel with the philosopher's analyses of regime change in cities (and there, too, his general account of the recurring conflict between the Oligarchic and the Democratic factions perfectly summarizes the many particular instances reported by the 'most politic' historian; 555b–557a). The young Democrat, raised within the stingy Oligarchic regime of his father, has had a scanted education. Thus, when he finally tastes the honey-sweet pleasures of the unnecessary desires, his soul becomes 'factionalized,' 'just as in a city,' with each faction being aided by outsiders (559d–e). He is tugged back and forth, as first the sober, more ascetic faction, then the other more profligate faction gains ascendancy. Thus it can happen that 'the Democratic party retreats before the Oligarchic, and with some of its desires destroyed and others exiled, shame arises in the youth's soul, and order is restored.' But other desires, akin to those exiled, invariably arise; and finally, they 'seize the acropolis of the youth's soul,' perceiving it to be inadequately guarded, such as only 'noble studies and practices and true arguments' can provide. In place of such guardians, the dronelike desires in him and in his like-minded associates promote false and vainglorious beliefs, and together they 'call shame "simplicity," and expel it, a dishonoured fugitive; they call moderation "cowardliness" and banish it, mud-spattered; persuaded to regard measured and orderly expenditure as "rustic and illiberal," the many unbeneficial desires combine to drive them over the border.' This done, 'arrogance (*hubris*), anarchy, prodigality, and shamelessness return from exile,' but are rechristened 'enlightment,' 'freedom,' 'magnificence,' and 'courage' (560d–e). This transformation in the meanings of words and ideas invites comparison with Thucydides' description of what happened as the example of Corcyra spread throughout Greece:

Words had to change their ordinary meaning and to take that which was now given them. Reckless audacity came to be considered the courage of a loyal supporter; prudent hesitation, specious cowardice; moderation was held to be a cloak for unmanliness; ability to see all sides of a question, incapacity to act on any. Frantic violence became the attribute of manliness; cautious plotting a justifiable means of self-defense. The advocate of extreme measures was always trustworthy; his opponent a man to be suspected. (3.82)

Thus the language – the *Greek* language, its honourable words still trailing their connotations of virtue and respectability – was used to rationalize acts of utter barbarity.[24]

But whence came these barbarous impulses? That is, what is their psychic source? Here one must turn to Sokrates's analysis of the Tyrannical Man, for in his soul are writ large the tyrannical inclinations that lurk in the depths of every man, being of a piece with man's *erotic nature*. As the philosopher reminds his interlocutors, 'Love [*Erōs*] has from antiquity been spoken of as a tyrant' (573b). Explaining the Tyrant – who is the furthest thing from Hobbes's rational King – requires that Sokrates provide a still more detailed account of the human soul. Specifically, it entails recognizing a further division in its Desiring part. Just as the class of Necessary desires is subdivided into the Irrepressible and the Beneficial, so the class of 'not necessary pleasures and desires' includes two kinds. There are those that are readily amenable to being regulated by *nomoi* (laws especially, but other rules as well, such as those of morals, customs, and conventions). However, there is another kind of Unnecessary desire, a kind that is inherently 'anti-rules' (*paranomoi*), and which 'probably arises in everyone.' When 'checked [or 'corrected,' 'chastized'; *kolazomenai*, lit. 'pruned'] by the *nomoi* and the better desires implanted with reason, in some humans they are entirely eliminated, or only a few weak ones left, while remaining stronger and more numerous in others' (571b). Asked which ones he means, Sokrates replies, 'Those that awaken when the rest of the soul, that of the calculating and gentle and ruling part, sleeps.' Then it is that the soul's 'beastly and savage part,' being released from all 'shame and prudence,' sallies forth to seek the satisfactions denied it in waking life. In the lawlessness of dreams, this part refrains from no kind of sexual intercourse, be it with one's mother or father, with god or beast; it is willing to murder *anyone*; 'and there is no food from which it abstains' – in short, there is nothing it will baulk at doing, however mindless or shameful (571c–d).

In light of this understanding of what moderns have learned to call the Subconscious, Sokrates prescribes a bedtime routine that would facilitate having only sweet and profitable dreams. Protesting that he has already said too much about this matter, he nonetheless concludes his analysis by reiterating its universality: 'that a terrible and savage and lawless form of desires is in each of us, even in some who seem so very measured; and this becomes quite plain in sleep' (572b).[25] Something similar may also be disclosed in inebriation: 'doesn't a drunken man have a somewhat tyrannical mind?' Likewise revealing are certain kinds of madness (*mania*), such that 'the one who is mad and deranged attempts and hopes to be able to rule not only humans, but gods also' (573b–c). The relevant point is this: what is true about the lawless realm of dreams can become true of waking life in the chaotic, anarchic conditions of the State of Nature that is a civil war.

Who, then, is truly a Greek, and who a Barbarian? And what relationship, if any, is there between Plato's *ideas* and the conventional notions of Greeks and Barbarians?

Given that a true Greek would, like Glaukon, agree with Sokrates's radical policies regarding factional fighting among Greeks and waging war against Barbarians, it is reasonable to suppose that a true Greek would be *Just*. That is, he would have formed a well-ordered, harmonious regime in his own soul, each part doing its natural work well: an educated reason ruling his life as a whole, aided by a disciplined and obedient spirit, both working together to control moderate, 'pruned' appetites. To be Just in this sense, a Greek would necessarily manifest the other cardinal virtues as well: prudent by virtue of his soul's rational part, courageous by virtue of an indomitable spirit, and moderate by virtue of an acceptance by all parts of the natural sovereignty of Reason.

A practical test as to whether or not a given person can fully accept the sovereignty of Reason is provided by his understanding of, and attitude toward, Sokrates's radical proposal with respect to women's eligibility for selection to the ruling class. Bearing in mind that the rationale for constructing a City in *logos* is to apply what is writ large there to the regime of an individual human soul (368e–369a), the various features introduced in Book Five, comical though they may be as applied to the City, imply quite reasonable analogues for the Individual. In this case of 'the equality of women' – meaning, recognition of the possibility that the souls of the best women may be equal to those of the best men – a true Greek would treat all women accordingly: as much potentially free and responsible

beings as are comparable men. With respect to the very perfection of justness and Greekness – the philosophical life – the Greek acknowledges
that one may find worthy dialogical partners for the pursuit of wisdom
among women, and that for the arduous task of freeing oneself from the
barbarous mire within (the precondition of self-knowledge), both sexes
could benefit from their baring their souls to each other. The true Barbarian, by contrast, is practically identified by how he treats women: as
fit only to be ruled despotically.[26]

In light of the foregoing, one can make some sense of conventional
notions. A political regime tends both to shape, and be shaped by, the
characters of those subject to it, but especially of those who rule it (cf.
338d–e, 435e, 544d–e). Thus, the *nomoi* of the Spartan *politeia* 'made'
Spartans; that is, the beliefs and practices demanded of people raised in
Sparta instilled a complementary regime in each one's soul. Through a
rigid education that was far more athletic than musical, spiritedness was
amplified and self-discipline emphasized, whereas the development of the
mind was neglected, even held suspect (547e–548b, 548e–549b). By contrast, the greater liberty afforded citizens of the Athenian democracy
allowed for greater nurturing of a person's rational faculties, if he was so
inclined; but it was also an environment of greater luxury and moral
laxity, hence 'softness,' resulting in less steadiness of soul in many Athenians. And the commitment to political equality is always in tension with
respect for excellence (557a–558c). Sokrates's City in *logos* is an attempt
to blend what is best in these two dominant poles of Greek political life.
But the general point is, some polities more so than others tend to instil
in the souls of those subject to them a *naturally just* regime, as judged by
the standard established in Plato's *Republic*.

By this standard, the typical citizen of a 'Greek' *polis* was apt to be
closer to being truly Greek than would be most of the peoples he denominates 'Barbarian' – such as the docile subjects of the Great King of Persia
or the wild, high-spirited horsemen of Thrace and Scythia. For simply by
virtue of being to whatever extent a participating *citizen* of an
autonomous polity, he would have been raised in an environment that
honoured and otherwise promoted the martial virtues of courage and
self-discipline expected of every able-bodied man, this being necessary
for his city's defence, and similarly encouraged to acquire sufficient prudence and public-spiritedness to manage his own household and to serve
responsibly in certain public offices. Moreover, as Sokrates himself
attests, the 'love of learning' (*philomathes*) was most characteristic of
Greece (435e). That love, if sufficiently strong in a person, can lead quite

naturally to philosophy (475c–e). Still, one should not make too much of all this. The typical citizen of a Greek *polis* was a long way from the moral autonomy that would fulfil Plato's idea of a true Greek. For as Thucydides' *History* so painfully shows, stripped of the external supports for decency provided by enforced laws, by common religious beliefs, by a code of honour, and by the concern for one's reputation – elevating refinements of behaviour that can flourish only within a stable environment of civil peace – the typical 'Greek' quickly sank back into his own Barbaric mire, or fell victim to someone who had.

A few 'Greeks,' of course, had never even partially extricated themselves, having no wish to (such people being present in every society). If true *evil* is the will to cause human suffering and to destroy things fine or useful – not in pursuit of some higher purpose, but gratuitously, a perverse glorying in an otherwise impotent power – then the hard truth is, some men turn out to be thoroughly, incorrigibly evil. Thus the unsentimental public health policy Sokrates proposes for their City in *logos*: those who are incurably ill or naturally defective in body they will let die, while those who are 'bad-natured and incurable in soul they will kill themselves' (410a). Whether because their brutish passions are preternaturally strong, and the high side of their spirits so much weaker than the low side (the mire at the base of their souls being particularly deep and viscous), and whether these misfortunes of their psychic composition were aggravated by misfortunes of breeding or circumstance – whatever conjunction of nature and nurture, choice and chance might explain it instance by instance – some men, thankfully only a few in normal times, end up Barbarians through and through. Intelligence presents no obstacle; quite the contrary: it renders them only the more dangerous. For in their case, reason truly is the slave of the passions. As a result, the Barbarian is himself enslaved, tyrannized by his basest impulses, and living only to gratify them: 'a soul teeming with much slavery and illiberality,' its potentially decent parts enslaved to a 'most depraved and maniacal master' – a nightmare come to life (577d). Within civil society, most of his kind are forced either to adopt a deceptive persona of normality, which severely limits the range of their malice, or to exist in the shadowy interstices of society competing with the rest of the criminals (whose motives are more ordinary), which also limits their activity. When civil society breaks down, however, the natural Barbarian is in his native element, a wolf among sheep.

But in light of that same Platonic analysis, grounded as it is in the universalities of human nature, one sees that it is possible for a human being, regardless of the society into which he happens to have been born, to *become* a true Greek. Provided, that is, he is naturally blessed with the requisite qualities of soul, or can through self-nurture acquire any that he lacks. Needless to say, fortune plays an irreducible role in this, much as it does in every life. While the rational faculties can be strengthened by exercise, the well-ordered, harmonious soul – the naturally just soul – presumes a basic intelligence that cannot simply be willed into existence. Equally important, it presumes a spirit that recognizes, or can be taught to recognize, the *beauty*, the natural *nobility*, of possessing such a soul, hence to desire it. The evidence for the natural superiority of this form of soul is in principle available to a thoughtful observer in any numerous association of people – evidence pointing towards a pattern of Greek citizenship laid up in Heaven for anyone who wishes to model himself upon it (592b).

Obviously, some political environments are more felicitous than others insofar as their laws and morals and religious beliefs nurture people to be moderate, courageous, respectful, and law-abiding, and insofar as thoughtfulness and inquiry are encouraged, whether purposefully or incidentally. People born into such environments are fortunate. And the possibility of a few reaching the pinnacle of true Greekness – of becoming genuinely philosophical – is more likely in these places. Yet the essential points are unaffected by such contingencies. First, that every soul harbours base, bestial, barbarous, tyrannical longings which must be mastered by its nobility-aspiring elements if a person's distinctly human potential is to be actualized (589c–d). Second, that the philosopher and perfectly just man is a natural possibility wherever there are civil societies. Third, that all such Greeks and potential Greeks are by nature friends; hence disputes that arise among them must not be allowed to undermine their far more important commonality of interests. Because, fourth, Greeks and potential Greeks will always be vastly outnumbered, a mere scattering among the countless Barbarians and semi-Barbarians who would readily subjugate them – whereas it would be best for everyone that Barbarians be ruled by Greeks (590c–d).

What about Hobbes – does he also see things this way? I shall suggest in the following chapters that it is far more likely than not. By way of concluding this chapter, however, I shall confine myself to the first matter: whence man's potential for the utmost barbarity. It is not possible to find in Hobbes's skimpy psychology a clear ratification even of Plato's basic tripartite analysis of the soul, much less of his finer differentiations. Nor, evidently, does Hobbes regard a deeper plumbing of the human psyche to be necessary for justifying his political prescription. On the surface, at least, he leaves it pretty much as does Thucydides, accounting for the potential brutality of civil war in terms of familiar passions that he contends would rule unrestrainedly in the absence of a power sufficient to police and enforce their containment by laws: 'So that in the nature of man, we find three principall causes of quarrel. First, Competition, Secondly, Diffidence; Thirdly Glory. The first, maketh men invade for Gain; the second, for Safety; and the third, for Reputation' (XIII/6–7, 61–2). Beyond that, Hobbes relies upon knowledge of history for empirical confirmation as to what can happen upon a complete breakdown of civil authority – for it has happened, and there is no good reason to believe it could not, so would not happen again and again. Moreover, strictly speaking, knowledge of 'the fact' should be sufficient for the credibility of his political doctrine; a deeper understanding of 'the cause' is not logically required.

Still, as I noted earlier, a more convincing explanation of 'why' may be psychologically required for those many readers inclined to believe 'it can't happen here.' That such an explanation is readily available, courtesy of Plato, and that it fits nicely with Hobbes's doctrine, only further legitimates that doctrine, quite apart from whether or not Hobbes himself had it in mind (as he so clearly did the wisdom of Thucydides). There are, however, a few indications that he may well have – bearing in mind that he evidently had studied Plato's *Republic* with the interest and insight of a fellow philosopher.

For example, in discussing the intellectual virtue of Discretion, he noted, 'The secret thoughts of a man run over all things, holy, prophane, clean, obscene, grave, and light, without shame, or blame' (VIII/10, 34). Their ultimate sources are the various passions 'annexed' to man's nature, which include of course those that, left unrestrained, are the sources of both folly and crime – especially 'Anger,' along with the all-too-human manifestations of *Erös*: 'Hate, Lust, Ambition, and Covetousnesse' ('And for Lust, what it wants in the lasting, it hath in the vehemence'; XXVII/17–18, 155; cf. VIII/16–21, 35–6). Obliquely bearing on this matter is Hobbes's rather strange inclusion of the following vignette abstracted from the beginning of Lucian's essay 'The Way [or 'How'] to Write History':

There was once a great conflux of people in *Abdera*, a City of the Greeks, at the acting of the Tragedy of *Andromeda*, upon an extream hot day: whereupon, a great many of the spectators falling into Fevers, had this accident from the heat, and from the Tragedy together, that they did nothing but pronounce Iambiques, with the names of *Perseus* and *Andromeda*; which together with the Fever, was cured, with the comming on of Winter: And this madnesse was thought to proceed from the Passion imprinted by the Tragedy. (VIII/25, 37)

Undoubtedly, a most interesting example of the *interaction* between body and soul! However, Hobbes leaves it for the classically educated to recall – or the doggedly curious to discover – what he himself necessarily knew, that the favourite 'Iambique' these people were reciting, according to Lucian, was from the great speech of Perseus: 'O *Erös*, tyrant of Gods and men!' And, speaking more expansively in a vein that might remind one of observations by Sokrates, Hobbes contends:

Again, that Madnesse is nothing else, but too much appearing Passion, may be gathered out of the effects of Wine, which are the same with those of the evill disposition of the organs. For the variety of behaviour in men that have drunk too much, is the same with that of Mad-men: some of them Raging, others Loving, others Laughing, all extravagantly, but according to their severall domineering Passions: For the effect of the wine, does but remove Dissimulation; and take from them the sight of the deformity of their Passions. For, (I believe) the most sober men, when they walk alone without care and employment of the mind, would be unwilling the vanity and Extravagance of their thoughts at that time should be publiquely seen: which is a confession, that Passions unguided, are for the most part meere Madnesse. (VIII/23, 36–7)

And if a man of discretion, though sober and awake, may have thoughts so 'vain and extravagant' that he would be chary of revealing them to others, presumably Hobbes would agree that the passion-driven dreams of that same man, unpoliced by either his reason or his sense of pride and shame, could be – and occasionally would be – even more disreputable, not to say maniacal.

Hobbes is certainly not naive about the dark side of human nature. He warns his reader that 'there be some, that taking pleasure in contemplating their own power in acts of conquest, which they pursue farther than their security requires' (XIII/4, 61). He does not elaborate. But it is worth thinking about, for it opens up a range of possibilities. If even within a precarious State of Nature some men's use of their power is not confined within an ever-urgent concern for personal security, if they derive positive pleasure from discharging their power in various acts of conquest per se, irrespective of manner and kind, this bespeaks the existence of *desires* for such pleasures. It is not open to Hobbes expressly to condemn any desires as simply, unqualifiedly evil, as that would contradict the popular hedonism he wishes to appear to endorse (fundamental to the 'realism' of his political science). The prospects of satisfying perverse, 'inhuman' desires within civil society are strictly limited, of course, being incompatible with maintaining civil peace, and policed accordingly. But not so in the State of Nature, wherein 'every man has a Right to every thing; even to one anothers body' (XIV/4, 64). Hobbes is amply aware that men, at least some, are not merely capable of extreme cruelty, but would positively enjoy causing it, given the opportunity. According to Aubrey, he said 'that if it were not for the Gallowes, some men are of so cruell a nature as to take a sport in Killing men no more than I should to kill a Bird.'[27] Hobbes is content to let the fact imply the existence of the cause. For as readers sufficiently familiar with rapacious martial societies throughout history would know, the idea of hunting and killing men for the sheer sport of it is far from fanciful.

Beyond these few explicit remarks directly pertinent to man's capacity for brutality, including sadistic cruelty, there are scattered indications that – despite his crafting appearances to the contrary – Hobbes does generally subscribe to Plato's psychology. Some occur in conjunction with his pseudo-materialistic adaptation of Plato's Man-Polity analogy. For example, Hobbes attributes to Commonwealths three distinct 'faculties' modelled upon those of individual humans: 'the Power of levying mony' is 'the Nutritive faculty'; 'the Power of conduct and command' is 'the Motive faculty'; and 'the Power of making Lawes' is 'the Rationall faculty' (XXIX/16, 172). These faculties correspond to Plato's tripartite division of the soul into its Appetitive, Spirited, and Rational parts. Of course, this alone does not license concluding that Hobbes accepts the fourfold taxonomy of desires basic to the more elaborate psychology Plato's Sokrates presents, much less its implications for the health of persons and polities. But he may have, given the need to explain otherwise unexplained phenomena he himself points to, given his obvious familiarity with the *Republic*, and given his personal identification with its central teaching. Nor is there any decisive reason why he would not.

Of greatest importance, however, are Hobbes's various endorsements of the propriety of Reason *ruling* – rather than *serving* – the soul's subrational parts, while at the same time conceding the difficulty that most people have in always abiding by this prescription: 'for the Passions of men, are commonly more potent than their Reason' (XIX/4, 96). Moreover, 'the most part of men, though they have the use of Reasoning a little way … yet it serves them to little use in common life' (V/18, 21). Among other implications, this means most people lack the minimum reasoning requisite for recognizing the natural authority of Reason. But what is commonly true, what is true of most men, is not true of all men. In particular, it is not true of those whom one must regard as the *best* men, presuming that Reason *ought* to rule. And Hobbes is unequivocal on that point: 'in all Deliberations, and in all Pleadings, the faculty of solid Reasoning is necessary: for without it, the Resolutions of men are rash, and their Sentences unjust' (R&C/1, 389). But the generality of men, in pursuing what they perceive to be their interests, set 'themselves against reason, as oft as reason is against them' (XI/21, 50). Thus, suppressing the pernicious effects of the most powerful crime-inducing passions (i.e., anger, hate, greed, lust, and such) generally requires reliance upon a still stronger passion, namely, the fear of severe punishment; some men, however, can control these same passions 'by extraordinary use of Reason' (XXVII/18, 155). Similarly, while 'most men choose rather to hazard their life, than not to be revenged' for signs of contempt, it nonetheless is not 'worthy of a man that hath the use of Reason' even to take notice of 'words of disgrace or some little injuries' (XXVII/20, 155).

As these passages suggest, the rule of right reason is all-important, yet its effectiveness varies greatly among people, with most being (at best) 'endued but with a mediocrity of reason' (cf. XXXVII/13, 237). This has major implications for the functioning of a regime supposedly founded upon the premise of human equality, matters I shall address in the following chapter.

Before proceeding further, however, I must return to the problem I acknowledged at the conclusion of the preceding chapter: that upon recognizing Hobbes is actually employing two distinct versions of a State of Nature, and yet has not only declined to make this as clear as he easily could have, but instead has intentionally invited – and largely achieved – their unwitting conflation, a reader is tacitly challenged to explain to himself 'why so?' Indeed, at first blush it would seem rhetorically advantageous to *emphasize* what Hobbes himself sees as the truth: that a collapse of civil society can propel people into a condition even *worse* than the primitive and savage situation out of which civil society first arose. So, what purpose (or purposes) is (or are) served by this rhetorical misdirection, and is it (or are they) primarily political, or philosophical? As the preceding sentence suggests, there may be a complexity to this question.

Thus, without meaning to account exhaustively for this remarkable feature of *Leviathan*, I would venture the following.

First of all, Hobbes does have both political and philosophical reasons for intentionally obscuring the distinction between mankind's original condition and that into which a people may descend should their civil society collapse for lack of a single strong sovereign. I shall reserve for the following chapter my suppositions about Hobbes's philosophical purpose. However, to avoid confusion, I wish it understood that by 'philosophical' I do not mean 'theoretical.' I can make the difference clear by suggesting that the paramount philosophical purpose of any philosopher worthy of the name is the promotion and protection of philosophy.

That said, I shall confine myself in what follows to what I see to be the political purpose served by Hobbes's rhetorical sleight of hand. Notice, the effect of conflating the two States of Nature is to make Mankind's *original* condition seem worse than it was – as if everyone *then* was isolated, utterly and solely dependent upon his, or her, own 'natural powers,' and in a state of war with everyone else (whereas most people would have been parts of extended families). Thus, the question becomes, why allow, or rather encourage, this mistaken view? Must it not be because people's seeing man's original condition in the manner Hobbes has inconspicuously indicated – that it certainly was not 'solitary,' nor consequently as 'poore, nasty, brutish, and short' as his famous epithet seemingly implies – would leave them sceptical as to how grave the threat posed by social collapse truly is? Perhaps the outrages of the Greek civil war have been exaggerated; or perhaps that conflict was a unique aberration.[28] Perhaps, as a rule, the breakdown of civil society merely returns people to the pre-civil way of life, which was not really all that bad. Indeed, might it even have been *better* in some respects: a free, healthy, honest, simple, leisurely existence within the affectionate bosom of one's family? How easy it is to glamorize the lives of 'noble savages' was shown before Hobbes by Montaigne, and after him by Rousseau and a host of others, including the young Melville. Thus Rousseau in his *Discourse on Inequality*:

The first developments of the heart were the effect of a new situation that brought husbands and Wives, Fathers and Children together in a common dwelling; the habit of living together gave rise to the sweetest sentiments known to man, conjugal love, and Paternal love. Each family became a small Society, all the better united as mutual attachment and freedom were its only bonds ...

...

Thus, although men now had less endurance, and natural pity had undergone some attenuation, this period in the development of the human faculties, occupying a just mean between the indolence of the primitive state and the petulant activity of our amour propre, must have been the happiest and most lasting epoch. The more one reflects on it, the more one finds that this state was the least subject to revolutions, the best for man, and that he must have left it only by some fatal accident which, for the common utility, should never have occurred. The example of the Savages, almost all of whom have been found at this point, seems to confirm that Mankind was made always to remain in it, that this state is the genuine youth of the World, and that all subsequent progress has been so many steps in appearance towards the perfection of the individual, and in effect towards the decrepitude of the species. (Part Two, pars. 12 and 18)

The allure of Rousseau's charming portrait even today proves the natural, hence enduring, appeal of this wishful, romanticized view of man's pre-civil condition[29] – that is, to people who chafe under the restrictions and artificialities of civilized life (which they could not do without). But to the extent people beguile themselves with a kinder, gentler view of the State of Nature, the natural *sanction* upon which rests Hobbes's entire body of Natural Laws and his consequent political prescription – namely, a profound and fully justified *fear* of Hell on Earth – is vitiated. Hobbes, in his wisdom, used his rhetorical skill to deny false grounds of hope to people who would seize upon any pretext for evading the harsh truth about a post-civil State of Nature. And, after all, the truth about man's condition in the original State of Nature is politically irrelevant. Admittedly, encouraging the false view of that State does generate some perplexing theoretical issues (first and foremost, concerning the origin of language). But once again, all this sort of thing is politically irrelevant – everyone knows that language did come into existence somehow, and most people care little about any conundrums associated with its origin. As for those who might care, let them examine Hobbes's text more carefully, and thereby discover for themselves that he has *not* in fact envisioned man's origins in such a way as would make impossible his subsequent social evolution.

21

The Nature of Men:
Equality as a Useful Lie

I have more than once in the preceding pages expressed doubts about the claim that people, stripped of their civil acquisitions, are by nature equal – doubts both about the claim itself and of Hobbes's own subscription to it. Even his initial statement of it is not as strong as rhetorically it seems; it begins the thirteenth chapter (the only one of the forty-seven whose first word, like that of the Introduction, is 'Nature':

Nature hath made men so equall, in the faculties of body, and mind; as that though there bee found one man sometimes manifestly stronger in body, or of quicker mind then another; yet when all is reckoned together, the difference between man, and man, is not so considerable, as that one man can thereupon claim to himselfe any benefit, to which another might not pretend, as well as he. For as to the strength of body, the weakest has strength enough to kill the strongest, either by secret machination, or by confederacy with others, that are in the same danger with himselfe.

Notice, there are two very different issues here, as well as a tacit acknowledgment that the one has a clear logical implication for the other. The first issue is the 'degree' to which men are approximately equal in '*Naturall Power*' ('the eminence of Faculties of Body, or Mind; as extraordinary Strength, Forme, Prudence, Arts, Eloquence, Liberality, Nobility'; X/2, 41).[1] The claim is that men are 'close enough' to equality of natural *powers* such that each can plausibly 'pretend' to an equality of *right* to whatever benefits are available (the second issue). This 'pretence' turns out to be of greater importance politically than the reality.

Hobbes several times contends that Right is correlative with Power. To cite merely one, but apparently definitive, instance:

Seeing all men by Nature had Right to All things, they had Right every one to reigne over all the rest. But because this Right could not be obtained by force, it concerned the safety of every one, laying by that Right, to set up men (with Soveraign Authority) by common consent, to rule and defend them: whereas if there had been any man of Power Irresistible; there had been no reason, why he should not by that Power have ruled, and defended both himselfe, and them, according to his own discretion. To those therefore whose Power is irresistible, the dominion of all men adhaereth naturally by their excellence of Power; and consequently it is from that Power, that the Kingdome over men, and the Right of Afflicting men at his pleasure, belongeth Naturally to God Almighty; not as Creator, and Gracious; but as Omnipotent. (XXXI/5, 187)

There is, of course, a broad range of possibilities *between* approximate equality of power and 'Power Irresistible' – just as there is between 'all men' *everywhere* and all of those in one's vicinity. Thus, were one to reject the notion that men in a State of Nature would be approximately equal in natural powers, believing instead that some men would be conspicuously 'stronger in body,' 'of quicker mind,' *and* – to add what Hobbes chooses here to ignore – of greater spiritedness (hence bolder, prouder, more aggressive, wrathful, and ambitious), then one would not so readily concede that all men are equally deserving of a 'Right to All things.'[2]

Hobbes's argument for recognizing a rough natural equality of bodily strength rests upon insinuating (without actually asserting) that, with respect to what everyone ought to care most about – staying alive – each man is equally dangerous to every other: 'For as to the strength of body, the weakest has strength enough to kill the strongest, either by secret machination, or by confederacy with others, that are in the same danger with himselfe.' But that any man, or woman, may pose *some* threat to any other is no ground for concluding that everyone is *equally* dangerous. Were that so, and bearing in mind that the best defence is a ruthless offence (for 'there is no way for any man to secure himselfe, so reasonable, as Anticipation; that is, by force, or wiles, to master the persons of all men he can, so long, till he see no other power great enough to endanger him'; XIII/4, 61), then the original State of Nature might indeed have been the universal war of 'every man, against every man' that Hobbes implies. And were *that* so, the natural emergence of social grouping would have been practically impossible. For the wily stronger men would have both the incentive and the means to eliminate everyone weaker (but equally dangerous, supposedly) that comes within their vicinity, with the fittest survivors living like cougars, widely dispersed.[3]

It is irrelevant to claim that the weaker could defeat the stronger by banding together, as if their foremost concern were not survival but that of protecting their 'equal rights,' and as if they were no (supposedly equal) threat to each other. The essential point is that the weaker men's very need to band together contradicts what it is supposed to demonstrate: all men's approximate equality in bodily faculties. Moreover, this is a plausible strategy only within an already existing society, with people accustomed to living communally according to established rules. Indeed, it is precisely the 'social contract theory' which Plato has Glaucon articulate: that so-called justice as determined by the law is in reality a conspiracy whereby the naturally weak Many band together, becoming artificially strong enough to constrain and rule over the naturally strong Few (*Republic* 358e–359b; more on this later). Whereas, in primitive, pre-societal circumstances, the obvious survival strategy for the many who are weaker, less courageous, less cunning and resourceful (and not only women and children) is to willingly – and faithfully – subordinate themselves to the leadership of the conspicuously strong, bold, prudent Few, gaining their protection for mere life on such terms 'as not to be weary of it' (cf. XIV/8, 66).

What, then, about the claim that, 'when all is reckoned together,' men are by nature roughly equal in mental abilities? Hobbes purports to establish this in the chapter's second paragraph:

And as to the faculties of the mind, (setting aside the arts grounded upon words, and especially that skill of proceeding upon generall, and infallible rules, called Science; which very few have, and but in few things; as being not a native faculty, born with us; nor attained, (as Prudence,) while we look after somewhat els,) I find yet a greater equality amongst men, than that of strength. For Prudence, is but Experience; which equall time, equally bestowes on all men, in those things they equally apply themselves unto. That which may perhaps make such equality incredible, is but a vain conceipt of ones owne wisdome, which almost all men think they have in a greater degree, than the Vulgar; that is, than all men but themselves, and a few others, whom by Fame, or for concurring with themselves, they approve. For such is the nature of men, that howsoever they may acknowledge many others to be more witty, or more eloquent, or more learned; Yet they will hardly believe there be many so wise as themselves: For they see their own wit at hand, and other mens at a distance. But this proveth rather that men are in that point equall, than unequall. For there is not ordinarily a greater signe of the equall distribution of any thing, than that every man is contented with his share. (XIII/2, 60–1)

'But man, whose Joy consisteth in comparing himselfe with other men, can relish nothing but what is eminent' (XVII/8, 86). Thus, 'such is the nature of men' that in their vanity they routinely, insistently misjudge their own intelligence compared with that of other men. And the fact that, partly as a consequence, virtually all men *reject* the notion of intellectual equality is alleged as 'proof' of intellectual equality! This must be one of the most amusing arguments in this frequently amusing book (that the joke is not even original only adds to the humour of its use here).[4]

As for the 'equality of prudence-as-experience' claim, Hobbes's two caveats strip it of practically all significance; for even were people of roughly equal mental abilities, few are of equal age, nor 'do they equally apply themselves unto' matters of equal importance. Hobbes's own 'prudential knowledge' attests to this, speaking of those 'whom necessity, or covetousnesse keepeth attent on their trades, and labour; and they, on the other side, whom superfluity, or sloth carrieth after their sensuall pleasures, (which two sorts of men take up the greatest part of Man-kind,) being diverted from the deep meditation, which the learning of truth … requireth' (XXX/14, 179); 'And wee see daily by experience in all sorts of People, that such men as study nothing but their food and ease, are content to beleeve any absurdity, rather than trouble themselves to examine it' (XLV/30, 363). Virtually from his first mention of prudence as 'conjecture' based on past experience, Hobbes subtly indicates that even men of equal experience are *not* equally prudent: 'the *best* guesser [is] he that is most versed *and studied* in the matters he guesses at' (III/7, 10; emphases added). Some men 'study' and reflect upon their experiences, others do not – just as some actively *observe* what others but passively 'see.' Thus, '*No man is presumed to be a good Counsellour, but in such Businesse, as he hath not onely been much versed in, but hath also much meditated on, and considered*' (XXV/13, 134; emphasis in original).

Admittedly, acceptance of Hobbes's bogus argument, so flattering to the vast herds of mediocre minds, would – ironically – bespeak a kind of 'equality' among those who subscribe to it, but clearly this does not include Hobbes himself. He is, after all, a philosopher. More than once he refers to something being 'intelligible,' or 'evident,' even to those of 'the meanest capacity' (XV/35, 79; XLII/67, 295). If that phrase does not imply significant differences in mental capacities, I cannot imagine what of relevance it might mean. At several crucial points in his text, Hobbes presumes – indeed, insists upon – recognition of the differences in people's reasoning power. Some of these I have cited previously, such as the first requirement of 'a good Judge,' namely, 'the goodnesse of a mans own naturall Reason' so as to have a right understanding of Equity (XXVI/28, 146–7), and how Impostors claiming a power of enchantment depend upon 'the ordinary ignorance, stupidity, and superstition of mankind' (XXXVII/10, 236). More is involved here, however, than reasoning ability; equally important is that *desire* peculiar to the rational soul, curiosity, and it too is a variable: whereas everyone is curious to some extent about 'the Causes of the Events they see,' they are *not* equally so, but rather 'some more, some lesse' (XII/2, 52) – those having 'lesse' being the rule, those having conspicuously 'more' the exception. This has countless consequences, not the least being widespread gullibility: 'For such is the ignorance, and aptitude to error generally of all men, but especially of them that have not much knowledge of naturall causes, and of the nature, and interests of men; as by innumerable and easie tricks to be abused' (XXXVII/12, 236).

For a clear enough indication of Hobbes own view of men's natures, however, one need look no further than the concluding sentence of a passage I have had various reasons to cite previously, namely, the rationale which precedes his 'putting this' as the Ninth Law of Nature: '*That every man acknowledge other for his Equall by Nature.*' The whole paragraph nicely illustrates his ironical style:

The question who is the better man, has no place in the condition of meer Nature; where, (as has been shewn before,) all men are equall. The inequality that now is, has bin introduced by the Lawes civill. I know that *Aristotle* in the first booke of his Politiques, for a foundation of his doctrine, maketh men by Nature, some more worthy to Command, meaning the wiser sort (such as he thought himselfe to be for his Philosophy;) others to Serve, (meaning those that had strong bodies, but were not Philosophers as he;) as if Master and Servant were not introduced by consent of men, but by difference of Wit: which is not only against reason; but also against experience. For there are very few so foolish, that had not rather governe themselves, than be governed by others: Nor when the wise in their own conceit, contend by force, with them that distrust their owne wisdome, do they alwaies, or often, or almost at any time, get the Victory. If Nature therefore have made men equall; that equalitie is to be acknowledged; or if Nature have made men unequall; yet because men that think themselves equall, will not enter into conditions of Peace, but upon Equall termes, such equalitie must be admitted. (XV/21, 76–7)

If sometimes 'Who is the better man' is a question best not raised 'in the condition of meer Nature,' it is *not* because therein 'all men are equal,' but rather for the reason Hobbes gave earlier: 'because in the condition of meer Nature, the *inequality* of Power is not discerned, but by the event of Battell' (XIV/31, 70; emphasis added). Other times, however, there would be no question as to who enjoys physical superiority; it would be obvious from how people *look*. In a chance meeting between two large, robust savages, both in their prime, each would doubtless tread warily around the other, not sure who is the better man. But no such doubt – on anyone's part – would affect their encounters with men much younger or older or smaller, to say nothing of women and children, the sick and the lame.

Upon reflection, however, what is curious in Hobbes's rationale requiring the recognition of equality is his snide allusion to Aristotle. Admittedly, on the face of it, the reference makes sense. For Aristotle argues that some people, lacking the wherewithal to rule themselves for their own good, are by nature suited to be *slaves* – virtually living tools or beasts of burden – of those who *are* capable of rational self-rule (though most would be what Hobbes calls 'servants'; cf. XX/10, 104). This amounts to the strongest conceivable rejection of natural human equality. But Hobbes's cleverly associates that (now infamous) contention with an altogether different idea: that philosophers, being of 'the wiser sort,' are in natural fact 'more *worthy* to Command,' regardless of what people would freely consent to – as if rejecting the one (slavery) entailed likewise rejecting the other (philosophical rule). Indeed, why is the notion of 'philosophers commanding' even raised in this context? Is Hobbes merely playing to the prejudices of the many non-philosophers? As I observed in an earlier chapter, the claim that the few Wise cannot 'by force' impose themselves politically on the many Unwise is utterly irrelevant to what is supposedly at issue here: mental competence for governing. Not only would the very attempt put the lie to their claim of wisdom, they might well regard the idea as unseemly. This is the spirit in which Plato's Sokrates responds to Adeimantos's charge that even most decent (or 'most equitable'; *epieikestatoi*) philosophers are 'useless to the Many':

However, bid [the accuser] blame their uselessness on those who do not use them, not on the decent [philosophers]. For it is not natural that a pilot beg sailors to rule over them, nor that the wise go to the doors of the wealthy; the crafter of that epigram lied. The truth naturally is, whether a sick person be rich or poor, it is necessary that he go to the doors of the doctors, and that everyone who needs to be ruled [go] to him who has the ability to rule – *not* for the Ruler, one who is truly of some benefit, to beg the Ruled [to let themselves] be ruled. (*Republic* 489b–c)

But Hobbes seems to ridicule the idea of rule by philosophers, however decent or equitable. And yet, he concludes the secular presentation of his political teaching with a recognition of the necessity of this very thing (most surprisingly, as I emphasized in discussing the Crucial Paragraph).

The appearance of Hobbes's contradicting himself on this matter is, however, just that: mere appearance. Sufficiently thought about, one sees his real point is that the possession of wisdom is in itself *politically* impotent. As he earlier noted, 'The Sciences, are small Power; because not eminent; and therefore, not acknowledged in any man; nor are at all, but in a few ... For Science is of that nature, as none can understand it to be, but such as in a good measure have attayned it' (X/14, 42). Truth is, it takes some considerable wisdom to *recognize* wisdom for what it is, and thereupon to accept its authority. Thus, if wisdom (or science, including a science of politics) is to *rule* more or less directly over actual political life, the philosopher must be known to have the means of *compelling* obedience to his will in the absence of voluntary compliance. He needs, in short, the support of those who *are* capable of 'contending by force and gaining the Victory' – a warrior class, say: men who have been carefully selected for spiritedness and intelligence and loyalty – well-trained, self-disciplined soldiers who will police the polity internally, and protect it from external enemies.

As for the fact that most people would rather govern themselves than be governed by others, it is of a piece with their 'vain conceit of ones owne wisdome, which almost all men think they have in a greater degree, than the Vulgar; that is, than all men but themselves.' Indeed, Hobbes cites a corollary of this trait in comparing men with so-called political insects (who lack 'the use of reason'): 'whereas amongst men, there are very many, that thinke themselves wiser, and abler to govern the Publique, better than the rest' (XVII/9, 86–7). The totality of such opinions and preferences, however, is worthless as evidence of people's equal competence for self-government, being evidence instead of how prevalent is human vanity (especially regarding that which bears directly upon a person's very humanity: rationality). Its true relevance is nonetheless profoundly political, as is implicit in Hobbes's shocking conclusion: 'If Nature therefore have made men equall; that equalitie is to be acknowledged; or if Nature have made men unequall; yet *because men that think themselves equall, will not enter in conditions of Peace, but upon Equall termes, such equalitie must be admitted.*' This in effect concedes that the previous arguments purporting to show the natural equality of men – which, in turn, is the basis for recognizing their 'pretense' to equality of rights – are so far from manifesting geometric certitude, as to be at best inconclusive (if not profoundly defective).[5] Furthermore, it amounts to a belated denigration of the importance of *truth* about the matter, such that whether or not those arguments are valid is *not decisive* for the overall validity of Hobbes's political teaching. *Whatever* the truth about natural human (in)equality, the politically relevant point is that the universal *ascription* of human equality is the most efficacious principle upon which to construct a stable, internally peaceful regime.

Why, then, has Hobbes bothered to provide these arguments in favour of the view that all men are by nature equal – and presumably they are the best he saw fit to supply – if the acceptance of their soundness is not strictly necessary to the validity of his political prescription? Simply stated, they provide *everyone*, whatever their own beliefs on the matter, a publicly acceptable rationale for *ascribing* a natural equality to all their fellows, thereby justifying the equality of rights and liberties that are essential to the Hobbesian regime's functioning as its designer intended. That everyone has reason to agree to honour this literally *fundamental* premise of the regime is, in turn, essential to securing the willing civil obedience that is the precondition of stability and civil peace, and thus of technical progress and material prosperity. But not everyone's reason for agreeing is the same. Tentatively, one might distinguish four classes of people according to the grounds of their acceptance of the egalitarian premise.

First, there are those who agree with the premise because they are persuaded by Hobbes's arguments that – 'when all is reckoned together' – '*Nature*' really and truly 'hath made men' roughly equal. Suffice it to suggest, many of such people would not be distinguished by the strength of their own reasoning power, nor by the care and thoughtfulness with which they read; they may, partly as a consequence, already prefer to believe what Hobbes purports to show.

Second, there are those who agree with the premise, but on some other basis or authority. For example, divinely revealed truth: that *God* has created all men equal, and endowed them with equal rights to life, liberty, and the pursuit of happiness. Both of these classes of people would be inclined to interpret Hobbes's equivocating conclusion as merely a rhetorical concession, dictated by the need to secure the agreement of foolish, self-important people who retain, as he so well expressed it, 'a vain conceit of ones owne wisdome,' and/or of people who are obtuse with respect to God's revealed truth.

Third, there are those who do indeed find 'such equality incredible,' and furthermore are sure that Hobbes does not believe it either. Moreover, that this is ironically confirmed by his very arguments supposedly showing it, which he shrewdly judged would persuade mediocre, superficial minds wishing to believe they are equal to the best, but which he could not possibly have supposed would convince anyone really intelligent and thoughtful. Thus, while his strangely ambivalent conclusion actually lets the cat out of the bag, it does so in such a way as will be easily dismissed by most readers, if it does not escape their notice entirely. Whereas, the minority who do recognize the implications of Hobbes's failure to ratify unconditionally the view of men's natures he had ostensibly argued for, should also be smart enough to see the advantages, both public and personal, of the polity being founded on this false premise, and so agree to subscribe to it. For they should see that, by offering everyone full citizenship on the same terms – equality before the law (thus equal justice; equal rights legally guaranteed; equal liberty, mainly in the silence of the law; equal civic 'respect') – one will most readily secure the loyalty and civil obedience of the many ordinary, naturally inferior men, who will view the arrangement as providing them an enhanced, if not strictly equal, prospect for a contented life. Whereas, those who are in fact naturally *superior* (stronger, healthier, smarter, bolder, more ambitious, more energetic, more imaginative and creative) stand to prosper 'disproportionately' in a regime institutionally structured *as if* everyone were naturally equal in mental and physical attributes – as if, that is, people's natures were more or less homogeneous. But as in milk that is *not* in fact homogenized, the cream will rise to the top. Moreover, anyone who cannot see that a regime premised on natural equality is advantageous for almost everybody, but especially advantageous for those who are naturally superior, is *not* by nature all that superior. So, whatever the particular height to which a naturally gifted person aspires – whether in commerce or industry, arts or letters, science or scholarship, civil or military office – it would be in his, or her, best interest to endorse the regime's premise of natural human equality.

Still, whether they realize it or not (though the best of them would), those of this third class, are not the crème de la crème. A minuscule class of men, epitomized by Hobbes himself, aware not merely of the great natural inequalities mankind manifests, but of the virtual chasm that separates minds and spirits such as theirs from those of the vast majority – minds and spirits capable, for example, of designing a *just* political architecture that can accommodate this vast diversity – have their own reasons for accepting a regime seemingly founded on the presumption that all humans are by nature equal.[6]

A useful lie – or so the egalitarian premise of Hobbes's *Leviathan* would be regarded by a Guardian of Plato's *Politeia*, being himself licensed to resort to lies 'for the benefit of the *polis*' (389b). The possibility that establishing and maintaining decent political life requires the judicious use of salutary lies and myths arises early in that dialogue. The interlocutors, having set about designing a City in *logos* in which to discern Justice writ large, soon become preoccupied with the key to its successful functioning: the education of its Rulers. As Sokrates tells it, the foundation of this education is a correct – that is, a politically salutary – understanding of gods and heroes (377e). If lies must be told about such things, they should at least be 'noble' (or, 'fine,' 'fair', 'beautiful'; *kalos*) lies. For although everyone in their City – including its Rulers – is nurtured to be a truth-teller (389b–c), the fact remains that lies can be politically useful, even necessary, hence justifiable: to deceive enemies, for example; or when dealing with those we call friends, when from madness or folly they are determined to do something bad; also, in telling tales (*mythologia*) about the origins of things, origins people may invest with much significance, but about which the truth, or the whole truth, is not, or best not, known (382c–d; cf. R&C/8, 392). But the right of resorting to lies when needed is reserved to the Rulers (cf. 459c).

The latter use, though perhaps also the second use, is illustrated in one of the most famous – or infamous – parts of Sokrates's narration, that of the so-called Well-bred (or 'Noble'; *gennaion*) Lie. It is intended as a persuasive ratification of the basic structure of the City that he and his young helpers have designed. And (ideally) it would be believed, or at least accepted, by all the citizens of the City. Of its two main parts, only the first is an outright 'lie' (*pseudos*). For it would have the first generation of citizens regard their actual historical origin as a dream, and to believe instead that they sprang directly from their land, fully grown and fully equipped.[7] Glaukon is rightly sceptical that there would be any way to convince the first generation of this, but concedes that subsequent generations might just be persuaded to accept this about their remote ancestors (414d); after all, people have believed stranger things. The second part Sokrates calls a 'myth' (*mythos*; 415a), and he had earlier in the discussion characterized 'myths' as tales that are false as a whole but which nonetheless contain truths (377a). This second part, the so-called Myth of the Metals, justifies the class hierarchy of the city – an arrangement that institutionalizes what is *true*: the natural *inequalities* among men – by invoking a divine sanction, such that those who are by nature suited to rule are said to have been fashioned by God with gold in their souls, and their martial auxiliaries with silver, whereas the souls of the wage-earning, producing class – the farmers and craftsmen (everyone from cobblers to neurosurgeons) – are infused with iron or bronze. All men are akin, as are all metals, sharing many formal characteristics; but so too does each class or kind have its distinctive characteristics, including that of it relative prevalence (415a–c).

Hobbes has reversed this arrangement. The *origin* of his Commonwealth in a Covenant among a sufficient multitude of men, heretofore denizens of the State of Nature, is a 'myth' in the Platonic sense – for it is false taken as a whole, but it nonetheless is meant to convey some essential truths about the nature of a political association properly conceived. However we happen to find ourselves in a polity that is maintaining law and order, we would be right to think of it 'as if' it were the result of a Social Contract obliging us all to each other to support the government and obey its laws:

[I]t is a reall Unitie of them all, in one and the same Person, made by Covenant of every man with every man, in such manner, as if every man should say to every man, *I Authorize and give up my Right of Governing my selfe, to this Man, or to this Assembly of men, on this condition, that thou give up thy Right to him, and Authorize all his Actions in like manner*. This done, the Multitude, so united in one Person, is called a COMMON-WEALTH, in latine CIVITAS. This is the Generation of that great LEVIATHAN, or rather (to speake more reverently) of that *Mortall God*. (XVII/13, 87)

To repeat, this origin of a commonwealth is mythical: it is an 'as if' account.

Its legal and institutional arrangement, however, is pervaded by an outright lie, albeit a supremely useful lie: that all men are roughly equal in faculties of body and mind, *Nature* having made them so. And for those who care to do so, they may regard 'Nature' (according to the first line of the book) as nothing more nor less than 'the Art whereby God hath made and governes the World.'

Despite his employing that fallacious premise, I earlier praised Hobbes for having designed a *just* political architecture. This is a most difficult and accordingly rare accomplishment precisely because humans are *not* substantially equal in mental and bodily strengths and weaknesses. The political problem would be much simpler if they were. As it is, an altogether acceptable regime must accommodate this manifold diversity in men's natures, for reasons of both justice and expedience. And, as I argued in chapter 15, Hobbes knows full well that synoptic judgments about the justness of regimes as a whole are not only inevitable, but entirely appropriate. Presuming, then, that he believes his own political architecture (in either its universal form, or its optimal form, or both) meets the test of true justice – though he never explicitly says as much – to what idea of justice does he look?

   In defending the Legal Positivist view, which he contends all citizen-subjects *within* a given regime should adopt, Hobbes ignores this 'external' or 'transcendent' issue concerning the justness of his (or any) regime as a whole, confining attention to 'The Foole' who would dispute the view's 'internal' adequacy. For the purpose of assessing this defence of Justice as defined by Enforced Law, it is useful to have in mind the problem as Glaukon and Adeimantos pose it to Sokrates in Plato's *Republic* (358b–367e). Together these two 'sons of Best [*Ariston*]' mount the most powerful assault on Justice in the history of political thought, for it is raised against the background of the only question that, practically speaking, really matters: Why Be Just?

The challenge of Plato's brothers is pertinent to any account of political justice – indeed, provides the perfect *test* for the adequacy of any putative Theory of Justice – and deserves to be thoroughly understood for that reason alone. But it has a special pertinence to the 'social contract' view, since that is the very conception the brothers expressly set about dissecting. It is a two-pronged attack, initiated by Glaukon, who – appealing directly to Nature – makes the positive case for the superiority of the unjust life over the just life; and is seconded by Adeimantos, who – having analysed what is commonly said in praise of behaving justly – demolishes the standard case in favour of justice. The first brother glorifies crime; the second brother raises serious doubts about the certainty, hence the efficacy, of punishment. Both claim to be speaking only as the Devil's Advocates in order to elicit from Sokrates his strongest defence of Justice. But as he observes upon their concluding, they must have been touched by something divine if they are not in fact persuaded by the case they articulate so powerfully (368a).

Glaukon's portion has three distinct parts. First, he gives his analysis of what so-called 'justice' actually *is*, and how it originates. Second, he proposes a mental experiment which he claims proves that no one not mentally defective is *willingly* just, which would clearly imply that *being* just (rather than merely appearing just) is *not* something intrinsically good. Third, he compares the likely fate of the truly Just Man with that of the successful Unjust Man.

Glaukon thinks of himself as the Natural Man, for whom injustice – not justice – comes naturally, since 'having more' is 'what any nature naturally pursues as good.' In this sense, the restraints imposed by a polity in the name of justice are profoundly unnatural. In another sense, however, this artificiality called 'justice' is natural in that it is naturally attractive to the many weaker individuals who, each lacking sufficient natural power to get more for himself, are content to settle for equal shares. Thus, banding together through the artifice of an agreement (or compact; *xunthesia*) to regulate by law the natural competition for life's good things, the many individually weaker men become collectively strong enough to lord it over the naturally stronger few. But these latter, recognizing that the whole artificial arrangement, though supposedly fair for everyone – which would be plausible if everyone were roughly equal in natural strengths and weaknesses – is primarily aimed at constraining *them*, the naturally *best* men, by denominating as 'criminal' any person's effort to get and have much more than anyone else. Seen for what it is, the naturally strong man need not feel *morally* bound by any covenant so obviously prejudicial to his own best interests; he is free to treat its provisions, the laws, as so many obstacles to be circumvented, and/or opportunities to be exploited. With the clearest conscience in the world, he can merely *appear* to abide by the conventions of political life, while selectively departing from them whenever he can profitably do so undetected. After all, the motivation of the many mediocre men in their erecting and abiding by their edifice of rules is entirely self-interested; they have no claim to moral superiority by virtue of their 'justness,' which is nothing but a self-flattering disguise for their natural inferiority.

For this is the one respect in which all men *are* equal: they are all equally self-interested, ruled by their selfish desires to have more for themselves, and 'obliged' to settle for whatever they can get by the balance among their comparative powers. Viewed in that light, no one is willingly just merely for the sake of being so, but rather out of a lack of sufficient power to commit injustice and get away with it. This is easily seen by imagining how *anyone* would behave were he provided a magic ring whereby he could become invisible whenever he found it advantageous to do so (such as, according to legend, was found by Gyges). He could steal without fear of apprehension, and thus become rich; evade various social conventions that restrict sexual gratification; assist others in escaping the trammels of 'justice,' if he saw some profit in doing so; and kill whomever he pleased. Indeed, presuming sufficient intelligence and courage, he could even usurp a throne and become a Tyrant whom people mistook for a glorious King. But in any case, given such a flexible power as selective invisibility, only a wretched fool would decline to use it to his own advantage (360d). And the behaviour of a fool hardly recommends the rationality of being just.

Now, setting magic rings aside, compare how just and unjust men actually fare in the real world. However, to judge the matter fairly as it pertains to the naturally superior individual (strong of both body and soul, hence proud, intelligent, courageous, ambitious) – the kind of man who can be politically troublesome, as Hobbes would be the first to insist – one must imagine each type of man to be wholly successful according to his own lights. With respect to the Unjust man, this means crime on a big scale; the superior man has nothing but contempt for pimps and pickpockets (cf. 344a–b). A clever criminal operates like a skilled artisan in that he does not overreach himself in attempting the impossible; moreover, should he make a mistake, he knows how to correct it and minimize the damage, especially to his reputation. A manly show of power will overcome whatever difficulties cannot be finessed with rhetoric and sophistry. For this is the ultimate of successful injustice: enjoying the fruits of crime while nonetheless preserving the *appearance* of being the perfectly Just Man, thereby gaining as well whatever benefits the reputation for justness brings. Such a person – wealthy, respected, politically well connected – can count on having many friends should he happen to get in a scrape. By contrast, the strictly law-abiding, hence *truly* Just Man not only forgoes all the advantages, both big and small, of selective injustice, he typically penalizes himself by his 'excessive' fairness. He pays more taxes than necessary, performs more onerous public duties (often to the neglect of his personal affairs), and refuses to favour friends and family. Moreover, this scrupulousness in matters both public and private, his unwillingness to cut corners and bend the rules, alienates many people, earning him only rancour and resentment (however much he may be praised to his face). In short, confronting the question of which way of life is best: that which sincerely honours Justice as defined by the Rule of Law *versus* that which treats such bodies of conventions for the unnatural partisan arrangements they truly are, a man of superior abilities has no difficulty in choosing.

As if Glaukon's indictment of conventional justice were not enough to carry the day, Adeimantos insists that his brother has left unsaid the most important considerations. He may be right, for his contribution both raises the accusation to the 'cosmic' level, and undermines the very possibility of anyone's rationally demonstrating the preferability of living justly. His most important points are these:

First of all, if one carefully analyses what is said by those who praise the Just Life, one sees that they do not praise being just as beneficial in and of itself, but only for its consequences. Indeed, they concede that the practice of justice, like that of moderation, is itself difficult, a kind of drudgery, whereas yielding to the temptations of injustice and intemperance can be pleasant and easy. Moreover, all the personal and political benefits the praisers promise actually come, not from the *reality* of being just, but exclusively from the *appearance* of being so. Similarly do the penalties and punishments for injustice, at least insofar as these depend on the perceptions and judgments of one's fellows. Therefore, if a man has whatever it takes to maintain a *reputation* for justness despite being selectively, surreptitiously unjust in his various dealings, he stands the best prospect of enjoying to the full whatever good things this life has to offer.

Ah, but what about the gods, or God? Divine Judgment is typically the last refuge of those who would defend the superiority of the Just Life. For presumably God is not taken in by mere appearances, for He (in Hobbes's words) 'knoweth the heart' (XLII/80, 300). On this basis, it is sometimes claimed that God rewards justice and punishes injustice here in this earthly life – that just people generally fare better than do the unjust. But confronted with the evidence that (as Hobbes more than once observes) '*Evill men often Prosper, and Good men suffer Adversity*' (XXXI/6, 188; cf. XXXIII/12, 202), the apologists for Justice allege Divinely distributed rewards and punishments in some existence *after* death. Notice, in this case, too, being just is not praised as good in itself, but only for its consequences. Of course, this whole fabric of belief presumes Divine omniscience, and a Divine interest in human affairs, and a

Divine endorsement of the invariably partisan arrangements that men call justice. Logically prior to these presumptions, however, is that of the very existence of a Divinity. But perhaps there are no gods; or if one or more do exist, perhaps he or they have no interest in human affairs – in either of which cases, one need not worry about Divine Judgment. On the other hand, if a god does exist who cares about what we do, we 'know' it only on the basis of the testimony of (supposedly) inspired men, so-called prophets. And these same authorities assure us that God can be propitiated by prayers and sacrifices. If this is so – and rational consistency requires that one believe both claims or neither – then the shrewdest course would be to resort to injustice whenever favourable opportunities arise, and later do whatever is necessary to secure Divine forgiveness. One can reasonably expect forgiveness from a *just* god, who would necessarily be aware of all the considerations that render the just life problematic and so would sympathize with an intelligent, ambitious, bold, 'conscientious' practitioner of injustice.

As for most of those praisers who actually practice justice themselves, they do so not willingly, but from a lack of courage or other weakness; and they blame injustice because they lack the power to engage in it successfully. They do not believe what they preach, as is readily seen whenever one of their kind somehow comes to some power: he immediately exploits it as much as he can (cf. XII/26, 58). And the reason is, nobody believes that the practice of justice is intrinsically beneficial to the practitioner, nor injustice intrinsically harmful. All praise and blame is in terms of consequences, and insofar as those consequences pertain to *this* world, they are determined by external appearances, not internal reality. So, unless someone can show that actually *being* just has beneficial *internal* consequences, that having a just soul makes one stronger and happier (say); and, correspondingly, that being unjust internally is harmful – quite regardless of whether noticed and approved by either gods or humans – no rational person concerned to get the most out of life will practise justice any more than necessary.

But it is Adeimantos's final twist to the challenge that so radicalizes the problem. He has witnessed and analysed enough arguments to have cultivated a healthy suspicion of argument. As often as not, the only 'truth' revealed in those dialogical contests called 'arguments' is who is the best arguer. Thus, he requires that the supposed superiority of justice be proven *not only in rational argument* [logos], but that it be somehow shown or otherwise demonstrated what each thing, justice and injustice, truly *is* and what it *does* to or for the man in whom it dwells.[8]

Suppose Hobbes to be confronting this challenge, how adequate is the response he addresses to 'The Foole [that] hath sayd in his heart, there is no such thing as Justice; and sometimes also with his tongue' (XV/4, 72)? The brothers would readily agree that anyone who openly *expressed* such a view was a fool indeed, as the first principle of successfully practising injustice is: always appear to be a fervent partisan of justice. But how would they regard Hobbes's explicit account of *natural* justice, upon which rests all conventional justice (all bodies of positive law defining in practical terms what is permitted, what required, and what forbidden): 'So that the nature of Justice, consisteth in keeping of valid Covenants: but the Validity of Covenants begins not but with the Constitution of a Civill Power, sufficient to compel men to keep them: And then it is also that Propriety begins' (XV/3, 72)? Given this admission that *external enforcement* is the material point, would they not merely nod and smile, saying to themselves, 'suspicions confirmed'?

For even if one were to agree completely that a stable, orderly, decent political environment requires the general acceptance of the rationale embodied in Hobbes's so-called Natural Laws; and that for all practical purposes, justice is defined by a set of policed and enforced conventions called 'Civill Laws'; and that the entire citizenry ought to be nurtured and otherwise encouraged to obey, willingly and scrupulously, all such laws, but especially those respecting the persons and property of their fellows – even if one agrees with all this and more of like kind, one need not be persuaded that living the best life available requires actually *being* just, rather than merely *appearing* so. For other than generating the appearance, the 'reality' provides no advantage not to be had from mere appearance however generated – at least so far as one can judge from Hobbes's explicit account. And given only that for a basis, the fact would remain: selectively resorting to unjust practices can be quite profitable, provided one has a ready eye for worthy opportunities, the energy and boldness to make the effort, and the intelligence and composure required to succeed without one's just appearance being compromised.[9]

Most people, not having such qualities, find it generally expedient to stick to the easier and safer course of abiding by the letter, if not always the spirit, of the Law (cf. XV/10–11, 74). They are easily governed. And as noted, if *everyone* were like them, equal enough in faculties of body and mind and spirit, the political problem would be much simpler. But they are not, so it is not. There will always be those, a significant few, who *do* have the requisite qualities for successfully combining crime with apparent civil obedience. They are *not* so easily governed. Apart from the injustice of their flourishing, they present a subtle, more insidious danger than does the presence of known criminals. And in any event, their line of reasoning occurs to many more people than have the qualities requisite for successfully acting upon it.

What response does Hobbes offer to those who think thus – who in effect treat Justice as hardly more than an honorific word? The preface he chose to frame his response leads one to suspect he has the challenge of Glaukon and Adeimantos particularly in mind:

The Foole hath sayd in his heart, there is no such thing as Justice; and sometimes also with his tongue; seriously alleaging, that every mans conservation, and contentment, being committed to his own care, there could be no reason, why every man might not do what he thought conduced thereunto: and therefore also to make, or not make; keep, or not keep Covenants, was not against Reason, when it conduced to ones benefit. He does not therein deny, that there be Covenants; and that they are sometimes broken, sometimes kept; and that such breach of them may be called Injustice, and the observance of them Justice: but he questioneth, whether Injustice, taking away the feare of God, (for the same Foole hath said in his heart there is no God,) may not sometimes stand with that Reason, which dictateth to every man his own good; and particularly then, when it conduceth to such a benefit, as shall put a man in a condition, to neglect not onely the dispraise, and revilings, but also the power of other men. The Kingdome of God is gotten by violence [i.e., in Matthew 11:12]: but what if it could be gotten by unjust violence? were it against Reason so to get it, when it is impossible to receive hurt by it? and if it be not against Reason, it is not against Justice: or else Justice is not to be approved for good. From such reasoning as this, Successfull wickednesse hath obtained the name of Vertue: and some that in all other things have disallowed the violation of Faith; yet have allowed it, when it is for the getting of a Kingdome. And the Heathen that believed, that *Saturn* was deposed by his son *Jupiter*, believed neverthelesse the same *Jupiter* to be the avenger of Injustice:[10] … From which instances a man will be very prone to inferre; that when the Heire apparent of a Kingdome, shall kill him that is in possession, though his father; you may call it Injustice, or by what other name you will; yet it can never be against Reason, seeing all voluntary actions of men tend to the benefit of themselves; and those actions are most Reasonable, that conduce most to their ends.

Does this not read as if Hobbes were summarizing the gist of the brothers' challenge, including the 'unjust' seizure of Sovereign Power (such as

Gyges effected, according to Glaukon)? To this, Hobbes responds in continuing:

This specious reasoning is neverthelesse false.

For the question is not of promises mutuall, where there is no security of performance on either side; as when there is no Civill Power erected over the parties promising; But ... where there is a Power to make [them] performe; there is the question whether it be against reason, that is, against the benefit of [either] to performe, or not. And I say it is not against reason ... where every one expects the same defence by the Confederation, that any one else does: and therefore he which declares he thinks it reason to deceive those that help him, can in reason expect no other means of safety, than what can be had from his own single Power. He therefore that breaketh his Covenant, and consequently declareth that he thinks he may with reason do so, cannot be received into any Society, that unite themselves for Peace and Defence, but by the errour of them that receive him; nor when he is received, be retayned in it, without seeing the danger of their errour; which errours a man cannot reasonably reckon upon as the means of his security: and therefore if he be left, or cast out of Society, he perisheth; and if he live in Society, it is by the errours of other men, which he could not foresee, nor reckon upon ... as all men that contibute not to his destruction, forbear him only out of ignorance of what is good for themselves. (XV/4–5, 72–3)

Is it conceivable that Hobbes could believe this to be an adequate response to the Glaukons and Adeimantuses of this world (to say nothing of the Caesars and Alexanders)? It amounts to little more than an insistence that 'Crime Does Not Pay *because* You Won't get Away With It (... Probably).' As such, it obviously begs the question, since the prospects of bold, intelligent, and otherwise *strong* men – natural winners – 'getting away with it' is precisely what is at issue (not the containment of natural losers). A thoughtful reader can only wonder about so weak a rebuttal of so powerful a challenge – as it is even in the attenuated version Hobbes supplies. Later, he returns to this same supposed 'defect in Reasoning'; but far from allaying one's doubts, he deepens them. Addressing the question of why 'men are prone to violate the Lawes':

First, by Presumption of false Principles: as when men from having observed how in all places, and in all ages, unjust Actions have been authorized, by the force, and victories of those who have committed them; and that potent men, breaking through the Cob-web Lawes of their Country,[11] the weaker sort, and those that have failed in their Enterprises, have been esteemed the onely Criminals; have thereupon taken for Principles, and grounds of their Reasoning, *That Justice is but a vain word: That whatsoever a man can get by his own Industry, and hazard, is his own: That the Practice of all Nations cannot be unjust: That Examples of former times are good Arguments of doing the like again*; and many more of that kind. Which being granted, no Act in it selfe can be a Crime, but must be made so (not by the Law, but) by the successe of them that commit it; and the same Fact be vertuous, or vicious, as Fortune pleaseth; so that what *Marius* makes a Crime, *Sylla* shall make meritorious, and *Caesar* (the same Lawes standing) turn again into a Crime, to the perpetuall disturbance of the Peace of the Common-wealth. (XXVII/10, 153)

If the ultimate *groundlessness* of so-called Justice based solely on the Law had never before occurred to a reflective reader – its amounting to nothing more than the capricious will of whoever at any given time is 'potent' enough to impose it; and that 'the Just' are merely the Winners in the struggle for Power, who then denounce as 'Unjust' and 'Criminals' the weaker challengers who have failed[12] – this passage ought to disabuse him of his innocence. Justice is indeed 'but a vain word' if it bespeaks nothing more substantial, or morally authoritative, than the current Will of the current Sovereign, as Hobbes seems several times to argue (e.g., 'For having power to make, and repeale Lawes, he may when he pleaseth, free himselfe from that subjection, by repealing those Lawes that trouble him, and making of new'; XXVI/6, 137–8; cf. /37, 148; XVIII/10, 91; XXIV/5, 128), such that what is meritorious today may as easily be criminal tomorrow. In which case, all that really matters – on the part of *both* Rulers and Ruled – is *power*: whether it be the power to impose one's will so far as one can, or the power to get away with whatever one can.[13] This alone cannot provide the basis for a peaceful, orderly, *stable* civil society.

Nor does Hobbes believe that it can. There must be more to the moral authority of the Law than merely its being the Law – that is, the enforced will of the Sovereign – if it is to command respect as *Justice* in any meaningful sense. So, while it would be best if everyone who is subject to the Law were encouraged to regard it as providing the very definition of Justice, the Law must itself manifest substantive principals of *natural* justice, beginning with a kind of *equality* ('that Justice be equally administered to all degrees of People,' be they 'rich, and mighty' or 'poor and obscure'; 'For in this consisteth Equity; to which, as being a Precept of the Law of Nature, a Soveraign is as much subject, as any of the meanest of his People'; XXX/15, 180). This does not preclude there being legally established distinctions among classes of people (e.g., between adults and minors, between authorized practitioners and laymen, between public officials and private persons, even between a Nobility and a Commons; cf. X/11, 41; /35, 43; XVIII/15, 92). But everyone is equally obliged to respect and obey the Law as it pertains to him, or her. Hobbes expands upon this matter in his 'Advice to the Prince':

> The Inequality of Subjects, proceedeth from the Acts of Soveraign Power; and therefore has no more place in the presence of the Soveraign; that is to say, in a Court of Justice, then the Inequality between Kings, and their Subjects, in the presence of the King of Kings. The honour of great Persons, is to be valued for their beneficence, and the aydes they give to men of inferiour rank, or not at all. And the violences, oppressions, and injuries they do, are not extenuated, but aggravated by the greatnesse of their persons; because they have least need to commit them. The consequences of this partiality towards the great, proceed in this manner. Impunity maketh Insolence; Insolence Hatred; and Hatred, an Endeavour to pull down all oppressing and contumelious greatnesse, though with the ruine of the Common-wealth. (XXX/16, 180)

In short, murder is murder, theft is theft, fraud is fraud, rape is rape, regardless of the status of either the victim or the perpetrator.

But while Natural Justice might be said to begin with the cliché, 'No one is above the Law,' it surely does not *end* there. Fortunately so, for were there no more to be cited in its favour than the social convenience and utility of law and order, no beneficial consequences beyond those wholly dependent upon external appearances, then Justice could not command the whole-hearted allegiance of any sensible person, much less of the naturally strongest, most talented men. Yet these are the very men – energetic, intelligent, clear-sighted, resolute – that Hobbes, or for that matter any sensible person, would *prefer* occupied the positions of power. Provided, that is, they ruled (legislated, commanded, administered, judged) with due regard for Hobbes's broader conception of '*the safety of the people*' (meaning 'not ... a bare Preservation, but also all other Contentments of life, which every man by lawfull Industry ... shall acquire to himselfe'; XXX/1, 175). If the Laws are to be framed to comport with this or whatever else is *naturally* Just, then whoever establishes them needs know what this *is*, and *why* it is Just: its *ground* in Nature. For the first lesson taught in Plato's *Republic* is that all general rules, hence all laws, admit of exceptions (331c–d). Thus, there must be something 'behind' a given rule by light of which one can determine the justness of both the rule, and occasional exceptions to it (and this cannot be another rule, to which one can always imagine legitimate exceptions, ad infinitum).

Beyond this, however, those who would govern a commonwealth in the optimal manner Hobbes indicates must *want* it to be Just; hence, they must want to be Just themselves. As such, they must have themselves met the challenge of Glaukon and Adeimantos, must have sought and found the true ground of Justice, and thus seen why *being* well and truly Just is inherently *good*. They will not have found this validating ground in Hobbes's *Leviathan*, however, except insofar as it points beyond itself to Plato's *Republic*. For it is therein that the touchstone of natural justice is shown to be the naturally best order of the human soul – specifically, the order whereby a person's soul is at its healthiest, strongest, and most beautiful – and that the ways of thinking and acting whereby such a psychic regime is instilled constitute the Just Life.[14]

Strange though it may seem, it is on the basis of this same foundational text that one may defend the overall justness of Hobbes's political prescription – and not *despite* its being based on a manifestly false principle, but precisely *because* of it. For put into motion, a polity premised on all men being roughly equal in natural powers of body and soul will function and configure itself very differently if that premise is factually false than if it were true. Given a citizenry that is not at all homogeneous with respect to natural inclinations and abilities, especially regarding various kinds of learning – as is invariably the case with any sizeable body of people – those with a more focused ambition, with greater natural and acquired abilities, will generally be the ones who rise to eminence in whatever field of endeavour they choose to pursue. Unless, that is, there are artificial obstacles to this natural outcome – all of which are, so far as possible, eliminated in Hobbes's design.

However, in a regime offering not only Equality before the Law, but a general equality of opportunity for all lawful talents to emerge – recognizing, for example, that 'he is Worthiest to be a Commander, to be a Judge, or to have any other charge, that is best fitted, with the qualities required to the well discharging of it' (X/54, 46–7); and that 'Good Counsell comes not by Lot, nor by Inheritance; and therefore there is no more reason to expect good Advice from the rich, or noble, in matter of State, than in delineating the dimensions of a fortresse' (XXX/25, 184); and that 'the use of Lawes ... is not to bind the People from all Voluntary actions; but to direct and keep them in such a motion, as not to hurt themselves by their own impetuous desires, rashnesse, or indiscretion; as Hedges are set, not to stop Travellers, but to keep them in the way. And therefore a Law that is not Needfull ... is not Good' (XXX/21, 182), since for the most part 'Lyberties ... depend on the Silence of the Law' (XXI/18, 113) – in a polity structured with these principles in view, people will generally pursue vocations which attract them, and succeed according to their talents. As to *why* a given person is attracted to this rather than that profession, the appeal of whatever kind and amount of remuneration it offers is apt to be a dominant factor. Typically, this would be some mix of money and status (or honour), with most people – but by no means all – caring more for the former than the latter. However, people also derive some satisfaction simply from 'a job well done'; this generally implies a task for which they have some natural ability that they enjoy exercising. Inherent satisfaction is an especially important factor for callings having to do with the pursuit and dissemination of knowledge.

Given people with varying abilities pursuing useful work of varying difficulty and 'value, or worth' ('a thing dependant on the need and judgement of another' – for 'as in other things, so in men, not the seller, but the buyer determines the Price'; X/16, 42), the result will be a civil society that manifests significant disparities of wealth and status, influence and power. That is to say, a society very different from what one would expect were it true that everyone is roughly equal 'in the faculties of body, and mind,' the ostensible premise of a Hobbesian commonwealth, licensing its equality of rights and obligations. Why, then, should the regime as it would actually work in practice be regarded as *Just*? The Legal Positivist's conception of justice-as-legality, something relative and internal to each particular regime, is irrelevant since it precludes judging the justness of the laws themselves, or of any regime as a whole. By what idea of Political Justice, then, *can* such a determination be made, and where is its validation to be found?

Ironically, in what most readers would suppose the least likely of places: Plato's *Republic*. For the distribution of tasks and rewards as would 'automatically' result in a Hobbesian commonwealth is an approximation of their intentional distribution in Sokrates's City in *logos* – indeed, it aims at the closest approximation that is practically feasible in polities of the size characteristic of modernity.

The regime of Plato's dialogical City is explicitly based on matching human inequalities to the diversity of kinds of tasks and roles necessary for the existence of a polity, or most advantageous to its flourishing. This is implicitly established in Sokrates's arguing for the utility of a rational division of labour, based on three considerations: 'first, each of us is naturally not quite like anyone else, but instead differs in his nature, one from another [with respect to] doing a job'; second, anyone would do finer work practising one art [*techně*] rather than many; third, a person must be free of other responsibilities to do his allotted work when it needs doing (agrarian pursuits providing the paradigm cases, but the principle is to some degree applicable to almost all occupations, from plumbing to medicine). By implementing this rationale, everything becomes more plentiful, is of finer quality, and more easily produced (370a–c). And though Sokrates does not mention it here, there is a fourth consideration: people are generally happier doing only the kinds of work for which they are naturally best suited, often indicated by the readiness with which they learn how to do it (cf. 455b–c, 536e).

But what is equally, if not more, important than differences in natural aptitudes are differences in people's primary motivations for pursuing whatever they pursue – that is, what they most desire to *gain* from the work they choose, or are required, to do – for it is differences in the intensity and kinds of people's dominant desires, or 'loves,' that provide the basis for their being *ranked* according to a hierarchy of natural classes. Most people, regarding pleasure to be the Good, are generally motivated to pursue wealth, money being the means whereby the desires for various pleasures are most readily indulged. One may further discriminate within this lowest class, however, between those who are mainly lovers of the pleasures of the body (i.e., food, drink, sex, and sleep), and a smaller but better part who expend as much or more on pleasures of the soul (cf. 475d–e). A higher and smaller class of men are those who are primarily motivated by desires rooted in the spirit, hence are lovers of victory (success in especially challenging enterprises) and lovers of honour (distinction, fame, glory). Highest and smallest of all is the class of those who love, hence pursue human excellence (virtue) for its own sake, especially Wisdom (i.e., such knowledge, or 'science,' as is deserving of that name).

The political structure of the City in *logos* – specifically, its class hierarchy – is based on these differences and inequalities in people's natural aptitudes and motivations. Its Producing class of farmers and artisans is made up of those who are primarily lovers of money; its Martial class, the so-called Auxiliaries who police and defend the City, are selected from among those spirit-driven men who love victory and honour; and in the first version of the City, its Rulers, Guardians of the City's regime (*politeia*), are patriotic elders selected from among the warriors for their proven virtue. In the second and higher (but paradoxical) version, the Rulers are philosophical Kings. As I noted before, the hierarchical relationships of the classes are ratified by that 'Well-bred Lie' in which those who are naturally suited to be Rulers are said to have mixed in their souls that most rare and precious of metals, *gold* (making them the 'most honoured'); whereas their Auxiliaries are to be thought of as *silver*-souled; and the Producers are characterized by souls with admixtures of a far more common but useful metal, *iron* or *bronze*. What is essential to the City's justness, however, is that the whole class system be radically 'open,' not hereditary. Sokrates is emphatic about this provision, insisting that the Guardians' foremost responsibility is that of ensuring that each child end up in the proper class as determined by its psychic metal, irrespective of its parentage or any other considerations (415b–c; cf. 412e–414a, 536e–537a).

Never in the course of constructing this City in *logos* is any feature introduced for the reason that it is *just*; in every case, it is adopted in response to some perceived need or advantage. Only when the City is judged to be essentially complete, and on the assumption that it is 'perfectly [or, 'completely'; *teleös*] good' (427e), do the philosopher and his young auxiliaries attempt to discern in their handiwork what makes it *Just*. They have some notion of what they are looking for, since purely formal definitions of both political justice and injustice emerged in the philosopher's earlier discussion with the sophist Thrasymachus: Justice is whatever produces unanimity and friendship among partners in a common enterprise, be it a city, an army, or even bands of thieves and pirates; whereas, Injustice is whatever produces factions, hatreds, and quarrels (351c–d). Presumably with that in mind, they conclude – albeit only provisionally since the same *form* of Justice must fit a single person, as well as account for the partial justness of ordinary views – that *political* justice is a matter of everyone in the city minding his own proper business, thus doing his own work *as best he can*, and not meddling in the business of others. For on that principle, everything that needs doing for a polity to flourish gets done in the finest manner (433b). Needless to add, the entire arrangement presumes that each able person perform some socially useful task – that 'he who can but does not work shall not eat' (cf. 406c–e; 371c–d; *Leviathan* XXX/18–19, 181; XXIV/10, 130–1). The essential thing with respect to political justice is that each person end up in his correct natural *class* as determined by his primary motivation – not necessarily that he be practising the very vocation for which he is optimally suited. As Sokrates observes, whether someone naturally best fitted to be a carpenter ends up a cobbler instead (or vice versa) is of little political consequence (434a) – and certainly not grounds for impugning the City's justness.

Moreover, by functioning in this Just manner, the city will be Courageous in its being stoutly defended; it will be Prudent because those best suited by nature and nurture are its rulers; and it will be Moderate by virtue of a practical unanimity amongst all the classes concerning this very thing: who ought to rule, including whose 'taste' ought to rule over the entire diversity of 'desires, pleasures, and pains' found in any heterogeneous collection of people composing a normal political community (431b-e). Bearing in mind that quarrels over who ought to rule (that is, what criteria entitle one to claim a right to rule, and thus make the laws) are the principal threat to political harmony, this agreement among virtually all citizens – even if merely passive on the part of most – is of primary importance for the maintaining of domestic peace. With respect to the justness of this distribution of political power, one might here invoke Hobbes's ironic evidence for 'the equall distribution of any thing': 'that every man is contented with his share.'

Given this idea of Political Justice, the case for the justness of a Hobbesian commonwealth as it would work in practice is not difficult to make. Indeed, it is obvious in light of the preceding discussion of the Idea of Justice which *informs* – literally – Sokrates's City in *logos*. For as I suggested earlier, the distribution of tasks among the citizenry and the currency in which each is paid (the particular mix of status, money, and personal satisfaction) that would automatically result in Hobbes's Commonwealth, approximates their purposeful distribution in Sokrates's City. This, of course, is the fundamental difference in the two regimes. What Sokrates explicitly made the paramount responsibility of the Rulers in his City: assignment of each individual citizen to the particular kind of socially useful work for which he is best suited by nature, devolves instead onto each individual in a Hobbesian commonwealth – a regime that, so far as practical, offers everyone an equal opportunity to pursue whatever lawful vocation he finds naturally attractive for whatever reason. But precisely because everyone else has that same opportunity, each aspirant must compete for success in his chosen field – must 'do his best' in an effort to succeed, with the result that those who naturally *prove* best for the chosen task tend to enjoy the most success, and polity as a whole is best served in all that needs doing.

To the extent this *is* the result, a just distribution of responsibilities and benefits – effected by wise Rulers in the City in *logos* – is brought about by the very structure of a political environment designed with that same just end in view. For that matter, one may be sceptical as to the practicality of any rulers being wise enough to so surely ascertain the natures of children as to predict with tolerable accuracy their mature talents and inclinations. They certainly could not do so for a polity of a scale beyond that wherein each individual could be personally known and assessed. Whereas, the regime Hobbes has conceived aims at the closest approximation of Platonic Justice that is feasible in polities of the size typical of modernity. And the fact that each person is himself accountable for his place therein has certain advantages: any resulting dissatisfaction cannot be credibly blamed on the Sovereign; the freedom of each individual to choose for himself contributes to the intuitive fairness of the arrangement; and it encourages self-reliance and a sense of personal responsibility. These advantages compensate somewhat for the inevitable imperfections – real and imagined – that are sure to be manifested in the actual resulting distribution of jobs and rewards, whether due to residual inequities in the political environment (e.g., the variable quality of familial nurture), or to lack of self-knowledge on the part of he who chooses (cf. *Republic* 617e).

But, generally speaking, a commonwealth established in the manner Hobbes prescribes, will order itself along the lines Sokrates lays out for his City, and accordingly enjoy civil peace and harmony. For high-spirited, honour-loving men will gravitate naturally to those especially challenging, exciting, and dangerous occupations (e.g., military, police, fire and rescue) which, when done well, naturally command people's admiration and respect. Whereas the majority of men will seek out some suitable money-making trade in commerce, industry, agriculture, or service (comprising a wide spectrum of vocations, from waiters and trash collectors to doctors and accountants). However, as I have noted before, a special feature of Hobbes's prescription is the subtle but unmistakable encouragement it gives to those with a natural talent for the pursuit of any kind of knowledge, but especially of the technologically useful kind of knowledge that has come to define modern Baconian science: for '*Reason* is the *pace*; Encrease of *Science*, the *way*; and the Benefit of man-kind, the *end.*' It is with respect to the pursuit of knowledge that the regime's offering equality of opportunity for everyone's natural abilities to come forth is especially important.

Still, a major question – *the* major question – remains: what sort of man will be drawn to the Government of such a polity? This, and related matters, is the subject of the chapter that follows.

22

The Place of Philosophy:
The Kingship of Hobbes

The treatment of Philosophy and Philosophers in *Leviathan* is apt to leave one perplexed. Neither is given a ringing endorsement, and yet philosophy turns out to be the one thing needful lest the labour Hobbes has invested in crafting his book come to naught.

Virtually from the outset, however, philosophers as a class seem singled out for disparagement, and often outright ridicule. They are themselves, Hobbes claims, especially subject to being confused by the vagaries of language – mainly of their own invention – and are consequently a source of confusion and fantastical beliefs in others who take 'upon credit' the 'absurd speeches' of these 'deceived Philosophers, and deceived, or deceiving Schoolemen' (III/12, 11). There has been an abundance of new words coined by 'Schoolemen, and Pusled Philosophers,' but insofar as their meanings have not been 'explained by Definition,' they amount to nothing but so many 'insignificant sounds' (IV/20, 16–17). Whereas:

[I]n the right Definition of Names, lyes the first use of Speech; which is the Acquisition of Science: And in wrong, or no Definitions, lyes the first abuse; from which proceed all false and senselesse Tenets; which make those men who take their instruction from the authority of books, and not from their own meditation, to be as much below the condition of ignorant men, as men endued with true Science are above it. For between true Science, and erroneous Doctrines, Ignorance is in the middle. (IV/13, 15)

True Science being 'the knowledge of Consequences, and dependance of one fact upon another' (V/17, 21), hence of *causes*, it is the stuff of Philosophy proper (IX/3, 40). If Hobbes is to be credited, however, there had not been much of it to brag about, Geometry being 'the onely Science that it hath pleased God hitherto to bestow on mankind' (IV/12, 15; but cf. XVIII/20, 94; XXXVII/12, 236). And perhaps with that in mind, Hobbes reiterates his own version of an old truth: 'yet they that have no *Science*, are in a better, and nobler condition with their naturall Prudence; than men, that by mis-reasoning, or by trusting them that reason wrong, fall upon false and absurd generall rules' (V/19, 21).

Indeed, judging by results thus far, the philosophical aspiration is a mixed blessing. For example, the form of senseless speech Hobbes calls 'absurdity' (any false general assertion), it is necessarily a 'priviledge' reserved to man as the only creature that uses language: 'And of men, those are of all most subject to it, that professe Philosophy' (V/7, 20). The confusions resulting from entertaining absurdities, as 'when men speak such words, as put together, have in them no signification at all,' may even 'be numbred amongst the sorts of Madnesse.' However, 'this is incident to none but those, that converse in questions of matters incomprehensible, as the Schoole-men; or in questions of abstruse philosophy' (VIII/27, 39). Thus, 'it is most true that *Cicero* sayth of them somewhere; that there can be nothing so absurd, but may be found in the books of Philosophers' (V/7, 20). This superlative 'truth' is important enough to bear repeating (though in a form tinged with paradox): 'there is nothing so absurd, that the old Philosophers (as *Cicero* saith, who was one of them) have not some of them maintained' (XLVI/11, 370).

As for Philosophy itself, that which then prevailed 'through all the Universities of Christendome,' according to Hobbes, was 'grounded upon certain Texts of *Aristotle*' (I/5, 4). As such, it was a misnomer: 'since the Authority of Aristotle is onely current there, that study is not properly Philosophy, (the nature whereof dependeth not on Authors,) but Aristotelity' (XLVI/13, 370). This faux-philosophy has thoroughly contaminated Christianity, with the result (Hobbes alleges) that 'Faith faile in the People.' For the Schoolmen's introduction of Aristotelian doctrine into Religion has been the source of 'so many contradictions, and absurdities, as brought the Clergy into a reputation both of Ignorance, and of Fraudulent intention; and enclined people to revolt from them' (XII/31, 59). Nor was the pernicious influence of philosophy confined to Christianity; something similar happened to the Jews: 'So that by their Lectures and Disputations in their Synagogues, they turned the Doctrine of their Law into a Phantasticall kind of Philosophy, concerning the incomprehensible nature of God, and of Spirits; which they compounded of the Vain Philosophy and Theology of the Grecians, mingled with their own fancies, drawn from the obscurer places of Scripture' (XLVI/12, 370).

Likewise, the influence upon politics of philosophy in general, and of Aristotle in particular, is mainly to be regretted. 'The Libertie, whereof there is so frequent, and honourable mention, in the Histories, and Philosophy of the Antient Greeks,' is not rightly understood by those many people who base their understanding of politics upon these texts, and who therefore confuse 'the Libertie of Particular men' with 'the Libertie of the Common-wealth' (which is the freedom of the State of Nature). 'But it is an easy thing, for men to be deceived, by the specious name of Libertie.' From defective educators such as Aristotle and Cicero, men are nurtured from childhood to rebel in the name of Liberty (XXI/8–9, 110). Similar remarks pertain to 'the Reading of the books of Policy, and Histories of the antient Greeks, and Romans,' whereby is cultivated a general prejudice against any monarchical form of government, inviting those subject to it to regard it as a tyranny, with the corollary that it is honourable for any man to kill a King, 'provided before he do it, he call him Tyrant ... From these same books, they that live under a Monarch conceive an opinion, that the Subjects in a Popular Common-wealth enjoy Liberty; but that in a Monarchy they are all Slaves' (XXIX/14, 170–1). Speaking summarily, 'there was never any thing so deerly bought, as these Western parts have bought the learning of the Greek and Latine tongues' (XXI/9, 111) – this from a man who himself published translations of Thucydides and Homer.

Arguably Hobbes's most prejudicial reference to philosophy, however, is implicit in the jeering remark about Aristotle that, as I have previously noted, is woven into his argument for a Natural Law requiring the 'acknowledgment' of natural human equality, non-compliance being denounced as the Original Sin of 'Pride.' The passage is a masterpiece of rhetorical misdirection, and deserves still another look:

I know that *Aristotle* in the first booke of his Politiques, for a foundation of his doctrine, maketh men by Nature, some more worthy to Command, meaning the wiser sort (such as he thought himselfe to be for his Philosophy;) others to Serve, (meaning those that had strong bodies, but were not Philosophers as he;) as if Master and Servant were not introduced by consent of men, but by difference of Wit: which is not only against reason; but also against experience. For there are very few so foolish, that had not rather governe themselves, than be governed by others: Nor when the wise in their own conceit, contend by force, with them that distrust their owne wisdome, do they alwaies, or often, or almost at any time, get the Victory. (XV/21, 77)

Notice, Hobbes first invites the reader to dismiss the very idea that some men are 'by Nature more worthy to Command' on *any* ground by immediately narrowing attention to *wisdom* as the ground, while simultaneously questioning whether those who (like Aristotle) pursue 'Philosophy' actually *are wiser*, either for doing so or as a consequence. Then the issue of who by virtue of natural worth *ought* to rule is not only subsumed within, but subordinated to, a series of question-begging claims about actual political life. First, that the Master-Servant relationship is based on mutual 'consent,' not 'difference of wit' – which even were it invariably true, would not preclude the possibility that the latter is a dominant consideration inducing the former (cf. X/10, 41). Second, that whoever would not prefer to 'govern himself rather than be governed by others' is a fool (further implying that anyone who does not see this for himself is also a fool) – whereas it is this 'preference' that is foolish *unless* it is construed *ironically*, as tacitly including a desire for the requisite *competence* for self-rule, such as has traditionally been associated with philosophy. Finally, the whole populist sneer is polished off with the logically irrelevant boast that when anyone who thinks himself wise is so unwise as to 'contend by force' (to establish his rulership over The People, presumably, who rightly or wrongly 'distrust' his problematic wisdom), he is seldom successful. The fact that the inclusion of this compounded conflation of issues involving Philosophy is largely gratuitous to the point Hobbes is supposedly arguing for – natural human equality – in no way diminishes its rhetorical effect, suggestive of philosophers being ridiculously pretentious and impractical. Whereas, critically analysed, it might help explain the shockingly ambiguous conclusion of that argument ('*If* Nature therefore have made men equall,' so be it; on the other hand, 'if Nature have made men *un*equall,' nonetheless …).

Suffice it to say, the typical reader of Hobbes's *Leviathan*, far from being persuaded of the grandeur of Philosophy and the nobility of Philosophers, is apt to have, at best, mixed feelings about both. True, Hobbes has included in the midst of his warnings about 'erroneous Doctrines' and 'misreasonings' an inconspicuous endorsement of Sokratic wisdom: that awareness of one's ignorance is preferable to believing one knows what one does not, for it leaves one open to learn. But on the whole, the book generates the impression that Philosophy thus far has contributed little of real value to human life, being a corrupting influence on Religion and a fecund source of pernicious notions about liberty and tyranny in Politics. As for Philosophers, even the most eminent – far from having realized their heart's desire of gaining wisdom – are mainly creators of their own confusions and perplexities. Whereas many of the rest seem almost silly in their pretensions, and others outright mountebanks. What a contrast to the exaltation of Philosophy and Philosophers in Plato's *Republic*!

... Or is it? Consider the 'apology for philosophy' with which Sokrates responds to Adeimantos's indictment of it (487b–497c). The context is as follows. The philosopher having made his 'very paradoxical' pronouncement that the only real solution to mankind's political problems is the rule of 'philosopher-kings' – or at any rate, some sort of 'coincidence [*xumpesë*]' of 'political power and philosophy [*dynamis te politikë kai philosophia*]' (473c–d) – he is immediately challenged to defend so seemingly outrageous a proposal. Sokrates's first step is to distinguish what *he* means by a 'lover of wisdom' (474b). This entails clarifying both what counts as a genuine 'lover' of *anything* (be it boys, wine, honour, or learning; 474c–475c), and what is meant by 'wisdom' (knowledge of the unchanging reality, i.e., 'science,' as distinct from 'opinion' or 'belief'; 476b–480a). Precise definitions of these freighted terms are essential if one is to correctly understand, and rationally appraise, this rightly famous, literally central pronouncement of Plato's *Republic*.

These definitions having been provided, Sokrates next addresses the question of whether a genuine philosopher – that is, someone who is clear-sighted by virtue of knowing what is permanently true (484b–d) – would be the best Guardian of a polity. Since those suited to be Guardians must be not only knowledgeable but virtuous in all respects, as well as sufficiently experienced in managing human affairs, this question also comprises two issues: does someone who is by nature a true lover of wisdom necessarily manifest, or acquire, all the human virtues (or facets of human excellence)? And is there some way he might also accumulate the requisite political experience? Taking up first the nature of someone who is genuinely philosophical, Sokrates argues that simply by his channelling all of his soul's power into learning the whole truth about permanent reality, the philosopher would not be a lover of money, hence he would be moderate, liberal, and magnificent (*megaloprepës*; 'of befitting greatness'); and fearless of death (485a ff.), he would be no coward; and having a soul ordered according to nature, he would be *just* and gentle, with a sure sense of grace and proportion (485d–486d). Speaking summarily, Sokrates contends that an adequate practitioner of the philosophical life is necessarily 'by nature of sound memory, a good learner, magnificent, gracious – altogether a friend and kinsman of truth, justice, courage, and moderation' (487a).

Before Sokrates can turn to the second requisite of a philosopher's being a suitable Guardian – namely, his acquiring the sorts of experience necessary for cultivating political prudence – Adeimantos objects. Based on what he has seen of the breed, he finds Sokrates's portrait of a philosopher to be, quite literally, *incredible*. Far from its being merely the sort of idealization that often results when one speaks in generalities (cf. 473a), this glowing description bears no resemblance at all to the so-called philosophers one encounters in actual life. Despite whatever a verbal chess master like Sokrates might seem to establish in *speech*, the truth in deed remains unaffected, namely, that of all those who stick with philosophy beyond youth, 'most become quite eccentric, not to say thoroughly vicious; while those who seem most decent [or, 'most equitable'; *epieikestatous*] become, as a consequence of the pursuit praised, useless to their polities' (487c–d). To Adeimantos's surprise – and confusion – Sokrates does *not* disagree with this. Instead, he explains *why* what the young man says is *true*. The essential thing to understand is that the very few genuine philosophers are not readily distinguishable in appearance from the far more numerous sophists and other false or merely incompetent pretenders, all being lumped together and tarred with same brush.

Sokrates chooses to address the last charge first, however, explaining why even decent philosophers seem politically useless (whereas they are potentially most useful). Supposedly because this point is so difficult to prove, he resorts to an 'image' which will illustrate it – but not an image drawn straight from the natural world; rather, he claims he must employ the sort of image that painters create by mixing together disparate components to portray, for example, a 'goatstag' (488a; cf. *Leviathan* II/4, 5). Sokrates's image is of a Ship-of-State, with a strong but ignorant ship owner; fractious sailors fighting over the role of pilot, none of whom possesses the requisite art (which they deny exists); the one competent pilot, preoccupied with the things of his art (especially the structure of the heavens and its bearing on earthly time and tide), ridiculed as a babbling stargazer; and so on (488a–e; cf. *Leviathan* XLVI/42, 380). The philosopher's situation in actual polities, Sokrates contends, is like that of the true pilot: supremely useful in principle, but utterly dismissed in practice. Nor, he adds, is it fitting that he should have to beg to rule the ship, any more than a doctor should have to beg the sick to let him cure them (489b).

That done, Sokrates turns to explaining why most of the few who have real natural potential for philosophy so seldom actualize it, but are instead corrupted while still young – not by philosophy, nor even so much by individual sophists, but ultimately by a far greater Sophistry: the regnant prejudices and dogmas, the orthodoxies and vanities, that pervade public life. The private sophists themselves know nothing of what is truly noble or base, good or bad, just or unjust; their 'wisdom' consists simply of knowing how to apply 'all of these *names*' – all of these ill-defined terms – according to the humours of the 'large, strong Beast,' this large composite Animal that is the Public (493b–c). Born into such an environment, it is hardly surprising that youths who are especially blessed by nature with the superior qualities requisite for genuine philosophy would attract the wrong kind of attention. And so, flattered by the proffered opportunities for worldly success, they end up corrupted – *not* by philosophy, but by *politics*. Thus it is that from the ranks of the most naturally talented individuals come 'the men who work the greatest evils to polities and individuals,' rather than doing the greatest good (495b).

So, with most of those for whom 'Love of *Sophia*' would be most fitting having instead gone into 'exile, leaving her abandoned and unfulfilled [*atelë*],' unworthy suitors take her up and disgrace her. Some are merely 'of no account, whereas many are "worthy" only of many evils.' But being quite *un*worthy of higher education, these manikins with their small, cramped, and maimed souls, can beget only 'bastard and paltry' notions, mere 'sophisms, nothing genuine nor truly sensible.' It is mainly such defective natures, full of pretensions that far outstrip their meagre abilities, who are responsible for philosophy's suspect reputation (495b–496a). Whereas the very few worthy candidates who somehow escape the usual fate of superior natures – those philosophers acknowledged to be decent, but nonetheless useless – prefer to lead a private, retired way of life (496b–e).[1]

In short, Plato makes it clear enough that Sokrates, too, could cite endless examples of meaningless distinctions, confused ideas, vacuous claims, and paltry truisms 'begotten' by sophists and philosophical mediocrities – the mere 'Schoolmen' of his and every day – were that to his purpose. But it is not. For therein lies a, if not *the*, essential difference between these complementary masterworks. The *Republic* aims at promoting a human good above politics; albeit fully accessible to only a precious few, it is of potential benefit to many more. Thus, explicating not merely the possibility, but establishing the nobility of the genuinely philosophical life is the ruling intention of the dialogue. Its political content is entirely contributory to that aim. For as Sokrates warns young Glaukon, those who rise to the challenge of the philosophical life should not imagine that they will thereby emigrate to the Isles of the Blessed (519c), much less become disembodied Spirits that can dwell perpetually outside the political Caves that confine lesser mortals. They remain embodied Spirits who may enjoy episodic sojourns 'above ground' but whose bodily needs tie them to one or another Cave to which they must ever return (cf. *Symposium* 174d, 220c–d). Hence, it behoves them to understand Cave life thoroughly, constituting as it does the everyday environment of philosophy (and depicted as such throughout Plato's dialogical Cosmos). This requires careful and extensive observation. But it also requires transcending the realm of ever-fluctuating Opinion (regnant of Cave life), gaining access to a realm of Knowledge – of permanently true forms grounded in the Nature of things, Man included – whereby a genuinely 'scientific' understanding of Politics is possible, allowing one to see Caves for what they are.

Hobbes, while at the very end admitting himself ever drawn to the higher realm of pure contemplation, has in *Leviathan* directed his attention down onto politics – returned to the Cave, as it were – to offer his own prescription for ordering political life, one that will harmonize so far as possible its requirements with the interests of philosophy. His rhetoric is crafted so as to establish his intellectual authority with the practically minded men to whom his prescription is primarily addressed. Thus, he endorses a healthy suspicion of so-called philosophers – most of whom in truth are at best journeymen thinkers, and not a few outright sophists, distinguished more by vanity than true wisdom, and productive (at best) mainly of quibbles and pointless arguments, nothing useful. All too often, moreover, they are propagators of outright pernicious views. By showing himself so critical of his own tribe, Hobbes reassures those practical men of his down-to-earth sensibleness – apparently confirming their own prejudices and suspicions, their own 'vain conceit' that they are wiser than everyone else except those who 'for concurring with themselves, they approve.' That Hobbes frequently, and not at all incidentally, derides Churchmen in the same breath may secretly endear him still further, to some at least. Nonetheless, he – like Sokrates – does defend and promote a certain kind of philosophy, not least by his example, tailoring its presentation to the tastes of those for whom political life is the be-all and end-all. In short, Hobbes, like Plato's Sokrates, sells philosophy on the grounds of its potential *political utility*: '*Reason* is the *pace*; Encrease of *Science*, the *way*; and the Benefit of man-kind, the *end*' – with this increasing of Science, the '*Knowledge of the Consequence of one Affirmation to another*,' being touted as the business of a genuine Philosopher (IX/1, 40).

Ironically, these claims are true, as manifested repeatedly in this magnanimous 'deed,' Hobbes's *Leviathan*, whereby he, like Plato, demonstrates the political utility of philosophy, and of his own competence to 'rule,' ruling in the only practical way a philosopher would wish to, by founding an enduring regime in the minds of other men, who will, according to their own lights, translate his 'Truth of Speculation, into the Utility of Practice.' This is the Philosophical Kingship of Thomas Hobbes.

The single most important chapter for understanding Hobbes's own conception of philosophy is numbered 46, and entitled '*Of* DARKNESSE *from* VAIN PHILOSOPHY, *and* FABULOUS TRADITIONS.' In this instance, too, however – as is so often true regarding matters treated in *Leviathan* – his view is not what it first seems. What he has *made* it seem, that is. The chapter begins with a definition that amounts to an unqualified endorsement of the Baconian conception, at least as usually interpreted: 'By PHILOSOPHY, is understood *the Knowledge acquired by Reasoning, from the Manner of the Generation of any thing, to the Properties; or from the Properties, to some possible Way of Generation of the same; to the end to bee able to produce, as far as matter, and humane force permit, such Effects, as humane life requireth.*'

However, to illustrate this utilitarian, technology-fostering notion of philosophy, Hobbes has chosen two of the least utility-*motivated* of all the sciences: Geometry and Astronomy. Admittedly, they have their practical uses, including those which he mentions (using geometry 'to measure Land, and Water' – which is, after all, the Greek origin of the word: *geö-metria*, 'earth-measuring'); and by virtue of astronomy, 'star-naming' (i.e., classifying), we not only 'keepeth an account of Time,' but attempt to 'findeth out the Causes of Day, and Night, and of the different Seasons of the Year.'[2] But most geometers do not pursue their inquiries for any utilitarian purpose;[3] quite the contrary: they are engaged in strictly intellectual explorations – of which there is no better example than the notorious controversy that so tarnished Hobbes's mathematical reputation, the search for a geometric procedure that would 'Square the

Circle.' As for astronomy, this has been regarded since antiquity – and rightly so, even today – as primarily a theoretical pursuit in the classical sense: knowledge sought simply for the sake of knowing, for contemplation or 'speculation' (to use Hobbes's term). Moreover, long before and after Hobbes wrote, astronomy was regarded as the one science in which *certain* knowledge is inherently *impossible* – that far from it ever yielding 'generall, eternall, and immutable Truth,' the best one might aspire to is a hypothetical account which 'saved the appearances.' There is the added irony that it is in this theoretical, and inherently speculative science (in both Hobbes's and our senses of the word, since astronomy leads naturally and seamlessly to cosmology), that geometrical knowledge is most indispensable.

The status of these two sciences merits a digression, in that their theoretical nature is intrinsic to the rationale for their being included in the 'Sciences Mathematical' that Hobbes refers to as required by 'Plato' in order that his 'Soveraigns be Philosophers.' That is, Plato has his Sokrates prescribe an ordered mathematical curriculum as the most suitable preparation for mastering dialectical analysis,[4] required by those who would rise to the kingship of his 'City in *logos*.' But ostensibly because all candidates for such training come from the Warrior class of that city, he also specifies that whatever is studied 'not be useless to warlike men.' The regimen begins, however, with an unconventional study of Arithmetic, treating it primarily as exercise whereby to strengthen one's power of reasoning: 'those who are by nature apt at calculation [*physei logistikoi*] are naturally quick [or 'sharp'; *oxeis*] in all studies [*mathēmata*], whereas ones who are slow, if given instruction and exercise in this, improve by becoming quicker.' But its benefit is not confined to training one's reason through becoming skilled at counting and calculating – skills, Sokrates notes, that are common to all arts (*technai*) and thinking (*dianoiai*) and sciences (*epistēmai*).[5] Beyond this, the contemplation of Number itself is a means of turning a soul from a 'night-like day to the true day' (that is, from a preoccupation with the realm of Becoming to a concentration on Being).

This mind training in Arithmetic is to be followed by Plane Geometry, for (as Glaukon puts it) 'geometrical knowing is of what *is* always,' hence (Sokrates adds) 'it would draw the soul towards truth.' Then, when Sokrates asks whether Astronomy comes next, Glaukon responds that it seems so to him, and in defending its utility, suggests, 'A better awareness of seasons and months and years is fitting not only for farming and navigation, but no less for generalship [*stratēgia*].' Sokrates, however, chides him for reasoning thus: 'You are amusing, like one who is afraid of the Many in not wanting to command useless studies. It's scarcely a paltry thing, but hard, to trust that in these studies a certain instrument of one's soul [*organon psychēs*], corrupted and blinded by other pursuits, is purified and rekindled, more important to save than myriad eyes. For only with it is truth seen.' However, he acknowledges that this is a 'use' which most people would scarce credit, and so they regard such studies as without benefit. Might Hobbes himself share the ancient philosopher's broader idea of utility?

Shortly thereafter, Sokrates announces that moving straight from Plane Geometry to Astronomy was a mistake, in that it amounts to prescribing the study of 'a solid in motion' before that of the solid in itself.[6] This prompts Glaukon's objection that a science of Solid Geometry does yet properly exist and Sokrates's explanation that because 'no polity honors it, it is feebly sought due to its difficulty'; moreover, there is a lack of knowledgeable supervisors for those who would nonetheless pursue it. Next, then, would come Astronomy, but studied not so much in order to understand the motions of astral bodies as ends in themselves. Rather, these problems would be used, like those of geometry, as a means 'to convert from useless to useful the natural sensibleness in the soul.' The philosopher's pre-dialectical curriculum concludes with the study of the mathematical basis of Harmony, treated as the 'complement' of Astronomy. For 'as the eyes fasten upon Astronomy, so the ears are fastened upon Harmonic movement, and these *are* somehow brethren sciences with each other, as the Pythagoreans say.'[7] But just as the visible heavenly bodies and their motions, for all of their beauty and precision, are not to be regarded as perfect, so audible harmonies are to be studied primarily as a means of determining which *Numbers* are themselves concordant and which not, and why so (531b–c).

We know that Hobbes is not merely familiar with this mathematical curriculum, thus with its purpose, but – more to the point – he has a practitioner's appreciation for its difficulty, even given a nature gifted for the labour involved. Thus, while he concludes his chapter on 'The Kingdome of God by Nature' by voicing his belief in the impossibility of civil disorders ever being eliminated – till the Second Coming of our Lord Jesus Christ, Prince of Peace? ... not exactly – 'till Soveraigns be Philosophers,' he nonetheless is prepared to excuse 'Soveraigns and their principall Ministers' from the necessity of mastering all those 'Sciences Mathematicall, (as [required] by *Plato*...,) further, than by good Lawes to encourage men to the study of them.' It will suffice if instead such Soveraigns and their principal Ministers have somehow acquired 'the Science of Naturall Justice.' But insofar as the practical *application* of this Science of 'Equity' requires the kind of deductive and proportional reasoning best perfected by training in Geometry, presumably Hobbes would agree that at least this much 'Science Mathematicall' is 'highly recommended' for prospective rulers. Still, given his own contention that having '*great* knowledge of Geometry' is virtually a prerequisite of Philosophy, one must suppose that his lessening of the mathematical requirements for acceptable Sovereigns represents a compromise with practicality: that such rulers might not be philosophers themselves, but sufficiently philosophical to appreciate the value of having philosophers as friends and advisers, be they living or dead.

By way of further clarifying what philosophy *is*, Hobbes distinguishes it from four things that it is *not*, devoting a single paragraph to each. First, it is not 'that originall knowledge called Experience, in which consisteth Prudence: Because it is not attained by Reasoning, [for] nothing is produced by Reasoning aright, but generall, eternall, and immutable Truth.' Second, then, genuine Philosophy results in no 'false Conclusions: For he that Reasoneth aright in words he understandeth, can never conclude an Error.' Third, the name 'Philosophy' does not pertain 'to that which any man knows by supernaturall Revelation; because it is not acquired by Reasoning.' Neither, fourthly, to whatever 'is gotten by Reasoning from the Authority of Books; because it is not by Reasoning from the Cause to the Effect, nor from the Effect to the Cause; and is not Knowledg, but Faith' (XLVI/2–5, 367).

Next follow four paragraphs in which Hobbes briefly sketches the History of Philosophy from what one might call its accidental origins, to the establishment of formal schools by Master practitioners, mentioning four by name: Plato, Aristotle, Zeno, and Carneades. It might seem curious that Sokrates – who is usually regarded as pivotal in that history, having 'brought Philosophy down from the Heavens and into the Cities' (the founder, in effect, of 'Civill Science,' as Hobbes elsewhere acknowledges) – is not mentioned. But Sokrates neither wrote nor established an actual *school*, in either the physical or the socio-historical sense.

Another four paragraphs, far more critical in tone and substance, carry the history up to the establishment of Universities. This latter half is, in effect, Hobbes's account of the *degeneration* of philosophy, such that what passes for philosophy in the universities ever bows before the 'Authority of Aristotle.' As a consequence, it is not truly Philosophy at all, '(the nature whereof dependeth not on Authors,) but Aristotelity' (XLVI/13, 370).

The balance of the chapter 'descends' to criticizing 'particular Tenets of Vain Philosophy, derived to the Universities, and thence into the Church, partly from Aristotle, partly from Blindnesse of understanding.' Much of this criticism is dubious, and some of it demonstrably wrong as attributed to Aristotle, but its purpose is primarily polemical, not philosophical. Hobbes tacitly acknowledges this in explaining its presence 'in a work of this nature': 'that men may no longer suffer themselves to be abused, by them, that by this doctine of *Separated Essences* ... would fright them from Obeying the Laws of their Countrey, with empty names' (XLVI/18, 372–3). Thus, since his criticism is aimed at undermining the doctrinal authority of the Church, and thereby its power, it is not necessarily indicative of Hobbes's own views. For example, his expounding still again what seems a strict Materialism – 'the *Universe*, that is, the whole masse of all things that are,' is 'Corporeall, that is to say, Body ... and that which is not Body, is no part of the Universe' (XLVI/15, 371) – may be solely for the purpose of confuting the existence of '*Abstract Essences, and Substantial Formes*' (hence 'spirits,' 'ghosts,' and 'an Incorporeall Soule, Separated from the Body' – notions too easily abused by Churchmen). When in this very context he asserts, 'But for Spirits, they call them Incorporeall; which is a name of more honour,' he could hardly himself believe that either names or honour, though a real 'part of the Universe,' are *bodies* in a materialist sense. If nothing else did, the penultimate sentence in the book should make a thoughtful reader suspect that Hobbes's idea of 'body' is not at all conventional: 'I return to my interrupted Speculation of Bodies Naturall; wherein, (if God give me health to finish it,) I hope the Novelty will as much please, as in the Doctrine of this Artificiall Body it useth to offend.' He must indeed have a 'novel' notion of 'body' in mind if a particular *form* of *polity* qualifies as an 'artificial' instance of it!

In summary, it is mainly the first thirteen paragraphs of the chapter that are of most *philosophical* (as opposed to political) importance – not for any doctrines advanced, but for what is indicated about the nature of Philosophy per se. Of no small significance is Hobbes's acknowledgment that philosophizing is intrinsic to human nature. As he explains, the close relationship between Thought and Speech made it a virtual inevitability 'that there should have been some generall Truthes found out by Reasoning, as ancient almost as Language it selfe' – including some elementary Arithmetic – such 'being the naturall plants of humane Reason, [albeit] at first but few in number.' However, this did not amount to Philosophy, inasmuch as relying mainly upon 'grosse Experience' and lacking a sound 'Method,' there was 'no Sowing, nor Planting of Knowledge by it selfe, apart from the Weeds, and common Plants of Errour and Conjecture.' These limitations were due to a lack of the one thing needful for the emergence of Philosophy: *Leisure.*

And the cause of it being the want of leasure from procuring the necessities of life, and defending themselves against their neighbors, it was impossible, till the erecting of great Common-wealths, it should be otherwise. *Leasure* is the mother of *Philosophy*; and *Common-wealth*, the mother of *Peace*, and *Leasure*: Where first were great and flourishing *Cities*, there was first the study of *Philosophy*. The *Gymnosophists* of *India*, the *Magi* of *Persia*, and the *Priests* of *Chaldaea* and *Egypt*, are counted the most ancient Philosophers; and those Countreys were the most ancient of Kingdomes. (XLVI/6, 368)

As he tells it, only later when political consolidation brought some peace, hence leisure, did philosophy arise among the Greeks, having acquired the fundaments of those philosophy-inducing subjects, Astronomy and Geometry, from 'the learning of the *Chaldeans* and *Egyptians*.'

Of the many implications of Hobbes's here endorsing what is in fact the ancient view – that Philosophy is a natural employment of leisure, indeed, perhaps the highest such, if 'humans by nature reach out to know'[8] – is the possibility that this obliquely indicates the deeper purpose of his *Leviathan*. That Hobbes has set out to persuade the world to adopt a form of regime which, though de jure dedicated to advancing the distinctly *modern* conception of philosophy qua science (the busy pursuit of technologically useful knowledge for 'the relief of man's estate'), is also de facto hospitable to philosophy in the *ancient* style (meaning the pursuit of knowledge for its own sake). Moreover – bearing in mind the extraordinary central paragraph of his book – the latter may be Hobbes's own principal concern. Recall his definition of 'Curiosity':

Desire, to know why, and how ... such as is in no living creature but *Man*: so that Man is distinguished, not onely by his Reason; but also by this singular Passion from other *Animals*; [it is] a Lust of the mind, that by a perseverance of delight in the continuall and indefatigable generation of Knowledge, exceedeth the short vehemence of any carnall pleasure. (VI/35, 26).

Knowledge simpliciter, notice, not necessarily technologically useful knowledge. And Hobbes had singled out this 'Desire of Knowledge' as one of only two desires that, along with fear, support forming and sustaining a political association that can provide civil peace: 'For such Desire, containeth a desire of leasure' (the other being the far more common desire 'of Ease, and sensuall Delight'; XI/4–5, 48). Hobbes apparently does not equate 'leisure' with 'ease' (cf. XVII/11, 87).

However, neither curiosity without leisure, nor leisure lacking curiosity, suffices to ignite philosophy – as Hobbes indicates by way of explaining the belated arrival of a political prescription such as his: 'The skill of making, and maintaining Common-wealths, consisteth in certain Rules, as doth Arithmetique and Geometry; not (as Tennis-play) on Practise onely: which Rules, neither poor men have the leisure, nor men that have had the leisure, have hitherto had the curiosity, or the method to find out' (XX/19, 107). He spoke similarly of 'the things that make a good Judge': 'first, *A right understanding* of that principall Law of Nature called *Equity*; which depending not on the reading of other mens Writings, but on the goodnesse of a mans own naturall Reason, and Meditation, is presumed to be in those most, that have had the most leisure, and had the most inclination to meditate thereon' (XXVI/28, 146–7). These statements put together suggest that the natural 'constituents' of philosophy are Leisure, Curiosity, a sound Method, and 'the goodnesse of a mans own naturall Reason.' As for a sound Method, we may presume its results are on display in *Leviathan*. But as I have been at pains to argue, whatever that method actually is, it is *not* simply modelled on Geometry, at least in the ordinary sense of the word.[9]

In any case, these four constituents do not dictate exclusively the 'Baconian' conception of philosophy. Accordingly, the endorsement which Hobbes offers in the first lines of the chapter may be regarded as ironic. Though genuine in its own way, it is misleading in the way it is apt to be generally understood. But by presenting philosophy as if it aimed *only* at discovering knowledge useful for manipulating material nature, thus furthering comfortable survival (catering to people's desire for 'Ease, and Sensuall Delight'), a twofold political purpose is served.

First, propagating this view is the most effective way of garnering popular support for the pursuit of knowledge per se, thereby providing security for the continuance of philosophy as classically conceived. Historically, there has been a need for such security, especially to prevent the persecution of philosophers by their natural rivals: those who act in the name of protecting an established religion.[10] Hobbes reminds us of that fact in this very chapter, citing an example whose implications reverberate from one end of his text to the other: regarding 'the *Entities*, and *Essences*' which he claims are so abused by Church thinkers, he muses that Aristotle himself may have known this 'to be false Philosophy; but writ it as a thing consonant to, and corroborative of their Religion [presumably, that of the Greeks]; and fearing the fate of Socrates' (XLVI/18, 373). This, perhaps not so incidentally, is the only mention of Sokrates in the book. And given that Hobbes had similar reason to fear a similar fate,[11] the reflexive possibilities that arise from this acknowledgment are surely worth pondering.

In his dialogue 'On Heresy,' which accompanied the later Latin edition of *Leviathan*, Hobbes shows further his recognition of the need for a prudential 'esotericism' in writings that bear on religion:

A. But if the act is against natural law, isn't it a crime, and can't it be punished, even if no manner of punishing is written in the law?

B. The natural law is eternal, divine, and written only in the heart. But few people know how to look into their hearts and read what is written there. So they learn what is to be done and what is to be avoided from the written laws. And they do and avoid as it seems to them, in light of the penalties they foresee, advantageous or harmful. ...

A. What if someone is an atheist, and there is no written law which defines the manner of punishment – will he not be punished?

B. Indeed he will be punished, and very severely. But first he must be accused, and heard, and condemned. Moreover, nothing can be made a ground of accusation except words or deeds. But what deeds will support an accusation of atheism? For what deed have you ever heard of which was so wicked or impious that its like has not at some time been committed by those who, not only are not thought to be atheists, but are even, as far as their profession goes, Christians? So an atheist is not judged by his acts. Therefore, the only ground on which he can be accused is something he has said, either orally or in writing, viz. if he has straightforwardly denied that God exists.

A. Will someone not also be called an atheist if he has said or written something from which it necessarily follows that God does not exist?

B. Of course he will, provided that when he said or wrote it, he saw the necessity of that implication ... For it is very difficult to judge the consequences of words. Therefore, if an accused person has said something against the letter of the law, because he did not know how to reason well, and has not harmed anyone, his ignorance will excuse him ...

So, even if the manner of punishment has not been prescribed in the law, he who denies that God exists, or who openly confesses that he doubts whether God exists or not, can be punished, but by exile, in accordance with natural equity. [i.e., 'because an atheist cannot be obliged by swearing' an oath to 'keep faith in covenants']¹²

As is fairly obvious, Hobbes has been ever careful in his treatment of religion to stay within the protective rationale he has speaker 'B' articulate. In particular, he has provided himself with what today would be called 'deniability' regarding the atheism that can be teased out as implicit in what he has written. There would not be a need for so much caution in a commonwealth such as he prescribes in *Leviathan*, with its radical revision in the common perception of philosophy's relation to political life.¹³ But Hobbes himself did not live and write in such a commonwealth.

There is a second political effect of benefit to genuine philosophy achieved by explicitly endorsing the 'Baconian' conception, namely, that its widespread acceptance will – as Bacon promised – generate a growing body of technologically useful knowledge, and an increasing prosperity based thereon. There will as a consequence be a commensurate increase in the amount and availability of leisure, and a more tolerant environment for discussion and inquiry by virtue of civil peace. Nor does this utilitarian conception necessarily conflict with the original idea of philosophy as simply the love of wisdom for its own sake – quite the contrary: much of what is discovered by men inspired by the Baconian project will surely be of interest to those whose desire for knowledge is primarily theoretical, even if the forms in which it comes to them will be only as so much grist for the mills of their own minds.¹⁴

Further evidence that Hobbes does not regard his own 'Baconian definition' as truly and exclusively *definitive* of philosophy per se is provided by his acknowledging various men to be philosophers despite their *not* subscribing to that conception. Although there is a certain equivocation in how he expresses it, he must wish to be understood as recognizing 'The *Gymnosophists* of *India*, the *Magi* of *Persia*, and the *Priests* [!] of *Chaldaea* and *Egypt*' as philosophers if they are to count as evidence for his claim that 'Where first were great and flourishing *Cities*, there was the first study of *Philosophy*.' In the first dialogue which he appended to the Latin edition of *Leviathan*, Hobbes observes that 'among the philosophers were the Sadducees,' and he refers to both Plato and Aristotle as 'founders of philosophy' ('On the Nicene Creed,' par. 56).¹⁵ And his second appended dialogue ('On Heresy') virtually begins with this conversation:

A. What were the sects? What men did they follow?

B. They followed the philosophers, viz. Plato, Aristotle, Zeno, Epicurus and others. And they were called Academics, Peripatetics, Stoics, and Epicureans. These were the principal sects of the Greek philosophers, or of those who sought to be seen as philosophers. For though I think the founders of the sects themselves (Plato, Aristotle, Zeno, and Epicurus) really were philosophers, so far as a pagan could be – i.e. men who were zealous in the pursuit of truth and virtue, for which their names were deservedly famous throughout almost the whole world, from the honor due to wisdom – I still do not think their followers ought to be called philosophers. They understood nothing (except that they knew what their masters' opinions were). For they did not know the principles and reasonings on which their doctrines rested, nor did they show in their lives that they were philosophers.

Of paramount importance for an understanding of Hobbes's idea of philosophy, however, is his flat declaration that '*Plato* ... was the best philosopher of the Greeks' (XLVI/11, 369). The comprehensive significance of this bears emphasizing. Not the materialist-determinist Democritus, not the hedonist Epicurus, not Empedocles, nor Anaxagoras, nor any other pre- or post-Sokratic, but *Plato* – who was neither a materialist nor a determinist, neither a nominalist nor a hedonist, and who confined the 'utility' of philosophy to the very proposition Hobbes endorses in his central paragraph: that philosophers be used as kings – Plato was the best philosopher of the Greeks. Why so? Because according to ancient sources he 'forbad entrance into his Schoole, to all that were not already in some measure Geometricians'? If true, was this because he himself religiously adhered to the 'method of Geometry,' and insisted that all his students do likewise? There is precious little evidence of that (not to say none). Admittedly, the Sokrates that Plato portrays is as fussy as Hobbes about clear definitions, but this is for the sake of the clarity and completeness in the synoptic thinking their establishment requires (cf. *Republic* 331d, 537b–c). And various geometrical truths do figure in Plato's texts. To mention only the most obvious case, he has Sokrates use the dialectical method to teach the Pythagorean Theorem to Meno's young Greek slave (*Meno* 82a–85b); and both the logically valid and invalid forms of the hypothetical-conditional mode of argument so basic to geometrical reasoning are illustrated in the course of the discussion. Yet this dialogue as a whole, just as all the others, bears no resemblance whatsoever to a Euclidean treatise.

Moreover, judging from Plato's writings – and whether despite or because of the influence of geometry on his own philosophizing – he was led to metaphysical conclusions quite *opposite* to those with which Hobbes is usually identified. But if Hobbes himself subscribed to the simplistic cosmology presented in his book's opening chapters, why in the world would he pronounce *Plato* to be 'the best philosopher of the Greeks,' when by *that* standard he was *wrong* about virtually everything 'on which all other Philosophy ought to depend,' namely, wrong in his *'Philosophia prima'*? I cannot conceive of any explanation for this other than that – contrary to the expressed views whereby his new Political science might seem of a piece with the modern Natural science it is designed to promote and exploit – he *agreed* with Plato. Agreed not only in his 'opinion that it is impossible for the disorders of State … ever to be taken away, till Soveraigns be Philosophers,' but with respect to much else of importance as well.

With that possibility in mind, a different interpretation of Hobbes's contention that Geometry is 'the Mother of all Naturall Science' presents itself. So too, then, his praise of Plato for requiring geometrical training of prospective students. It is convenient to address this latter point first. Presuming geometry was as vital for the studies undertaken at the Academy as traditional accounts attest, it most likely was so for the rationale Plato has Sokrates sketch in his *Republic*. Glaukon having drawn attention to some of the military advantages of knowing geometry, Sokrates accepts his point, but notes that only a minor portion of geometry would suffice for that purpose. Its greater utility lies in its compelling the soul to turn from the sensory realm of things that are ever-changing, to the intelligible realm of unchanging Being.[16] The soul is thereby drawn upwards towards what is permanently true, and so towards philosophical understanding. Moreover, the mental training that results from advanced work in geometry facilitates eventually discerning 'the idea [or, 'sight,' 'look'] of the Good.' Indeed, Sokrates contends that with respect to the reception of *all* studies, someone who is *'geometrias'* – and whose powers of reasoning, and of deduction in particular, have thus been refined and strengthened – differs as a whole and in every way from someone who is not (526d–527c).[17] Plato's rationale for emphasizing geometrical training, especially for those who are trusted with political power, may be Hobbes's as well.

In that case, Hobbes's claim that Geometry is 'the Mother of all Naturall Science' must be considered afresh.[18] However, it might be best to retreat a step or two, as Hobbes has an entire 'matrilineal' derivation of Science and Philosophy. It begins in his chapter on language, wherein he endorses a view as old as antiquity: that 'need [is] the mother of all inventions' (IV/2, 12). But his idea of 'invention' is apparently much broader than ordinary, as it includes what would normally be thought of as the *discovery* of natural truths, such as those of geometry (cf. IV/9, 14). In fact, 'discovery' seems the primary meaning he gives to the word when defining it: 'In summe, the Discourse of the Mind, when it is governed by designe, is nothing but *Seeking*, or the faculty of Invention … a hunting out of the causes, of some effect, present or past; or of the effects, of some present or past cause' (III/5, 9–10). This does not square with most of his own uses of the term, however, beginning with the first: his characterizing exorcism, crosses, holy water, and such, as the 'inventions of Ghostly men' (II/8, 7). In fact, fully a third of his uses of the word are similarly in connection with Religion (e.g., XII/12, 54; X/48, 45; XLVII/19, 384). Otherwise, Hobbes most frequently associates the word 'invention' with language itself; the chapter '*Of* SPEECH' begins thus:

The Invention of *Printing*, though ingenious, compared with the invention of *Letters*, is no great matter. But who was the first that found the use of Letters, is not known. He who first brought them into *Greece*, men say was *Cadmus*, the sonne of *Agenor*, King of Phaenicia. A profitable Invention for continuing the memory of time past, and the conjunction of mankind, dispersed into so many, and distant regions of the Earth; and with all difficult, as proceeding from a watchful observation of the divers motions of the Tongue, Palat, Lips, and other organs of Speech; whereby to make as many differences of characters, to remember them. But the most noble and profitable invention of all other, was that of SPEECH, consisting of *Names* or *Appellations*, and their Connexion. (IV/1, 12)

Hobbes's description of the invention of Letters does not fit his 'discovery-of-causes' definition any better than does the invention of Printing, or of Language itself,[19] though all of these *do* comport with the ordinary meaning of 'invention.' Presumably, Hobbes has some reason for encouraging the assimilation of what is ordinarily meant by 'discovery' with that of 'invention.' In the case of language, discovery typically precedes invention, in that someone has to have discovered a need for a new term prior to coining it. This is especially common in the sciences: discovering a previously unknown (or undistinguished) life form, mineral, element, or astral body; or natural process, quality, or relationship; or taxonomic class, or analytical distinction – the list is practically as endless as the progress and proliferation of the sciences themselves. And as Hobbes is at pains to emphasize, and mostly disparage, Philosophers have proven themselves especially fertile inventors of abstruse and recondite language, much of it (he insists) meaningless or nonsensical. He does concede, however, that the language of Adam would be only so much 'as he had found use for; though not so copious, as an Orator or Philosopher has need of' (IV/1, 12) – that is, has *discovered* the need of, and so invented.

Need, then, being the 'mother of *all* inventions,' need of some sort is the mother of all polities, or 'commonwealths' (cf. *Republic* 369c ff.). As for what that need is: '*Common-wealth*' is 'the mother of *Peace*, and *Leasure.*' And Leisure, in turn, 'is the mother of *Philosophy*' (XLVI/6, 368). Genuine Philosophy, however, presumes 'great knowledge in Geometry,' for 'Geometry ... is the Mother of all Naturall Science' (XLVI/11, 369). And Science, 'the Knowledge required in a Philosopher; that is to say, of him that pretends to Reasoning' (IX/1, 40), is the 'true Mother' of the 'Arts of publique use, as Fortification, and making of Engines, and other Instruments of War; [which] because they conferre to Defence, and Victory, are Power' (X/15, 42). Does not this genealogy suggest that a, if not *the*, primary purpose of political life – if properly ordered – is the promotion of Philosophy, whether for its own sake (in the Ancient mode), or for its utility (in the Modern mode), or (as I argued above) for both? Moreover, that the philosopher's *Political* Science would be the 'true Mother' for the *supreme* 'Art of publique use,' namely the Statesman's Art, or better still, the Royal or Kingly Art?

This, as I suggested earlier, is the Philosophical Kingship of Thomas Hobbes: his having invented-qua-discovered 'by industrious meditation' the rationale that rules the design and management of the liberal techno-commercial republic (XXX/5, 176), variously imperfect approximations of which dominate so much of the modern world. As such, it illustrates the place of Philosophy in political life: genuinely political Philosophy is ministerial, being an original source of prudential wisdom for the founding of regimes, and a continuing source of wisdom to actual rulers who have wisdom enough themselves to take advantage of that which is available to them. Seen in light of his prescription's full potential, Hobbes may well regard himself as truly a King of Kings and Prince of (civil) Peace.

The important question remains: philosophical natures being both rare and disinclined to participate directly in political life, what sort of person is Hobbes's political design intended to draw into government? Simple though the question may seem, the answer is bound to be complicated because of the complexity of that design, admitting as it does of both a universally applicable interpretation and a uniquely best interpretation. Moreover, the universal version allows for three basic kinds of commonwealth as formally defined by the numerical make-up of the Sovereign: One, Some, or All. The Rule of One is, of course, some sort of Monarchy (that being the literal meaning of the word). The Rule of a subset of the totality of Citizen-Subjects would typically be less than a majority of them, hence literally an Oligarchy ('Rule of the Few'); but since whatever the qualification for inclusion in the Few would be touted as rendering a person most 'worthy,' it will likely style itself as an 'Aristocracy' (from *aristos*, 'best'). The Rule of All the Citizens collectively over themselves as individual Subjects is known as Democracy (from the Greek *ho dëmos*, 'The People') or as a Popular commonwealth (from the Latin *popularis*, 'of the People').

But as I noted in chapter 15, this taxonomy hardly does justice to the substantive diversity possible *within* each of these numerical categories. To take the most obvious case, Oligarchy-qua-'Aristocracy': as formally defined, this class of regime is quite broad, comprising ranges of both quantitative and qualitative diversity, either of which admits differences that have great practical consequence. Quantitatively – that is, how inclusive or exclusive is the 'Some' who participate in sovereignty – it could be a large number (such as the brief rule of Athens by 'The Four Hundred' in the midst of the Peloponnesian War), or very few (such as the even briefer reign of the so-called Thirty Tyrants in Athens at the conclusion of that war; or of the thirty-member *Gerousia* of Sparta).[20] Indeed, if the qualifying criterion were sufficiently generous (for example, including even the smallest property owners), such an 'aristocracy' might not differ much from an outright Democracy. As for qualitative diversity, this obviously is determined by the criterion for inclusion in the ruling class, who in turn impart a certain character to the whole regime; thus, a military aristocracy is bound to differ from a theocracy, a republic ruled by a commercial elite from one dominated by large landowners.

Given any one of these types, however, it could also vary enormously by what Hobbes would regard as the most important 'variable' of all: how closely it does, or does not, conform to the arrangements and policies he prescribes in chapters 21 through 30. For this points to the implicit relationship between the universal version of his regime and the uniquely best version: that of a Philosophical Kingship. A king sufficiently philosophical to read *Leviathan* and interpret it himself in the spirit Hobbes intended, a spirit akin to that in which Hobbes wrote it, would see for himself the rationale pervading that prescription, the necessity of its every element, thus subscribe to it himself, and rule accordingly. Such a Kingship serves as the implicit standard against which all actual regimes (Hobbesian or otherwise) can and should be judged, even if conceived merely as 'a pattern laid up in Heaven.' But lest this be dismissed as an inappropriate standard precisely for that reason – that it is not really mortal but divine, hence hopelessly Utopian – Hobbes insists that it remains a human possibility, that his expressed hope for such a Sovereign is not irrational. After all, its advent would amount to neither more nor less than the full actualization of the regime prescribed in his *Leviathan*, converting his Truth of Speculation into the Utility of Practice.

Indeed, herein lies an important – though unspoken – reason for generally preferring the Monarchical form to that of most Aristocracies and virtually all Democracies: the possibility, however remote, of an individual coming into Sovereign power who is, or may become, genuinely philosophical, or at least sufficiently respectful of philosophy as to be counselled by philosophers, living or dead. Of enduring regimes, hereditary Kingships would seem to provide the greatest likelihood of such an unlikely happening, as they offer the possibility of 'a true *erös* for genuine philosophy taking possession of the sons of those now in power or holding kingship' (*Republic* 499b–c; cf. 502a). Recall, this is not utterly without precedent: King Phillip of Macedon sought out a philosopher to educate his son – with world-shaping consequences. Whereas, given the rarity of such natures, it is practically impossible that there would ever be a numerous assembly of people genuinely philosophical, to say nothing of an entire citizenry (cf. 491a–b, 503b–d). This ground of preference for Monarchy must remain unexpressed, however, as Hobbes has no wish to compromise the attractiveness of the universal version, some variant of which would be the only regime practically possible in almost all times and places.

Restricting attention to these practically possible variants, then, what sort of person is Hobbes's design intended to draw into government or, speaking more generally, into 'politics'? Again, this will necessarily vary according to the extent a given regime accurately manifests that design – most importantly, perhaps, on how *just* it is. This factor has both passive and active consequences. Of major importance would be the openness of its various echelons of leadership to their being filled by people of proven 'worthiness,' those having 'the qualities required to the well discharging' of a given office or role. Obviously, if all higher governmental positions of power and status are limited to the blood relations of a Royal Family or small hereditary Nobility, or otherwise subject to pervasive nepotism, or restricted to a closed guild, then an outsider of superior talent and ambition will seek some other venue in which to excel (which may be in another polity altogether). However, a regime in which every office, possibly excepting only the very highest, is open to whoever is prepared to rise through talent, effort, diligence, loyalty, and proven ability – with incumbents being publicly respected accordingly – will attract some of the so-called best and brightest to compete for positions of rule. Moreover, a Hobbesian commonwealth that is basically just, and decent in other respects as well, would positively attract good men for that very reason, men who are proud to participate in the political life of a just and rational order; whereas most men of honour and integrity would shun active participation in a disorderly polity rife with corruption, whose squalid 'politics' tended instead to attract only clever, amoral opportunists.

However, this is to acknowledge that the kind of person who is attracted to politics depends also on the kinds of remuneration it offers, both de jure and de facto. Hobbes's skimpy treatment of this matter is curious, as he is clearly aware of its great practical importance. For the most part, it is dealt with only obliquely, figuring directly in but three of twenty-seven paragraphs near the end of his chapter 'Of PUNISHMENTS *and* REWARDS,' and in a few other observations and admonitions scattered throughout the text; whereas it is the dominant factor guiding Plato's Sokrates in designing his City in *logos* – and as I have been at pains to show, Plato's *Republic* is a text which Hobbes kept constantly in mind.

The 'Wages of Rule' is a topic that arises early in that dialogue. Sokrates has manoeuvred Thrasymachus to admit that insofar as a craftsman practises his art in accordance with its governing purpose, he 'rules' for the sake of the Ruled (his client), not for that of the Ruler (himself). This is why, generally speaking, he has to be *paid* for doing so. Thus, if ruling a whole polity is an *art* like the other arts, then an artful political Ruler also rules for the benefit of those he rules, and (so) must also be appropriately rewarded – for one must suppose that he, like any rational person, would not willingly *choose* to take on the task of straightening out other people's problems, and generally promoting *their* good, for *free*. Presumably, then, anyone who has this ability would demand 'wages' for his efforts, 'either money [literally, 'silver'], or honour, or a penalty if he refused to rule' (347a).

When Glaukon protests that he does not understand how a penalty can be a kind of 'wage,' the philosopher replies that he therefore does not understand 'the wage of the Best, for which the most decent [or, 'most equitable'; *epieikestatoi*] rule, when they are willing to rule.' Since these 'best, most decent' types are primarily motivated neither by money nor honour (which need not mean they are totally indifferent to these goods), 'there must in addition be necessity and a penalty, if they're likely to be willing to rule.' As for the penalty, 'the greatest' is 'to be ruled by a worse [man]' simply because 'oneself is not willing to rule' (347b–c). This permanent, inevasible truth, relevant to communal life at all levels, may move decent men to challenge for leadership even in indecent regimes. Be that as it may, Sokrates supposes that if ever there were a '*polis* of good men,' they would fight over the privilege of *not* having to rule, rather than is commonly the case: fighting over the opportunity to rule. The reason is, any knowledgeable person would choose to be benefited by another, rather than be bothered benefiting another (347d) – the implication being that a knowledgeable person is concerned first and foremost, if not exclusively, with his own good. Needless to add, Hobbes completely agrees.

Sokrates here, however, seems to have ignored a fourth kind of 'wage': the inherent *gratification* that may come simply from the exercise of power – though he later acknowledges sheer 'love of ruling' (*philarchos*) to be a prominent constituent in the *psychē* of the archetypal great-spirited man, one who loves hunting and athletics, but also music and fine rhetoric, though he is most conspicuously a lover of victory and of honour (548d–549a). His spirit-grounded love of ruling is to be distinguished, however, from a more overtly 'erotic' kind, such as that manifested by men who constantly fight with each other for the opportunity to rule, viewing political office as a means of selfish gain, mainly of a material kind (cf. 521a–b).

It is the high-spirited kind of soul that is to be recruited as a raw youth for potential membership in the ruling warrior class of the City in *logos*, and who is then subjected to a strict and demanding regimen of nurture aimed at his becoming practically indifferent to things of the body in order that an harmonious regime be instilled in his soul. A naturally *just* regime, that is, each of his soul's parts doing well what it is naturally best suited to do: his reason ruling in accordance with sound beliefs, aided in its control of moderated appetites by an obedient spirit. The actual Rulers are chosen from among those who have long lived the simple warrior's life in service to the City, and who have proven themselves the 'most skillful at guarding it,' as well as prudent, powerful, and caring of it

(412c). The philosopher gives special attention to this matter of 'caring' for the City, plausibly arguing that one cares *most* for 'that which one happens to love [*philön*],' and suggesting, furthermore, that one would most *love* something with which, or whom, one's own well-being was congruent, each faring as well or ill as did the other. Those who are to be the complete Guardians of the City are extensively tested as to the strength of this 'conviction [*dogma*]': that their own good and that of the City are identical, so that they will be eager to do whatever is advantageous to the City, and adamantly unwilling to do what is not (412e).

However, Sokrates does not rely solely on the firmness of the Rulers' beliefs to ensure that they invariably rule in the interests of the City as whole. He also deprives them of the most common temptations for doing otherwise by denying them all means of enjoying any extrinsic benefits from their monopoly of power – beyond what is rightly due them, that is, namely, honour and respect from everyone for their virtue and service. For although he affirms that a fine education provides the surest protection against an abuse of power by them or their auxiliaries, he warns it is not prudent to rely entirely on this (416b). Thus, the whole ruling class of Guardians and Auxiliaries are to be allowed no private property 'beyond what is entirely necessary' (and it would seem that nothing is, other than their own bodies). Nor are they to have any place of privacy wherein to enjoy private pleasures (other than within their own souls). Their material needs for simple food, clothing, and shelter are all provided them at public expense – that is, they will be housed together in barracks open to the public, they will be fed together a plain spartan fare in common mess halls, and they will draw from the commissary their uniforms and equipment as needed. And not only may they not *possess* gold and silver, they may not so much as *touch* it (hence they cannot *use* costly implements and ornaments, despite not technically owning them, and thereby evade the intent of the proscription). Their lives open books, they would be made, so far as humanly possible, wholly public-serving, public-spirited men (416d–417b).

Some arrangement such as this is what would be required for a polity to have Rulers that were, so far as humanly possible, completely dedicated to protecting and promoting the common good. Logically required, that is. But thinking *psycho*-logically, *does* this remain within the realm of the 'humanly possible'? Is it realistic to expect that the prospect of living in this ascetic manner for one's entire life would attract – and retain – enough naturally suitable individuals to meet all the civil and military responsibilities of a Ruling Class? If one has doubts, then one must be prepared to accept certain compromises that are, in effect, dictated by inclinations of human nature which remain present in virtually all individuals, however strenuously 'pruned' by nurture.

But the logic of the problem – as revealed in the philosopher's requirements – does not change: the Private is in tension with the Public. And that tension is most dangerously manifested in the desire for private property, for wealth and all it can buy, which includes the *privacy* of enjoyment that is possible within the private homes of 'moneymakers' (in contrast to the communal barracks of soldiers; 415e). As Sokrates later argues, it is those 'private nests' with their treasuries and walled pleasure gardens that eventually corrupt the Honour-and-Victory-loving Rulers who define a martial Timocracy, transforming them into Wealth-loving Oligarchs (547c, 548a). Admittedly, they are apt to be products of a defective nurture – 'having been educated not by persuasion but by force, through neglect of the true Muse of *logos* and philosophy, and honouring athletics with greater distinction than music' – hence not unalterably convinced that virtue truly is more precious than 'mortal gold' (548b; cf. 416e). But inasmuch as moral certainty attends only genuine *knowledge*, and is gained only over time and through philosophy, and philosophical natures are few and far between, it is impossible to nurture an entire ruling class that will be permanently impervious to all temptations of the flesh. Practically speaking, then, one should wish to reduce those temptations to the greatest extent consistent with maintaining a belief among its members that they have not forgone their own good in furthering that of the rest of the citizenry. But this means they must be allowed some private property and private life. Thus the political problem becomes that of establishing an institutional structure whereby the ruling elite as a whole polices itself, ensuring that private aggrandizement remains subordinate to, and dependent upon, public service.

Though doubtless aware of the problem, Hobbes never explicitly addresses it. To be sure, doing so might well require greater rhetorical delicacy than even Hobbes can muster. For tackling it directly would risk exposing one and all to the peculiar *paradox* implicit in his teaching '*both* how to govern, *and* how to obey,' to wit: preaching that Subjects owe unconditional obedience to their Sovereign, the quality of whose governing they are to regard as beyond their criticism, while at the same time providing the Sovereign a substantial description of how a rational, well-ordered commonwealth *ought* to be structured and ruled – which necessarily provides anyone who can read a detailed template for criticizing his Sovereign. Of course, in Hobbes's day, that would have been a much smaller proportion of the population, and the proportion of those likely to read a book such as his much smaller still, and the proportion of those able to grasp its 'main Designe' very small indeed. But also, and related, there would be proportionally greater sympathy then than now for the prudence of a doctrine which discourages the Ruled from criticizing the Sovereign, and which denies them any rational ground for doing so – knowing that people are ready enough to do that without either encouragement or grounds, since 'amongst men, there are very many, that thinke themselves wiser, and abler to govern the Publique, better than the rest' (XVII/9, 87).

Beyond this, however, the whole set of issues involved in maintaining the integrity of Rulers is complicated by the complexity inherent in the many permutations comprised by the universal version of his prescription. Whatever arrangement a martial Aristocracy might adopt to sustain its warrior ethos, for example, is sure to differ from that which would be most effective in providing a Commercial Republic with good government, to say nothing of a Theocracy concerned to sustain the piety and suppress the avarice of its members.

What little a reader can piece together of Hobbes's view confirms, first, his basic agreement with Plato's Sokrates that Private interests exist in tension with the Public interest, that this tension is not entirely eradicable, and that it is most dangerously manifested in the desire for private property and wealth; and, second, that all ways of ameliorating this problem support the superiority of the Monarchical form of commonwealth, more precisely, of a rational Kingship. Thus, having insisted that the 'three kindes of Common-wealth' differ not in the Power each must exercise, 'but in the difference of Convenience, or Aptitude to produce the Peace, and Security of the people,' he proceeds to survey the reasons why by that criterion the Monarchical form is superior. And his first argument – which I have had reasons to quote more than once before – addresses the very point at issue: the tension between private and public good. Everyone involved in exercising sovereign power bears both 'his own naturall Person' and that of the whole People (as their Representative):

And though he be carefull in his politique Person to procure the common interest; yet he is more, or no lesse carefull to procure the private good of himselfe, his family, kindred and friends; and for the most part, if the publique interest chance to crosse the private, he preferrs the private: for the Passions of men, are commonly more potent than their Reason. From whence it follows, that where the publique and private interest are most closely united, there is the publique most advanced. Now in Monarchy, the private interest is the same with the publique. The riches, power, and honour of a Monarch arise onely from the riches, strength and reputation of his Subjects. For no King can be rich, nor glorious, nor secure; whose Subjects are either poore, or contemptible, or too weak through want, or dissension, to maintain a war against their enemies: Whereas in a Democracy, or Aristocracy, the publique prosperity conferres not so much to the private fortune of one that is corrupt, or ambitious, as doth many times a perfidious advice, a treacherous action, or a Civill warre. (XIX/4, 95–6)

Notice, however, this rationale presumes a monarch who is sufficiently rational himself to be ruled by it. History, and not least of all England's, is replete with instances of Kings and Queens who squandered the resources of their realms to finance their own pleasures and a vainglorious appearance.

Even with respect to a problem which at first glance might seem to count against Monarchy, further consideration reveals that it actually favours it:

[I]n Monarchy there is this inconvenience; that any Subject, by the power of one man, for the enriching of a favourite or flatterer, may be deprived of all he possesseth; which I confesse is a great and inevitable inconvenience. But the same may as well happen, where the Soveraigne Power is in an Assembly: For their power is the same; and they are as subject to evill Counsell, and to be seduced by Orators, as a Monarch by Flatterers; and becoming one an others Flatterers, serve one anothers Covetnesse and Ambition by turnes. And whereas the Favorites of Monarchs, are few, and they have none els to advance but their owne Kindred; the Favourites of an Assembly, are many; and the Kindred much more numerous, than of any Monarch. (XIX/8, 96–7)

The overwhelming power of Sovereignty, constituted with authority to do as it pleases 'without stint' (XVI/14, 82), is subject to all sorts of what would ordinarily be regarded as 'abuse' – 'being [as Hobbes concedes] obnoxious to the lusts, and other irregular passions of him, or them that have so unlimited a Power in their hands' (XVIII/20, 94). While not the worst that could happen, one might regard a Sovereign's confiscating all of one person's property in order to fuel his own profligacy, or to bestow it on some sycophant, as the epitome of an abuse of power. And though Hobbes insists that a sitting King (say) has every *right* to do such a thing – 'that whatsoever he doth, it can be no injury to any of his Subjects; nor ought he to be by any of them accused of Injustice' (XVIII/6, 90) – he argues that a King's actually doing so is irrational, since he cannot damage or weaken his subjects without undermining his 'own strength and glory.' Hobbes's example is especially apt, since the arbitrary seizure of one subject's property casts into doubt the security of every subject's property, and *that* – irrespective of the 'logic' of Sovereignty – is flirting with rebellion, the 'Naturall Punishment' for the 'Negligent government of Princes' (XXXI/40, 193).[21] So, however threatening to the maintenance of civil society may 'in theory' be the notion '*That every private man has an absolute Propriety in his Goods; such, as excludeth the Right of the Soveraign*' (XXIX/10, 169) – requiring a king to ensure that his subjects are taught instead a more responsible view, one allowing for reasonable taxation[22] – he must not forget that 'in practice' the wholesale expropriation of what any 'man by lawfull Industry, without danger, or hurt to the Common-wealth, shall acquire to himselfe' will be regarded as the act of an oppressive Tyrant, not of a legitimate King.

The rest of Hobbes's recipe for preventing or mitigating the corrupting effects of power follows this same pattern of showing what is rational in terms of a sovereign's own self-interest. But obviously, as I have several times emphasized, his advice will be only as effectual as the sovereign is rational, meaning not only capable of fully *understanding* the 'why' of it, but sufficiently master of himself always to *act* upon it.

To illustrate Hobbes's strategy with a few important examples: Whereas any Aristocratic or Democratic assembly counsels itself from among its own members (who have counselling as a right simply by virtue of belonging), *choosing* competent counsel is a problem peculiar to Monarchy. It is obviously in the interest of even a self-indulgent monarch to get the best information and advice he can. But it is worth noting that Hobbes makes this *also* a *moral* requirement: 'the Soveraign that endeavoureth not to make choyce of those, that in every kind are the most able, dischargeth not his Office as he *ought* to do.' But precisely because power, hence opportunity for personal profit, attends the role of a King's Counsellor, there is always the potential for a conflict of interest between that of the Counsellor and that of the King (and therefore of the Public). Consequently, 'The most able Counsellours, are they that have the least hope of benefit by giving evill Counsell, and most knowledge of those things that conduce to the Peace, and Defence of the Common-wealth.' Both criteria, however, while easy to state, are difficult to apply. With respect to the first desideratum, Hobbes allows for a 'just suspicion' of those 'men whose estates are not sufficient to discharge their accustomed expenses.' He leaves the reader to trace out for himself the several implications of this warning.

As for the second qualification, 'to know, who has the most knowledge of the Publique affaires, is yet harder; and they that know them, need them a great deale the lesse.'[23] That said, 'the best signes of Knowledge of any Art, are, much conversing in it, and constant good effects of it.' The difficulty with following this advice is that proof of possessing the Statesman's Art by producing 'constant good effects' is not nearly so straightforward as in the case of, say, the Art of Medicine, or even of Generalship. It would seem to presume some sort of apprenticeship in government. This is perhaps confirmed by the warning Hobbes adds: 'Good Counsell comes not by Lot, nor by Inheritance; and therefore there is no more reason to expect good Advice from the rich, or noble, in matter of State, than in delineating the dimensions of a fortresse; unless we shall think there needs no method in the study of the Politiques, (as there does in the study of Geometry,) but onely to be lookers on; which is not so. For the Politiques is the harder study of the two' (XXX/25, 184; cf. X/15, 42).

Of only slightly less importance than a king's choice of Counsellors is his choice of Judges, that is, of 'Interpreters of the Law,' and as such dispensers of his Justice. In specifying the qualities that make for a good Judge, Hobbes lists '*Contempt of unnecessary Riches*, and Preferments' as second only to 'the goodness of [his] own naturall Reason' whereby he recognizes what is equitable in particular cases (XXVI/28, 147). Needless to add, that second-place requirement would in itself eliminate from consideration the vast majority of people. Moreover, presuming that the first quality alone will not ensure the second, good judges must be recruited from a subset of that minority distinguished by 'a certain Noblenesse or Gallantnesse of courage, (rarely found,) by which a man scorns to be beholding for the contentment of his life, to fraud, or breach of promise' (XV/10, 74). Add to this the third requirement – '*To be able in judgement to divest himself of all feare, anger, hatred, love,* and *compassion*' – and still a fourth set of qualities (patience, attentiveness, retentive memory, synthetic judgment) – and Hobbes's idea of a 'good Judge' approaches that of the philosophical nature as described (and illustrated) by Sokrates in Plato's *Republic* (484c–487a; cf. 409a–e). Indeed, too closely so, one might protest, since such natures are admitted to be exceedingly rare, certainly much rarer than would be needed to fill the number of judgeships typically required in large polities. Thus, unless a regime is purposefully structured to select and nurture such natures, while at the same time cultivating moderation in the entire citizenry (such that crime and litigation are minimized; cf. *Republic* 405a–b, 409a–c), there is sure to be a serious shortfall of 'good judges.' Still, the idea is relevant with respect to both the recruitment and the supervision of the judiciary, since it makes clear what surrogate arrangements ought to aim at.

The remuneration of Judges is singled out as a matter for a Sovereign's particular concern in maintaining integrity in the administration of Justice:

And whereas some Salaries are certain, and proceed from the publique Treasure; and others uncertain, and casuall, proceeding from the execution of the Office for which the Salary is ordained; the later is in some cases hurtfull to the Common-wealth; as in the case of Judicature. For where the benefit of Judges, and Minis-ters of a Court of Justice, ariseth from the multitude of Causes that are brought to their cognisance, there needs must follow two Inconveniences: One, is the nourishing of sutes; for the more sutes, the greater the benefit; and another that depends on that, which is contention about Jurisdiction; each Court drawing to it selfe, as many Causes as it can. (XXVIII/26, 166)

This is of a piece with Hobbes's observation that 'Unnecessary Lawes are not good Lawes; but trapps for Mony' (XXX/21, 182). One can hardly help noticing how prominent in his various discussions of properly staffing and running a government are the problems posed by the temp-tations of wealth.

What one could regard as Hobbes's basic statement on 'remuneration' for political service comes not until the twenty-fourth paragraph of chapter 30. It presumes, however, his earlier but equally brief general treatment of the Sovereign's power of Reward:

REWARD, is either of *Gift*, or by *Contract*. When by Contract, it is called *Salary*, and *Wages*; which is benefit due for service performed, or promised. When of Gift, it is benefit proceeding from the *grace* of them that bestow it, to encourage, or enable men to do them service. And therefore when the Soveraign of a Common-wealth appointeth a Salary to any publique Office, he that receiveth it, is bound in Justice to performe his office; otherwise, he is bound onely in honour, to acknowledgement, and an endeavour of requitall. For though men have no lawfull remedy, when they be commanded to quit their private businesse, to serve the publique, without Reward, or Salary; yet they are not bound thereto, by the Law of Nature, nor by the Institution of the Common-wealth, unlesse the service cannot otherwise be done; because it is supposed the Soveraign may make use of all their means, insomuch as the most common Souldier, may demand the wages of his warre-fare, as a debt. (XXVIII/24, 166)

It bears adding, however, that unpaid public service may still attract good men whose private situation allows them to afford providing it, insofar as they find the honour of being called upon payment enough (cf. X/35, 43). Moreover, they are apt to be the very kind of men who will regard themselves as honour-bound to do their best as a matter of noblesse oblige. Speaking more broadly, however:

[I]t belongeth to the Office, and Duty of the Sovereign, to apply his Rewards alwayes so, as there may arise from them benefit to the Common-wealth: wherein consisteth their Use, and End; and is then done, when they that have well served the Common-wealth, are with as little expense of the Common Treasure, as is possible, so well recompenced, as others thereby may be encouraged, both to serve the same as faithfully as they can, and to study the arts by which they may be enabled to do it better. (XXX/24, 183)

A nice task for prudential judgment, this: striking the balance of 'just so much compensation as necessary, but no more' – not merely to recruit and retain faithful public servants, however, but to encourage prospects to seek to qualify for such service by virtue of education.

The contexts of both of the above-quoted statements, however, caution against confusing 'reward' with 'bribery.' And though these warnings are most pertinent to a Monarchy, they nonetheless further emphasize it as Hobbes's 'regime of choice':

The benefits which a Sovereign bestoweth on a Subject, for fear of some power, and ability he hath to do hurt to the Common-wealth, are not properly Rewards; ... because they be extorted by fear, which ought not to be incident to the Sovereign Power: but are rather Sacrifices, which the Sovereign (considered in his naturall person, and not in the person of the Common-wealth) makes, for the appeasing the discontent of him he thinks more potent than himselfe; and encourage not to obedience, but on the contrary, to the continuance, and increasing of further extortion. (XXVIII/25, 166)

Thus the imprudence of attempting 'To buy with Mony, or Preferment, from a Popular ambitious Subject, to be quiet, and desist from making ill impressions in the mindes of the People.' Moreover, by making seditious ambition profitable, one simply creates a Hydra: for every man bought off, three more are encouraged to 'the same Mischiefe, in hope of like Benefit' (XXX/24, 183).

Not that a Subject's popularity is invariably bad. Indeed, 'A Commander of an Army in chiefe, if he be not Popular, shall not be beloved, nor feared as he ought to be by his Army; and consequently cannot performe that office with good successe.' Hobbes nonetheless warns – doubtless with Caesar in mind – 'this love of Souldiers, (if caution be not given of the Commanders fidelity,) is a dangerous thing to Soveraign Power; especially when it is in the hands of an Assembly not popular' (XXX/28, 185; presumably, Hobbes has the Roman Senate in mind). Whereas, 'when the Soveraign himselfe is Popular; that is, reverenced and beloved of his People, there is no danger at all from the Popularity of a Subject.' As for the soldiers, they are 'never so generally unjust, as to side with their Captain; though they love him, against their Soveraign, when they love not onely his Person, but also his Cause' (XXX/29, 185). Of course, to 'make assurance double sure,' it would be best if the Sovereign were himself a proven soldier, and so could credibly himself serve as Commander-in-Chief of the Army.[24] Then there would be no doubt but that 'whoever is made Generall of an Army, he that have the Soveraign Power is always Generallissimo' (XVIII/12, 92).

A final word of clarification is perhaps necessary. The name 'democracy' raises a still further complication in regards to the universal version of Hobbes's prescription. For by the term 'Democracy,' he does *not* mean any of the variants of 'Commonwealth' as has become virtually universal in the West, and touted as desirable for the rest of the world: what is today called '*Representative* Democracy' – all of which variants Hobbes would regard as Elective Aristocracies. There is no need to speculate on what sorts of people are drawn into 'electoral politics' of these regimes (or for that matter, into one or another of the enormous administrative apparatuses whereby their governments actually govern). Anyone who cares to look, and think about what he sees, can judge that for himself.[25]

23

A Colossus of Irony:
The Latent Platonism of *Leviathan*

By way of a summary, let me return to the beginning, where I observed that only near the very end of *Leviathan* does Hobbes explain why he begins as he does: 'There is a certain *Philosophia prima*, on which all other Philosophy ought to depend; and consisteth principally, in right limiting of the significations of such Appellations, or Names, as are of all others the most Universall; Which Limitations serve to avoid ambiguity, and aequivocation in Reasoning' (XLVI/14, 371). I took his belated emphasis on the fundamental importance of First Philosophy – and on what in practice is so closely bound up with it: Epistemology – as, whatever else, a tacit invitation to *re*-examine the metaphysical context he has provided for his new Science of Politics. Doing so, however, simply highlighted the manifest inadequacy of his explicit treatment of those issues he chooses to address; his conspicuous silence on other matters that it would seem imperative to address; and the extent to which his political prescription does not square with the principles upon which it is supposedly based. Moreover, as one ranges more widely through his text, one encounters indications, some quite explicit, others subtle or indirect, that Hobbes himself does not subscribe to the positions he establishes as a framework for his revolutionary political teaching. Critical examination of those views is nonetheless warranted, I believe, for the sake of better understanding not simply *Leviathan*, but also the modern world it has been so instrumental in shaping. For versions of these premises about reality, despite their evident deficiencies, remain widely accepted today, with consequences far from trivial.

Hobbes, however, never really tries to make a case for any of the metaphysical or epistemological claims he propounds. Not surprisingly, since that would entail addressing the more obvious objections which could be raised, as well as refuting alternative views. He simply declares things to be as he says they are, in effect endorsing the intellectual presuppositions shared by most of those who took up the Baconian-Cartesian challenge to pursue a new Science of Nature. And he does so, I contend, not because he regards those same metaphysical principles as truly adequate for understanding and ordering human life, but to create the appearance that his new Science of Politics is of a piece with the new Natural Science it is designed to promote: sharing the same premises about the basic character of reality, founded on the same sensory empiricism, proceeding through the same rigorous geometrical reasoning, and partaking of the same practical certitude. As such, it preserves the appearance of a unified understanding of the world, reflective of its real unity that we all somehow intuit.

Nonetheless, there are several reasons why I find it most unlikely that Hobbes himself subscribes to the premises he would have his trusting reader accept as the basis for the political teaching that follows. First and foremost, the positions he stakes out about Nature, including Human Nature – plausible though they might seem to readers who do not, and probably cannot, subject such claims to thorough critical analyses – are philosophically indefensible (as I argued at length in Part One, and will briefly review below). I can only presume, given such ample evidence of Hobbes's mental acuity, that he understands this at least as well as I do. He is, after all, a philosopher. More to the point, he is a *political* philosopher, hence not merely an accomplished ironist, but willing and only too able to employ rhetoric and sophistry in a worthy cause.

Second, as I mentioned above, these same positions do not fully cohere with the political doctrine supposedly based thereupon; indeed, in some cases they are clearly in conflict not only with various practical necessities of Hobbes's political prescription, but with any conceivable alternative that one could take seriously. Again, I presume he is well aware of this but (being a political philosopher) knows equally well that the contradictions in question are not merely compatible with, but requisite to, the viability of his commonwealth – and that in any case, political life typically abounds with logical contradictions which trouble most people not the least bit.

Third, certain of Hobbes 'official' positions logically conflict with other claims he makes, thereby calling the former into question, and obliging a thoughtful reader to determine as best he can what *must* be Hobbes's real views. But this cannot be done apart from deciding for oneself what position best makes sense overall. For surely one is not to presume that a philosopher worth reading would settle for anything less. As Hobbes warns, 'it is not the bare Words, but the Scope of the writer that giveth the true light, by which any writing is to bee interpreted; and they that insist upon single Texts, without considering the main Designe, can derive no thing from them cleerly' (XLIII/24, 331).

Fourth, Hobbes's own use of certain key terms does not always square with the basic premises and principles he explicates – whereas he is so emphatic about the importance of clear definitions and consistent usage. In my attempt to understand his doctrine, I did nothing less than take his admonitions at face value: 'a man that seeketh precise *truth*, had need to remember what every name he uses stands for; and to place it accordingly'; and 'how necessary it is for any man that aspires to true Knowledge, to examine the Definitions of former Authors; and either to correct them ... or to make them himselfe' (IV/12–13, 15). Presuming he is as fastidious in his choice of language as he insists the pursuit of truth requires, his usage must reflect how he actually understands things, or more cautiously put, how he intends an attentive reader to refine, qualify, and even 'correct' his own initial understanding of the teaching Hobbes has put forth.

At the risk of trying the patience of some readers, I must briefly review the major metaphysical tenets upon which Hobbes has appeared to found his new science of politics. For the established, but I believe mistaken, view is that it rests upon an 'Empiricist' First Philosophy that is diametrically opposed to the supposed 'Idealism' of Plato.

So, begin with *Materialism*.[1] The notion that Matter and its motions is the fundamental reality, the ultimate cause of whatever happens, and of why anything and everything is the way it is – that everything *real* is composed of matter, and that (conversely) if it is not material it is not real – will not withstand even a cursory examination. One might begin by asking whether the Doctrine of Materialism, communicable from his mind to mine, is itself 'made of matter.' The world consists of much that is not materially embodied, beginning with the truths of geometry, which – as with all knowledge, all truths – must have a prior existence in order to be discovered (for the general truths themselves are not to be confused with their particular representations in material things, including people's brains, any more than is the meaning of these words to be equated with the paper and ink by means of which they are expressed).

Indeed, even with respect to embodied things, the inadequacy of Materialism as a metaphysical doctrine was shown millennia ago by Aristotle simply through pointing to the fact that what is meant by 'matter' is always *relative* to particular level of analysis. One never observes matter simpliciter, but always some particular *form* of matter, all of whose distinctive characteristics are due to its form, not the stuff on which the form is imposed (or imposes itself). And since each particular form of matter is reducible to a still simpler form, it necessarily terminates in some homogeneous 'prime matter' that is itself inert – and so could not conceivably be the cause of the virtual infinitude of heterogeneous kinds that make up the natural world. As I noted in chapter 2, Hobbes is actually rather coy about Materialism, speaking mainly of 'bodies' (i.e., *formed* matter) rather than 'matter' simply; and though he insists that the World is a body, as is everything real found in it, that even 'spirits' are bodies, he informs us in the book's penultimate sentence that he is working on a pleasingly novel theory of Bodies.

The radical *Nominalism* that Hobbes expounds in connection with his account of Language – or so is generally regarded his claim of 'there being nothing in the world Universall but Names; for the things named, are every one of them Individuall and Singular' – is as indefensible as the materialism with which it is implicated, and grossly misleading about language, human rationality, and 'the real world.' For the simplistic account of sensation and thought provided in the chapters preceding that '*Of* SPEECH' cannot begin to account for the ability to *recognize* the 'similitude' whereby one correctly applies even such a familiar Universall as 'tree.' In this, as in most cases, there is a multiplicity of 'similitudes' involved which must be integrated into a coherent whole, *none* of which are primarily, much less exclusively, congruences of sense data; even the recognition that trees have leaves involves the intellect in 'seeing' the similarity between leaves as different in *appearance* as those of the willow, the birch, and the maple – to say nothing of the palm or the fir.

The metaphysical flaw with Nominalism, however, is its failure to account for the similitudes of the things themselves, allowing for their being rightly recognized as of the same kind: what makes all maple trees *maples*, oak trees *oaks* – that is, shared *forms* (and not only of *visibility*), in which each thing's unique *nature* inheres, whereby it is a specific *kind* of thing. These forms of Nature have a reality independent of their ever-changing sets of incarnations, as is tacitly shown whenever we speak of an extinct species. It is to these forms, or rather to their mental representations, *ideas*, that the common nouns or 'universals' actually refer (not to one or another of their particular instances). The name 'swan' refers to the (invariably incomplete, and often inaccurate) *idea* of the *form* of swan. Thus, Hobbes is ironically correct in asserting that there is 'nothing in the world Universall but Names; for the things named, are every one of them Individuall and Singular.'

As for the strict *Determinism* that is the necessary presupposition of all Natural Science,[2] its application to the activities of the human mind is self-negating. First, however, one must not misconstrue the issue as that of 'Free Will *versus* Determinism' – as so many people do, a mistake Hobbes skilfully exploits. For what is at stake is not a freedom of the *will* (practically an incoherent idea), but of mind or thought, whence willing and acting take direction. Properly focused, then, the claim that all thought is predetermined by antecedent causes is in principle insupportable (literally), since applying it reflexively – as one must – renders irrelevant all evidence and argument pro or con, on this or any other issue. If the mind is not free in its rational activities of analysing, assessing, and concluding, presumedly on the perceived merits of each case, but is instead predetermined to think whatever it thinks *irrespective* of whatever might be true (as shown whenever two people hold conflicting views), then thinking – and truth itself – lose all meaning. And humans, far from being partially autonomous by virtue of their rational souls, are actually deluded automatons.

Seen in that light, one can hardly take seriously *any* so-called thinking – whether about Determinism or anything else. Thus, Determinism is bewilderingly paradoxical: upon assuming oneself to be strictly determined, one should no longer take the idea seriously. When one attempts to do so – attempts to manage the compound reflexivity and resulting schizophrenic existence, that of an automaton subject to irrepressible delusions of autonomy – one learns that the human soul is not constructed to cope with such a baffling mode of self-consciousness. Hobbes, for his part, argues strenuously against the notion of 'free *will*,' but expressly (if inconspicuously) acknowledges, 'A private man has alwaies the liberty, (because *thought* is free,) to beleeve, or not beleeve in his heart' (XXXVII/13, 238); moreover, men's 'Consciences [are] free' (XLVII/19, 384); and 'a mans Conscience, and his Judgement is the same thing' (XXIX/7, 168).

Arguably, however, it is Hobbes's apparent endorsement of *Hedonism* that is most consequential, both philosophically and politically. With respect to political effects, it is far more significant than Determinism. For despite the fact that Determinism is 'in principle' a greater distortion of the truth about human nature – infinitely greater, I would say – its impact on actual political life is fairly limited (confined mainly to excusing human failings). Even people who profess to believe in it do not 'live it,' because no one *can*. But Hedonism is not paradoxical, and is supported by both experience and observation; thus, most people need very little convincing that the Good is Pleasure, and little persuasion to live accordingly. While this view tends to encourage people's industriousness so as to obtain the means for their own 'ease and sensual delight' (cf. XXX/1, 175), it also thereby promotes a preoccupation with their private lives – with 'minding of one's own business' (cf. *Republic* 433a–b, 441d–e, 443c–e) – to the proportional exclusion of a concern with public affairs.

However, were *everyone* strictly ruled by the pursuit of pleasure and avoidance of pain and death; were there not some men who regarded the noble and honoured life as *better* than the merely pleasant life, hence were willing to sacrifice personal interests, even risk life and limb for a *common* good, the polity would be deprived of services essential to its very existence, much less to its flourishing. Hobbes has allowed for this choice by a clever piece of sophistry that licenses *both* a mandatory Natural Law forbidding 'that, which is destructive of [one's] life' (upon which his entire edifice of derivative Natural Laws is based), *and* a permissive Natural Right which 'consisteth in the liberty to do, or to *forbeare*' using one's own power solely in the interest of one's own preservation.

As a metaphysical postulate, the notion that The Good *is* Pleasure – something subjective and relative to each sentient being, whether man or beast – is inadequate not merely in its moral form (as Hedonism). It trivializes what is actually one of the most taxing philosophical problems. The claim derives its plausibility from being confused with a quite different proposition: that Pleasure is Good (more accurately, pleasure 'feels good' – virtually by definition), which, according to vast amounts of empirical evidence, is *a* ruling principle of all animate creation, man included, and *the* ruling principle of beasts. But one cannot explain *why* creatures are pleased (and pained) in the particular way they are apart from the recognition that there is an *objective* good relevant to each and every sentient being, epitomized by its optimum condition of health, strength, and beauty, which in turn determine reproductive success. On that basis one sees that, generally speaking, the pleasures sought by the lower animals – 'their quotidian Food, Ease, and Lusts' (XII/4, 52) – lead them towards that optimum condition, as individuals and as species.[3]

This, in turn, contributes species by species to sustaining the whole natural order, which is good in itself, and points beyond to the Goodness of Being (cf. *Republic* 508e–509b, 534b–c).

There are literally dozens of times in *Leviathan* where Hobbes's use of 'good' or 'evil' (or 'bad') clearly indicates that he does *not* himself regard the Good as radically subjective and relative (determined by 'whatsoever is the object of any mans Appetite or Desire'; VI/7, 24). One example suffices: 'A good Law is that, which is *Needfull*, for the *Good of the People*, and withal *Perspicuous*' (XXX/20, 182). Of course, the governing premise of Hobbes's entire political science is that there is an objective Good for humans: that, whatever else, it consists of living law-abiding lives in a stable, peaceful Civil Society; and likewise, an objective Evil: falling back into that anarchic 'condition of meer Nature' wherein every man is enemy to every other, resulting in their lives being generally 'solitary, poore, nasty, brutish, and short.'

Closely allied to Hedonism is the principle of strict and universal *Egoism*: the conception of human nature as profoundly self-centred, radically *individualistic*, each person being concerned, not merely for the most part (a reasonable view), but *exclusively* with his own good: that 'of the voluntary acts of every man, the object is some *Good to himselfe.*' Presuming this to be so, each man cares about others only insofar as they somehow bear on his own good. Apart from the fact that this view would square with only some, even if much, but *not all* of any normal person's experience; and that it would render practically meaningless expressions of praise, honour, gratitude, love, and much else; apart from these and other objections, a strict and narrow egoism does not seem to conform with some of Hobbes's own definitions (e.g., of 'good will' or 'charity' or 'good nature'; nor especially of 'indignation': '*Anger* for great hurt done to another, when we conceive the same to be done by Injury'; VI/21, 26).

Most significantly, however, egoism does not comport with certain essential features of his political prescription. For example, it rules out the possibility of the Sovereign (or anyone else) receiving genuinely disinterested advice or counsel, as there would be no motive for either seeking or giving it; nor if provided, could it be credibly received for what Hobbes defines genuine counsel to be: 'directed to … the benefit of another man.' But egoism has an even more troubling implication: it precludes all practical possibility of there being Sovereigns who are genuinely concerned with *Equity* in the framing and administering of the Laws. Whereas Hobbes insists that everyone is to presume that the will of the Sovereign is 'always consonant to Equity and Reason' (XXVI/15, 141). Similarly, a strictly selfish Egoism is inconsistent with all four of Hobbes's requirements of 'a good Judge, or good Interpreter of the Lawes.' One can only conclude that, just as Hobbes recognizes fear of violent death is the most powerful passion of *most*, but *not all*, human beings, so too does the possibility of Justice and Equity depend on there being people of probity, who are both willing and able to rise above the selfish egoism that rules most people most of the time.

Speaking of Justice, the *Legal Positivism* Hobbes propounds – that all political justice exists only as enforced rules, and as such is always relative to time and place – presumes that the metaphysical status of Justice, its mode of being, is purely *conventional*. As such, there is justice within established regimes, but no transcendent standards of justice whereby to judge the justness of a given regime itself: its actual distribution of power and privilege, rights and duties, wealth and property – which may or may not strictly conform to its 'official' laws; that would depend upon how faithfully, how 'justly,' they are administered. But, as I previously argued, it is exceedingly difficult to understand the Natural Law of Equity, much less how it can be substantially applied in actual cases, apart from the existence of a *natural* Justice to which humans have access.

And, sure enough, Hobbes does acknowledge there *is* a form of Justice whose status is *not* that of mere conventions, changeable as the Sovereigns who enforce them – a Justice that is neither relative nor mutable because grounded in Nature. And while there is 'no *Court* of Naturall Justice, but in the Conscience onely' (XXX/30, 185; emphasis added), it is nonetheless pertinent to political life. The '*Fidelity*' of conscientious officials, for example, 'is a branch of naturall Justice' (XXVI/14, 141). Hobbes's most important declaration, however, is made in the very centre of his treatise – in the Crucial Paragraph – where he declares that 'the Science of Naturall Justice' is the one thing needful 'for Soveraigns, and their principall Ministers.' But since 'the learning of the truth [about] Naturall Justice' requires study and 'deep meditation' – which 'the greatest part of Man-kind' is too preoccupied either with labours or pleasures to engage in (XXX/14, 179) – positive laws must define what is just for almost all practical purposes. If, however, those laws are framed and applied by Rulers who are learned in the Science of Natural Justice, they will not be mere conventions, but partake of what is Just by Nature.

Finally, the simplistic view of *Reason as Calculation* – reducing the whole of Reason not merely to Deduction, but exclusively to arithmetical-type '*Reckoning* of the Consequences of *generall* names' (i.e., Universals) – amounts to a, literally, incredible diminution of human rationality. As if deducing conclusions about *individuals* (Hobbes's religious views, say), or particular things (such as the English Civil War), were not strictly rational. As if *inducing* generalizations, and *recognizing* individuals as instances of kinds, were not also rational activities. As if the human *imagination* – whereby people create, invent, hypothesize, empathize, evaluate, envision the future, understand the past – is not a rational faculty, reliant upon both deduction and induction. As if *memory*, similarly, does not operate on rational principles. Suffice it to observe, were one to accept Hobbes's explicit account of Reason as truly definitive (plausible enough, perhaps, to the many who equate Reason with the effort of 'reasoning'), one could not regard his political prescription, much less *Leviathan* as a whole, as a product of Reason. Whereas we may be fairly sure that Hobbes would have it so regarded: 'So, long time after men have begun to constitute Commonwealths, imperfect, and apt to relapse into disorder, there may Principles of Reason be found out, by industrious meditation, to make their constitution (excepting by externall violence) everlasting. And such are those which I have in this discourse set forth' (XXX/5, 176).

Whatever Hobbes's metaphysical views, at least two things are clear. First, they are *not* what they are usually taken to be – happily so, as it would be difficult to regard him as a pre-eminent thinker if he actually subscribed to the positions he sketches as the context wherein to situate his political prescription (being plausible enough to readers having little interest in metaphysics per se). Second, since he is *not* a Materialist, nor a Nominalist, nor a Determinist, nor a Hedonist, nor an Egoist, nor a Legal Positivist, none of these commitments rule out the possibility of his agreeing on fundamentals with Plato. For whatever Plato's actual metaphysical views, no serious student of the dialogues would contend that he maintained any of those positions I have denied to Hobbes.[4] On the other hand, it does seem that what one can fathom of Plato's ontology and epistemology (ignoring all the precious nonsense written about some putative 'Theory of Forms')[5] would meet Hobbes's requirements, resolving problems that his supposed principles cannot. But it is not my intention to attempt to show that here.

My case for a 'Platonian Leviathan' consists mainly of two parts. The first has this negative character of demonstrating that Hobbes did *not* hold various positions which could readily, and rightly, be seen as diametrically opposed to Plato's – such as those briefly reviewed in the preceding paragraphs, and fully argued in various chapters of Part One. Or more cautiously put, that so far as one can judge from the form and substance of his *Leviathan*, this is so. For I am not attempting to prove that, appearances to the contrary, Hobbes can be fairly described as a Platonist; that is, as holding essentially the same views as Plato regarding Knowledge and Nature, the City and Man, and (what is most important) with respect to Philosophy and the Art of Writing. My aim is the more modest one of showing the Platonic character of Hobbes's masterpiece, that the inspiration for *Leviathan* is taken from the dialogue which is in effect its complement: Plato's *Republic*. I do not deny that I believe this has broader implications, but the reader will judge this for himself.

As for the positive half of the case, it too has already been made, mainly in the preceding chapters of Part Two, the principal elements of which I shall briefly review in the paragraphs that follow. The significance of what I call 'the Crucial Paragraph' is indeed crucial in several respects. First of all, the rhetorical effect of its very presence, though perhaps slight upon first reading, grows in proportion to its further consideration. For its content seems at odds with everything that preceded it: the rigorously logical, practical, universally adaptable blueprint for establishing and administering political life scientifically, a design supposedly intelligible to almost anyone of ordinary capacity. All of this is retroactively called into question by Hobbes's melancholy confession of doubt. Will it, he wonders, ever be converted from a pure 'Truth of Speculation, into the Utility of Practice,' or has his been all so much 'uselesse' labour? Why would he think so? Because of 'how different this Doctrine is'? In what respect? In 'how much *depth of Morall Philosophy* is required, in them that have the Administration of the Soveraign Power'! To be sure, *Leviathan* is not a brisk or easy read, but I doubt that it leaves many readers of the preceding thirty-one chapters with the impression that implementing its political prescription would require great *philosophical* 'depth.' Is not this the virtue of the book, that Hobbes has solved all of the more taxing moral and practical problems – that 'the pains left another, will be onely to consider, if he also find not the same in himself'?

Truth is, no, he has *not* – although the lacuna in his treatment is not immediately evident, being concealed by a superficial resolution of the central problem of political life, hence of political philosophy: *Justice*. As

I noted earlier in discussing Legal Positivism, the claim that, for all practical purposes, justice is whatever the laws of a given regime declare it to be is not a resolution, but a trivialization – when not an outright evasion – of the defining issues of politics: what *ought* the law to declare, including what ought to fall within the purview of law (and what left to individual discretion); and what is the right overall arrangement of political life – a *just* form of regime, in light of which one may judge all actual and proposed regimes, including the various versions which Hobbes's prescription allows for. As one tries to imagine, concretely, framing those 'good laws' required for Hobbes's enlarged idea of the people's 'safety,' for rightly arbitrating disputes, adjudicating cases, distributing property, applying natural law where positive law is silent, and much else, one realizes the extent to which Hobbes has shifted the substantial problems of justice onto an undefined – and undefinable, but not unknowable – idea of *Equity* (accessible to those of exceptional 'goodnesse of naturall Reason,' and who are inclined 'to meditate thereon'). Moreover, and perhaps most important of all, if justice is merely *conventional*, nothing more than rules made by some men with sufficient power to impose their will upon the rest, then there is no convincing answer to 'Why be Just?' apart from the prudence of abiding by rules one cannot safely evade, though occasions arise when one might wish to. If 'justice' has no reality beyond convention, then 'the Foole' is *not* he who 'hath sayd in his heart, there is no such thing as Justice,' but he who hath said there *is*.

In the Crucial Paragraph, however, Hobbes – despite having himself explicitly provided only a conventionalist account of justice – declares 'the Science of *Naturall* Justice' to be the one thing needful 'for Soveraigns, and their principall Ministers.' Where is *that* 'Science' to be found, if not in the book obliquely referred to in the sentence immediately preceding this declaration: Plato's *Republic*, as famous for its defence of *natural* justice as *Leviathan* for the conventionalist alternative. But 'conventionalist *application*' would perhaps be a more accurate characterization of its status, if viewed in light of the form of political justice discovered in Sokrates's City in *logos* – what Hobbes calls 'the Commonwealth of *Plato*.' For one thereby recognizes the natural justice *implicit* in the overall design of 'the Commonwealth of *Hobbes*': that in actual operation it would automatically tend to achieve what Sokrates designates as the pre-eminent responsibility of Guardians, namely, the distribution of socially useful tasks and rewards according to the natural differences in people's talents and motivations. Moreover, it is in that same dialogue that is to be found the only convincing answer to the most important question of all: Why be Just? If there are to be Rulers of a commonwealth whose own first concern is that the laws and policies they frame be Just and Equitably administered, it is essential that they be persuaded of the inherent *goodness* of actually *being* Just themselves. Their police may as necessary enforce a law-defined justice upon the Ruled; but the Rulers must police themselves – or, rather, have little or no need to, inasmuch as being Just is their own ruling desire.

However, even more startling than Hobbes's reference to *natural* justice is the revelation that he is in agreement with Plato's most famous pronouncement, the very proposition that pragmatic readers are apt to regard as emblematic of his 'utopian Idealism': 'that it is impossible for the disorders of State, and changes of Governments by Civill Warre, ever to be taken away, till Soveraigns be Philosophers.' Ridiculous as others might find the idea, Hobbes does not find it so, because he understands the rationale that leads to this conclusion – which is not necessarily an advocacy of Philosophers ruling as Kings. It may as plausibly be construed as a veiled recognition that there is no perfect, much less permanent, solution to the problems of political life (cf. XXIX/1, 167). One must bear in mind that this revelation concludes a chapter entitled 'Of the Kingdome of *God* by Nature.'

Be that as it may, Hobbes also makes it clear that he has not overlooked what is so easily missed in Sokrates's pronouncement: that not only does he disqualify those who are not capable of philosophy from the rulership of his City in *logos*, but also *excludes from philosophy* those who would not be capable of ruling – and first of all, of ruling themselves – in the right kingly manner. Thus, Hobbes specifies that his hoped-for Sovereign would, 'by the exercise of *entire* Soveraignty,' which includes as its central Right that of judging what 'Opinions and Doctrines' are in any way published, protect 'the Publique teaching' of what he has written.

It is not merely Hobbes's endorsement of this view that is so significant, however. Its placement in his text – precisely in the centre, concluding the secular, scientific half of the book 'derived from the Principles of Naturall Reason' – greatly amplifies its importance. For that is where the original pronouncement is found in Plato's *Republic*: precisely in the centre, a fact that is easily established but not generally noticed. This in itself suggests Hobbes has studied that dialogue with sufficient care and insight to apply the dialogue's emphasis on Geometry to the physical text, and so has not merely understood the rational centrality of Plato's most famous pronouncement, but affirmed his agreement with it by the exact same arrangement of his own text. He cannot have supposed that many readers would make the connection. But neither should we suppose he thought *no one* would, nor that he did not intend it to have special significance for the few who did. To this and other geometrical likenesses of *Leviathan* and *Republic*, one may add certain arithmetical likenesses involving special numbers (most notably, the prevalence of sets of Four, the number traditionally symbolizing Justice).

Admittedly, Hobbes no sooner expresses his concurrence with Plato concerning the importance of Sovereigns being Philosophers than he qualifies his agreement, or so it would seem. For he contrasts Plato's requirement that potential Guardians master a demanding curriculum of 'Sciences Mathematicall' as preparation for becoming expert in the dialectical method, with his own insistence that Sovereigns themselves need only 'the Science of Naturall Justice' (though they are to encourage other men in the study of those same mathematical sciences by enacting 'good Lawes' to that purpose – which, whatever else, would amount to the political cultivation of philosophy and philosophers). Hobbes, having clearly set out the 'Theoremes of Morall Doctrine' whereby men may learn 'both how to govern, and how to obey,' it remains for an otherwise suitable Sovereign simply to study *Leviathan*; he need not be a philosopher in the full sense, merely sufficiently respectful of philosophy to learn from philosophers.[6] Hobbes, who has no interest in ruling directly himself – quite the contrary: he hopes to return to philosophy full-time (R&C/17, 396) – would happily settle for the *indirect* rule of philosophers. However, as I discussed previously, this is also the implicit teaching of Plato's *Republic*, exemplified by the character of Sokrates *in* the dialogue, and by Plato himself through the writing of it.

Once alerted by the Crucial Paragraph to the special relationship between the foundational work of political philosophy, Plato's *Republic*, and the single greatest influence on modern political life, Hobbes's *Leviathan*, one recognizes echoes of the former elsewhere in the latter, for example, in its Dedicatory Letter, which speaks of a pair of brothers in ways that may remind a reader of the two brothers who serve as Sokrates's primary interlocutors in the dialogue, and in Hobbes's likening himself to a sacred goose whose noise awakens those responsible for defending the Civil Power – a piece of ironic humility reminiscent of Sokrates's characterizing himself as a god-sent insect charged with awakening the citizenry with his stinging criticisms. Hobbes warns that the Scriptural interpretations he advances are apt to be regarded as offensive to those wedded to the established views, but that these latter are used in ways that endanger the Civil Power. Similarly, the first reform undertaken by Sokrates in designing a suitable education for the Guardians of his City in *logos* – concerned that they be nurtured in only politically salutary beliefs – is focused on the traditional ideas about gods and their relationship with men as depicted in Greek 'Scripture' (i.e., the poetry of Homer and Hesiod).

Hobbes introduces his *Leviathan* as does Sokrates his City in *logos*: by positing an analogy between a Man and a State. The apparent difference between the two analogies – that the former bases his on the human body, whereas the latter on the human psyche – turns out to be irrelevant, since Hobbes does not actually derive his political prescription from the mechanistic physiology he sketches (glaringly inadequate, and disposable), but from a phenomenological psychology: his analysis of people's passions, perceptions, and reasoning, from his own 'searching of human hearts,' and confirmable likewise by 'whosoever looketh into himself, and considereth what he doth, when he does *think, opine, reason, hope, feare*, &c, and upon what grounds' (spoken of in the Introduction's third paragraph).

The regime Hobbes describes, like that of Plato's Sokrates, is founded on an Official Lie about its origins and its social structure. But whereas the account Sokrates provides of the origin of his City in *logos* is the outright *lie* (a *pseudos* about the citizens being born of their land), and the ratification of its hierarchical social structure a 'truthful fiction' (a *mythos* about people's differing abilities being due to God's distribution of various spiritual 'metals'), Hobbes's version reverses the status of these components. The idea of a Commonwealth first *originating* in a plurality of covenants among all its composing members, heretofore denizens of a State of Nature, is a fictional way of rightly conceiving the rationale for civil obedience, sovereign authority, and of the members' mutual obligations; it is an 'as if' account. Whereas the official premise of social life – the (approximate) natural physical and mental equality of all humans – is a lie, albeit a supremely useful one, as it legitimates everyone's recognizing equality of Civil Rights as the basis of the regime's objective justness, and the source of people's subjective sense of its legitimacy.

As for Hobbes's basic idea of human nature, careful attention to his scattered comments about mankind's original, pre-civil existence clearly shows that he does *not* regard humans as beings whose natural condition is *solitary* – the notorious 'atomic individual' – but rather as proto-political in that originally they lived in more or less extended families, being animated by certain 'Passions that encline [them] to Peace' as well as by those that foment war, and dominated by mutual needs (cf. *Republic* 369b–c). And that so far as the State of Nature was nonetheless a chronic condition of War (meaning not perpetual fighting, 'but in the known disposition thereto'), it was not that 'of every man against every man,' but among families and alliances of families – out of which grew tribes, and eventually nations, each unified not least by a common language (cf. IV/2, 12; cf. *Republic* 373e). Hobbes's famous formula – 'and which is worst of all, continuall feare, and danger of violent death; And the life of man, solitary, poore, nasty, brutish, and short.' – applies to a far worse State of Nature than that out of which mankind first emerged, namely, that into which people may descend should Civil Society give way to the anarchic chaos of Civil War, a condition in which freely emerge the brutish and tyrannical impulses latent in human nature (as are revealed in our dreams and nightmares, according to Plato's Sokrates), but rendered the more voracious by the calculating mentality nurtured in ordinary political life.

Finally, and of greatest importance, consider the treatment of Philosophy itself in these two, apparently very different, Masterworks of truly *political* philosophy. For the most part, Hobbes refers to philosophers in tones of scorn and ridicule, as sources of endlessly silly views about Nature and pernicious views about Politics ('there can be nothing so absurd, but may be found in the books of Philosophers'). Up to his precisely centred Crucial Paragraph, that is. Whereupon, one is surprised to learn that nothing less than a *union* of Philosophy and Sovereignty is required if the design found in the book of *this* Philosopher is to be fully realized. Plato's *Republic*, however, though deservedly celebrated as the paradigm Apology for Philosophy, is *also* scathingly critical of most of those who pose as philosophers, mainly incompetent tinkers if not downright rogues, while the best of the breed are politically useless. The pernicious political effects of shallow and bogus 'philosophers' are so serious as to be the focus of half of Sokrates's famous pronouncement concerning the ills of mankind. That just as we will see no rest from evils until philosophers are kings, or so-called kings and lords genuinely and adequately philosophize (and conversely, those who are *not* capable of philosophy are excluded from positions of supreme political power), so also 'the many natures' drawn to philosophy, but not capable of political responsibility – that is, of pursuing wisdom with due regard for the possible political consequences of their activity (cf. 538c–539c) – must be denied the standing of philosophers (cf. XLVI/42, 380).

Only very late in his book (part way into the penultimate of forty-seven chapters) does Hobbes expressly declare that '*Plato* ... was the best Philosopher of the Greeks.' In order to appreciate the *full* significance of this statement, one must bear in mind both the form and the substance of Plato's philosophizing, at least as manifested in his dialogues. Hobbes never ventures any criticism of Plato, and tacitly excludes him from the judgment that the 'naturall Philosophy of [the Greek] Schools, was rather a Dream than Science ... which cannot be avoided by those that will teach Philosophy, without having first attained great knowledge in Geometry.' For Plato was the exception, forbidding 'entrance into *his* Schoole, to all that were not already in some measure Geometricians.' And yet, Plato's preferred 'method' of philosophizing was not Geometrical, but Dialectical. According to his *Republic*, the study of Geometry is merely preparatory to Dialectics, though it is also the best means of strengthening one's reasoning for all kinds of studies. But this might as well explain Hobbes's emphasis on Geometry as the model of scientific reasoning. Whereas, despite some limited portions of his treatise wherein he mimics the geometric method of deducing conditional knowledge from definitions, by no stretch of his or anyone else's imagination does *Leviathan* as a whole manifest a geometrical character. But it does prove Hobbes capable of attaining an 'overall view' (*synopsis*) of political life, the defining 'test' of a 'dialectical nature' (*Republic* 537c).

Like Plato, Hobbes treats Philosophy as the perfection of an impulse unique to human nature: the '*Desire* to know why, and how,' a certain 'Lust of the mind' for knowing the *causes* of things. However, this curiosity about causes, and the causes of causes, is a variable among men, 'some more, some lesse.' He who would 'plunge himselfe profoundly into the pursuit of causes' will be led eventually to the questions of *Philosophia prima* ('on which all other Philosophy ought to depend'). But besides a strong desire to know, and an intellect equal to the challenge, success requires two other factors: proper method, of course; but especially *leisure*. Indeed, the *desire* for leisure – distinct from the desire for '*Ease*, and sensuall Delight' – is implicit in the desire for *knowledge*, and as such is one of the only two positive motivations Hobbes cites for the founding and sustaining of Civil society; the Many seek a happiness of ease and sensual delight, whereas the Few seek knowledge (XI/4–5, 48; cf. *Republic* 520b–e). And there are a number of subtle but unmistakable indications that Hobbes, like Plato, ranks the latter motive as much the higher of the two (e.g., XX/19, 107; XXVI/28, 146–7; XXX/14, 179; cf. *Republic* 505b). For those capable of it, the *philosophical* life is *the good* life; and those who lead it, the best of mankind. Not incidentally, then, the form of regime Hobbes prescribes, like the City in *logos* of the Platonic Sokrates, is one in which genuine philosophers would be at home.

However, there are two versions of the regime Hobbes prescribes: a universal version, which (in keeping with the universality of modern Baconian science) can in principle be enacted anywhere, anytime; and an optimal version that requires a philosophically inclined Sovereign, along with other congenial conditions, and thus is subject to the vagaries of Chance. The 'at-homeness' of philosophy differs accordingly. In the unlikely realization of the latter version, philosophers would have a privileged, if inconspicuous, position in Society, and a similarly privileged relationship with the actual ruling Sovereign; whereas in the various incarnations of the universal version, any genuine philosophers and philosophical scholars and teachers are free to lead lives outwardly indistinguishable from those of the far more numerous scientists and scholarly specialists, artisans and writers, that staff the enormous universities and numerous research institutes, laboratories, libraries, museums, journals, and other such honoured features of contemporary Hobbesian commonwealths. This is perhaps not entirely alien to the depiction of actual political life in Plato's *Republic*. For he has Sokrates expressly acknowledge that Philosophy is present, along with almost every other imaginable way of life, in that parti-coloured regime which offers to one and all the same kind of personal freedom as does Hobbes: a minimum of legal constraints, leaving individuals to pursue whatever life they please (557c–e, 561c–e). And if such philosophers and quasi-philosophers have no special status therein, neither do they bear any special political responsibilities beyond those they take upon themselves (520a–c).

Still, a major question remains: Why has Hobbes not been more forthright about the broader relationship between his *Leviathan* and Plato's *Republic* – as he quite easily could have been? Why has he left so few, mainly elliptical, hints of that relationship, and of a sort apt to be noticed only by readers who are themselves more than just casually acquainted with Plato's dialogues? Since Hobbes, for all of his public engagement in controversial matters, was apparently a very close, very private man as far as his personal views were concerned (only occasionally, briefly, partially opening a window on his mind); since we retain comparatively few of his letters (and far fewer still any that illuminate his political philosophy); since, according to Aubrey, he destroyed many of his personal papers when loomed the danger of being tried for heresy; since his own autobiographical statements seem intended more to furbish a public persona than to reveal the private man – and since in discussing '*Persona*' ('the *disguise* or *outward appearance* of a man') his quoting Cicero to no clear purpose in the context leaves one much to ponder: 'I beare three Persons; my own, my Adversaries, and the Judges' (XVI/3, 80) – since, in short, we cannot confidently claim to know the deeper thoughts and motives of Hobbes the philosopher, one necessarily resorts to 'speculation' in answering this question.[7]

First, however, there may be a danger of underestimating the proportion of readership that in Hobbes's day could and would respond to those few Platonic allusions in his text, and be led thereby to notice the broader Platonic parallels. I am not suggesting that it would have been anything but small, merely that it would not necessarily have been quite so small as one might carelessly presume. After all, Plato had been 'rediscovered' in the preceding two centuries, and much was made of the fact. He was the darling of the Florentine Renaissance, epitomized by Cosimo Medici's founding of a new Platonic Academy and commissioning Marsilio Ficino to produce a complete Latin translation of the dialogues, making Plato accessible to all of educated Europe. He was widely regarded (rightly or wrongly) as a powerful alternative to Aristotle – hence as a most valuable resource for combating the Aristotelianism that Hobbes complains had so corrupted Christianity, and the 'Aristotelity' that dominated philosophy in the Universities. Plato was especially admired by the most prominent English poets of the sixteenth and seventeenth centuries. The works of Marlowe, Dryden, Donne, and Spenser reveal a more than passing acquaintance with Plato's views and writings. As a leading scholar of the period has recently shown, Sir Philip Sidney's *An Apology for Poetry* is based primarily on his understanding of Platonic philosophy.[8] The presence of Platonic influences on, and allusions in, Shakespeare's plays has been extensively documented.[9] And references to 'the divine Plato' abound in Milton's writings, both poetry and prose – not always approvingly, but displaying his close familiarity with at least ten of the dialogues.[10]

But it was not just poets that were admirers of Plato. 'Humanists' in general, including several of the prominent natural philosopher-scientists of the day, were as well.[11] Copernicus invokes the authority of Plato on the first page of Book One of his *Revolutions of the Heavenly Spheres*. Kepler, quoting from the *Timaeus* in its original Greek, famously (or infamously) based his ingenious explanation for the spacing of the planetary orbits on the five Platonic solids. Scholars debate whether Galileo was much or little influenced by Plato's mathematical cosmology,[12] but there is no doubt that he was well aware of it; and he *did* cast his major philosophic-scientific writings in the form of dialogues (though this had become a common literary form, along with the revival of Platonism). Hobbes's friend, William Harvey, introducing his treatise *On the Generation of Animals*, writes knowingly and approvingly of Seneca's insightful application to portraits of Plato's doctrine about forms (*eidë*) in their relation to *ideas*, which Harvey (in turn) adapts to the problem of understanding reproduction in general. And as one scholar of the period has noted, 'The *Opticks* shows more clearly than the *Principia* the strong neo-Platonic streak that ran through Newton's thought. It can be seen, for example in his attempt to link the visual spectrum with the musical octave.'[13] The list could easily be extended.

Whether or not Plato's views were a common topic among Hobbes's circle of friends (which is certainly possible), the fact remains that Hobbes does not exactly advertise his *Leviathan*'s special – I would say, comprehensive – relationship to Plato's *Republic*. One can hardly help wondering why not. It may simply be part of his rhetorical strategy, wishing to appear a thoroughgoing modern, firmly committed to the metaphysical premises of the new Baconian natural science. Or perhaps he was concerned that the practicality of his political prescription would be fatally compromised were he to indicate more openly the scope of its complementary relationship with a book so widely perceived as the very archetype of 'utopian' imaginings. Or, perhaps he (and his friends) had no wish to be in any way publicly associated with the so-called Cambridge Platonists, whose leading figures were all 'tainted' by their theological backgrounds and intentions.[14] Or, perhaps there were other reasons instead, or in addition. We may never know.

Whatever else Hobbes might have intended by his two brief endorsements of Plato – the one in the very centre of his treatise; the other almost at the end, in the chapter providing his most extensive treatment of philosophy – this much is clear to me: they are sufficient to increase the book's *philosophical* value by a whole order of magnitude. For these surprising references to Plato (the more intriguing the more one ponders them) suggest a *dialectical* relationship between Hobbes's *Leviathan* and Plato's *Republic*, though it remains the reader's responsibility to bring the dialogue between them to life. The effect is to stimulate philosophical *activity* far beyond that which is evoked simply by the attempt to generate a coherent interpretation of *Leviathan* unto itself (challenging as that doubtless is). Seeing each book in light of the other raises questions about each, and both, that would be less likely to occur to a reader of either work alone. One is thereby led to consider still more deeply – and if one is fortunate, understand more thoroughly – the permanent problems of politics, and of philosophy, and of the uneasy relationship between these two ruling activities of human beings. In particular, one comes to appreciate how vital to a Hobbesian commonwealth's working in the manner its architect hoped is the presence of a Sovereign of requisite quality – one whose paramount political concern is *equity* in procuring '*the safety of the people*,' because his paramount personal concern is that of maintaining a *naturally just soul* himself. Hence, how resounding is Hobbes's silence on the nature and nurture of such rulers. Reviewing Part Two of *Leviathan*, on the other hand, leaves one struck by how many practical issues of political life are finessed in Plato's *Republic* by his Sokrates's casual assertion that all such matters will be 'easily' resolved by the rulers, being 'sensible men' (*metrioi andres*) as a result of a proper education and rearing.

Hobbes is a philosopher who knows his business. The highest priority for any philosopher who knows his business is that of promoting and safeguarding the well-being of philosophy. It is inconceivable to me that Hobbes could have crafted that crucial central paragraph of his treatise, indifferent – much less, oblivious – to its broader, practically inexhaustible, implications for both politics and philosophy.

A Melvillian Coda:
Moby-Dick as Fourfold Allegory

... the visible surface of the Sperm Whale is not the least among the many marvels he presents ...

Melville has gone to some lengths to make the challenge of interpreting *Moby-Dick* allegorically well-nigh irresistible.[1] And doubtless his story presents multiple possibilities. Apropos my purpose here, however, I should like to suggest a set which, so far as I have been able to determine, has not previously been considered: that his novel is, whatever else, a fourfold allegory, offering a double view of both Hobbes's political prescription and Plato's conception of philosophy. In each case, that is, we are provided an indication of its proper fulfilment – the Hobbesian Commonwealth as it is supposed to function, and the Platonic idea of a true philosopher – but seen mainly in juxtaposition with their respective perversions, which are the primary foci of Melville's tale.

The Pequod is a contractarian 'common-wealth' in the most literal sense. For not only are its constituting members bound to a common enterprise by contracts each have entered into as individuals – originally 'each *Isolato* living on a separate continent of his own,' they are 'now, federated along one keel' (ch. 27, 121); subjected to the single will of their sovereign, 'They were one man, not thirty' (ch. 134, 557).[2] But also, their Ship of State is organized primarily with material prosperity – that most 'common' kind of 'wealth' – in mind. So, while all crew members understand that everyone's physical security is dependent upon their cooperation within a structure of enforced rules, each man is also presumed to be motivated, not solely by the 'Feare of Death,' but as much or more by the common desire to provide him and his 'such things as are necessary to commodious living, and a Hope by [his] Industry to obtain them' (XIII/14, 63). Lest there be any doubt of this, Melville has crafted a circumstance wherein Ishmael can say plainly yet inconspicuously, 'the entire ship seems great leviathan himself' (ch. 98, 428). That both the regime of the ship and the mighty sea monster it hunts are at various times denominated 'leviathan' no more than reminds us of the very reason Hobbes chose this epithet for his vision of the well-ordered polity.

Melville's story confirms that man is so much 'a money-making animal' (ch. 93, 413) that men such as sail in the *Pequod* are willing, for the dream of gain, to expose their lives to the very considerable dangers of whale hunting. He quite purposefully portrays this commonwealth of hunters as exemplifying what Hobbes subtly acknowledged: that *not all* men are ruled by their fear of violent death; that despite the alleged irrationality of doing so, there are and always will be some who are willing to risk their lives in pursuit of things that matter enough to them (wealth, power, honour, faith, love, including sheer love of adventure and challenge). Moreover, that all political life, including a regime organized according to Hobbes's own prescription, presupposes this: that always a polity's security, and often its continuing prosperity, presupposes *courage* on the part of some of its members. But Hobbes's explicit treatment of courage is coarse, as Melville tacitly shows. For the ruling elite of the *Pequod* manifests, in rank order, the various *kinds* of courage that will naturally be found among a suitably representative sampling of people – and for whom fitting kinds of employments must be available in a commonwealth, lest they do it mischief.

The indomitable courage of Ahab is best considered later in conjunction with his misbegotten philosophizing. As for that of his three subordinate officers, the King's 'knights,' the courage of the first and chief mate, Starbuck, a 'staid, steadfast man' of 'hardy sobriety and fortitude,' is explicated most fully:

'I will have no man in my boat,' said Starbuck, 'who is not afraid of a whale.' By this, he seemed to mean, not only that the most reliable and useful courage was that which arises from the fair estimation of the encountered peril, but that an utterly fearless man is a far more dangerous comrade than a coward.

...

Starbuck was no crusader after perils; in him courage was not a sentiment; but a thing simply useful to him, and always at hand upon all mortally practical occasions. Besides, he thought, perhaps, that in this business of whaling, courage was one of the great staple outfits of the ship, like her beef and her bread, and not to be foolishly wasted ... For, thought Starbuck, I am here in this critical ocean to kill whales for my living, and not to be killed by them for theirs. (ch. 26, 116)

Ishmael describes the second mate, Stubb, as 'Good-humored, easy, and careless,' an 'unfearing man,' who 'presided over his whale-boat as if the most deadly encounter were but a dinner, and his crew all invited guests':

Long usage had, for this Stubb, converted the jaws of death into an easy chair. What he thought of death itself, there is no telling. Whether he ever thought of it at all, might be a question; but, if he ever did chance to cast his mind that way after a comfortable dinner, no doubt, like a good sailor, he took it to be a sort of call of the watch to tumble aloft, and bestir themselves there, about something which he would find out when he obeyed the order, and not sooner. (ch. 27, 118)

The third mate, Flask, is accounted 'very pugnacious concerning whales, who somehow seemed to think that the great Leviathans had personally and hereditarily affronted him; and therefore it was a sort of point of honor with him, to destroy them whenever encountered.' Devoid of any reverence for 'the many marvels of their majestic bulk and mystic ways,' his was an 'ignorant, unconscious fearlessness [that] made him a little waggish in the matter of whales; he followed these fish for the fun of it' (ch. 27, 119). Each of these 'knights' has an attending 'squire,' namely, the ship's harpooneers: Queequeg, the South Seas 'cannibal'; Tashtego, a purebred Indian from Massachusetts; and Daggoo, 'a gigantic, coal-black negro-savage' straight from Africa, who 'retained all his barbaric virtues.' These three alien mercenaries brought to their allotted task a savage, state-of-nature courage which complemented that of the men they served.

Given whale hunters' practical proof that even Feare of Death does not operate on human beings with anything like the universal force of gravity, it is hardly surprising that Love of Gaine – especially when nurtured in a regime dedicated to it – may also compromise a man's religious convictions. So Ishmael observes in the case of the old Quaker Captain Bildad: 'very probably he had long since come to the sage and sensible conclusion that a man's religion is one thing, and this practical world quite another. This world pays dividends' (ch. 16, 74). Each of the *Pequod*'s citizen-sailors' commitment to the commercial gamble rests on his awareness that he will prosper only so far as his ship is successful in filling its hold with whale oil – the peculiar wealth of their polity – since each individual shares in its proceeds according to the market '*Value*' of his 'WORTH' (i.e., 'his Price; that is to say, so much as would be given for the use of his Power ... And as in other things, so in men, not the seller, but the buyer determines the Price'; *Leviathan* X/16, 42). Ishmael is at pains to make clear the standard arrangement in ships with regimes like that of the *Pequod*:

I was already aware that in the whaling business they paid no wages; but all hands, including the captain, received certain shares of the profits called *lays*, and that these lays were proportioned to the degree of importance pertaining to the respective duties of the ship's company. I was also aware that being a green hand at whaling, my own lay would not be very large. (ch. 16, 75)

Queequeg, having adopted Ishmael as his bosom companion, is determined to ship aboard whatever whaler his friend chooses. However, he is first excluded on the grounds that the owners allow 'no cannibals on board, unless they previously produced their papers' – meaning, 'He must show that he's converted' to Christianity. But upon Queequeg's instead demonstrating his uncanny skill with a harpoon, the owners promptly amend their policy: 'Quick, I say, you Bildad, and get the ship's papers. We must have Hedgehog there, I mean Quohog, in one of our boats' (ch. 18, 88–9).

   To be sure, not everyone aboard is dominated by the 'sordidness' Ahab believes to be 'the permanent constitutional condition of the manufactured man' – Queequeg, Ishmael, and Ahab himself each being in his own way conspicuous exceptions. Nonetheless, everyone is expected to comport himself in a manner consonant with the ostensible purpose of their voyage, which is but part of an endless sequence: 'one most perilous and long voyage ended, only begins a second; and a second ended, only begins a third, and so on, for ever and for aye. Such is the endlessness, yea, the intolerableness of all earthly effort.'[3] Even Ahab must cloak his subversive intention in a certain outward conformity in order to achieve his monomaniacal ambition: 'Ahab plainly saw that he must still in a good degree continue true to the natural, nominal purpose of the Pequod's voyage; observe all customary usages; and not only that, but force himself to evince all his well known passionate interest in the general pursuit of his profession' (ch. 46, 212–13).

Ostensibly, the regime of the *Pequod* is that of an Absolute Monarchy. Ishmael signs on knowing this full well, and moreover does so irrespective of his ignorance concerning the designated monarch ('without once laying my eyes on the man who was to be the absolute dictator'; ch. 20, 97; cf. *Leviathan* XVIII/5, 90). Ahab himself, in a moment of high passion, invokes the ultimate analogy to proclaim most emphatically his own absolute authority: 'There is one God that is Lord over the earth, and one Captain that is lord over the Pequod' (ch. 109, 474).[4] But despite the Pequodian commonwealth's government being monarchical, it nonetheless rests upon the radical egalitarianism implicit in the requirement that every individual, whatever his status and station, personally consent to the regime in signing on. He need not do so; it is a voluntary act, the natural right of each man to pursue his own good as he sees fit. Melville, however, makes clear that this natural equality of right is *not* out of a recognition that 'Nature hath made men so equal in faculties of body, and mind' (XIII/1, 60) – for that is false, as Ishmael repeatedly attests. Indeed, he not only acknowledges a natural hierarchy among human souls, he insists that the range of difference is far greater than is generally appreciated.

Ishmael describes one such grand and wondrous individual, clearly modelled on the Captain he has yet to meet at this point in his story. By way of explaining the apparent anomaly of supposedly pacifistic Quakers being 'the most sanguinary of all sailors and whale-hunters' ('They are fighting Quakers; they are Quakers with a vengeance') Ishmael observes:

[T]here are instances among them of men, who, named with Scripture names ... and in childhood naturally imbibing the stately dramatic thee and thou of the Quaker idiom; still, from the audacious, daring, and boundless adventure of their subsequent lives, strangely blend with these unoutgrown peculiarities, a thousand bold dashes of character, not unworthy a Scandinavian sea-king, or a poetical Pagan Roman. And when these things unite in a man of greatly superior natural force, with a globular brain and a ponderous heart; who has also by the stillness and seclusion of many long night-watches in the remotest waters, and beneath constellations never seen here at the north, been led to think untraditionally and independently; receiving all nature's sweet or savage impressions fresh from her own virgin, voluntary, and confiding breast, and thereby chiefly, but with some help from accidental advantages, to learn a bold and nervous lofty language – that man makes one in a whole nation's census – a mighty pageant creature, formed for noble tragedies. Nor will it at all detract from him, dramatically regarded, if either from birth or other circumstances, he have what seems a half wilful over-ruling morbidness at the bottom of his nature. For all men tragically great are made so through a certain morbidness. (ch. 16, 73–4)

Men differ greatly, more so than most men can imagine. As Melville indicates, the true purpose behind founding a regime on the premise of human equality – practically manifested in equality before the law, the foundation of equality of opportunity insofar as politically achievable – is twofold: first, to endow every socially useful role with some recognition of its worth, thereby encouraging practitioners of all vocations, from the lowest to the highest, to perform their own respective work well, and be appreciated for doing so; and second, to ensure that there are no artificial, no merely conventional obstacles to natural differences – natural *in*equalities – asserting themselves, especially of talent and ability, ambition and dedication.

The latter desideratum relates especially to he Hobbesian Commonwealth's fulfilling its promise to 'relieve Man's estate' by liberating everyone who can contribute to advancing a science such as Bacon envisioned, one that would provide all sorts of technological power whereby men may become (in Descartes's beguiling phrase) 'masters and possessors of Nature.'[5]

This important facet of the Hobbesian prescription is represented in the Pequodian commonwealth by Ishmael's serio-comic efforts to establish a true 'cetology, or the science of whales': 'a matter almost indispensable to a thorough appreciative understanding of the more special leviathanic revelations and allusions of all sorts which are to follow' (ch. 32, 134). In formal terms, Ishmael's method is pure Baconianism: prior to deriving valid generalizations ('axioms') on any subject, we require a complete assembling of the relevant phenomena, systematically classified.[6] This provides what Bacon calls 'the primary material of philosophy and the stuff and subject matter of true induction': 'they who shall hereafter take it upon them to write natural history should bear this continually in mind – that they ought not to consult the pleasure of the reader, no, nor even that utility that may be derived immediately from their narrations, but to seek out and gather together such store and variety of things as may suffice for the formation of true axioms' [274].[7]

Hence, Ishmael sets himself to provide 'some systematized exhibition of the whale in his broad genera,' while cautioning it is 'no easy task' – nothing less than 'the classification of the constituents of a chaos' (134). Given the magnitude of this 'ponderous task,' he promises 'nothing complete,' but only 'an easy outline ... hereafter to be filled in all its departments by subsequent laborers' (136). By so construing his own contribution, Ishmael echoes Bacon, who warns: 'For a history of this kind ... is a thing of very great size and cannot be executed without great labor and expense, requiring as it does many people to help, and being ... a kind of

royal work' [271]. And, as Bacon admonishes, Ishmael is careful to indicate regarding the information he supplies whether it is 'certainly true,
doubtful ..., or certainly not true,' and whether taken 'from report, oral
or written,' or 'affirmed it of his own knowledge' [280–1]. Thus,
Ishmael's entry on the 'Razor Back': 'Of this whale little is known but his
name. I have seen him at a distance off Cape Horn. Of a retiring nature,
he eludes both hunters and philosophers ... Let him go. I know little
more of him, nor does anybody else' (140–1). Moreover, Melville understands that the 'incompleteness' of the Baconian scientific project
(reflected in the admittedly 'unfinished' character of Ishmael's cetology)
is necessarily *permanent*: 'For small erections may be finished by their
first architects; grand ones, true ones, ever leave the copestone to posterity' (145). Ever.

So much for Ishmael as 'theoretical scientist.' On the side of 'applied
technology,' there is his detailed account of the mechanics of all that is
involved in supplying the whale oil that illuminated the lives of his contemporaries. However, in order to appreciate this fully, it helps to bear in
mind what Hobbes teaches concerning the 'NUTRITION of a Common-
wealth':

For the Matter of this Nutriment, consisting in Animals, Vegetals, and Minerals,
God hath freely layd them before us, in or neer to the face of the Earth; so as there
needeth no more but the labour, and industry of receiving them. Insomuch as
Plenty dependeth (next to Gods favour) meerly on the labour and industry of men.
...
[A] man's Labour also, is a commodity exchangeable for benefit, as well as any
other thing: And there have been Common-wealths that having no more Territory, than hath served them for habitation, have neverthelesse, not onely maintained, but encreased their Power, partly by the labour of trading from one place
to another, and partly by selling the Manifactures, whereof the Materials were
brought in from other places. (XXIV/3–4, 127)

Combined with Hobbes's contention that 'the *Value*, or WORTH of a
man, is ... his Price' (X/16, 42), one has the essence of the 'Labour Theory
of Value' famously associated with John Locke – and basic to the classical economic theory which complements and completes the liberal-scien-
tific-capitalist political order.
    In making the case that human labour is the source of almost all *value* in
things useful to the life of man, Locke suggests that one but 'trace some of

the ordinary provisions of life, through their several progresses, before they come to our use, and see how much they receive of their *value from human industry.*' What Locke himself sketches with the example of bread (*Second Treatise*, §43), Melville's Ishmael provides in exhaustive detail with respect to what is directly involved in appropriating whale oil. We learn about the organization of a whale ship, and the elaborate efforts involved in fitting it out for three years of self-sufficient cruising; how it prowls the sea in search of promising hunting grounds; both the physical and social structure of the several whaleboats it lowers upon spotting its prey (e.g., how the line is coiled, how attached to the harpoon and how to the boat, who of the boat's crew does what, when); about chasing, harpooning, playing out and hauling back a speared whale, lancing and killing the exhausted beast, towing it back to the ship, securing it alongside – and the various complications and misadventures that can arise at any of these stages; and then about all the 'labour and industry' involved in extracting from the carcass the marketable commodity that is the reward of the whole enterprise: cutting and stripping off the blanket of blubber, hoisting it aboard, chopping it into manageable chunks, boiling it down (using the whale's own fat to fuel the try works), stowing the oil in casks; and finally, how the fouled ship is cleansed once the reduction process is completed.

What justifies Melville's burdening his epic with this seemingly excessive technical detail about the business of whaling?[8] To be sure, seeing the story of the *Pequod* not only as a microcosm of the larger Hobbesian commonwealth, but also as merely a very small yet representative *part* of one, deepens and enlivens one's appreciation of the ever-increasing material complexity of modern political life, as well as of the materialistic spirit that pervades it. That behind the ready availability of familiar products and facilities that almost everyone takes for granted – be it bread in the seventeenth century, whale oil in the nineteenth, or electronics in the twenty-first – is a socio-economic order inherently configured to become ever more extensive, intricate, specialized, and accordingly opaque. For it is made up of myriads of interlocking technical specialties about which the typical democratic citizen knows no more than he does about whaling. And for the vast majority of people whose understanding of the source of their many necessities and superfluities extends barely beyond each item's purchase price, their appreciation of them is determined exclusively by the relative cost of their enjoyment.

There is one more feature of the *Pequod*'s allegoric significance that is especially worth mentioning. It sails the oceans as but one commonwealth among many, all in vigorous competition with each other to extract for themselves as much of this world's resources as each can. And though occasionally it has to deal with violent predatory regimes (as signified by the *Pequod*'s brush with 'the piratical proas of the Malays'; ch. 87), competition remains for the most part peaceful despite there being no super-leviathan to enforce the peace. That 'the most vexatious and violent disputes,' which could readily arise from conflicting claims to a captured whale, rarely do so, is a consequence of a pair of 'universal, undisputed,' hence international 'laws' that whalers find mutually advantageous to adhere to (based simply on the distinction between 'Fast-fish and Loose-fish'; ch. 89). Nonetheless, that such competition can sometimes be quite direct and head-on, as it were, is exemplified in Ishmael's account of his ship's encounter with the German whaler *Jungfrau* (ch. 81). Both ships' lookouts having spotted the same pod of whales, all their boats were lowered, and the race was on. The American crews were ultimately triumphant in first fastening onto the prize (a maimed and blind old bull), but it proved a pyrrhic victory, as not only did the carcass begin to sink once grappled to the ship's side, it nearly dragged down the *Pequod* with it. Presumably there is a moral to this episode.

Ahab's Usurpation, for so Ishmael calls it (ch. 46, 213), is a cautionary tale about the regime Hobbes prescribes, focusing upon a peculiar perversion to which this artificial leviathan is inherently vulnerable. Melville is *not*, however, dramatizing the commonplace objection that Hobbes 'legitimates' monarchical absolutism irrespective of the character of the monarch and the quality of his rule – that he justifies Tyranny, being neither willing nor able to distinguish it from legitimate Kingship. As I endeavoured to show in the preceding chapters, this is a superficial and decidedly 'unpolitical' understanding of his prescription. The fact that this view is nonetheless so widely held (and not only by first-time readers of *Leviathan*) is a testament to the ingenuity of Hobbes's rhetoric.[9] As Hobbes belatedly makes explicit, the Sovereign is responsible for '*the safety of the people*': 'But by Safety here, is not meant a bare Preservation, but also other Contentments of life, which every man by lawfull industry, without danger, or hurt to the Common-wealth, shall acquire to him-selfe' (XXX/1, 175).

Ironically, then, in the very course of insisting that the Sovereign is answerable to no one but God, Hobbes informs whoever can read that the proper purpose for 'entrusting' anyone with sovereign power is to establish an environment where 'every man by lawful industry' may pursue his own happiness. Having made that explicit, it is futile – not logically, but psychologically – to insist that civil obedience and quality of rule are two utterly separate matters, or that the difference between Monarchy and Tyranny is merely semantic. Thus, Hobbes time and again subtly reminds Sovereigns, and those who govern in their name, to rule with justice, moderation, and all due regard for 'the safety of the people' as he has construed it – to do so out of self-interest, if nothing higher. For however 'irrational' rebellion may be, or can be made to seem, it remains a perennial danger of political life, given the limited rationality of most people.[10]

Suffice it to say, Hobbes is not an apologist for despotism, nor are regimes inspired by the essentials of his prescription made to order for tyrants. He has written his treatise in order 'that men may learn thereby, *both* how to *govern, and* how to *obey.*' Balancing his argument for strict civil obedience on the part of Subjects with a template for the rational, responsible rule of Sovereigns – by which they know they will be judged, humans being humans, not logicians – he has designed a regime in which the power of government is both moderated and directed by a certain 'low but solid' conception of the common good: material prosperity, promoted through science and industry, commerce and liberty, pursued and practised within the safe and stable rule of no more laws than necessary for the purpose. All this should be readily apparent to any reader who brings to *Leviathan* some practical insight into human nature, or who can synthesize as much from Hobbes's own dispersed account of it. And for those who need the inner rationale of Hobbes's teaching made more explicit, there is Locke's *Second Treatise*, as well as the writings of the American Founders, who bother to express clearly and unequivocally the view 'that all men are created equal, that they are endowed by their Creator with certain unalienable Rights, that among these are Life, Liberty, and the pursuit of Happiness. That to secure these rights, Governments are instituted among Men, deriving their *just* powers from the consent of the governed.'

Nurtured in this view, the crew of the American ship *Pequod*, including Ahab's own 'officials,' regard his rule, not as absolute, but as conditional to the purpose for which they gave their willing consent: to further their own safety and prosperity. This is several times indicated by the words and deeds of both Ruler and Ruled. Thus, First Mate Starbuck protests Ahab's declared intention to hunt down the monster that 'dismasted' him: 'I am game for his crooked jaw, and for the jaws of Death too,

Captain Ahab, if it fairly comes in the way of the business we follow; but I came here to hunt whales, not my commander's vengeance' (ch. 36, 163). And thus Ishmael's 'Surmises' about Ahab's thinking manifest both the Lockean mode of expression congenial to the citizen-subject's perspective, and a Hobbesian political realism reflective of a ruling monarch who understands his practical situation:

Having impulsively, it is probable, and perhaps somewhat prematurely revealed the prime but private purpose of the Pequod's voyage, Ahab was now entirely conscious that, in so doing, he had indirectly laid himself open to the unanswerable charge of usurpation; and with perfect impunity, both moral and legal, his crew if so disposed, and to that end competent, could refuse all further obedience to him, and even violently wrest from him the command. From even the barely hinted imputation of usurpation, and the possible consequences of such a suppressed impression gaining ground, Ahab must of course have been most anxious to protect himself. (ch. 46, 213)

Ishmael presumes that not only he, common sailor, but Captain Ahab himself recognizes that he has usurped, not his position of ruler, but the purpose – 'The finall Cause' – for which it is instituted; and that he has thereby 'laid himself open' to a justified rebellion by the ruled, even to being deposed. Moreover, that Ahab, aware that his motive and object were hardly sane, had from the beginning been consciously dissembling in order to gain command of a ship under the falsest of pretences. Thus Ahab was obliged to proceed with caution, and 'still in a good degree continue true to the natural, nominal purpose of the Pequod's voyage,' biding his time, ever cognizant of the need to secure at least the acquiescence of the sailors he rules. This being so, the *Pequod*'s boats were lowered whenever whales were sighted, and in the course of one such chase, Starbuck nicely encapsulated the mentality of a proper Hobbesian citizen: 'There's hogsheads of sperm ahead, Mr. Stubb, and that's what ye came for. (Pull, my boys!) Sperm, sperm's the play! This at least is duty; duty and profit hand in hand!' (ch. 48, 219).

So, while the story of Ahab's peculiar despotism and misappropriation of his authority is not that of Shakespeare's Richard the Second – who presumes he rules by Divine Right, unchallengeable whatever course he might choose – neither does it exemplify the normal functioning of a monarchy as Hobbes rationally envisions it. Ahab *is* a kind of usurper of his own authority, and perverter of the very regime that authorizes him. Moreover, he is *emblematic* of what Melville sees as the special, if not strictly peculiar, nemesis of the Hobbesian commonwealth in its 'popular' or democratic form. To understand what this is, one must trace out how Ahab contrives to persuade his crew to sacrifice pursuit of their common material interest – hazardous enough, to be sure – and join with him in attempting a malign, quixotic conquest. Not just any man called 'Captain' could do so.

Ishmael attests to a factor in Ahab's extraordinary power the first time he lays eyes on him, namely, his *imposing appearance*. Our narrator confesses he had anticipated this dramatically delayed event with certain 'colorless misgivings,' but when it finally came to pass, 'foreboding shivers ran over [him]. Reality outran apprehension.' Lean of limb, of 'compacted aged robustness, [his] whole high, broad form, seemed made of solid bronze, and shaped in an unalterable mould,' except that a livid white scar ran down one side of his face and body:

So powerfully did the whole grim aspect of Ahab affect me, and the livid brand which streaked it, that for the first few minutes I hardly noted that not a little of this overbearing grimness was owing to the barbaric white leg upon which he partly stood ... fashioned from the polished bone of the sperm whale's jaw ...

I was struck by the singular posture he maintained ... Captain Ahab stood erect, looking straight out beyond the ship's ever-pitching prow. There was an infinity of firmest fortitude, a determinate, unsurrenderable wilfulness, in the fixed and fearless, forward dedication of that glance. Not a word he spoke; nor did his officers say aught to him; though by all their minutest gestures and expressions, they plainly showed the uneasy, if not painful, consciousness of being under a troubled master-eye. (ch. 28, 124)

Who would not be intrigued, even awed by the sight Ishmael describes? The mysterious sense of majesty, power, and purpose Ahab radiated – that he, like King Lear, had in his countenance that which lesser men 'would fain call master' – doubtless, this was instrumental in his bending the wills of *Pequod*'s crew to his own.[11]

However, a forbidding yet inspiring persona was but the first contributor to Ahab's utterly personal ascendancy. His manner reinforced it. For example, when his three mates dined with him, 'Ahab presided like a mute, maned sea-lion ... surrounded by his war-like but still deferential cubs ... They were as little children before Ahab; and yet, in Ahab, there seemed not to lurk the smallest social arrogance.' His own behaviour tacitly militated a respectful reticence, even outright silence in his presence. As a result, the captain's table, we are told, was characterized by 'hardly tolerable constraint and nameless invisible domineerings' – all without his so much as lifting a finger of enforcement. In brief, 'socially, Ahab was inaccessible' (ch. 34, 150–2).

Chapter 36 is the first of a set of five chapters that commence with and afterwards employ stage directions, and include 'asides'; three are chapter-long soliloquies, and the last is cast wholly as the script of a scene in a play. Their stylistic peculiarities suggest that they constitute a five-act drama unto themselves.[12] And rightly so, for therein is depicted the pivotal moment in the story. It is immediately followed by the chapter that bears the title of the book, 'Moby Dick.' The opening Act portrays Ahab's initial seduction of his crew. The four that follow offer various perspectives on and reactions to this subversive event: first Ahab's own, then Starbuck's, then Stubb's, and finally the crew gathered in the forecastle at midnight.

The drama begins 'one morning shortly after breakfast.' On this occasion, the always pensive Captain seemed especially burdened as he paced the quarter deck: 'so full of his thought was Ahab, that at every uniform turn that he made ... you could almost see that thought turn in him as he turned, and pace in him as he paced; so completely possessing him, indeed, that it all but seemed the inward mould of every outer movement.' He continued in this semi-Sokratic, thought-possessed state until the day was drawing to a close, whereupon he ordered the entire ship's company assembled. After a pregnant silence, he began to address them with a series of elementary questions about their profession, to which they enthusiastically responded in unison. This collective interrogation, more ritual than inquiry, had pronounced effects on both cantor and chorus: 'More and more strangely and fiercely glad and approving, grew the countenance of the old man at every shout; while the mariners began to gaze curiously at each other, as if marveling how it was that they themselves became so excited at such seemingly purposeless questions.' Ahab then nails a gold doubloon to the mainmast, and announces that it shall go to 'Whosoever of ye raises me a white-headed whale with a wrinkled brow and a crooked jaw.'

The crew cheer the proclamation, but it leaves the mates puzzled. From questions by the *Pequod*'s three savage harpooners ('as if each was separately touched by some specific recollection'), it is established that the sought-after whale is of sufficiently distinct characteristics and longevity so as to have acquired a name among experienced whale hunters: Moby Dick. Upon learning this, First Mate Starbuck suspects he has solved the mystery of the curious behaviour he has just witnessed: 'Captain Ahab, I have heard of Moby Dick – but it was not Moby Dick that took off thy leg?' Ahab's response suggests that he would have preferred that this not be known. Its having been revealed, however, he confirms it in terms of mounting passion:

'Aye, aye! it was that accursed white whale that razeed me; made a poor pegging lubber of me for ever and a day! ... And this is what ye have shipped for, men! to chase that white whale on both sides of land, and over all sides of earth, till he spouts black blood and rolls fin out. What say ye, men, will ye splice hands on it, now? I think ye do look brave.' (163)

The harpooneers and the crew shout their agreement with this radical reinterpretation of their contracts, but the mates, especially Starbuck, manifest disapproval – as Ahab notes and addresses: 'But what's this long face about, Mr. Starbuck; wilt thou not chase the white whale?'

It is at this point that Starbuck protests that he signed on to hunt whales, not his commander's vengeance, that vengeance 'will not fetch ... much in our Nantucket market.' Ahab scorns the idea that 'money's to be the measurer.' Starbuck changes tack: 'Vengeance on a dumb brute! ... that simply smote thee from blindest instinct! Madness! To be enraged with a dumb thing, Captain Ahab, seems blasphemous.' Ahab rejects the charge: 'Talk not to me of blasphemy, man; I'd strike the sun if it insulted me.' Ahab then denigrates the degree to which his intention departs from the nominal purpose of their voyage, while flattering Starbuck's virtue: 'Reckon it. 'Tis but to help strike a fin; no wondrous feat for Starbuck. What is it more? From this one poor hunt, then, the best lance out of all Nantucket, surely he will not hang back, when every foremast-hand has clutched a whetstone?' Upon noting that, despite his lingering misgivings, Starbuck no longer protests aloud, Ahab knows he has at least neutralized this last source of opposition to his hijacking their Ship of State. As a finale, Ahab leads the entire company in a pagan ceremony of ratification under the setting sun, the king-captain bidding his three knights and their squires drink a toast of grog from the harpoon sockets and swear 'Death to Moby Dick.' And so 'to cries and maledictions against the white whale, the spirits were simultaneously quaffed down with a hiss,' while a large pewter of liquor 'went the rounds among the frantic crew.'

In the chapters that follow, we are privy, first, to Ahab's musings once alone in his cabin. He expresses some surprise at his own success: ''Twas not so hard a task. I thought to find one stubborn, at the least; but my one cogged circle fits into all their various wheels, and they revolve' (ch. 37, 167). Ahab's soliloquy is followed by those of the First and Second Mates. And in considering their diverse perspectives, one needs bear in mind what, near the bitter end, Ahab says to their faces: 'Ye two are the opposite poles of one thing; Starbuck is Stubb reversed, and Stubb is Starbuck; and ye two are all mankind; and Ahab stands alone among the millions of the peopled earth, nor gods nor men his neighbors!' (ch. 133, 553). Starbuck's meditation '[*by the Mainmast*]' is first of all a confession: 'My soul is more than matched; she's overmanned; and by a madman! Insufferable sting, that sanity should ground arms on such a field! But he drilled deep down, and blasted all my reason out of me! I think I see his impious end; but feel that I must help him to it. Will I, nill I, the ineffable thing has tied me to him' (ch. 38, 169). The ineffable thing. Stubb has retreated to the Fore-Top, where he mends a brace while thinking everything over and chuckling to himself: 'Why so? Because a laugh's the wisest, easiest answer to all that's queer; and come what will, one comfort's always left – [namely,] it's all predestinated ... I know not all that may be coming, but be it what it will, I'll go to it laughing' (ch. 39, 171). Meanwhile, the crew of this ostensibly American whaler, drawn from all four quarters of the globe, make merry in the night.

Once Ahab has turned the ship's company, his authority grows with their continuing complicity in his redefinition of their collective purpose, becoming virtually irresistible, not least because internalized in everyone subject to him. The consequences, for both him and them, are profound.

How has this happened? Ahab is no Louis XIV brazenly declaring '*l'état, c'est moi!*' Nor is his a Norman Conquest, imposed by intimidation, coercion, violence. For though Ahab has secretly brought aboard his own personal boat crew of aliens that might serve as a Praetorian Guard, they play no part whatsoever in his initial usurpation. Indeed, their existence on board is at this point still unknown to the rest of the ship's company. Thus one must see Ahab's success as a personal tour de force, albeit in circumstances perhaps especially congenial to a man like him succeeding.

First, then, *ecce homo*: large-souled, great-spirited especially, of powerful intellect, but concentrated rather than dispersed, focused on a single clear, grand goal; moreover, not totally civilized in the tame, domestic sense (ironically symbolized by the 'barbaric white leg upon which he partly stood'). To grasp the psychic effect of all this on people, one must appreciate its rarity. The vast majority of people are small- and shallowsouled, as revealed in the meagreness of their ambitions, their petty greed, their short-sightedness, their changeability and irresolution, their frequent spitefulness, their various envies and resentments – and not least in the ease with which they become discouraged, in their indifference to the many confusions and contradictions in their own views, and in their readiness to seek solace in pleasure. Each living his paltry life immersed in the evidence of his and his fellows' mediocrity, most people are aware, if only subconsciously, that this *is* how they are: that taken 'in mass, and for the most part … a mob of unnecessary duplicates' (cf. ch. 107, 466). In their workaday experience with their familiars as well as themselves, passions and purposes are in constant flux, enthusiasms and commitments wax only to wane again, dissipated amid the tempting and threatening distractions that invariably arise. Almost everyone, in his heart of hearts, recognizes the explanation for all this: that humanity at large is characterized by manifold *weaknesses*, especially of *will*. There's nothing good to be said for weakness; hence, reason readily validates one's instinctive despising of it, and commensurate honouring of strength, of power. This is the deeper truth undergirding Hobbes's entire discussion of Power and Honour (ch. X).

Confronted, then, with their very antithesis: a man of indomitable will, who radiates determination, clear and far vision, unity of soul and fixity of purpose, seemingly possessed of 'an infinity of firmest fortitude' – it is hardly surprising that he arouses in people both fascination and admiration on the one hand, but also envy and fear on the other. Thus, if he has the ability to amplify the former and mollify the latter, and has a reason to do so – that is to say, if he understands human nature in both its commonality and significant diversity; has sufficient self-mastery to translate this knowledge into fitting words and deeds and demeanour; and has some use to which he would put people, be it creative or destructive – he may become a great leader of men, a conqueror perhaps, or a founder, or reformer, even a Caesar.

Captain Peleg describes Ahab to Ishmael in terms distinctly Caesarean: 'He's a grand, ungodly, *god-like* man' (ch. 16, 79). In his soliloquy, Ahab describes himself as 'demoniac' (ch. 37, 168).[13] Like Shakespeare's King Henry the Fifth, Ahab understands men, men of all kinds, all nationalities, the savage as well as the civilized, whether pagan and Christian, Old Testament men as well as New. His aloof, remote manner discourages familiarity, and thus insulates him from any taint of the contempt that 'familiarity' famously breeds in small-souled, envious men. Still, his natural sense of his own superiority, of his own nobility, manifests itself without grating arrogance, much less with contrived pomp. Again like Shakespeare's Henry, Ahab possesses the common touch:

[T]hough the only homage he ever exacted, was implicit, instantaneous obedience; though he required no man to remove the shoes from his feet ere stepping upon the quarter-deck; and though there were times when, owing to peculiar circumstances ... he addressed them in unusual terms, whether of condescension or *in terrorem*, or otherwise; yet even Captain Ahab was by no means unobservant of the paramount forms and usages of the sea.

Nor, perhaps, will it fail to be eventually perceived, that behind these forms and usages, as it were, he sometimes masked himself; incidentally making use of them for other and more private ends than they were legitimately intended to subserve. That certain sultanism of his brain, which had otherwise in a good degree remained unmanifested; through those forms that same sultanism became incarnate in an irresistible dictatorship. For be a man's intellectual superiority what it will, it can never assume the practical, available supremacy over other men, without the aid of some sort of external arts and entrenchments, always, in themselves, more of less paltry and base. ... Such large virtue lurks in these small things when extreme political superstitions invest them, that in some royal instances ... the plebian herds crouch abased before the tremendous centralization. (ch. 33, 147–8)

However, Ahab's political circumstances are not those of Rome's first Caesar, much less those of a Russian Tsar – quite the contrary: he faces men nurtured in a Hobbesian mentality. He cannot avail himself of 'outward majestical trappings and housings' invested with mystic significance by long history and dogmatic religion. In dealing with this or that individual, Ahab tailors his speech, manners, and actions according to his always shrewd assessment of the man's character and ruling concerns. But when addressing men collectively, as on the occasion of his successful subversion of the *Pequod*'s crew, he speaks to them simply as men: a man's man appealing directly to the universal manliness of men. Because he comports himself generally as a man of few words – indeed, for the most part, of pregnant, intense, preoccupied silence – he can count on everyone's complete attention when he does speak. Able to articulate lesser men's own ideals, especially of themselves, he can convince them that they are special, the chosen few who can defeat Moby Dick, much as against all odds were Henry's soldiers victorious at Agincourt.

His appeal is the more effective in that those he addresses already have reason to think of themselves as more select than ordinary landsmen. As did the Romans. As did King Henry's Britons. As do Americans, and those who would become Americans, whether in America or elsewhere. For the foremost constituent of citizenship in a Hobbesian commonwealth is the state of one's mind, believing firmly in certain principles: the Rights of Man, Equality before the law, Consent of the governed, a maximum of Liberty and minimum of Laws – principles that in practice are meant to underwrite a Commercial Republic, ready and able to exploit the ever-advancing technological science the regime is especially designed to favour. Not the least of Ahab's perversions of the polity placed in his care is his rejection of the science intended to be the foundation of the commonwealth's ever-increasing prosperity: 'Science! Curse thee, thou vain toy; and cursed be all the things that cast man's eyes aloft to the heaven.' Then, dashing to the deck his means of celestial navigation, 'Curse thee, thou quadrant! … no longer will I guide my earthly way by thee … thus I trample on thee, thou paltry thing that feebly pointest on high; thus I split and destroy thee!' (ch. 118, 501). This action as much as any disturbs the sober, pious, nicely named Starbuck, pondering assassination: 'Has he not dashed his heavenly quadrant? and in these same perilous seas, gropes he not his way by mere dead reckoning of the error-abounding log? and in this very Typhoon, did he not swear that he would have no lightning-rods?' (ch. 123, 514).

The troubling question that *Moby-Dick* obliquely raises concerns the typical way of life in a Commercial Republic. Does it offer full satisfaction to the human soul? Or does it leave people, men especially perhaps, longing for something 'higher,' for some higher purpose to life than simply living it out in safety and comfort? Does there remain deep inside men a formless yearning to which an Ahab may appeal? The more so, the manlier the man? As religious belief erodes – and the Hobbesian regime is practically designed to ensure that it will erode, its intellectual authority contracting proportional to the growth of modern science, its moral authority increasingly undermined by both the inherent 'worldliness' of commerce and the amorality of modern science – a vacancy opens up in people's lives. Vaguely longing for some 'cause' that seems worthy of dedication, of self-sacrifice, hence repeatedly embracing and discarding popular enthusiasms in search of an honourable challenge that can engage them body and soul, and thereby impart a larger meaning to their routinized, money-driven lives (whether of bank clerks or whale hunters), they are ripe to follow a magical, mysterious charismatic who seems able finally to supply what they yearn for. Inspired by an 'Ahab' who can, by 'the ineffable thing,' bind them to him, and through him to each other, they are willing to subordinate their individualized lives of petty purpose to his grand vision of conquest, to the challenge of overcoming some great White Whale, be that what it may. Does not the Hobbesian regime, in short, constitute a fertile seedbed for Caesarism?[14]

Caesarism requires a *demos*. This need not mean that the regime be formally a democracy, but simply that it include a large and potent plebian class whose members feel free to bestow their allegiance where they will, as their own spirits move them – or are moved.[15] But Caesarism also requires a Caesar. The real thing, however, is exceedingly rare; ages may pass without one gracing or cursing the scene. Most claimants who offer themselves are more or less ridiculous pretenders, if not outright charlatans and imposters. Only someone akin to the original can bring Caesarism to life. However, as the career of Melville's Ahab so emphatically illustrates (to say nothing of history), there is no assurance that the mission of a Caesar be either wholesome or feasible. Or even that he himself be altogether what normal people regard as sane; a certain monomaniacal temper – a 'bloody-mindedness' – may be intrinsic to both his inner strength and outer mystique.

Ahab's appeal to pursue Moby Dick to the ends of the earth, whatever its commercial cost, falls on receptive ears. For not only does he speak to fellow 'warrior whalemen,' bold hunters of the watery frontier who have been nurtured to share his view of whales and the world they swim in: that they are dangerous monsters inhabiting a fickle, unpredictable environment. But also, and more fundamental, they are *modern* men, sharing his view of Nature as a whole: that it is an alien order, indifferent when not simply antagonistic to human well-being. Accordingly, they see 'meer Nature' as something to be mastered, for the most part forcibly – a vast fund of otherwise worthless resources which human artifice can transform for the sake of ameliorating man's estate (lest his life be poor, nasty, brutish, and short). A plausible, no-nonsense view, to be sure.

What is perhaps more disturbing, however, is that to one degree or another, men of the Pequodian commonwealth are already subconsciously infected with the *resentment* so hypertrophied in Ahab: of a world that is cold, unjust, meaningless, and wholly indifferent to mankind's righteous preferences. That the one attitude naturally reinforces the other – that the resentment of the natural order is both a cause and an effect of choosing to regard Nature as but so much base matter to be exploited – is a likelihood not to be ignored, pregnant as it is with nihilistic implications.

How it was that they so aboundingly responded to the old man's ire – by what evil magic their souls were possessed, that at times his hate seemed almost theirs; the White Whale as much their insufferable foe as his; how all this came to be – what the White Whale was to them, or how to their unconscious understandings, also, in some dim, unsuspected way, he might have seemed the gliding great demon of the seas of life, – all this to explain, would be to dive deeper than Ishmael can go. The subterranean miner that works in us all, how can one tell whither leads his shaft by the ever-shifting, muffled sound of his pick? (ch. 41, 187)

Nor was the young Ishmael exempt from Ahab's spell: 'my shouts had gone up with the rest; my oath had been welded with theirs; and stronger I shouted, and more did I hammer and clinch my oath, because of the dread in my soul. A wild, mystical, sympathetical feeling was in me; Ahab's quenchless feud seemed mine' (ch. 41, 179).

Whatever more precisely the various other individuals may have thought about Moby Dick, or felt rather, Ishmael – who, recall, is telling his story 'some years' after the fact – is sure that for Ahab the great White Whale represented in summary form the entirety of a malignant universe, inveterately hostile to man, if only in its amoral indifference to mankind's weal.

Small reason was there to doubt ... that ever since that almost fatal encounter, Ahab had cherished a wild vindictiveness against the whale, all the more fell for that in his frantic morbidness he at last came to identify with him, not only all his bodily woes, but all his intellectual and spiritual exasperations. The White Whale swam before him as the monomaniac incarnation of all those malicious agencies which some deep men feel eating in them, till they are left living on with half a heart and half a lung ... All that most maddens and torments; all that stirs up the lees of things; all truth with malice in it; all that cracks the sinews and cakes the brain; all the subtle demonisms of life and thought; all evil, to crazy Ahab, was visibly personified, and made practically assailable in Moby Dick. He piled upon the whale's white hump the sum of all the general rage and hate felt by his whole race from Adam down. (ch. 41, 184)

Ahab's view of the world into which he has been thrown, or dumped, is the predominant modern one, and compared with Ishmael's own, it is a perversely partial, hence unjust, view. In the final analysis, Ahab's warped ambition is a product of misbegotten philosophy.

A Bastard's Philosophy: for so one may justly call Ahab's jaundiced view of Nature, of the Divine, and of the all-too-Human. It is a conception reached by a man who has taken upon himself the challenge of philosophy – to understand and assess the whole of things – but who is not quite up to the task. Despite prodigious natural gifts of both mind and spirit, and despite having striven mightily to find an intelligible ground beyond the weltering appearances, Ahab has clearly failed to do so. This is partly the cause and partly the effect of his inability to attain the synoptic perspective – the calm, balanced, and measured overview of the whole – that is the defining goal of a Platonic philosopher, and the mark of one who is, or has become, by nature *dialektikos*.[16] For Melville's purposes, Ishmael, both as actor in and narrator of his tale, approximates such a person. Judging from the textual evidence, some of which I marshalled in the Overture to this book, Ishmael is by nature and self-nurture a Platonist, having been naturally drawn to and shaped by his Master's dialogical portrayal of the true philosopher. Ishmael's contrasting presence accentuates the perversion of the philosophical nature in the figure of Ahab. Hobbes would recognize each man for the type he is, and there can be little doubt which type he would prefer holding a professorship in a university.

To be sure, Ishmael is himself no romantic idealist about Nature and the cosmos, any more than is Plato. For example, in trying to explain why it was the *whiteness* of the whale that he found so disturbing, he wonders about whiteness per se: 'Is it that by its indefiniteness it shadows forth the heartless voids and immensities of the universe, and thus stabs us from behind with the thought of annihilation, when beholding the white depths of the milky way?' (ch. 42, 195).[17] And as manifested by the Sea, Ishmael sees clearly the voracity and violence that pervade Nature, and is aware that 'by vast odds, the most terrific of all mortal disasters have immemorially and indiscriminately befallen tens and hundreds of thousands of those who have gone upon the waters':

But not only is the sea such a foe to man who is an alien to it, but it is also a fiend to its own offspring ... sparing not the creatures which itself hath spawned ... No mercy, no power but its own controls it ... Consider also the devilish brilliance and beauty of many of its most remorseless tribes, as the dainty embellished shape of many species of sharks. Consider, once more, the universal cannibalism of the sea; all whose creatures prey upon each other, carrying on eternal war since the world began. (ch. 58, 274)

Ishmael, however, appreciates that the Sea and its creatures are not the whole of Nature. Though ocean covers 'two thirds of the fair world,' there is also the land; and it has denizens, such as the dog and the horse, that do not seem to partake of the same life-instinct as those of the sea: 'does the ocean furnish any fish that in disposition answers to the sagacious kindness of the dog?'[18] To reach a fair assessment of the natural order – and, indeed, of man himself – one must balance the 'full awfulness of the sea' with the character of the land, 'this green, gentle, and most docile earth.'

Consider all this ... consider them both, the sea and the land; and do you not find a strange analogy to something in yourself? For as this appalling ocean surrounds the verdant land, so in the soul of man there lies one insular Tahiti, full of peace and joy, but encompassed by all the horrors of the half known life. God keep thee! Push not off from that isle, thou canst never return! (ch. 58, 274)

Ahab, however, has pushed off, has irrevocably turned the back of his mind upon the verdant land, and so ascribes to the whole the 'universal cannibalism' that Ishmael attributes only to the sea – as if the entire life world were nothing more than an enormous, voracious, insatiable Eating Machine. Ahab regards the amoral indifference of the sea as exemplifying the pervasive injustice of the natural order per se. As if exhorting a Sperm whale's severed head suspended from his ship's boom, he voices his own summary judgment:

'Speak, thou vast and venerable head,' muttered Ahab ... '[that] has moved amid this world's foundations. Where unrecorded names and navies rust, and untold hopes and anchors rot; where in her murderous hold this frigate earth is ballasted with bones of millions of the drowned ... O head! thou hast seen enough to split the planets and make an infidel of Abraham, and not one syllable is thine!' (ch. 70, 311–12)

No one in Melville's story expressly articulates a convincing theodicy whereby to rebut Ahab's indictment of the world. But bearing in mind the entire crew's willing complicity in Ahab's mad and blasphemous project, the fate of the *Pequod* itself might be interpreted as a not altogether unjust outcome, whether attributed to God or Nature. That the philosophical Ishmael alone escaped, whereby 'the tale was saved,' may convey its own message.[19]

However, it is not the amoral callousness of this 'frigate earth' – perpetually carving its furrow through the heavens, yet ever going nowhere – that most estranges Ahab. It is the world's mute opacity, its stubborn resistance to man's questioning, that most exasperates the old Captain. His obsessive hunting of the White Whale is a quest for knowledge. This is first hinted in the course of his dramatic subversion of the ship's company, diverting them from their constituted purpose of commercial whale fishing in favour of wreaking vengeance on the 'accursed white whale' that had previously crippled him. Conscientious Starbuck alone openly protests, warning that Ahab's intention is not merely unprofitable, but mad and blasphemous. Moreover, and not least important: that Ahab's sense of *justice* – so narrowly self-centred, as if he, Ahab, were the measure of all things – is profoundly warped. 'Vengeance on a dumb brute! ... that simply smote thee from blindest instinct!' That is, the whale was acting naturally, in self-defence, which one might acknowledge to be the 'natural right,' not just of man, but of any living thing. That it did not tamely submit to Ahab's mortal assault upon it, but responded in kind, hardly legitimates the wild justice of vengeance. To all these accusations, Ahab replies with a rant that must puzzle the First Mate, revealing though it is of his Captain's obsession:

All visible objects, man, are but as pasteboard masks. But in each event – in the living act, the undoubted deed – there, some unknown but still reasoning thing puts forth the mouldings of its features from behind the unreasoning mask. If man will strike, strike through the mask! How can the prisoner reach outside except by thrusting through the wall? To me, the white whale is that wall, shoved near to me. Sometimes I think there's naught beyond. But 'tis enough. He tasks me; he heaps me; I see in him outrageous strength, with an inscrutable malice sinewing it. That inscrutable thing is chiefly what I hate; and be the white whale agent, or be the white whale principal, I will wreak that hate upon him. (ch. 36, 164)

As Ahab sees it, the perceptible world – a surface 'inscrutable,' hence perplexing in itself – hides but nonetheless conforms to a powerful, malicious, yet presumably intelligible Reality. This reality does not reveal itself to the passive observer, however patient and assiduous. An understanding of reality, and thereby the meaning of one's own place in it, is to be gained only through an aggressive 'thrusting through the wall' of appearances. The white whale represents this wall, this mask concealing an intelligible reality, and Ahab would strike through it with harpoon and lance – not so much to satisfy a gnawing hunger to know the truth, as to assuage his hatred of living in a world that does not make perfect sense to him, especially concerning what he views as its amoral inhospitality to man. It is this mortal hatred of living in ignorance (not fervent love of immortal wisdom) that drives him, that motivates his pursuit of Moby Dick, intent on breaching the obscuring wall, thereby opening a personal vista on the Truth. Ahab considers the possibility 'that there's naught beyond' the wall, no coherent meaning to reality, after all – that the wall of the White Whale is not mere 'agent,' representing the inscrutable mask of a rationally meaningful reality, but 'principal': brute representation of brutish reality itself. Still, since there is but one way to find out which it is, and since both alternatives are hateful to Ahab, ''tis enough' for him that there be a white whale to hunt, a wall to assault.

Ishmael confirms that the Sperm whale's 'battering ram' of a forehead 'is a dead, blind wall,' but composed of such tough material that 'the severest pointed harpoon, the sharpest lance darted by the strongest human arm, impotently rebounds from it' (ch. 76, 336–7). Moreover, it is a wall in motion: 'there swims behind it all a mass of tremendous life'; the Ahab-led Pequodian commonwealth perishes in collision with it. But Ishmael attests that there is something precious beyond the impregnable wall: an enormous chamber filled with 'the most delicate oil,' the highly prized spermaceti – to be reached, however, in a different way and from a different direction. The thought of 'perishing' immersed in this sweetly fragrant substance, 'tombed in the secret inner chamber and sanctum sanctorum of the whale' (as accidentally was almost the fate of the harpooneer Tashtego) prompts Ishmael to wonder, 'How many, think ye, have likewise fallen into Plato's honey head, and sweetly perished there?' (ch. 78, 344).

The mention of Plato, however, may prompt one to wonder whether Melville's allegorical image of a wall of appearances is meant to point beyond his text to the most famous allegory in all of philosophical literature: the Cave Allegory recounted by Plato's Sokrates.[20] By reflecting on what it teaches about 'our nature concerning its education and lack of education,' one sees how and why Ahab's attempt to gain sure knowledge is misbegotten. Ahab appreciates well enough that we are somehow 'prisoners,' and that the flickering shadows on the wall of his Cave in themselves offer no solid understanding of reality – that they are somehow 'shaped' by that reality, but nonetheless mask and mislead concerning its true character. But whereas Sokrates teaches that one must first unshackle oneself from the conventional opinions and language of one's Cave, and then turn around in order to face its mouth – a natural opening whereby one may exit to the sunlit reality exposed above ground – Ahab mistakenly believes that the reality he seeks is on the far side of the wall, which must perforce be violently attacked and hewn through ('How can the prisoner reach outside except by thrusting through the wall?').

Ahab possesses the warrior spirit requisite to a genuine philosopher.[21] But to the disadvantage of his philosophical aspirations, he is possessed *by* this warrior spirit, ruled by it. The natural ruling relationship, in which a strong spirit is the subordinate ally of the soul's rational part, is reversed in Ahab. As a result, he is, one might say, courageous to a fault. Not having had the 'musical' education that would tame his spirit, rendering it obedient to rational rule, he lacks the psychic harmony that a philosopher requires if he is to view the truth, the whole truth, dispassionately. The nurture implicit in Ahab's forty years a whaleman has been, almost exclusively, violently 'athletic' ('for a thousand lowerings old Ahab has furiously, foamingly chased his prey – more a demon than a man!'; ch. 132, 544). His way of life has been too much that of a Spartan, not enough of the Athenian. As a result, his spirit has been 'raised to a higher pitch' than is good for him, rendering him imperious (and not only towards other men), apt to be easily angered, overly sensitive to slights, too ready to resort to force, and animated largely by hate, little by love. Most significantly, however, it has made him vengeful.[22]

With a nature already so disposed, his previous crippling encounter with Moby Dick simply fixed in monomania his spirit's ascendancy, but in such a way that 'not one jot of his great natural intellect had perished. That before living agent, now became the living instrument' (ch. 41, 185). Thus, all his striving after knowledge is warped, corrupted, by this overpowering desire seated in his soul's spirited part: the desire for vengeance, dominating and embittering his entire posture towards life and its cosmic setting. In his hostile, antagonistic view of Nature, Ahab is modern to the core. But beyond that, he is a classic illustration of why seeking the truth about justice is essential to philosophy, lest a misguided sense of righteous indignation distort all of one's observations, prejudice all of one's analyses, and pervert all of one's judgments – not only about political life, but about the character of the whole natural order and one's own just deserts therein, including what one has a right to know.

What the White Whale finally means to Ishmael is never made perfectly clear. But it is possible that he hints at something in reporting that the 'superstitiously inclined' entertained the 'unearthly conceit that Moby Dick was ubiquitous,' having been simultaneously 'encountered in opposite latitudes,' and 'not only ubiquitous, but immortal (for immortality is but ubiquity in time).' Nor, he adds, 'was this conceit without some faint show of superstitious probability. For as the secrets of the currents in the seas have never yet been divulged, even to the most erudite research; so the hidden ways of the Sperm Whale when beneath the surface remain, in great part, unaccountable to his pursuers' (ch. 41, 182). In the exact centre of the book's central chapter ('The Blanket'), Ishmael, speaking for himself, informs us that 'the visible surface of the Sperm Whale is not the least among the many marvels he presents,' being cross-hatched with a rich array of 'hieroglyphical' lineations that defy decoding; thus, 'the mystic-marked whale remains undecipherable' (ch. 68, 306). Ishmael in his wisdom can accept that the universe presents mysteries that are beyond mere human capacity to penetrate and comprehend. Blessed by the natural piety that such acceptance brings, Ishmael can live with his ignorance. Ahab, plagued by his own unruly spirit, could not.

Still, for all his pious wisdom, Melville's precocious Ishmael may be wrong in claiming so unqualifiedly that anyone who is willing to resort to those 'paltry and base external arts' – which even a Caesar must employ in order to acquire and maintain 'supremacy over other men' – would necessarily be so 'infinitely inferior' to 'God's true princes of the Empire.' These true princes, he implies, are distinguished even more by their 'intellectual superiority' than by their fastidious taste (ch. 33, 148).

But what if one of them were sufficiently philanthropic, and artistic, to say to himself, 'The devil take my good taste,' and so – against all odds – be willing to demean himself for the sake of political creation?[23] What might a philosophical Caesar make of a Hobbesian commonwealth?[24] For that matter, can one altogether rule out the possibility that this was Hobbes's own fondest hope, given that wonderful paragraph in the very centre of his *Leviathan*: 'that one time or other, this writing of mine, may fall into the hands of a Soveraign, who will consider it himselfe'? If he is to understand it as its author understood it, however, he would have to be, or become, sufficiently philosophical himself, thereby fulfilling Plato's prescription announced in the very centre of his *Republic*.

Postlude

The level of social development required by democracy as it is known in the West has existed in only a minority of places – and even there only during certain periods of history. We are entering a troubling transition, and the irony is that while we preach our version of democracy abroad, it slips away from us at home.

          – Robert Kaplan, *The Coming Anarchy*

I undertook this re-examination of Hobbes's most famous and influential book partly out of curiosity, and partly out of my growing unease about the political health of contemporary liberal democracies. My curiosity was initially stimulated by the book's strange central paragraph, being fascinated and yet perplexed by both its surprising substance and its precise placement. Pondering its implications led me to notice other, similarly strange features of the form and matter of the text – and to a proportional dissatisfaction with the standard interpretations of 'Hobbes's Political Thought.'[1] My curiosity was intensified by successive readings of Melville's masterpiece, which set me to mulling what all he might mean by characterizing whales as 'leviathans' – a term so loaded with political connotations – and knowing Melville to be a declared admirer of Hobbes. I was especially intrigued by his having Ishmael contend that the most awesome of the genus, the Sperm whale (instantiated by the seemingly indestructible Moby Dick), deserves to be regarded as a '*Platonian* Leviathan.' Why ever would such an idea occur to anyone?

My uneasiness about the form of regime virtually all Westerners take for granted – basically Hobbesian, but departing from his prescription in two crucial respects: with regard to censorship, and the Church-State relationship – arises from what I see as a triple threat to its continuing viability.[2] I hoped that by virtue of understanding Hobbes's political reasoning more fully, more deeply than is evident in those standard interpretations, I (or anyone) would be the better prepared to address the problems now confronting our liberal-democratic, techno-commercial republics. Whereas, given the nature of these threats, most academic political philosophy seems to me irrelevant at best, and too often pernicious in its effects.

I spoke briefly in my Prelude about the massive disruptive consequences of high-tech terrorism – vastly disproportionate to the resources required to perpetrate it – and of its proven potential to effect major dislocations and alterations in the commercial, industrial, financial, military, transportational, communicational, and educational policies and practices of modern liberal democracies. Similarly, the perceived need for increased domestic surveillance and intelligence-gathering impact their citizenries' lives in a multitude of ways, few of them appealing. I will not repeat myself here except to emphasize that it may well prove a more serious long-term threat than is generally appreciated. Vast swaths of the populations in Africa, Asia, and Latin America are infected with anti-Western (or anti-capitalist, or anti-globalist, or anti-modern, or – symbolic of everything they both covet and resent – anti-American) sentiment. Suffice it to say, they have at best an equivocal attitude towards the realization of Hobbes's political project thus far. Such animosity will not be sufficient to overcome most people's habitual passivity, but compounded with resurgent tribalisms and sectarianisms, it will activate enough (mainly) young men to provide an ample reservoir of terrorist recruits. And while future nihilists may not be able to exploit suicidal agents so readily in the execution of their murderous and destructive schemes (that seems generally to require some misbegotten religious faith), they will nonetheless derive a perverse inspiration from the all-too-evident vulnerabilities of liberal societies. Step by step efforts to counteract permutations of this threat may distort the structures and practices of their present regimes beyond recognition. But so too, albeit in very different ways, may a burgeoning set of *internal* problems, problems apparently inherent in the basic principles upon which these societies operate, though they come to sight only over time.

Consider, first of all, the accelerating decay of what is called popular culture, since so many of these polities' other current domestic troubles – from drug abuse and irresponsible violence, especially among increasingly unruly children and youths, to the decay of basic morality, especially sexual morality, but including the civility, politeness, and respectful behaviour that make such a difference to the social comfort and general tone of life. These and related political problems are greatly exacerbated, if not simply caused, by the abject state of popular culture.[3] Now, as ever, most people's, particularly young people's, ideas of how to behave, their understandings of how their world 'really' works, and their judgments about what is important – their so-called values – are profoundly shaped by the primary constituents of this culture, especially by the various modes and enormous amounts of visual entertainment (not just the farces and melo-dramas of films and television, but also professional sports and pseudo-sports, news and pseudo-news, video games, and the ever-proliferating sources of amusement available on the internet). And by music of a quality and content that beggars description, and would have defied credulity a bare half-century ago. And by all-pervasive commercial advertising appealing to, hence encouraging and ratifying, the very hedonism and acquisitiveness that a wholesome morality would seek to restrain. More-over, one must suppose that the influence of these cultural components is increasing simply because of their increasing presence and availability, thanks mainly to inexpensive new technical modes and devices, many aimed directly at the disposable wealth that today's youth command (derivative of an unprecedented general level of material prosperity).

The issue is not primarily that of 'high-brow' versus 'low-brow' – though Gresham's law seems as pertinent to culture (and journalism) as to money. It is worth recalling there was a time and place where ordinary citizens packed theatres to be entertained by the likes of Sophocles; and not so very long ago, unlettered common folk paid their precious pence to see performances of Shakespeare. The main point, however, is that popular entertainment does not have to be high-brow in order to be morally and politically wholesome, even edifying. And conversely, offer-ings aimed at a sophisticated cultural elite can be decadent in the extreme. But who other than a natural fool could seriously believe that a steady diet of witty insolence, slick pornography, celebrations of hedonism, and spectacular violence does not have a cumulative effect on human souls – on minds and hearts, passions and desires – especially on the souls of life's most eager imitators: youths. It is revealing that those who publicly pretend to deny any such causal effect (mainly those who profit from producing it) are never so audacious as to claim that their productions actually make people *better*; merely that there is no incontrovertible proof that they do harm.[4]

The rapidity with which popular culture has spiralled downward is a consequence of freedom of the marketplace conjoined with what is today often called (apparently without irony) 'freedom of artistic expression' – a recent, wildly implausible expansion of liberal democracy's defensible commitment to the freedom of speech essential to an informed citizenry. The widespread, largely passive acceptance of this expansion has culmi-nated in the almost total relaxation of all formal and informal censorship of public entertainment, mild though it long had been. Applied commer-cially, this freedom of expression, and consumption, has meant the licence for some to make mountains of money by pandering ever more flagrantly to the lower impulses of human nature. The effects, inconceivable to people but two or three generations ago, have not been slow in appearing. Whether as a result of ever more explicit portrayals of sexual ingenuity, glamorous criminality, wholesale killings, and the noisiest, most fiery modes of destroying property, the public's taste has been corrupted beyond recovery is debatable. But given people's fondness for the pleasures to which they have grown accustomed, it is difficult to imagine any practical way that decency can be restored to popular culture by democratic means.

Not the least consequence of cultural decay is its effect upon stable family life, eroding both moral standards and the discipline required to inculcate and maintain them. Divorce, and the single-parent or otherwise fractured families that result, is becoming as normal as the traditional arrangement that is being proportionally supplanted. The threat this poses to any regime's political viability needs no exaggeration, families (not individuals) being the true 'atoms' of social life,[5] and the principal seat of moral education – doubly important in a regime that explicitly disavows responsibility for the cultivation of any virtue beyond law-abidingness (and decreasingly even that). The adverse effects of family breakup on the educability of children has been documented ad nauseum; similarly, its correlation with learning and behavioural disorders, juvenile delinquency, drug use, and depression.[6]

But equally if not more disturbing is the decline in the overall birth rate in these polities, well below that required for population stability. While there doubtless are various factors contributing to this dangerous trend, the insecurity bred by the prevalence of divorce is one factor; another is the self-centred – and self-satisfied – hedonism that underlies the typical rationales of prosperous couples choosing to remain childless (or 'child-free,' as some so revealingly prefer to put it). The effects of both are amplified by the ready availability, and broad public acceptance, of abortion (in countries where it is legal, it terminates anywhere from 15 to 50 per cent of pregnancies).[7] The resulting political situation, that of a proportionally aging population dependent upon an array of welfare state programs financed by a shrinking workforce, is potentially explosive. But what are the prospects of restoring by purely democratic means the conditions that once sustained stable, two-parent families of moderate size?

The strategy of maintaining an adequate tax-paying workforce through the adoption of generous immigration policies – seemingly the only feasible remedy, hence increasingly relied upon by liberal societies, despite the inflow rate being beyond any polity's capacity for assimilation – is fast revealing itself to be a Faustian bargain. As the proportion of population made up of mainly Third World immigrants grows, their need and motive and opportunity to assimilate diminish, leaving the host country with large enclaves of people who retain the non-liberal mindsets of the nations whence they came. Moreover, they soon enough become aware of their potential power to compromise and, in effect, undermine a political system for which they have little affection or respect. And they *do* produce children. Children who, nurtured amid social prejudices and limited economic prospects, and ignorant of the reality their parents fled (though perhaps fed upon romanticized memories thereof), are more apt to mature into alienated opponents than loyal citizens of a regime they regard as decadent, feckless, and hypocritical. Not that their ever more intrusive presence will be accepted with equanimity by the more reactionary constituents of the native population. It is unlikely that beholden politicians relentlessly touting the glories of multiculturalism will suffice to defuse this time bomb.

To be sure, problems such as these are not strictly necessary consequences of a commitment to liberty and equality. Neither the political liberty indispensable to the functioning of representative democracy, nor the personal liberty requisite to the pursuit of happiness, logically implies the decay of popular entertainment, the deterioration of family structures, gambling addiction, rampant drug abuse (and the crimes it breeds), gang 'culture,' or any other of the growing list of social problems. But the practical question is, are they the *psycho*-logical consequences? That is, given the normal inclinations of human nature in the absence of intentional countervailing efforts, do people's expectations of liberty have a natural tendency over time to expand in degenerative ways, the commitment to rationally desirable, hence defensible liberties devolving so as to include pernicious, indefensible ones? And as a consequence, the very conception of liberty, unqualified as it invariably is in popular praise, itself become degraded, licensing freedom from external constraints for everyone, however irresponsible or morally repulsive their behaviour? Ultimately, however, such developments may result in something other than a thoroughly decadent social environment – but an outcome no less alarming. Plato's Sokrates contends that, in the long run, Democracy's honouring a permissive conception of freedom as the highest good, married with a widespread acceptance of the belief that all desires are 'equal' (even those of brutes),[8] leads naturally to an anarchic situation that is ripe for tyranny (*Republic* 562d–563e). For as everyday life becomes increasingly chaotic, a growing majority of people will support whoever can plausibly promise to restore law and order, and thereby some decency and civility. History, both ancient and modern, supplies ample confirmation of this possibility.

The regime's commitment to equality raises another kind of internal problem (or set of problems, rather), resulting from divergent interpretations, hence expectations, of 'equal justice.' There can be no question but that the original understanding – of Hobbes, and of those following in his footsteps, such as Locke and the American Founders and all the thousands and millions who agreed with them – understood it to mean 'equality of opportunity': that with equality before the law, and with there being no unnecessary laws, there would be no artificial obstacles to each individual's using his abilities and resources to pursue what seems to him the best life of which he is capable, or is willing to exert himself to achieve. And let the chips fall where they may. With people having different conceptions of the good life, not all of which are equally attainable; with chance still a significant factor in human affairs; and with innumerable other variables in circumstances and natures affecting actual outcomes, there is no reason to expect that everyone will be equally successful in whatever they choose to pursue. But so far as practical, people will, generally speaking, get to live the life they themselves have chosen and earned, and in that sense the life they deserve. And what more can be reasonably asked in the way of a just political arrangement? Nurtured in such an environment, people acquire a sense of personal responsibility and self-reliance, thus an implicit desire for the virtues requisite to any successful pursuit of happiness – become citizens, that is, better suited for liberty.

Over time, however, a very different notion of 'just equality' has been gaining ground, what is usually referred to as 'equality of result', a principle that pretty much inverts the former idea, and not infrequently crashes head-on with the commitment to individual freedom. Each view traced to the bottom, it becomes plain that not merely are they incompatible, but that partisans of the one must regard the other view as profoundly *unjust*.[9] Now, it can be shown in several different ways that, quite apart from its suspect justness, no society can be made to work well, or even work at all, on the basis of the notion that everyone has the 'right' to an equally comfortable and satisfying life,[10] much less, that a given polity's commitment to equal rights, however conceived, pertain 'equally' to citizens and non-citizens alike. But impractical or undesirable as a thorough analysis might show it to be, most people will never undertake a thorough analysis of this (or any other) conception of justice. Moreover, there will always be people who prefer to believe that they are equally deserving, not merely of opportunity, but of happiness, and plenty more who see that they can personally benefit from the selective application of the notion. Consequently, this false standard can be rhetorically effective for impugning the justness of any and all existing arrangements, insisting that they be 'reformed' in its direction. To the extent such efforts succeed, contradictions are introduced into the functioning of the modern liberal regime, with all the frustrations, incriminations and recriminations, resentments and bitterness that contradictory views of justice are bound to generate (precisely the situation that Hobbes sought so strenuously to preclude).

The theoretical question here is not which view of equality can be consistently applied in a viable polity – that's open and shut – but whether there is not the same sort of problem with the public commitment to equality as there is with liberty. That is, an inherent tendency, whether in the regime as Hobbes prescribed it, or merely in the imperfect versions that have been implemented, for the idea of equality to devolve as historically it has, from that 'of opportunity' to that 'of result.' Such that, given certain propensies of human nature, this transformation in many people's understanding, hence in political expectations and feelings of entitlement, was bound to happen. And that this was only the more likely, given also the ready availability of arguments purporting to show that people are 'by nature' roughly equal in faculties of body and mind (thus, that their observable differences are all due to the advantages and disadvantages of nurture), perhaps abetted by some vague notion of determinism as 'scientific.' Whatever the case, are the resulting problems remedial within the quasi-Hobbesian regimes as presently constituted?

Profoundly complicating liberal democracy's capacity to cope either with the threat of terrorism or with the political consequences of these internal developments are the problems arising from the increasingly unmanageable growth of scientific technology: unprecedented ethical and practical quandaries, mortal dangers, and socio-economic vulnerabilities. This is the more ironic inasmuch as promoting scientific progress is the primary, albeit tacit, raison d'être its architect envisioned for this form of regime (as I have argued at length in the preceding chapters). One may doubt whether *any* version of Hobbes's prescribed commonwealth would prove equal to controlling the consequences of an unlimited growth of scientific knowledge, but for sure the Popular version is not.

The threat posed by modern science has three analytically distinct but practically related components. One has to do with the deeply perplexing – and politically very divisive – issues being spawned by the once barely conceivable technological possibilities in genetics and other biological sciences, as well as in micro-electronics. A second concerns the practical difficulties of controlling access to an ever-expanding catalogue of powerful, hence dangerous, technologies, ensuring that they are not appropriated for malign uses. Third is a quite different sort of challenge: that which arises from an increasing reliance on scientific expertise in framing laws and public policies, compromising still further the democratic principles on which the modern liberal regime is supposedly founded, while tainting the intellectual authority of science itself. I shall expand a bit on each of these in turn.

I need say little about the first sort of problem, since its salience has already become the subject of considerable public discussion (e.g., concerning the various ethical issues involving reproductive technologies, cloning, genetically modified foods, electronic invasion of privacy, inter alia). One commentator's observation, though already passé, will suffice as a mild illustration of the novel issues such technologies can raise:

Within a decade, biotechnology companies will be offering hundreds, if not thousands, of predictive genetic tests. Given the character of the practice of medicine in much of the affluent world, it is highly likely that a significant number of people will confront information that is psychologically devastating, or be excluded from a job on genetic grounds, or be denied insurance through genetic discrimination, or face an acute dilemma about continuing a pregnancy.[11]

It does not take much imagination to conceive of far more problematic uses to which such genetic testing might be put. But it is much less easy to see how, given a liberal democracy's commitment to economic and personal liberty, the further development and employment of this – and dozens of other emerging technologies – are to be controlled. How are 'legitimate' uses to be determined, given the complex pros and cons of, say, prenatal screening, further compounded by the always controversial problem of balancing the value of personal freedom with the perceived necessity of some government regulation to protect the common good? Moreover, even if some medical procedure (say) is prohibited in Polity X, it may be readily available in Polity Y, hence to people with the means to go there. For the same reason, legal restrictions on particular lines of research may be pointless, or practically impossible to enforce, especially without jeopardizing the freedom of inquiry essential to scientific progress in general. Of course, none of this is a problem only for liberal democratic regimes. The sobering truth may be that there is *no* politically decent way of coping with the quasi-anarchy of modern science and its unforeseeable technological applications.

Given what mayhem terrorists have recently caused, their callous disregard for human lives (including their own), the numbers and resources of those still at large in the world today – and lacking any reason to believe their ranks will not be regularly replenished – little reflection is required to appreciate the dangers implicit in open access to the arsenal of vast destructive powers that ever-advancing technology provides. Nor are political terrorists the only concern; there are other sorts of people, from the deranged to the criminal, whom one would prefer never get their hands on such powers. Preventing this from happening, however, is exceedingly difficult and becoming ever more so. For it is not simply a matter of denying access to materials and hardware, but also to information and skills, perhaps even to certain curricula of education. This would be difficult for an autocracy, given that wonder of technology: the personal computer connected to the internet via satellite communication. How much more so, then, for a liberal democracy, with its expanded conception of civil liberties, its freedom of expression, of movement and of association, its openness to immigration and visitation?

Finally, consider the tension between every modern polity's need for scientific expertise in identifying various sorts of problems and threats to its well-being, and in formulating policies whereby to deal with them (on the one hand), and liberal democracy's adherence to its defining principles, including majority rule via elected representatives (on the other). The practical problem, briefly stated, is this: how to incorporate scientific expertise in political decision making when and as necessary, but without unduly privileging a tiny minority of experts to the prejudice of democratic majoritarian rule. Moreover, this problem has an obverse side: as scientific expertise grows in political salience, it becomes ever more subject to political pressure, exploitation, and partisanship. This undermines the status – the perceived objectivity, hence the intellectual authority – of science itself, and consequently the credibility of scientists. And yet the polity's need for objective scientific knowledge is no way diminished.

Arguably, the ultimate politicization of science – influencing research agenda and theoretical modelling; biasing the gathering, assessment, and analysis of evidence; introducing political partisanship into the relations among scientists – is the natural consequence of the accumulating successes of the Baconian-Hobbesian project. The more techno-science-saturated political life becomes, the more science impinges on public policy issues (when not the very focus thereof); and the more scientific expertise is drawn into political debate, the more that scientists themselves become implicated, whether as lionized allies or vilified opponents. What can be done? Typically, liberal democracies favour procedural answers – that the Public's interest will be ensured if a certain procedure is followed – being loath to trust in anyone's disinterested prudential judgment. After all, a basic premise of the regime's rationale is that people are motivated primarily by self-interest. But is there any liberal-democratic procedure whereby to marry scientific knowledge and political responsibility? Any politically *realistic* way, that is, not some utopian fantasy featuring idealized scientists and statesmen.

In light of the troubles I see overtaking Hobbes's variously imperfect political progeny, I cannot pretend a high regard for contemporary academic political philosophy. It seems to me that most practitioners have failed to recognize, or lack the courage to address, the real problems threatening the Popular version of Hobbes's prescription – problems of such scale as may well require the liberal regimes's being profoundly modified, if not replaced with some new political form altogether. In considering that possibility, it is important to bear in mind two truths.

First, regimes per se are merely *means*, not ends in themselves. As such, they are to be judged in light of the ends for which they are instituted, maintained, and defended. Hence, one needs clarity on what these ends properly are, and of the extent to which a given political arrangement effectively secures these ends, not something else instead. The conception dominant in modern liberal democracies remains that which Hobbes specified as the 'finall Cause' for which people form commonwealths: some combination of physical security, prosperity ('commodious living'), liberty, and justice (as defined mainly by the Rule of Law). This conception is notable for what it does *not* include: the cultivation of human virtue, either personal or civic – indeed, its silence on this matter may actually contribute to its rhetorical appeal, since 'the good is hard,' and most people prefer the easy. And yet, given the external and internal threats to these societies, both courage and moderation are needed as much as ever, probably more.

Second, Western civilization is *not* coterminous with democracy, liberal or otherwise. Indeed, most of Western civilization's greatest *cultural* achievements – as distinct from the bulk of scientific progress, but including Hobbes's *Leviathan* and most of the other greatest works of philosophy – antecede the emergence of even the earliest glimmering of liberal democracy. Historically, democracy has had many intelligent, insightful critics other than Hobbes, and reviewing their critiques could be helpful.

Envisioning what changes would suffice, and – equally challenging – how the transition could be accomplished, is not likely to come from divine inspiration. It will necessitate clear, rigorous thought, both about the problems and about what of greatest value needs to be protected and promoted. With respect to the latter, there is sure to be some significant disagreement between the Many and the Few. As the security and civility of everyday life deteriorate, this becomes most people's primary political concern: the safety of their persons and property – as Hobbes knew well. Accordingly, they will accept, even demand, greater surveillance by State authorities of all public space,[12] and tolerate ever more monitoring of private transactions and curtailment of liberty (at least so long as the enjoyment of their favourite pleasures are unaffected). But they will do so largely ignorant of the dangers lurking in an indiscriminate acceptance of just anything (or anyone) that promises to answer their legitimate concerns – dangers evident to the minority of people who have some foresightful understanding of political life (and of bureaucratic rule in particular), and who are concerned with more than merely comfortable survival. In any event, we may be sure that major changes in the regimes of Western-style societies are on the horizon, and that they are more apt to be of an 'authoritarian' than a 'libertarian' kind. They will come about willy-nilly, absent an intentional effort to institute, in a duly prudent manner (itself a testing problem), some rationally coherent modification or replacement for the present regime. With this prospect in mind, revisiting Hobbes's broader case for a rational Monarchy or Aristocracy, as manifested throughout Part Two of *Leviathan*, is not a waste of time.[13]

By contrast, much of what today passes for political philosophy remains wedded in its fundamentals to the present form of regime, tacitly if not expressly, even while producing critiques and proposals that aggravate rather than alleviate its real problems. For example, by a misplaced emphasis on attaining 'greater real equality' through some explicit or covert scheme of reverse discrimination. Or by treating 'rights' as the conceptual medium whereby political problems are to be resolved – often by discovering, that is, imagining and ascribing, various new rights, and even new kinds of rights. Or by defending the 'equal value/legitimacy' of all traditions and *Weltanschauungen* as a justification for promoting the largely illusory benefits of some oxymoronic notion called 'multiculturalism.'

What is more significant, however, is that these criticisms and proposals, whatever their merit, reflect the conception of political philosophy that is currently dominant in academe, one which effectively discourages the *comprehensive* reconsideration of the established regime, realistically assessing both its virtues and its failings, identifying what is most important to preserve and what most needs remedy. The mode of thinking that this requires, however – at once radical and synoptic – is attained only through extensive practice of a kind that working within the regnant conception of political theorizing does not readily provide. Instead, the tacit assumption is that philosophizing about politics can be done piecemeal, and valid conclusions drawn about a particular issue from an analysis confined to factors bearing more or less directly on that issue (about healthcare policy, say, or fair wages, capital punishment, conscription, civil disobedience, etc.).

While such analyses are not invariably without value, they typically bespeak a misunderstanding of politics, and consequently of what is entailed in valid philosophizing about it. As Hobbes indicates, politics is – virtually by definition – architectonic: that 'politics,' properly conceived, comprehends *whatever* establishes the practical architecture within which all of life's more particular activities take place, and are allotted such place as they have.[14] Thus, to understand politics is to understand how this is accomplished, and why one arrangement is better than another. Given this architectonic requirement, pursuing a coherent account of the *whole* of political life is the sine qua non of genuinely *political* philosophy. True, one cannot address everything at once, but one has to bear everything in mind as one focuses attention on any particular aspect. This is why genuinely political thinking is so difficult, and why *fully coherent* political thinking is exceedingly rare. One can count on the fingers of one's hands those who are in a league with Plato and Aristotle, Hobbes and Rousseau.

Secondly, much academic theorizing manages to be *both* excessively 'rationalistic' *and* profoundly irrational. For the prevalent conception of Reason is woefully impoverished (as I argued in chapter 11), being roughly equivalent to formal rules of logic. So conceived, reason is seen as merely a tool whereby one may calculate the most effective means to ends that reasoning itself does not, and allegedly cannot, determine or establish (as these belong instead to some arational realm of 'values').[15] But while such theorists thus underrate the power of reason to determine appropriate ends and governing principles, they at the same time analyse political problems as if a typical person's foremost concern is to be 'rational' according to that narrow 'means to ends' conception. This betrays, I believe, a failure to appreciate what Hobbes knew well: how limited is the actual influence of rational calculation with most people in comparison with passions and desires, and how little they care about truth compared with what they would prefer to believe.[16] The foremost problem for genuine *political* reasoning is how to cope with the various irrationalities that pervade political life, most of them incorrigible.

However, utopian reasoning, egalitarian prejudice, and a piecemeal approach are not the worst faults undermining the value of so much academic political philosophy. Some practitioners espouse one or another sort of Materialism; others profess to be Determinists. Suffice it to say, they know not of what they speak – a singular liability, I should think, for this sort of work. More serious, however, is the widespread passive acceptance, and even active promulgation, of both moral and epistemological relativisms, rendering its subscribers incapable of defending the superiority of their own philosophizing to the obscurantist ravings of any intoxicated ignoramus claiming prophetic powers. And this despite the fact, easily shown and seen, that every conceivable form of radical relativism, whatever its ostensible basis (e.g., history, culture, language, sex), dissolves into incoherent mush upon reflexive application. And if publicly funded philosophy cannot manage to lay to rest such inherently vulnerable yet practically dangerous opponents of civilization – at the very least in academe, self-proclaimed bastion of reason and truth, bailiwick of people who supposedly think for a living – one has to wonder what it could possibly be good for.

The net result of these various deficiencies is that most of what today calls itself 'political philosophy' is profoundly ideological (indeed, often unashamedly so, being self-characterized as 'democratic theory'), and much of it practically indistinguishable from sophistry. Not altogether incidentally, it verges upon amazing how often the positions espoused by prominent members of the academic establishment manage to remain synchronous with whatever views are currently in political or intellectual fashion among the elites with whom they identify. As for contradictions that happen to be noticed, these are not treated as indications that the regnant premises are flawed. Rather, convinced of the essential correctness of contemporary enlightenment, practitioners simply resign themselves to the impossibility of fully articulating, much less defending, the higher truth whence such views derive – rather as theologians wrestling with conflicting revelations perforce conclude that the wisdom of God surpasseth human understanding. The resultant orthodoxy that pervades such so-called philosophizing begs comparison with its own caricature of Medieval Scholasticism, such that a serious political thinker in our day finds himself in a situation akin to that of Thomas Hobbes in his.

Doubtless some readers will be offended by the dismissive tone of the foregoing remarks. To them, I apologize, and offer in mitigation my having communed too much of late with the spirit of Hobbes, falling under the spell of his mode of plain speaking. In any event, my criticisms of professional academic philosophy, which pertain as well to the related social sciences and humanities, are by no means gratuitous. For the dominant strains of thought in these academic professions are hardly incidental to the intellectual confusion and deepening moral malaise affecting modern liberal-democratic societies. Quite the contrary. In fact, I believe it no exaggeration to say that the primary source of some of the most serious problems of these societies, and contributing to the rest, is the intellectual and moral failure of their universities. Like the 'Divines' of Hobbes's day, the vast majority of those who staff the various agencies that play any significant role in shaping public opinion – clerics, teachers, governmental officials, pundits and journalists, judges and lawyers, novelists and script writers, advertisers and publicists – themselves owe their views in large part, whether directly or indirectly, to what passes for higher education in the hugely expensive institutions responsible for providing it:

They whom necessity, or covetousnesse keepeth attent on their trades, and labour; and they, on the other side, whom superfluity, or sloth carrieth after their sensuall pleasures, (which two sorts of men make up the greatest part of Mankind,) being diverted from the deep meditation, which the learning of truth, not onely in the matter of Naturall Justice, but also of all other Sciences necessarily requireth, receive the Notions of their duty, chiefly from Divines in the Pulpit, and partly from such of their Neighbours, or familiar acquaintance, as having the Faculty of discoursing readily, and plausibly, seem wiser and better learned in cases of Law, and Conscience, than themselves. And the Divines, and such others as make shew of Learning, derive their knowledge from the Universities, and from the Schooles of Law, or from the Books, which by men eminent in those Schooles, and Universities have been published. It is therefore manifest, that the Instruction of the people, dependeth wholly, on the right teaching of Youth in the Universities. (XXX/14, 179–80)

The decline in ethical business practices, undercutting people's trust in the very professions of which trust is the essence; the deterioration in the aesthetic and moral standards manifest in popular culture, and thus in everyday life; the increasingly explicit glorification of passions at the expense of respect for reason, thus of reliance on force by default; the downward-spiralling hedonism (propelled by an increasing use of pleasure-enhancing and/or anxiety-relieving drugs); the broadening acceptance of bigotry and intellectual intolerance imposed in the name of combating bigotry and intolerance – these and a host of related problems, are all, to one extent or another, practical consequences of misbegotten conceptions, distinctions, analyses, models, theories, and unreasonable expectations generated by modern academics. But most seriously troublesome of all have been the successive incarnations of radical relativism and the resulting irrationalism and prevalence of sophistry that flourish in the last place one might expect: the modern university, whence their miasmic influence eventually spreads throughout the supporting society.

In the penultimate chapter of the first half of *Leviathan*, Hobbes addressed to himself a couple of 'Hard questions.' The first had to do with whether the universities of his day were in fact competent to accomplish their ostensible mission: 'the right teaching of Youth.' Citing evidence that implied the contrary, he answered in the negative. This raised the second question. Did he, then, himself 'undertake to teach the Universities'? I have long admired his ironic answer: 'it is not fit, nor needfull for me to say either I, or No: for any man that sees what I am doing, may easily perceive what I think.'

Notes

Prelude

1 All citations of *Leviathan* are by chapter/paragraph, followed by the page of the original 1651 text, which is indicated in all the readily available scholarly editions. I have generally relied upon the critical edition of G.A.J. Rogers and Karl Schuhmann (London: Thoemmes/Continuum, 2003/2005), though the differences between it and my long-time favourite, that edited by Richard Tuck (Cambridge: Cambridge University Press, 1991), are few and minor, as are my own departures from it. Noel Malcolm is severely critical of Rogers's and Schuhmann's analysis of the relationships among the three main versions of *Leviathan*: 'Head,' 'Bear,' and 'Ornaments' (which they discuss in Volume One of their edition); but none of the issues he raises materially affect my interpretation of the book. See Malcolm's review of the Rogers-Schuhmann edition in *Times Literary Supplement*, 3 December 2004, 'Changing the Sheets'; also his 'The Making of the Bear: Further Thoughts on the Printing of the Second Edition of *Leviathan*,' *Hobbes Studies* 20 (2007): 2–39; and 'The Making of the Ornaments: Further Thoughts on the Printing of the Third Edition of *Leviathan*,' *Hobbes Studies* 21 (2008): 3–37.

2 Moreover, the disproportion between 'cause' and 'effect' was stupendous: in commandeering four high-tech marvels (jumbo jets loaded with jet fuel) and careening them into some other high-tech marvels (a pair of super skyscrapers and the headquarters of the most powerful military in the world), a couple dozen men backed by a few million dollars did not simply kill several thousand people and destroy some expensive buildings. They temporarily disabled the commercial and financial heart of the leading nation of the modern world, vaporized trillions of dollars of fiscal assets, caused that

nation and a score of others to commit hundreds of billions of dollars and man-hours in an effort to provide 'security' against future such attacks, and otherwise profoundly affected the foreign and domestic policies of every important nation on Earth.

3 As Mark Lilla rightly observes by way of beginning his history of the relationship between political theology and political philosophy, *The Stillborn God: Religion, Politics, and the Modern West* (New York: Alfred A. Knopf, 2007):

> Today we have progressed to the point where we are again fighting the battles of the sixteenth century – over revelation and reason, dogmatic purity and toleration, inspiration and consent, divine duty and common decency. We are disturbed and confused. We find it incomprehensible that theological ideas still inflame the minds of men, stirring up messianic passions that leave societies in ruin. We assumed that this was no longer possible, that human beings had learned to separate religious questions from political ones, that fanaticism was dead. We were wrong. (3)

4 So Leo Strauss contends in *Natural Right and History* (Chicago: University of Chicago Press, 1953), that Hobbes, as 'the creator of political hedonism,' has produced 'a doctrine which has revolutionized human life everywhere on a scale never approached by any other teaching' (169). This is not to say, however, that it has everywhere taken the 'Popular' (i.e., Liberal Democratic) form.

5 The idea that the modern novel at its best is a 'prose poem' might be said to originate with Henry James, though it was shared by D.H. Lawrence and given its fullest exposition by critics such as F.R. and Q.D. Leavis and Yvor Winters. See, e.g., F.R. Leavis's *The Great Tradition* (New York: New York University Press, 1973), ch. 1.

6 Apparently, Melville was largely self-taught; that is, he educated himself by extensive reading of great books, integrating what he learned from them with reflections on his own quite varied experience. We must assume that he was something of a prodigy, bringing forth his masterpiece when not quite thirty-two years of age – perhaps rather like de Tocqueville, who published the first volume of his now-classic *Democracy in America* at the ripe old age of thirty.

7 Melville's profound appreciation of Hobbes's special brilliance is made most explicit in *Israel Potter*, his novel of the American Revolution and its aftermath. Israel has been sent on a secret mission conveying intelligence to Ben Franklin in Paris. At the beginning of chapter 8, Melville provides the fol-

lowing description of this leading founder of the American regime (variously referred to as a 'serene, cool and ripe old philosopher,' a 'homely sage, and household Plato'):

> The First, both in point of time and merit, of American envoys was famous not less for the pastoral simplicity of his manners than for the politic grace of his mind. Viewed from a certain point, there was a touch of primeval orientalness in Benjamin Franklin. Neither is there wanting something like his scriptural parallel. The history of the patriarch Jacob is interesting not less from the unselfish devotion which we are bound to ascribe to him, than from the deep worldly wisdom and polished Italian tact, gleaming under an air of Arcadian unaffectedness. The diplomatist and shepherd are blended; a union not without warrant; the apostolic serpent and dove. A tanned Machiavelli in tents.
>
> ...
>
> Franklin all over is of a piece. He dressed his person as his periods; neat, trim, nothing superfluous, nothing deficient. In some of his works his style is only surpassed by the unimprovable sentences of Hobbes of Malmsbury, the paragon of perspicuity. The mental habits of Hobbes and Franklin in several points, especially in one of some moment, assimilated. Indeed, making due allowance for soil and era, history presents few trios more akin, upon the whole, than Jacob, Hobbes, and Franklin; three labyrinth-minded, but plain-spoken Broadbrims, at once politicians and philosophers; keen observers of the main chance; prudent courtiers; practical magicians in linsey woolsey.

How carefully, how thoroughly and thoughtfully, must Melville have read Hobbes that he would offer these particular encomiums? Incidentally, Shakespeare also noted the biblical Jacob's eye for 'the main chance,' making an instance of it the centrepiece of Shylock's defence of usury (*The Merchant of Venice*, 1.3.66–85).

Melville's insight about Hobbes and Franklin has been recently confirmed. According to Jerry Weinberger, *Benjamin Franklin Unmasked* (Lawrence: University of Kansas Press, 2005), 'Franklin, of course, knew Locke's *Second Treatise*. And he knew Hobbes's *Leviathan* very well' (227). 'Franklin was almost a full-blown Baconian and Hobbesian, and what kept him from going with them all the way was the issue of religion' (273).

8 For example, by Professor Quentin Skinner in *Reason and Rhetoric in the Philosophy of Hobbes* (Cambridge: Cambridge University Press, 1996); and in ch. 4 of *Visions of Politics*, vol. 3: *Hobbes and Civil Science* (Cambridge:

Cambridge University Press, 2002). While most of the analysis Professor Skinner provides is tangential to my own, the study of his books has been especially valuable. Somewhat closer to my own treatment of Hobbes's rhetoric is that of Jerry Weinberger, 'Hobbes's Doctrine of Method,' *American Political Science Review* 69 (1975): 1336–53.

9 Machiavelli achieves the opposite rhetorical effect in *The Prince*: almost everyone reads that book from the perspective of a political ruler.

10 The term 'natural rights' has been largely supplanted of late by 'human rights,' but so far as I can tell, either their meaning is the same or the latter is imaginary.

11 The caprices of Hobbes's spelling are so numerous as to make explicit indications thereof utterly impractical.

12 In practice, the execution of this sovereign responsibility can vary in three quite different ways. One is in the range of matters that are judged pertinent to the political purpose of censorship; another is in the degree of intelligent discretion and good taste manifested by those doing the censoring. What results will depend ultimately on the qualities of whoever exercises sovereign power in choosing and instructing censors. The third variable is the degree of tolerance, or stringency, with which censorship is applied; this should depend primarily on the state of the citizenry, on what is needed to maintain (or restore) its moral character, especially moderation and law-abidingness.

13 'It is therefore manifest, that the Instruction of the people, dependeth wholly, on the right teaching of Youth in the Universities' (XXX/14, 180). I believe these words remain as true today as when Hobbes first penned them.

14 The governing premise of my treatment of Hobbes's masterpiece is that it was written with all the care its author was capable of bestowing upon it. Accordingly, I have taken to heart the warning Hobbes addressed to those 'Professors of Mathematics' (i.e., Wallis and Ward) by way of concluding his *Six Lessons*: 'take heed of speaking your mind so clearly in answering my *Leviathan*, as I have done in writing it.'

A Melvillian Overture

1 Melville used this same image to hint at his esotericism in the final chapter of *White-Jacket*. The narrator, speaking ostensibly of the man-o'-war on which he served, but exploiting the ambiguity in the meaning of 'craft,' observes: 'Outwardly regarded, our craft is a lie; for all that is outwardly seen of it is the clean-swept deck, and oft-painted planks comprised above

the waterline; whereas the vast mass of our fabric, with all its storerooms of secrets, for ever slides along far under the surface.'

2   Chapter 55 of *Moby-Dick; or, The Whale*. Since so many editions of the book exist, all references to it will be by chapter, but also by page according to the authoritative Northwestern-Newberry edition, Harrison Hayford, Herschel Parker, G. Thomas Tansell, eds (Evanston, IL: Northwestern University Press, 1988). Thus: (ch. 55, 263–4).

3   Curiously, the name is hyphenated in the title, but with a single exception not when referred to in the text.

4   Melville has not numbered his collection of 'extracts,' but he gives various subtle indications in his text that numbers matter; hence, the curious reader is prompted to number them for himself.

5   *Leviathan* XXVIII/27, 166–7. It may not be a coincidence that the forty-first chapter of *Moby-Dick* is itself entitled 'Moby Dick.'

6   Or so Hobbes renders it, supplying a translation of the Hebrew that differs considerably – especially in poetic quality – from that of the Authorized English text of his day (the King James version).

7   The term 'leviathan' is a transliteration of a Hebrew word (variously transliterated, e.g., 'livyathan.' 'liweyatan') meaning 'twisted,' 'coiled,' 'crooked.' In at least one Biblical instance, the term suggests a many-headed serpent (Psalms 74:14). Augustine identifies Leviathan with Satan (*The City of God* 11:15); Origen identifies Leviathan as the 'great fish' that swallowed Jonah and treats its belly as the locus of Fallen Humanity (Luther likewise). In Bunyan's *The Pilgrim's Progress*, Leviathan is symbolic of ultimate Evil, defeated only by the Shield of Faith. Cf. Shakespeare's *Henry V* (3.3.26) and *Two Gentlemen of Verona* (3.2.79).

   Carl Schmitt begins his monograph on Hobbes's masterpiece with a chapter-long discussion of the term, observing that 'numerous interpretations and transformations belong to the nature of mythical images ... In the instance of the leviathan, the wealth of theological and historical interpretations is simply immense.' However, during 'the Middle Ages two major categories of interpretation' emerged: Christian and Jewish. Speaking of the latter, he says: 'They are produced by cabbalists and have naturally an esoteric character. Without losing their immanent esoteric nature they also became known outside of Jewry, as can be gathered from Luther's *Table talks*, Bodin's *Demonomanie*, [etc].' *The Leviathan in the State Theory of Thomas Hobbes: Meaning and Failure of a Political Symbol*, trans. George Schwab and Erna Hilfstein (Westport, CT: Greenwood Press, 1996), 7–8 – cited hereafter as 'Schmitt.'

   Johan Tralau has a useful essay treating the name and related matters,

'Leviathan, the Beast of Myth: Medusa, Dionysus, and the Riddle of Hobbes's Sovereign Monster,' in *The Cambridge Companion to Hobbes's Leviathan*, ed. Patricia Springborg (Cambridge: Cambridge University Press, 2007). Springborg likewise provides a valuable discussion in 'Hobbes's Biblical Beasts: *Leviathan* and *Behemoth*,' *Political Theory* 23, no. 2 (May 1995): 353–75. I believe Roberto Farneti does not give Hobbes sufficient credit for understanding the consequences of his choice of the name 'Leviathan,' but he nonetheless provides useful historical information in 'The "Mythical Foundation" of the State: Leviathan in Emblematic Context,' *Pacific Philosophical Quarterly* 82 (2001): 362–82. Keith Brown provides an especially interesting discussion of Hobbes's frontispiece: 'The Artist of the *Leviathan*,' *British Library Journal* 4 (1978): 24–36.

8 Specifically, this is Isaiah 27:1. Although Hobbes invokes the authority of Isaiah no less than nine times in his *Leviathan*, quoting extensively from the book on 'The State of Salvation' (XXXVIII/17–23, 246–7) and on 'the *Office* of a *Redeemer* (XLI/2, 261–2), he – not surprisingly – never refers to *this* verse from 'Isaiah's Apocalypse.' One of his references, conjoined as it is with another to Job, is especially pertinent to Melville's book. Speaking about 'the place of the Damned' as being the same as that to which 'Giants' are confined (according to Scripture), Hobbes cites: 'Job 26.5. *Behold the Giants groan under water, and they that dwell with them.* Here the place of the Damned, is under the water. And *Isaiah* 14.9. *Hell is troubled how to meet thee*, (that is, the King of Babylon) *and will displace the Giants for thee*: and here again the place of the Damned, (if the sense be literall,) is to be under water' (XXXVIII/7, 242). Cf. XXXIV/6, 209; XXXV/10, 218; XXXVI/10, 227; XXXVIII/14, 244; XLII/45, 286.

9 The line comes from Bacon's free rendering of the 104th Psalm, one of the seven that serve as inspirations for a small but elegant set of poems, each in a different metrical style. Dedicated to 'his very good friend, Mr. George Herbert,' who had translated Bacon's *Advancement of Learning* into Latin (and who, along with John Donne, would himself become one of the two most highly esteemed poets of his age), Bacon's poems were first published in 1625.

10 One should not accept this claim on faith, given Melville's cautionary observation at the beginning of chapter 82: 'There are some enterprises in which a careful disorderliness is the true method.'

11 In fact, that was the sole title of the book as published first in London, 1851 (exactly 200 years after the London publication of *Leviathan*), followed later that year by publication in New York under the title *Moby-Dick; or, The Whale*. Thus, a simple formula suggests itself: *Moby-Dick = The Whale = Leviathan*.

12 John Locke is obviously the more immediate philosophical authority for the American regime, but his political prescription – as Melville saw clearly – is essentially that of Thomas Hobbes (a matter to be discussed more fully in the Coda). John Alvis has provided an insightful interpretation of *Moby-Dick* as a dramatization of problems inherent in Locke's political doctrine: '*Moby-Dick* and Melville's Quarrel with America,' *Interpretation* 23, no. 2 (Winter 1996): 223–47.

13 Andrew Delbanco's recent literary biography of Melville, which draws upon much of the best Melville scholarship, thoroughly documents his relationship to the political issues of his day: *Melville: His World and Work* (New York: Alfred A. Knopf, 2005).

14 Stanton Garner provides a detailed account of the relation between these poems and the circumstances of Melville's life during this period of national agony: *The Civil War World of Herman Melville* (Lawrence: University of Kansas Press, 1993). Although he favoured the Democrat party, Melville was essentially a political conservative. As Garner observes: 'Herman was committed to his country despite its failures, believing that the social perfection envisioned by the Founding Fathers could be approached only through slow, laborious effort, not by radical reform ... His conservatism was manifested in a desire to conserve the radicalism of the nation's founders, the revolutionary zeal of Jefferson and Madison' (26). Speaking summarily, Garner states: 'His position was not very different from that of Abraham Lincoln, who, although privately opposed to slavery, was willing to defer emancipation if by doing so he could preserve the United States' (27).

15 Carl Rollyson and Lisa Paddock, *Herman Melville A to Z* (New York: Checkmark, 2001), 214.

16 As William Bartley observes by way of concluding his excellent essay on Melville's novella, 'Few besides Melville had the imaginative courage to countenance [this] kind of impasse latent in antebellum America – an America, that is, in the shadow of the Fugitive Slave Law and the constitutional protection of slavery and an America haunted by the historical precedents of insurrection.' '"The creature of his own tasteful hands": Herman Melville's *Benito Cereno* and the "Empire of Might,"' *Modern Philology* 93, no. 4 (May 1996): 445–67.

   In the Introduction George Schwab wrote for the English translation of Schmitt's book on Hobbes's *Leviathan*, he contends that Schmitt is speaking of 'passive resistance' to an indecent regime (such as that of Nazi Germany) when he says in chapter 5: 'But when public power wants to be only public, when state and confession drive inner belief into the private domain, then the soul of a people betakes itself on the "secret road" that leads inward. Then grows the counterforce of stillness and silence' (61). And in an endnote expanding on this point, Schwab observes: 'This is obviously an allusion to Herman Melville's *Benito Cereno*. Immediately after World War II Schmitt returned to the so-called inward migration and spoke of Benito Cereno as having become a symbol of the predicament of an individual in a mass totalitarian system' (xix, xxviiin48).

17 However, scholars have debated the intended correlations of this satire. For one interpretation, see Helen Trimpi's *Melville's Confidence Men and American Politics in the 1850's*, Transactions of the Connecticut Academy of the Arts and Sciences (Hamden, CT, 1987). A.P. Martinich is one of the few Hobbes scholars who recognizes the philosopher's presence in Melville's writings, calling attention to a couple of relevant passages in *The Confidence Man*: 'Two Uses of Thomas Hobbes's Philosophy in Melville's *The Confidence-Man*,' *ANQ* 16, no. 3 (Summer 2003): 37–40. However, as my present work attests, I believe that his summary appraisal – 'If there is a general Hobbesian tenor to some of Melville's books, nonetheless, specific arguments from Hobbes do not seem to play a significant role in them' (37) – greatly underestimates Hobbes's importance for Melville.

18 As Delbanco observes about the posthumously published *Billy Budd*, '[It] was a book about politics – or at least about the manipulation of truth for political purposes. And ever since it became part of our literary heritage in the 1920s, it often has been cited in debates over the perennial question of what makes authority legitimate and what justifies resistance. Like Conrad's *Heart of Darkness*, it is one of those texts that has generated a body of critical responses ... so rich and varied that they may be read as a chronicle of modern intellectual life.' *Melville*, 312–13.

19 Hobbes cites Hagar's second angelic visitation (Genesis 21:17–18), but not the first (16:7–13), as part of the scriptural evidence that God communicates with mortals by means of apparitions, visions, and dreams (XXXVI/10, 293). One verse from the first passage would seem to have special, albeit different, significance for both Hobbes and Melville: 'And he [Ishmael] will be a wild man; his hand *will be* against every man; and every man's hand against him [rather as Hobbes would have us conceive *all* men in a State of Nature]; and he shall dwell in the presence of all his brethren' (16:12). The *Revised Standard Version* (Oxford University Press, 1962; ed. Herbert G. May and Bruce M. Metzger) renders the same verse thus: 'He shall be a wild ass of a man, his hand against every man and every man's hand against him; and he shall dwell over against all his

kinsmen,' and includes the gloss, 'A *wild ass of a man* describes the
bedouin freedom of the Ishmaelites in the southern wilderness.'

20 So Jews refer to all Gentiles as 'Hagar's offspring' (for example, Shylock in
The Merchant of Venice 2.5.44). Paul, in his Letter to the Galatians
(4:22–31), interprets this story as an allegory concerning carnality and
spirituality: 'For it is written that Abraham had two sons, one by a slave
and one by a free woman. But the son of the slave was born according to
the flesh, the son of the free woman through promise. Now this is an allegory: these women are two covenants.' According to Muslim tradition,
Arabs are descended from Abraham via Ishmael, and it was he (not Isaac)
whom the father was prepared to sacrifice, but whom God intervened to
save.

21 The sole exception is Captain Peleg in accepting our narrator as a member
of the *Pequod*'s crew: 'Now then, my young man, Ishmael's thy name,
didn't ye say? Well then, down ye go here, Ishmael, for the three hundredth
lay' (ch. 16, 78).

22 Cf. *Republic* 347d.

23 Cf. ibid., 549a, and Craig, *The War Lover: A Study of Plato's* Republic
(Toronto: University of Toronto Press, 1994), 71–2.

24 For a variety of reasons, the number Seven is associated with Plato. In that
light, it is of some interest that upon signing aboard the *Pequod*, Ishmael is
offered but a 'seven hundred and seventy-seventh lay' (1/777 of the net
profits of the voyage) by one of the ship's managing owners, though he is
subsequently assigned a three hundredth lay (ch. 16, 76–7).

25 Cf. *Phaedo* 109c–e, 67c–e, 82d-83d, 115c. Plato's *Phaedo* apparently
occupies a special place in Melville's own soul. For example, in a letter he
wrote to his editor and friend, Evert Duyckinck (dated 5 April 1849), he
includes the following: 'I bought a set of Bayle's Dictionary the other
day, & on my return to New York intend to lay the great old folios side
by side & go to sleep on them thro' the summer, with the Phaedon in
one hand and Tom Brown in the other.' *Tales, Poems, and Other Writings*, ed. John Bryant (New York: Modern Library, 2001), 34. As a previous letter to Duyckink makes clear, the 'Tom Brown' referred to is Sir
Thomas Browne (1605–82), a Baconian whose *Religio Medici* (*The Religion of a Physician*) has been described as a 'conjunction between religious meditation and an enduring fascination with observation of the
most minute details of the physical world,' evidencing a 'determination
to refute ideas commonly entertained by the credulous.' *Penguin Guide
to English Literature*, ed. Marion Wynn-Davies (London: Penguin,
1989), 372.

26 'Bowditch' is common shorthand for *The American Practical Navigator*, successive editions of which have served as virtually the mariner's bible since it was first published by Nathan Bowditch in 1802.

27 Tradition associates Plato with a visit to Egypt (cf. *Gorgias* 511d), and his dialogues do contain some intriguing allusions to the Egyptians (e.g., *Phaedo* 80c, *Timaeus* 21e, *Critias* 113a), including the credit for having invented writing (*Phaedrus* 274d ff), and as being the source of Sokrates's unique oath: 'By the dog' (cf. *Gorgias* 482b). As for the tower of Babel, cf. *Leviathan* IV/2, 12.

28 Cf. Hesiod, *Works and Days* 106–201; Plato's *Republic* 546e–547a, 415a–c.

29 Cf. *Republic* 529b–c.

30 *Apology* 30a, e, 36d–e.

31 Cf. *Republic* 486a–b, 500b–c, 604b, 608c–d.

32 Cf. ibid., 514a.

33 Cf. *Theaetetus* 149c–151d.

34 *Republic* 544b, *Laches* 185a–e and passim.

35 Cf. *Apology* 29a, 40c–41d; *Republic* 486a, 500b–c, 604b–c, 608c–d; see also Montaigne's essay so titled, Book One, no. 20, in *The Complete Essays of Montaigne*, ed. and trans. Donald Frame (Stanford: Stanford University Press, 1958).

36 But not entirely; there is a scattering of pithy pronouncements on matters generally recognized as central to political philosophy, such as the American whalers' terse theory of property: 'these two laws touching Fast-fish ['belongs to the party fast to it'] and Loose-fish ['fair game for anybody that can soonest catch it'], I say, will, on reflection, be found the fundamentals of all human jurisprudence' (ch. 89, 396–7).

37 This possibility might seem to be precluded by Ishmael's tacit warning against it: 'So ignorant are most landsmen of some of the plainest and most palpable wonders of the world, that without some hints touching the plain facts, historical and otherwise, of the fishery, they might scout at Moby Dick as a monstrous fable, or still worse and more detestable, a hideous and intolerable allegory' (ch. 45, 205). Thought about, however, the actual rhetorical effect of this disclaimer is to suggest the very possibility it supposedly denies (rather like Marc Antony's plea that the plebs not make him read Caesar's will). And, of course, Ishmael – accomplished ironist that Melville makes him to be – has not actually said what he gives the impression of saying: he has not denied that his story is an allegory, nor even a hideous and intolerable one. Indeed, the book almost begins with a hint that comprehending it may present a challenge. Ishmael recounts what arrested his attention upon first

entering the Spouter-Inn (where he would later meet with the 'cannibal' Queequeg):

> On one side hung a very large oil-painting so thoroughly besmoked, and every way defaced, that in the unequal cross-lights by which you viewed it, it was only by diligent study and a series of systematic visits to it, and careful inquiry of the neighbors, that you could any way arrive at an understanding of its purpose. Such unaccountable masses of shades and shadows, that at first you almost thought some ambitious young artist, in the time of the New England hags, had endeavored to delineate chaos bewitched. But by dint of much and earnest contemplation, and oft repeated ponderings, and especially by throwing open the little window towards the back of the entry, you at last came to the conclusion that such an idea, however wild, might not be altogether unwarranted.
>
> …
>
> But at last all these fancies yielded to that one portentous something in the picture's midst. *That* once found out, and all the rest were plain. But stop; does it not bear a faint resemblance to a gigantic fish? even the great leviathan himself? (ch. 3, 12–13)

38 I have been unable to track down the precise source of this quote in Parker's works; it was supplied to me by the Melville scholar Helen Trimpi.
39 Vol. II, ch. LVII.
40 Perhaps Melville noticed Hobbes's strange quoting from the most problematic of the Apocrypha, the Second Book of Esdras (14:45): '*And it came to passe when the forty dayes were fulfilled, that the Highest spake, saying, The first that thou hast written, publish openly, that the worthy and unworthy may read it; but keep the seventy last, that thou mayst deliver them onely to such as be wise among the people*' (XXXIII/19, 203; cf. XLII/41, 284; VIII/10, 34).
41 As Melville later expressed it in the concluding stanza of '*The Coming Storm*' (written in the wake of Lincoln's assassination): 'No utter surprise can come to him / Who reaches Shakspeare's [*sic*] core; / That which we seek and shun is there – / Man's final lore.' *Selected Poems of Herman Melville*, ed. Robert Penn Warren (Boston: David R. Godine, 2004), 141.
42 'Hawthorne and His Mosses,' in *Pierre, Israel Potter, The Piazza Tales, The Confidence-Man, Uncollected Prose, Billy Budd* (New York: Library of America, 1984), 1159–60.

Charles Colson, *Call Me Ishmael: A Study of Melville* (copyright by the author, 1949; reprinted in San Francisco: City Lights Books, no date), reports that Melville's copy of Shakespeare's plays survives, that he has examined it, and offers the following judgment: 'The set exists, seven volumes, with passages marked, and comments in Melville's hand. The significant thing is the rough notes for the composition of *Moby-Dick* on the fly-leaf of the last volume. These notes involve Ahab, Pip, Bulkington, Ishmael, and are the key to Melville's intention with these characters' (39). Colson contends: 'As the strongest literary force Shakespeare caused Melville to approach tragedy in terms of the drama. As the strongest social force America caused him to approach tragedy in terms of democracy' (69).

Ivor Winters – surely one of the more exacting of critics – contends that *Moby-Dick* is 'less a novel than an epic poem' and belongs in a class with *Hamlet, Macbeth*, and *Paradise Lost. In Defense of Reason* (Denver: University of Denver Press, 1947), 219.

43 I have discussed in detail both the political and the philosophical reasons for the use of esotericism, and have documented a wide variety of the literary devices (and authors who used them), in my prologue to *The War Lover*.

44 Charles Robert Anderson, *Melville in the South Seas* (New York: Columbia University Press, 1939), 5.

45 Writing to Nathaniel Hawthorne in the summer of the year *Moby-Dick* was published (1851), Melville avers: 'I have come to regard this matter of Fame as the most transparent of all vanities. I read Solomon more and more, and every time see deeper and deeper and unspeakable meanings in him ... It seems to me now that Solomon was the truest man that ever spoke, and yet that he a little *managed* the truth with a view to popular conservatism.' *Tales, Poems, and Other Writings*, 41. Melville shows an extensive familiarity with the writings of Francis Bacon, revolutionary founder of modern science. Note, e.g., the passing comment in ch. 55: 'In the title-page of the original edition of the "Advancement of Learning" you will find some curious whales' (261). How many people would make a point of examining the *original edition* of the *Advancement of Learning*? Ishmael's ironic attempt to provide an adequate 'Cetology' is a self-consciously Baconian task of natural history. It begins with the chapter so named, no. 32, which just happens to be the number Bacon assigned in his catalogue of 'Particular Histories' to a history that included 'Ambergris' – the only one of the 130 such histories accompanying his *New Organon* that directly touches on whales. I shall discuss this matter more fully in the Coda.

46 That Melville's Ahab represents 'a man who is obsessed with the problem of knowledge' is argued by C.Q. Drummond in 'Nature: Meek Ass or White Whale,' *Sage* 2, no. 1 (Spring 1966): 71–84, reprinted in the collection of Drummond's writings, *In Defence of Adam*, ed. John Baxter and Gordon Harvey (Harleston, Norfolk: Edgeway Books, 2004). I shall treat this matter more fully in the Coda.

47 Hobbes presents both 'positive' ('*Whatsoever you require … that* do *ye*'; XIV/5, 65; cf. XVII/2, 85) and 'negative' ('Do *not* that … which thou thinkest unreasonable'; XXVI/13 140; cf. XVII/4, 152) variations of the Golden Rule, as if they were practically equivalent. But a moment's thought confirms that they are not, as the positive versions enjoin us to actively care for our fellows, whereas the negative versions allow for an entirely passive, 'mind-your-own-business,' posture. Stimulating such thinking may be Hobbes's very point, having conveniently – not once, but twice – provided both versions sequentially (XIV/5, 65; XLII/11, 272). And notice, it is a *negative* version that Hobbes offers as 'one easie sum' of the entirety of 'the Laws of Nature, dictating Peace' ('intelligible, even to the meanest capacity'; XV/35, 79). Geoffrey M. Vaughan has a useful discussion of Hobbes's use of the Golden Rule in *Elements of Law* and *De Corpore* as well as in *Leviathan* (though he speaks as if there were only two instances in the latter work, rather than seven English versions and one Latin). Vaughan shows that 'the positive version is used outside the context of education, whereas the negative version is used exclusively in this context. This is consistent throughout his three books.' *Behemoth Teaches Leviathan: Thomas Hobbes on Political Education* (Lanham, MD: Lexington, 2007), 50–3.

Part One: The Problematical *Leviathan*

1 In the wake, moreover, of several soporific chapters offering tendentious Biblical exegesis of marginal interest to the '*Worldly men*' Hobbes seems primarily concerned to persuade of his political teaching – making those chapters ideal places for revelations apt to be overlooked by all but the most dogged of readers.

2 Hobbes does analyse 'cause' elsewhere (e.g., in chapter 9 of *De Corpore*, and chapter 27 of *Thomas White's* De Mundo *Examined*), but this simply makes his failure to do so in *Leviathan* the more curious, given the importance with which he invests it in the latter work.

3 *Physics* 195b31, 196a25.

4 Given the way Hobbes has dispersed his claims on various topics, it is prac-

tically impossible to avoid quoting certain passages more than once, though to different purposes in each case. Still, some redundancy results. Exploring his text presents a problem somewhat like that Wittgenstein complained of in the 'Preface' to his *Philosophical Investigations*, that he was compelled 'to travel over a wide field of thought criss-cross in every direction,' such that 'the same or almost the same points were always being approached afresh from different directions.'

1: Curiosity about Causes and the Problem of *Religion*

1 Cf. *Republic* 476d–478e, *Meno* 97b–98c.
2 Note, curiosity (as Hobbes here defines it) is the desire to know *why*, and *how* – not *what* or *that*. Thus, it excludes the sort of 'curiosity' proverbially fatal to cats.
3 Here, then, is a clue to Hobbes's philosophical rhetoric. By providing their definitions in a single paragraph, Hobbes subtly indicates the essential identity of religion, superstition, and true religion. For the most part, each of the forty-odd passion-based phenomena Hobbes defines in chapter 6 are each given separate paragraphs. Only in two other cases does he name three passions in a single defining paragraph, and in both instances (pars. 22 and 29) he indicates that they are practically synonymous names for the same passion. Of course, the very fact that 'religion' is defined as a *passion*, a certain fear, is prejudicial to its intellectual standing.
4 Basic to any political science worthy of the name is a realistic understanding of human nature – or rather, so much of an understanding as is adequate for all political purposes. This Part One of *Leviathan* ('Of Man') is intended to supply, presumably. Among the most important manifestations of human nature in need of explanation for purposes of political understanding, if not the most philosophically challenging to provide, is religion in all its protean forms. Thus, appropriately enough, it is the last topic Hobbes addresses prior to his summary appraisal of what he would have us imagine human life to be like in a State of Nature, namely: Hell on Earth.
5 Hobbes warns in his Dedication that what some people may find most offensive in the book are his interpretations of 'certain Texts of Holy Scripture'; but he goes on to explain why nonetheless they are necessary for an adequate defence of 'the Civill Power.' And he returns to the subject in the thirteenth paragraph of 'A *REVIEW*, and *CONCLUSION*': 'For I ground the Civill Right of Soveraigns, and both the Duty and Liberty of Subjects, upon the known naturall inclinations of Mankind, and upon the Articles of the Law of Nature; of which no man, that pretends but reason enough to

govern his private family, ought to be ignorant. And for the Power Ecclesiasticall of the same Soveraigns, I ground it on such Texts, as are both evident
in themselves, and consonant to the Scope of the whole Scripture.'

6 This points to a recurring problem in *Leviathan*: the apparent inadequacy of
Hobbes's account of Reason, compared with that of Aristotle. I will discuss
this problem extensively in chapter 11, which is devoted to it.

7 There is an ambiguity here: does Hobbes mean the mental 'image' of an
effect actually perceived; or does he mean an imagined effect? Given the
other two uses of the term in this very quote, it may be either.

8 Still, the peculiarity of Hobbes's use of *Prometheus* to illustrate his ostensible point – that while everyone is subject to anxiety about the future, especially about 'the evill he feares,' some people worry excessively – may do
more than remind the reader of the original myth: it could call to mind
Francis Bacon's unique interpretation of that story. 'Prometheus; or The
State of Man' is the twenty-sixth, and longest, of the thirty-one Fables
included in Bacon's *Wisdom of the Ancients*, a quite popular book in its day.
Bacon interprets the myth as a parable that, among other things, warns
against extravagantly admiring the arts and sciences in their current condition, as if there were no more knowledge needed or to be had: 'that conceit
of plenty is one of the principal causes of want.' Hobbes, however, has
appropriated for his purpose what would seem the most fanciful portion of
Bacon's interpretation, hence the feature that would most readily point to it.
Bacon suggests that Prometheus and his brother Epimetheus ('After-
thought') represent two divergent 'models of human life.' Whereas the 'followers of Epimetheus are the improvident, who take no care for the future
but think only of what is pleasant at the time,'

> The school of Prometheus on the other hand, that is the wise and fore-
> thoughtful class of men, do indeed by their caution decline and remove
> out of their way many evils and misfortunes; but with that good there is
> this evil joined, that they stint themselves of many pleasures and of the
> various agreeableness of life, and cross their genius, and (what is far
> worse) torment and wear themselves away with cares and solicitude and
> inward fears. For being bound to the column of Necessity, they are trou-
> bled with innumerable thoughts (which because of their flightiness are
> represented by the eagle), thoughts which prick and gnaw and corrode the
> liver: and if at intervals, as in the night, they obtain some little relaxation
> and quiet of the mind, yet new fears and anxieties return presently with
> the morning. Very few therefore are they to whom the benefit of both
> portion falls, – to retain the advantages of providence and yet free them-

selves from the evils of solicitude and perturbation. Neither is it possible for anyone to attain this double blessing, except by the help of Hercules; that is, fortitude and constancy of mind, which being prepared for all events and equal to any fortune, foresees without fear, enjoys without fastidiousness, and bears without impatience. (*The Works of Francis Bacon*, vol. 6, James Spedding and Robert Leslie Ellis, eds [London: Longmans, 1870], 751–2)

Judging from a letter F. du Verdus wrote in August 1654, no. 68 in *The Correspondence of Thomas Hobbes*, vol. 1, Noel Malcolm, ed. (Oxford: Oxford University Press, 1994), Hobbes was well versed in Bacon's *Wisdom of the Ancients*. Du Verdus asks Hobbes to send him an English translation of Bacon's book, if one is available.

I would not ask this of you if I did not know how highly you regard Mr Bacon's writings, and if I had not, for my own part, done some work on this book ... I have written explanations of various passages in it, and throughout my explanations I have elaborated on the interpretations which you gave me. Above all, on the subject of Typhon I have written at length about the unity of the power of the state, constantly citing you and explaining your views so that ordinary people can understand them. Moreover, the friendship which I feel towards you ... has made me put forward the following claim in my commentary on the subject of Prometheus, concerning the small amount of progress achieved in the sciences. (196–7)

Plato's dialogical character Protagoras also presents an intriguing version of the Prometheus story in the dialogue Plato named after this first and most famous Sophist. It is a dialogue that has a special pertinence to *Leviathan*, a point to which I will return in chapter 14; cf. Leo Strauss, *Natural Right and History* (Chicago: University of Chicago Press, 1953), 117, 168.

9 Melville's Ishmael matches Hobbes's wry humour: 'I cherish the greatest respect towards everybody's religious obligations, never mind how comical' (ch. 17, 81).

10 'Piety' is a term that does not appear in the first half of the book (and a mere half-dozen times in the second half), though Hobbes twice associates 'pious' with people's intention to *honour* God, in much the same way as they honour human beings (XII/7, 53; XXXI/33, 191). Hobbes does use the term 'sanctity' in regard to people; and although he never defines it, he implies that it (like Faith) is neither a natural attribute nor infused supernat-

urally, but that – contrary to what is 'commonly taught' – is in fact '*attained by Study and Reason*': 'Faith, and Sanctity, are indeed not very frequent; but yet they are not Miracles, but brought to passe by education, discipline, correction, and other naturall wayes' (XXIX/8, 169; but cf. XXXIV/25, 215).

11 No one has captured this point more poignantly than Shakespeare's Shylock in his immortal rant, 'Hath not a Jew eyes? hath not a Jew hands, organs, dimensions, senses, affections, passions?' (*The Merchant of Venice,* 3.1.52–60).

12 While there are things to be said in favour of the Roman practice of broad religious tolerance, at least for purposes of peacefully governing an empire (or perhaps any polity comprising a multiplicity of religions), it would not seem to be Hobbes's view of the optimum political arrangement (cf. XXXI/37, 192).

13 Here using the term 'theoretical' in its original, Aristotelian sense, derived from *theoria*, 'contemplation.' Theoretical knowledge is that sought simply for the satisfaction of knowing, in fulfilment of Man's essential nature as a being that 'by nature reaches out to know' (first line of his *Metaphysics*). Thus, it contrasts with both Practical knowledge (e.g., of politics, ethics, economics – knowledge whose primary purpose is to guide human practice) and Productive knowledge (principles and skills of the various arts and crafts).

14 The issues involved will be examined in detail later (in chapter 9).

15 Melville's almost-philosophical Ahab seems to have become entangled in the confusions Hobbes's argument gives rise to:

> Is Ahab, Ahab? Is it I, God, or who, that lifts this arm? But if the great sun move not of himself; but is as an errand-boy in heaven; nor one single star can revolve, but by some invisible power; how then can this one small heart beat; this one small brain think thoughts; unless God does that beating, does that thinking, does that living, and not I. … Who's to doom, when the judge himself is dragged to the bar? (ch. 132, 545)

16 This is, of course, a widely debated issue among Hobbes scholars, some seeing him as a sincere Christian of some Protestant stripe (even as a model Anglican); others are sure he was simply a deist; still others would agree with Douglas M. Jesseph, who begins his useful analysis of the question by stating bluntly, 'Thomas Hobbes was an atheist' ('Hobbes's Atheism,' *Midwest Studies in Philosophy* 24 [2002]). Jesseph dismisses Hobbes's many apparent professions of Christian faith as evidence of his irony: 'Hobbes was really a sly and ironic atheist who concealed his disbelief behind a

screen of disingenuous theological verbiage while constructing a philosophical system that makes the concept of God inadmissible' (140). Moreover, as I intend to show in the following chapters, Hobbes's use of irony is not confined to religious matters. Needless to add, recognition of Hobbes's 'Atheism' (which might be more strictly termed 'Agnoticism' since Hobbes treats the existence of a supreme Deity and its properties and dictates as primarily an epistemological issue) profoundly compromises interpretations that treat the *obligation* to obey Natural Laws as based on their being commanded by God – as does, for one famous example, Howard Warrender in *The Political Philosophy of Hobbes* (Oxford: Oxford University Press, 1957).

Pierre Manent characterizes Hobbes as 'the most sober, reasonable and persuasive enemy of the Christian name in European history' and rightly observes: 'He proposed the modern state, for which he drew up the plan. He grasped with perfect clarity that this state would mean the end of the church as it had been understood up to then.' *Democracy without Nations? The Fate of Self-government in Europe* (Wilmington, DE: ISI Books, 2007), 100. Similarly, Mark Lilla observes, 'Hobbes's political teaching ... brooked not a single compromise with the basic assumptions of Christian political thinking. His great treatise *Leviathan* (1651) contains the most devastating attack on Christian political theology ever undertaken and was the means by which later modern thinking was able to escape from it.' *The Stillborn God: Religion, Politics, and the Modern West* (New York: Alfred A. Knopf, 2007), 75.

17 Cf. *Republic* 508e–509b.

18 As Nietzsche, ever insightful, observes, 'who could mistake the *optimistic* element in the nature of dialectic, which celebrates a victory with every conclusion, and can breathe only in cool clarity and consciousness' (*The Birth of Tragedy*, ch. 14).

19 Hobbes's argument for this claim is almost laughable. He purports to explain 'different Dreams' by diversity of bodily distempers, given 'the motion from the brain to the inner parts, and from the inner parts to the Brain being reciprocall'; thus:

> [A]s Anger causeth heat in some parts of the Body, when we are awake; so when we sleep, the over heating of the same parts causeth Anger, and raiseth up in the brain the Imagination of an Enemy. In the same manner; as naturall kindness, when we are awake causeth desire; and desire makes heat in certain other parts of the body; so also, too much heat in those

parts, while wee sleep, raiseth in the brain an imagination of some kind-ness shewn. In summe, our Dreams are the reverse of our waking Imagi-nations; The motion when we are awake, beginning at one end; and when we dream, at another. (II/6, 6)

As anyone adequately schooled in elementary logic should recognize, Hobbes here commits (repeatedly) the fallacy of Affirming the Consequent. Since the number of things that can arouse a person's anger (generating heat in some bodily part) is practically infinite, becoming heated in that 'inner anger part' cannot determine what source of anger *in particular* one might dream about – as if because seeing crows makes one have the sensation of blackness, so blackness being somehow aroused in the imagination (by some peculiar bodily stimulation while asleep) makes one dream of crows, rather than pots or kettles, licorice or London taxis. This, in turn, reveals the fallacy of explaining anger, or any other emotion, simply in terms of some bodily condition or motion – unless one is willing to believe that there is some unique inner bodily part keyed to every conceivable particular object (which are countless) of every one of the forty-odd passions Hobbes cata-logues in chapter 6!

20 The conclusion Melville provided Father Mapple's sermon beautifully illus-trates the problem posed by politically autonomous divines: 'Delight is to him, who gives no quarter in the truth, and kills, burns, and destroys all sin though he pluck it out from under the robes of Senators and Judges. Delight, – top-gallant delight is to him, who acknowledges no law or lord, but the Lord his God, and is only a patriot to heaven' (ch. 9, 48).

21 Despite his ironic disclaimers to the contrary, Hobbes's explanation of the natural basis of Religion tacitly precludes any practical possibility of reliable revelations. As will be shown in a subsequent chapter, Hobbes in effect con-tends that the only faith humans need is a faith in Reason.

22 In *Leviathan*, that is. As previously noted, Hobbes does discuss causation elsewhere, notably in *De Corpore*. About this, A.P. Martinich writes in *A Hobbes Dictionary* (Oxford: Blackwell, 1995):

The primary discussion of causality occurs in Part II of *De Corpore* after the discussion of body and accident. This is the logical place for it, because, according to Hobbes, only bodies cause things ....

For Hobbes, only moving bodies cause effects; and every effect is the motion of some other body. Hobbes considers this his own revolutionary discovery, notwithstanding the work of Galileo, upon which it is probably based. A body is a cause 'not because it is a body, but because [it is] ... so moved' (*DCo* 9.3). All changes, qualitative or quantitative, are explainable in terms of the motions of bodies. (56)

Suffice it to say, this treatment of 'cause' does not square with Hobbes's own usage in *Leviathan*, such as his catalogue of seven causes why people, especially those who 'professe Philosophy,' so often reach 'Absurd conclusions,' all traceable ultimately to miscast or misused definitions (V/7–15, 20–1). This is but one of numerous examples, others of which I shall cite in the main text in connection with the 'causes' of commonwealths (chapter 5).

Cees Leijenhorst, 'Hobbes's Theory of Causality and Its Aristotelian Background,' *The Monist* 79, no. 3 (1996), provides a useful analysis of Hobbes's treatment of Cause in various writings other than *Leviathan*. He does not, however, attempt a critical assessment of the adequacy of Hobbes's account, nor undertake a systematic comparison with that of Aristotle. Thus he reports without comment Hobbes's reduction of Final Cause to a constituent of Efficient Cause (as if 'purpose' were confined to human intentionality – a view Aristotle decisively rebuts, for reasons I will review in chapter 6).

23 According to the usual understanding of the analysis provided by the great Scottish philosopher David Hume – often regarded as continuing the British Empiricist 'school' or 'tradition' begun by Bacon and Hobbes – when we assert a causal relationship between two events, 'A' and 'B,' we are implicitly claiming three things: Constant Conjunction (no B without A), Temporal Antecedence (A always precedes B), and Necessary 'Connexion.' Hume argues that this third element, and the only one that really counts, can never be established simply through empirical observation, since there is always the logical possibility of an unobserved 'C' that first causes the A, then the B. Thus, one is always justified in regarding the empirical generalizations of science with a measure of scepticism. Something like this, at least, would be the usual schematic summary of the analysis found (e.g.) in Bk I, Sec xii of *A Treatise of Human Nature*. And certainly the history of natural science is littered with cases where what were originally thought to be causal connections were subsequently concluded to be incidental, if not altogether spurious, correlations. And most of what passes today for 'social science' is made up almost entirely of such problematic correlations. In that Hume's analysis raises basic psychological issues, I shall return to it later. Hobbes's strategy for circumventing this troubling issue of establishing valid causal connections seems to be purely linguistic. This, too, will be examined further in conjunction with a critique of Hobbes's account of Language.

Parenthetically, it is worth noting that Hobbes implicates the natural human tendency to mistake mere correlation for causal connection in the most common misconception about Justice: 'Ignorance of the causes, and originall constitution of Right, Equity, Law, and Justice, disposeth a man to make Custome and Example the rule of his actions; in such manner, as to think that Unjust which it hath been the custome to punish; and that Just, of the impunity and approbation whereof they can produce an Example, or (as the Lawyers which onely use this false measure of Justice barbarously call it) a Precedent' (XI/21, 50).

24 *Politics* 1253a7–17; *Republic* 371d, 372b.

25 Hobbes's own treatment of this beautiful phenomenon, the rainbow – imbued since antiquity with both profound religious significance and intense philosophic-scientific interest – is perplexing, not to say provoking. For he seems to argue in his chapter on miracles that the rainbow was *originally* purposive (being an intentional communication from God), but now is not (having *become* simply a natural phenomenon!):

> The first Rainbow that was seen in the world, was a Miracle, because the first; and consequently strange; and served for a sign from God, placed in heaven, to assure his people, there should be no more an universall destruction of the world by Water. But at this day, because they are frequent, they are not Miracles, neither to them that know their naturall causes, nor to them that know them not. (XXXVII/4, 233)

However, according to the Biblical account (Genesis 9:8–17), the rainbow is both a permanent sign to *all* living creatures *and* a reminder to God Himself of His *covenant* with them: 'And God said, This *is* the token of the covenant which I make between me and you and every living creature that *is* with you, for perpetual generations: I do set my bow in the cloud, and it shall be for a token of the covenant between me and the earth' (9:12–13). Cf. Descartes, *Optics*, 'Discourse Six: Vision.'

2: Reality and the Problem of *Materialism*

1 One must wonder, then, about *space* (the 'room' or 'place' *into* which a body may move, and thereupon 'filleth' or 'occupyeth') – is it no part of reality?

2 Hobbes's classifying mirror images with dreams and hallucinations is at least odd, and not apt to further a scientific understanding of phenomena seemingly so very different in kind. The former was recognized in his own day as

a challenging problem of 'Opticks,' whereas the latter has been treated since antiquity as a subject for depth psychology (cf. *Republic* 571c–d). Hobbes's real purpose here, however – as in the other two times he makes the same association (XII/7, 53; XLV/14, 358) – may be to counteract the fear people have of disembodied spirits and phantoms, and thus its exploitation by 'Ghostly men.' So, irrespective of whether reflections in mirrors have any-thing more in common with dreams and hallucinations than that both might be called 'images,' people may rest assured the latter are illusions no more substantial than the former.

3   Most revealingly in the chapter on Speech, in describing one of four general sources of the 'diversity of names': 'First, a thing may enter into account for *Matter*, or *Body*; as *living, sensible, rationall, hot, cold, moved, quiet*; with all which names the word *Matter*, or *Body* is understood; all such, being names of Matter' (IV/15, 16). That is, Hobbes speaks here as if 'matter' and 'body' were perfectly synonymous. Later, however, in listing some of the 'Names' of First Philosophy that require clear definitions in order 'to avoid ambiguity, and aequivocation in Reasoning,' he implies that the two are to be distinguished ('such as are the Definitions of Body, Time, Place, Matter, Forme, [etc.]'; XLVI/14, 371).

To be sure, any discrete batch of matter would constitute a body, but that body would have some form as well, however vague and changeable. As such, bodies must be distinguished from 'The unformed matter of the World' Hobbes elsewhere refers to (XII/14, 55).

In his chapter '*Of the* NUTRITION, *and* PROCREATION *of a Common-wealth* (XXIV), Hobbes speaks repeatedly of 'matter' and 'materials,' but there means '*Materials* conducing to Life,' i.e., the various 'commodities' humans eat or otherwise use – in every case, *formed* matter.

4   There is no entry for either 'form' or 'matter' in Martinich's *A Hobbes Dictionary* (Oxford: Blackwell, 1995). In the entry 'bodies and accidents,' he notes, 'Hobbes does not distinguish between the form and matter of a sub-stance as Aristotelians do. Rather, he distinguishes between body and acci-dents' (53).

5   *Physics* (first sentence of Book Two) 192b9–11.

6   That something could come from nothing (*creatio ex nihilo*), or that some-thing could become nothing, is rationally inconceivable. Hence, it could be accepted only on faith, and on the presumption that it is a mystery which is not actually contrary to reason, but is simply 'above reason' (to resort to Hobbes's clever distinction), and thus revealing the limitation of merely human reason. But, considered within the limits of human reasoning, we must conclude that through all transformations of matter, the basic 'stuff' is

preserved. Needless to add, the mutual convertibility of matter and energy (such that the basic stuff is now thought of as matter-energy) in no way affects this old 'conservation of matter' principle.

7 *Physics* 193b.
8 Ibid., 185a21–2.
9 As described in *Van Nostrand's Scientific Encyclopedia*, 5th ed., Douglas M. Considine, ed. (New York: Van Nostrand Reinhold, 1976):

> **BONE.** The hard, calcified tissue which forms the major part of the skeletal system of the body. The bones and cartilage are referred to as *connective* or *supporting* tissue because their chief function is structural. The distinction should be made between the terms *bone* and *bones*. Bone is a *tissue*, derived from connective tissue cells which become specialized in function. Bones are *organs*, such as the skull, pubis, tibia, fibula, and so on ...
>
> Bone tissue consists of two permanent components: (1) the *osteocytes*, which are the specialized cells of the bone; and (2) the surrounding *matrix*, which is composed of minute fibers and a cementing substance. This cementing substance contains mineral salts, mainly calcium phosphate ...
>
> Mature bone of mammals is *lamellated*, i.e., it is made up of thin plates (*lamellae*) of bone tissue. The plates occur in bundles. This arrangement offers increased resistance to shearing forces. The shape and arrangement of the lamellae differ in the two major types of mature bone (1) *spongy*, and (2) *compact*. In spongy bone, the matrix consists of a lamellated network of interlacing walls resembling the structure of a sponge. This form can be found in the skull and ribs. In compact bone, the bundles of lamellae are arranged in vertical cylinders around a central canal. This bone is found in the long bones of the arms and legs. (336)

Notice the pertinence of the following terms for an understanding of this matter called 'bone': form, system, structure, function, shape, matrix, substance, and arrangement (of which plates, cylinders, sponges, and such are examples).

10 When an atom of uranium-235 is split, the result is not two halves of uranium-235, since its distinctive atomic form, which is the basis of the identity of this element (with its distinctive properties), requires the structured combination of protons and neutrons that give it the atomic weight of 235. Rather, the splitting results in two different chemical elements made up of new *formations* of the same parts as previously composed the uranium atom, with a bit left over as 'radiation.'

Practitioners of the new, post-Newtonian physics have reached the same conclusion about the nature of matter as did Plato and Aristotle. As one of it architects, Werner Heisenberg, writes in 'Natural Law and the Structure of Matter,' in *Across the Frontiers* (New York: Harper and Row, 1974), 'the inherent difficulties of the materialist theory of the atom, which had become apparent even in the ancient discussions about smallest particles, have also appeared very clearly in the development of physics during the present century' (113):

> We can say that all particles are made of the same fundamental substance, which can be designated energy or matter; or we can put things as follows: the basic substance 'energy' becomes 'matter' by assuming the form of an elementary particle. In this way the new experiments have taught us that we can combine the two seemingly conflicting statements: 'Matter is infinitely divisible' and 'There are smallest units of matter,' without running into logical difficulties ...
>
> During the coming years, the high-energy accelerators will bring to light many further interesting details about the behavior of elementary particles. But I am inclined to think that the answer just considered to the old philosophical problems will turn out to be final. If this is so, does this answer confirm the views of Democritus or Plato?
>
> I think that on this point modern physics has definitely decided for Plato. For the smallest units of matter are in fact not physical objects in the ordinary sense of the word; they are forms, structures or – in Plato's sense – Ideas, which can be unambiguously spoken of only in the language of mathematics. (115–16)

In *The Matter Myth* (New York: Simon and Schuster, 2007), Paul Davies and John Gribbin observe that 'science is throwing off the shackles of three centuries of thought in which a particular paradigm – called "mechanism" – has dominated the world view of scientists ... the belief that the physical Universe is nothing but a collection of material particles in interaction, a gigantic purposeless machine, of which the human body and brain are unimportant and insignificant parts' (7–8), and that 'The paradigm shift that we are now living through is a shift away from reductionism and toward holism: it is as profound as any paradigm shift in the history of science' (29).

11 However, not in *De Corpore*, where he writes, '*Materia prima*, therefore, is body in general, that is, body considered universally, not as having neither form nor any accident, but in which no form nor any other accident but quantity are at all considered' (8.24 – as quoted in Martinich, *A Hobbes Dictionary*, 54).

12 Thus, when the various 'materialists' – 'dialectical,' 'historical,' 'cultural,' or whatever – that are so common in contemporary social science and literary studies (of all places) attribute causal power to 'material factors,' they necessarily mean certain kinds of *formed* matter. But since there is no basis for believing that matter per se is more real than the forms that are the source of everything distinctive about one or another *kind* of matter – nor, consequently for regarding any Materialism as more realistic than the most unabashed Idealism (whatever that might mean) – a rational defence of any plausible materialistic theory of human life would have to show *why* one ought to grant causal *priority* to certain kinds of formed matter over other kinds. This task is virtually never taken up, for in their naivety about Matter, the partisans of materialistic explanations are unaware of any need for doing so.

13 Hobbes's extreme 'Nominalism' creates additional – and equally insoluble – difficulties for the metaphysical position he asserts in *Leviathan*; but these are more conveniently explicated in connection with his account of language (to be examined in chapter 12).

14 In his edition of *Leviathan*, Curley comments on this claim: 'The only work Hobbes had published on the subject by 1651 was his *Tractatus opticus*, published by Mersenne in 1644 in his *Cogitata physico-mathematica*' (p. 6, n1). And in the penultimate sentence of *Leviathan*, Hobbes himself speaks as if his 'novel' account of 'Bodies Naturall' remained unfinished at that time (R&C/17, 396).

15 Of course, the structural advantages of the arch form occur in Nature, e.g., in the skeletal structures of many animals, as in the human foot.

16 And doubtless scientific research will discover still more forms that can be artificially imposed on existing matter – new forms of plastics, ceramics, fibres, alloys, lubricants, adhesives, conductors, etc – which will only be *new* relative to human knowledge and utility.

17 We are told by experts who somehow make these stupendous calculations that 99.9 per cent of all life forms that have ever existed on earth are now extinct. But that the *forms* did not perish with their last instantiations is self-evident from the fact that (in principle, at least) some of the more recently extinguished species might, through genetic technology applied to recovered DNA, be resurrected.

18 This broaches upon a fundamental controversy in modern Evolutionary theory, namely, whether the results of the evolutionary process are due to chance, or whether (alternatively) it is actually a goal-directed process whereby ever-higher forms of life are actualized (i.e., whether the evolutionary process is itself form-governed).

19 Jacob Klein, *A Commentary on Plato's* Meno (Chapel Hill: University of

North Carolina Press, 1965). Plato's Sokrates treats meditation on numbers as almost equivalent to contemplation of pure Being; cf. *Republic* 510c–511d, 522c ff.

20 Nor, of course, are they purely subjective (i.e., idiosyncratic 'fancies' caused, supposedly, by vibrating grey matter), as Hobbes seems to suggest: 'for one man calleth *Wisdome*, what another man calleth *feare*; and one *cruelty*, what another *justice*; one *prodigality*, what another *magnanimity*' (IV/24, 17). Here, however – as I have previously cautioned – it may be essential to distinguish what this or that man '*calleth*' (whatever) from Hobbes's own views: notice, elsewhere in *Leviathan* he provides definitions of some of these same things, apparently intending that they be regarded as authoritative (e.g., VI/27, 26; XV/2, 71).

3: The Aristotelian Analysis of Cause

1 *Physics* 194b18–20. I have generally followed the translations of Aristotle provided in the Revised Oxford edition of his complete works, though sometimes (as here) modified in light of my own examination of the Greek texts. Unless my departures are fairly substantial, however, I have not expressly noted them.

2 Ibid., 194b6–195b30, *Metaphysics* 983a24 ff.

3 This contrasts with certain modern accounts, such as that of Logical Positivism (or Logical Empiricism, as it subsequently came to be called), whose advocates insisted that there is a clear line of demarcation between Science and Metaphysics, the latter being concerned strictly with logico-linguistic issues on which factual matters have no bearing (since those belong exclusively to one or another domain of 'empirical' science).

   According to Plutarch, the expression *hë meta ta physika* is how Aristotle himself referred to his treatises on First Philosophy in a letter to Alexander ('The Life of Alexander,' VII 4–9).

4 While the same sort of reductive analysis can be applied to this 'incorporeal matter' of story and song (e.g., reducing paragraphs to sentences, sentences to words, words to syllables, syllables to phonemes), it obviously does not terminate in prime matter. But it does nicely reveal how something significant is lost at each step of reduction – indeed, everything truly significant of the linguistic properties characteristic of each level of composition.

5 Formal mathematical relations do, however, figure in explanations of natural phenomena, as already noted in regard to musical harmony. Similarly, one explains why maximum projectile range is achieved by a cannon elevated at

a forty-five degree angle, that being a formal consequence of the parabolic trajectory of free projectiles. And one explains 'the Causes of Day, and Night' as well as the seasonal variations in night and day in terms of the properties of spherical bodies and the geometry of the Heavens (XLVI/1, 458). Quite how much of Nature is explicable by mathematical formulas – and why that which is, is, and why that which is not, is not – is a question that takes one deep into the heart of the metaphysical problems that attend Modern Science. Hobbes's own thinking on these matters has been extensively examined by scholars; see, for example, the daunting bibliography of an excellent study by Douglas M. Jesseph, *Squaring the Circle: The War between Hobbes and Wallis* (Chicago: University of Chicago Press, 1999).

6   Briefly discussed in note 23 of chapter 1.

7   As both Bacon and Descartes saw clearly, people's pervasive concern with (mainly) bodily health makes the claim to promote it one of the most rhetorically effective means of cultivating public support for our modern, technology-oriented science: that it can and will provide enormous medical benefits, greatly easing and prolonging life. In his *Discourse on Method*, in *The Philosophical Writings of Descartes*, vol. 1, J. Cottingham, R. Stoothoff, and D. Murdoch, trans. (Cambridge: Cambridge University Press, 1985), Descartes touts his revolutionary principles of physics thus:

> For they opened my eyes to the possibility of gaining knowledge that would be very useful in life ... [A]nd we could use this knowledge ... not only for the invention of innumerable devices which would facilitate our enjoyment of the fruits of the earth and all the goods we find there, but also, and most importantly, for the maintenance of health, which is undoubtedly the chief good and the foundation of all the other goods in this life. For even the mind depends so much on the temperament and disposition of the bodily organs that if it is possible to find some means of making men in general wiser and more skilful than they have been up till now, I believe we must look for it in medicine. (pt. 6, par. 2, 142–3)

Moreover, there are grounds for suspecting that a good part of Bacon's preoccupation with the problem of Heat stems from his own suspicion that it somehow holds the key to life.

8   *Nikomachean Ethics* 1094a2–3; *Rhetoric* 1362a21–7, 1365a1.

9   Cf. *Republic* 508e ff. I shall develop this point further in discussing teleology (chapter 6).

10   *Physics* 195a9–10; cf. *Republic* 444c–e.

4: The Human Psyche and the Problem of *Chance*

1 *The Prince*, ch. XXV, par. 1, Harvey Mansfield, ed. and trans. (Chicago: University of Chicago Press, 1998), 98. Certainly not to be overlooked in this passage is the initial identification of God with fortune, and the subsequent silence about God.

2 Discussing Hobbes's use of 'accident' is complicated, however. For roughly half of the forty-odd times it appears, its meaning is only remotely related to that which happens by chance. Instead, it is used in a quasi-technical sense to refer to the contingent properties or qualities of objects. For example, his first use of the term is to speak of 'some quality, or other Accident of a body without us' (I/1, 2). Whereas with respect to people's '*Sudden Dejection* ... that causeth WEEPING,' Hobbes explains that it 'is caused by such accidents, as suddenly take away some vehement hope, or prop of their power' (VI/43, 27).

3 This is implicit in Bacon's famous formula for the governing purpose of his revolutionary new kind of science ('the relief of man's estate'), as in Descartes's promise to make us 'lords and masters of nature.'

4 Cf. *Republic* 499b–d, 502a, 592a; *Politics* 1288b21–41.

5 Martinich has no entry for 'Chance,' 'Fortune,' or 'Luck' in his useful *A Hobbes Dictionary* (Oxford: Blackwell, 1995).

6 *Physics* 196b5–6. Given, then, both ancient and modern testimony, it would seem that a tendency to assimilate Divinity and Fortune – e.g., to refer to accidents as 'acts of God' – is a natural tendency of humans.

7 This is addressed in connection with the issue of 'free will' (chapter 9).

8 It is this that Hobbes so egregiously misrepresents in the passage quoted earlier: 'And in many occasions [Aristotelians] put for cause of Naturall events, their own Ignorance; but disguised in other words: As when they say, Fortune is the cause of things contingent; that is, of things whereof they know no cause' (XLVI/29, 375). What Aristotle actually teaches is that Fortune is sometimes a contingent cause of things, meaning 'concurrent' with the primary causes – *not* 'the cause of *contingent things*.'

9 To further complicate matters, we may be mistaken in our presumption that what happened was unintentional, thus an accident. This is an especially significant possibility where humans are involved, artful manipulators of appearances as we all are (indeed, employing actual arts for the purpose, everything from cosmetics and tailoring to sophistry and statistics). The 'staged accident' figures prominently in the repertoire of arsonists, secret agents, professional killers, and mystery writers. It also plays no small role

in politics, from the lowest to the highest levels. Diplomats often invoke chance to 'explain' actions taken quite intentionally.

10 199b19–21.

11 According to Diogenes Laertius, who records various versions of this piece of world-historical good luck (III, 17–21), 'Annikeris the Cyrenaic happened to be present and ransomed him for twenty minae – according to others, thirty – and dispatched him to Athens to his comrades, who immediately remitted the money. But [Annikeris] declined it, saying that the Athenians were not the only ones worthy of the privilege of providing for Plato' (III, 20; translation based on that of R.D. Hicks in the Loeb edition).

12 *Physics* 198a9–12.

13 Cf. Nietzsche, *Beyond Good and Evil*, aphs. 19 and 21, in *The Basic Writings of Nietzsche*, Walter Kaufmann, ed. and trans. (New York: Modern Library, 1966). I do not mean to suggest, however, that Hume's complete account of our causal thinking and how it actually operates in life is as simplistic as my schematic version (like that of most textbooks) makes it seem. For a especially insightful treatment of this issue, and virtually all others in Hume's thought, see Donald W. Livingston, *Philosophical Melancholy and Delirium: Hume's Pathology of Philosophy* (Chicago: University of Chicago Press, 1998); chap. 7, 'True Philosophy and the Skeptical Tradition,' is particularly relevant.

14 Bearing in mind the profound significance of pride-related phenomena in political life, and the special problems they pose for the civil peace at which Hobbes's political science is aimed (he acknowledges that he chose the name 'Leviathan' because the Bible affirms this fearsome creature to be 'King of the Proud'; XXVIII/27, 166–7), the glaring absence of any reference to the Spirited part of the soul (*thumos*) is perhaps the most suspicious omission in Part One of *Leviathan*. According to Platonic and Aristotelian psychology, the spirit is not only the seat of pride and love of glory, but also of anger, indignation, pity, love, hate, grief, joy, and all the emotions, the source of courage and resolve, of confidence, self-assertion and self-respect, of humility and vanity, and of the desires for honour and victory, for freedom and mastery. Thus, the nice irony Leo Strauss imparted to the title of his seminal essay, 'The Spirit of Hobbes's Philosophy,' *Revue Internationale de Philosophie* (October 1950): 405–31. For a detailed analysis of Platonic psychology, with special attention given to the importance of the spirited part of the soul, see chapter 4 and the first half of chapter 5 of my study of Plato's *Republic, The War Lover: A Study of Plato's* Republic (Toronto: University of Toronto Press, 1994).

15 Beginning with the 'law of contradiction,' basic to all reasoning: that logically contradictory claims cannot both be true. As I shall argue more fully in chapter 11, the absence of any acknowledgment of Rational Intuition, or 'Intellection' (*noësis*), is as serious a defect in Hobbes's account of Reason as his omission of Spirit is in his psychology. It is practically impossible to deny that we possess this power of immediate recognition, since we employ it repeatedly every day of our lives in recognizing particular objects to be the *kinds* of things they are (e.g., in counting the books on a table, I am counting objects that I immediately recognize meet my understanding of the criteria whereby something qualifies as a book). Were it not for this power, there would be no way 'Universall names' ('imposed on many things, for their similitude in some quality, or other accident'; IV/7, 13) could ever be applied. And were this power of immediate recognition not a part of Reason, not itself a *rational* power, then all the rules of logic and calculation would themselves be without rational justification, as that depends upon the immediate recognition of their validity, as does our ability to learn them. To take the simplest example: how could one *know* which two forms of Hypothetical-Conditional argument are valid and which fallacious (If A, then B; A; therefore, B. Or, If A, then B; not A; therefore, not B. Or, If A, then B; not B; therefore, not A. Or, If A, then B; B; therefore, A), except by instantiating them and then 'seeing' – immediately recognizing – which hold true and which do not? So, accepting the major premise, 'If it's a crow, then it's black,' we see that 'affirming the antecedent' (A; therefore, B) is a valid form ('it is a crow; therefore, it is black'); as is 'denying the consequent' (not B; therefore, not A – 'it is not black, therefore it is not a crow'). Whereas, upon recalling that many things are black, we see immediately that 'affirming the consequent' (B; therefore, A – 'it is black, therefore it is a crow') is a fallacy.

5: The Causes of a Commonwealth

1 To speak of 'the *Nature* of this *Artificial* man' entails a radical revision of a distinction basic to previous philosophy – so basic, indeed, as to justify regarding recognition of the distinction as the *origin* of philosophy: the 'discovery' of Nature as something distinct from the Whole of things, that not everything which exists does so 'by nature'; cf. Leo Strauss, *Natural Right and History* (Chicago: University of Chicago Press, 1953), chap. 3. Later, in discussing Bacon's new form of science and the Baconian character of Hobbes's political science, I shall address the reason for their blurring this distinction. For the present purpose of discussing Hobbes's account of

Commonwealths, however, it is useful to employ the stronger contrast between the Natural and the Artificial.

2   Hobbes reiterates this in accounting for why polities 'come to be dissolved' by internal causes: 'the fault is not in men, as they are the *Matter*; but as they are the *Makers*' (XXIX/1, 167).

3   In a posthumously discovered commentary (in Latin), which Hobbes is thought to have written in the early 1640s, and now published under the title *Thomas White's* De Mundo *Examined*, Harold Whitmore Jones, trans. (London: Bradford University Press, 1976), Hobbes presents a simplified analysis of causation:

> Some causes *sine qua non* or hypothetically necessary lie ... in the body that acts [the agent], some in the body acted on [the patient]; so all properties present in the agent, if taken collectively, are termed 'an efficient cause,' and those causes in the patient, taken collectively, are called 'a material cause.'
>
> Both an efficient cause, then, and a material cause are but part of an integral cause, or of a cause that produces an effect. Only that which is necessarily followed by an effect is rightly termed a cause, for cause and effect are related things. Where there is no effect, anything that exists or will have existed is not called a cause. A cause, therefore, whether *simpliciter* or integral, I define thus: 'a cause is one act or more acts through which another act is produced or destroyed.' An efficient cause is 'the acts of the agent, taken collectively, through which another act is produced or destroyed.' A material cause is 'all the acts of the patient, taken collectively, that produce another act within the patient itself.'
>
> It is usual to point to two other kinds of cause: the formal and the final. The latter, as far as man can understand it, is exactly the same as an efficient cause: from something pleasant arises the thought of enjoying it; from the thought arises the notion of the path to secure it; [etc.] ... The former, i.e. the formal cause, is properly, i.e. correctly speaking, not a cause ... Correctly speaking, that the angles are right angles is not a consequence of the square's form; rather, our understanding of the proposition: 'Those angles are right angles' follows from our knowing that proposition: 'That figure is a square.' (314–16)

This is clearly inadequate as a theoretical account, though it may suffice for purposes of scientific practice. Collapsing final cause into a component of efficient cause presumes that the only final causes (purposes) are human intentions. This is demonstrably false, as will be shown in the following chapter.

And Hobbes's 'psychological' argument against the existence of formal causes completely misses the meaning of formal cause, even in the case of geometrical relations. Nor can it be applied to the full range of formal cause, as the formal requirements of valid contracts prove. As does indeed the very title page of the book, which reads, LEVIATHAN, / or / The Matter, Forme, & Power / OF A / COMMON-WEALTH / ECCLESIASTICAL / AND / CIVILL.

6: Nature and the Problem of *Teleology*

1 A teleological perspective is characteristic of Aristotle's whole corpus of writings. His most systematic discussion of teleology, however, is in his *Physics* 198b10–199b33 (Book II, ch. 8).
2 *Physics* 198b24–32. As anyone versed in Evolutionary theory would recognize, the dominant modern view today is similar to that of Empedocles: that generation by generation, chance combinations of genetic material, along with mutations, produce variations in the individuals of existing species. And those variations that enhance survival or reproductive success in the competitive environment of Nature tend to be selected for continuation through the offspring of the advantaged individuals, whereas those that do not so contribute tend not to persist. The major difference is that the modern view includes a theory of genetics that can plausibly explain the persistence of advantageous variations.
3 Cf. *Leviathan* XXIII/12, 126; XXV/16, 136.
4 Much modern biological research, particularly at the micro level, tacitly relies on this knowledge of function and fulfilled form in order to carry out anatomical and physio-chemical analyses of mechanisms. Thus, many microbiological researchers working in their highly specialized areas mistakenly believe that modern biology does not essentially differ from inorganic chemistry and physics, and that teleological explanations are not necessary to account fully for biological phenomena. There are a couple of amusing ironies here. First, the 'Complementarity Principle' that Niels Bohr introduced in Quantum physics (whereby electromagnetic radiation may be treated as either wave-like or particle-like, depending on the explanatory context) actually originated with his father, who as a physiologist had argued that biology requires both teleological-functional and mechanistic forms of explanation, and that they are not contradictory, but (rather) complementary. Aristotle would agree, of course, for that is the status of all four kinds of cause he identified: that they complement each other and only collectively provide a complete account. The second irony is that the Quantum physicists' use of this principle is not at all analogous to that of biologists

who use both functional and mechanistic explanations. To treat the same phenomenon as now a particle, now a wave, is as if a biologist were to treat the same phenomenon as both living and dead.

5 *De Incesso Animalium* 704b15, 711a16–17. This judgment remains valid regardless of *how* the diversity of life forms were 'made' or 'came to be' – whether designed by an omniscient, omnipotent Divine Power (such as Hobbes pretends to endorse), or as the net result of an almost inconceivably long evolutionary process. As a measure of how poorly understood teleology is today, even the ranks of biologists include people who presume that it has been 'disproved' by modern Evolutionary theory. Whereas it is hard to imagine a theory of life on earth – of how it arose, proliferated, and diversified, and why the results are what we can observe today – that could be more thoroughly and emphatically teleological than that of (neo)Darwinian Evolution. According to this view (touched upon in note 2 above), from the inexhaustible supply of morphic and behavioural variation produced by 'chance' (in the form of occasional genetic mutations and the regular genetic combining intrinsic to sexual reproduction), the regimen of natural competition automatically 'selects' for the features most advantageous to survival and/or reproduction by favouring the reproductive success of the individuals who bear these traits – i.e., traits that, comparatively speaking, *best* serve those *purposes*. The essential vocabulary of Evolutionary theory ('fitness,' 'adaptive,' 'survival value,' 'developmental stability,' 'heritability,' 'selection pressure,' etc.) attests to the pervasive importance of purpose in its explanation of the life world as presently constituted.

What remains controversial is whether the overall process is teleological, necessarily generating ever higher forms of life (culminating in Man). It seems to me that the evidence of its overall teleological character is undeniable: after all, if the process begins with life somehow arising out of non-life, there is only one direction for it to go, and that is up. Accordingly, I am somewhat puzzled by supposed experts on the subject who insist on denying what seems to me virtually self-evident, and I cannot help suspecting that extraneous factors are involved (see following note). Admittedly, the 'mechanisms' whereby the process could be so directed are hard to conceive. However, so-called Chaos theory, which highlights the fact that *forms* of order can spontaneously arise out of disorder, may dispel some of the mystery here. John J. Reilly briefly sketches some of the implications of Chaos or Complexity theory for evolution in 'After Darwin,' *First Things* (June/July 1995): 14–17. Where Evolutionary theory conflicts with the Aristotelian view is *not* with respect to the teleological character of the life world, but rather in regards to the eternality of the species.

Not altogether incidentally, the reigning 'paradigm' in Evolutionary biology is almost surely going to undergo major modifications as the result of another growing field of research: Epigenetics (the study of *heritable* changes in the *regulation* of genes without affecting DNA sequences; by transmission of various agents that suppress the activation of certain genes or that stimulate others, there is some allowance for the inheritance of *acquired* characteristics – the rebirth of a limited Lamarckian view).

6   I am of course aware that there is an increasing number of people who profess to reject any such prioritizing of life forms, insisting that all are equal (and have 'rights,' no less) – in effect requiring that Nature ratify their own dogmatic Democratism. Suffice it to say, such views are simply so much evidence of the ravages wreaked on people's common sense by a succession of fashionable moral and epistemological relativisms (every one of which when applied reflexively dissolves into incoherence), along with the other kinds of bogus social science and pseudo-philosophy that have come to dominate contemporary life. Still, put to the test, most of these people would concede that there is something wrong with a truck driver who, given a choice, would run over a child in order to avoid squashing a half-dozen frogs. They may even agree that doing so ought to be a crime.

7   *Physics* 199a34–b4.

8   And this remains the case regardless of how the whole natural order originated. If, as per modern Evolutionary theory, the life forms evolved in adaptation to their inanimate material base, the net result is nonetheless an overall purposive system.

9   Paul Colinvaux, *Why Big Fierce Animals Are Rare* (Princeton, NJ: Princeton University Press, 1978), 32.

10   *Physics* 199b31–2.

11   There is among contemporary physicists *cum* cosmologists a school of thought that contends that the very laws of physics came into existence along with the Big Bang supposedly determined by those laws. Suffice it to say, the reasoning whereby this is supposedly possible is like the Love of God in one respect: it surpasseth all understanding, including (one suspects) that of those who claim it.

12   In recent times, some academic philosophers of science (mainly Logical Positivists and fellow travellers) have argued that there is no need for teleological explanations. They contend that any teleological claim can be recast in non-teleological terms without loss of content (thereby obviating the claims of macrobiologists and those working in the human sciences that they *need* forms of teleological explanations to render their phenomena intelligible). Insofar as their underlying concern is for a unified scientific view, reflecting

the unity of the world, their ambition is perfectly legitimate. But the scheme simply does not work. And it is rather amusing that anyone ever thought it could. After all, if the whole point of the translation is to eliminate a certain constituent of the original claim (namely, purposiveness), how could the two statements be logically equivalent? Moreover, there would be a nice irony to this translation strategy if it *did* work: since logical equivalence is a two-way street, one could as readily use it to translate the non-teleological statements of physics and chemistry into teleological statements and thereby achieve a 'unified science' that was teleological throughout!

13 Manipulating Nature for technological purposes requires precisely detailed knowledge as can only be had by concentrating on some fairly narrow slice of it. For example, the general understanding of Chemistry that would be sufficient for satisfying one's curiosity about the material composition of the world (e.g., about which kinds of matter combine, and why and how; why some are gases whereas others are liquids or solids; the commonalities shared by salts, or metals, or acids, etc.) will not suffice for inventing synthetic fibres, dyes, flavours, plastics, paints, fuels, explosives, drugs, glues, cleansers, lubricants, fire retardants, or a myriad of other useful products that are the results of highly specialized research laboratories.

14 This is true even for those sectors of modern science – such as astronomy, evolutionary studies, archaeology, anthropology – that provide little or no technical payoff. The generous public respect and support they receive comes courtesy of the general aura of sacro-sanctity that has grown up around science generally. That the findings of these 'impractical' disciplines is of interest to more than just fellow specialists, but to some lesser extent is shared by a small but significant minority of the general public, is evidence in favour of Aristotle's conclusion concerning Man's natural *telos*: that we are beings who by nature strive to know simply for the sake of knowing – as most fully realized in the philosopher.

15 This was certainly the case in Bacon's own time, as attested by the controversies surrounding certain clubs (such as the notorious 'Mermayd') and private societies that tainted major figures of the English Renaissance (e.g., Walter Raleigh, John Dee, Thomas Harriot, Christopher Marlowe, et al.). Cf. John Winton, *Sir Walter Ralegh* (London: Michael Joseph, 1975), 142–57; Peter French, *John Dee: The World of an Elizabethan Magus* (London: Routledge and Kegan Paul, 1972). The case of Galileo, which Hobbes alludes to without naming the principal, is the most notorious, though the fiery end of Bruno's heterodoxical career more emphatically illustrates the dangers.

16 We know from Aubrey's brief biography of Hobbes that he served for a time as a secretary for the great Sir Francis Bacon (Lord Verulam), principal

visionary and architect of modern science, and of its political requirements –
the 'Lord Chancellor of England' whom Rousseau in his First Discourse
suggested was 'the greatest, perhaps, of Philosophers.' *The Discourses and
Other Early Political Writings*, Victor Gourevitch, ed. and trans. (Cambridge: Cambridge University Press, 1997), 27. François du Verdus asks
Hobbes about his service with Bacon in a letter dated 3 August 1664: no.
168 in *The Correspondence of Thomas Hobbes*, vol. 2, Noel Malcolm, ed.
(Oxford: Oxford University Press, 1994), 624, 628. Unfortunately, we do
not have Hobbes's reply.

7: The Essentials of Baconian Science

1 All quotes from Bacon's *New Organon* are according to the translation supplied by the editors (James Spedding, Robert Ellis, and Douglas Heath) in
   vol. 8 of the complete *Works*, with minor modifications to it in the edition
   by Fulton H. Anderson (Indianapolis: Bobbs-Merrill, 1960), to which my
   page references refer.
2 The notion that the natural science of Aristotle and genuine Aristotelians is
   not rigorously empirical is simply a fantasy of the mythologizing histories of
   modern science. However, the role of experimentation as a means of augmenting empirical evidence is significantly restricted in Aristotelian science, since
   its goal is an understanding of Nature behaving naturally, which requires its
   being 'free and at large' to do so (hence not being interfered with in the
   manner that the artificially 'controlled experiment' requires). This is of a piece
   with the primarily theoretical purpose of such science: that it is knowledge
   sought for its own sake (i.e., to satisfy the human desire to know).
3 This matter will be treated more fully in chapter 12.
4 That one might, in turn, share such knowledge with others in no way mitigates the 'offence' in the eyes of anyone who agrees with Bacon's insistence
   on inquiry being guided by potential utility (and there will always be plenty
   of people who do). Indeed, it must rather be seen as aggravating the offence.
   For if seeking knowledge for its own sake is an illegitimate self-indulgence,
   it is hardly an effective apology to attest that one encourages a similar corruption in others. Hence, the fact that a philosopher might teach or otherwise share his wisdom does not in itself justify his presence in the polity
   unless that wisdom has some intrinsic value – which, according to the utilitarian conception of wisdom, strictly theoretical knowledge 'by definition'
   does not have.
   However, Bacon, though he obviously knows better himself, has misrep-
   resented the motivation for seeking theoretical knowledge, as if it were

nothing more than a refined hedonism (pursuing 'pleasure of the mind'). Such knowing may indeed yield a unique pleasure or 'delight' (as Hobbes attests; VI/35, 26), but this need not mean that it is sought simply for that purpose, any more than eating is solely for sake of the pleasures that attend it. There are deeper necessities at work in both cases, and the legitimacy of eating to live is in no way compromised by the fact that there doubtless are shallow souls who seem to live only for eating.

5 *New Organon*, Book One, aph. 3, 39.

6 This despite the fact that most of the numbered entries of Book Two do not very well fit Bacon's descriptions of aphorisms in *The Advancement of Learning*, G.W.Kitchin, ed. (Philadelphia: Paul Dry Books, 2001) – unlike, say, the first thirty-nine of Book One. In *The Advancement*, he contrasts the use of aphoristic style of 'delivery' with the methodical style of a treatise:

> 7. For first, it trieth the writer, whether he be superficial or solid: for Aphorisms, except they should be ridiculous, cannot be made but of the pith and heart of sciences; for discourse of illustration is cut off: recitals of examples are cut off; discourse of connection and order is cut off; descriptions of practice are cut off. So there remaineth nothing to fill the Aphorisms but some good quantity of observation: and therefore no man can suffice, nor in reason will attempt to write Aphorisms, but he that is sound and grounded. (II.17.6–7, 133)

Here one might add that aphoristic delivery, 'carrying the show' of a *lack* of system, may nonetheless conceal a rigorously systematic treatment, such that a writer as solidly knowledgeable and as clever as Bacon so clearly is, can have it both ways: provide useful practice of the sort necessary to reach valid conclusions about Nature (wherein the evidence is similarly 'dispersed'), while at the same time providing a coherent esoteric teaching about Nature (the assembling of which requires the reader to philosophize actively himself).

Given the seminal importance of Bacon's writings for instigating the modern Scientific Revolution, and thus for our own understanding of how this radical transformation of the world was brought about, one must know 'how to read' Bacon. That this is not as straightforward as one might suppose is indicated by the fact that, with the possible exception of Nietzsche, no other philosopher has spoken so explicitly so often about the uses of esoteric (or 'acroamatic,' or 'epoptic') communication. All fourteen sections of chapter 17, Book Two, of *The Advancement* are relevant here, as they provide a survey of the various 'methods of delivery' (i.e., of communication, as opposed to 'methods of inquiry'), including those that screen out 'vulgar capacities from being admitted to the secrets of knowledges,' reserving them for 'selected auditors, or wits of such sharpness as can pierce the veil' (II.17.5, 133).

In *De Augmentis*, Bacon speaks of the 'higher character' of 'Parabolical Poesy,' such being commonly employed in religion 'as a means of communication between divinity and humanity': 'It is of double use and serves for contrary purposes; for it serves for an infoldment; and it likewise serves for illustration. In the latter case the object is a certain method of teaching; in the former an artifice for concealment.' Its use for concealment is especially appropriate in treating such things 'the dignity whereof requires they should be seen as it were through a veil; that is when the secrets and mysteries of religion, policy, and philosophy are involved in fables or parables.' *The Works of Francis Bacon*, vol. 9, cited in note 1, 122–7. Judging by the first two paragraphs of his Preface to *De Cive*, Hobbes (like Bacon) approves of what 'the wise men of remotest antiquity' believed about political understanding: given that its intrinsic difficulty is not readily appreciated by most men (rather 'as if it were easy and accessible without effort'), political teachings 'should be given to posterity only in the pretty forms of poetry or in the shadowy outlines Allegory, as if to prevent what one might call the high and holy mystery of government from being contaminated by the debates of private men.'

Bearing in mind that Hobbes served as a secretary to Bacon in his forced retirement, and that (according to John Aubrey), 'The Lord Chancellor Bacon loved to converse with him,' is it not merely prudent, then, to presume that Hobbes was at least privy to Bacon's views about esotericism, as well as about science and politics? And might he have agreed with them? One could conclude as much from an observation he makes in the prefatory material to his translation of Thucydides (Hobbes's first major publication, 1629). Speaking of that ancient author's style, Hobbes contends that whatever 'obscurity' it manifests

> proceedeth from the profoundness of the sentences; containing contemplations of those human passions, which either dissembled or not commonly discoursed of, do yet carry the greatest sway with men in their public conversation. If then one cannot penetrate into them without much meditation, we are not to expect a man should understand them at the first speaking. Marcellinus saith, he was obscure on purpose; that the common people might not understand him. And not unlikely: for a wise

man should so write, (though in words understood by all men), that wise men only should be able to commend him. (as per the modernized version of the text, *Hobbes's Thucydides*, edited by Richard Schlatter [New Brunswick, NJ: Rutgers University Press, 1975], 25)

In his *Miscellanies of Literature* (London: Edward Monon, 1840), Isaac D'Israeli points to this passage as evidence that Hobbes himself adopted an esoteric approach virtually from the outset of his literary career: 'Thus early in his life Hobbes had determined on a principle which produced all his studied ambiguity, involved him in so much controversy, and, in some respects, preserved him in an inglorious security' ('Hobbes and His Quarrels,' 263).

   Schlatter notes that Bacon regarded Thucydides' *History* as 'the most perfect type of historical writing,' and that in *The Advancement of Learning*, 'Thucydides is mentioned as one of the historians worthy of being incorporated without alteration or omission into a Universal History. Thus it is entirely possible that Hobbes's translation is a part of Bacon's grand plan for collecting and digesting all knowledge for its advancement' (xix).

7 In *The Advancement of Learning*, Bacon offers an explanation – who knows whether sincere or ironical – of this practice of employing traditional terms in novel ways: 'wheresoever my conception and notion may differ from the ancient, yet I am studious to keep the ancient terms. For hoping well to deliver myself from mistaking, by the order and perspicuous expressing of that I do propound, I am otherwise zealous and affectionate to recede as little from antiquity, either in terms or opinions, as may stand with truth and the proficience of knowledge' (II.7.2, 88).

8 This is not strictly true, for (as noted earlier) only in awareness that some purpose is served can one then investigate 'how so.' Still, of the resulting knowledge, only the 'how so' knowledge is useful, allowing one to see ways to manipulate natures in pursuit of human purposes.

9 However, whereas Hobbes contends that this is so of the World, the Universe, by which he means *all* things that are, Bacon speaks here of 'nature.' And he may regard nature as simply the *embodied part* of the world. His proposed distinction between 'physics' and 'metaphysics' could be so interpreted.

10 Because the Baconian prescription for scientific inquiry is what has been largely followed, Cause per se has tended to 'disappear' from whole bodies of scientific knowledge, inasmuch as it has come to be expressed in mathematical formulas. This, too, is as Bacon prescribed: 'And inquiries into nature have the best result when they begin with physics and end in mathe-

matics' (129). But whereas Bacon, like Aristotle, regarded these formulas as symbolic expressions of Formal causes (as the very word 'formula' would suggest), contemporary usage no longer recognizes them as such (confining the idea of cause in Nature to Efficient causation). Instead, expressions such as pV=RT (the Ideal Gas Law, relating the variables Pressure, Volume, and Temperature), or $E=mc^2$ (Einstein's famous formula relating Energy to mass and the speed of light), are seen simply as economical *descriptions* of fixed relations among phenomena, which can be *used* causally (i.e., to cause effects, such as increasing the temperature of a body of gas by increasing the pressure), but having no specific causal content themselves.

11 Bacon's position, however, is a far cry from the dogmatic Fact-Value distinction that has since become so ingrained in the social sciences and other academic disciplines – and consequently throughout popular culture – for he recognized that there is such a thing as moral *knowledge* (not merely subjective preferences). I have provided a commonsense critique of the Fact-Value distinction in an endnote of *The War Lover: A Study of Plato's* Republic (Toronto: University of Toronto Press, 1994), 326–36.

12 For a useful discussion of why the very conceptions of 'fact' and 'value' reflect a misunderstanding about modern science, see Roger Trigg, *Understanding Social Science* (Oxford: Basil Blackwell, 1985), especially ch. 6.

8: The Baconian Character of Hobbes's Political Project

1 *New Organon*, Fulton H. Anderson, ed. (Indianapolis: Bobbs-Merrill, 1960), 23–4.

2 Similarly, Descartes concedes that carrying out his version of the Baconian project is beyond both his personal abilities and his financial resources, 'were it even a thousand times greater than it is,' that this project is plainly a task 'for a king or a pope.' *Discourse on Method*, VI/3, in *The Philosophical Writings of Descartes*, vol. 1, J. Cottingham, R. Stoothoff, and D. Murdoch, trans. (Cambridge: Cambridge University Press,1985), 144.

3 In his monumental study of Western political thought and practice, Paul A. Rahe, *Republics Ancient and Modern* (Chapel Hill, NC: University of North Carolina Press, 1992), deals at some length with Hobbes's new political teaching and its legacy. And while I believe his interpretation of Hobbes is somewhat compromised by a reliance on the validity of what I regard as actually a rhetorical veneer, Rahe sees more clearly than most scholars the significance of modern Baconian science for Hobbes's political project:

Thus, if one may term the ancient republics aristocracies dedicated to the pursuit of virtue and honor, one may in contrast call the Hobbesian state a bourgeois regime – though not as Marxists use the term ... [It] is neither dedicated to the protection of property per se nor designed to promote the interests of those already in possession of great fortunes; it is, rather, devoted to the fostering of natural science, to the encouragement of labor, and to the provision of commodious living for all those capable of profiting from the economic opportunities opened up by a political regime liberated from religious and moral illusions. (393–4)

4 For what it is worth, the described location of 'mythical' Bensalem in Bacon's *New Atlantis* would usually be thought of as 'the Antipodes.' There are grounds, however, for suspecting that 'the antipodes' has some significance beyond the strictly geographical. In *The Advancement of Learning*, G.W.Kitchin, ed. (Philadelphia: Paul Dry Books, 2001), Bacon addresses 'those particular seducements or indispositions of the mind for policy and government, which Learning is pretended to insinuate,' arguing that if it sometimes causes 'indisposition or infirmity,' it also provides the 'medicine or remedy.' By way of illustrating this curative power of Learning, he includes: 'Let him look into the errors of Cato the second, and he will never be one of the *Antipodes*, to tread opposite to the present world' (I.2.4, 13).

5 In his *Annales Veteris Testamenti, a Prima Mundi Origine Deducti* ('Annals of the Old Testament, deduced from the first origins of the world'); a follow-up volume continuing the story, *Annalium Pars Postierior*, was published in 1654.

6 Cf. Matthew 25:14–30. Although 'talent' in Scripture means a unit of money, the lesson of using one's means to 'turn a profit' has a special pertinence for the techno-science–based Commercial Republic that Hobbes has designed.

9: Philosophy and the Problem of *Determinism*

1 Pierre Simon de Laplace, *A Philosophical Essay on Probabilities* (New York: Dover, 1951), 4. About this oft-cited statement, James Gleick, *Chaos: Making a New Science* (New York: Penguin, 1987), observes:

In these days of Einstein's relativity and Heisenberg's uncertainty, Laplace seems almost buffoon-like in his optimism, but much of modern science has pursued his dream. Implicitly, the mission of many twentieth-century scientists – biologists, neurologists, economists – has been to break their universes down into the simplest atoms that will obey scientific rules. In all these sciences, a kind of Newtonian determinism has been brought to bear. The fathers of modern computing always had Laplace in mind, and the history of computing and the history of forecasting were intermingled ever since John von Neumann designed his first machines. (14)

2 Einstein's Theories of Relativity render half the Laplacean ideal impossible in principle, since the apparent 'state of the Universe at any one instant' varies with one's position in it; nor can there be any way to correct for the varying lag times in information arriving without knowing precisely what the information is meant to reveal: the position of everything at a given instant.

This part of the ideal is not to be confused with the very different Laplacean notion that all this knowledge could be reduced to a single formula. Something to this effect has become the ambition of modern physicists: to provide an integrated account of nuclear, electromagnetic, and gravitational phenomena by showing their derivability from a single formulas set (of what, is not clear). This has come to be referred to popularly as 'the Theory of Everything,' though it would be much more aptly named 'the Theory of Almost Nothing,' since it would actually *explain* almost nothing that an intelligent human might be curious about – the ecosystem of a rain forest, say, or price fluctuations in commodity markets, the migration cycles of wildebeests, or the rapturous sonic qualities of Stradivarius instruments – much less explain an intelligent human being.

The claim that such a theory would in principle explain everything 'real' falsely presumes the validity of Reductionism: that the properties and the behaviour of the complex is fully explicable in terms of the properties and behaviour of its simpler constituents (consequently, that Political Science is fully reducible to Psychology, that to Physiology, that to Biology, that to Chemistry, that to Atomic Physics). But as the Aristotelian analysis of the relativity of Matter so clearly establishes, there are properties which emerge at each more complex level of organization, and which are due precisely to the *organization* of the parts, not to the parts themselves. Everything distinctive about water is lost when it is reduced to the elements that compose it. Similarly, there is all the difference in the world between an armed mob and a disciplined army. Thus the first rule of effective politics: 'get organized.' This is exemplified by the difference in the conditions of Hobbes's State of Nature, understood as a war of all against all precisely because populated by 'atomic individuals' constantly competing at cross-purposes, and Civil Society, which is a condition of peace, thus graced by all that peace makes possible, because those same competitive individuals have been organized into an effective unity.

3 No more comprehensible is the claim, based on an Operationalist interpretation of Relativity and employing non-Euclidean geometry, that Space itself is 'curved' so as to be both finite and yet endless. This may somehow be so, but the issue is whether such a notion is comprehensible to the human mind. That it is not is suggested by the fact that all attempts to explain it rely, tacitly if not explicitly, on an intuitive grasp of a three-dimensional Euclidean framework in order to explicate it analogically, e.g., by likening it to two-dimensional existence on what is actually the surface of a (three-dimensional) sphere.

4 I suspect most people's posture towards time is rather like Augustine's (and mine): they presume they understand it perfectly well until they are asked to explain it, and thus have to think about it. Cf. *Confessions*, Bk. XI, par. 14.

5 Although Robert Boyle identified the distinction in these terms, and Locke provided the fullest exposition of it, the distinction itself was earlier recognized by Galileo and Descartes.

6 Reflecting on Hobbes's account of sensation, Jan Blits draws out some implications in particularly provocative terms: 'while coloring the world, sense also conceals what it appears to reveal. While it makes us think that sensory experience gives us direct access to the world around us, it actually cuts us off from the outside world. Limited to the deceptive surface of things, it closes us up within ourselves, hiding what truly exists behind a screen of representation. Contrary to what sense tells us, the world literally lies hidden in darkness. Sensory experience is the true Kingdom of Darkness … The sun does not light the world. Nothing does.' 'Hobbesian Fear,' *Political Theory* 17, no. 3 (August 1989): 419.

7 Melville's Ishmael, attempting to account for the uncanny feeling 'The Whiteness of the Whale' aroused in him, gives this doctrine of Secondary Qualities a morbid, Hamlet-like twist:

> And when we consider that other theory of the natural philosophers, that all other earthly hues – every stately or lovely emblazoning – the sweet tinges of sunset skies and woods; yea, and the gilded velvet of butterflies, and the butterfly cheeks of young girls; all these are but subtile deceits, not actually inherent in substances, but only laid on from without; so that all deified Nature absolutely paints like the harlot, whose allurements cover nothing but the charnel-house within. (ch. 42, 195)

Ishmael, notice, does not declare this 'theory of the natural philosophers' to be valid. From a humane perspective, the very repugnancy of the world so described suggests its inadequacy.

8 Much of what follows is expanded from a discussion of this issue in my essay on *Macbeth* in *Of Philosophers and Kings: Political Philosophy in Shakespeare's* Macbeth *and* King Lear (Toronto: University of Toronto Press, 2001), 72–5.

9 Hence, the best (I believe, only effective) defence of 'free will' – meaning, of mental freedom – is an exposé of the indefensibility of Determinism.

10 What is most curious to me is the extent to which this conclusion is apparently not recognized by those who discuss the Free Will versus Determinism question: that whatever their position, *debating* the issue only makes sense on the assumption that Determinism is *false* – that the human mind is free to discover the truth on the basis of objective evidence and rational argument. But if on that basis one were somehow to conclude that the human mind is strictly determined as to whatever one concludes, it would immediately render irrelevant everything that supposedly implied that conclusion. So, while it is logically possible that Determinism could be true, it would be unknowable as such, hence could only be believed as a matter of dogma, and in indifference to the confusing welter of implications of such belief being itself determined. However, most scholars who debate the issues do so as if they had somehow managed to 'step outside the problem,' viewing it from an Olympian rather than a human perspective.

11 Thus, there is nothing paradoxical in my presenting a critique of Determinism, as there would be were I offering a defence of it, since I presume the reader is free to reach conclusions on the basis of rationally assessing the merits of my arguments.

12 This problem is more fundamental than that which Hobbes explicitly addresses in stressing the importance of public education to the Sovereign's maintaining his 'Rights entire':

> [I]t is against his Duty, to let people be ignorant, or mis-informed of the grounds, and reasons of those his essentiall Rights; because thereby men are easie to be seduced, and drawn to resist him, when the Commonwealth shall require their use and exercise.
>
> And the grounds of these Rights, have the rather need to be diligently, and truly taught; because they cannot be maintained by any Civill Law, or terror of legall punishment. For a Civill Law, that shall forbid Rebellion, (and such is all resistance to the essentiall Rights of Soveraignty,) is not (as a Civill Law) any obligation, but by vertue onely of the Law of Nature, that forbiddeth the violation of Faith; which naturall obligation if men know not, they cannot know the Right of any Law the Soveraign maketh. And for the Punishment, they take it but for an act of Hostility; which

when they think they have strength enough, they will endeavour by acts of Hostility, to avoyd. (XXX/3–4, 175–6)

The effectiveness of such teaching, however, will depend on the power of Reaon: not only on the rational soundness of what is taught, but crucially on the strength of reason in the souls of those to whom it is addressed.

13 *Beyond Good and Evil*, aph. 21, in *The Basic Writings of Nietzsche*, Walter Kaufmann, ed. and trans. (New York: Modern Library, 1966). Indeed, 'freedom of the *will*' is virtually an incoherent notion.

14 In an effort to finesse the inconsistency in the meaning of 'liberty,' such that it covers both bodily and legal restraint, Hobbes resorts to flagrant sophistry: 'But as men, for the atteyning of peace, and conservation of themselves thereby, have made an Artificiall Man, which we call a Common-wealth; so also have they made Artificiall Chains, called *Civill Lawes*' (XXI/5, 108). Suffice it to say, to liken Laws to 'Chains' is merely to use the word metaphorically; it does not transform Laws into physical bodies capable in themselves of restricting the motion of other physical bodies (as real chains do). Of a similar status is his later reference to 'the Opinion of men' as a 'restraint' on liberty (XXXI/12, 189). However, the fact that in the penultimate sentence of his book Hobbes speaks of this 'Artificiall Man' as an 'Artificiall *Body*' requires a radical reconsideration of what he includes within the rubric 'Body,' hence what actually is meant by his insistence that 'when the words *Free*, and *Liberty* are applied to any thing but *Bodies*, they are abused.' Hobbes does himself speak of 'the Libertie of the Common-wealth' (XXI/8, 110).

15 Since the real issue concerns the freedom of *thought* – *not* of the *will* – Hobbes's celebrated dispute with Bishop Bramhall over whether 'not only the *man* is free to choose what he will *do*, but the *will* also to choose what it shall *will*,' is largely irrelevant. *The Questions Concerning Liberty, Necessity, and Chance*, vol. 5 of *The English Works of Thomas Hobbes*, Sir William Moleworth, ed. (London: John Bohn, 1841). Hobbes uses the dispute mainly to show off his superior knowledge, or interpretations, of Scripture.

Hobbes seems to acknowledge both the power and the freedom of a rational mind also in his 'Preface to the Readers' of *De Cive*. Speaking of peevish children: 'Unless you give infants everything they want, they cry and get angry, they even beat their own parents, and nature prompts them to do so. But they are not to blame, and are not evil, first, because they cannot do any harm, and then because, not having the use of reason, they are totally exempt from duties.' Translation as in *On the Citizen*, Richard Tuck and Michael Silverthorne, eds (Cambridge: Cambridge University

Press, 1998), 11. Apparently, 'having the use of reason' makes all the difference with respect to culpability and obligation. But why so, unless one thereby has the freedom to choose rightly or wrongly?

16 *Nikomachean Ethics* 1119a23–5.

17 To be sure, in strict logic, 'nothing changes' for the rigorously consistent determinist (provided he could ignore the schizoid implications of accepting this view of oneself): given an identical awareness of a present set of factors, thus confronting the same whole world, there is no *practical* difference between asking oneself 'what ought I to do,' and asking 'what am I determined to do.' However, virtually no one in practice *is* rigorously consistent in this respect. Instead, the supposed determinist employs his determinism selectively. For the most part he lives in the way that comes naturally to a human being: as a 'free agent,' autonomous, expecting to be respected and treated as such, and to be given full credit for any admirable accomplishments. And for most of his dealings with other people, he views them likewise – not as so many determined mechanisms, but as beings responsible for their own actions (especially any that bear adversely on him). But when he finds it convenient to renounce moral responsibility for indulging his appetites and passions, or to excuse his or anyone else's moral failing – or to deny anyone credit for virtuous action – he invokes his determinism. So, in practice, his determinism licenses an easy-going, shame-free, guilt-free hedonism.

10: Reason and the Problem of *Revelation*

1 Cf. VIII/27, 39; XXIX/16, 172; XVI/3, 80–1. In its entry 'Trinity,' *The Oxford Companion to the Bible*, Bruce M. Metzger and Michael D. Coogan, eds (New York: Oxford University Press, 1993) notes: 'Because the Trinity is such an important part of later Christian doctrine, it is striking that the term does not appear in the New Testament. Likewise, the developed concept of three coequal partners in the Godhead found in later creedal formulations cannot be clearly detected within the confines of the canon.' For all the perplexity this causes for a religion that nonetheless professes to be monotheistic, 'the idea of a Trinity – one God subsisting in three persons and one substance – ultimately prevails' (782). The closest Scriptural authority for the doctrine would seem to be that found in Matthew 28:18–19: 'And Jesus came and spake unto them, saying, All power is given unto me in heaven and in earth. Go ye therefore, and teach all nations, baptizing them in the name of the Father, and of the Son, and of the Holy Ghost.'

Hobbes is coy in his treatment of the Trinity doctrine. For example, in discussing the idea of 'Mixt Government,' he allows, 'In the Kingdome of God, there *may* be three Persons independent, without breach of unity in God that Reigneth; but where men Reigne, that be subject to diversity of opinions, it cannot be so' (XXIX/16, 172; emphasis added). Hobbes is clearly aware that the Scriptural basis for the doctrine is shaky: 'But a Person, (as I have shewn before, chapt. 13 [*sic*; presumably a printer's error, as the relevant chapter is 16]) is he that is Represented, as often as hee is Represented; and therefore God, who has been Represented (that is, Personated) thrice, may properly enough be said to be three persons; though neither the word *Person*, nor *Trinity* be ascribed to him in the Bible' (XLII/3, 268; again, note the 'may'). And in discussing the unknowability of God's attributes, Hobbes supplies his own idea of 'unity in trinity': 'For there is but one Name to signifie our Conception of his Nature, and that is, I AM: and but one name of his Relation to us, and that is *God*; in which is contained Father, King, and Lord' (XXXI/28, 191).

2 The major premise uniting the two halves of *Leviathan* is that whatever issues from these three sources must be consistent, and ensuring that this be so serves as the main criterion for 'skillful interpretation' of Scripture.

3 In discussing the practical basis of the authority exercised by rulers of the Jewish people, according to the 'Holy History' of the Old Testament, Hobbes notes that for them, at least, a somewhat different equivalency obtained: 'great miracles, or (which is the equivalent to a miracle) great abilities, or great felicity in the enterprises of their Governours' (XL/12, 255).

4 In only one instance does Moleworth's edition of *Leviathan* depart from Hobbes's own paragraphing (and Curley's numbering of paragraphs in his edition follows Moleworth, though Curley also subdivides some of the longer of the numbered paragraphs). The single exception occurs in chapter 26, at the twenty-ninth paragraph, which Moleworth splits into two. As a result, the paragraph I quote – which is actually the thirty-ninth in Hobbes's text – is numbered forty in Molesworth and Curley. I bother to note this on the off chance that the arithmetical distribution of textual material matters to Hobbes (as the geometric distribution surely does).

5 Hobbes was by no means alone in his efforts to do so. As Leo Strauss, *Thoughts on Machiavelli* (Seattle: University of Washington Press, 1958) explains:

We have devoted what at first glance seems to be a disproportionately large space to Machiavelli's thought concerning religion. This impression is due to a common misunderstanding of the intention, not only of Machiavelli but also of a whole series of political thinkers who succeeded him. We no longer understand that in spite of great disagreements among these thinkers, they were united by the fact that they all fought one and the same power – the kingdom of darkness, as Hobbes called it; that fight was more important to them than any merely political issue. This will become clearer to us the more we learn again to understand those thinkers as they understood themselves and the more familiar we become with the art of allusive and elusive writing which all of them employ, although to different degrees. The series of those thinkers will then come to sight as a line of warriors who occasionally interrupt their fight against the common enemy to engage in a heated but never hostile disputation among themselves. (231)

6   According to I Kings 22:19–23 (which Hobbes treats as Micaiah's 'Vision'):

> And the LORD said, Who shall persuade Ahab, that he may go up and fall at Ramoth-gilead? And one said on this manner, and another said on that manner. And there came forth a spirit, and stood before the LORD, and said, I will persuade him. And the LORD said unto him, Wherewith? And he said, I will go forth, and I will be a lying spirit in the mouth of all his prophets. And he said, Thou shalt persuade *him*, and prevail also: go forth and do so. Now therefore, behold, the LORD hath put a lying spirit in the mouth of all these thy prophets, and the LORD hath spoken evil concerning thee.

7   For good reason, then, the role of supernatural Deceiver came to be ascribed to the great Enemy of God and Man, the fallen angel, Satan.

8   When one assembles and meditates upon Hobbes's many scattered indications of radical scepticism about things supposedly divine, and the weakness of his arguments purporting to support the existence of God, a pattern emerges that strongly – I think overwhelmingly – suggests that Hobbes was at least an agnostic, if not indeed an atheist (as so many of his contemporaries claimed). To be sure, the case is largely circumstantial – a matter of adding two and two together. Atheism being a basis for capital prosecution in his day, and sure to alienate a broad swath of potential readers, Hobbes is careful never to say anything that would clearly and directly amount to a denial of the existence of God. I shall address this further in Part Two.

9   Hobbes's treatment of this all-important point invariably begs the question. For instance, in addressing the dispute, *'From whence the Scriptures derive*

their Authority: which question is also propounded sometimes in other terms, as, *How wee know them to be the Word of God*, or, *Why we beleeve them to be so*':

> As far as they differ not from the Laws of Nature, there is no doubt, but they are the Law of God, and carry their Authority with them, legible to all men that have the use of naturall reason: but this is no other Authority, then that of all other Morall Doctrine consonant to Reason; the Dictates whereof are Laws, not *made*, but *Eternall*. (XXXIII/21–2, 205)

10 Cf. *Republic* 439d.

11: Rationality and the Problem of *Reason*

1 Insofar as the Lawyer deals in both '*Lawes*, and *facts*,' as in my example, his reasoning will necessarily be a *mix* of general principles and particular facts. As such, then, his argument will *not* exemplify Reason as Hobbes describes it: 'nothing but *Reckoning* (that is, Adding and Subtracting) of the Consequences of *generall* names agreed upon.'

2 Hobbes's equating deductive logic with the whole of Reason is quite common in modern times. It is a view that has been especially prominent in Philosophy of Science over the past century. The Logical Positivists, for example, argued that 'concept formation,' being part of the invention of scientific theories, belongs to the so-called Context of Discovery, and as such is essentially non-rational. On this view, reason can be brought to bear only in the Context of Justification, wherein the adequacy of theories (including their 'conceptual frameworks') is assessed in light of empirical evidence. The very influential Karl Popper is famously associated with the contention that there is no such thing as Induction. Thomas Kuhn's much-debated claim that fundamental 'paradigm shifts' in the sciences are non-rational similarly presumes that only deduction is rational. Cultural relativists employ a formally identical view to argue that one can reason only *within* the standards of a given way of life, but that one cannot rationally assess whole cultures.

3 As this analogy, along with the rest of Hobbes's Introduction, is rich with implications for adequately interpreting the whole text, I shall offer a fuller consideration of it in a subsequent chapter (18).

4 The formality of this claim might remind one of Sokrates's inquiry into what Polemarchos thought the poet Simonides meant by saying 'That it is just to give to each what is owed,' which under interrogation the young man interpreted to mean 'that it is just to give to everyone what is *fitting*' –

something else entirely, at least compared with what is ordinarily meant by 'owed' (*Republic* 331e–332c). The idea of Equity in relation to Reason and natural Justice will be treated extensively in chapter 16.

5 *The* classical account of Prudence is, of course, that which Aristotle presents most systematically in Book Six of his *Nikomachean Ethics*. Prudence is especially important to his understanding of the moral virtues, being the power of judgment whereby one recognizes the appropriate mean between extremes. Hobbes obviously intends his simplistic account of prudence and virtue to contrast with that of Aristotle, but to what deeper purpose one can only speculate.

6 Why Hobbes chooses to treat Prudence in this fashion is puzzling. Perhaps he regards this as merely a formalization and 'politic' ratification of the popular understanding, akin to his treatment of Reason as nothing but deduction/calculation. And he could have found support in Plato's *Republic* for this being the popular view of Prudence; speaking of one who has escaped the Cave and so now despises what passes for wisdom there, Sokrates asks Glaukon: 'If then there were some honours and praises among them which they bestowed on one another, and prizes for the one who is quickest to make out the things that go by, and most remembers which are accustomed to pass before, and which after, and which at the same time, and [so] is most able to divine what is to come, do you opine he would be desirous of these [rewards], and envy those who were so honoured and empowered?' (516c–d).

7 Is this not a somewhat curious view for a supposed Determinist, who must believe the Future to be preordained, hence implicit in the Past, much as the conclusions of a deductive argument are implicit in its premises?

8 As for this last point, Hobbes seemingly maintains it to the end. Discussing 'What Philosophy is' ('*the Knowledge acquired by Reasoning*') in his penultimate chapter, he insists 'that we are not to account as any part thereof, that originall knowledge called Experience, in which consisteth Prudence: Because it is not attained by Reasoning, but found as well in Brute Beasts, as in Man; and is but a Memory of successions of events in times past, wherein the omission of every little circumstance altering the effect, frustrateth the expectation of the most Prudent: whereas nothing is produced by Reasoning aright, but generall, eternall, and immutable Truth' (XLVI/2, 367).

9 Cf. *Phaedrus* 265d–266b.

10 *Republic* 537c. With the Platonic account in mind, Hobbes's treatment of Reason in *De Corpore* is of more than passing interest – and not only for the substance of the account found there, but for what it shows about his writing technique. The book virtually begins with definitions of philosophy and of reasoning:

> 2. PHILOSOPHY *is such knowledge of effects or appearances, as we acquire by true ratiocination from the knowledge we have first of their causes or generation: And again, of such causes or generations as may be from knowing first their effects ...* By RATIOCINATION, I mean *computation.* Now to compute, is either to collect the sum of many things that are added together, or to know what remains when one thing is taken out of another. *Ratiocination,* therefore, is the same with *addition* and *subtraction*; and if any man add *multiplication* and *division*, I will not be against it, seeing multiplication is nothing but addition of equals one to another, and division nothing but a subtraction of equals one from another, as often as is possible. So that all ratiocination is comprehended in these two operations of the mind, addition and subtraction.

Thus the second numbered article of the first chapter of Book One of *De Corpore*. It closely resembles the first half of the first paragraph of chapter 5 of *Leviathan* ('*Of* REASON, *and* SCIENCE'). But compare both with what is said in the first numbered article of the *sixth* chapter of Book One ('Of Method'):

> The first beginnings, therefore, of knowledge, are the phantasms of sense and imagination; and that there be such phantasms we know well enough by nature; but to know why they be, or from what causes they proceed, is the work of ratiocination; which consists (as is said above, in the 1st Chapter, Art. 2) in *composition*, and *division* or *resolution*. There is therefore no method, by which we find out the causes of things, but is either *compositive* or *resolutive*, or *partly compositive*, and *partly resolutive*. And the resolutive is commonly called *analytical* method, as the compositive is called *synthetical*. (translation that of vol. 1 in *The English Works of Thomas Hobbes*, William Molesworth, ed. [London: John Bohn, 1836])

Not incidentally, Hobbes's use of the terms 'phantasm' and 'idol' in *Leviathan* squares with Sokrates's use of 'phantasm' (φάντασμα: appearance, image, phantom) and 'idol' (ἐίδωλον: image, spectre; esp. an image in the mind, a vision) in Plato's *Republic* (cf., e.g., 510a1, 516a7, b5, 532c1, c2; but also 443c4). Hobbes himself hints at the relationship, speaking of 'Images, which are originally and most properly called *Ideas*, and IDOLS, and derived from the language of the Graecians, with whom the word *Εἴδω* signifieth to *See*. They are also called PHANTASMES, which is in the same language, *Apparitions*. And from these images it is that one of the faculties of mans Nature, is called the *Imagination*' (XLV/14, 358).

11 *The New Organon*, Fulton H. Anderson, ed. (Indianapolis: Bobbs-Merrill, 1960), Book One, aph. LV, 54–5.

12 Cf. *Republic* 331e ff.

13 As I shall argue in a subsequent chapter (19), this must be Hobbes's actual view of pre-civil history.

14 Rightly or wrongly, Hobbes later would seem to call this claim into question by observing, 'To have a known Right to Soveraign Power, is so popular a quality, as he that has it needs no more, for his own part, to turn the hearts of his Subjects to him, but that they see him able absolutely to govern his own Family' (XXX/29, 185).

15 The 'solitary' claim seems particularly questionable on both logical and empirical grounds, not to mention certain indications elsewhere in Hobbes's text – a point I shall address at length in chapter 19.

16 Strictly speaking, one must use this formulation to distinguish the Natural laws that Hobbes presents in the fourteenth and fifteenth chapters (those being the 'means of the conservation of men in multitudes; and which onely concern the doctrine of Civill Society') from the countless other 'dictates of Reason' that tend merely to 'the destruction of particular men; as Drunkenness, and all other parts of Intemperance; which may therefore also be reckoned amongst those things which the Law of Nature hath forbidden' (XV/34, 78). For the sake of convenience, however, most references to 'the Laws of Nature' simply mean those 'Lawes of Nature dictating Peace' which Hobbes specified. The slight ambiguity in their number arises from the rather problematical 'law' that Hobbes adds in his '*REVIEW* and *CONCLUSION*' (par. 5, 390).

17 I believe there is, and I will explore the differing implications of the various versions in chapter 13. But in any case, if 'adding' is all that is involved, one ought always to arrive at the same formulation.

18 Aristotle argues that humans alone (a) can perceive good and bad, just and unjust, and (b) have language especially *in order* to deliberate about what is just and mutually advantageous, and that this is evidence that man is by nature a political animal (*Politics* 1253a14–18). In his typically oblique way, Hobbes acknowledges Aristotle's argument:

> It is true, that certain living creatures, as Bees, and Ants, live sociably one with another, (which are therefore by *Aristotle* numbred amongst Politicall creatures;) and yet have no other direction, than their particular judgements and appetites; nor speech, whereby one of them can signifie to another, what he thinks expedient for the common benefit: and therefore some man may perhaps desire to know, why Man-kind cannot do the same. (XVII/6, 86)

I shall examine certain implications of Hobbes's six-element response in later chapters.

19 By so narrowing the conception of Reason to relations among general terms, it would seem that Hobbes is intent upon the closest possible identification of Reason with Science (thus their being treated in a single chapter).

20 As I discussed in note 15 of chapter 4.

21 Cf. *Republic* 369b–370c ff.

22 In comparison with the traditional account, Hobbes's treatment of Trust, or Faith, is conspicuously thin. First of all, though Hobbes uses 'trust' and its cognates over four dozen times, and 'faith' over fourteen dozen, he neither describes nor fully defines either term. Nor does he expressly and unqualifiedly identify them (i.e., as two names for the same thing); the closest he comes is in speaking '*Of the* Ends, *or* Resolutions of Discourse':

> When a mans Discourse beginneth not at Definitions ... [but] at some saying of another, of whose ability to know the truth, and of whose honesty in not deceiving, he doubteth not; and then the Discourse is not so much concerning the Thing, as the Person; and the Resolution is called Beleefe, and Faith; *faith, in* the man; *Beleefe,* both *of* the man, and *of* the truth of what he sayes. So that in Beleefe are two opinions; one of the saying of the man; the other of his virtue. To *have faith in,* or *trust to,* or *beleeve a man,* signifie the same thing; namely, an opinion of the veracity of the man: But to *beleeve what is said,* signifieth only an opinion of the truth of the saying. (VII/5, 31)

In any case, it is clear from Hobbes's first use of 'trust' that he regards it as a variable in both of the ways I have specified: 'And though by mens actions wee do discover their designes sometimes; yet to do it without comparing them with our own, and distinguishing all circumstances, by which the case may come to be altered, is to decypher without a key, and be for the most part deceived, by too much trust, or by too much diffidence; as he that reads, is himself a good or evil man' (Introd/3, 2).

12: Science and the Problem of *Language*

1 *Politics* 1253a7–17. That Man is a *political* animal means much more than that he is a 'social' or 'herd' animal (i.e., gregarious). It implies that everything requisite for well-ordered political life – such as the use of money, common units of measure, manners, ceremonies, and a multitude of other conventions – is in a sense natural to man; so, too, the use of *logos* ('rational

speech') as the primary means of ordering and conducting community life.

2 The recent controversy about the possibility/impossibility of there being a private language arose from the analysis Wittgenstein provides in *Philosophical Investigations* (New York: Macmillan, 1953), arts. 241–315. Reactions, both pro and con, can be conveniently sampled in E.D. Klemke, ed., *Essays on Wittgenstein* (Urbana: University of Illinois Press, 1971). One of the more trenchant critiques of Wittgenstein's position is that of Stanley Rosen in *Nihilism* (New Haven: Yale University Press, 1969), ch. 1.

3 Albeit his dubious treatment of Thought as something entirely separate from Reason will not suffice for the task of inventing language.

4 In fact, remembering what names refer to seems to increase rather than diminish the demands on one's memory. For example, when a teacher meets a new class of students, he must first learn to recognize them, then in addition learn their names. Still, there is something right about Hobbes's claim, which would imply that we are biologically pre-adapted to 'process' information 'for storage' in verbal terms.

5 Pt I, par. 32. of *Discourse on Inequality* in *The Discourses and Other Early Political Writings*, Victor Gourevitch, ed. and trans. (Cambridge: Cambridge University Press, 1997), 149).

6 The complexity of Hobbes's 'State of Nature' is the subject of chapters 19 and 20 in Part Two.

7 While the *correspondence* of the fourth 'abuse' of Speech works tolerably well, the rationale for *why* it is actually an *abuse* is puzzling: 'for seeing nature hath armed living creatures, some with teeth, some with horns, some with hands, to grieve an enemy, it is abuse of Speech, to grieve him with the tongue' (IV/4, 13). What kind of argument is *that*? Surely one has 'the Right by Nature' to use any and all means one has – teeth, horns, hooves, claws, hands, feet, rocks, clubs, as well as the most dispiriting, demeaning, altogether painful insults conceivable – 'to grieve an *enemy.*' True, Hobbes's Eighth Natural Law forbids expressing hatred or contempt towards one's fellow *citizens*. But he several times assures us that in a condition of war, one has a right 'of doing any thing,' that one 'may seek, and use, all helps, and advantages of war,' etc.

8 Charles Cantalupo observes, '*Leviathan* brandishes more metaphors about sovereignty than any work of English Literature other than Shakespeare's *Richard II.*' *A Literary* Leviathan: *Thomas Hobbes's Masterpiece of Language* (Lewisburg, PA: Bucknell University Press, 1991), 33.

9 The term 'metaphor' comes directly from classical Greek rhetoric, *metaphora*, from the verb *metapherein*: 'to carry over,' 'carry across,' hence

'transfer,' 'change,' 'alter.' Thus, the very term 'metaphor' originates as a metaphoric usage.

10 For a sampling, see the bibliography supplied for the discussion of 'metaphor' in Paul Edwards, ed., *The Encyclopedia of Philosophy* (New York: Macmillan, 1967), 284–9.

11 In the dialogical essay 'On Heresy,' which Hobbes appended to the Latin version of *Leviathan*, he argues that proven atheists deserve to be exiled because they cannot be obliged to keep faith in covenants by swearing an oath (par. 38). On the other hand, in *Leviathan* he observes, somewhat equivocally, 'It appears also, that the Oath addes nothing to the Obligation. For a Covenant, if lawfull, binds in the sight of God, without the Oath, as much as with it: if unlawfull, bindeth not at all; though it be confirmed with an Oath' (XIV/33, 71; in the Latin version, 'by force of natural law' replaces 'in the sight of God').

12 One would not conclude this from examining Hobbes's own use of 'universal' and its cognates (which occur some four dozen times in his text). For example, he speaks of men abandoning their 'universal Right' to all things upon entering a Commonwealth (XV/3, 72), and states that 'Naturall Lawes being Eternall, and Universall, are all Divine' (XXVI/ 39, 148); as for *supernatural* revelations of God's will, 'there have not been any Universall Lawes so given' (XXXI/3, 187). And in speaking about 'the whole number of Christians,' he insists there is not 'an Universall Church that hath any authority over them,' nor any 'Universall Soveraigne of all Christendome' – claiming this on political, historical, and Scriptural grounds, not as a matter of either ontology or linguistics (XXXIII/24, 206; cf. also XLVII/7, 382; /21, 386; /23, 386). Now, this may be simply a semantic matter, Hobbes carelessly using the word 'universal' in two entirely different ways (despite his emphatic pronouncement on what he knows is a major metaphysical issue in philosophy); or, it is *not* simply a matter of semantics, which opens up other possibilities.

13 Dedicatory Letter of *De Cive*: '*There are two maxims which are surely both true*: Man is a God to Man, *and* Man is a wolf to Man. *The former is true of the relations of citizens with each other, the latter of relations between commonwealths*' (3–4). Francis Bacon provides his own rationale for the view: 'Again, let a man only consider what a difference there is between the life of men in the most civilized province of Europe, and the wildest and most barbarous districts of New India [i.e., America]; he will feel it be great enough to justify the saying that 'man is a god to man,' not only in regard to aid and benefit, but also by comparison of condition. And this difference comes not from soil, not from climate, not from race, but from the arts.' *New*

Organon, Fulton H. Anderson, ed. (Indianapolis: Bobbs-Merrill, 1960), Book One, aph. 129.

14 This is sufficient to show the inadequacy of the 'arithmetical' notion of Reason, such as is supposedly illustrated in the case of 'Logicians ... adding together *two Names* to make an *Affirmation*' (V/1, 32), which would imply that the order in which they were combined is as irrelevant as in adding together two numbers.

15 The notion that Imagination and Memory are essentially the same thing, simply the decaying motions first introduced into the brain by motions in the objects sensed – 'From whence it followeth, that the longer the time is, after the sight, or Sense of any object, the weaker is the Imagination ... So that distance of time, and of place, hath one and the same effect on us' (II/3, 5) – is so preposterous that one is at a loss to explain why Hobbes bothered to introduce it. Anyone who gave it a moment's thought would immediately notice that it in no way squares with one's psychic experience. Memories do not decay with anything like the uniformity this mechanistic account implies (as nicely shown by the truism that most everyone remembers how and where they first learned of some major historical happening, e.g., 'Pearl Harbor,' 'the assassination of President Kennedy,' 'the terrorists' attack on the World Trade Center,' whereas they could not remember most of what went on right next to them yesterday).

16 Noam Chomsky, while acknowledging that there are many legitimate reasons for studying language, continues:

> [F]or me personally the most compelling reason ... is that it is tempting to regard language, in the traditional phrase, as 'a mirror of the mind.' I do not mean by this simply that the concepts expressed and distinctions developed in normal language use give us insight into the patterns of thought and the world of 'common sense' constructed by the human mind. More intriguing, to me at least, is the possibility that by studying language we may discover abstract principles that govern its structure and use, principles that are universal by biological necessity and not mere historical accident, that derive from mental characteristics of the species. A human language is a system of remarkable complexity. To come to know a human language would be an extraordinary intellectual achievement for a creature not specifically designed to accomplish this task. A normal child acquires this knowledge on relatively slight exposure and without specific training. ... For the conscious mind, not specifically designed for the purpose, it remains a distant goal to reconstruct and comprehend what the child has done intuitively and with minimal effort. Thus lan-

guage is a mirror of mind in a deep and significant sense. It is a product of human intelligence, created anew in each individual by operations that lie far beyond the reach of will or consciousness. [Aristotle would agree.]

By studying the properties of natural languages, their structure, organization, and use, we may hope to gain some understanding of the specific characteristics of human intelligence. We may hope to learn something about human nature; something significant, if it is true that human cognitive capacity is the truly distinctive and most remarkable characteristic of the species. (*Reflections on Language* [New York: Pantheon Books, 1975], 4–5)

I am aware of no other writer who expresses with such clarity the so-far-intractable problem of developing a plausible scientific theory either of how language works or of how it is learned. As Chomsky notes, 'Even the relevant concepts seem lacking; certainly, no intellectually satisfying principles have been proposed that have explanatory force, though the questions are very old. It is not excluded that human science-forming capacities simply do not extend to this domain, *or any domain involving the exercise of the will*, so that for humans, these questions will *always* be shrouded in mystery' (25; emphasis added). The whole second half of his valuable book is devoted to expounding 'The Problems and Mysteries in the Study of Human Language.' For all of the excellent research of the past three decades since Chomsky offered his assessment, there has been little that challenges its essentials and much that confirms his thesis on biological pre-adaptation.

Appreciative of what a (perhaps impossible) challenge it is to explain what language is and how it works, one may excuse Hobbes's failure to provide a convincing account. Still, the theoretical inadequacies of his attempt are so glaring – and by extension, so too the superficiality of his treatment of the human mind – that one must presume he is aware that such is the case and merely intends his account to be sufficient for the purpose of presenting his political prescription.

17 While there is a vast amount of recent research providing evidence of the extent to which interpretation is an intrinsic part of both visual and aural perception (and especially of the human mind's natural aptitude for recognizing significant form), it merely confirms what a careful analysis of ordinary perceptual experience readily reveals: that perception relies heavily on one's antecedent understanding of, and familiarity with, one's own portion of the world – an understanding initially shaped by the language one learns.

18 Cf. *Phaedrus* 265e.

19 Perhaps Hobbes's scepticism about the utility and/or the possibility of truly

understanding such Forms, and especially their causal efficacy in governing every aspect of the individuals they comprise, accounts for his radical disclaimer about knowing 'natures.' Alternatively, he may see it as the implication of the distinction between Primary and Secondary qualities (discussed in chapter 9 above), or of the 'conditionall' character of all scientific knowledge, or because one can truly know only that which one makes (i.e., causes). Whatever the case, the disclaimer comes in the context of his insistence that we have no basis for disputing about the attributes of God: 'For it is supposed, that in this naturall Kingdome of God, there is no other way to know any thing, but by naturall Reason; that is, from the Principles of naturall Science; which are so farre from teaching us any thing of Gods nature, as they cannot teach us our own nature, nor the nature of the smallest creature living' (XXXI/33, 191).

20 When later Hobbes explains, 'Of which Words, some are the names of the Things conceived; as the names of all sorts of Bodies, that work upon the Senses, and leave an Impression in the Imagination: Others are the names of the Imaginations themselves; that is to say, of those Ideas, or mentall Images we have of all things wee see or remember' (XLVI/16, 372), his radical nominalism still obtains. For these named 'Ideas, or mentall Images' are all of particular things sensed. Thus, A.P. Martinich would seem to have accurately rendered Hobbes's expressed position in the entry on 'Ideas' in *A Hobbes Dictionary* (Oxford: Blackwell, 1995), 141–2: 'Unlike Plato's ideas, Hobbes's are all individuals and only refer to individuals.'

21 A posture conveniently laid out by Richard von Mises in the introductory chapter of *Positivism: A Study in Human Understanding* (New York: Dover, 1968). Moreover, given the natural appeal of a 'no-nonsense' approach to life, there will always be 'positivists' of one stripe or another.

22 Hobbes frequently appeals to ordinary usage himself for ratification of his claims, citing what 'we say,' or what 'men call [whatever].' However, because his doing so can have the – possibly misleading – rhetorical effect of implying that his own views on a subject are the same as those he cites, one should guard against this presumption, as well as scrutinize carefully what he presents as ordinary usage. For example – as I shall later show – Hobbes does not himself subscribe to the radical subjectivism implicit in what he rightly contends most people mean when they say something is 'good': that it gives them pleasure.

23 The Latin version of this chapter differs considerably (included in Curley's edition of *Leviathan*, 49–50).

24 This seems of a piece with the definition of 'Philosophy' that begins the penultimate chapter of *Leviathan*, so steeped in Baconian rhetoric: 'By PHI-LOSOPHY, is understood *the Knowledge acquired by Reasoning, from the*

Manner of the Generation of any thing, to the Properties; or from the Properties, to some possible Way of Generation of the same; to the end to bee able to produce, as far as matter, and humane force permit, such Effects, as humane life requireth' (XLVI/1, 367). I shall have much more to say about this passage in the beginning chapter of Part Two.

25   Some, such as Rudolph Carnap, went further, formally distinguishing kinds of concepts, and arguing for the inherent superiority of Quantitative concepts over Comparative and Classificatory ones. See *The Philosophic Foundations of Physics*, Martin Gardner, ed. (New York: Basic Books, 1966), ch. 5.

26   This is a common misconception about Hobbes – one that I for a long time shared – that he has a 'Humpty Dumpty' theory of linguistic meaning, as J.W.A. Watkins so amusingly put it in *Hobbes's System of Ideas* (London: Hutchinson, 1965), 104–5. And in mitigation of my and other scholars' culpability, this mistake is quite easy to make, given the impression left by many things Hobbes says, especially about the role of the Sovereign in establishing whatever *authoritative* definitions are necessary for the orderly functioning of a regime. And we may all take comfort from the fact that no less a critic than Leibniz seems to have wrongly interpreted Hobbes in the same manner (from 'Meditations on Knowledge, Truth, and Ideas,' in *Philosophical Essays*, Roger Ariew and Daniel Garber, eds and trans. [Indianapolis: Hackett, 1989]):

> And so we also have a distinction between *nominal definitions*, which contain only marks of a thing to be distinguished from other things, and *real definitions*, from which one establishes that a thing is possible. And with this we give our due to Hobbes, who claimed that truths are arbitrary, since they depend on nominal definitions, without considering the fact that the reality of a definition is not a matter of decision and that not just any notions can be joined to one another. Nominal definitions are insufficient for perfect knowledge [*scientia*] except when one establishes in another way that the thing defined is possible. (26; cf. 57)

27   It is somewhat curious that this is *not* how Hobbes originally characterized the first 'corresponding' abuse of Speech, warning then only of 'the *inconstancy* of the signification of [one's] words' (IV/4, 13). This is but one of many statements that could be seen as fitting the conventionalist view, and so has contributed to the mistaken assessment referred to in the preceding note.

28   Bacon warns time and again against the hazard of casting definitions prematurely, that is, on the basis of an inadequate assemblage of relevant particu-

lars. He stresses the philosophic virtue of *patience*, and most of all patience in collecting adequate Natural Histories upon which to base one's concepts and 'axioms,' rising inductively a careful step at a time to the highest generalities. In his *New Organon*, for example:

> There are and can be only two ways of searching into and discovering truth. The one flies from the senses and particulars to the most general axioms, and from these principles, the truth of which it takes for settled and immovable, proceeds to judgment and the discovery of middle axioms. And this way is now in fashion. The other derives axioms from the senses and particulars, rising by a gradual and unbroken ascent, so that it arrives at the most general axioms last of all. This is the true way, but as yet untried. (Book One, aph. XIX)

Hobbes, as noted, says nothing about the conduct of empirical inquiry, nor even so much as mentions induction. Perhaps this is because he believes that Bacon said all that needs saying about the matter, and thus he focuses attention exclusively on the results.

29   And is not something like this true of much of what today is studied scientifically? For an ethologist to study the territorial requirements of cougars (say), he must have some preliminary knowledge of what is a 'cougar.' Upon further study, he may discover there are actually several distinguishable versions of these big cats, subspecies that are not distinguished in ordinary language; in this case, he may himself affix to each kind a scientific name that indicates both its distinctness and its kinship with the others. But the fact remains, it is only on the basis of 'pre-scientific' knowledge of how 'cougars' *look* (the original meaning of the Greek words ἰδέα and ἐῖδος) that he knows what he is 'looking for.' Similar remarks apply to meteorologists studying 'hurricanes,' astronomers studying 'comets,' agronomists seeking the causes of various forms of 'blight,' mineralogists studying the composition of 'granite' or 'marble,' and a host of other scientific specialties that have developed since Hobbes's day.

30   In the course of speaking about laws, however, Hobbes himself casts some doubt on the realism of this provision: 'For the signification of almost all words, are either in themselves, or in the metaphoricall use of them, ambiguous; and may be drawn in argument, to make many senses' (XXVI/26, 145). And in arguing that 'the Law is more easily understood by few, than many words,' he observes: 'For all words are subject to ambiguity; and therefore multiplication of words in the body of the Law, is multiplication of ambiguity' (XXX/22, 182). However, one might suggest that in these

instances Hobbes means to speak only of ordinary language, not to the technical vocabularies of the sciences. Still, the language of the law is also expected to be quite precise; and Hobbes does say 'all words are subject to ambiguity.'

31 The Latin version is a bit more nuanced, characterizing Geometry as 'virtually the only precise science.'

32 Hobbes knows precisely where: in Cicero's dialogue, *De Divinatione*, II.lvii.119. The context is that of 'Marcus Cicero' addressing earlier claims by 'Quintus Cicero,' who defends the Stoic assimilation of divination with philosophy. Quintus had invoked the authority of Plato in support of the possibility that dreams may be a reliable source of certain truths, citing the pre-sleep regimen Plato has Sokrates recommend at the beginning of Book Nine of his *Republic* (571d–572b). To this Quintus adds the reported practice of the Pythagoreans of avoiding beans so that one's sleep not be disturbed by flatulence (I.xxix–xxx.60–3). It is with respect to the latter notion that Marcus observes, 'Somehow or other no statement is too absurd for some philosophers to make' (as per the Loeb translation by William Armistead Falconer [London: William Heinemann, 1946]. Hobbes's entire critique of Revelation would seem to be indebted to this work by Cicero – who, needless to add, did *not* rely therein upon geometry.

33 Important truths nicely illustrated in Plato's *Meno* by his having Sokrates help a slave boy discover for himself the Pythagorean theorem, and by a process, moreover, that depends crucially on the boy's being able to recognize mistakes in reasoning, and so not persist in them (82b ff). There are several indications that Hobbes especially valued this dialogue. I have discussed its profound – but generally overlooked – *political* significance in 'The Strange Misperception of Plato's *Meno*,' in *Politics, Philosophy, Writing*, Zdravko Planinc, ed. (Columbia: University of Missouri Press, 2001).

34 This distinction, traceable more or less directly to Kant, was near and dear to Logical Positivists. As such, it received a lot of critical attention over the years. The doctrine that all valid judgments and knowledge claims are of one kind or the other leaves the validity of the Analytic-Synthetic distinction itself in limbo. For in claiming that all knowledge is of one kind or the other, it must itself be one or the other. If it is regarded as analytic, one must be able to establish whether it is true simply from the meaning of the terms, which in this case goes nowhere, and in any event – according to the distinction – would say nothing about the world (i.e., about the kinds of knowledge that actually exist). Whereas, if it is regarded as synthetic, it requires empirical investigation to establish whether it is true. However, such an investigation

would necessarily be circular, since its validity would be presumed in determining whether something was or was not knowledge (and if so, what kind); and even were this investigation somehow possible, its status would still be inconclusive since, like any empirical generalization, it would remain open to refutation by a single, as yet undiscovered, counterexample. Thus the claim, 'All knowledge is either Analytic or Synthetic,' is self-refuting, since for it to be true there must be a third kind of knowledge – as Plato and Aristotle allow for by virtue of 'rational intuition' (*noësis*), and as Euclid presumes with respect to the basic, 'self-evident' truths on which geometry is based.

35 *Posterior Analytics* 89b23–4.

36 Thus, as that great Deducer, Descartes, acknowledges, deductions from 'the principles or first causes of all that is or can be in the world' and 'from certain seeds of truth that are in our souls' can carry one only so far. To determine from among the logical possibilities which ones actually exist in Nature, one must turn to empirical investigation, including making use of 'many particular experiments.' *Discourse on Method* in *The Philosophical Writings of Descartes*, vol. 1, J. Cottingham, R. Stoothoff, and D. Murdoch, trans. (Cambridge: Cambridge University Press,1985), Part Six, par. 3.

37 Hobbes returns to this example in his all-important penultimate chapter, there expressing himself differently, and somewhat more clearly: 'when we say *a Man, is, a living Body*, wee mean not that the *Man* is one thing, the *Living Body* another, and the *Is*, or *Beeing* a third: but that the *Man*, and the *Living Body* is the same thing; because the Consequence, *If hee bee a Man, hee is a living Body*, is a true Consequence, signified by that word *Is*' (XLVI/17, 372).

38 According to Noel Malcolm, *Aspects of Hobbes* (Oxford: Oxford University Press, 2002), Hobbes spent some of his free time 'in the stimulating company of the lawyers John Selden and John Vaughan, and the physicians William Harvey and Charles Scarborough' (21). Malcolm notes that Hobbes engaged in various empirical as well as theoretical scientific work, for example in optics and chemistry, adding: 'It also seems likely that he had dissected deer with William Harvey' (320). Hobbes lauds Harvey in the Dedicatory Letter of *De Corpore*: 'the science of *man's body*, the most profitable part of natural science, was first discovered with admirable sagacity by our countryman Doctor Harvey, principal Physician to King James and King Charles, in his books of the *Motion of the Blood*, and of the *Generation of Living Creatures*.' Clearly, then, Hobbes was aware of the potential benefits a sound understanding of human anatomy could bring.

39 Cf. *Posterior Analytics* 90b2–25 ff.

40 *Republic* 511b–d.

41 As in the sixth part of his 'Plan of the Great Instauration,' which precedes his *New Organon*, 28–9.
42 *On the Lodestone and Magnetic Bodies*, P. Fleury Mottelay, trans., vol. 28 of *Great Books of the Western World* (Chicago: Encyclopaedia Britannica, 1952).
43 Andrew Motte's translation, as revised by Florian Cajori (Berkeley: University of California Press, 1934).
44 Silvanus P. Thompson, trans., vol. 34 of *Great Books of the Western World* (Chicago: Encyclopaedia Britannica, 1952), 551.

13: Honour and the Problem of *Natural Law*

1 This view of Justice in relation to Nature will be more fully treated in subsequent chapters (mainly in 16).
2 A question worth asking is *why* Hobbes *divided* his Natural Laws as he did, introducing the first two in chapter 14, the remaining seventeen in the following chapter. An obvious possibility is that we are to see the first two as universally applicable (thus, an individual is *'to seek Peace, and follow it'* regardless of whether in the State of Nature or Civil Society), with the Second Law showing the way *out* of the former and into the latter: *'That a man be willing, when others are so too, as farre-forth, as for Peace, and defence of himselfe he shall think it necessary, to lay down this right to all things; and be contented with so much liberty against other men, as he would allow other men against himselfe'* (XIV/5, 64–5); whereas the *'other Lawes of Nature'* all pertain directly to the well-ordering of a Commonwealth.
     There is another possibility, however, itself suggested by Hobbes's characterizing his Second Law as itself equivalent to 'that Law of the Gospell,' which he expresses as *'Whatsoever you require that others should do to you, that do ye to them'* – one of the several times Hobbes invokes the so-called Golden Rule in connection with the Natural Laws, expressing it sometimes in the positive ('do unto others,' as *per* both instances in the Gospels: Matthew 7:12 and Luke 6:31), other times in the negative ('do not to others,' as in the Latin version which Hobbes supplies immediately following the English version quoted above). According to the synoptic Gospels, Jesus also singled out two divine 'Laws' as fundamental when a lawyer, attempting to entrap him, asked, 'Which is the great commandment in the law?' Jesus answered, 'Thou shalt love the Lord thy God with all thy heart, and with all thy soul, and with all thy mind. This is the first and great commandment. And the second is like unto it. Thou shalt love thy neighbour as thyself. On these two commandments hang all the law and the prophets' (Matthew 22:36–40; cf. Mark 12:28–31; Luke 10:25–8; Romans 13:8–10).

Comparing Hobbes's two basic 'dictates of Reason' with the two summary commandments of Jesus is instructive.

3 The one possible exception comes in his discussion of subjects' liberties, where he speaks of 'allowing [the Sovereign] to kill me.' But the context implies that this is nothing more than the implication of 'my' having authorized all of a Sovereign's actions (XXI/14, 112). Typical of Hobbes's invocation of Natural Right is his clarifying that, while no subject has the liberty 'To resist the Sword of the Common-wealth, in defence of another man, guilty, or innocent,' the case is altogether different with respect to a multitude of men who 'have already resisted the Soveraign Power unjustly, or committed some Capital crime, for which every one of them expecteth death.' They *do* have the liberty to defend each other: 'For they but defend their lives, which the Guilty man may as well do, as the Innocent' (XXI/17, 112–13).

4 In his chapter on 'Civill Lawes,' Hobbes reiterates both the distinction and the warning that other writers fail to understand it properly:

> I find the words *Lex Civilis*, and *Jus Civile*, that is to say, *Law* and *Right Civil* , promiscuously used for the same thing, even in the most learned Authors; which neverthelesse ought not to be so. For *Right* is *Liberty*, namely that Liberty which the Civil Law leaves us; But *Civill Law* is an *Obligation*; and takes from us the Liberty which the Law of Nature gave us ... Insomuch as *Lex* and *Jus*, are as different as *Obligation* and *Liberty*. (XXVI/43, 150)

5 This is the case regardless of whether there is anything historical that might count as instituting a Commonwealth by explicit covenant. As I shall discuss in Part Two, the basic issue concerns how one properly understands one's relationship to an existing civil society, irrespective of how it came into being.

6 The dangers inherent in the pursuit and capture of desperate men is to be distinguished from the unsavouriness of carrying out executions and lesser forms of corporal punishment. Hobbes belatedly saw a need to address the latter in his 'Review and Conclusion':

> But I have omitted to set down who were the Officers appointed to doe Execution; especially in Capital Punishments; not then thinking it a matter of so necessary consideration, as I find it since. Wee know that generally in all Common-wealths, the Execution of Corporeall Punishments, was either put upon the Guards, or other Souldiers of the

Soveraign Power; or given to those, in whom want of means, contempt of honour, and hardnesse of heart, concurred, to make them sue for such an Office. (R&C/10, 392)

Hobbes apparently endorses this arrangement for discharging what he implies is a 'dishonourable Office.'

7 It is not as if Hobbes has ignored the importance of education. It is cited in his Introduction as a source of diversity in the objects of people's passions, hence of their 'difference of Witts' (VIII/14, 35; cf. XXV/13, 134). And he assures his readers that 'Faith, and Sanctity ... are not Miracles, but brought to passe by education, discipline, correction, and other naturall wayes' (XXIX/8, 169). However, there is no discussion of the inculcation of any of the virtues requisite to decent political life.

8 Cf. *Republic* 545a ff., 548c ff.; and Craig, *The War Lover: A Study of Plato's Republic* (Toronto: University of Toronto Press, 1994), passim.

9 In one of the most surprising passages in this often surprising book, Hobbes himself praises the person who has the courage to choose death rather than break faith or otherwise disgrace himself: 'For an unlearned man, that is in the power of an Idolatrous King, or State, if commanded on pain of death to worship before an Idoll, hee detesteth the Idoll in his heart, he doth well; though if he had the fortitude to suffer death, rather than worship it, he should doe better' (XLV/27, 362).

10 That a fear of dishonour can sometimes be a stronger motivation than fear of death is confirmed, albeit rather perversely, by the story of the suicidal maidens which Hobbes himself provides, apparently appropriated from Plutarch's *Moralia* ('Virtues of Women,' ch. XI). In what seemed a contagious demonic possession, many of the maids of Miletus hanged themselves, despite the best efforts of their families to prevent them. 'But one that suspected, that contempt of life in them, might proceed from some Passion of the mind, and supposing they did not contemne also their honour, gave counsel to the Magistrates, to strip such as so hang'd themselves, and let them hang out naked. This the story says cured that madnesse' (VIII/25, 37).

11 Thus, in buttressing with Scriptural interpretation his case for the unity of Church and State, he writes:

The maintenance of Civill Society, depending on Justice; and Justice on the power of Life and Death, and other lesse Rewards and Punishments, residing in them that have the Soveraignty of the Common-wealth; It is impossible a Common-wealth should stand, where any other than the Soveraign, hath a power of giving greater rewards than Life; and of inflicting greater punishments, than Death. Now seeing *Eternall Life* is a greater reward, than the *life present*; and *Eternall torment* a greater punishment than the *death of Nature*; It is a thing worthy to be well considered, of all men that desire (by obeying Authority) to avoid the calamities of Confusion, and Civill war, what is meant in holy Scripture, by *Life Eternall*, and *Torment Eternall*; and for what offences, and against whom committed, men are to be *Eternally tormented*; and for what actions, they are to obtain *Eternall life*. (XXXVIII/1, 238)

12   Somewhat curiously, Hobbes elsewhere suggests that a certain 'kind of Publique Ministers resembleth the Nerves, and Tendons that move the severall limbs of a body naturall' (XXIII/3, 124). There is no contradiction here insofar as rewards and punishments (versus patriotism, loyalty, philanthropy, or fear of enemies) are what move the ministers. Such is the view Hobbes proclaims in the first paragraph of his treatise: '*Reward* and *Punishment* (by which fastned to the seate of the Soveraignty, every joynt and member is moved to perform his duty) are the *Nerves*, that do the same in the Body Naturall' (Introd/1, 1).

13   Obviously, these *conventional* 'Lawes of Honour' must be distinguished from those Hobbes spoke of in describing conditions in the State of Nature:

> And in all places, where men have lived by small Families, to robbe and spoyle one another, has been a Trade, and so farre from being reputed against the Law of Nature, that the greater spoyles they gained, the greater was their honour; and men observed no other Lawes therein, but the Lawes of Honour; that is, to abstain from cruelty, leaving to men their lives, and instruments of husbandry. (XVII/2, 85)

One can see, however, some kinship between these 'natural' Laws of Honour, and those things Hobbes acknowledges to be 'Honourable by Nature,' such as magnanimity.

14: Nobility and the Problem of *Hedonism*

1   Frederick Vaughan, *The Tradition of Political Hedonism: From Hobbes to J. S. Mill* (New York: Fordham University Press, 1982), vii. The label 'political hedonism' was originally affixed to Hobbes's doctrine by Leo Strauss in *Natural Right and History* (Chicago: University of Chicago Press, 1953), 169.

2   *Republic* 508e–509b, 505a–b, 540a.

3 In the subsequent paragraph, Hobbes distinguishes three ways in which things can be good: 'Good in the Promise, that is *Pulchrum*; Good in Effect, as the end desired, which is called *Jucundum, Delightfull*; and Good as the Means, which is called *Vtile, Profitable*; and as many of Evil: for *Evill* in Promise is that they call *Turpe*; Evil in Effect, and End, is *Molestum, Unpleasant, Troublesome*; and Evil in the Means, *Inutile, Unprofitable, Hurtful*' (VI/8, 24–5). This tripartite scheme of classification invites comparison with that which Plato has Glaukon articulate and Sokrates approve in *Republic* 357b–d, and with Aristotle's three motives of choice and three of avoidance in *Nikomachean Ethics* 1104b30–3.

4 To cite but two important examples:

> For Morall Philosophy is nothing else but the Science of what is *Good*, and *Evill*, in the conversation, and Society of man-kind. *Good*, and *Evill*, are names that signifie our Appetites, and Aversions; which in different tempers, customes, and doctrines of men are different: And divers men, differ not onely in their Judgement, on the senses of what is pleasant, and unpleasant to the tast, smell, hearing, touch, and sight; but also of what is conformable, or disagreeable to Reason, in the actions of common life. Nay, the same man, in diverse times, differs from himselfe; and one time praiseth, that is, calleth Good, what another time he dispraiseth, and calleth Evill. (XV/40, 79)

> In the second place, I observe the *Diseases* of a Common-wealth, that proceed from the poyson of seditious doctrines; whereof one is, *that every private man is Judge of Good and Evill actions*. This is true in the condition of meer Nature, where there are no Civill Lawes; and also under Civill Government, in such cases as are not determined by the Law. (XXIX/6, 168)

5 In that case, then, Hobbes can be read as essentially agreeing with Sokrates, who elliptically makes this same point in the simplified psychology he provides in Book Four of Plato's *Republic* (435c–441c). Having established that the various desires are understandable only in terms of their distinct objects (e.g., 'hunger' as the desire for *food*, 'thirst' as the desire for *drink*; 437d–e), Sokrates himself introduces a complication: 'that no one desires drink [i.e., *simpliciter*], but *good* [or 'beneficial,' valuable'; *chrēstou*] drink, nor food, but *good* [*chrēstou*] food; for everyone desires the good things [*tōn agathōn*]' (438a). He responds with a discussion of what we might call relational qualities, such as greater/smaller, more/fewer, heavier/lighter, etc. To quote from

the more detailed analysis of this matter that I have provided elsewhere, 'The implication seems to be that good and bad, beneficial and harmful, when applied to the various objects of one's desires, are 'relative' in this same way. A given portion of a given kind of food at a given time for a given person is more-or-less beneficial, or a given drink more or less harmful, just as it is more or less large or small. None of these particular objects of desire is purely and absolutely good, just as none of them is absolutely large.' *The War Lover*, 89.

6 Cf. *Republic* 409a–d.

7 Hobbes uses the term 'bad' only seven times in the book; in most instances, it can be read as synonymous with 'evil' (which occurs 123 times); e.g., compare 'And that which is alternate Appetite, in Deliberating concerning Good and Evil' with 'And as the whole chain of Appetites alternate, in questions of Good, or Bad, is called *Deliberation*' (VII/2, 30; cf. XLVI/11, 369), and with 'from Daemons, or Spirits, either good, or bad' (VIII/24, 37; cf. XXXIV/15, 210). In the two instances concerning the quality of counsel, however, the synonymity may be questionable (XIX/9, 97; XLII/43, 284).

8 So Shakespeare has his Gratiano warn the Merchant Antonio against 'a willful stillness entertain, / With purpose to be dress'd in an opinion / Of wisdom, gravity, profound conceit' so as to be 'reputed wise' (*Merchant of Venice* 1.1.90–6).

9 'Happiness' occurs six times, all but one (at XXXI/9, 189) associated with the beneficence of God. 'Felicity' is used twenty-five times in the text (twenty-seven, if one includes 'felicities'), most notably in the title of notorious chapter 13, 'Of the NATURALL CONDITION of Mankind, as concerning their Felicity, and Misery.'

10 Having to do with claims of the supposed '*Universall Church*' (XXXIII/24, 206). Also, Hobbes does once distinguish the 'Common benefit' of the whole Polity from that of 'Bodies of Merchants' (XXII/20, 120).

11 Later, reviewing those same Rights, he reiterates that they include 'examining what Doctrines are conformable, or contrary to the Defence, Peace, and Good of the people' (XXX/3, 175; cf. /1, 175; /20, 182), while insisting that 'the good of the Soveraign and People, cannot be separated' (XXX/21, 182).

12 Reading Machiavelli should persuade one otherwise. With a wealth of history on his side, he insists 'that nothing is more difficult to handle, more doubtful of success, nor more dangerous to manage, than to put oneself at the head of introducing new orders.' Accordingly, he praises these four men as exemplifying great political founders. *The Prince*, Harvey Mansfield, ed. and trans. (Chicago: University of Chicago Press, 1985), ch. 6, 23–4).

13 Elsewhere in his text, Hobbes does employ 'indifference' in connection with our passionate reaction to things, but he attaches to it a pejorative connotation: 'And therefore, a man who has no great Passion for any of these things; but is as men terme it indifferent; though he may be so farre a good man, as to be free from giving offence; yet he cannot possibly have either a great Fancy, or much Judgement … For as to have no Desire, is to be Dead: so to have weak Passions, is Dulnesse'; on the other hand, 'to have Passions indifferently for every thing [is] GIDDINESSE, and *Distraction*; [whereas] to have stronger, and more vehement Passions for any thing, than is ordinarily seen in others, is that which men call MADNESSE' (VIII/16, 35). This last category might include Philosophy insofar as it presumes a passion for knowledge far beyond the ordinary. Plato's Sokrates, speaking as one who knows, characterizes it as a 'divine madness' (*Phaedrus* 245a, 249a–e ff).

14 'Admire(d)' is used four times, 'admiration' five times, and 'admirable' six times; a majority of these occur in some connection with God. For example, Hobbes's first mention of 'admire' is in dismissing those who mistakenly believe themselves divinely inspired, and so 'admire themselves; as being in the speciall grace of God Almighty' (VIII/22, 36; cf. XXXVII/6, 234).

15 Leo Strauss concludes his essay 'What Is Liberal Education?' by observing, 'Liberal education is liberation from vulgarity. The Greeks had a beautiful word for 'vulgarity'; they called it *apeirokalia*, lack of experience in things beautiful. Liberal education supplies us with experience in things beautiful.' *Liberalism Ancient and Modern* (New York: Basic Books, 1968), 8.

16 As does the sophist Protagoras in the Platonic dialogue that bears his name. Plato has Sokrates ask him, 'Then living pleasantly is good and living unpleasantly is bad?' Protagoras replies, 'If, that is, one lived taking pleasure in the noble [or, 'beautiful'; *kalois*] things' (351c). But since Protagoras relies upon nothing but genteel prejudice in distinguishing pleasures, Sokrates compels him to accept the validity of unqualified, 'vulgar' hedonism, and then proceeds to expose – most amusingly – its bizarre implications. The dialogue is a comic masterpiece, but surely also one of the most profound explorations ever crafted of the relation between *To Kalon* and Hedonism.

17 The two dozen ingredients of the Witches' brew in Shakespeare's *Macbeth* (4.1.4–38) provide an especially effective illustration of the repulsive power of the Ugly. Plato's Sokrates presents a more complicated example in his parable of Leontius and the Corpses (*Republic* 439e–440a). I have discussed the latter example in *The War Lover*, 97, 100–2.

18 *Beyond Good and Evil*, in *The Basic Writings of Nietzsche*, Walter Kaufmann, ed. and trans. (New York: Modern Library, 1966), aph. no. 78.

19 This presumes, moreover, that there are other than prudential grounds for concerning oneself with the pleasures and pains of other sentient beings, hence for attempting such a calculation. However, the main point is, if one cannot qualitatively rank pleasures, one cannot privilege those that are uniquely human (i.e., those of the mind and spirit).

20 And (then) is justice to others *good* only insofar as it is *pleasing* to *oneself*; and injustice bad merely because feeling indignation is painful (cf. VI/21, 26)?

21 The word 'noble' is not heard in Democratic societies as often as 'admirable' or synonymous terms (mainly for historical reasons, though egalitarian indoctrination figures as well).

22 While some female animals will vigorously defend their young, the notion that they will do so to the death is largely myth. As for the sometimes mortal combat of males competing to breed, this is clearly selfish.

23 Also for that same reason, there can be no legal *obligation* to attempt dangerous rescues of this sort. But this being so, it shows why The Noble is *higher* than The Legal. As Anthony Trollope has the Duke of Omnium admonish his rather feckless son, Lord Silverbridge (*The Duke's Children*, ch. 61):

> Do you recognise no duty but what the laws impose upon you? Should you be disposed to eat and drink in bestial excess, because the laws would not hinder you? Should you lie and sleep all the day, the law would say nothing! Should you neglect every duty which your position imposes on you, the law could not interfere! To such a one as you the law can be no guide. You should so live as not to come near the law – or to have the law to come near to you. From all evil against which the law bars you, you should be barred, at an infinite distance, by honour, by conscience, and nobility. Does the law require patriotism, philanthropy, self-abnegation, public service, purity of purpose, devotion to the needs of others who have been placed in the world below you? The law is a great thing – because men are poor and weak, and bad. And it is great, because where it exists in its strength, no tyrant can be above it. But between you and me there should be no mention of law as the guide of conduct. Speak to me of honour, and duty, and of nobility; and tell me what they require of you.

24 This is not a merely 'academic question.' Most professional militaries establish a hierarchy of awards (decorations and citations) for different degrees of proven valour or other martial prowess. So do civilian police forces and other emergency response agencies.

25 *Republic* 386a–b, 387b.

26 Such would seem to be the teaching of Plato's *Phaedo*.

15: Justice and the Problem of *Regimes*

1 Being one of 'two principles prior to reason' that together allegedly rule primitive man, namely that which 'inspires in us a natural repugnance to seeing any sentient Being, and especially any being like ourselves, perish or suffer.' *Discourse on Inequality* in *The Discourses and Other Early Political Writings*, Victor Gourevitch, ed. and trans. (Cambridge: Cambridge University Press, 1997), Preface, par. 9; cf. Pt I, par. 35 ff.

2 Hobbes never uses this phrase in *Leviathan*, though he once speaks of 'the state of meer Nature' (XX/4, 103), and of 'the condition of meer Nature, (which is a condition of Warre of every man against every man)' (XIV/18, 68), and of 'the ill condition, which man by meer Nature is actually placed in' (XIII/13, 63). He refers several times to man's 'natural condition,' and to the 'condition of Nature,' invariably equating it to a 'condition of Warre.'

3 Consider also the dialogue 'On Heresy' appended to the Latin edition of *Leviathan*, where Hobbes has 'B' say, 'The natural law is eternal, divine, and written only in the heart. But few people know how to look into their hearts and read what is written there. So they learn what is to be done and what is to be avoided from the written laws' (par. 34; as per the translation in Curley's edition of *Leviathan*, 528).

4 358b–367e. As I argue in *The War Lover: A Study of Plato's* Republic (Toronto: University of Toronto Press, 1994), 118–29, this is 'the most powerful one-two punch in the history of political philosophy. For first bold, musical, erotic Glaukon – appealing directly to nature – delivers a positive attack on the just life and eulogizes the unjust life. Then Adeimantos – that most careful, thoughtful, skeptical listener of what other men say – rips to shreds the conventional defence of the just life.'

5 There are certain clear *dis*-analogies between the situation of an individual in the State of Nature and that of a polity. States are not 'mobile' in the way that individual men are; thus it is usually only adjacent polities that are threats. Also, whatever the merits of Hobbes's arguments for there being a rough natural equality of individuals' faculties, nothing comparable can be claimed about polities – nor does Hobbes try to suggest otherwise. Instead, he again tacitly invokes immediate 'neighbours' in answering how large a commonwealth needs be: 'The Multitude sufficient to confide in for our Security, is not determined by any certain number, but by comparison with the Enemy we feare' (XVII/3, 86).

These dis-analogies are sufficient to invalidate Kant's argument that 'distress must force the states to make exactly the same decision (however difficult it may be for them) as that which man was forced to make, equally unwillingly, in his savage state – the decision to renounce his brutish freedom and seek calm and security within a law-governed constitution.' 'Seventh Proposition' of his 'Idea of a Universal History with a Cosmopolitan Purpose,' as per the translation by H.B.Nisbet in *Kant's Political Writings*, Hans Reiss, ed. (Cambridge University Press, 1970), 48.

6 In discussing how to deal with surplus population, Hobbes does subsequently declare in favour of the more humane alternative, though not expressly as a matter of justice: 'The multitude of poor, and yet strong people still encreasing, they are to be transplanted into Countries not sufficiently inhabited: where neverthelesse, they are not to exterminate those they find there; but constrain them to inhabit closer together, and not range a great deal of ground, to snatch what they find; but to court each little Plot with art and labour, to give them their sustenance in due season' (XXX/19, 181).

7 *Republic* 338e.

8 *Politics*, 1279a22–1281a2, though all of Book Three is pertinent. Hobbes's pairing 'Democracy' with 'Anarchy' rather than with the blend of claimants to rule that Aristotle calls 'Polity' (*politeia*), of which democracy is the degenerate counterpart, is another instance of Hobbes's rhetoric of misdirection. But also, by suggesting that one man's democracy is easily seen to be another man's anarchy, he rhetorically compromises the attractiveness of democracy relative to monarchy and aristocracy.

9 This is akin to Aristotle's warning that men who are not willing and able to defend themselves are in effect natural slaves, since 'those who cannot face danger courageously are slaves of those who assault them' (*Politics* 1334a19–21).

10 This view of political matters may be seen as in keeping with a statement Hobbes makes in *The Elements of Law* (I.17.15):

> The sum of virtue is to be sociable with them that will be sociable, and formidable to them that will not. And the same is the sum of the law of nature; for in being sociable, the law of nature taketh place by way of peace and society; and to be formidable, is the law of nature in war, where to be feared is a protection a man hath from his own power; and as the former consisteth in actions of equity and justice, the latter consisteth in actions of honour. And equity, justice, and honour, contain all the virtues whatsoever. (as in the modernized text edited by J.C.A.Gaskin [Oxford: Oxford University Press, 1994], 99)

16: Equity and the Problem of *Egoism*

1 In 'Hobbes and Psychological Egoism,' as reprinted in *Hobbes's* Leviathan: *Interpretation and Criticism*, Bernard H. Baumrin, ed. (Belmont, CA: Wadworth, 1969), Bernard Gert attempts 'to show that the almost unanimous view that Hobbes held psychological egoism is mistaken.' While there is much in his essay with which I agree, what is curious is that Gert never confronts any of the textual evidence that gives rise to that 'almost unanimous view' – which is not only ample, but clearly intended by Hobbes to create the rhetorical effect that it has. Hence, Gert makes no attempt to explain the discrepancy between appearance and reality in this matter.

2 Presumably, Hobbes means here that this 'sufficient rule' is derivable from one or more of the Natural Laws he has specified (perhaps, e.g., the eighteenth), or at least from the same general rationale.

3 Cf. *Republic* 440c–d; Craig, *The War Lover: A Study of Plato's* Republic (Toronto: University of Toronto Press, 1994), 98–9.

4 But it is worth emphasizing that however strong a person's feelings in such matters – which can be very powerful, affecting practically all aspects of life – they provide no assurance that what he or she happens to regard as just or unjust truly is so. One's feelings are guided by one's beliefs, however well or ill considered. Hence the importance of pursuing a correct understanding of justice – and not least of all for philosophy, such that one's judgment is not distorted by inappropriate passion. Accordingly, Plato's *Republic*, which is ostensibly about justice, is the dialogue the philosopher chose for his most extensive treatment of philosophy.

5 That is, no explanation beyond the empty tautology that if a person desires 'good to another' it must ipso facto also be 'Good to himselfe' simply because he desires it, and whatever one desires one regards as good. If the logic of egoism is sound, and if all a person regards as good is his own pleasure, then this must be his exclusive motivation. He may not be averse to his actions incidentally benefiting someone else, but their doing so would not figure in his motivation unless he expects some direct or indirect benefit thereby.

6 Cf. *Republic* 387d–e; 605c–606b.

7 How one reacts to being pitied – whether consoled, or offended – seems to be an important respect in which people differ, and even the same person differs according to circumstance (e.g., when, by whom, concerning what). Cf. Nietzsche, *Beyond Good and Evil*, aphs. 29, 62, 171, 225, 293.

8 One is reminded here of the Dedicatory Letter of Machiavelli's *The Prince* – and for that matter, of Hobbes's own dedication of *Leviathan*.

9   As was previously noted in my chapter on 'Honour and the Problem of Natural Law,' Hobbes late in the book acknowledges that genuine honour is to be distinguished from these external *shows* of honouring which could be motivated by pure egoism: 'And thus Honor is properly of its own nature, secret, and internall in the heart. But the inward thoughts of men, which appeare outwardly in their words and actions, are the signs of our Honoring, [thus] whether those words and actions be sincere, or feigned ... because they appear as signes of Honoring, are ordinarily also called *Honor*' (XLV/12, 357). However, as this statement tacitly concedes, only because there is *sincere* honouring – which defies analysis in strictly egoistic terms – are these 'signes of Honouring' available for egoistic exploitation.

10   Thus, 'Revenge is sweet,' and 'is a dish best served cold.' 'He who laughs last, laughs best' is one of the milder expressions of this amply attested truth. Proverbial wisdom also recognizes the baseness in human nature that is manifested in spitefulness, and in the enjoyment people derive from contemplating other people's misfortunes. Ambrose Bierce neatly captures both sides of this baseness: 'Calamities are of two kinds: misfortunes to ourselves and good fortune to others' (*The Devil's Dictionary*). But while there is nothing good to be said for these feelings, the desire for revenge, suitably channelled, is a major – perhaps indispensable – constituent of people's insistence that justice be done.

11   Might Hobbes have Hamlet in mind here, or any of several other Shakespeare characters (e.g., Othello, Titus, Coriolanus, or even Macduff), inasmuch as so-called Revenge Tragedies were a staple of the English theatre in Hobbes's younger days, and revenge figures thematically in at least half of Shakespeare's plays?

12   Hobbes expressly cites at least one striking exception to this dictum: 'The best Counsell, in those things that concern not other Nations, but onely the ease, and benefit the Subjects may enjoy, by Lawes that look onely inward, is to be taken from the generall informations, and complaints of the people of each Province, who are best acquainted with their own wants, and ought therefore, when they demand nothing in derogation of the essentiall Rights of Soveraignty, to be diligently taken notice of' (XXX/27, 184–5).

13   Elsewhere, however, Hobbes acknowledges otherwise: 'And because the first instruction of Children, dependeth on the *care* of their Parents; it is necessary that they should be *obedient* to them, whilst they are under their tuition; and not onely so, but that also afterwards (as gratitude requireth,) they acknowledge the *benefit* of their education, by externall signes of honour' (XXX/11, 178; emphasis added).

14   Cf. *Gorgias* 520d–e; *King Richard the Second* 2.1.93–208.

15 The status of the Decalogue is discussed more fully in the chapter 'Of POWER ECCLESIASTICALL,' where Hobbes distinguishes between the two Tables, arguing that the first four Commandments 'containeth the law of [God's] Soveraignty,' and 'were peculiar to the Israelites,' whereas the final six Commandments of the Second Table are 'indeed the Laws of Nature,' and as such are pertinent 'to all people' (XLII/37, 282).

16 Cf. *Republic* 433e.

17 This would seem to be the most unproblematic illustration 'that they that have Soveraigne power, may commit iniquity; but' – Hobbes hastens to add – 'not Injustice, or Injury in the proper signification' (XVIII/6, 90). And the line just quoted exemplifies a semantic point that may be worth noting: the four times Hobbes uses 'iniquity' in a secular context, it is as an antonym of 'equity' (cf. XV/38, 79; XXI/7, 109; XXVI/9, 139). While this meaning of 'iniquity' is now obsolete, it was (according to the *Shorter Oxford English Dictionary*) an established meaning of the word in Hobbes's day.

18 Essential to the plausibility of this claim is Hobbes's reductionist analysis of what the Ancient authors regarded as *differentiating* people into distinct natural *classes*: 'The Passions that most of all cause the differences of Wit, are principally, the more or lesse Desire of Power, of Riches, of Knowledge, and of Honour. All which may be reduced to the first, that is Desire of Power. For Riches, Knowledge, and Honour are but severall sorts of Power' (VIII/15, 35).

19 Cf. *Republic* 369b–370c ff; Craig, *The War Lover*, 150–66.

20 As Michael Oakeshott sensibly concludes in *Hobbes on Civil Association* (Indianapolis: Liberty Fund, 1937/1975):

> In short, if we have to choose between an explanation of the more important discrepancies in Hobbes's writing in terms of mere confusion or an explanation in terms of artful equivocation, I think the probability lies with the latter.
>
> And if we do settle for an explanation of this sort, which recognizes Hobbes to have two doctrines, one for the initiated (those whose heads were strong enough to withstand the giddiness provoked by his scepticism) and the other for the ordinary man who must be spoken to in an idiom and a vocabulary he is accustomed to, and to whom novelties (both in respect of duties and in respect of their grounds) must be made to appear commonplaces, we are not attributing a unique and hitherto unheard of character to *Leviathan*. Numerous other writers on these topics (Plato, for example, Machiavelli, and even Bentham) were the authors of works that contain at once, and imperfectly distinguished from

one another, an esoteric and exoteric doctrine; and the view that matters of this sort (indeed, political questions generally) are 'mysteries' to be discussed candidly and directly only with the initiated goes back to the beginning of political speculation and was by no means dead in the seventeenth century. (126)

Many scholars have, like Oakeshot, dismissed the Metaphysical context in which Hobbes chose to appear to embed his new Political Science. Their reasons vary. Some ignore it because they recognize respects in which it is not consistent with a political teaching that is fully persuasive on its own terms, and which, moreover, is all that is really of continuing interest in Hobbes's work. Others treat that context as merely so much window dressing for an age increasingly captivated by the newly emerging (Baconian) Natural Science, but make no real effort to explain *why* Hobbes adopted it *despite* the predictable opposition it would arouse to that teaching (e.g., treating man as merely a physical machine determined by the stimuli of pleasure and pain). As a measure of how little attention is now paid to what Hobbes insisted is that 'on which all other Philosophy ought to depend' – namely '*Philosophia prima*' (XLVI/14, 371) – only one of the twenty-one essays in the recently published *The Cambridge Companion to Hobbes's Leviathan*, namely that by Cees Leijenhorst ('Sense and Nonsense about Sense: Hobbes and the Aristotelians on Sense Perception and Imagination') is directly relevant.

However, as I indicated at the beginning of this Part One, I took Hobbes's belated emphasis on the importance of *Philosophia prima* as an invitation to re-examine that which he supplies. I did so partly out of dissatisfaction with what I have seen of most other scholarly treatments of its relationship with his political prescription; in particular, with the lack of much substantial analyses of how these metaphysical premises may serve political purposes *within* that prescription. In endeavouring to *show* that these various premises, however plausible they may seem to those for whom they are intended, are in reality rationally indefensible, even absurd, but also that Hobbes has inconspicuously indicated that he does not subscribe to them himself – that with this shown, I intended to open the way to an alternative interpretation of his actual metaphysical views. But since these same premises – Materialism, Determinism, Hedonism, Egoism, Nominalism, and such – continue to attract adherents, by virtue mainly of the Techno-Scientism that pervades modern political life and theorizing about it, I believe a common-sensical exposure of their manifold inadequacies is valuable in itself.

A Conradian Intermezzo

1   There are several very good studies that do treat the work comprehensively, but I have encountered none better than that of Ian Watt in his *Conrad in the Nineteenth Century* (Berkeley: University of California Press, 1979), 126–253. Watt's analysis of the historical context in which *Heart of Darkness* was written, of the intellectual perspective it expresses, and of its stylistic mode (a synthesis of impressionism and symbolism) shows quite convincingly why it is indeed 'one of the earliest and greatest works in the tradition of modern literature' (135). He observes: 'On the one hand Conrad disclaimed, and rightly, that he possessed anything approaching a conscious intellectual system ... But if Conrad disclaims being a thinker, he strikes us as very thoughtful; and if we cannot call him a philosopher, the intimations of his fictional world steadily invite ethical and even metaphysical response' (147). Moreover, Watt judges that *Heart of Darkness* 'is Conrad's nearest approach to an ideological summa' (148). As I have argued here and elsewhere, possessing an 'intellectual system' is *not* the defining requisite of a philosopher; a dedication to pursuing the important questions is the primary thing, and a writer capable of inspiring a like dedication in his reader – as Conrad surely does – may fairly be judged philosophical in this most important respect.

2   And controversy, one should add. Chinua Achebe's much-anthologized attack – 'An Image of Africa: Racism in Conrad's *Heart of Darkness*,' *Massachusetts Review* 18 (1977): 782–94 – has achieved the notoriety he doubtless sought, generating reams of response, pro and con. More recently, various feminists have raised their predictable hue and cry about Conrad's ratification of 'patriarchal stereotypes.' Since in neither case is truth the issue, argument is pointless.

Robert D. Kaplan, in one of the more sobering analyses of the contemporary world – *The Coming Anarchy: Shattering the Dreams of the Post Cold War* (New York: Random House, 2000) – includes an essay entitled 'Conrad's *Nostromo* and the Third World.' Precisely because 'in the guise of fiction a writer can more easily tell the truth,' especially unpleasant truth about portions of the world radically different from our own, Kaplan laments 'the separation of literature from history and of both from political science in this age of academic specialization' (158–9).

3   E.g., by F.R. Leavis: 'The great English novelists are Jane Austen, George Eliot, Henry James, and Joseph Conrad' – so begins *The Great Tradition* (New York: New York University Press, 1973). And Leavis sees much good in the story. 'The details of the voyage to and up the Congo are present to

us as if we were making the journey ourselves.' But Leavis nonetheless regards Conrad's language as occasionally overwrought (174–82).

Among Conrad's staunchest and most admiring defenders, and of *Heart of Darkness* in particular, was André Gide, who oversaw the translation into French of Conrad's collected works (translating several stories himself). Gide's own *Voyage au Congo* (1927) is dedicated to the memory of Conrad. The influence of Conrad's tale has not been simply literary, however. Hardly any historian writing about 'the scramble' of colonial powers in West Africa, and the eventual public reaction to the atrocities committed there, fails to note the novella, both as historical evidence and as a contributor to the reform movement. One of the most complete recountings of the history of the Congo, exploiting access to official Belgian documentary material only recently made available, is that of Adam Hochschild, *King Leopold's Ghost* (Boston: Houghton Mifflin, 1998). It is laced throughout with dozens of references to *Heart of Darkness*, invariably validating the accuracy of Conrad's portrait of incidents, practices, attitudes, and policies.

4   Accordingly, many commentators before me have recognized that *Heart of Darkness* is about man in a 'State of Nature.' So far as I know, however, there has been no systematic treatment of it in terms of Hobbes's political philosophy, such as I present here. It is clear that Conrad was conversant with Plato and Nietzsche and had given considerable thought to Rousseau (most evident in *Under Western Eyes*). And that he was fairly steeped in Shakespeare is well documented. As Frederick R. Karl observes in his monumental biography, *Joseph Conrad: The Three Lives* (London: Faber and Faber, 1979), 'Shakespeare's words remained with Conrad for the rest of his life, the one book he has Lord Jim take into Patusan with him. Conrad himself carried a five-shilling one-volume edition of the plays' throughout his years at sea (67–8). By contrast, there is no hard evidence that Conrad was deeply familiar with Hobbes (as Melville obviously was) or had even read him. But for reasons I hope to make clear, I am practically certain that he was.

5   All page citations refer to *Heart of Darkness* as it appears in volume 5 of *The Works of Joseph Conrad* (London: William Heinemann, 1921).

The complex narrative frame Conrad has crafted for his novella – which I shall subsequently argue serves a philosophical purpose – makes quoting from it somewhat complicated. The arrangement I have adopted is as follows: when quoting our anonymous narrator's own contributions, I use double quotes; when quoting from our narrator's reproduction of Marlow's narration, I use just single quotes (unless inset), i.e., not single within double (these are reserved for our narrator's using single quotes for some purpose other than quoting Marlow); Marlow's quoting of speakers within his story are in double quotes within the single quotes indicating his narrative (unless inset, where single quotes suffice). Also, because Conrad himself uses ellipses for various purposes, whenever I use them to indicate elisions from quoted material, I have enclosed them within brackets.

6 Indeed, Marlow later suggests that insofar as Kurtz's name was itself a word with a common, everyday meaning, it was positively misleading ('Kurtz – Kurtz – that means "short" in German – don't it? Well, the name was as true as everything else in his life – and death. He looked at least seven feet long'; 163). Insofar as most of the characters in Marlow's story, as well as those listening to it, are not identified by name, but by occupation or some other descriptive character – the aunt, the doctor, the Company's chief accountant, its manager of the Central Station, his expedition-leading uncle, the brickmaker, the chief mechanic, Kurtz's half-caste clerk, his motley-clad disciple, his Intended, the journalist, etc. (instances of Hobbes's 'universals,' as well as a standard technique of modern symbolist literature) – given this 'anonymity' of most of the characters, both Marlow's and Kurtz's names take on potential significance.

7 In speaking of 'Plantations, or Colonies' – 'which are numbers of men sent out from the Common-wealth, under a Conductor, or Governour, to inhabit a Forraign Country, either formerly voyd of Inhabitants, or made voyd then, by warre' – Hobbes merely allows for empire. However, reflection on the inner rationale of the polity he prescribes – devoted to techno-scientific progress, ostensibly for the sake mainly of economic development – suggests what subsequent history amply confirmed: that empire would be a natural development (Leviathan XXIV/14, 131; cf. XXX/19, 181). And this despite his warning against political 'Bulimia' (XXIX/22, 174).

8 Conrad also suffered several bouts of illness during his six months in the Congo, the last nearly fatal, and believed that their legacy was a permanent constitutional weakness that underlay all of his subsequent health problems.

9 Here the Harlequin expresses Conrad's own avowed intention as a novelist, stated in his Preface to The Nigger of the Narcissus: 'My task which I am trying to achieve is, by the power of the written word, to make you hear, to make you feel – it is, before all, to make you see. That – and no more, and it is everything.'

10 Marlow's image here refers unmistakably to the lacerating words Jesus addressed to the Pharisees who sought to entangle him with their sophistries: 'Woe unto you, scribes and Pharisees, hypocrites! for ye are like unto whited sepulchres, which indeed appear beautiful outward, but are within full of dead men's bones, and of all uncleanliness. Even so ye also

outwardly appear righteous unto men, but within ye are full of hypocrisy and iniquity' (Matthew 23: 27–8).

11 Cf. Rousseau's *Discourse on Inequality*, in *The Discourses and Other Early Political Writings*, Victor Gourevitch, ed. and trans. (Cambridge: Cambridge University Press, 1997), Pt II, par. 19: 'property appeared, work became necessary, and the vast forests changed into smiling Fields that had to be watered with the sweat of men, and where slavery and misery were soon seen to sprout and grow together with the harvests.'

12 Must not this unflattering comparison be an intentional reminder of Samuel Johnson's notorious characterization of 'a woman preaching'?

13 As Ian Watt, *Conrad in the Nineteenth Century*, notes, this stylistic technique of using an anonymous narrator, who in turn is recounting Marlow's narration, effectively precludes the reader's presuming 'full authorial understanding.' Instead, it restricts itself 'to showing an individual consciousness in the process of trying to elicit some purely relative and personal meaning from its experience. What Marlow says is not lucidly pondered but random and often puzzled, leaving contradictions unresolved and allowing the less conscious elements of the mind, including those of reverie and dream, to find expression' (209).

In his *The Life of Joseph Conrad* (Oxford: Blackwell, 1994), John Batchelor makes a similar point somewhat more concretely: 'All we as readers, looking over Marlow's shoulder at the dying Kurtz, can say confidently about "The horror! The horror!" is that we don't know what is going on in Kurtz's mind and therefore we cannot say what his dying words mean. The moral reading of Kurtz's final words is Marlow's invention, authorized by nothing but Marlow's innate moral balance' (92).

It should be emphasized, however, that none of this need suggest that Marlow's ambiguities, contradictions, randomness, and puzzlement were not carefully and coherently plotted by Conrad. Having written the whole, his own view of things can no more be reduced to that of one of his 'parts,' this or that character, than in the case of Plato or Shakespeare.

14 Marlow's words remind one of Nietzsche's: 'He who fights monsters should see to it that he himself does not become a monster. And when you gaze long into an abyss, the abyss also gazes into you.' *Beyond Good and Evil* in *The Basic Writings of Nietzsche*, Walter Kaufmann, ed. and trans. (New York: Modern Library, 1966), aph. 146.

15 Thus the acute discomfort he experiences at the conclusion of his visit to The Intended. Cf. *Republic* 382a–d, 389b, 413a, 535e.

16 One of the most intriguing of those who chose to live among the African

natives became known by the name of Trader Horn, who as a young man in his late teens moved to West Africa from Lancashire (c. 1871). He spent much of the rest of his life as either a hunter or freelance trader or company clerk in that area. Near the end as a old peddler in South Africa, he encountered the housewife and sometime novelist, Ethelreda Lewis, who encouraged him to write his memoirs, which she lightly edited and published as *Trader Horn, Being the Life and Works of Alfred Aloysius Horn* (New York: Simon and Schuster, 1927). What is striking is the extent Trader Horn reached several of Hobbes's subtler views about Nature and human nature based simply on his experience of living 'amongst [cannibals] for many years.' For example:

> But looked at from all angles I've always arrived at the notion that Nature's a great big unknown god we've got to make terms with without the humiliation of prayer. This constant nudging of the Almighty is a mistake. *Homo sapiens* with a spear or a gun will go as far, and with less trouble to the great Onlooker. (151)

> Whenever you lose a fight in Africa you're lost. There's no softness about Nature. When you're driven from the herd it's for good. I've seen a beaten old chief weep. Cover his eyes like a child. No wounds, mind you. But his heart broken. Aye, he knows there's no redress, in the state of Nature. No newspaper talk to prop him up again. None of this so-called diplomacy. He sees finis all over the sunlight, same as an old elephant.
>   Aye, pity's a fancy article Nature in her wisdom can't afford to handle. Pity versus preservation of the race. That's all it is. (230)

17 'Africa ... long figured in European thought as the Dark Continent. But Marlow also gives the wilderness much larger metaphysical connotations. It is an actively malign force; and it is also, Marlow senses, impenetrable to human thought, because it has a primal inclusiveness which confounds the categories man has constructed as the basis of his civilization' (Ian Watt, *Conrad in the Nineteenth Century*, 250).

18 Norman Sherry, in his exemplary work of biographical reconstruction, provides a detailed comparison of Conrad's actual experience on the Congo with that which he creates for his Marlow. *Conrad's Western World* (Cambridge: Cambridge University Press, 1971).

19 In the name 'Freleven' one can easily detect the original upon which it was based: 'Freiesleben' (i.e., 'free, open, out-of-doors life') – which by a happy

quirk of fate was the actual name of the Dane whom Conrad succeeded as captain of a Congo riverboat, the career move that provided the experiential basis for this exotic novella. Norman Sherry devotes a short chapter in his *Conrad's Western World* to 'The Death of Freiesleben' (15–22).

20 Despite – or rather, because of – Hobbes's beguiling rhetoric, it is worth emphasizing that the difference between Natural Woman and Civil Woman is at least as important for our understanding of political life as is the contrast of Civil with Savage Man.

21 The fact that many modern women reject Conrad's portrait of a truly civilized woman is not decisive for determining its accuracy; in a sense, it begs the question, since the contemporary deterioration of civility is precisely what is at issue. Marlow's views here are strikingly similar to Nietzsche's: cf. *Beyond Good and Evil*, aph. 232; cf. aphs. 127, 144, 145, 148; also 85, 131.

22 A persuasive case can be made – has been made by Geoffrey Miller, in *The Mating Mind: How Sexual Choice Shaped the Evolution of Human Nature* (London: William Heinemann, 2000) – that virtually everything distinctive about human nature (e.g., language, art, morality, humour, creativity) is primarily the result of female preference for certain mental qualities in the males with whom they choose to mate, 'sexual ornaments' of the mind reflective of overall fitness.

23 Cf. *Republic* 382a–c, 331d, 377a, 389b, 414b–c.

24 One cannot help suspecting that in crafting Kurtz, Conrad had in mind various of Nietzsche's equivocal observations about 'we good Europeans,' e.g.: 'In an age of disintegration that mixes races indiscriminately,' occasionally are produced individuals of surpassing potential (*Beyond Good and Evil*, aph. 200; cf. 199, 214, 242).

25 Cf. *Republic* 491a–e.

26 Ian Watt, discussing novels of symbolic quest as a literary genre, observes: 'The most famous of them, *Moby Dick* and *Heart of Darkness*, have two important features in common: they do not subordinate everything to the hero's quest; and the symbolic objects which the protagonists seek – the whale or Kurtz – are both dangerous and ambiguous. *Heart of Darkness*, then, belongs to a specifically symbolic tradition of fiction, and it is the only one of Conrad's novels which does' (*Conrad in the Nineteenth Century*, 188).

27 Cf. *Republic* 538c–539a. The psychoanalysis of Kurtz proposed here is based on the psychology presented in that dialogue. I have expounded it at some length in chapter 4 of *The War Lover: A Study of Plato's* Republic (Toronto: University of Toronto Press, 1994).

17: The Crucial Paragraph: Platonic Intimations

1 Still, does this not seem a curious sentiment for someone ostensibly a Determinist, who must believe that whether it will or it will not is a foregone certainty? And how different must be a *political* science from, say, physics or chemistry (or even medicine) if the effects it purports to explain – whether of 'good' politics or 'bad' – are dependent upon human understanding and volition? Hobbes himself elliptically acknowledges the difference in suggesting, 'Reason, and Eloquence, (though not perhaps in the Naturall Sciences, yet in the Morall) may stand very well together' (R&C/34, 390; cf. XI/21, 50; also, the concluding two sentences of the book).

2 The title, *Politeia*, would be more accurately translated as 'Regime,' rather than 'Republic,' the name that has become affixed to the dialogue, apparently as the result of Cicero's references to it in his own *De Re Publica*. However, Sokrates treats the term as pertinent not only to the ordering of 'things public,' but also to that of the most private thing: the soul (cf. 592b).

3 This all-important question will be addressed extensively in chapter 21.

4 The most obvious place is Plato's *Republic*, of course, for this is precisely the problem Sokrates directs attention to upon first introducing warriors into the City in *logos*. Naturally, suitable candidates must be courageous, 'if they are to fight well.' But, he asks, 'will horse, or dog, or any animal whatsoever, be willing to be courageous if it's not spirited [lit., 'spirit-formed; *thumoeides*]? Have you not observed how irresistible and invincible is spirit [*thumos*], so when present every soul is fearless and indomitable?' Still, such men must be 'gentle to their own,' and only 'harsh to enemies': 'But where will we find a disposition [*ēthos*] at once gentle *and* great-spirited?' (375a–c). The answer is, nowhere. Such men are not 'found,' they are nurtured into existence. One begins with high-spirited youths and subjects them to a rigorous education designed to tame and discipline their spirits while informing their reason. The lion's share of the dialogue is devoted to expounding just such an education.

Geoffrey M. Vaughan, *Behemoth Teaches Leviathan: Thomas Hobbes on Political Education* (Lanham, MD: Lexington Books, 2007), is one of a minority of scholars who have recognized the significance of the broader 'educational problem' being left largely untouched in *Leviathan*. He argues that Hobbes's *Behemoth* fills the need precisely because it, like Thucydides's work, comes in the form of history (with its power to convey precepts 'secretly,' 81; and because history is manipulable, 87). But Vaughan deals mainly with education of the Ruled (which includes a society's intellectual elite), with how a Hobbesian understanding of political life would be conveyed to the public: 'from those who attended universities' – after those institutions have been suitably reformed, that is (42).

5 In this respect, *Leviathan* differs from Hobbes's earlier *Elements of Law Natural and Politic*. Having in a previous chapter (VII.1) spoken of love in the most general terms, Hobbes later indicates that this would include 'the love men bear to one another, or pleasure they take in one another's company [presumably, the kind of love Greeks called *philia*, though Hobbes does not use the name]; and by which men are said to be sociable by nature.' This latter would seem to be what Greeks would call *agapē*, and figures in the New Testament as the love Christians are enjoined to show towards all men. That said, Hobbes adds:

> But there is another kind of LOVE, which the Greeks call Ἔρως, and is that which we mean, when we say: that man or woman is in love. For as much as this passion cannot be without diversity of sex, it cannot be denied but it participateth of that indefinite love mentioned in the former section. But there is a great difference between the desire of a man indefinite, and the same desire limited *ad hanc* ['towards her'], and this is that love which is the great theme of poets. But notwithstanding their praises, it must be defined by the word need; for it is a conception of the need a man hath of that one person desired. (IX.16; as per the modernized text in the Oxford University Press edition, J.C.A. Gaskin, ed., 56)

> Hobbes goes on to speak of a fourth distinct kind of love, 'which the Greeks call Στοργή,' manifested, e.g., in parental love, and which Hobbes himself suggests amounts to 'good will or CHARITY.' Notably, he speaks in this connection of Plato's *Symposium* and 'the then noted love of Socrates wise and continent, to Alcibiades young and beautiful; in which love, is not sought the honour, but issue of his knowledge; contrary to common love … it should therefore be this charity, or desire to assist and advance others' (IX.17, 56–7).
>
> I have discussed more extensively the four types of love – *philia*, *agapē*, *storgē*, and *erōs* – in chapter 3 of *The War Lover: A Study of Plato's Republic* (Toronto: University of Toronto Press, 1994).

6 Disregarding, for the purpose of this calculation, the unpaginated prefatory material (Frontispiece, Dedicatory Letter, Table of Contents), as well as the 'Introduction' and the 'Review and Conclusion' – which, for all of their (very considerable) philosophical importance, are not strictly speaking integral to the argument structuring the sequence of numbered chapters.

However, if one includes the eight pages which precede the main text, and the eight pages of the 'Review,' obviously the same placement results. The total of 385 pages (rather than 387, as per the last numbered page of chapter 47) makes allowance for certain aberrations in the book's pagination – which Hobbes manipulated in order to achieve this precise placement (see note 30 below).

7 Hobbes had previously referred to Plato by name only once, and in a context that seemed nothing special ('my designe being not to shew what is Law here, and there; but what is Law; as *Plato, Aristotle, Cicero*, and diverse others have done'; XXVI/1, 137). Altogether, he refers explicitly to Plato seven times: three in this central paragraph, and three more times in chapter 46.

This is an opportune point at which to acknowledge that the corresponding 'crucial' paragraph in the later Latin edition of *Leviathan* differs from that of the English edition. Most notably, Hobbes expands the 'useless' category to which his treatise might be relegated: 'I fear that this writing of mine will be numbered with Plato's *Republic*, [More's] *Utopia*, [Bacon's New] *Atlantis*, and similar amusements of the mind' (as per Curley's edition of *Leviathan*, 244n15). That is, Hobbes here associates his book with *two other Plato-inspired writings*! That the two added authors happen to have been Lord Chancellors of England may not be altogether irrelevant either. As for the fact that Hobbes does not in the Latin version *expressly* declare his agreement with Plato regarding the desirable conjunction of Philosophic Wisdom and Political Sovereignty, this in no way affects his having quite clearly done so in the English edition. There are any number of reasons why he may later have chosen to be less explicit, including certain reactions to his having earlier been more explicit.

8 For so Sokrates's dialogical partners regard it, and assure him almost everyone else would as well. Cf. 473e–474a, 487b–d.

9 Speaking of the typical philosophy schools of ancient Greece: 'The naturall Philosophy of those Schools, was rather a Dream than Science, and set forth in senselesse and insignificant Language; which cannot be avoided by those that will teach Philosophy, without having first attained great knowledge in Geometry.' By contrast, '*Plato* that was the best Philosopher of the Greeks, forbad entrance into his Schoole, to all that were not already in some measure Geometricians' (XLVI/11, 369).

10 In his prose autobiography, Hobbes tells us only that 'he began to look at Euclid's *Elements*; delighted with its method, not so much because of the theorems as because of the way of reasoning, he read it through most carefully.' Aubrey specifies that Hobbes happened upon a volume of Euclid's

geometry open at 'the forty-seventh proposition in the first book.' However Aubrey gained this information, Hobbes must have been the original source. And he may have had his own reasons for pointing to this, the 'Pythagorean theorem,' knowing he had fashioned *Leviathan* to have forty-seven chapters.

11 I have done so, fairly thoroughly I believe, in *The War Lover*. While the entire argument of the book bears on these matters, see especially: 22–6, 34–6, 112–29, 241–4, and ch. 7.

12 Cf. *Republic* 519b–521b, 540b, 592a–b. The practical approximation of Sokrates's City in *logos*, namely, a polity ruled by gentlemen friendly and open to philosophy, would provide philosophers their most congenial political environment.

13 Including this central paragraph, Hobbes refers to 'Naturall Justice' four times in his text. The first is in speaking about the duty of a Minister (such as an Ambassador) with respect to matters not covered by his written instructions. He is to do 'that which Reason dictates to be most conducing to his Soveraigns interest': 'All which Instructions of naturall Reason may be comprehended under one name of *Fidelity*; which is a branch of naturall Justice' (XXVI/14, 141). Then in explaining why most people are easily misled about a range of political issues: 'being diverted from the deep meditation, which the learning of truth, not onely in the matter of Naturall Justice, but also of all other Sciences necessarily requireth' (XXX/14, 179). And with respect to 'the *Law of Nations*' being the same as the Law of Nature: no sanction exists outside the consciences of Sovereigns, 'there being no Court of Naturall Justice' (XXX/30, 185).

14 This will be examined more fully in chapter 21. Few scholars have addressed the question of Hobbes's relationship to Plato. One of those who has is Karl Schuhmann, 'Hobbes and the Political Thought of Plato and Aristotle,' in *Selected Papers on Renaissance Philosophy and on Thomas Hobbes*, Piet Steenbakkers and Cees Leijenhorst, eds (Dordrecht: Kluwer, 2004). Unhappily, he manages to be almost entirely mistaken in his assessment of virtually every reference in the Hobbesian corpus to either Plato or Sokrates, concluding: '*Republic* and *Leviathan* are therefore to be contrasted as the wrong and the right project of political thought' (199). How he could have given any serious thought to the central paragraph of *Leviathan*, or to Hobbes's references to Plato in chapter 46, and nonetheless come to such an extreme conclusion is puzzling, to say the least.

Richard Flathman, *Thomas Hobbes: Skepticism, Individuality and Chastened Politics* (Walnut Creek, CA: Altamira Press, 2000), is one of a small minority of scholars who has recognized 'Hobbes's admiration for Plato'

(147) or who has attached any significance to the reference to Plato in Hobbes's central paragraph (112). His treatment of it, however, is very limited, and has almost no commonality with mine.

15 As he made clear when he first introduced them, they are legitimately referred to as *Laws* only 'if we consider the same Theoremes, as delivered in the word of God, that by right commandeth all things' (XV/41, 80).

16 In a later work (*De Principiis et Ratiocinatione Geometrarum*, 1666), Hobbes himself insists upon this: 'The certitude of all sciences is equal, and otherwise they are not sciences, since *to know* does not admit of more and less. [Thus,] physics, ethics, and politics, if they are well demonstrated, are no less certain than the pronouncements of mathematics, just as mathematics is no more certain than other sciences unless its pronouncements are properly demonstrated.' Quoted in Douglas M. Jesseph, *Squaring the Circle: The War between Hobbes and Wallis* (Chicago: University of Chicago Press,1999), 282. One cannot overemphasize the importance of the 'if' in this statement.

17 Aristotle argues this by way of beginning his *Nicomachean Ethics*: that the degree of precision it is reasonable to expect depends on the subject, and that since the premises of ethical and political demonstrations are only more or less probable generalizations admitting of exceptions, so too the conclusions. He implies that the degree of precision that a sufficiently knowledgeable person would expect from political science (*politikë*) falls somewhere between mathematics and rhetoric (1094b11–27).

18 This is typically the case with the writings of political philosophers, that their books are 'treatise-tracts,' i.e., partly a timeless treatise and partly a tract for the times – though not usually presented as such. See Leo Strauss, 'Political Philosophy and History' in *What Is Political Philosophy* (New York: Free Press, 1959), 63.

19 Because such opinions come not just from books, Plato's Sokrates requires that the rulers of his City supervise the whole cultural environment in which the citizenry's souls are nurtured (401b–d). It is reasonable to suppose that Hobbes would have his Sovereign do likewise, insofar as it is required to 'protect' the public acceptance of his doctrine.

20 This is the same possibility – the conversion of a young but already well-established tyrant, one who is courageous, a quick learner with a strong memory, and of a magnificent nature – that the Athenian Stranger cites as the readiest means of bringing into existence a regime such as that described in Plato's *Laws* (709e; cf. 710c–e). Hobbes is careful to inform his reader that 'A *Tyrant* originally signified no more simply, but a *Monarch*' (XLVI/35, 377). Incidentally, in Plato's dialogues 'stranger' (*xenos*) seems to

serve as a metaphor for 'philosopher' inasmuch as in four dialogues wherein the principal interlocutor is not Sokrates, he is pointedly so identified – the Athenian Stranger in *Laws* and *Epinomis*, the Stranger from Elis in *Statesman* and *Sophist.* Plato has Sokrates identify himself at the beginning of his 'Apology' as a 'stranger' to the Law Courts of Athens, and who accordingly speaks in a foreign dialect (17d; cf. *Leviathan* XIX/23, 101).

21 Thucydides, 2.65.8–9. Plato, *Phaedrus* 269e–270a.

22 Caesar's discussion of the Druids nicely illustrates these qualities (VI, 14). Bacon cites 'Alexander the Great and Julius Caesar the Dictator' as best exemplifying the fact that both 'Learning and Arms' can flourish and excel 'in the same men and in the same ages.' *The Advancement of Learning*, G.W. Kitchin, ed. (Philadelphia: Paul Dry Books, 2001), 11. 'As for Julius Caesar, the excellency of his learning needeth not to be argued from his education, or his company, or his speeches; but in a further degree doth declare itself in his writings and works' (49).

According to Aubrey, after leaving Oxford and entering into service as companion to the young son of Lord Cavendish, Hobbes found that 'he had almost forgotten his Latin. He therefore bought him books of an Amsterdam print that he might carry in his pocket (particularly Caesar's *Commentaries*), which he did read in the lobby, or ante-chamber, whilst his lord was making his visits.'

23 Hobbes mentions Alexander's *name* two other times, but in contexts that have little or nothing to do with Alexander himself (II/4, 5; XLI/8, 265), whereas, each of the four references to Alexander the man is of some special interest. The first figures in Hobbes's discussion of the difference between *knowing* and merely believing out of 'faith' in some authority, such as believing that 'the Scriptures are the word of God' because 'the Church' says so: 'And so it is also with all other History. For if I should not believe all that is written by Historians, of the glorious acts of *Alexander*, or *Caesar*; I do not think the Ghost of *Alexander*, or *Caesar*, had any just cause to be offended; or any body else, but the Historian' (VII/7, 32). What, then, must we suppose Hobbes believes about the 'glorious acts' written of Moses, or of Jesus? Or, more to the point, *who* has 'just cause to be offended' if he believes them not? Be that as it may, I shall suggest in my Coda that there is a sense in which the 'ghost' of Caesar, if not that of Alexander also, haunts Hobbes's political prescription. Plutarch famously 'paralleled' the lives of these two history-shaping conquerors.

Hobbes employs some of what is written about Alexander as a rather curious image of his point that, for the Sovereign as Legislator, 'there can not be any knot in the Law, insoluble; either by finding out the ends, to undoe it by; or else by making what ends he will, (as *Alexander* did with his sword in the Gordian knot,) by the Legislative power' (XXVI/21, 143). And though he had a nobleman's vast library from which to choose illustrations of his claim that, with respect to the various books of the Bible, in some cases the title indicates the author whereas in others the subject, he chose thus: 'The *History of Livy*, denotes the Writer; but the *History of Alexander*, is denominated from the subject' (XXXIII/4, 200; here I follow Richard Tuck's Cambridge Text edition rather than that of Rogers and Schuhmann). The latter example is curious, in that any such history would, as Hobbes well knows, feature prominently what he conspicuously ignores: the Aristotle connection.

Thus, Plutarch's *Life of Alexander* – with which Hobbes was well acquainted – is pertinent here for more than one reason:

> And since Phillip saw that, whereas his son's nature was unyielding such that he could not be compelled, but was easily led to his duty by reasoning, he tried to persuade rather than to command; and because he did not wholly entrust [his son's] education to the care of teachers of music and general studies, being matters of more importance ... he sent for the most renowned and learned of philosophers, Aristotle, and paid him a fine and fitting tuition-fee ... And it seems that Alexander received not only his ethical and political doctrine [*logon*], but also forbidden [or, 'mysterious,' 'sacred,' 'secret,' 'not to be spoken of'; *aporrëton*] and deeper teachings, which men privately call 'acroamatic' and 'epoptic' and do not convey to many. For after he had already crossed into Asia, and happened to learn that Aristotle had published certain discourses [*logous*] about these things in books, he wrote a letter to him speaking plainly in defense of philosophy, of which this is a copy: 'Alexander to Aristotle, fair well. You have not done rightly in making public the acroamatic of your doctrines [*logon*]; for in what shall I surpass others if those doctrines in which I am trained are to become common to all? I would wish [rather] to excel in my experience with the best things than in my powers. Be well [lit., 'be strong'].

Aristotle responded by assuring Alexander that the doctrines about which he spoke had been both published and yet not published, 'for in truth the metaphysical matters [*hë meta ta physika pragmateia*] are of no use for either teaching or learning, but written as memoranda for those who have first been trained in them [i.e., by him]' (VII. 1–9).

Hobbes's conspicuous silence about the Aristotle connection contrasts markedly with how it is regarded by Bacon, who makes much of Alexander's having been 'Aristotle's scholar in philosophy,' treating the fact that 'Alexander was bred and taught under Aristotle, the great philosopher' as perhaps equal in importance to his conquests (*The Advancement of Learning*, 11, 46–9).

24 Definitions listed as '*arch.*' and 'Now *rare* or *obsolete*' by the *Oxford Shorter English Dictionary*, 2949.

25 There are also four references to the city Alexander founded, and named in his own honour: XLII/41, 284; XLV/4, 353; XLV/37, 366; XLVI/10, 369.

26 It is well established that numerological and geometrical features were commonplace in the literature of the centuries preceding and succeeding Hobbes's writing, just as there was an elaborate language of symbolism employed in frontispieces and other ornaments of books. Carl Schmitt, *The Leviathan in the State Theory of Thomas Hobbes: Meaning and Failure of a Political Symbol*, George Schwab and Erna Hilfstein, trans. (Westport, CT: Greenwood Press, 1996), commenting on the parallel columns of icons that figure in the frontispiece of Hobbes's *Leviathan*: 'The fortresses and cannons correspond to the contrivances and intellectual methods of the other side [i.e., being various 'symbols for sharpened distinctions, syllogisms, and dilemmas'], whose fighting ability is by no means inferior … The important realization that ideas and distinctions are political weapons, in fact, specific weapons of wielding "indirect" power, was thus made on the first page of the book' (18).

As Russell A. Peck writes in his entry on 'Numerology' in *A Dictionary of Biblical Tradition in English Literature*, David Lyle Jeffrey, ed. (Grand Rapids, MI: Eerdmans, 1992), concerning numerological techniques of Renaissance poets: 'sometimes it is so craftily developed as to follow predetermined stanza and line count and in some instances even syllable count … The fruit of such an intricate poetic is works like Dante's *Divine Comedy*, Chaucer's *Troilus and Criseyde*, the ME *Pearl*, Spenser's *Epithalamion* and *Faerie Queene*, and Milton's *Paradise Lost*, all of which employ various forms of numerology extensively' (556–7). So, too, do various prose writers, including philosophers (notably Machiavelli and Francis Bacon), and the greatest philosopher poet: Shakespeare.

A useful survey of these aspects of literature in the Western tradition, derived from the two distinct but interwoven strands of Pythagorean-Platonic philosophy and Biblical exegesis, is that of Christopher Butler, *Number Symbolism* (London: Routledge and Kegan Paul, 1970). In his words: 'We can safely conclude that numerological exegesis as practiced from Philo on, must have made some knowledge of number symbolism the possession of every educated Christian in those centuries, well up to the close of the Renaissance, in which an allegorical mode of understanding a literary text was intellectually respectable' (30). He goes on to warn, however, of a special obstacle to this sort of analysis: 'Attempts to trace with any exactitude the features of numerological Pythagoreanism and Platonism are further complicated by the Renaissance liking for the occult' (53).

There have undoubtedly been vast quantities of numerological nonsense written by those of a mystical bent, but this should not obscure its importance for serious literary analysis of works by authors who used numbers and symbols for their own purposes. See, for example, *Silent Poetry: Essays in Numerological Analysis*, Alastair Fowler, ed. (London: Routledge and Kegan Paul, 1970); also, the bibliography Peck included with his discussion of numerology (cited above).

27   Cf. the sixth of Bacon's *Essays*, 'Of Simulation and Dissimulation,' which discusses the 'three degrees of this hiding and veiling of a man's self, and concludes: 'The best composition and temperature is to have openness in fame and opinion [i.e., in *reputation*]; secrecy in habit; dissimulation in seasonable use; and a power to feign, if there be no remedy.'

28   This is not simply a numerologically convenient but otherwise fanciful suggestion. The so-called Egerton Manuscript – the ornate scribal version Hobbes had prepared for presentation to King Charles II ('engross'd in Vellam in a marvelous fair hand,' according to Edward Hyde) – has the 'Review and Conclusion' labelled as 'CHAP. 48' (Rogers and Schuhmann, Volume One, 50).

29   In Hobbes's own day, it might have been of interest to those who regarded him as in league with the Anti-Christ that 396 = 66 × 6.

30   One result of this fiddling with pagination is that the whole of chapter 39, '*Of the signification in Scripture of the Word* CHURCH,' consists of duplicated pages. Another is that chapter 40 is bracketed by these aberrations: preceded by the duplicated pages, succeeded by the 'missing' pages. In connection with chapter 39, it may be noteworthy that, according to Rogers and Schuhmann, 'it also seems that Ch. XXXIX was stylistically more heavily revised than most other chapters. At least the number of divergences between the [Egerton] MS and the print [i.e., the first printed edition] is in this chapter quite high' (Volume One, 82). Charles Cantalupo observes, 'Few chapters in *Leviathan* are as exacting and pointed as 39, so much so much so that the chapter's number becomes a pun on the Anglican church's Thirty-nine Articles.' *A Literary Leviathan – Thomas Hobbes's Masterpiece of Language* (Lewisburg, PA: Bucknell University Press, 1991), 170.

31 The aforementioned Egerton MS provides further evidence that the printed
    text's pagination was intentionally manipulated, since something similar was
    done with this manuscript version. As one example noted by Rogers and
    Schuhmann, 'The pages numbered 242, 243, and 244 are blank, and again the
    last leaf of this quire was cut off.' Summarizing the consequences of these
    irregularities in the manuscript: 'Let us note here a curious fact about the
    text of *Leviathan*, namely that – as to its distribution over the quires – it
    can be neatly divided into two halves,' such that 'the text of Part III begins
    exactly half way through, namely on the first page of quire 32. That this is
    not mere coincidence, but has something deliberate about it, is suggested by
    the blank pages cut out' (vol. 1, 49–50).

32 I shall address this matter more fully in chapter 20.

33 I have provided the evidence for this division in the Spirited part of the soul,
    and traced its far-reaching implications for both politics and philosophy, in
    the fourth chapter of *The War Lover*. Some of the psychic significance of
    this division is exemplified by Sokrates's two primary interlocutors.

34 If one includes both versions of Sokrates's City in *logos* (cf. 544a), his com-
    plete political taxonomy comprises six types of regimes.

35 There is, however, an unacknowledged complication to this psychological
    taxonomy. As discussed previously, there are two kinds of Timocrats, one
    properly so-called because Honour is his foremost desire; whereas the other,
    often indistinguishable by outward behaviour, is misnamed in that Victory
    (*nikë*) – i.e., success of all kinds – is his primary motivation. Accordingly, he
    would more properly be designated 'nikocratic.' And as a further complica-
    tion, it would seem that the man who corresponds to each City in *logos* is
    one and the same, in that the true Aristocrat (after all, the name means 'best')
    is 'the one that is kingliest and king of himself' (580b–c) – an exceedingly
    rare type of man, to be sure, as rare as a Plato or a Sokrates. And much as
    they are not accommodated within the fourfold taxonomy, neither is
    Hobbes. The analytically complete taxonomy actually consists of six psychic
    archetypes: Aristocrat, Nikocrat, Timocrat, Plutocrat, Democrat, Tyrant.

36 Hobbes was not wedded to the Treatise format, however. *Behemoth*,
    although ostensibly an historical commentary on the English Civil War, is
    cast as four dialogues. The Appendices to the Latin edition of *Leviathan* are
    all in the form of dialogues. So, too, his critique of Boyle, *Dialogus physicus
    de naturae aerae*. There is also *A Dialogue between a Philosopher and a
    Student of the Common Laws of England*, and Hobbes's *Decameron Physio-
    logicum*, or *ten Dialogues of Natural Philosophy*.

37 To be sure, Hobbes presents much of his analysis in sets *other* than of four
    (or multiples thereof). And there are other numbers that seem to have

special significance in his book, notably Twelve. Twelve figures importantly in the Christian tradition by virtue of the twelve Apostles. Hobbes managed to have Chapter Twelve be his general 'causal' – hence, scientific-philosophical – account 'Of Religion.' As noted before, Part Three ('OF A CHRISTIAN COMMON-WEALTH') is divided into twelve chapters; together, they comprise a total of 324 paragraphs (i.e., 12 × 27, or 4 × 3^4). And according to his explicit tabulation, there are twelve 'Rights of Soveraigns by Institution,' which centrally include control over 'what Opinions and Doctrines' are publicly disseminated (XVIII/3–15, 88–92). In the concluding chapter of the Treatise, Hobbes specifies twelve doctrinal errors contributing to 'Spirituall Darknesse' that 'we may justly' attribute to 'the Pope, and Roman Clergy' (XLVII/2–17, 381–3), which he likens to 'The Kingdome of Fairies' in twelve respects (XLVII/21–33, 386–7). Hobbes himself emphasizes the special significance of the number Twelve: 'For as Moses chose twelve Princes of the tribes, to govern under him; so did our Saviour choose twelve Apostles, who shall sit on twelve thrones, and judge the twelve tribes of Israel' (XLI/7, 264–5).

The number Twelve has a subtle but profound importance in Plato's *Republic* as well. Since tracing out this particular subterranean story would take us far astray, a few observations will have to suffice. It begins with Sokrates's curious rejoinder to Thrasymachus, who in challenging the philosopher to say what he himself believes 'the Just' to be, disallowed a handful of purely formal answers (336d). Sokrates protests against being prohibited from answering in any of these terms: 'You well knew that if you asked someone how much "twelve" is, and prefaced in asking, "don't be telling me, O [mere] human, that it's two times six, or three times four, or six times two, or four times three; for I'll not accept such drivel from you" – it was plain to you, I suppose, that no one could answer when asked in this way' (337a–b). Incidentally, since the six archetypes of regimes (as per note 34 above) can be paired with the six archetypes of souls (listed in note 35 above) – twelve archetypes altogether – they could be expressed as either 'two times six' (two sets of six), or as 'six times two' (six pairs). Including the slave boy who speaks in the Prologue, there are twelve identified participants in the dialogue, though only eight of them have speaking parts. Plato's 'story of Twelve' concludes with 'the Tale of Er,' a 'strong man' slain in war but whose corpse did not decay; instead, he came back to life 'on the twelfth day,' and told of what he had seen in the nether world.

38 *A Survey of Mr Hobbes His Leviathan*, as reproduced in *Leviathan: Contemporary Responses to the Political Theory of Thomas Hobbes*, G.A.J. Rogers, ed. (Bristol: Thoemmes Press, 1995), 181. Hyde indicates that he

'finished this discourse ... in April One thousand six hundred and seventy'; it was not published, however, until 1676, nearly three years after his death. He had, however, been actively – and proudly – opposing Hobbes for over two decades. As Johann P. Sommerville relates: 'Sir Edward Nicholas, a very well informed source, spoke of Hobbes' exclusion from court as a recent event in 1652. He was happy that the "father of atheists" had at last been removed from court since he had already done much to spread his atheism there. Writing to Hyde, Nicholas mentioned the report that it was the English Catholics, ... who were responsible for the fall from royal favour of "that great atheist." Hyde, however, denied that the Catholics had been involved and took upon himself much of the credit "for the discountenancing of my old friend, Mr H."' *Thomas Hobbes; Political Ideas in Historical Context* (New York: St Martin's Press, 1992), 24–5. Sommerville's detailed discussion of Hobbes's views on religion in their historical context is valuable (105–67), though he remains agnostic on the question of whether Hobbes was an atheist.

39 'A Survey of Mr Hobbes *His* Leviathan,' 183–4.

40 As luck would have it, Plato has Glaukon offer to provide money for the always impecunious Sokrates (*Republic* 337d).

41 In introducing his 'Survey,' Hyde proposes to speak about 'such particulars, as may in my judgment produce much mischief in the World, in a Book of great Name, and which is entertain'd and celebrated (at least enough) in the World; a Book which contains in it good learning of all kinds, politely extracted, and very wittily and cunningly digested, in a very commendable method, and in a vigorous and pleasant Style: which hath prevailed over too many' (180).

42 For what it's worth, Plato's Sokrates seems generally to identify with 'wily Odysseus' rather than with the more popular Homeric hero, Achilles (cf. *Republic* 388a, 390e–391c, 620c–d; but also *Apology* 28c–d).

43 'A Survey ...,' 183, 185. Hyde's attack on Hobbes's *Leviathan* is fairly representative of many right-thinking gentlemen's reaction to the book – indeed, it is restrained compared with some (e.g., Ward, Wallis, inter al.). Bishop Bramhall advertises his *The Catching of Leviathan, or the Great Whale* as 'Demonstrating, out of Mr. Hobs his own Works, That no man who is thoroughly an Hobbist, can be a good Christian, or a good Common-wealths man, or reconcile himself to himself. Because his Principles are not only destructive to all Religion, but to all Societies; extinguishing the relation between Prince and Subject, Parent and Child, Master and Servant, Husband and Wife: and abound with palpable contradictions.' In *Leviathan: Contemporary Responses*, 115.

44 XLVI/18, 373. George Lawson cites Hobbes's pernicious effect on the youth
    as what precipitated his undertaking to publish a critique (*An Examination
    of the Political Part of Mr. Hobbs His* Leviathan). Based on his initial
    perusal, he presumed 'that as little good was to be expected, so little harm
    was to be feared from that book. Yet after that I understood by divers
    learned and judicious friends, that it took much with many Gentlemen and
    young Students in the Universities, and that it was judged to be a rational
    piece, I wondered.' *Leviathan: Contemporary Responses*, 15).

45 I have provided the evidence for this claim, along with a detailed compari-
    son of the natures of these two brothers and of their respective relationships
    with Sokrates, in *The War Lover*, especially in the first half of chapter 5.

46 According to Aubrey's 'brief life' of Lucius Cary (Viscount Falkland), his
    estate at Great Tew not far from Oxford 'was like a college, full of learned
    men,' which included 'Ben Jonson, Edmund Waller, Mr Thomas Hobbes
    and all the excellent wits of that peaceable time.' And in his 'brief life' of
    Waller, Aubrey on Waller's testimony associates Sidney Godolphin with the
    others: 'He told me he [Waller] was not acquainted with Ben Jonson (who
    died about 1638), but familiarly with Lucius, Lord Falkland; Sidney Godol-
    phin, Mr Hobbes, etc.' Noel Malcolm twice refers to Sidney as a poet in the
    'Biographical Register' addendum to *The Correspondence of Thomas
    Hobbes* (Oxford: Oxford University Press, 1994), 777, 913. Like Glaukon,
    then, Sidney was 'musical' (cf. *Republic* 398e).

47 In his *History of the Great Rebellion*, Edward Hyde (Earl of Clarendon)
    describes the actions undertaken by the cavalry of Sir John Berkeley to
    disrupt the recruiting efforts of the Parliamentary forces in the Devon area,
    and devotes a paragraph to the death of Sidney Godolphin:

    In these necessary and brisk expeditions, falling upon Chagford (a little
    town in the south of Devon) before day, the king lost Sidney Godolphin,
    a young gentleman of incomparable parts. Being of a constitution and
    education more delicate, and unacquainted with contentions, upon his
    observation of the wickedness of those men in the House of Commons of
    which he was a member, out of the pure indignation of his soul and con-
    science to his country he had with the first engaged himself with that
    party in the West: and though he thought not fit to take command in a
    profession he had not willingly chosen, yet as his advice was of great
    authority with all the commanders, being always one in the council of
    war, and whose notable abilities they still had use of in their civil transac-
    tions, so he exposed his person to all action, travail and hazard. By too
    forward engaging himself in this last, he received a mortal shot by a

musket a little above the knee, of which he died in the instant, leaving the ignominy of his death upon a place that would never otherwise have had a mention to the world. (from the Oxford University Press edition for The Folio Society, 1967, 93–4)

18: The Heartless Introduction: Hobbes's Disposable Physiology

1 As Hobbes might call it, since he several times emphasizes that Adam, but for his sinful disobedience in eating from the Tree of Knowledge of Good and Evil, would have enjoyed eternal life (e.g., XXXI/6, 188; XXXV/3, 216; XXXVIII/2, 238–9; XLIV/14, 339; /23, 343; /28, 345), but mentions Eden by name only once (XXXVIII/2, 238). Needless to say, a being who had no reason to fear death would be radically different from humans as we know them. Hobbes points to one consequence that has endless implications: 'For seeing Adam, and Eve, if they had not sinned, had lived on Earth Eternally, in their individuall persons; it is manifest they should not continually have procreated their kind. For if Immortalls should have been generated, as Mankind doth now; the Earth in small time, would not have been able to afford them place to stand on' (XXXVIII/3, 239).

2 Hobbes refers to this 'Sokratic turn' in his Preface to *De Cive*:

> This book sets out men's duties, first, as men; then as citizens and lastly as Christians …
>
> The wise men of remotest antiquity believed that this kind of teaching (with the exception of anything relating to the Christian religion) should be given to posterity only in the pretty forms of poetry or in the shadowy outlines of Allegory, as if to prevent what one might call the high and holy mystery of government from being contaminated by the debates of private men … Sokrates is said to have been the first to fall in love with this civil science; it had not yet been conceived as a whole at the time but was, so to speak, showing a bit of itself through the clouds in the matter of civil government. He is said to have valued this science so much that he spurned and rejected every other part of Philosophy, judging only this part to be worthy of his intellect. (7–8)

3 In the Preface he later (1647) added to *De Cive* (1642), which was originally planned to be the third part in his three-element system, Hobbes tacitly acknowledged that in publishing it before both *De Corpore* (eventually published in 1655) and *De Homine* (1658), his political teaching is in fact logically independent of both his metaphysics and his physiology:

I took up Philosophy for intellectual enjoyment, and in every branch of it I was assembling the first Elements. I arranged them into three Sections, and was gradually writing them up, so that the first Section would discuss body and its general properties; the second, Man and his particular faculties and passions; the third, the Commonwealth and the duties of citizens. And so the first Section contains first Philosophy and some elements of Physics ... The second Section is concerned with imagination, memory, understanding, reasoning, appetite, will, Good, Evil, Moral and Immoral, and other such topics. [Because of political turmoil in my county, however], I put the rest aside and hurried on the completion of [the] third part. And so it has come about that the part which was last in order has come out first; especially as I saw that it did not need the preceding parts, since it rests upon its own principles known by reason. (13)

As Leo Strauss observes, Hobbes here indicates that 'the science of man and human things, being based on principles of its own ... is not in need of natural science.' 'On the Basis of Hobbes's Political Philosophy,' in *What Is Political Philosophy* (New York: Free Press, 1959), 179. And since Hobbes's own political teaching *requires* neither natural science's mechanistic-materialistic account of man nor its deterministic cosmology, its validity is not dependent thereupon.

4 Accordingly, I am sceptical of claims such as those of Norberto Bobbio (and Carl Schmitt): 'Except for its name, Leviathan, Hobbes's state was not at all monstrous, as Carl Schmitt remarked. It was merely a great machine, the *machina machinarum*, in an age dominated by the mechanistic conception of the universe.' *Thomas Hobbes and the Natural Law Tradition*, Daniela Gobetti, trans. (Chicago: University of Chicago Press, 1993), 69. Rather, it seems to me that this 'mechanical' appearance is an aspect of the rhetorical illusion Hobbes intended to perpetrate (with some success, apparently).

Gary B. Herbert is one of few commentators I have read who bothers to analyse Hobbes's Man-State analogy. *Thomas Hobbes: The Unity of Scientific and Moral Wisdom* (Vancouver: University of British Columbia Press, 1989), 15–16. While he notes some of its curious features, he does not (to my mind) correctly interpret their implications, as I mean to show in what follows.

5 Nor has Hobbes neglected to suggest *political* (*versus* mechanical) analogues for other features of natural life, speaking of 'the *Plenty*, and *Distribution* of *Materials* conducing to Life' as the 'Nutrition' of the commonwealth (XXIV/1, 127; of course, the 'life' in question here is not that of the Artificial Man, but of the natural men who compose it). A similar caveat applies

to his treating '*Plantations*, or *Colonies*' as 'The Procreation, or Children of a Common-wealth (XXIV/14, 131).

6 Actually, if taken at his word, Hobbes's idea of a commonwealth synthesizes not merely three, but *four* distinct modes of Being, inasmuch as he later characterizes it as a '*Mortall God*' (XVII/13, 87). Thus Carl Schmitt observes, 'What appears to have been attained is a mythical totality composed of god, man, animal, and machine. This totality assumes the Hebrew Bible name, "leviathan."' *The Leviathan in the State Theory of Thomas Hobbes* (Westport, CT: Greenwood Press, 1996), 19. Schmitt, however, treats its 'mechanical' character as what is, or at least becomes, most distinctive about Hobbes's prescription:

> The intrinsic logic of the manmade, artificial product 'state' does not culminate in a person but in a machine. Not the representation by a person but the factual, current accomplishment of genuine protection is what the state is all about ... That, however, can only be attained by an effectively functioning mechanism of command. [Such a State] differs from all earlier kinds of political units. It may even be regarded as the first product of the age of technology, the first modern mechanism in the grand style ... [W]ith that state was not only created an essential intellectual or sociological precondition for the technical-industrial age that followed but also the typical, even prototypical, work of the new technological era – the development of the state itself. (34)

Rather, I would say, Hobbes has crafted the *illusion* thereof, as if his political science really were of a piece with the mechanistic, materialistic, deterministic techno-science it is designed to promote and exploit.

7 Noel Malcolm, *Aspects of Hobbes* (Oxford: Oxford University Press, 2002), 21, 320, 329. Malcolm notes that Hobbes engaged in various empirical as well as theoretical scientific work, for example in optics and chemistry (320). As for the claim that 'it was probably through Harvey that Hobbes met John Aubrey,' Malcolm must mean in Aubrey's adulthood, since Aubrey himself relates first meeting Hobbes as 'a little youth' in the summer of 1634, upon what turned out to be the philosopher's last visit to Malmesbury.

8 Although Hobbes expressly leaves open the possibility that the '*One Person*' serving as the '*Soveraign Representative*' (XXX/title, 175) can itself be a multiplicity of natural men, obviously the problem of *their* unity recurs. Thus the logic of how a multiplicity of people becomes a real *unity*, as presented in chapter 16, points towards Monarchy, whether de jure or de

facto. A small coterie of like-minded, like-hearted (hence, like-feeling) men – in effect, a singular kind of Aristocracy – might approximate the life-giving unity of a single man. But not so a large legislative assembly as such, much less could a Sovereign composed of the entire populace. Only insofar as such aggregations are more or less strictly led by a single person can a commonwealth experience the unified, 'single-hearted' sovereignty Hobbes argues for (cf. XXIX/15–17, 171–3).

9   Translation that of Robert Willis in *Great Books of the Western World* (Chicago: Encyclopaedia Britannica, 1952), vol. 28, 267.

10   Carl Schmitt, *Leviathan in the State Theory,* maintains that Hobbes's doing so was a mistake:

> Hobbes was for centuries regarded as the notorious representative of the absolute 'power state,' the image of the leviathan having been distorted to be a horrible Golem or Moloch. It still serves today as the prototype of what western democracy perceives to be a polemical horror picture of a 'totalitarian' state and of 'totalism.' The specific law-state elements of Hobbes' theory of state and jurisprudence were almost always misjudged. (71)

> When an author employs an image like that of the leviathan, he enters a domain in which word and language are no mere counters that can be used to calculate worth and purchasing power ... Hobbes used this image because he considered it to be an impressive symbol. He failed to realize, however, that in using this symbol he was conjuring up the invisible forces of an old ambiguous myth. His work was overshadowed by the leviathan, and all his clear intellectual constructions and arguments were overcome in the vortex created by the symbol he conjured up. No clear chain of thought can stand up against the force of genuine, mythical images. (81)

I am not persuaded that Hobbes was as naive as Schmitt here presumes, and who ignores the implications of the fuller textual context whence the name was chosen.

11   I have been unable to identify the translation Hobbes uses here (or elsewhere); it is not the King James version (despite declaring his 'submission ... to the interpretation of the Bible authorized by the Common-wealth, whose subject I am'; XXXVIII/2, 238). All of the verses I quote here *are* from that version.

12   This is clearly so in case of 'Commonwealth by Institution.' But as I shall discuss in the following chapter, the matter is somewhat more complicated

in the case of 'Commonwealth by Acquisition,' though in the final analysis this is how the Subjects of such commonwealths should regard their civic obligation.

13 Hobbes's subtle strategy for Man's declaring his independence of God begs to be compared with Sokrates's very different, but equally subtle, way of disengaging the gods from Man's political life: reform man's conception of the gods such that they are regarded as motionless, passionless, unchanging, undeceiving, non-interfering powers (*Republic* 377e–383c) – not unlike the 'negative' portrait of God with which Hobbes concludes his rational political teaching (XXXI/14–28, 190–1).

The best treatment of the significance of the Book of Job for *Leviathan* that I have come across is Norman Jacobson's *Thomas Hobbes as Creator* (New York: General Learning Press, 1971).

19: The Original State of Nature: Hobbes's Palaeoanthropology

1 This pertains not only to *Leviathan*, but to *The Elements of Law* and *De Cive* as well, though in these latter two works Hobbes provides less indication of how humans *did* live before the emergence of civil societies.

2 Still, there can be no question but that Hobbes intends that life in Civil Society be seen as infinitely preferable to that of the original State of Nature. As such, it would seem that his view is meant to oppose diametrically the rosy picture of savage life that Montaigne presents in his famous essay 'Of Cannibals,' along with its unequivocal endorsement of the superiority of Nature over Art:

These nations, then, seem to me barbarous in this sense, that they have been fashioned very little by the human mind, and are still very close to their original naturalness. The laws of nature still rule them, very little corrupted by ours; and they are in such a state of purity that I am sometimes vexed that they were unknown earlier, in the days when there were men able to judge them better than we. I am sorry that Lycurgus and Plato did not know of them; for it seems to me that what we actually see in these nations surpasses not only all the pictures in which poets have idealized the golden age and all their inventions in imagining a happy state of man, but also the conceptions and the very desire of philosophy. They could not imagine a naturalness so pure and simple as we see by experience; nor could they believe that our society could be maintained with so little artifice and human solder. This is a nation, I should say to Plato, in which there is no sort of traffic, no knowledge of letters, no science of numbers, no name for a magistrate or for political superiority, no custom of servitude, no riches or poverty, no contracts, no successions, no partitions, no occupations but leisure ones, no care for any but common kinship, no clothes, no agriculture, no metal, no use of wine or wheat. (I.31, in *The Complete Essays of Montaigne*, Donald Frame, ed. and trans. [Stanford: Stanford University Press, 1958], 153)

One cannot be sure how seriously Montaigne, a connoisseur of irony, meant this eulogy; after all, it is an essay about *cannibals*. As for the portion of the portrait quoted above, it has too much similarity to what Glaukon in the *Republic* rightly dismissed as a 'city of pigs' to believe Plato would have preferred it to his own idea of the best human environment (a matter to which I shall return in a later chapter). It is widely recognized that Gonzalo's fantasizing about an ideal commonwealth in *The Tempest* (2.1.138–63) is inspired by Montaigne's essay. And the fact that Gonzalo, though 'honest,' is something of a fool indicates that Shakespeare is closer in agreement with Hobbes and Plato than with Montaigne's romance.

   According to Noel Malcolm, *Aspects of Hobbes* (Oxford: Oxford University Press, 2000), Hobbes was almost surely familiar with Montaigne: 'The evidence of the earliest Hardwick library catalogue – compiled by Hobbes – suggests that his reading in the 1620s and 1630s included Machiavelli, Bodin, Botero, Boccalini, Huarte, Montaigne, Sarpi, de Dominis, and Grotius' (458).

3 'Above all, let us not conclude with Hobbes that because he has no idea of goodness, man is naturally wicked, that he is vicious because he does not know virtue, that he always refuses to those of his kind services which he does not believe he owes them, or that by virtue of the right he reasonably claims to the things he needs, he insanely imagines himself to be the sole owner of the entire Universe.' *Discourse on Inequality* in *The Discourses and Other Early Political Writings* (Cambridge: Cambridge University Press, 1997), Part I, par. 35, 151). Of course, Hobbes never argued for any of these four 'conclusions,' though he may leave this impression on careless readers – of which Rousseau, most definitely, is *not* one. But as I shall argue in the following chapter, Rousseau has rightly seen that the 'solitary' premise applied (counter-factually) to an *original* State of Nature would *not* result in the 'Hell on Earth' of universal war that most readers understand Hobbes to be claiming.

4 Noel Malcolm, in an essay piecing together some historical evidence that early in the seventeenth century Hobbes had been marginally involved in one or more companies that sponsored plantations in America ('Hobbes, Sandys, and the Virginia Company' in *Aspects of Hobbes*), suggests that

Hobbes may thereby have had first-hand information about the Indian populations found in the New World. If so, Malcolm concludes that it did not come to much (76).

5 Or, as Hobbes expresses it in *De Cive* (IX/5): '[I]f a *woman* gives herself to a man to share her life with him, on terms that power be in the hands of the *man*, their common *children* belong to the *father* because of his power over the *mother*' (as per the translation, *On the Citizen*, Richard Tuck and Michael Silverthorne, eds [Cambridge: Cambridge University Press, 1998, 109]).

6 As Locke expresses it in his *Second Treatise* (V.27): 'Though the Earth, and all inferior Creatures be common to all Men, yet every Man has a *Property* in his own *Person*. This no Body has any Right to but himself. The *Labour* of his Body, and the *Work* of his Hands, we may say, are properly his.'

7 *The Discourses*, 126–7.

8 Geoffrey Vaughan puts it thus: 'the move out of the state of nature – the first step in the creation of a commonwealth – had already been achieved in many times and many places before Hobbes ever wrote a word. In a pragmatic sense, therefore, Hobbes did not need to concern himself with the creation of commonwealths as with the maintenance of commonwealths.' *Behemoth Teaches Leviathan: Thomas Hobbes on Political Education* (Lanham, MD: Lexington, 2007), 31.

9 In *De Cive*, Hobbes refers to this as 'the natural origin of the commonwealth' (V/12, 74), resulting in 'the *natural commonwealth* [*Civitas naturalis*]; which may also be called the commonwealth *by Acquisition* [*Acquisita*] since it is acquired by natural power and strength' (VIII/1, 102).

There has been a lot of ink spent (and in my view, wasted) in an attempt to reconstruct the logic whereby pre-civil men might actually bring about a 'Commonwealth by Institution' out of the original State of Nature – an historical prospect Hobbes never took seriously for a moment. Thus, for example, the irrelevance of Michael Oakeshott's ingenious efforts in the Appendix to his generally insightful 'The Moral Life in the Writings of Thomas Hobbes,' in *Hobbes on Civil Association* (Indianapolis: Liberty Fund, 1937/1975), 133–40. Similarly irrelevant is most of Jean Hampton's *Hobbes and the Social Contract Tradition* (Cambridge: Cambridge University Press, 1986).

10 At this point, something similar to Hobbes's anomalous 'Third Right of Sovereignty' – otherwise irrelevant to 'Commonwealth by Conquest,' hence conveniently ignored in summarizing 'the same' (supposedly) 'Rights and Consequences of Soveraignty' (XX/3, 102) – would come into play: 'because the major part hath by consenting voices declared a Soveraigne; he that dissented must now consent with the rest; that is, be contented to avow

all the actions he shall do, or else justly be destroyed by the rest ... And whether he be of the Congregation ['of them that were assembled'], or not; and whether his consent be asked, or not, he must either submit to their decrees, or be left in the condition of warre he was in before; wherein he might without injustice be destroyed by any man whatsoever' (XVIII/5, 90). 'And whatsoever is not Unjust, is *Just*' (XV/2, 71).

11 In this respect, there is a formal similarity between Hobbes's procedure and that of Plato's Sokrates in his 'founding' of the City in *logos*. Sokrates also does not bring it into being as it might arise historically (i.e., from a natural grouping together of families, such as Aristotle describes). Instead, he builds it up from successive recognitions of the various technical specialties required for a fully functioning, self-reliant polity. He thereby shows the foundation of political life – the inner *rationale* of its cohering as a *political* association – to be the rational division of labour (*Republic* 369b–371e). But this could not conceivably be the cause of polities arising historically (as grouping together for mutual defense surely is).

12 Apart from minor alterations based on my own examination of the original text, I have here generally followed the translation of Peter L. Phillips Simpson, *The Politics of Aristotle* (Chapel Hill, NC: University of North Carolina Press, 1997).

13 *On the Citizen*, 24–5. It is with profound reservations that I resort to *De Cive* on this or any other point, since the governing assumption of my book is that *Leviathan* supersedes all earlier presentations of Hobbes's political thinking, and that it clearly differs in several important respects from them. Indeed, there is no better illustration of the difference than the presence of this statement in *De Cive* – addressing what Hobbes himself concedes is such an obvious objection – and the conspicuous absence of anything like it in *Leviathan*. Moreover, it requires very little reflection on the description of 'The Naturall Condition of Mankind' given in chapter 13 to see how its psychic effect would be in large measure nullified by a discussion comparable to that of the note in *De Cive*. Whereas generating that psychic effect – namely, fear – is fundamental to establishing the rationality of Hobbes's Natural Laws (and consequent political prescription), since each and all of those Laws are premised on the State of Nature being the horror of horrors.

The marked difference in tone between the thirteenth chapter of *Leviathan* and the longer but less alarming first chapter of *De Cive* ('On the State of Man without Civil Society') might itself be sufficient evidence that Quentin Skinner is correct in arguing that Hobbes underwent 'a remarkable change of mind' with respect to the place of rhetoric in political science:

One of his principal aims in *The Elements* and *De Cive* is to discredit and replace the Renaissance ideal of a union between reason and rhetoric, and hence between science and eloquence. This ambition is reflected with particular clarity in *The Elements* … He maintains that, so long as we reason aright from premises based in experience, we shall be able not merely to arrive at scientific truths, but to teach and beget in others exactly the same conceptions as we possess ourselves … This is because the methods of *recta ratio*, and hence the procedures of all the genuine sciences, serve in themselves to dictate the acceptance of the truths they find out …

If we turn from these pronouncements of 1640 to the *Leviathan* of 1651, we encounter a remarkable change of mind – a change of mind later consolidated and even extended in the Latin *Leviathan* in 1668 ['at some points an even more rhetorical text']. Hobbes now endorses in large measure the humanist analysis of the relations between reason and rhetoric which he had earlier sought to challenge and supercede. [Not expressly, of course; he continues to *profess* adherence to his earlier view.] He acknowledges that 'the Sciences are small Power', and cannot hope in themselves to persuade us of the findings they enunciate. He accepts in consequence that, if reason is to prevail, we shall need to supplement and enforce its findings by means of the rhetorical arts. Finally, and most dramatically, he proceeds to practise his own precepts in the body of his texts. The outcome is astonishingly different from the self-consciously scientific austerities of *The Elements* and *De Cive*. The *Leviathan* constitutes a belated but magnificent contribution to the Renaissance art of eloquence. (*Reason and Rhetoric in the Philosophy of Hobbes* [Cambridge: Cambridge University Press, 1996], 3–4)

It may not be amiss to note that in the intervening years, people throughout the British Isles witnessed first-hand the death, destruction, and anarchic turmoil of civil war. Regardless of what role (if any) it might have played in Hobbes revising his own thinking, it lent immediate plausibility to the more scarifying depiction of the State of Nature he employed in *Leviathan*.

However, as I noted in first citing Skinner's important book, I see a more comprehensive and deeper purpose in the rhetoric of *Leviathan* than that which he so usefully demonstrates. Some indication of this purpose has by now, I should hope, become clear.

14 Hobbes's primary source, however, is almost surely Thucydides (I.5): 'For the Grecians in old time, and such barbarians as in the continent lived near unto the sea, or else inhabited the islands, after once they began to cross over one to another in ships, became thieves, and went abroad under the

conduct of their most puissant men, both to enrich themselves and to fetch in maintenance for the weak; and falling upon towns unfortified and scatteringly inhabited, rifled them, and made this the best means of their living; being a matter at that time nowhere in disgrace, but carrying with it something of glory' (Hobbes's translation, as per Schlatter's modernized edition [New Brunswick, NJ: Rutgers University Press, 1975], 30).

15 That it is to be understood as generic is strongly suggested by the Latin version of *Leviathan*, where in stating the Ninth Law the term used is 'humans' (*homines*), not 'men' in the distinctly male sense (*viri*): 'all humans among themselves are by nature equal.'

20: The Ever-Present State of Nature: Greeks versus Barbarians

1 *Hobbes's Thucydides*, Richard Schlatter, ed. (New Brunswick, NJ: Rutgers University Press, 1975), 7.

2 Ibid., 18.

3 Ibid., 25.

4 *Poetics* 1451b7–11. Leo Strauss, *The City and Man* (Chicago: Rand McNally, 1964), regards this as but one more point upon which Hobbes simply did not agree with Aristotle. Strauss's own statement about the matter is prefaced by a particularly interesting parallel with Plato (whom no one regards as an 'historian'):

> Thucydides has discovered in the 'singulars' of his time (and of 'the old things') the 'universal.' It is not altogether misleading to refer to the Platonic parallel: Plato too can be said to have discovered in a singular event – in the singular life of Socrates – the universal and thus to have become able to present the universal through presenting a singular.
>
> At the time when the tradition stemming from Aristotle was being decisively shaken, Hobbes turned from Aristotle to Thucydides. He too understood Thucydides as an historian as distinguished from a philosopher. But he understood the relation between the historian and the philosopher differently than did Aristotle. The philosopher's part is 'the open conveyance of precepts' whereas history is 'merely narrative.' History too then conveys precepts; to take the most important example, according to Hobbes, Thucydides' work teaches the superiority of monarchy to any other form of government but especially to democracy. (143–4)

Strauss's prefatory reference to Plato, however, serves to remind the reader that not *all* philosophers write in forms that 'openly convey precepts.'

5 Clifford Orwin, *The Humanity of Thucydides* (Princeton, NJ: Princeton University Press, 1994), 3.
6 Ibid., 184.
7 Thus Hobbes's seemingly paradoxical Eighth Natural Law *'against Contumely'*: 'because all signs of hatred, or contempt, provoke to fight: insomuch as most men choose rather to hazard their life, than not to be revenged' (XV/20, 76).
8 Despite the obvious reservation, I have chosen in preference to Hobbes's own translation the version of Richard Crawley as slightly modernized in Robert B. Strassler, ed., *The Landmark Thucydides* (New York: Free Press, 1996), 198–201. While by no means literal, Crawley is somewhat more accurate and clear; but of primary importance, his rendering is rhetorically more effective for the modern reader – which is the point, after all: to experience something akin to Thucydides' rhetorical effect.

The bloodletting among the Corcyreans did not end with the events in the war's fifth year. The remnants of the exiled oligarchic faction, having established a base of operations on Mount Istone in the north of the island, fought on but were eventually defeated, with substantial Athenian assistance. Under the terms of the exiles' capitulation to the discretion of the Athenians, they were to be kept safely in custody; but if any were caught attempting to escape the small island on which they were held awaiting decision from Athens about their fate, all would be turned over to the Corcyreans. The leaders of the *dēmos*, 'afraid that the Athenians might spare the lives of the prisoners,' lured a few to make the fatal attempt.

> The prisoners thus handed over were shut up by the Corcyraeans in a large building, and afterwards taken out by twenties and led past two lines of hoplites, one on each side, being bound together, and beaten and stabbed by the men in the lines whenever any saw pass a personal enemy; while men carrying whips went by their sides and hastened on the road any who walked too slowly.
>
> As many as sixty were taken out and killed in this way without the knowledge of their friends in the building, who fancied they were merely being moved from one prison to another. At last, however, someone opened their eyes to the truth … and refused any longer to go out of the building, and said they would do all they could to prevent anyone coming in. The Corcyraeans, not wishing themselves to force a passage through the doors, got up on top of the building, and breaking through the roof, threw down the tiles and let fly arrows at them, from which the prisoners sheltered themselves as well as they could. Most of their number, meanwhile, were

engaged in killing themselves by thrusting into their throats the arrows shot
by the enemy, and hanging themselves with the cords taken from the beds
that happened to be there, and with strips made from their clothing; adopt-
ing, in short, every possible means of self-destruction, and also falling
victim to the missiles of their enemies on the roof. Night came on while
these horrors were taking place, and most of it had past before they were
concluded ... In this way the Corcyraeans from the mountain were
destroyed by the People; and so after terrible excesses the party strife came
to an end ... for of one party there was practically nothing left. (4.46–8)

It is easy to see why for Thucydides, and thus for all subsequent history,
Corcyra became emblematic of this increasingly voracious civil war.

9 As Nietzsche observes, it is in such circumstances that certain natural
   *in*equalities would become most evident:

   Vanity as an offshoot of the antisocial. – For the sake of their security,
   men have founded the community on the basis of positing themselves as
   being *equal* to one another; but this conception is at bottom repugnant to
   the nature of the individual and something imposed upon him; and so it
   happens that, the more the general security is guaranteed, the more do
   new shoots of the ancient drive to domination assert themselves: in the
   division of classes, in the claim to special dignities and privileges, and in
   vanity in general (in mannerisms, costumes, modes of speech, etc). ... If,
   however, the communality collapses completely and everything dissolves
   into anarchy, then there at once breaks through that condition of unreflecting, ruthless inequality that constitutes the state of nature: as, according to the report of Thucydides, happened on Corcyra. There exists
   neither a natural right nor a natural wrong. (*The Wanderer and His
   Shadow*, aph. 31, Part Two of *Human, All Too Human*, R.J.Hollingdale,
   trans. [Cambridge: Cambridge University Press, 1986], 316)

10 Thus Rousseau's insight: 'By reasoning on the basis of the principles
    [Hobbes] establishes, this Author should have said that, since the state of
    Nature [the *original* state of Nature, that is] is the state in which the care for
    our own preservation is least prejudicial to the self-preservation of others, it
    follows that this state was the most conducive to Peace and the best suited
    to Mankind. He says precisely the contrary because he improperly included
    in Savage man's care for preservation the need to satisfy a multitude of pas-
    sions that are the product of Society and have made Laws necessary' (*Dis-
    course on Inequality*, Part I, par. 35, 151).

11 Brian Barry, while writing to a quite different critical purpose (what he sees as Warrender's misreading of Hobbes), nicely captures this point: 'Hobbes does not argue that the covenant obliges you because "there is a power set up to constrain" *you*; he says the covenant obliges you because "there is a power set up to constrain" the *other* parties to it, thus taking away the "reasonable suspicion" of being double-crossed that would otherwise invalidate such a covenant.' 'Warrender and His Critics,' in *Hobbes and Rousseau: A Collection of Critical Essays*, Maurice Cranston and Richard S. Peters, eds (Garden City, NY: Doubleday, 1972), 54.

12 A few infamous names suffice to make the point: Afghanistan, Algeria, Bosnia, Cambodia, Chechnya, Colombia, Congo, Darfur, East Timor, Ghana, Iraq, Iran, Ivory Coast, Kenya, Liberia, Nicaragua, Nigeria, Rwanda, Sierra Leone, Somalia, Sri Lanka, Sudan, Tibet, Togo.

In *The Coming Anarchy: Shattering the Dreams of the Post Cold War* (New York: Random House, 2000), Robert D. Kaplan provides a sobering ratification of Hobbes's essential truth. As he writes: 'We are entering a bifurcated world. Part of the globe is inhabited by Hegel's and Fukuyama's [actually, Nietzsche's] Last Man, healthy, well fed, and pampered by technology. The other, larger part is inhabited by Hobbes's First Man, condemned to a life that is "poor, nasty, brutish and short"' (24). But the latter will increasingly impinge on the former. Based on what he has observed in extensive travels through and sojourns in the most volatile parts of the world, Kaplan endorses Martin van Crewald's thesis that warfare itself is being transformed, such that in the future it will increasingly 'have more in common with the struggles of primitive tribes,' meaning that it will be fought by '*re-primitivized* man: warrior societies operating at a time of unprecedented resource scarcity and planetary overcrowding' (48): 'In many of these countries Hobbesian realities – in particular, too many young, violence-prone males without jobs – have necessitated radical action. [Such that] democrats must be increasingly ingenious and dictators increasingly tyrannical in order to rule successfully. Surveillance, too, will become more important on an urbanized planet' (76).

13 Among the fragments we retain of the first and most famous Sophist, Protagoras of Abdera, is the beginning of his essay 'On the Gods': 'About the gods, I am not able to know whether they exist or do not exist, nor what they are like in form; for the factors preventing knowledge are many: the obscurity of the subject, and the shortness of human life.' And from 'Truth' or 'Refutatory Arguments': 'Of all things the measure is Man, of things that are, that they are, and of things that are not, that they are not.' From Kathleen Freeman, ed., *Ancilla to the Pre-Socratic Philosophers* (Oxford: Basil

Blackwell, 1952), 125–6. Protagoras was on friendly terms with much of the Athenian elite, including Pericles, as well as having achieved renown throughout Greece; cf. *Republic* 600c–d.

14 In the prefatory essay to his translation of Thucydides' *History*, Hobbes refers to both philosophers in connection with the historian: 'Agreeable to his nobility, was his institution in the study of eloquence and philosophy. For in philosophy, he was the scholar (as also was Pericles and Socrates) of Anaxagoras; whose opinions, being of a strain above the apprehension of the vulgar, procured him the estimation of an atheist: which name they bestowed on all men that thought not as they did of their ridiculous religion' (11).

15 *Discourse on Inequality* in *The Discourses and Other Early Political Writings*, Victor Gourevitch, ed. and trans. (Cambridge: Cambridge University Press, 1997), Part One, par. 37, 153–4.

16 Hobbes several times refers to what we all know: that most people's views on most matters of importance are derivative of those held by a minority who enjoy a reputation for being learned or wise: 'For all men whom the truth concernes, if they rely not on their own, must rely on the opinion of some other, whom they think wiser than themselves, and see not why he should deceive them' (XI/17, 49; cf. XII/4, 52; /9, 54). His most explicit discussion comes in the context of cautioning Sovereigns about their special responsibility for supervising universities, since virtually all so-called opinion leaders 'derive their knowledge from the Universities, and from the Schooles of Law, or from the Books, which by men eminent in those Schooles, and Universities have been published' (XXX/14, 179–80).

17 In modern times, a similar question was asked about the Germans, ostensibly the best-educated, the most cultivated people in Europe if not the world: how could they of all people be seduced by Nazism, and so many Germans become willing instruments of its barbaric practices?

In his popular book reporting the latest research on the astonishing 'plasticity' of the human brain (*The Brain That Changes Itself* [New York: Penguin, 2007]), Norman Doidge has an appendix on the brain-shaping influence of Culture. He concludes an especially pertinent section on 'How We Civilize Our Animal Instincts' with the following observation:

> Civilization is a series of techniques in which the hunter-gatherer brain teaches itself to rewire itself. And the sad proof that civilization is a composite of the higher and lower brain functions is seen when civilization breaks down in civil wars, and brutal instincts emerge full-force, and theft, rape, destruction, and murder become commonplace. Because the plastic brain can always allow brain functions that it has brought together

to separate, a regression to barbarism is always possible, and civilization will always be a tenuous affair that must be taught in each generation and is always, at most, one generation deep. (298)

18 While Hobbes does not include Envy among the 'principall causes of quarrel' in the State of Nature (XIII/6–7, 61–2), he does refer to it later in his analysis of the differences between humans and so-called political insects: 'First, that men are continually in competition for Honour and Dignity, which these creatures are not; and consequently amongst men there ariseth on that ground, Envy and Hatred, and finally Warre' (XVII/7, 86; cf. XXXI/41, 193).

19 Or so he is characterized by the most questionable growth of modernity, Nietzsche (*Beyond Good and Evil*, Preface).

20 According to Thucydides's *History*, 'The number of the killed and prisoners taken in the island was as follows: of the four hundred and twenty hoplites who had passed over originally, two hundred and ninety-two were taken alive to Athens; the rest were killed. About a hundred and twenty of the prisoners were Spartiates' (4.38). Retrieving them from captivity was a major preoccupation of Sparta for the balance of the first ('Archidamian') half of the war, motivating its agreement to the so-called Peace of Nicias that provided some respite from hostilities until the war formally resumed (5.15).

21 One might interpret Sokrates's reference to 'Anacharsis the Scythian' in company with 'Thales the Milesian' (600a) as evidence that this is already a proven possibility, both men being numbered among the 'Seven Sages' famous among Greeks. Cf. Herodotus IV.46, 76–7.

22 Cf. *Phaedrus* 274c–275b.

23 *Borboros*, literally 'mire' or 'mud,' is also used idiomatically to mean 'foul or filthy abuse'; it occurs only three times in the Platonic corpus (cf. *Phaedo* 69c, 110a).

24 Churchill, discussing the polarizing effect of the Irish Home Rule Bill of 1909, similarly attests to the distortion in perspectives and language that can arise in the midst of intense political conflicts in democracies: 'To fall behind is to be a laggard or a weakling, not sincere, not courageous; to get in front of the crowd, if only to command them and to deflect them, prompts often very violent action. And at a certain stage it is hardly possible to keep the contention within the limits of words and laws. Force, that final arbiter, that last soberer, may break upon the scene.' *The World Crisis 1911–1918* (London: Macmillan, 1941), 105.

25 The Philosopher's subsequent offer to 'pretend' to be someone fit to judge the Tyrant, as one who 'has the power in thought to insinuate himself in a

man's disposition and see through it ... adequately,' as one who 'has lived together with the tyrant' (577a–b), suggests that there may be an especially intimate relationship between Philosophy and Tyranny. Here one is reminded of Nietzsche's provocative claim that 'philosophy is this tyrannical drive itself, the most spiritual will to power, to the "creation of the world," to the *causa prima*' (*Beyond Good and Evil*, aph. 9).

26 The preceding sketch is based on the extensive analysis I present in *The War Lover: A Study of Plato's* Republic (Toronto: University of Toronto Press, 1994), chapters 4, 5, and the first part of 6.

27 'The Life of Mr Thomas Hobbes of Malmesbury,' in John Aubrey, *Brief Lives* (New York: Penguin, 2000), 441.

28 Whereas events of the Thirty Years War on the Continent, and of the English Civil War – especially as the conflict spilled over into Ireland – would prove to Hobbes's contemporaries that the behaviour of the Greeks was *not* unique in its barbarity.

29 There are two points pertinent to Hobbes's argument that are especially worth noting about Rousseau's ironical portrayal of savage life. First, despite its familial basis, he still refers to it as 'a simple and *solitary* life' (par. 13). Second, at this 'stage reached by most of the Savage Peoples known to us,' vengeances were 'terrible, and men bloodthirsty and cruel' (par. 17).

21: The Nature of Men: Equality as a Useful Lie

1 In his summary description of human life in the State of Nature, Hobbes excludes the possibility of Arts. But the context ('no Arts; no Letters'; XIII/9, 62) suggests that here he means fine arts, rather than all productive or practical skills.

2 The qualities distinguishing the generality of men from women, which Hobbes cites by way of explaining the presumption that a monarch would prefer to be succeeded by a son than by a daughter (XIX/22, 101), can obviously be used as well for distinguishing *among* men, ranking each according to his fitness 'for actions of labour and danger.'

3 Cf. Rousseau's *Discourse on Inequality* in *The Discourses and Other Early Political Writings* (Cambridge: Cambridge University Press, 1997), Part One, par. 13.

4 Montaigne may be the first to advance a version of it: 'It is commonly said that the fairest division of her favors Nature has given us is that of sense; for there is no one who is not content with the share of it that she has allotted him.' 'Of Presumption,' *The Complete Essays of Montaigne*, Donald Frame, ed. and trans. (Stanford: Stanford University Press, 1958), 499.

Descartes offers his version in the same spirit as does Hobbes, beginning his first published work (*Discourse on Method*, 1637) with these words: 'Good sense is the best distributed thing in the world: for everyone thinks himself so well endowed with it that even those who are hardest to please in everything else do not usually desire more of it than they possess. In this it is unlikely that everyone is mistaken. It indicates rather that the power of judging well and of distinguishing the true from the false – which is what we properly call "good sense" or "reason" – is naturally equal in all men.' *Discourse on Method*, in vol. 1 of *The Philosophical Writings of Descartes*, J. Cottingham, R. Stoothoff, and D. Murdoch, eds and trans. (Cambridge: Cambridge University Press, 1985), 111. But Descartes begins the very next paragraph by declaring himself an exception to the claim that everyone is content with his share of good sense: 'indeed, I have often wished to have as quick a wit, or as sharp and distinct an imagination, or as ample or prompt a memory as some others.' Later, he distinguishes 'Those with the strongest reasoning and the most skill at ordering their thoughts' (I/9, 114). And he declares that 'a majority vote is worthless as proof of truths that are at all difficult to discover' (II/4, 119). And in addressing the question of 'the difference between man and beast': 'For it is quite remarkable that there are no men so dull-witted or stupid – and this includes even madmen – that they are incapable of arranging various words together ... to make their thoughts understood; whereas there is no other animal, however perfect and well-endowed it may be, that can do the like ... This shows not merely that beasts have less reason than men, but that they have no reason at all. For it patently requires very little reason to be able to speak' (V/11, 140). As for the status of what is merely 'likely' or 'unlikely,' Descartes prudently decided to regard 'as well-nigh *false* everything that was merely probable' (I/12, 115).

5 Given that this equivocal conclusion of Hobbes's argument for a Natural law tacitly admits the weaknesses of the case, it is curious to me how few commentators address it. C.B. Macpherson, for example – preoccupied with how Hobbes in this very instance derives 'right and obligation from fact' ('a leap in political theory as radical as Galileo's formulation of the law of uniform motion was in natural science, and not unrelated to it') – ignores it completely. *The Political Theory of Possessive Individualism: Hobbes to Locke* (Oxford: Oxford University Press, 1962), 74–8.

6 Carl Schmitt, *The Leviathan in the State Theory of Thomas Hobbes* (Westport, CT: Greenwood Press, 1996), asks rhetorically, 'Who is this god who brings peace and security to people tormented by anguish, who transforms wolves into citizens and through this miracle proves himself to be a god,

obviously a "mortal god," a *deus mortalis*, as Hobbes calls him?' (31–2). Schmitt seems to be referring to a successful founding Sovereign, or Prince. But in a prior, and higher, sense, it is Hobbes himself who performs this demi-divine feat, and who, if not exactly immortal, lives on, centuries after having shuffled off his mortal coil.

7 In *De Cive*, Hobbes employs a variation of this idea in order to analyse the ways whereby 'the right of *Dominion* [*Dominium*] is acquired over men's *persons*': 'To return once again to the natural state and to look at men as if they had just emerged from the earth like mushrooms' (VIII/1, 102).

8 The preceding synopsis of the brother's challenge to Sokrates is largely based on my fuller discussion of it in *The War Lover: A Study of Plato's* Republic (Toronto: University of Toronto Press, 1994), 118–36.

9 It is worth adding that this sort of person, presuming his ambitions remain 'personal' (as opposed to political), will appreciate that so long as his various injustices go undetected, he is not setting a bad example nor otherwise undermining other people's respect for justice – not fouling his own nest, as it were. After all, an intelligent criminal wants a safe, law-abiding environment in which to enjoy the fruits of his labours every bit as much as does an honest citizen – indeed, more so, since the more trusting and just are other people, the more the opportunities for surreptitious exploitation.

10 Bearing in mind the scepticism Adeimantus displayed about the gods and their relationship to human ideas of justice, it is worth noting that this same story of Saturn and Jupiter (Chronos and Zeus in Hesiod's Greek version) is the first 'ugly' tale about the gods that Sokrates repudiates in his response to the brothers' challenge to defend the inherent goodness of being just (377e–378a).

  One of the better treatments of Hobbes's argument with his Foole is that of Marshall Missner in his sprightly introductory text *On Hobbes* (Belmont, CA: Wadsworth, 2000). Missner clearly recognizes the broader implications of the Hobbes's treatment, including its implicit allusion to the Gyges story in Glaukon's portion of the brothers' challenge to Sokrates (49–57).

11 This tacit allusion to Plutarch's *Life of Solon* is all the more interesting in light of the context from which Hobbes has lifted it:

> Anacharsis, on learning what Solon was about, laughed at him for thinking that he could check the injustice and greed of the citizens by written laws, which were like spiders' webs; they would hold the weak and insignificant who might be caught in their meshes, but would be torn in pieces by the powerful and rich. To this Solon is said to have answered that humans keep their agreements with each other when neither party

profits by the breaking of them, and he was adapting his laws to the citizens in such a manner as to make it clear to all that the practice of justice was more advantageous than the transgression of the laws. But the results justified the conjecture of Anacharsis rather than the hopes of Solon. It was Anacharsis, too, who said, after attending a session of the assembly, that he was amazed to find that among the Greeks, the wise pleaded causes, but the ignorant [or, 'unlearned'; *amatheis*] decided them. (V.1–3; translation based on that of Bernadotte Perrin, *Plutarch's Lives*, vol. 1 [London: Heinemann/Loeb Classical Library, 1932])

Apparently Hobbes had a special fondness for this particular vignette, since he used it in a later work to illustrate a different point: 'For speech has something in it like to a spider's web, (as was said of old of *Solon's* laws) for by contexture of words tender and delicate wits are ensnared and stopped; but strong wits break easily through them' (*De Corpore* III.8, as per vol. 1, p. 36 of Moleworth's edition).

12 This is essentially the first view of justice that Thrasymachus expresses in Plato's *Republic* (338e). As have many others, Bernard H. Baumrin attributes this view to Hobbes himself by way of beginning his Introduction to *Hobbes's* Leviathan: *Interpretation and Criticism* (Belmont, CA: Wadsworth, 1969): 'Not since Machiavelli had any philosopher made so bold as to propound in updated form the ancient view of Thrasymachus that "Justice is the interest of the stronger."'

13 This is essentially the second view of justice that Thrasymachus advances (cf. 343c).

14 Cf. *Republic* 443c–444e. I have discussed this matter at length in chapter 5 of *The War Lover*; see especially 166–76.

22: The Place of Philosophy: The Kingship of Hobbes

1 The preceding sketch of Sokrates's 'apology for philosophy' is based on my fuller discussion in *The War Lover: A Study of Plato's* Republic (Toronto: University of Toronto Press, 1994), 250–63.

2 Cf. *Hamlet* 2.2.88–9.

3 Hobbes claims that 'the Geometrician, from the Construction of Figures, findeth out many Properties thereof.' This is of course true of the geometric figures themselves, but it leaves the false impression that one could learn the *structural* properties of (say) the Arch from geometry. A military engineer will use geometry in 'delineating the dimensions of a fortress' (XXX/25, 184) – for example, in laying out protective fields of crossfire, or in comput-

ing the capacity of vaults. But the solidity of his construction will depend upon his understanding of materials, the distribution of static forces in materials variously configured, etc. – knowledge that comes from experimental physics, not geometry.

4 *Republic* 521c–531e.

5 Here the kinship with Hobbes's account of Reason per se is especially close (V/1, 31–2). That this 'Calculation' view pretty much exhausts most people's understanding of what Reason essentially *is* likely accounts for Hobbes's propounding it.

6 This is something of a joke, in that the relevance of Solid Geometry to Astronomy is not that of understanding the heavenly 'solids' themselves, but of their *motions* – their trajectories as various curves that result from transecting regular geometrical solids (which, of course, have no material solidity at all, being purely forms).

7 All the more interesting, then, that in his schematic classification of the Sciences (chapter 9), Hobbes has directly paired 'Consequences from *Vision* … OPTIQUES' with 'Consequences from *Sounds* … MUSIQUE.' On a personal note, Aubrey tells us that Hobbes 'had always books of prick-song [i.e., written music] – e.g. of H. Lawes', etc, *Songs* – which at night, when he was abed, and the doors made fast, and was sure nobody heard him, he sang aloud (not that he had a very good voice, but for his health's sake).'

8 As Aristotle asserts in the first line of his *Metaphysics*. A couple of quotes from Plato's *Republic* are particularly apposite here: 'Then insofar as the work of the Guardians is greatest [*megiston*; i.e., 'most important'], it would require the most leisure from the other tasks, as well as the greatest art and attention' (374d–e); 'Come, then, as if telling tales in a tale and at leisure, let us in *logō* [i.e., 'in description'] educate the men [i.e., the potential Guardians]' (376d–e).

9 The supposedly 'geometrical' character of *Leviathan* has been much discussed. For example, Richard Peters, *Hobbes* (Baltimore: Penguin Books, 1967) – who shows more awareness of a 'Platonic connection' than do most scholars – nonetheless treats the book's spotty geometrical appearance as genuinely indicative of Hobbes's method, and as lifted straight from Plato (43–8). As such, I believe he misunderstands the actual significance of Geometry for both philosophers. Jürgen Overhoff accepts the genuineness of Hobbes's reliance on geometry, but argues that Galileo was his true inspiration. *Hobbes's Theory of the Will: Ideological Reasons and Historical Circumstances* (Lanham, MD: Rowman and Littlefield, 2000), 33–41. With respect to this latter point, see also Douglas M. Jesseph, 'Galileo, Hobbes, and the Book of Nature,' *Perspectives on Science* 12, no. 2 (2004): 191–211.

10 In Hobbes's day, the newly developing scientific philosophy of Bacon and
   Descartes was also in need of security, as shown by the controversial case of
   Galileo, which Hobbes alludes to in the concluding paragraph of this
   chapter: 'With the Introduction of False, we may joyn also the suppression
   of True Philosophy, by such men, as neither by lawfull authority, nor sufficient study, are competent Judges of the truth ... And every day it appeareth
   more and more, that Years, and Dayes are determined by Motions of the
   Earth. Nevertheless, men that have in their Writings but supposed such
   Doctrine, as an occasion to lay open the reasons for, and against it, have
   been punished for it by Authority Ecclesiasticall.' Descartes similarly
   alludes to the infamous Galileo case (though also without mentioning the
   man's name) as justification for his own caution in presenting his revolutionary doctrine (*Discourse on Method*, Part Six, par. 1).
      It is worth noting that Hobbes's forty-sixth chapter both begins and con-
   cludes with references to Astronomy. In his first paragraph, however, he
   speaks of 'the Rising, Setting, and Moving of the *Sun*,' implying *that* to be
   'the Causes of Day, and Night' – the orthodox view of the age. Whereas, by
   the *end* of the chapter, he sounds suspiciously like a Copernican. As I have
   noted before, Astronomy – unlike Geometry – is a politically sensitive
   subject, carrying cosmological, hence theological, implications. And Hobbes
   is well aware that how one stands on this scientific question concerning the
   structure of the Heavens – whether the Earth or the Sun is the centre of the
   World – implies much more than how one conceives the causes of day and
   night.

11 I alluded to this fact earlier in discussing Hobbes's Dedication. As Douglas
   Jesseph writes, '[Hobbes's] feelings of isolation and vulnerability were by no
   means confined to the fields of natural philosophy and mathematics. The
   Monster of Malmesbury faced powerful and determined opposition from
   other quarters as well, and they could do him considerably more harm.
   Much of London had been destroyed in the great fire of September 1666
   and in October the House of Commons concluded that the fire was probably divine punishment for the country's toleration of the (alleged) atheism
   of Hobbes and Thomas White. Parliament empowered a committee to
   examine their writing and determine whether they should be tried for
   heresy. Hobbes was spared further investigation or harm by the action of
   his patron Henry Bennet, baron of Arlington, who intervened on his behalf
   to stop the proceedings. Still, Hobbes was sufficiently concerned by the
   episode that he destroyed a large number of his papers.' *Squaring the Circle:
   The War between Hobbes and Wallis* (Chicago: University of Chicago
   Press, 1999), 281–2.

12 Translation that supplied in the Curley edition of *Leviathan*, 528–9. And as Curley shrewdly observes about the last quoted exchange between 'A' and 'B,' 'There is a curious asymmetry between Hobbes' treatment of atheism here and his treatment of Christianity in xliii, 18, where someone who holds that Jesus is the Christ is to be credited with holding all the consequences of that doctrine, whether or not she sees that they are consequences.' Hobbes included a similar discussion '*Of Heresie*' in his *A Dialogue between a Philosopher & a Student of the Common Laws of England*, Joseph Cropsey, ed. (Chicago: University of Chicago Press, 1971), 122–32.

13 Still, Hobbes explicitly acknowledges that the *teaching* of philosophy per se must remain subject to political control: 'For disobedience may lawfully be punished in them, that against the Laws teach even true Philosophy' (XLVI/42, 380).

14 I refer to this utilitarian conception as 'Baconian' even though I believe that Bacon himself argued for it in the same spirit as did Hobbes: that whatever its intrinsic merits, it provides the most effective political envelope for the preservation of the ancient Platonic conception of philosophy. For a thorough expounding of Bacon as himself a 'Platonic philosopher,' see Laurence Lampert's seminal *Nietzsche and Modern Time:s A Study of Bacon, Descartes, and Nietzsche* (New Haven: Yale University Press, 1993), 17–141.

15 Translation that supplied in the Curley edition of *Leviathan*, 510. Given this characterization of the Sadducees as philosophers, Hobbes's comment on them in the main text is all the more interesting: 'whosoever behaved him-selfe in extraordinary manner, was thought by the Jewes to be possessed either with a good, or evill spirit; except by the Sadducees, who erred so farre on the other hand, as not to believe there were at all any spirits, (which is very neere to direct Atheisme;)' (VIII/25, 38; cf. XXXIV/18, 211).

16 Hobbes endorses the importance of this distinction in his *Thomas White's De Mundo Examined*, Harold Whitmore Jones, trans. (London: Bradford University Press, 1976): 'Rightly, then, did Plato distinguish two kinds of thing: one, namely *tò ón*, he said existed but did not come into being; the other, *tò einai*, did not exist but did come into being, unless *tò ón* could also be made by God, and in the Creation was made, by a method we do not understand' (313–14). There are several of Plato's dialogues in which this distinction figures, but it is most prominently discussed and employed in the central analogical images of his *Republic* (the Sun-Good Analogy, the Divided Line, and the Cave Allegory) along with the non-imagistic Proportion (533e–534a). All analogies are adaptations of the formal idea of 'proportion' (*analogon*) in Geometry.

17 This is reason, of course, that geometry became an established part of the 'liberal education' in the West and subsequently was incorporated in virtually all grammar school curricula.

18 That there is *more* to be considered is not to deny the validity of what Hobbes emphasizes: the role of deductive reasoning (as exemplified by geometry) for generating scientific theories and explanations, and the '*Conditional*' character of the resulting knowledge: *If* X, *then* Y. As I discussed in chapter 12, his explicit view of what Science *is* (a logico-linguistic construction), and of how it 'works' (the hypothetical-deductive model of explanation), is to this extent congruent with the view propagated in the twentieth century, mainly by Logical Positivists.

19 For all the enormous political significance of the mass reproduction of written speech made possible by mechanical printing, Hobbes's ranking the accomplishment of the unknown Inventor of Letters far above that of the known Inventor of Printing is easily justified – and not merely because the former presupposes the latter. Basing a mode of writing on purely formal symbols for the various phonetic components of aural activity was truly revolutionary. But in order to appreciate the ingenuity involved, entailing as it does a reversal of what comes more 'naturally,' one must compare it with the form of writing that it replaced: hieroglyphics, pictographs – representation of whole words, 'names,' usually a stylized image of the 'look' of a given name's referent – a step in linguistic history which Hobbes, most strangely, chose to skip over. This is unlikely to have been an oversight on Hobbes's part, since his mentor used the comparison between pictographs and letters in various analogies, e.g., 'For as hieroglyphics came before letters, so parables came before arguments.' Francis Bacon, *Wisdom of the Ancients*, in *The Works of Francis Bacon*, vol. 6, James Spedding, Robert Leslie Ellis, and Douglas Denon Heath, eds (London: Longmans, 1870), 698.

20 Hobbes claims that in Sparta, 'Soveraignty was in the *Ephori*' (XIX/12, 99). Judging the issue is difficult, inasmuch as our information about the regime may be incomplete or otherwise problematic. The five *Ephors* were guardians of Sparta's laws and served as its chief executives, including the overseeing of its two hereditary Kings; however, they were elected by the entire citizenry for only one-year, non-renewable terms. As such, their status would seem the same as that of an elected King, who (according to Hobbes; XIX/18, 100) 'have not the Soveraign Power in propriety, but in use only'; 'But if he have no Power to elect his Successor, then there is some other Man, or Assembly known' who *does*, and who would seem the 'ultimate' sovereign ('For none have a right to give that which they have not

right to possesse, and keep to themselves, if they think good'; /11, 98). But the Spartan assembly, though they elected the *Ephori*, did *not* have the right to exercise the *Ephori*'s powers themselves. The thirty members of the Spartan *Gerousia*, on the other hand, were elected for life from among citizenry over sixty years old (as vacancies occurred), and apparently functioned perpetually as a kind of Senate. In short, it is very hard to say who, or what, was *sovereign* in the Spartan constitution. Despite this confusing complexity (at least to us), the Spartan regime was famous for its stability and longevity. As such, its example would seem to present a plausible challenge to Hobbes's doctrine of the indivisibility of sovereign power (XVIII/18, 93; XIX/1, 94) – which perhaps explains his flatly declaring the *Ephori* to be sovereign.

21 A lesson most beautifully shown by Shakespeare in his *The Life and Death of King Richard the Second*. He has Richard's uncle Gaunt, Duke of Lancaster, warn his royal nephew: 'A thousand flatterers sit within thy crown, / Whose compass is no bigger than thy head, / And yet, incaged in so small a verge, / The waste is no whit less than thy land' (2.1.100–3). Richard, however, chooses to regard old Lancaster as but 'A lunatic lean-witted fool,' and upon learning of his death, immediately orders the confiscation of his entire estate, which by legal right and tradition should pass to his eldest son, the recently exiled Henry Bolingbroke. This stirs the King's last surviving uncle, the feckless Duke of York, normally so mild and accommodating, to voice an extended admonition and warning:

> Seek you to seize and gripe into your hands
> The royalties and rights of banish'd Herford?
> ...
> Let not to-morrow then ensue to-day:
> Be not thyself. For how art thou a king
> But by fair sequence and succession?
> Now afore God – God forbid I say true! –
> If thou do wrongfully seize Herford's rights,
> ...
> You pluck a thousand dangers on your head,
> You lose a thousand well-disposed hearts,
> And prick my tender patience to those thoughts
> Which honour and allegiance cannot think. (2.1.189–208)

While Shakespeare has much else to teach in this play, he does mean to ratify Machiavelli's warning that in becoming feared, a Prince must nonetheless avoid becoming hated, which is possible so long as 'he abstains from the property of his citizens and his subjects': 'because men forget the death of a father more quickly than the loss of a patrimony.' *The Prince*, Harvey Mansfield, ed. and trans. (Chicago: University of Chicago Press, 1985), ch. 17, par. 4, 67.

22 But taught in such a manner as does not allow Subjects to presume themselves capable judges of what is reasonable, since 'all men are by nature provided of notable multiplying glasses, (that is their Passions and Selfe-love,) through which, every little payment appeareth a great grievance; but are destitute of those prospective glasses, (namely Morall and Civill Science,) to see a farre off the miseries that hang over them, and cannot without such payments be avoyded' (XVIII/20, 94).

23 In this, as is in so much, Hobbes is in agreement with Machiavelli: 'The choice of ministers is of no small importance to a prince; they are good or not according to the prudence of the prince. And the first conjecture that is to be made of the brain of a lord is to see the men he has around him; and when they are capable and faithful, he can always be reputed wise because he has known how to recognize them as capable and to maintain them as faithful' (so begins chapter 22 of *The Prince*, 92).

24 For so Machiavelli also advises: 'The prince should go in person, and perform himself the office of Captain' (ch. 12, par. 3, 49; cf. ch. 14, par. 1).

25 I have my own views, of course, which are apt to be offensive to partisans of these regimes; indeed, my reservations about the quality of leadership typical of modern democracies contributes to my doubts about their continuing viability. And that concern, as I indicated in my Prelude, is partly what motivated my re-examination of Hobbes's political teaching. Some further discussion of what I see as the deepening problems confronting these regimes is provided in my concluding Postlude.

23: A Colossus of Irony: The Latent Platonism of *Leviathan*

1 What I intend here is merely a reminder to readers of conclusions reached on the basis of analyses argued at length in the relevant chapters of Part One.

2 Some would except quantum physics. But so far as I can tell, the basis for doing so is an insistence that epistemological indeterminism be regarded as the ontological reality; I find the arguments for doing so unpersuasive.

3 The problem of the human good is far more complex, of course, partly because of the diversity of human types stemming from the complexity of the rational soul, with its capacity for appreciating and creating beauty, for

pursuing and enjoying knowledge, and for acting morally and nobly; and partly because of man's political nature, such that a common good is implicated in each individual's good.

4 Insofar as Plato's own views are fairly represented by those he has Sokrates express in his *Republic* – which is by no means certain – I have ventured some of my own understanding of them in *The War Lover: A Study of Plato's* Republic (Toronto: University of Toronto Press, 1994), mainly in ch. 7.

5 There is no 'theory' of forms, or of anything else in Plato. There is no word in classical Greek for what we mean by 'theory,' which is essentially a concept derived from Kant's formalization of the method of Newtonian physics. This widespread misunderstanding of Plato is a result of reading him through Kantian lenses, thus misconstruing *ideas* and 'forms' (*eidē*) as 'ideals.' Plato uses the term *theoria* a total of fourteen times (three in *Republic*), and in every instance it simply means 'contemplation,' as it does for Aristotle whenever he speaks of 'theoretical knowledge': knowledge that is sought purely for the sake of knowing.

6 That is, he needs at least what Machiavelli treats as a 'second-class brain': 'And since there are three kinds of brains: one understands by itself, another that discerns what others understand, the third that understands neither by itself nor through others; the first is most excellent, the second excellent, and the third useless.' *The Prince*, Harvey Mansfield, ed. and trans. (Chicago: University of Chicago Press, 1985), ch. 22., par. 2, 92).

7 A recent biographer of Hobbes, Arnold Rogow, has observed: 'The reliance on Aubrey is not difficult to explain. Hobbes was a somewhat secretive man who rarely confided in others, and apparently never discussed with anyone his early years in Malmesbury and at Oxford. Unlike Pepys and Evelyn, whose lives overlapped his own, Hobbes left behind no diary; to make matters even more arduous for a biographer, only a small number of his letters survive, none of them written before he was forty.' *Thomas Hobbes: Radical in the Service of Reaction* (New York: W.W. Norton, 1986), 11. In this guarding of his privacy, however, Hobbes was surpassed by his junior contemporary, Descartes, who concealed his own birthday, and about whom Stephen Gaukroger writes: 'Descartes was intensely secretive, taking as his motto *bene vixit, bene qui latuit* – "he lives well who is well hidden."' *Descartes: An Intellectual Biography* (Oxford: Oxford University Press, 1995), 16.

Noel Malcolm, editor of *The Correspondence of Thomas Hobbes* (Oxford: Oxford University Press, 1994), has himself conceded that the collection suffers from serious limitations: 'The first is the one-sidedness of what survives' (xxxi). Of the 211 letters comprised by these two volumes, fully two-thirds are letters *to* him, the remainder *from* him. But even this is misleading in that so many of the latter are short, and of negligible philosophical interest (e.g., most of those to one or another of his noble patrons; the half dozen to John Aubrey; and those to various other personal friends, discussing mainly incidental matters). I would say there is barely a dozen that would qualify as philosophically important, including here those dealing with mathematics.

However, one does encounter in the collection odd indications that some of Hobbes's correspondents presumed he would recognize a Platonic allusion. For example, compare Sokrates's explanation of Philosophy's being disgraced by the 'bastard and paltry offspring' of pretentious tinkers (there being such a very small number who are worthy of the calling; *Republic* 495c–496e) with Samuel Sorbière's lament, 'how few people there are who philosophize at all deeply … who are strong in learning, judgement, and discrimination, without which philosophy is handled with dirty fingers, and authors give birth to malformed embryos, disgracing our most learned discipline' (Ltr. 105, 389–90), or the same author's assuring Hobbes that the present 'age of iron will not last forever,' and that 'despite the barbarism in the midst of which we have lived,' there remain 'a number of worthy people who have not lost their love of philosophical studies' (Ltr. 133, 494; cf. *Republic* 546e–547b).

8 Wesley Trimpi, *The Cambridge History of Literary Criticism*, vol. 3: *The Renaissance*, Glyn P. Norton, ed. (Cambridge: Cambridge University Press, 1999), ch. 18.

9 I have cited some important examples of relevant scholarship in the endnotes of my study of Shakespeare's political philosophy, *Of Philosophers and Kings: Political Philosophy in Shakespeare's* Macbeth *and* King Lear (Toronto: University of Toronto Press, 2001); see, e.g., 390–1.

10 While Milton repeatedly objects in *Areopagitica* to Plato's defence of censorship, he nonetheless refers to Plato as 'divine' in his *Defense of the People of England* in *Areopagitica and Other Political Writings of John Milton*, John Alvis, ed. (Indianapolis: Liberty Fund, 1999), 234. See also his poem *De Idea Platonica Quemadmodum Aristoteles Intellexit* ('On the Platonic Idea as Understood by Aristotle'), wherein he satirizes Aristotle's apparent objections in his *Metaphysics* to Plato's doctrines.

11 As Marie Boas writes in *The Scientific Renaissance: 1450–1630* (New York: Harper and Row, 1966): 'Overtly in rebellion against the dead hand of the past in the person of Aristotle, humanists everywhere turned to Platonist (and neo-Platonist) doctrines' (43):

Pure mathematics, in Platonic doctrine, because it dealt with the world of perfect, unchanging, abstract ideas, was the best possible training for the philosopher who wished to study the nature of ideas, forms, and essences. Mathematics reflected the unchanging reality behind the flux and uncertainty of the world of the senses; hence for the Platonist to study nature was to search for the mathematical laws which govern the world ... The fifteenth century's intensification of interest in Platonic and neo-Platonic doctrine helped to encourage the view that mathematics was not only the key to science, but included within its competence the greater part of what the seventeenth century was to call natural philosophy. (198)

This has by no means become an outmoded view. In *The Emperor's New Mind* (Oxford: Oxford University Press, 1989), Roger Penrose, discussing changes in thinking about geometry since Einstein's revolutionary theories, explains:

In Plato's view, the objects of pure geometry – straight lines, circles, triangles, planes, etc. – were only approximately realized in terms of the world of actual physical things ... Plato's [different] world consists not of tangible objects, but of 'mathematical things'. This world is accessible to us not in the ordinary physical way but, instead, via the *intellect*. One's mind makes contact with Plato's world whenever it contemplates a mathematical truth, perceiving it by the exercise of mathematical reasoning and insight. ... By some miraculous insight Plato seems to have foreseen, on the basis of what must have been very sparse evidence indeed at that time that: on the one hand, mathematics must be studied and understood for its own sake, and one must not demand completely accurate applicability to the objects of physical experience; on the other hand, the workings of the actual external world can ultimately be understood only in terms of precise mathematics – which means in terms of Plato's ideal world 'accessible via the intellect'! (158–9; cf. 428)

12 Herbert Butterfield, *The Origins of Modern Science* (New York: Free Press, 1965), is one who thinks he was: 'Galileo said that the book of the universe was written in mathematical language, and its alphabet consisted of triangles, circles, and geometrical figures. There is no doubt that, in both Kepler and Galileo, Platonic and Pythagorean influences played an important part in the story' (102).

13 A.J.Meadows, *The High Firmament: A Survey of Astronomy in English Literature* (Leicester, UK: Leicester University Press, 1969), 133.

14 As Paul D. Cooke, *Hobbes and Christianity: Reassessing the Bible in Leviathan* (Lanham, MD: Rowman and Littlefield, 1996), observes, 'the Cambridge Platonists were among Hobbes's most virulent opponents' (127). Cooke does an admirable job of showing 'that the religion Hobbes teaches does not constitute Christianity and that, indeed, Hobbes's theology aims at something else entirely.' Cooke's thesis is one with which I have considerable sympathy: 'Hobbes authored a kind of conspiracy against authentic Christianity in the name of his science of natural justice and the rights of man, and that those who accept Hobbes's treatment of religion as ingenuous have been taken in by his deception' (xiv).

Samuel Mintz speaks of 'Ralph Cudworth, the Master of Christ's and a Cambridge Platonist' as being 'Hobbes's most intellectually formidable opponent.' Mintz recounts the trials of one Daniel Scargill, who was expelled from the university for asserting certain Hobbesian views (Cudworth signing the expulsion order), and who was only partially restored to his previous standing upon publicly recanting for his having 'gloried to be an *Hobbist* and an *Atheist*.' Mintz observes: 'Here we see a university scholar submitting (with what disingenuousness we cannot at this distance tell) to the overwhelming pressure of university and Church opinion, united in their detestation of Hobbes.' *The Hunting of Leviathan* (Bristol: Thoemmes Press, 1996), 50–1.

A Melvillian Coda

1 In November 1851, a few months after *Moby-Dick* was first published, Melville wrote Hawthorne (the book's dedicatee):

> [Y]our joy-giving and exultation-breeding letter is not my reward for my ditchers's work with that book, but is the good goddess's bonus over and above what was stipulated for – for not one man in five cycles, who is wise, will ever expect appreciative recognition from his fellows, or any one of them. Appreciation! Recognition! Is Jove appreciated? Why, ever since Adam, who has got to the meaning of his great allegory – the world? Then we pygmies must be content to have our paper allegories but ill comprehended. (In Herman Melville, *Tales, Poems, and Other Writings*, John Bryant, ed. [New York: Modern Library, 2001], 42)

2 Some might protest that the crew of this ship cannot plausibly represent a viable commonwealth because of the simple fact that all are men: there are

no women. True. And this is an objection not to be lightly dismissed, in that human sexuality presents what is both the foremost necessity of political life, and (arguably) the single most troubling complication of it. Two points in response will have to suffice. First, women as such are similarly absent from Hobbes's *Leviathan*; one can read that book and almost forget that we are sexual beings. In both texts, women are occasionally mentioned, but almost invariably in connection with men to whom they are attached. Second – and this may at least partially justify the first – one might argue that the assumption of substantial human equality, taken seriously, renders the objection nugatory.

3 This and like statements serve as Melville's ratification of Hobbes's famous formula: 'So that in the first place, I put for a generall inclination of all mankind, a perpetuall and restlesse desire of Power after power, that ceaseth onely in Death' (XI/2, 747). For it is the same *within* each voyage: 'many is the time the poor fellows, just buttoning the necks of their clean frocks, are startled by the cry of "There she blows!" and away they fly to fight another whale, and go through the whole weary thing again. Oh! my friends, but this is man-killing! Yet this is life' (ch. 98, 429).

4 One might hear in Ahab's words an echo of Hobbes's claim that 'the Multitude so united in one person' – in whom 'consisteth the Essence of the Common-wealth,' and who 'is called SOVERAIGNE, and said to have *Soveraigne Power*' – can be regarded as a '*Mortall God*' (XVII/13–14, 87–8).

5 Ishmael expresses profound doubt, however, about the complete success of this Baconian-Cartesian project: 'however baby man may brag of his science and skill, and however much, in a flattering future, that science and skill may augment; yet for ever and for ever, to the crack of doom, the sea will insult and murder him' (ch. 58, 273).

6 As noted in my Overture, in making this 'Cetology' his thirty-second chapter, Melville has aligned it with the catalogue of natural histories that Bacon appended to his *Novum Organum*, as needed for the foundation of his revolution in Science. The only one of the 130 such histories that refers to whale matters is number thirty-two, which includes 'ambergris' – a precious substance which figures significantly in Ishmael's story (ch. 92).

7 The square-bracketed page references in this section are to Bacon's *Description of a Natural and Experimental History Such as May Serve for the Foundation of a True Philosophy* included in the version of *The New Organon* edited by Fulton F. Anderson (Indianapolis: Bobbs-Merrill, 1960). The rounded parentheses refer to pages in ch. 32 of *Moby-Dick*.

8 In '*Moby-Dick* and Melville's Quarrel with America,' *Interpretation* 23, no. 2 (Winter 1996), John Alvis suggests, 'Melville devotes lengthy passages to

explaining the whaling industry so as to keep in sight the image of the *Pequod* as an epitome of a society organized for the sake of commercial venturing' (230). Alvis stresses the Lockean character of the political environment in which the story proceeds; in placing the emphasis instead on Hobbes, I need not be understood as greatly disagreeing, inasmuch as I maintain that Locke's teaching is derivative of Hobbes's – even on the matter of toleration. See Edwin Curley's 'Hobbes and the Cause of Religious Toleration,' in *The Cambridge Companion to Hobbes's Leviathan*, Patricia Springborg, ed. (Cambridge: Cambridge University Press, 2007).

9   Scholars who fail to see how Hobbes's prescription would work in actual practice – who fail, that is, to 'think politically – also fail to recognize the extent to which Hobbes is the true founder of Liberalism. See, e.g., Lucien Jaume, 'Hobbes and the Philosophical Sources of Liberalism,' in *The Cambridge Companion to Hobbes's* Leviathan,' 199–216.

10   On this view, one may say that Locke merely articulates a moral ratification for what Hobbes acknowledges is naturally true: that faced with what they judge to be gross misrule (the criteria of which Locke, following Hobbes's implicit indication, has conveniently supplied), not only will people rebel, they will believe they have a *right* to rebel, irrespective of any doctrines to the contrary. Locke expressly characterizes as tyrannical the use of power 'for [one's] own private separate advantage,' such as when a ruler's 'commands and actions are not directed to the preservation of the properties of his people, but the satisfaction of his own ambition, *revenge*, covetousness, or any other irregular passion' (*Second Treatise*, §199; emphasis added).

11   As Machiavelli teaches he who would be a prince, 'Men in general judge more by their eyes than by their hands, because seeing is given to everyone, touching to few. Everyone sees how you appear, few touch how you are.' *The Prince*, Harvey Mansfield, ed. and trans. (Chicago: University of Chicago Press, 1985), ch. XVIII, 71. Cf. *King Lear* 1.4.27–8.

12   Melville several times resorts to this Shakespearean mode of writing later in his book (e.g., chs. 108, 119–22, 127, 129), complementing his dozens of allusions to various of Shakespeare's plays, e.g., Ahab's echoing of King Lear with his 'Oh, take medicine, take medicine!' ch. 120, 509 (cf. *King Lear* 3.4.33); and the double echo of Macbeth in his 'What I've dared, I've willed; and what I've willed, I'll do!' Ch. 37, 168 (*Macbeth* 1.7.46 and 4.1.147–8, 153–4); and his reference to *Hamlet* (5.1.65 ff.) when addressing the ship's Carpenter: 'Hark ye, dost thou not ever sing working about a coffin? ... the grave-digger in the play sings, spade in hand.' Ch. 127, 528.

13   The English term 'demoniac' is derived ultimately from the Greek *daimōn*. As Plato has Sokrates in his *Apology* remind the Athenians at his trial, he is

attended by a *daimōn*, which according to some accounts is a part-human, part-divine being, whereas according to other accounts, altogether divine (27c–d).

14 The inhabitants of pre- and post-Revolutionary America were keenly sensitive to the political threat posed by Caesarism, a concern aroused not least by the unparalleled popularity of Joseph Addison's *Cato: A Tragedy*. Depicting the last efforts of Cato the Younger to protect the Roman Republic from usurpation by Julius Caesar, the play was first published and performed (repeatedly) in London in 1713. An immediate success, its popularity continued throughout the eighteenth century, not only in England but on the continent, and especially in colonial America. As Forest McDonald writes in the Foreward to a new edition of Addison's writings, *Cato: A Tragedy and Selected Essays*, Christine Dunn Henderson and Mark E. Yellin, eds (Indianapolis: Liberty Fund, 2004),

> [A]t least eight editions were published in the British-American colonies by the end of the century. The play was also performed all over the colonies, in countless productions from the 1730s until after the American Revolution.
>
> That most of the founding generation read it or saw it or both is unquestionable, and that it stuck in their memories is abundantly evident. Benjamin Franklin, as a young and aspiring writer, committed long passages from it to memory … Patrick Henry adapted his famous 'Give me liberty or give me death' speech directly from lines in *Cato*. Nathan Hale's last celebrated words, 'I only regret that I have but one life to lose for my country,' echoes a remark by Cato, 'What a pity it is that we can die but once to save our country.'
>
> *Cato* was the favorite play of George Washington, who saw it many times and quoted or paraphrased lines from it in his correspondence over the course of four decades. (vii–viii)

In short, the American founders were not unaware of a republic's vulnerability to subversion by a charismatic demagogue. Alexander Hamilton, arguing in *Federalist No. 21* the inadequacy of the existing Articles of Confederation, warns that as things (then) stood:

> A successful faction may erect a tyranny on the ruins of order and law, while no sucour could constitutionally be afforded by the union to the friends and supporters of the government. The tempestuous situation from which Massachusetts has scarcely emerged, evinces, that dangers of

this kind are not merely speculative. Who can determine what might have been the issue of her late convulsions, if the malcontents had been headed by a Caesar or by a Cromwell?

Notice, Hamilton seems here not to distinguish tyranny from Caesarism. One may rightly insist that this is a theoretical mistake, that, as Leo Strauss observes (in *On Tyranny*, revised and expanded edition, Victor Gourevitch and Michael S. Roth, eds [New York: Free Press, 1991]), 'genuine Caesarism is not tyranny,' that indeed it may be necessary and thus legitimate at a certain stage of political decay:

> Caesarism belongs to a degraded society, and thrives on its degradation. Caesarism is just, whereas tyranny is unjust. But Caesarism is just in the way in which deserved punishment is just. It is as little choiceworthy for its own sake as is deserved punishment. Cato refused to see what his time demanded because he saw too clearly the degraded and degrading character of what his time demanded. It is much more important to realize the low level of Caesarism ... than to realize that under certain conditions Caesarism is necessary and hence legitimate.
>
> ...
>
> To stress the fact that it is just to replace constitutional rule by absolute rule, if the common good requires that change, means to cast a doubt on the absolute sanctity of the established constitutional order. It means encouraging dangerous men to confuse the issue by bringing about a state of affairs in which the common good requires the establishment of their absolute rule. The true doctrine of the legitimacy of Caesarism is a dangerous doctrine. The true distinction between Caesarism and tyranny is too subtle for ordinary political use. It is better for the people to remain ignorant of that distinction and to regard the potential Caesar as a potential tyrant. No harm can come from this theoretical error which becomes a practical truth if the people have the mettle to act upon it. No harm can come from the political identification of Caesarism and tyranny: Caesars can take care of themselves. (179–80)

Thus, Strauss implicitly endorses Hamilton's practical conflation of Caesarism and tyranny. And, as Strauss notes, potential Caesars do not restrict their ambitions to circumstances which truly require, hence legitimate, their absolute rule. Still, one may wonder whether polities framed in accordance with Hobbes's political prescription may not be peculiarly susceptible to degradation.

15 Hobbes is clearly aware of this problem, warning of its dangers more than once:

> [T]he Popularity of a potent Subject, (unlesse the Common-wealth have very good caution of his fidelity,) is a dangerous Disease; because the people (which should receive their motion from the Authority of the Soveraign,) by the flattery, and by the reputation of an ambitious man, are drawn away from their obedience to the Lawes, to follow a man, of whose vertues, and designes they have no knowledge. And this is commonly of more danger in a Popular Government, than in a Monarchy; because an army is of so great force, and multitude, as it may easily be made to believe, they are the People. By this means it was, that *Julius Caesar*, who was set up by the People against the Senate, having won to himselfe the affections of his Army, made himselfe Master, both of Senate and People. And this proceeding of popular, and ambitious men, is plain Rebellion; and may be resembled to the effects of Witchcraft. (XXIX/20, 173–4; cf. XXX/28, 185)

16 *Republic* 537d; cf. 531e–532a, 534b.
17 Drawing on philosophers from Locke and Newton to Burke, Addison, and Kant, Richard S. Moore provides a particularly useful discussion of 'whiteness' in Melville's writings: *That Cunning Alphabet: Melville's Aesthetics of Nature* (Amsterdam: Rodopi, 1982), 156–65.
18 Ch. 58, 273; cf. *Republic* 375a–d.
19 Cf. ibid., 619d–e, 621b.
20 Ibid., 514a–518e.
21 That this is the teaching of Plato's *Republic*, and that it is fraught with radical implications for the very ideas of philosophy and philosophers, is extensively argued in my interpretive study of that dialogue, *The War Lover: A Study of Plato's* Republic (Toronto: University of Toronto Press, 1994), passim.
22 Cf. *Republic* 548b, 549a, 586c–d.
23 Cf. Nietzsche, *Beyond Good and Evil*, aph. 26.
24 Cf. *Republic* 499b–500e.

Postlude

1 Although his essay 'Hobbes: The Problem of Interpretation' is now somewhat dated, it seems to me that W.H. Greenleaf's general description of 'three main types of interpretation of Hobbes's ideas' still encompasses the

vast majority of scholarly approaches. What he calls 'The *traditional case*, or orthodox interpretation' is certainly still alive and well: 'that [Hobbes] is a materialist imbued with the ideas of the "new" natural science and that he methodically applies its themes and procedures (the laws governing bodies in motion and their deductive elaboration) to the elucidation of a civil and ethical theory cast in the same mould.' In *Hobbes and Rousseau: A Collection of Critical Essays*, Maurice Cranston and Richard S. Peters, eds (Garden City, NY: Doubleday, 1972), 6.

2 I have treated these matters more extensively in two separate but related essays: 'The Liberal Regime under Attack,' in *The West at War*, Bradley C.S. Watson, ed. (Lanham, MD: Rowman and Littlefield, 2006); and *'New Atlantis* Reconsidered,' in *Public Science in Liberal Democracy*, Jene M. Porter and Peter W.B. Phillips, eds (Toronto: University of Toronto Press, 2007). Also in this regard, Paul A. Rahe's 'Introduction' to his monumental study of the Western political tradition, *Republics Ancient and Modern* (Chapel Hill: University of North Carolina, 1992), makes for sober reading. He warns that 'over the last few decades a noiseless revolution has been under way; and as countless commentators on both left and right have repeatedly pointed out, domestic developments in all of the modern republics have been disheartening in one critical regard. There is a drift toward a species of soft, administrative despotism nearly everywhere – not least in the United States, the oldest, the least centralized, and most democratic republic in the world.' In light of various symptoms of international vulnerability and domestic malaise, Rahe wonders 'whether modern republicanism suffers somehow from a debilitating, genetic disorder' (6–7).

3 Non-Western critics readily exploit an often exaggerated portrayal of the 'decadence' of life in Western societies by way of justifying their opposition to being co-opted into the Hobbesian project. This is but one respect in which the internal problems of liberal democratic societies connect with external threats to them.

4 In this, they remind one of what the tobacco companies long claimed about smoking: not that cigarettes are actually *good* for people, merely that there is no conclusive scientific evidence that they are addictive, nor that they cause any of the deadly illnesses that virtually everyone, and most of all manufacturers themselves, know that they do.

5 I have discussed this at length in connection with an analysis of Shakespeare's *King Lear* in *Of Philosophers and Kings: Political Philosophy in Shakespeare's* Macbeth *and* King Lear (Toronto: University of Toronto Press, 2001), 133–68. Hobbes would emphatically agree with my claim, as I argued (in ch. 19) a careful reading of his *Leviathan* shows.

6 As of 2005, roughly one-quarter of North American adults between the ages of eighteen and thirty-five had grown up in families that had experienced divorce. The consequences are seldom happy. See, e.g., David Popenoe's thoroughly documented *Life without Father* (New York: Free Press, 1996), and Elizabeth Marquardt's *Between Two Worlds: The Inner Lives of Children of Divorce* (New York: Crown, 2005).

7 According to the most recent data, Russia heads the list with 52 per cent, with most of the former USSR satellites in the 30–40 per cent range; the rate of abortion-terminated pregnancies in the Western democracies is lower, most being in the 20–25 per cent range.

8 The 'equality of desires' is, practically speaking, the necessary premise of a belief in substantial human equality, and of whatever equality of rights and liberties is based thereupon (cf. *Republic* 559d–561e). For if, instead, it is possible to *rank* desires – such that some desires are regarded as higher, nobler, more befitting; other desires as low, vulgar, base, even bestial – one thereby tacitly ranks people accordingly, that is, according to their ruling desires.

9 Rousseau expresses this clearly in the final note of his *Discourse on Inequality*. Moreover, matters are merely muddied by the introduction of a third variant that is sometimes argued for: 'equality of condition,' referring to the totality of circumstances in which 'opportunity' is exercised – insisting that equality of opportunity is a sham, if not simply meaningless, unless people's 'initial conditions' are equal. Given the practical impossibility of this proviso being met, the consequence of accepting it is the endorsement of 'equality of result' by default. Still, bearing in mind that equality of opportunity is not simply an end in itself, but also a means of achieving other politically desirable outcomes (e.g., political stability, economic productivity, scientific discovery and invention), there is considerable latitude for attempting to establish such conditions as will facilitate those outcomes, beginning with equal access to basic education.

10 To see why, one might begin with Aristotle's critique of its impracticality in Book Two of his *Politics*, which takes due cognizance of the fact that gross disproportions in the distribution of wealth and property raise political problems that in themselves *justify* measures for their amelioration in the names of civility, charity, humanity, and peaceful stability:

> Some ... think that the greatest thing is have matters to do with possessions nobly arranged, for they say it is about possessions that everyone creates factions. It was for this reason that Phaleas of Chalcedon first introduced such a policy, for he says that the possessions of the citizens should be equal ...

Human beings, however, do wrong not only because of necessities, for which Phaleas thinks equality of property is the remedy (to prevent cold or hunger driving them to thievery), but also in order to enjoy themselves and not be in a state of longing. For if they have a desire for things above what they need, they will do wrong as a way of curing it, and indeed not only for this purpose but also if their desire is for the enjoyment of pleasures that are without pain. What then is the remedy for these three? A little property with hard work for the first, and moderation for the second. But as regards the third, if there are some who want to get enjoyment relying on themselves alone, they are not going to find a remedy except in philosophy, for the other pleasures require human beings. The greatest wrongs, at any rate, are committed for the sake of excess, and not because of need (tyrants, for instance, are not people trying to avoid the cold) …

So then, equalizing of possessions of citizens is among the ways that are of some benefit for preventing faction, but it is not, to speak truly, one of any great significance … Moreover, the wickedness of human beings is insatiable … For it is in the nature of desire to have no limit, and satisfying desire is what the Many live for. Ruling over such people is a matter not so much of leveling possessions as of training those who are equitable [*epieikeis*] by nature not to *wish* to have excess, and of insuring that the base are not able to. (1266a37–1267b8) (translation, with minor emendations, that of Peter L. Phillips Simpson, *The Politics of Aristotle* [Chapel Hill: University of North Carolina Press, 1997])

And, of course, there is the added practical difficulty that, even if citizens were somehow to begin with equal property holdings, such equality could be maintained only if property were regularly redistributed to compensate for some citizens being more wastrel of their property while others were more frugal of theirs, thus penalizing frugality in order to reward indulgence – not a recipe for harmonious civic relations.

11   Philip Kitcher, *Science, Truth, and Democracy* (Oxford: Oxford University Press, 2001), 5.

12   Britain leads the world in this respect, having an estimated 4.2 *million* closed-circuit cameras currently in operation, with the number steadily continuing to increase year by year (incredible as this may seem).

13   To repeat a bit of what I wrote elsewhere, addressing the larger problem (from 'The Liberal Regime Under Attack'):

We should begin by acknowledging a simple fact: today's liberal democracy isn't actually very democratic. If the point of sovereign power resting

with 'the People' (*ho dēmos*) is that government will thereby be in accordance with their wishes, especially regarding the things that most directly engage their lives – and a strong case can be made for the value of their judgment on those matters (unlike, say, on foreign affairs) – the actions of liberal regimes today are as apt to be contrary to majority views as consonant. Whether it is with respect to administering the criminal justice system, the content of public education, the management of sexual relations, or the regulating and funding of scientific research, laws and policies are as apt to reflect the wishes of various well-organized minority interests as they are 'the will' of even a sizable majority of 'the People.'
...

The net result is that the basic premise of democracy – that periodic elections will ultimately ensure that the preferences of the majority of citizens determine public policies – is undermined. Moreover, the growing public perception that such is the case: that the will of the majority is routinely subverted by 'special interests,' generates political cynicism, thereby eroding support for the regime. Similar remarks pertain to the increasing politicization of the court system, whereby narrow minority interests exploit the regime's commitment to the rule of law in order to circumvent the normal political process entirely, such that the rule of law becomes the rule of lawyers. This results in further attrition of the citizenry's respect for the law and for those they perceive to be professional exploiters of it (self-aggrandizing lawyers, mainly).

I most emphatically do not mean to suggest that I believe 'returning power to the people' is the solution to these and the other problems I discuss. But it is important in assessing hypothetical alternative regimes, including those that would seem insufficiently responsive to popular will, that one bear in mind how little this is presently the case in contemporary liberal democracies. (86–7)

14 This is one respect at least in which Hobbes agrees with Aristotle. Repeatedly in *Leviathan* he refers to the political problem in terms of architecture. For example, in speaking 'Of those things that Weaken, or tend to the DISSOLUTION of a Commonwealth' (ch. 29), he begins by observing:

For men, as they become at last weary of irregular justling, and hewing one another, and desire with all their hearts, to conforme themselves into one firme and lasting edifice; so for want, both of the art of making fit Lawes, to square their actions by, and also of humility, and patience, to suffer the rude and combersome points of their present greatnesse to be taken off, they cannot without the help of a very able Architect, be compiled, into any other than a crasie building, such as hardly lasting out their own time, must assuredly fall upon the heads of their posterity. (XXIX/1, 167; cf. XXX/5, 176)

In this connection, see also Descartes's *Discourse on Method* II/1–2, III/1; and Rousseau's *Discourse on Inequality*, Pt II, par. 36.

15 As I previously noted, a detailed critique of the chimerical 'fact-value' and 'is-ought' distinctions, and of the misconception of reason upon which they are based, is provided in a long endnote to my study of Plato's *Republic*, *The War Lover* (Toronto: University of Toronto Press, 1994), 326–36.

16 This as much as anything distinguishes the greatest political philosophers: their appreciation of how *different* they are from most people with respect to the rule of reason and the importance of truth. And arguably the most important gain from studying them is the acquisition of a perspective on politics that transcends politics, allowing one to see the human limitations on even the best imaginable regime, limitations of rationality in particular. The result is a tempering of one's expectations about what can be achieved through politics. No political change will ever bring perpetual peace, prosperity, and perfect justice, much less heaven on earth. And since means can be rationally justified only as they are proportional to the worthiness of *achievable* ends sought, some means – indiscriminate terrorism, for example – can never be justified. But rational justification has little bearing on whether or not certain people will resort to such means, and others sympathize with their doing so.

Bibliography

Editions of Hobbes's *Leviathan*

Edwin Curley. Indianapolis: Hackett, 1994.
Facsimile of 1651 ('Head') edition. Menston, England: Scolar Press, 1969.
G.A.J.Rogers and Karl Schuhmann (vols 1 and 2). London: Thoemmes/Continuum, 2003/2005.
Richard Tuck. Cambridge: Cambridge University Press, 1991.

Other Writings of Hobbes

De Corpore. In vol. 1 of *The English Works of Thomas Hobbes*. Edited by Sir William Moleworth. London: John Bohn, 1839.
A Dialogue between a Philosopher and a Student of the Common Laws of England. Edited by Joseph Cropsey. Chicago: University of Chicago Press, 1971.
The Elements of Law Natural and Politic. Edited by J.C.A.Gaskin. Oxford: Oxford University Press, 1994.
Hobbes's Thucydides. Edited by Richard Schlatter. New Brunswick, NJ: Rutgers University Press, 1975.
On the Citizen. Edited by Richard Tuck and Michael Silverthorne. Cambridge: Cambridge University Press, 1998.
The Questions Concerning Liberty, Necessity, and Chance. In vol. 5 of *The English Works of Thomas Hobbes*. Edited by Sir William Moleworth. London: John Bohn, 1841.
Six Lessons to the Professors of the Mathematics. In vol. 7 of *The English Works of Thomas Hobbes*. Edited by Sir William Moleworth. London: John Bohn, 1841.
Thomas White's De Mundo *Examined*. Translated by Harold Whitmore Jones. London: Bradford University Press, 1976.

Other Works Cited

Note: Classics of philosophy and literature – e.g., works of Plato, Aristotle, Bacon, Shakespeare – are not listed unless use has been made of a particular edition or translation.

Achebe, Chinua. 'An Image of Africa: Racism in Conrad's *Heart of Darkness.*' *Massachusetts Review* 18 (1977): 782–94.

Addison, Joseph. *Cato: A Tragedy and Selected Essays*. Edited by Christine Dunn Henderson and Mark E. Yellin. Indianapolis: Liberty Fund, 2004.

Alvis, John. '*Moby-Dick* and Melville's Quarrel with America.' *Interpretation* 23, no. 2 (Winter 1996): 223–47.

Anderson, Charles Robert. *Melville in the South Seas*. New York: Columbia University Press, 1939.

Aristotle. *The Complete Works of Aristotle: The Revised Oxford Translation*. Edited by Jonathan Barnes. Princeton: Princeton University Press, 1984.

– *The Politics of Aristotle*. Edited and translated by Peter L. Phillips Simpson. Chapel Hill, NC: University of North Carolina Press, 1997.

Aubrey, John. 'The Life of Mr Thomas Hobbes of Malmesbury.' In John Aubrey, *Brief Lives*. New York: Penguin, 2000.

Bacon, Francis. *The Advancement of Learning*. Edited by G.W. Kitchin. Philadelphia: Paul Dry Books, 2001.

– *New Organon*. Edited by Fulton H. Anderson. Indianapolis: Bobbs-Merrill, 1960.

– *Wisdom of the Ancients*. In *The Works of Francis Bacon*, vol. 6. Edited by James Spedding, Robert Leslie Ellis, and Douglas Denon Heath. London: Longmans, 1870.

Barry, Brian. 'Warrender and His Critics.' In *Hobbes and Rousseau: A Collection of Critical Essays*, ed. Maurice Cranston and Richard S. Peters, 37–65. Garden City, NY: Doubleday, 1972.

Bartley, William. '"The creature of his own tasteful hands": Herman Melville's *Benito Cereno* and the "Empire of Might."' *Modern Philology* 93, no. 4 (May 1996): 229–39.

Batchelor, John. *The Life of Joseph Conrad*. Oxford: Blackwell, 1994.

Baumrin, Bernard H., ed. *Hobbes's* Leviathan: *Interpretation and Criticism*. Belmont, CA: Wadsworth, 1969.

Blits, Jan H. 'Hobbesian Fear.' *Political Theory* 17, no. 3 (August 1989): 417–30.

Boas, Marie. *The Scientific Renaissance: 1450–1630*. New York: Harper and Row, 1966.

Bobbio, Norberto. *Thomas Hobbes and the Natural Law Tradition.* Translated by Daniela Gobetti. Chicago: University of Chicago Press, 1993.

Bramhall, John. 'The Catching of Leviathan, or the Great Whale.' In *Leviathan: Contemporary Responses to the Political Theory of Thomas Hobbes,* ed. G.A.J. Rogers, 115–79. Bristol: Thoemmes Press, 1995.

Brown, Keith. 'The Artist of the *Leviathan.*' *British Library Journal* 4 (1978): 24–36.

Butler, Christopher. *Number Symbolism.* London: Routledge and Kegan Paul, 1970.

Butterfield, Herbert. *The Origins of Modern Science.* New York: Free Press, 1965.

Cantalupo, Charles. *A Literary Leviathan – Thomas Hobbes's Masterpiece of Language.* Lewisburg, PA: Bucknell University Press, 1991.

Carnap, Rudolph. *The Philosophic Foundations of Physics.* Edited by Martin Gardner. New York: Basic Books, 1966.

Chomsky, Noam. *Reflections on Language.* New York: Pantheon Books, 1975.

Churchill, Winston. *The World Crisis 1911–1918.* London: Macmillan, 1941.

Cicero. *De Divinatione.* Translated by William Armistead Falconer. London: William Heinemann (Loeb Classical Library), 1946.

Colinvaux, Paul. *Why Big Fierce Animals Are Rare.* Princeton: Princeton University Press, 1978.

Colson, Charles. *Call Me Ishmael: A Study of Melville.* Copyright by author, 1949; reprinted San Francisco: City Lights Books, no date.

Conrad, Joseph. *Heart of Darkness.* In *The Works of Joseph Conrad,* vol. 5. London: William Heinemann, 1921.

– *The Nigger of the Narcissus.* In *The Works of Joseph Conrad,* vol. 3.

– *Under Western Eyes.* In *The Works of Joseph Conrad,* vol. 9.

Considine, Douglas M., ed. *Van Nostrand's Scientific Encyclopedia,* 5th ed. New York: Van Nostrand Reinhold, 1976.

Cooke, Paul D. *Hobbes and Christianity: Reassessing the Bible in* Leviathan. Lanham, MD: Rowman and Littlefield, 1996.

Craig, Leon Harold. 'The Liberal Regime under Attack.' In *The West at War,* ed. Bradley C.S. Watson, 73–98. Lanham, MD: Rowman and Littlefield, 2006.

– 'New Atlantis Reconsidered.' In *Public Science in Liberal Democracy,* ed. Jene M. Porter and Peter W. B. Phillips, 149–73. Toronto: University of Toronto Press, 2007.

– *Of Philosophers and Kings: Political Philosophy in Shakespeare's* Macbeth *and* King Lear. Toronto: University of Toronto Press, 2001.

– 'The Strange Misperception of Plato's *Meno.*' In *Politics, Philosophy, Writing*, ed. Zdravko Planinc, 60–79. Columbia: University of Missouri Press, 2001.

– *The War Lover: A Study of Plato's* Republic. Toronto: University of Toronto Press, 1994.

Curley, Edwin. 'Hobbes and the Cause of Religious Toleration.' In *The Cambridge Companion to Hobbes's Leviathan*, ed. Patricia Springborg, 309–34. Cambridge: Cambridge University Press, 2007.

Davies, Paul, and John Gribbin. *The Matter Myth*. New York: Simon and Schuster, 2007.

Delbanco, Andrew. *Melville: His World and Work*. New York: Alfred A. Knopf, 2005.

Descartes, René. *Discourse on Method*. In vol. 1 of *The Philosophical Writings of Descartes*, ed. and trans. J. Cottingham, R. Stoothoff, and D. Murdoch. Cambridge: Cambridge University Press, 1985.

D'Israeli, Isaac. 'Hobbes and His Quarrels.' In *Miscellanies of Literature*. London: Edward Monon, 1840.

Doidge, Norman. *The Brain That Changes Itself*. New York: Penguin, 2007.

Drummond, C.Q. 'Nature: Meek Ass or White Whale.' In *In Defence of Adam*, ed. John Baxter and Gordon Harvey, 238–53. Harleston, Norfolk: Edgeway Books, 2004.

Edwards, Paul, ed. *The Encyclopedia of Philosophy*. New York: Macmillan, 1967.

Farneti, Roberto. 'The "Mythical Foundation" of the State: Leviathan in Emblematic Context.' *Pacific Philosophical Quarterly* 82 (2001): 362–82.

Flathman, Richard E. *Thomas Hobbes: Skepticism, Individuality and Chastened Politics*. Walnut Creek, CA: Altamira, 2000.

Fowler, Alastair ed. *Silent Poetry: Essays in Numerological Analysis*. London: Routledge and Kegan Paul, 1970.

Freeman, Kathleen, ed. *Ancilla to the Pre-Socratic Philosophers*. Oxford: Basil Blackwell, 1952.

French, Peter. *John Dee: The World of an Elizabethan Magus*. London: Routledge and Kegan Paul, 1972.

Garner, Stanton. *Melville: His World and Work*. New York: Alfred A. Knopf, 2005.

Gaukroger, Stephen. *Descartes: An Intellectual Biography*. Oxford: Oxford University Press, 1995

Gert, Bernard. 'Hobbes and Psychological Egoism.' In *Hobbes's* Leviathan: *Interpretation and Criticism*, ed. Bernard H. Baumrin, 107–26. Belmont, CA: Wadsworth, 1969.

Gibson, Gregory. *Demon of the Waters: The True Story of the Mutiny on the Whaleship Globe*. Boston: Little, Brown, 2002.

Gilbert, William. *On the Lodestone and Magnetic Bodies.* Translated by P. Fleury Mottelay. Chicago: Encyclopaedia Britannica, 1952.

Gleick, James. *Chaos: Making a New Science.* New York: Penguin, 1987.

Greenleaf, W.H. 'Hobbes: The Problem of Interpretation.' In *Hobbes and Rousseau: A Collection of Critical Essays,* ed. Maurice Cranston and Richard S. Peters, 5–36. Garden City, NY: Doubleday, 1972.

Hampton, Jean. *Hobbes and the Social Contract Tradition.* Cambridge: Cambridge University Press, 1986.

Harvey, William. *Anatomical Disquisition on the Motion of the Heart and Blood in Animals.* Translated by Robert Willis. Chicago: Encyclopaedia Britannica, 1952.

Heisenberg, Werner. *Across the Frontiers.* New York: Harper and Row, 1974.

Herbert, Gary B. *Thomas Hobbes: The Unity of Scientific and Moral Wisdom.* Vancouver: University of British Columbia Press, 1989.

Hochschild, Adam. *King Leopold's Ghost.* Boston: Houghton Mifflin, 1998.

Horn, Alfred A. *Trader Horn, Being the Life and Works of Alfred Aloysius Horn.* New York: Simon and Schuster, 1927.

Huygens, Christiaan. *Treatise on Light.* Translated by Silvanus P. Thompson. Chicago: Encyclopaedia Britannica, 1952.

Hyde, Edward, Earl of Clarendon. *History of the Great Rebellion.* Oxford: The Folio Society, 1967.

– 'A Survey of Mr Hobbes His Leviathan.' In *Leviathan: Contemporary Responses to the Political Theory of Thomas Hobbes,* ed. G.A.J.Rogers, 180–300. Bristol: Thoemmes Press, 1995.

Jacobson, Norman. *Thomas Hobbes as Creator.* New York: General Learning Press, 1971.

Jaume, Lucien. 'Hobbes and the Philosophical Sources of Liberalism.' In *The Cambridge Companion to Hobbes's* Leviathan, ed. Patricia Springborg, 199–216. Cambridge: Cambridge University Press, 2007.

Jesseph, Douglas M. 'Galileo, Hobbes, and the Book of Nature.' *Perspectives on Science* 12, no. 2 (2004): 191–211.

– 'Hobbes's Atheism.' *Midwest Studies in Philosophy* 24 (2002): 140–66.

– *Squaring the Circle: The War between Hobbes and Wallis.* Chicago: University of Chicago Press, 1999.

Kant, Immanuel. 'Idea of a Universal History with a Cosmopolitan Purpose.' Translated by H.B. Nisbet. In *Kant's Political Writings,* ed. Hans Reiss. Cambridge University Press, 1970.

Kaplan, Robert D. *The Coming Anarchy: Shattering the Dreams of the Post Cold War.* New York: Random House, 2000.

Karl, Frederick R. *Joseph Conrad: The Three Lives.* London: Faber and Faber, 1979.

Kitcher, Philip. *Science, Truth, and Democracy.* Oxford University Press, 2001.

Klein, Jacob. *A Commentary on Plato's* Meno. Chapel Hill: University of North Carolina Press, 1965.

Klemke, E.D., ed. *Essays on Wittgenstein.* Urbana: University of Illinois Press, 1971.

Lampert, Laurence. *Nietzsche and Modern Times A Study of Bacon, Descartes, and Nietzsche.* New Haven, CT: Yale University Press, 1993.

Laplace, Pierre Simon de. *A Philosophical Essay on Probabilities.* New York: Dover, 1951.

Lawson, George. *An Examination of the Political Part of Mr. Hobbs His* Leviathan. In *Leviathan: Contemporary Responses to the Political Theory of Thomas Hobbes,* ed. G.A.J. Rogers. Bristol: Thoemmes Press, 1995.

Leavis, F.R. *The Great Tradition.* New York: New York University Press, 1973.

Leibniz, G.W. *Philosophical Essays.* Edited and translated by Roger Ariew and Daniel Garber. Indianapolis: Hackett, 1989.

Leijenhorst, Cees. 'Hobbes's Theory of Casuality and its Aristotelian Background.' *The Monist* 79, no. 3 (1996): 426–47.

– 'Sense and Nonsense about Sense: Hobbes and the Aristotelians on Sense Perception and Imagination.' In *The Cambridge Companion to Hobbes's* Leviathan, ed. Patricia Springborg, 82–108. Cambridge: Cambridge University Press, 2007.

Lilla, Mark. *The Stillborn God: Religion, Politics, and the Modern West.* New York: Alfred A. Knopf, 2007.

Livingston, Donald W. *Philosophical Melancholy and Delirium: Hume's Pathology of Philosophy.* Chicago: University of Chicago Press, 1998.

Machiavelli, Niccolò. *The Prince.* Edited and translated by Harvey Mansfield. Chicago: University of Chicago Press, 1985.

Macpherson, C.B. *The Political Theory of Possessive Individualism: Hobbes to Locke.* Oxford: Oxford University Press, 1962.

Malcolm, Noel. *Aspects of Hobbes.* Oxford: University of Oxford Press, 2002.

– 'Changing the Sheets,' *Times Literary Supplement,* 3 December 2004.

– ed. *The Correspondence of Thomas Hobbes.* Oxford: Oxford University Press, 1994.

– 'The Making of the Bear: Further Thoughts on the Printing of the Second Edition of *Leviathan,*' *Hobbes Studies* 20 (2007): 2–39.

– 'The Making of the Ornaments: Further Thoughts on the Printing of the Third Edition of *Leviathan.*' *Hobbes Studies* 21 (2008): 3–37.

Manent, Pierre. *Democracy without Nations? The Fate of Self-government in Europe.* Translated by Paul Seaton. Wilmington, DE: ISI Books, 2007.

Marquardt, Elizabeth. *Between Two Worlds: The Inner Lives of Children of Divorce.* New York: Crown, 2005.

Martinich, A.P. *A Hobbes Dictionary*. Oxford: Blackwell, 1995.

– 'Two Uses of Thomas Hobbes's Philosophy in Melville's *The Confidence-Man*.' *ANQ* 16, no. 3 (Summer 2003): 37–40.

Meadows, A.J. *The High Firmament: A Survey of Astronomy in English Literature*. Leicester, UK: Leicester University Press, 1969.

Melville, Herman. 'Hawthorne and His Mosses.' In *Pierre, Israel Potter, The Piazza Tales, The Confidence-Man, Uncollected Prose, Billy Budd*. New York: Library of America, 1984.

– *Israel Potter*. New York: Library of America, 1984.

– *Moby-Dick; or, The Whale*. Evanston, IL: Northwestern University Press, 1988.

– *Selected Poems of Herman Melville*. Edited by Robert Penn Warren. Boston: David R. Godine, 2004.

– *Tales, Poems, and Other Writings*. Edited by John Bryant. New York: Modern Library, 2001.

– *White-Jacket*. New York: Library of America, 1983.

Metzger, Bruce M. and Michael D. Coogan, eds. *The Oxford Companion to the Bible*. New York: Oxford University Press, 1993.

Miller, Geoffrey. *The Mating Mind: How Sexual Choice Shaped the Evolution of Human Nature*. London: William Heinemann, 2000.

Milton, John. *Areopagitica and Other Political Writings of John Milton*. Indianapolis: Liberty Fund, 1999.

Mintz, Samuel I. *The Hunting of Leviathan*. Bristol: Thoemmes Press, 1996.

Missner, Marshall. *On Hobbes*. Belmont, CA: Wadsworth, 2000.

Montaigne, Michel de. *The Complete Essays of Montaigne*. Edited and translated by Donald Frame. Stanford, CA: Stanford University Press, 1958.

Moore, Richard S. *That Cunning Alphabet: Melville's Aesthetics of Nature*. Amsterdam: Rodopi, 1982.

Newton, Isaac. *Mathematical Principles of Natural Philosophy*. Translated by Andrew Motte, rev. by Florian Cajori. Berkeley: University of California Press, 1934.

Nietzsche, Friedrich. *Beyond Good and Evil*. In *The Basic Writings of Nietzsche*. Edited and translated by Walter Kaufmann. New York: Modern Library, 1966.

– *The Birth of Tragedy*. In *The Basic Writings of Nietzsche*.

– *Human, All Too Human*. Translated by R.J. Hollingdale. Cambridge: Cambridge University Press, 1986.

Oakeshott, Michael. *Hobbes on Civil Association*. Indianapolis: Liberty Fund, 1937/1975.

Orwin, Clifford. *The Humanity of Thucydides*. Princeton, NJ: Princeton University Press, 1994.

Overhoff, Jürgen. *Hobbes's Theory of the Will: Ideological Reasons and Historical Circumstances*. Lanham, MD: Rowman and Littlefield, 2000.

Peck, Russell A. 'Numerology.' In *A Dictionary of Biblical Tradition in English Literature*, ed. David Lyle Jeffrey, 555–7. Grand Rapids, MI: Eerdmans, 1992.

Penrose, Roger. *The Emperor's New Mind*. Oxford: Oxford University Press, 1989.

Peters, Richard. *Hobbes*. Baltimore: Penguin Books, 1967.

Plutarch. *Lives*. 11 vols. Translated by Bernadotte Perrin. London: William Heinemann (Loeb Classical Library), 1932.

Popenoe, David. *Life without Father*. New York: Free Press, 1996.

Rahe, Paul A. *Republics Ancient and Modern*. Chapel Hill, NC: University of North Carolina Press, 1992.

Reilly, John J. 'After Darwin.' *First Things*, June/July 1995.

Rogow, Arnold A. *Thomas Hobbes: Radical in the Service of Reaction*. New York: Norton, 1986.

Rollyson, Carl, and Lisa Paddock. *Herman Melville A to Z*. New York: Checkmark, 2001.

Rosen, Stanley. *Nihilism*. New Haven: Yale University Press, 1969.

Rousseau, Jean-Jacques. *Considerations on the Government of Poland*. In *The Social Contract and Other Later Political Writings*, ed. and trans. Victor Gourevitch. Cambridge: Cambridge University Press, 1997.

– *Discourse on the Arts and Sciences*. In *The Discourses and Other Early Political Writings*, ed. and trans. Victor Gourevitch. Cambridge: Cambridge University Press, 1997.

– *Discourse on Inequality*. In *The Discourses and Other Early Political Writings*.

Schmitt, Carl. *The Leviathan in the State Theory of Thomas Hobbes: Meaning and Failure of a Political Symbol*. Translated by George Schwab and Erna Hilfstein. Westport, CT: Greenwood Press, 1996.

Schuhmann, Karl. 'Hobbes and the Political Thought of Plato and Aristotle.' In *Selected Papers on Renaissance Philosophy and on Thomas Hobbes*, ed. Piet Steenbakkers and Cees Leijenhorst, 191–218. Dordrecht: Kluwer, 2004.

Sherry, Norman. *Conrad's Western World*. Cambridge: Cambridge University Press, 1971.

Skinner, Quentin. *Reason and Rhetoric in the Philosophy of Hobbes*. Cambridge: Cambridge University Press, 1996.

– *Visions of Politics*, vol. 3: *Hobbes and Civil Science*. Cambridge: Cambridge University Press, 2002.

Sommerville, Johann P. *Thomas Hobbes; Political Ideas in Historical Context*. New York: St Martin's, 1992.

Springborg, Patricia. 'Hobbes's Biblical Beasts: *Leviathan* and *Behemoth*.' *Political Theory* 23, no. 2 (May 1995): 353–75.

– ed. *The Cambridge Companion to Hobbes's Leviathan*. Cambridge: Cambridge University Press, 2007.

Strassler, Robert B., ed. *The Landmark Thucydides*. New York: Free Press, 1996.

Strauss, Leo. *The City and Man*. Chicago: Rand McNally, 1964.

– *Natural Right and History*. Chicago: University of Chicago Press, 1953.

– 'On the Basis of Hobbes's Political Philosophy.' In *What Is Political Philosophy?* New York: Free Press, 1959.

– *On Tyranny*. Revised and expanded edition. Edited by Victor Gourevitch and Michael S. Roth. New York: Free Press, 1991.

– 'Political Philosophy and History.' In *What Is Political Philosophy?*

– 'The Spirit of Hobbes's Philosophy.' *Revue Internationale de Philosophie* 4, no. 14 (October 1950): 405–31.

– *Thoughts on Machiavelli*. Seattle: University of Washington Press, 1958.

– 'What Is Liberal Education?' In *Liberalism Ancient and Modern*, 3–8. New York: Basic Books, 1968.

Tralau, Johan. 'Leviathan, the Beast of Myth: Medusa, Dionysus, and the Riddle of Hobbes's Sovereign Monster.' In *The Cambridge Companion to Hobbes's Leviathan*, ed. Patricia Springborg, 16–81. Cambridge: Cambridge University Press, 2007.

Trigg, Roger. *Understanding Social Science*. Oxford: Basil Blackwell, 1985.

Trimpi, Helen. *Melville's Confidence Men and American Politics in the 1850's*. Hamden, CT: Transactions of the Connecticut Academy of the Arts and Sciences, 1987.

Trimpi, Wesley. 'Sir Philip Sidney's *An Apology for Poetry*.' In *The Cambridge History of Literary Criticism*, vol. 3: *The Renaissance*, ed. Glyn P. Norton. Cambridge: Cambridge University Press, 1999.

Trumble, William R., and Angus Stevenson, eds. *New Shorter Oxford English Dictionary*, 5th ed. Oxford: Oxford University Press, 2002.

Tuck, Richard. *Hobbes*. Oxford: Oxford University Press, 1989.

Vaughan, Frederick. *The Tradition of Political Hedonism: From Hobbes to J.S. Mill*. New York: Fordham University Press, 1982.

Vaughan, Geoffrey M. *Behemoth Teaches Leviathan: Thomas Hobbes on Political Education*. Lanham, MD: Lexington Books, 2007.

von Mises, Richard. *Positivism: A Study in Human Understanding*. New York: Dover, 1968.

Warrender, Howard. *The Political Philosophy of Hobbes*. Oxford: Oxford University Press, 1957.

Watkins, J.W.N. *Hobbes's System of Ideas*. London: Hutchinson, 1965.

Watt, Ian. *Conrad in the Nineteenth Century*. Berkeley: University of California Press, 1979.

Weinberger, Jerry. *Benjamin Franklin Unmasked*. Lawrence: University of Kansas Press, 2005.

– 'Hobbes's Doctrine of Method.' *American Political Science Review* 69 (1975): 1336–53.

Winters, Ivor. *In Defense of Reason*. Denver, CO: University of Denver Press, 1947.

Winton, John. *Sir Walter Ralegh*. London: Michael Joseph, 1975.

Wittgenstein, Ludwig. *Philosophical Investigations*. New York: Macmillan, 1953.

Wynn-Davies, Marion, ed. *Penguin Guide to English Literature*. London: Penguin, 1989.

Index of Names

The following list includes only the proper names of persons and peoples that appear in the preceding text; the names of fictional characters are italicized. Four names are excluded, however, since they are mentioned so frequently that listing their separate occurrences would serve little practical purpose: 'Hobbes' (of course), 'Plato,' 'Sokrates,' and 'Aristotle.'